Reading Faulkner

COLLECTED STORIES

I0808404

Reading Faulkner Series

Noel Polk, *Series Editor*

Reading Faulkner

Collected Stories

Glossary and Commentary by

Theresa M. Towner and James B. Carothers

University Press of Mississippi / Jackson

www.upress.state.ms.us

The University Press of Mississippi is a member
of the Association of American University Presses.

Copyright © 2006 by University Press of Mississippi
All rights reserved
Manufactured in the United States of America

First edition 2006
∞
Library of Congress Cataloging-in-Publication Data

Towner, Theresa M.
Reading Faulkner. Collected stories : glossary and commentary / by Theresa M. Towner and James B. Carothers.— 1st ed.
p. cm. — (Reading Faulkner series)
Includes bibliographical references and index.
ISBN 1-57806-812-6 (alk. paper) — ISBN 1-57806-813-4 (pbk. : alk. paper)
1. Faulkner, William, 1897–1962—Criticism and interpretation. 2. Faulkner, William, 1897–1962—Language—Glossaries, etc. 3. Yoknapatawpha County (Imaginary place). 4. Southern States—In literature. 5. Mississippi—In literature. 6. Short story. I. Title: Collected stories. II. Carothers, James B. III. Title. IV. Series.
PS3511.A86Z97826 2006
813′.52—dc22 2005023608

British Library Cataloging-in-Publication Data available

CONTENTS

IV. THE WASTELAND

V. THE MIDDLE GROUND

VI. BEYOND

SERIES PREFACE

This volume is one of a series of glossaries of Faulkner's novels which is the brainchild of the late James Hinkle, who established its principles, selected the authors, worked long hours with each of us in various stages of planning and preparation, and then died before seeing any of the volumes in print. The series derives from Jim's hardcore commitment to the principle that readers must understand each word in Faulkner's difficult novels at its most basic, literal level before hoping to understand the works' "larger" issues. In pursuit of this principle, Jim, a non-Southerner, spent years of his scholarly life reading about the South and things Southern, in order to learn all he could about sharecropping, about hame strings, about mule fact and lore, about the Civil War, about blockade running, duelling, slavery and Reconstruction, Indian culture and history. When he had learned all he could from published sources, he betook himself to county and city archives to find what he could there. He was intrigued by Faulkner's names, for example, and over the years compiled a fascinating and invaluable commentary on their etymologies, their cultural and historical backgrounds, and, not least, their pronunciations: Jim is the only person I know of who listened to all of the tapes of Faulkner's readings and interviews at the University of Virginia, in order to hear how Faulkner himself pronounced the names and words he wrote. In short, for Jim, there was no detail too fine, no fact or supposition too arcane to be of interest or potential significance for readers of Faulkner: he took great pleasure in opening up the atoms of Faulkner's world, and in exploring the cosmos he found there.

It was my great fortune and pleasure to be Jim's friend and colleague for slightly more than a decade. In the late seventies, I managed to tell him something he didn't know; he smiled and we were friends for life. Our friendship involved an ongoing competition to discover and pass on something the other didn't know. I was mostly on the losing end of this competition, though of course ultimately the winner because of what I learned from him. It was extremely agreeable to me to supply him with some arcana or other because of the sheer delight he took in learning something—anything, no matter how large or small.

On numerous occasions before and after the inception of this series, we spent hours with each other and with other Faulkner scholars reading the novels aloud, pausing to parse out a difficult passage, to look up a word we didn't understand, to discuss historical and mythological allusions, to work through the visual details of a scene to make sure we understood exactly what was happening, to complete Faulkner's interruptions, to fill in his gaps, and to be certain that we paid as much attention to the unfamiliar passages as we did to the better-known ones, not to let a single word escape our scrutiny; we also paused quite frequently, to savor what we had just read. These readings were a significant part of my education in Faulkner, and I'm forever grateful to Jim for his friendship and his guidance.

This series, Reading Faulkner, grows out of these experiences in reading Faulkner aloud, the effort to understand every nuance of meaning contained in the words. The volumes in the series will try to provide, for new readers and for old hands, a handy guide not just to the novel's allusions, chronologies, Southernisms, and difficult words, but also to its more difficult passages.

Jim's death in December 1990 was a great loss to Faulkner studies; it was especially grievous to those of us embarked with him on this series. Absent his guidance, the University Press of Mississippi asked me to assume editorship of the series; I am happy to continue the work he started. The volumes in the series will not be what they would have been had Jim lived, but they all will bear his stamp and his spirit, and they all will try to be worthy of his high standards. And they will all be lovingly dedicated to his memory.

Noel Polk

INTRODUCTION

Whether limping down the road with Sarty Snopes or falling through darkness with Tom-Tom, whether gasping in the dust of Miss Emily Grierson's bedroom or retching on the outskirts of Jefferson with Hawkshaw, whether chasing the mule in Mrs. Hait's tiny yard or tracking enemy aircraft over France, countless readers of William Faulkner have first entered his world through one of the forty-two doors in *Collected Stories.* He began his literary life as a poet and fabulist but, as he told an interviewer in 1955, "I soon found I wasn't a poet." He offered himself as an example of his lifelong insistence that "every novelist is a failed poet. I think he tries to write poetry first, then finds he can't. Then he tries the short story, which is the most demanding form after poetry" (*Lion in the Garden* 217). In that form, Faulkner achieved splendid success by any measure save the strictly remunerative: he wrote over a hundred short stories, published nearly all of them during his lifetime, and became one of the most frequently anthologized writers in the genre.

Publishing short stories was one important way for Faulkner to pay his bills, especially in the Depression era of the 1930s, when he was, as he put it, "the sole, principal and partial support—food, shelter, heat, clothes, medicine, kotex, school fees, toilet paper and picture shows—of my mother . . . [a] brother's widow and child, a wife of my own and two step children, my own child," while he had "inherited my father's debts and his dependents, white and black without inheriting yet from anyone one inch of land or one stick of furniture or one cent of money; the only thing I ever got for nothing, after the first pair of long pants I received (cost: $7.50) was the $300.00 O. Henry prize last year" (*Selected Letters* 122–23). Desperate for money, he wrote as much as fast as he could and begged his agents to flog it all: "I can use money right now to beat hell"; "I hope to hell you can gouge somebody for a thousand for GOLDEN LAND. That will give me two months to work at the novel before I have to boil the pot again"; "The man who said that the pinch of necessity, butchers and grocers bills and insurance hanging over his head, is good for an artist is a damned fool" (*SL* 87, 88, 91). He obsessed over $25 owed him for the reprint of one story and claimed in 1935, "I am writing two stories a week now. I don't know how long I can keep it up" (*SL* 91). Not at a pace of one or two a week, but keep it up he did, producing the last-published of his collected stories in 1948. The least he seems to have earned for a story is twenty-five dollars, from *Story*, his last resort after better-paying magazines rejected his work; the most, $2500 from the *Saturday Evening Post* for "Race at Morning" (Skei, *Short Story Career* 69; Blotner 1974; 1150, 1513). And as angry as Faulkner often was at the exigencies of the fiction market in the United States, as bitter his assessments of its strategies and audiences, he held to his own aesthetic principles and standards in the actual production of his own fictions. When *Vanity Fair* asked him for "a lynching article," for example, he told Harrison Smith "Tell them I never saw a lynching and so couldn't describe one" (*SL* 89); and during a misunderstanding with the *Saturday Evening Post*, he wrote to Morton Goldman, "As far as I am concerned, while I have to write trash, I dont care who buys it, as long as they pay the best price I can get; doubtless the Post feels the same way about it; anytime that I sacrifice a high price to a lower one it will not be to refrain from antagonizing the Post; it will be to write something better than a pulp series like this" (*SL* 84).

Collected Stories was born at Random House publisher Albert Erskine's suggestion and passed to Faulkner through editors Robert Haas and Saxe Commins (Blotner 1974; 1270). Faulkner himself finalized the table of contents, the order of the stories, and the titles of the collection's subheadings. He wrote to Malcolm Cowley that "even to a collection of short stories, form, integration, is as important as to a novel—an entity of its own, single, set for one pitch, contrapuntal in integration, toward one end, one finale" (*SL* 278). He therefore had his reasons for exclusion as well as for inclusion: "No. Already in a book"; or "No. Topical, not too good" (*SL* 274). He settled early on the overall organization, and he immediately saw the possibilities for another collection of stories, "a 'Gavin Stevens' volume, more or less detective stories" (*SL* 280), which became *Knight's Gambit* (1949). He wrote the title novella for that volume much as he had "An Odor of Verbena" as a coda for the previously published stories in *The Unvanquished* (1938), although that book saw extensive revision into its new life as a novel. He voiced some doubt in the planning stages about producing a collection at that point in his career, but the finished product delighted him: "It's all right; the stuff stands up amazingly well after a few years. . . . I spent a whole evening laughing to myself about the mules and the shingles" (*SL* 304). As James Carothers has pointed out, *Collected Stories* represents virtually the end of Faulkner's work in the genre: "Fewer than half a dozen stories followed it"; it is "at once an index to Faulkner's judgment of his previously published short story texts, and an original text in its own right, organizing a diverse body of material in contrapuntal and thematic patterns" (58). Beginning with the poor white sharecroppers of "Barn Burning" and ending with the artist *manqué* beneath his roofing paper in "Carcassonne," each individual story in the collection pulses with a unique life force, echoing the original creative power channeled into them by a writer who knew he had made "the most demanding form after poetry" his own.

Faulkner's short stories have received nowhere near the amount of critical attention that his novels have, a condition that we hope the present volume will help to redress. Some of his most famous stories—"Barn Burning," "Dry September," and "A Rose for Emily," for instance—have generated most of the criticism that exists; but the fortunes of some stories have been changed by the perspicuity of individual critics, with "Carcassonne" at the top of that list. We have read and benefited from the existing criticism on the stories, particularly from the volumes by Hans Skei, Diane Brown Jones, Lisa Paddock, James Ferguson, and Edmond Volpe. However, we have not attempted to address fully in these pages the specifics of the range of criticism on the stories. Neither have we attempted to resolve major ongoing critical debates in Faulkner scholarship—about race or gender issues, say, or questions of intertextuality. We believe that the present volume is what Robert Scholes describes as "work that is useful to other scholars, especially teachers and students." Distinguishing between progressive-minded "research" and "scholarship," Scholes argues that scholarship "is more about recovery than discovery. It is about understanding more clearly or more richly the meaning of texts or events from the past, including how we got to our present cultural situation" (123). In our annotations of individual stories, we have tried first of all to recover and explain exactly what Faulkner was thinking about, looking at, or remembering when he made his allusions, crafted his dialogue, described his landscape. We have therefore paid as much attention to the description of a froe as to *The Waste Land,* quoted "Mademoiselle from Armentières" as extensively as Shakespeare. Each chapter of this book includes an introduction, with a composition and publication history of the story at hand as well as a discussion of the thematic and textual issues raised in each; however, since it is sometimes as difficult to determine exactly when Faulkner wrote a given piece as it is to determine when that other William wrote his, we have had to resort to informed speculation in some places. We have discovered during the process of annotating the short stories that Faulkner knew what he was talking about when he referred even casually to aesthetic, political, and historical persons, objects, events, or movements. His audience, by contrast, might not have ever known of the existence of a Robert Ingersoll, never mind the significance of his philosophy to the main character of "Beyond," or heard the lovely rhythms of T. S. Eliot's drowned sailor's bones "knocking together and together," or known how to use a middlebuster. Faulkner knew these things. If we have done our work well, readers will know them, too.

With Scholes, we hope that "the end product of this scholarship" is "a pedagogy enhanced by the best knowledge that is available," "learning in the service of teaching" (123). Perhaps more than any other writer, reading Faulkner means learning Faulkner, and our own learning in the course of writing the present volume has been enhanced by the hard work of many fellow-learners. We wish to acknowledge the contributions of our students at the University of Texas at Dallas and at the University of Kansas, many of whom provided material for the annotations here as well as lots of challenges to our collective notions about Faulkner. We thank Dianne Berrett for explanations of surgical and diagnostic procedures; Walter Berrett for information on ships, trains, and boilers; Eric Carlson for help with aviation in World War I; Gary L. Dirks for work on Faulkner's botany, meteorology, and mechanics; Glenna Dunning of the Los Angeles Public Library for the circulation of L.A. newspapers in the 1930s; R. David Edmunds for explanations of Native American culture, history, and customs; David

Fincannon for the history of pesticide use, particularly arsenic; Pamela S. Gossin, Sue Lederer, and Victor Wilson for explanations of medical conditions and the history of science; the late Edward Grier for the airplane in "Pennsylvania Station"; Gavin Hambly for medieval European lore; Anne Goodwyn Jones for help with Rincon; Lynn Nelson for World War I materials and many good questions; the family of Ensign Elmer Leroy Parkes for permission to quote in full the notice of his death in World War II; reference librarians everywhere for choosing their profession; D. Charles Towner for history of the automobile industry and information on hunting; UTD for a generous Special Faculty Development Assignment. Series editor Noel Polk was steadfast in his support of this project and unremitting in his examination of its details. Our work in these pages owes great debts to the published work of Calvin Brown and Robert Harrison, whose research helped us untangle much confusion regarding the two areas of Faulkner's world that are fading most quickly from modern memory; *A Glossary of Faulkner's South* and *Aviation Lore in Faulkner* saved us many times from outright errors of fact, and we apologize for any errors on those or other topics that might remain here. We do not exaggerate when we say that our greatest expression of gratitude belongs to our research assistants, Elizabeth D. Berrett and Kima Sheldon Dirks. Without them, the present volume would not exist, but with them, the journey to its completion has been a joyful collaboration among equals.

Theresa M. Towner
James B. Carothers

HOW TO USE THIS BOOK

The chapters in this book are arranged according to Faulkner's table of contents for *Collected Stories*, and entries in chapters are keyed to page and line numbers of the first edition of that text, published in 1950 by Random House and reprinted many times since then, most often in the Vintage paperback edition. The introduction sets the stories in the collection within the contexts of Faulkner's career and the criticism of it, while the series preface explains the history and goals of the *Reading Faulkner* project as a whole. Each individual chapter begins with an introduction that includes information regarding the plot and thematic concerns of the story, its composition and textual history, critical responses to it, and its place among Faulkner's other work. Annotations of individual passages then appear, with Faulkner's text quoted in bold print. In a very few instances, long passages from the stories have been shortened with ellipses. Intended to recover Faulkner's world as fully as possible for the contemporary reader, the annotations vary greatly in length and in supporting detail. In an effort to limit the size of what could have been a thoroughly unwieldy volume, we have not usually included definitions of "hard words"; instead, we have assumed that our readers have access to dictionaries but not, for instance, to Voltaire's *Philosophical Dictionary* or out-of-print dime novels that Faulkner also read. The chapters stand independent of one another; readers can therefore move from a reading of an individual story directly to the chapter in this volume, or they can consult the volume as they read Faulkner's stories. Where Faulkner repeats himself, then—on the impermanence of celluloid, the shirt collars of the 1930s, the unreliability of the Sopwith Camel, Chickasaws, Choctaws, Malbrouck, corn whisky—we repeat ourselves.

I. THE COUNTRY

"Barn Burning"

"Barn Burning," among the best and best-known of Faulkner's short stories, captures in extraordinary detail and immediacy the ultimately insoluble dilemma of an intelligent, sensitive ten-year-old boy, Sarty Snopes, who is profoundly divided between his allegiance to his father, Abner, a poor, proud, and violent man, embittered by years of economic exploitation, and his own aching desire for a more comprehensive justice, which, he hopes, will bring peace among his father and his kind and men of the more privileged classes. Widely anthologized and assigned, the story is for many readers their first experience with Faulkner, and its themes and techniques also serve as an introduction to the world of *Collected Stories.* Conflicts personal, familial, class- and race-based, political and sexual mark these forty-two stories, and to some degree "Barn Burning" contains them all. It describes Sarty's initiation into the adult world, not so much to its evils but to the cold fact that in life one cannot always travel two paths simultaneously. Sarty feels equally strongly "the old fierce pull of blood" and the lure of security represented by the De Spain house even as he fears the terrible outcome of their irreconcilable opposition. Whether his father and brother are dead at the end of the story, as he assumes, or alive, as the Snopes saga that continues beyond the short story indicates, Sarty cannot go home again. Because he cannot choose between the two paths and two codes available to him, he loses both. He finally walks out of the story and out of Faulkner's fiction.

Thematic ambiguity aside, the story also stands in a complex relation to the rest of the complex relations among Faulkner's texts. It emerges from the matrix of Snopes material that Faulkner had begun creating with *Father Abraham* in the mid-1920s and that would continue to engage him through the completion of *The Mansion* (1959). After carefully considering the textual evidence, Hans Skei concludes that Faulkner wrote "Barn Burning" in manuscript as the opening of what was to become *The Hamlet,* where it remained until late in the composition process of that novel, and then later excised the story for submission as a separate short story (*Reading* 55–57). Faulkner's agent, Harold Ober, had the typescript of "Barn Burning" by mid-November 1938, but the story was rejected five times before its acceptance by *Harper's,* which published it in June 1939. Writing to Malcolm Cowley in 1945, Faulkner offered a tantalizing account of the relations of "Barn Burning" to his projected Snopes trilogy: "THE HAMLET was incepted as a novel. When I began it, it produced Spotted Horses, went no further. About two years later suddenly I had THE HOUND, then JAMSHYD'S COURTYARD. . . . Meanwhile, my book had created Snopes and his clan, who produced stories in their saga which are to fall in the later volume: MULE IN THE YARD, BRASS, etc. This over about ten years, until one day I decided I had better start on the first volume or I'd never get any of it down. So I wrote an induction toward the spotted horse story, which included BARN BURNING, and WASH, which I discovered had no place in that book at all" (*SLWF,* 197). The "explanation" raises questions that remain unresolved: which is "my book"? (*Flags in the Dust? Father Abraham?*); did both "Barn Burning" and "Wash" have no place in *The Hamlet,* or just "Wash," and if so why isn't Sarty's story there, either?; and what role could he possibly have envisioned for "Wash" in *The Hamlet,* anyway? We might never have those answers, but the Snopes material offers us evidence both of Faulkner's "indefatigable persistence" in working at his short stories and his willingness—even eagerness—to re-envision his Yoknapatawpha County (Blotner, "Notes" 689). He even at first suggested omitting "Barn Burning" from *Collected Stories,* reasoning to his editor, Robert K. Haas, that the story "was in the first chapter of THE HAMLET, wasn't it?" (*Selected Letters* 274). He later not only reversed this decision, but gave "Barn Burning" the place of first honor in his most important short story collection. The story has had some small life in the popular culture, too, then and now. It won the first O. Henry short story award for the best short story published in 1939 and was adapted for television, airing 17 March 1980 on PBS, directed by Peter Werner and starring Tommy Lee Jones.

"Barn Burning" demonstrates Faulkner's considerable narrative skills, with detailed descriptions of the immediate scenes of the action juxtaposed with subtle and complex manipulations of time and point of view. From the opening line of the story, Sarty Snopes is confronted by his own immediate appetites and the larger social context in which he is situated, and early critics and interpreters of "Barn Burning" and many beginning readers have focused their attention primarily or exclusively on him and his ethical dilemma. Interestingly, the first major overview of Faulkner's work, George Marion O'Donnell's "Faulkner's Mythology," appeared in the *Kenyon Review* in the summer of 1939, just as "Barn Burning" made its debut in *Harper's*. In his essay, O'Donnell distinguished between the Sartorises and the Snopeses, "whatever the family names may be": "The Sartorises act traditionally; that is to say, they act always with an ethically responsible will. They represent vital morality, humanism." The Snopeses, he continues, "do not recognize this point of view; acting only for self-interest, they acknowledge no ethical duty. Really, then, they are amoral; they represent naturalism or animalism" (83). In "Barn Burning," however, Faulkner has already gone beyond the somewhat simplistic dualism that O'Donnell posits. In "Barn Burning," De Spain acts in self-interest as much as Abner Snopes does; and in recent years, some readers have highlighted the story's presentation of the harsh and archaic economic system that produced Abner Snopes and his bitterness and destructiveness. As John T. Matthews puts it, "Ab understands his economic situation as a tenant farmer to be a straightforward case of class disadvantage" (172); but, he continues, "Barn Burning" appears at the time that wage labor and mechanization were ending the system of sharecropping: although "Sarty is just old enough to inherit the legacy of hostility between rednecks and aristocrats," he intuits that "blackmail and revenge, based on an ethos of clan and individual dignity," are "irrelevant to the future" (173). Other contemporary critics keep Sarty center stage. Edmond Volpe says that the story "is not really concerned with class conflict," but is "centered on upon Sarty's emotional dilemma" (233). Joseph Blotner identifies Sarty as "by any standards an abused child" but notes that "there is hope for him, too, at the end," presumably because he has taken action to dissociate himself from his father ("Children" 87). Karl Zender argues that "Barn Burning" is more than a simple validation of Sarty's Oedipal act of dissociation from his father. By "emphasizing the social and economic sources of Ab's anger," Zender and others "tend to question the ideological sophistication and ethical correctness of Sarty's rebellion" (Hamblin and Peek 28, 29). Finally, locating a telling detail in this story full of the same, James Ferguson notes Sarty's final "stiff" walking and quite rightly calls it "one of the master touches of this extraordinary story" because it echoes the repeated descriptions of Abner Snopes's "stiff" gait. He concludes that "this suggestion of Sarty's heritage, of his blood ties, carrying with it the implication that there is something in him that must always be loyal to Abner Snopes, is one of the most moving moments in all of Faulkner's work" (138). And perhaps Faulkner himself invited such readings from the beginning, by giving his central character the name—whether oxymoron, amalgam, or synthesis—"Colonel Sartoris Snopes."

3:TITLE **Barn Burning** Barn burning was (and is) a serious offense in a farming community, since a barn provides not only protection and shelter for a farmer's animals, but storage for feed, corn, hay, tools, and implements needed for farming. Also, at story's end, there is a barn in the process of burning.

3:1–2 **The store in which the Justice of the Peace's court was sitting** A Justice of the Peace is a minor court official in charge of civil actions at the local level; the fact that this trial takes place in the town's general store indicates that the small town has no courthouse. The informality of the "courtroom" does not mean that the proceedings are frivolous or the results nonbinding.

3:2 **nail keg** large barrel used to hold nails, sold either by the pound or penny's worth

3:6–7 **the lettering which meant nothing to his mind** Sarty is either illiterate or in such a state of anxiety that he can't read. See also 8:32–34.

3:7–8 **the scarlet devils and the silver curve of fish** the logos from different Underwood products: deviled ham and canned mackerel or sardines. The Underwood company was granted a patent on its red "devil" logo in 1870 after decades of producing canned foods:

"Advertising showing the little red devil began to appear nationally as early as 1895. Today, the Underwood devil is the oldest existing trademark still in use in the United States" ("Underwood History"). This timing, with the reference to Abner's war wound of "thirty years ago" (5:25) would date the story at 1895. According to Hugh Ruppersburg, "sardines, sold in small flat tins, were considered a delicacy by rural Americans [during this time]—about the only delicacy inexpensive enough for many of them to be acquainted with" (21–22).

3:15 ***ourn! Mine and hisn*** ours; mine and his

4:2 **dollar pound fee** "a fee of one dollar which the owner of any strayed livestock must pay to the person who takes up the animal and returns it to him" (Brown 155)

4:3–4 **He was a strange nigger** a black person not known by the white members of the community

4:24 **his black Sunday coat donned not for the trial but for the moving** Christine Ammer explains "Sunday" clothes as "one's finest clothes, as in *They were all in their Sunday best for the photographer.* This expression alludes to reserving one's best clothes for going to church; indeed, an older idiom is *Sunday-go-to-meeting clothes* (*meeting* here meaning "prayer meeting") [Mid-1800s]" (625). Abner, however, has no respect for the court; he has made plans to move no matter what the verdict and wears his best coat for that alone.

4:28 **Colonel Sartoris Snopes** The Snopes family has a great many interesting and often telling names. Sarty has been named after one of the Confederate heroes of Faulkner's Jefferson, Colonel John Sartoris—a member of the class that Sarty chooses to protect at the end of the story.

4:30 **anybody named for Colonel Sartoris** see 4:28

5:4–7 **it was as if he had swung outward at the end of a grape vine, over a ravine, and at the top of the swing had been caught in a prolonged instant of mesmerized gravity, weightless in time** As Calvin Brown explains, "The vines of the WILD GRAPE are the regular improvised swings of country children and the improvised ropes of adults" (94); this is a brilliantly literal metaphor for the suspense that Sarty feels at the moment that might put him on the witness stand against his father.

5:23–24 **a Confederate provost's man's musket ball** A provost during the Civil War was in charge of detachments of military police and assigned to stop pillage, among other things; Brown explains that in Faulkner's South a musket was a "a smooth-bore gun with a very long barrel, used primarily for military purposes" (135). Abner was shot as he fled (probably in the act of pillage) by a minor officer and fellow Confederate soldier.

5:25 **thirty years ago** evidence to set the story in 1895 (see 3:7–8)

6:1 **half again his size** one and a half times bigger than Sarty

6:7 **the wagon** "In spite of superficial variations, farm wagons are basically much alike. The usual one is the two-mule wagon, with a TONGUE that extends forward between the mules and is attached to the pivoted front axle for steering. The running gear consists of the tongue and wheels and the framework that holds them together. The wheels have wooden spokes joined to a projecting metal-bound hub at the center and to a wooden rim. Outside this rim there is a flat iron tire. A loose tire is fixed by driving into a creek or pond so that the wood of the rim swells inside the tire. . . . On the running gear is the wagon bed, or wagon box. Strictly speaking, the bed is merely a platform, and the box is this platform with vertical sides attached to it, but the box is often loosely called the bed, or wagon bed. There are normally no springs in the running gear or between it and the bed. The seat, however, is as wide as the wagon box and is mounted on springs on the edges of the box" (Brown 209–10).

6:8 **a grove of locusts and mulberries** Locusts are fast growing trees that can thrive in poor soil and can tolerate drought. Although not considered trash trees, locusts reach their mature height in as few as 20 years and may start declining in as early as 40 years. Similarly, mulberries grow quickly and do well in "areas with long hot summers or extended droughts" (Crockett, *Trees* 128).

6:9 **Sunday dresses** see 4:24

6:10 **calico and sunbonnets** in their working clothes; calico is a type of cotton cloth, coarser than muslin, and sunbonnets are hats with projecting bills and "a flap [behind] to protect the back of the neck, worn by women as a protection against the sun" (Brown 193)

6:22 **the tail-gate** "the removable plank forming the back of a wagon box" (Brown 196)

6:24 **the peeled willow** a willow branch from which Ab has removed the bark and is using as a whip

6:26–27 **over-run the engine** rev up the engine while it's still in neutral gear; see 15:24–28

6:31–32 ***Maybe he's done satisfied now, now that he has*** **. . . stopping himself, not to say it aloud even to himself** has burned the barn

7:7–16 **Likely his father had already arranged to make a crop on another farm before he . . . Again he had to stop himself** see 6:31–32

7:17–18 **a grove of oaks and beeches where a spring ran** Faulkner has moved the Snopeses into a grove of nice trees, the quality and longevity of which may indicate that the land on which they camp belongs to an established landowner. As their name implies, water oaks grow near streams; the life spans of live oaks, which also do well in moist soil, are "measured in centuries" (Crockett, *Trees* 139). Likewise, beech trees of the American variety are large, slow-growing, and, as Brown puts it, "similar to the European beech" but with "larger and more sharply serrated leaves and lighter-colored bark, and grows over twice as high (up to 100′). Beeches tend to grow just at the junction of hills and creek bottoms, and since they seek out underground water, springs frequently flow from under their roots" (27).

7:18–19 **they had a fire against it, of a rail lifted from a nearby fence** further evidence that they camp on someone else's well-kept land (see 7:17–18). Brown explains that "fence rail is normally about 10′ long and 2″–4″ in diameter, though the accidents of the grain and splitting make the cross-section almost any conceivable shape" (158–159). Although Abner and his family are camped in a grove of trees, they don't pick up any fallen timber or dry wood for their fire; they damage someone's property instead.

7:22–23 **Older, the boy might have remarked on this and wondered** one of several points in the story at which Faulkner highlights the limitations in Sarty's understanding that exist solely because of his youth

7:27 **Then he might have gone a step farther** see 7:22–23

7:29–31 **those four years in the woods hiding from all men, blue or gray, with his strings of horses (captured horses, he called them)** During the Civil War, Abner stole horses from both the Union (blue) and Confederate (gray) armies and sold them to whoever might be willing to pay for them. As a renegade, eventually shot by a member of his own army (see 5:23–24), he would have been wanted by both sides, a fact which necessitated his hiding in the woods at night.

7:31–32 **And older still, he might have divined the true reason** see 7:22–23; an older Sarty could look back on his father's actions and understand that his use of fire stemmed from the great respect that he felt for it as a weapon, as a sniper might regard his gun—or a writer his words.

8:11–12 **a frockcoat which had not been made for him** "a knee-length, double-breasted dress coat" (Brown 86) that he has either bought secondhand or received as a hand-me-down

8:19–22 **You're getting to be a man. You got to learn. You got to learn to stick to your own blood or you ain't going to have any blood to stick to you** Abner's central lesson on adulthood and manhood for his son

8:22–23 **Do you think either of them, any man there this morning, would?** **either of them** = the Justice of the Peace and Mr. Harris

8:23–25 **Don't you know all they wanted was a chance to get at me because they knew I had them beat? Eh?** apparently the question that Sarty answers at 8:29

8:25 **Later, twenty years later, he was to tell himself, "If I had said they wanted only the truth, justice, he would have hit me again." But now he said nothing. He was not crying. He just stood there. "Answer me," his father said** an indication of how traumatic and life-changing this episode was in Sarty's life, since he recalls it and mulls it over after twenty years

8:29 **Yes** Sarty's answer to his father's question at 8:23–25

8:32–34 **a paintless two-room house identical almost with the dozen others it had stopped before even in the boy's ten years** As Brown explains, this is a "'dog-trot cabin,' consisting of two rooms with an open breezeway between them" (176; see also Newton 498–99). Moving at least twelve times in ten years would mean that the Snopeses move, on average, every ten months, which is a bit more often than was common in the sharecropping system: "With a great surplus of unskilled labor at hand, planters usually felt little need to hold dissatisfied or unwanted tenants. Most landless farmers were highly mobile, moving as often as every year or two. This transience was socially and economically wasteful; it deprived tenants of any role in their communities and reinforced illiteracy by preventing regular schooling of their children" (Mertz 31).

9:5 **fit it will and you'll hog it and like it** Abner's only advice to his daughters, an order to take whatever he provides them

9:18 **Abner** Sarty's father named for the first time

9:21–23 **I reckon I'll have a word with the man that aims to begin tomorrow owning me body and soul for the next eight months** Abner Snopes is a sharecropper, a tenant who pays his rent with part of the crop he makes rather than cash: "The landlord often provides seeds, stock, and equipment in return for a fixed proportion of the output. Share-cropping usually shows low yields in comparison with owner-occupied farms or cash tenancies since the incentives are less. In the United States, share-cropping replaced the plantation system after the Civil War. . . . Economic control was maintained by creating a class of landless tenants, by keeping the 'share' retained at subsistence level, and by encouraging indebtedness through company stores; social control took the form of segregation, violence, and paternalism" (*Oxford Reference Online: A Dictionary of Geography*; also Brown 173–74). In 1890, Mississippi had a tenancy rate of 62.4% (Mertz 30). Abner's contract with Major de Spain should be over in January of the next year (eight months from May). See also 16:8–11 and 19:6–7.

9:29–34 **divulging nothing to him save the terrible handicap of being young, the light weight of his few years, just heavy enough to prevent his soaring free of the world as it seemed to be ordered but not heavy enough to keep him footed solid in it, to resist it and try to change the course of its events** another evocation of Sarty's youth and its limited perspective

10:1 **oaks and cedars** see 7:17; as Crockett explains, "Many unrelated trees are called cedars, usually because of their aromatic wood, but only five are true cedars and only three grow in the United States" (*Trees* 91), and all in north Mississippi.

10:2 **the other flowering trees and shrubs** probably crepe myrtle among them; a landscaped yard—the owners have enough money to plant and care for ornamental vegetation

10:4 **honeysuckle and Cherokee roses** Honeysuckle is "a Japanese vine (*Lonicera japonica*), evergreen, bearing tubular white flowers with an almost oppressive fragrance in the spring. It has run wild and become a great nuisance, forming dense thickets, overrunning trees, etc." (Brown 105); a Cherokee rose is "a climbing rose (*Rosa laevigata*) with simple white flowers about 3″ across. The savage thorns plus the fact that there are no long stems make it 'unpickable,' but it has a delicate fragrance and is not 'scentless.' In spite of its name, it is a native of China, but it had been taken across Asia and then (by the Arabs) across Africa and into Spain, and to the southeastern part of this country by the Spaniards, so that the English colonists found it growing [in Mississippi] as a wild plant" (Brown 50).

10:13–16 ***Hit's big as a courthouse* he thought quietly, with a surge of peace and joy whose reason he could not have thought into words, being too young for that: *They are safe from him*** Sarty, who is not "safe from" Abner, immediately associates the big house with impunity from his father; the events of the story show that it and the people who live there are no safer than Sarty is.

10:30 **the stiff foot** the foot in which he was shot during the war

10:33 **it ebbed** Sarty's feeling that the house and its inhabitants are safe from his father and the threat of fire; see 10:21–22

11:3 **ravening and jealous rage** see 12:22–24

11:14–15 **friction-glazed greenish cast** from lack of brushing and proper care, perhaps including ironing while it is dirty

11:19 **a linen jacket** The servant is better dressed than Abner; see 12:31.

11:20 **fo** before

11:21 **Major** first mention of the landowner for whom Abner will be working—Major de Spain

11:22 **nigger** Abner insists on his superiority to everyone else—his family, black people, his employers, other sharecropping farmers—and is ruthless in his methods, as the episode of the rug demonstrates.

11:28–29 **Miss Lula!** According to Brown, "miss" is "a title with various special uses when employed with the given name rather than the surname. It is used by servants for the daughters of their employers. It is a general term of respect from younger to older, and since the given name does not change with marriage, it continues to be applied to married women" (129). Here, of course, it marks racial difference, too.

11:33 **a lady** In Faulkner's South, the term carries racial as well as class and gender connotations. A "lady" was by definition white, and the protection of her honor by (white) gentlemen a trap for both races and sexes.

12:22–24 **"Pretty and white, ain't it?" he said. "That's sweat. Nigger sweat. Maybe it ain't white enough yet to suit him. Maybe he wants to mix some white sweat with it"** Abner understands the socioeconomic structure of his country very well; it fills him with the "ravening and jealous rage" at 11:3.

12:31 **the linen-clad man on a fine sorrel mare** Major de Spain, wearing better fabric than Abner's family and better mounted as well

12:33–34 **the Negro youth following on a fat bay carriage horse** Even riding horses that usually pull carriages, De Spain's servants have better mounts than Abner's family.

13:2 **the two tilted chairs** Abner and the older son are not working; they are leaning back in two chairs watching Sarty chop wood while Sarty's mother and aunt prepare dinner.

13:6 **shout one of the sisters' names** We only learn one of them: Net (22:34).

13:10–11 **the wash pot** Brown describes this as a large rounded pot with short legs that could be set on "bricks or stones to raise the pot far enough off the ground so that a fire can be built under it. These pots are used not only for washing but for various other purposes, especially for scalding the carcasses when hogs are killed" (211).

13:32–33 **the harsh homemade lye** strong, highly corrosive alkaline solution used for washing; Brown says it was "made from leaching wood ashes with water. This process gives a strong alkaline solution, and there is no control over its exact strength or chemical composition" (105).

14:7 **the whippoorwills** As Brown says, this bird is "not the true whippoorwill" but "a nocturnal goatsucker seldom seen, but the cry of which its name is an imitation is constantly heard at dusk in the spring and early summer" (214).

14:13–16 **The tracks of his father's foot were gone. Where they had been were now long, water-cloudy scoriations resembling the sporadic course of a lilliputian mowing machine** The scrubbing with lye and the piece of field stone (14:4) have removed the horse droppings at the expense of the nap and pattern of the rug. The invocation of Swift's Lilliput has an interesting echo at 24:33–25:2.

14:19–21 **the two rooms, his mother in one bed, where his father would later lie, the older brother in the other, himself, the aunt, and the two sisters on pallets on the floor** This is another clear instance of the way patriarchy works in this family: the oldest son gets a bed while the aunt must sleep on the floor with the children.

15:20 **kin** can

15:24 **horse block** a platform used for getting on or off a horse (Brown 106)

15:24–25 **he doubled the reins over and slashed the mule across the neck** He has taken the reins together in one hand and hit the mule to hurry it along, but see 15:27–28.

15:27–28 **the hard, knotted hand jerking the mule back to a walk** He then with the other hand immediately pulls either the base of the reins or the mule's mane to make it stop. These are the same competing and contradictory impulses described at 6:26–27.

15:31–32 **collarless and even bareheaded** Major de Spain has left the house in such a hurry that he hasn't put on his shirt collar, which at the time was detachable from the shirt, or his hat; he must have just discovered the ruined rug on the porch.

16:1 **hame** A hame attaches the horse's collar to the traces that allow it to pull something—a plow, in this case—and the hame strings hold the hames together at the top and bottom of the collar. Abner must be fastening the lower hame string or else the lower part of the hame to its trace (see Brown 98).

16:3–4 **Wasn't there anybody here, any of your women . . .** "who could have washed it properly?" De Spain and Snopes might be separated by economic status, but they share an unquestioning allegiance to patriarchy.

16:8–11 **So I'm going to charge you twenty bushels of corn against your crop. I'll add it in your contract and when you come to the**

commissary you can sign it A commissary was the general store on a plantation frequented by its tenants (Brown 37); the most famous one in Faulkner's fiction is the McCaslins' in *Go Down, Moses.* As a sharecropper, Abner has already agreed to turn over a certain amount of his crop as rent; de Spain arbitrarily decides on a penalty of twenty extra bushels to pay for the damaged rug. In effect, he tells Abner that he will agree to this penalty whether he likes it or not. See 9:21–23.

16:16 **adjusting the logger-head in the hame** the U-shaped hook that attaches the hame (16:1) to the traces (Brown 122)

16:23 **I kin watch . . .** to make sure no one takes it

16:24 **the cutter** actually the colter, the blade ahead of the plow share, which makes a vertical cut to be followed by the horizontal cut of the share itself, thus clearing the way for it (see Brown 66)

16:24 **that straight stock** the plow stock; the "basic frame of a plow" (Brown 151)

16:33–34 **the half-size axe** "a boy's axe, a standard implement used both to teach a boy to use an axe and to let him cut wood effectively long before he can wield a man-sized axe" (Brown 97)

17:3–4 **the shoat and the cow which were a part of his father's contract with the landlord** De Spain has provided the Snopes family with two animals as part of their sharecropping arrangement. The shoat (a young weaned pig) could be fattened up over the course of the summer and slaughtered in the winter to provide meat for the family; the cow would provide milk year-round, which could be drunk, used for cooking, or consumed otherwise as cream, butter, buttermilk, or cheese.

17:7 **middle buster** Brown specifies this as a "middle-breaker, a shallow plow that throws earth to both sides, used to bank earth from the MIDDLES between the rows against the cotton plants, after they have attained a fair size" (128). Brown's definition implies that Sarty and his brother are working on a field that has already been plowed and planted by someone else.

17:9 **the rich black soil** alluvial soil (Brown 31)

17:13–14 ***what he used to be*** a barn burner

17:18 ***the being pulled two ways like between two teams of horses*** Sarty's divided allegiance to his father and to the security represented by De Spain's house

17:22 **The wagon gear** "the gear used to harness a mule to a wagon, as opposed to the plow gear mentioned two pages earlier" (Brown 210)

17:23 **the wagon bed** see 6:7

17:25–27 **the weathered paintless store with its tattered tobacco- and patent-medicine posters and the tethered wagons and saddle animals below the gallery** Patent medicines are not pharmaceuticals but commercial endeavors, so these posters are advertisements, and the people have gathered for another trial like the one that opens the story.

17:28 **gnawed steps** worn or chewed up, perhaps by the tethered animals, or simply worn by customers' feet

17:33–34 **the man in collar and cravat now** Major de Spain, in the attire expected of him

18:5–6 **He ain't done it! He ain't burnt . . .** he hasn't burned the barn

18:31–19:3 **October corn will be worth about fifty cents. I figure that if Major de Spain can stand a ninety-five dollar loss on something he paid cash for, you can stand a five-dollar loss you haven't earned yet. I hold you in damages to Major de Spain to the amount of ten bushels of corn over and above your contract with him, to be paid to him out of your crop at gathering time** See 9:21–23, 16:8–11, and 19:6–7. The Justice of the Peace cuts in half the amount that De Spain wanted, but Abner has won the real victory here—robbing De Spain of his omnipotence on his own land.

19:6–7 **since they were late, far behind all other farmers** they had started planting late in the season; early corn should have been planted in the beginning of March. As Crockett explains, "Oldtimers used to say, 'Plant corn when the leaves on the oak trees are as big as a mouse's ear.' This advice is still accurate, since oak leaves generally become that big soon after the last spring frost" (*Vegetables and Fruits* 91–92). If the corn crop was planted in mid-May, it would be ready at the middle to end of August.

19:13 **We'll . . .** very likely the beginning of a repetition of what Sarty said in response to De Spain's first fine at 16:23: "We'll gether hit and hide hit! I kin watch. . ."

19:17 **Well, we'll wait till October anyway** Ab doesn't let on to Sarty that he's already thinking about burning down de Spain's barn, but why he mentions October is unclear. October could be the very end of the growing season for corn and the last chance to sell it in large quantities, most likely to be dried and used for animal feed in the winter.

19:18–19 **The matter of the wagon—the setting of a spoke or two and the tightening of the tires—did not take long either, the business of the tires accomplished by driving the wagon into the spring branch behind the shop and letting it stand there** see 6:7

19:24–25 **the slow hammer** of the blacksmith as he works in his shed

19:25–26 **an upended cypress bolt** "a piece of log, cut off square at both ends, for splitting into shingles, etc. A shingle-length bolt makes a convenient seat" (Brown 34).

19:32–33 **the ammoniac dust and hoof-parings and scales of rust** ammoniac because of the urine scent of the horses; hoof-parings (rather like nail clippings) from the process of shoeing them; scales of rust from the tools, the forge, and perhaps even the building itself

19:33–20:2 **his father tell a long and unhurried story out of the time before the birth of the older brother even when he had been a professional horsetrader** If Abner is not lying about this former profession, then he could be making ironic reference to his wartime experience described at 6:28–30.

20:4–6 **the scarlet horses, the incredible poisings and convolutions of tulle and tights and the painted leers of comedians** Sarty has something of Huck Finn's astonishment in the face of the spectacle of a circus.

20:10 **a segment of cheese** Stores at this time would have bought cheese in large wheels with a hardened rind; pieces of cheese could be cut off the wheel and sold to individuals by the penny's worth. Abner is making a holiday for himself and his sons.

20:14–15 **they drank from a tin dipper tepid water smelling of the cedar bucket and of living beech trees** see 7:17

20:16 **a horse lot** a pen where horses are traded (see Brown 106)

20:17 **rail fence** see 7:18–19

20:18–19 **walked and trotted and then cantered** three speeds for horses; a kind of horse test drive

20:20 **the slow swapping and buying** intricate bargaining involved in horsetrading

20:30–31 **saw the altered light through the door where a candle stub now burned in a bottle neck** Abner has taken the kerosene from the lamp and replaced the lamp with a candle.

20:32 **still in the hat and coat** dressed to go out, not to go to bed

20:32–34 **at once formal and burlesque as though dressed carefully for some shabby and ceremonial violence** a reminder of Abner's reverence for fire: 7:22–8:3

20:34 **the reservoir of the lamp** the lower part of a kerosene lamp that contains the oil, which is then wicked upward into the burner

21:11 **"What . . ." he cried. "What are you . . ."** are you doing? going to do?

21:18 **it** the blood he has inherited from his father

21:21 **sploshing** onomatopoeic "blend of *splash* and *slosh*" (Brown 185)

22:13 **Lennie** Sarty's mother

22:30 **Lizzie** Sarty's aunt, his mother's sister (see 22:13)

22:34 **Net** one of Sarty's twin sisters

23:9–11 **the pale ribbon unspooling with terrific slowness** the road

23:25–26 **the entire sleeve, rotten with washing, carried away** The "harsh homemade lye" (13:32–33) that Abner uses to clean Major de Spain's rug is likely the same soap that Sarty's mother uses to wash the family's laundry. Sarty's shirt has been washed so often in this soap that it is literally "rotten with washing," a nice example of Faulknerian paradox and irony.

23:31 **the park** an enclosed piece of land, in this instance by a "vine-massed fence" (23:32), at an estate, used for recreation

23:33 **he dared not risk it** Sarty does not know the terrain in the park, so he sticks to the road he knows to try to find his father.

24:8 **early summer night sky** May is technically late spring, since the summer solstice occurs on June 21; see 25:21.

24:10 **stained abruptly and violently upward** the silhouette of De Spain and his horse

24:10–11 **a long, swirling roar incredible and soundless, blotting the stars** again, the silhouette of De Spain and his horse

24:13–14 **the shot and, an instant later, two shots** shots fired at Abner and Sarty's brother

24:18 **at the glare** from the burning barn

24:23 **But there was no glare behind him now** Sarty has outrun the sight of the burning barn.

24:32 **Colonel Sartoris'** Sarty's namesake (see 4:28)

24:33–25:2 **a private in the fine old European sense, wearing no uniform, admitting the authority of and giving fidelity to no man or army or flag, going to war as Malbrouck himself did: for booty** Malbrouck was John Churchill (1650–1722), the First Duke of Marlborough, known for embezzlement and taking bribes, whom Jonathan Swift had publicly criticized for greed. Swift's broadside *The Conduct of the Allies* (November 1711) "charged that the Whigs had prolonged the War of the Spanish Succession (1701–1714) out of self-interest. The pamphlet was instrumental in procuring the dismissal of John Churchill, 1st Duke of Marlborough, the commander in chief of the British armies" (see "Swift, Jonathan"). Upon his death, Swift wrote "A Satirical Elegy on the Death of a Late Famous General" (1722), which concludes: "Let pride be taught by this rebuke,/How very mean a thing's a duke;/From all his ill-got honours flung,/Turned to that dirt from which he sprung" (Swift, "A Satirical Elegy"). Given the allusion to Swift at 14:13–16, we think this is the context of the Malbrouck Faulkner had in mind. The perversion "Malbrouck" comes from a French nursery song dating from the eighteenth century popular throughout Europe, "*Malbrouck s'en va-t-en guerre,*" or "Malbrouck Goes Off to the War," sung to the tune we know as "For He's a Jolly Good Fellow." (See "John Churchill.")

25:4 **his own** spoils taken from the troops he should be fighting alongside

25:12–13 **the dark trees below him, constant and inflectioned and ceaseless** the activity of the whippoorwills

25:20 **quiring** from *choir, quire*: "to resound, as music sung by a choir" (*OED* online)

25:21 **the late spring night** perhaps a correction to the "early summer night sky" at 24:8

25:21 **He did not look back** The finality of the line underscores the importance of this episode in Sarty's life; it marks the destruction of his family, whether or not his father and brother were killed, and sets him on the road to an uncertain future. Yet 8:25 tells us that Sarty would relive the incident "twenty years later," so his adult self obviously locates its identity in the events of this story.

"Shingles for the Lord"

Res Grier of "Shingles for the Lord" is one of Faulkner's great comic overreachers. His complicated efforts to outsmart "Mr. Solon Work-Unit Quick" of half a dog result in spectacularly catastrophic consequences for himself and his community—indeed, for everyone except the dog—yet by story's end we know that all will be well in this small corner of Yoknapatawpha. Not so much a trickster tricked as a trickster tripped mid-trick, Res maneuvers the central situation in the story entirely to his advantage. His son, the young first-person narrator, records the progress of his father's scheme without knowing exactly what he's up to; consequently, his own shock and surprise at finding himself suspended over a burning church so that his father can beat a man in a deal registers equally with us, the bemused readers. As James Ferguson reminds us, the story is one of Faulkner's "swindle stories" that reflects its writer's love of "the kind of complexity that we associate with games, stratagems, tricks, reversals, puzzles, or surprises" (136). "Shingles for the Lord" has each one of those elements, and Joseph Urgo observes that it also "concerns the changing understanding of work and its relation to personal profit and community service, as well as the relationship of grace and works" ("Shingles" 351). If comedy, as James Thurber said, is "emotional chaos recollected in tranquility," then this little boy's rendering of a single eventful day is surely one of Faulkner's masterpieces in the comic tradition.

"Shingles for the Lord" has not often been approached as an autonomous story. Rather, it has been read, with "Two Soldiers" and "Shall Not Perish," as merely the funny one of Faulkner's three tales of the Grier family; as an encomium to the yeoman farmers of Yoknapatawpha County; and as a trivial coda to "Barn Burning." Readers have noted

Faulkner's adaptation of the tall tale and his uses of the traditions and conventions of Southwestern humor, and the story has interested some readers principally because it shares characters with several other Faulkner texts. A Reverend Whitfield appears in *As I Lay Dying* (1930), and the names of Armstid, Bookwright, Quick, Snopes, Tull, and Varner suggest *The Hamlet* (1940), while another Res (a Snopes this time, Orestes) appears in *The Mansion* (1959). Res Grier, however, comes in for some rather harsh criticism, and not just from Reverend Whitfield. "The narrator," says Hans H. Skei, "and the implied author—may pity him, but there is no doubt that Res Grier's hard luck is a result of his bad planning, his lack of discipline, and his impatience" (*The Novelist* 271–72). Grier, Lisa Paddock maintains, "is up against not only what Faulkner saw as the escapist logic of the WPA, but also the force of the community, which is symbolically represented by the church." Although Grier "recognizes the authority of the Church, he conflates its demands with those he feels are wrongly imposed upon him by the WPA-inspired wrangling of the aptly-named Quick" (140–41). John Longley concludes that Grier finally comes to feel "that his manhood or his self-respect or something demands that he somehow redress the balance of things and, if possible, come out ahead of the others in some dramatic and startling fashion" (121). Other readers have examined the cultural significance of the story. John T. Matthews, for example, reads the story as one of those in which "Faulkner's commercial fiction absorbs and formalizes the problems confronting the author in the modern marketplace" ("Faulkner's Stories" 223). "Shingles for the Lord," he says, illustrates the conflicts generated when modern ideas about the commodification of labor are juxtaposed with "work for the Lord," which, "perhaps like the work of the mind, however, expects exemption from the laws of the labor market." "In a story that superficially appears uncomplicated in its opposition to the modernization represented by the New Deal," he concludes, "we can detect Faulkner's usual critical intelligence, an intelligence so constitutive of the great works bracketing these years, that [it] would be harder believing its absence than granting its presence" (225, 227). Charles Reagan Wilson looks away from commerce to praise the story for its "marvelous evocation of the landscape and spirit of Southern rural folk religion" ("William Faulkner" 36). Citing the Grier boy's warm tribute to his church—"there was something that even that fire hadn't even touched" (*CS* 42)—he notes that "without describing any worship service Faulkner conveys the spiritual significance of this small institution to its people" (37).

"Shingles for the Lord" was written early in the summer of 1942 and received by Faulkner's agent, Harold Ober, on 17 July of that year; it appeared in *The Saturday Evening Post* on 13 February 1943, after considerable minor revision by the magazine's editors. In 1948, Faulkner agreed with Robert K. Haas that it should be included in *Collected Stories*; but he asked for an opportunity to revise the text, principally, as it turned out, to address such details as the spelling of "froe," "fyce," and "modern." He placed the story second in "The Village," the opening section of the volume, thus juxtaposing it most immediately with "Barn Burning." Some critics have read the parallels and differences between the two stories to the detriment of the later one, belittling or dismissing its humor and its comic achievement. Faulkner and his editors valued it highly, however; Commins chose it for inclusion in *The Faulkner Reader* (1954), and Faulkner readily assented. At the time of the publication of *Collected Stories,* Faulkner mentioned the story specifically in praising his editors for proposing the collection, which he had originally resisted: "You and Don [Klopfer] were both right about the collection and I was wrong," he wrote Saxe Commins. "It's all right; the stuff stands up amazingly well after a few years, 10 and 20. I had forgotten a lot of it; I spent a whole evening laughing to myself about the mules and the shingles" (*Selected Letters* 304). Whatever it implies about character, cultural forces, and modern life, "Shingles for the Lord" asks us first and foremost to join Faulkner in the laughing.

27:2–3 **borrow the froe and maul** Pap (Res Grier; see 36:16 and 40:25) either does not have or will not save enough money to buy his own tools. **froe** = cleaving tool used for splitting shingles from a block of wood. It has a heavy blade and handle set at right angles to one another, like the letter L. **maul** = heavy, long-handled hammer used to drive stakes, wedges, etc.

27:6 **in a lather** ridden so hard that it is covered with heavy sweat

27:6 **thumps** technically, synchronous diaphragmatic flutter, a condition in horses in which the diaphragm and heart contract at the same time. Thumps occur in heavily sweating horses and indicate an electrolyte imbalance.

27:7 **fox hunting** According to Calvin Brown, "Mississippi fox hunting is essentially a spectator sport. It is done at night, and the participants may ride horses from place to place trying to intercept the pursuit, but usually they simply build a fire on a commanding hilltop and stay by it with a jug of whiskey. In either case, their principal pleasure is in following the chase by ear and admiring the 'music' of the hounds. . . . In Virginia, fox hunters ride to hounds in the English manner" (85–86).

27:12 **ear trumpet** A form of hearing aid dating to prehistoric times, an ear trumpet is a funnel with its small end held inside the user's ear and its large end held toward the source of sound. In light of Killegrew's deafness and the nature of Mississippi fox hunting (see 27:7–11), Res implies that Killegrew is wasting everybody's time and not just his own.

27:14 **board tree** a tree harvested to be cut into boards or shingles (see Brown 34)

27:18 **dinner bucket** the chief meal of the day, eaten at noontime and carried to fields and work sites in a pail

27:19 **wedges** tapered pieces of wood or metal, used either to split material or to brace two surfaces

27:22 **upended cuts** pieces of cut logs set up as makeshift chairs

27:23 **boiled shirt** Probably white, a shirt cleaned by dropping it into a pot of boiling water and lye soap and stirring it with a stick, a highly labor-intensive process. Poor men and farmers would not have worn such clothing for everyday work.

28:5–7 **And naturally, the cook wasn't going to lend none of Killegrew's tools out, and Mrs. Killegrew was worser deaf than even Killegrew** Res could be deliberately sarcastic here, or the passage could reflect a race and class reality: as a servant, perhaps a black one, the cook would not have the authority to lend the tools out; and Mrs. Killegrew couldn't hear well enough to ask her in her husband's absence.

28:22 **owns** Whitfield views God as a property owner, and people on earth much like his crops.

28:23 **mizzling** "muddled, confused" (Brown 130)

28:27 **I Godfrey** an oath, euphemism for "by God" (Brown 108)

28:33 **we all taken off our hats except him** Whitfield exempts himself from this gesture of respect.

29:3 **split out** come loose from the log without getting tangled in the other shingles

29:13–14 **Then I seen that Homer was whittling on a stick** Homer's whittling indicates that he has been deliberately idle in Res's absence.

29:22 **work units** Here begins another of Faulkner's math and gambling games. Solon here posits an equation between work time and arbitrary value that Res accepts and tries to manipulate—both to his advantage and to beat Solon at his own game.

29:23 **WPA** The Works Progress Administration, approved by Franklin D. Roosevelt and signed into law in 1935, stipulated that "WPA jobs . . . are designed to provide employment for needy unemployed workers. Need and employability, therefore, are the two primary—though by no means the only—considerations in determining eligibility" (Howard 269). Howard also reports that "various attempts [were] also made to discourage WPA workers from owning and operating automobiles" (180). Since he would not give up his farm or his homemade schoolbus-truck, Solon was not eligible for WPA support on the grounds of employability.

29:24 **jobs and grub and mattresses** Perhaps a reference to the fact that Congress attempted to pass legislation to make WPA workers unable to cash their paychecks at liquor stores or buy liquor with the money (Howard 179–80). The narrator may be expressing a widely held community view that the WPA, while claiming to finance subsistence living, was really interested in controlling every aspect of the lives of the citizens on its rolls. **Grub**: slang for food

29:26 **twenty-two miles in to town** the distance from Jefferson, the county seat

30:5 **two units of twelve three-unit hours** Solon argues that he, Homer, and Res are each one "unit," each responsible for twelve hours of work on the new roof. See 29:22.

30:11 **modren** modern, either a regionalism or a deliberate mocking of Solon

30:23–24 **highway juke joint** a casual, inexpensive bar (perhaps a brothel as well) featuring music, live or recorded and available on a jukebox, food, and drinks

31:1–5 **There's six units left over. Six one-man-hour units. Maybe you can work twice as fast as me and Homer put together and finish them in four hours, but I don't believe you can work three times as fast and finish in two** Three men could have done six units of work in two hours, but now the work will have to be done in six hours by one man—Res.

31:16 **bolts** wood the correct size to cut into laths, to which the finished shingles will be nailed. In this context, a bolt is also the piece of wood from which shingles are directly split.

31:17 **riving** splitting wood in the direction of the grain

31:25 **rove** past tense of **riving**; see 31:17

31:30 **helve eye** The helve is the handle of a weapon or tool; the helve eye is a hole or opening in the wide end of the head (the blade) to admit the handle to be inserted. In Book XXI of Homer's *Odyssey*, Penelope devises a test for the suitors that requires them to string Odysseus's massive bow and shoot an arrow straight through the helve eyes of twelve axe blades in a row.

32:24 **a considerable** a considerable amount

32:26 **hant** regionalized spelling of "haunt"; a ghost

32:29 **treed** taken refuge in a tree while being hunted. Once he trees his prey, a hunter can shine his light up into the tree and spot it by looking for the light reflected in its eyes.

33:11 **fyce** small, worthless dog, usually a mongrel

34:17 **farm bell** Because clocks and watches were rather expensive during the time and place of this story, the farm bell, either rung hand-held or suspended and struck, was used by someone in the farmhouse to alert workers in the field or barn. The bell might announce dinner, quitting time, or some emergency.

35:13 **snicked** made a short, sharp strike

35:22 **I be dog** "I will be, in expressions like 'I be durn' . . . and 'I be dog'" (Brown 108). Similar to "I'll be dog-gone," which is a euphemism for "I'll be damned."

36:16 **Grier** Pap's last name and the first time he is identified by his proper name in the story; see also 40:25

38:23 **decking** in a roof, "the parallel planks, with spaces between them, which run at right angles to the rafters, and to which the shingles are nailed" (Brown 69)

39:5 **shuck a corn nubbin** A nubbin is usually an imperfect piece of corn, but can also be just a small ear of it; to shuck corn is to remove its husk.

39:20 **overhalls** narrator's pronunciation of "overalls," the one-piece denim work clothing held in place by shoulder straps; favored by farmers and others who perform rigorous labor resulting in head-to-toe grime

39:21 **water barrel** large barrel, usually made of wood, for collecting rainfall and water from other sources and storing it conveniently for later use. Due to the typically low levels of rainfall in northern Mississippi and in the absence of indoor plumbing, a water barrel was a necessity.

39:32 **cold out as a wedge** out cold, or unconscious

40:1 **two fire buckets to the spring** buckets, usually made of wood, reserved for holding water in case of fire, in this instance kept filled from the nearest source of fresh water

40:8 **old colored-picture charts** Brown explains that these were "gaudy illustrations of biblical scenes, etc. of the sort that were widely used for church decorations and Sunday-school prizes" (56).

40:11 **nightshirt** What the narrator compares to a man's sleeping garment is probably a special vestment worn for full-immersion baptism. Elmo Howell long ago noted that this detail was more appropriate to Baptists than to Methodists (see "Faulkner's Country" 208).

40:16 **Archangel Michael** Revelations 12:7–9: Michael is the archangel who battled the devil, in the form of a dragon, in heaven and cast him out.

40:17 **fit** fought

40:25 **Res Grier** Pap's full name

41:3 **all** The Grier, Bookwright, Quick, Armstid, Snopes, and Tull families comprise the church that Whitfield leads. The narrator omits the Killigrews.

42:25–26 **the devil can have the hindmost** a popular proverb originating in the 1608 play *Philaster: Or, Love Lies A-Bleeding* by Francis

Beaumont and John Fletcher, which was published in 1620. It expresses complete self-interest: the devil was said to chase his pupils through the halls of his academy; and he grabs the slowest one to be his imp. (See also Ammer 160.)

42:28 **liniment** medicine applied to the skin in order to ease pain

"The Tall Men"

Faulkner wrote "The Tall Men" early in 1941 with the expressed intention of making money to pay off his back taxes (*Selected Letters* 139). His agent, Harold Ober, received the story on 19 March; the *Saturday Evening Post* bought it in less than a week (Skei, *Short Story Career* 97) and published it on 31 May, only about ten weeks after Faulkner had sent it to Ober—after the first peacetime draft in United States history but before the nation's formal entrance into World War II. Largely forgotten in these days, that location in historical time crucially informs the story's actions and themes. The McCallum twins, Anse and Lucius, have failed to respond to previous notices to register for the draft because the country is not at war, as it was when their ancestors enlisted in the Civil and First World Wars. The story begins as the local deputy marshal, Gombault, an older man, brings the younger state investigator, Pearson, who intends to serve a warrant for Anse's and Lucius's arrest, to the McCallum farm in rural Yoknapatawpha County. By its end, the investigator's preconceptions about country people's behavior and motives have been debunked, if not completely stripped bare.

Various members of the McCallum family had previously figured in *Sartoris/Flags in the Dust* (1929, 1973), *As I Lay Dying* (1930), and *The Hamlet* (1940), and would appear again, at least briefly, in the title story of *Knight's Gambit* (1949), *Intruder in the Dust* (1949), *The Town* (1957), and *The Mansion* (1959). A brief reference to Gavin Stevens invokes the myriad appearances of that ubiquitous character. In fact, a good many discussions of "The Tall Men" center on its relations with other Faulkner texts rather than on the story in its own right. Most who do comment on it have emphasized its patriotic theme and its apparent celebration of the traditional independence, integrity, courage, and stoicism of the McCallum family. Elmo Howell, for example, reads the story as Faulkner's "deliberate attack on the social policies of the New Deal administration": "The McCallum farm is to Faulkner an Arcadian retreat, a country of tall men with clean minds and pure hearts and nature in a state of innocence" ("William Faulkner" 324, 325). In Joseph Blotner's opinion, writing this story allowed Faulkner to make a "sweeping" critique of modernization, "describing the concomitant weakening he saw in the moral fiber of the descendants of once-independent Scotch-Irish settlers who had emigrated to find freedom as well as to make better lives for themselves" (1974; 1071). Robert H. Brinkmeyer agrees that "their uncompromising individualism and their loyalty to family and community, particularly when in opposition to the incursions of the modern state, [are] seen here in the government investigator . . . and the illogic and mismanagement of New Deal initiatives" (308), while Peter Nicolaisen contends that "The Tall Men" "echoes Jefferson's creed of the independent farmer more strongly than any other Faulkner text" (69).

Not all readers, however, see the McCallums as exemplary. Albert J. Devlin, who treats of the same family in both "The Tall Men" and *Sartoris* (where they are called *Mac*Callum), calls them "a paradigm of arrested development," pointing out that the boys are all subservient to Buddy, and none of them has married: "Debilitating psychological effects—frustration, arrested development, dubious masculinity, neurotic symptoms— . . . strongly imply that the MacCallums are less than well-adjusted" (84, 85). Although John T. Matthews describes "The Tall Men" as "one of Faulkner's bluntest stories about the federal government's latest invasion of the South," he also cites details of the story—such as the boys' enrolling at an agricultural college to learn to raise cattle—that "work to disturb the author's position." The investigator's apparent indifference to Gombault's "windy paean to yeomanry" also "deflates his pronouncement" ("Faulkner's Stories" 227, 228). We note that structurally, Gombault's sermon balances Pearson's lengthy opening interior monologue against *"These people who lie about and conceal the ownership of land and property in order to hold relief jobs which they have no intention of performing"* (46). The story's patriotic themes come in for praise and blame by turns. Hans H. Skei calls the story "a strong, at times sentimental, story of patriotism and self-sufficiency" (*Short Story*

Career 97), while Sylvia Jenkins Cook says it "represents the extreme crystallization of attitudes less polemically expressed in the earlier works; in its assertion of the supremacy of individual rights over those of the group, it is certainly no less propagandistic than the novels of the Communist writers who proposed a contrary philosophy" (59). Subjects and theme aside, the story's tone has been roundly condemned as "didactic" (Ferguson 42; Volpe 248). Perhaps Brinkmeyer provides the most telling analysis of the problem of tone: "The story's structure mirrors that of classic American humor—the city slicker comes to the country and gets his comeuppance—but the story lacks humor. And without humor, we've got little else but a simplistic tract attacking big government and extolling the virtues of the simple folk" (310).

Faulkner had an obvious commercial motive for "The Tall Men," and for once he successfully gauged the market interest in his subject matter. When Robert K. Haas suggested including the story in the projected collection of stories, Faulkner agreed (*SL* 274) and included it as the third story in "The Country" section of *Collected Stories*. In that position, it extends the volume's exploration of the complex and often invisible dynamics of family.

45:1 **cotton gin** in this instance, the building containing the cotton gin, the machine that separates cotton fiber from its seeds

45:2 **coupé** a closed two-door automobile

45:7 **state draft investigator** In 1940, Congress reinstituted the draft, or compulsory military service, by passing the Selective Service Act; the Act represented the first time that United States civilians had been conscripted during peacetime. The Federal Bureau of Investigation was responsible for finding and arresting those who would avoid service, but each state also had investigators charged with similar duties.

46:14–15 ***relief jobs*** jobs created by the federal and state governments during the Great Depression. The Depression caused job losses across the country, and government-sponsored relief jobs were a way to provide subsistence living for citizens and to boost the economy as well. These relief jobs came from programs such as the Civilian Conservation Corps and the Works Progress

Administration (see entry 29:23–35 in "Shingles for the Lord"). These programs were woefully inadequate in Mississippi. During one single day in April 1932, "one-fourth of the real property in Mississippi, including 20 percent of all farms and 15 percent of town property, went under the auctioneer's gavel and was sold to pay taxes. The sales, conducted by 74 sheriffs, included about 40,000 farms. Most of the property went to the state of Mississippi which already owned about one million acres" (McCarty).

46:18 ***free mattress*** a gift from the government; also mentioned in "Shingles for the Lord" (see 29:24).

46:22 ***seed loans*** On 8 November 1930, President Herbert Hoover recommended to Congress an emergency appropriations bill, "to be included in the intensification of public works, public buildings and other forms of public construction," which included a program of loans to farmers in drought-stricken areas of the country (Hoover).

46:26–27 ***selective-service list*** the official roster of men eligible for the draft (see 45:7).

47:4 **foursquare** literally, having four equal sides set at four right angles to one another. "Foursquare" was also the name of the Gospel church and religious movement founded by Aimee Semple McPherson (1890–1944) in 1922. The first woman in the U.S. to own a radio station, over which she broadcast sermons nationwide, McPherson was a prominent presence in Depression-era America.

47:9 **horseman's hands** hands strong enough to control a horse but gentle and sensitive enough to nurture it

47:11 **Gombault** The name marks the deputy as a descendant of French pioneers in Yoknapatawpha.

47:14 **hammer mill** a machine for grinding corn or other kinds of feed for animals. Owning one kept the farmer from the expense and inconvenience of relying on store-bought food for the stock; in the MacCallums' case, it is another example of their self-reliance and independence.

47:24 **Jackson. From the draft board** Based on the model in effect from 1917–1919, the Selective Service Act established state and local draft boards charged with the task of keeping track of who had and had not registered. These boards also decided individual cases of exemptions and issued warrants for arrests and summonses to appear before them.

47:29–30 **You mean we have declared war?** The public made much of "the first peacetime draft," and there was a publicly generated conscription campaign in its favor. The Selective Service Act marked an end to the isolationist U.S. foreign policy of the 1930s, so there is great irony in the double isolationism of the MacCallums. See Clifford and Spencer.

48:9 **beetling** knitting together and protruding

49:30 **cob pipe** pipe for smoking tobacco, the bowl of which is made from a dried corncob

49:30 **wicker-covered demijohn** a large bottle with bulging body and narrow neck, encased in wickerwork, which held about five gallons of what in Faulkner is usually homemade whisky or moonshine

50:1 **that frame I was using** the casing for the hammer mill (see 47:14). Buddy seems to have been standing above the mill with his leg braced on the frame as he poured the grain. Apparently, his leg slipped into the grinding mechanism.

51:11 **ether** a general anesthetic, first successfully demonstrated in surgery in 1846 and in common medical and dental use during the time of this story

51:20 **One day in France** Buddy served in the Army during World War One.

51:28–29 **a heap of us racked up along a bank outside a field dressing station** Buddy takes a hunting metaphor to describe the triage area (the field dressing station) outside a battlefield hospital in France: on a hunt, felled deer are gutted (field-dressed) in order to make them lighter to transport and to keep the meat fresher for longer; to transport more than one dead deer, they are bound together side by side, or "racked up."

51:32 **got a-holt of this johnny-jug** took hold of the demijohn (and started drinking); see 49:30

53:1–2 **Gayoso Feed Company** Gayoso is an avenue in Memphis that Brown describes as "once elegant but sadly decayed by the 1920s" (90). A feed company is a store where farmers can buy equipment, seed, and food for their animals.

53:3 **Sixth Infantry** Buddy fought with the infantry division that joined the Fifth near the end of the Great War during the last offensive along the Western front, running from the English Channel and Ypres, Belgium, on the northern end to Verdun and St. Mihiel on the southern end.

54:10 **Indian summer** a period of calm, dry, mild weather in the late autumn or early winter

54:12 **cicadas** large flying insects sometimes called locusts; the males produce a high-pitched, buzzing whine.

54:18 **the old war** the Civil War

54:20 **his ma was a Carter** The marshal is saying that old Anse's mother was from a well-established and respected Virginia family, and Anse could not disgrace her name either by avoiding enlistment or by enlisting with strangers in Mississippi. Faulkner was related to a family of Carters: his aunt Willie Medora Falkner married Nathanial G. Carter and had two daughters, Natalie and Vance (Vanny). As a child, Faulkner once went to spend the night with them but was overcome with homesickness; his two cousins carried him home, and the memory remained one of his most cherished (Williamson 142).

54:24–30 **Stonewall Jackson's army and stayed in it all through the Valley, and right up to Chancellorsville, where them Carolina boys shot Jackson by mistake, and right on up to that morning in 'Sixty-five when Sheridan's cavalry blocked the road from Appomattox to the Valley, where they might have got away again** Born in 1824, Confederate General Thomas Jonathan Jackson earned the nickname "Stonewall" at the first battle of Manassas (Bull Run) in 1861 for his refusal to yield in battle; he commanded the Shenandoah Valley (Virginia) District in 1862, and he died during the battle of Chancellorsville in May of 1863 when he was mistakenly shot by one of the troops under his command. Union General Philip Henry Sheridan (1831–1888) had major victories in the Shenandoah Valley during the last two years of the War, including the defeat of J. E. B. Stuart. He also cut off Robert E. Lee's retreat from Appomattox Court House, Virginia, which resulted in the Confederate leader's surrender to General Ulysses S. Grant on 9 April 1865.

54:34 **Raphael** Interestingly, Anse has named his middle son with the full name of the Italian Renaissance painter Faulkner admired and not with the region's common nickname, Rafe. Raphael is also identified by many as the "angel of the Lord" who troubled the waters of the pool in John 5.

55:3 **an American medal and a French one** Although the context isn't fully clear, Buddy's wounds probably earned him the American Medal of Honor and the French Croix de Guerre, which could be awarded to foreign nationals. Both medals are earned for bravery and wounds incurred during battle, and both require specific documentation of the act that earned them; Buddy's refusal to talk about them probably reflects his modesty, rather than shellshock.

55:6–7 **them numbers on his uniform and the wound stripes and them two medals** The patches signifying his Army unit and wounding in battle; see 55:3

55:12 **thriblets** triplets

55:13 **spikehorn bucks** young male deer whose antlers have not yet fully grown

55:14 **pack of coon dogs** dogs assembled for hunting

55:19 **agricultural college** either a land-grant university, such as Mississippi State University, or a local junior college specializing in agriculture

55:20 **whiteface cattle** the Polled Hereford breed, so called because it is hornless. The breed was registered in 1901.

55:22–33 **It was when the Government first begun to interfere with how a man farmed his own land, raised his cotton. . . . and so they would actually be better off than trying to farm by themselves** before the federal government's regulation of agriculture and, from the marshal's view, subsequent interference into private matters

56:4–5 **no papers nor no cards nor nothing** agricultural contracts with the federal government

57:9 **bales** large bundles, in this case of cotton ginned and ready to sell. Depending on such variables as location and climate changes, the productivity of farms at the time varied from one-half to one bale per acre; the MacCallums' farm was notably productive during the Depression, the marshal implies, due to their efforts and not the government's help.

57:28 **make out** manage; get by

58:7 **grabble and snatch** groping and grabbing suddenly

58:7–9 **AAA and WPA and a dozen other three-letter reasons for a man not to work** Agricultural Adjustment Administration and Works Progress Administration—two of the so-called "alphabet soup" programs instituted by the Roosevelt administration during the Depression. See also 46:14–15.

58:24 **carrying something in a bloody sheet** Buddy's amputated leg

59:4–5 **shadow of his striding scissoring and enormous along the earth** the title passage of the story

59:33 **coping** in this context, the top part of a low wall, this one enclosing the family burial ground

60:6–10 **They was to run from left to right, beginning with Jackson. But after the boys was born, Jackson and Stuart was to come up here by their pa and ma, so Buddy could move up some and make room. So he will be about here** The marshal is locating Buddy's eventual gravesite by reciting (again) MacCallum family history.

60:32 **Growned** a regionalism; combination of "grown" and "growed" [*i.e.*, grew]

61:5 **tall, lean old man** a reference linking the marshal to the title passage; see 59:4–5

"A Bear Hunt"

Many readers of *Collected Stories* who turn to "A Bear Hunt" expect to find "The Bear." The latter, among Faulkner's best and best-known fictions, appears in *Go Down, Moses* (1942) as the fifth chapter in that richly constructed book; and a shorter version, intended for a popular audience, is reprinted in Joseph Blotner's edition of Faulkner's *Uncollected Stories* (1979). Those who are willing to accept "A Bear Hunt" on its own terms will find first of all a rough and ready practical joke. The story is doubly narrated: first, in an open frame by an anonymous, articulate, and self-conscious narrator; and second, in the vernacular by Ratliff, a sewing-machine agent who emerges as a central character in Faulkner's Snopes trilogy, *The Hamlet* (1940), *The Town* (1957), and *The Mansion* (1959). The literate narrator introduces the cast of characters in Major de Spain's hunting camp twenty miles from Jefferson, focusing especially on Luke Provine, a former bully and ruffian, now forty, with most of his teeth gone and, at present, an apparently interminable and noisy case of hiccups. Ratliff takes over the narration to describe his observation of Provine's comeuppance at the hands of the black attendant at the camp, and what began as a case of "the trickster tricked" from the point of view of the would-be perpetrator-turned-victim becomes a subtle narrative of cooperation between African- and Native Americans that results in their momentary revenge on some of the whites who have victimized or exploited them.

Most critics, Gene M. Moore asserts, "have dismissed ['A Bear Hunt'] as a minor comic story in the tradition of the tall tale" ("Faulkner's Incorrect" 6); James Ferguson, for example, calls it "little more than a rather elaborate but crude joke" (39). John Longley early christened the story "a comedy of manners," but stipulated that "stupidity, greed, excess, affectation, folly, and hypocrisy are sinful . . . and common sense, moderation, tolerance, and wit are moral qualities" in comedy; and "Lucius Provine is guilty of the gravest offenses against the morality of comedy: gluttony, dim-wittedness, and pointless, stupid, cruelty" (116). Hans H. Skei agrees, calling the story "a social comedy" and pointing to its "good-humoured jokes and friendly retributions" (*The Novelist* 220). Others have focused less on the story's tone and more on its narrative method. Edmond Volpe identifies the open-frame narrator as Quentin Compson and emphasizes that "by structuring his story as he does, Faulkner establishes an equation between Ratliff's tale and the Indian mound as elements in the boy's heritage that excited his imagination" (193). Lisa Paddock reads "A Bear Hunt" as a precursor to *Go Down, Moses*: "The contrast engendered by the juxtaposition of a humorous narrative with a somber framing device—related by a narrator who is either implicitly or explicitly identified as Quentin—prefigures the novel's careful counterpoise of comic and tragic elements" (146). Edwige Pluyaut says the role of the first narrator is "to make the teller of the tale [Ratliff] friendly and reliable even before he starts telling his story" so that he can get on with the business of "victimizing Lucius Provine and thereby acting out the wish of the white community of the hunting camp, but also that of the Negroes and Indians who join forces to turn the tables on him" (272, 273). Some very recent criticism takes Faulkner to task for the accuracy of his representation of Native Americans—"In Faulkner's Mississippi there were very few identifiable Indians, and his approach to portraying them was an amalgam of received stereotypes and modernist orientalism" (Galloway 13)—but some read the "Indian" material as revelatory of his continuing engagement with fragmented American history. Jay S. Winston, for example, argues that "To gain a truer, more autochthonous sense of connection with the land, he sees a need to forge a bond with its native inhabitants, to transcend the history that began in 1492" (129). He emphasizes the complex connections between the experiences and memories of the open-frame narrator and the story of Ratliff, Luke Provine, and Old Man Ash. "A Bear Hunt," he says, "captures the contradictory mystique of the first Yoknapatawphans perhaps more completely than any of the other 'Indian' stories" (131). The mound, in the opening narrative, "is associated with an untameable wildness, but also with a humanity that is one with that wildness, 'aboriginal.'" The narrator, a reader of dime novels who has also spent a memorable night at the mound with another adolescent, is "caught up in the popular discourse of 'the primitive'—the unpredictable violence and strange ritual, the mystery of 'dark' people's savage cultures—at the same time that he acknowledges that this sense of menace is not based on any knowledge of the actual Chickasaws" (132). "The story leaves us," Winston concludes, "with the contrast between the boyish fascination, awe, and terror evoked by the mounds in the introductory frame and the far more cynical narration of an adult which makes up the main story" (134).

The first-published of Faulkner's short stories about hunting, "A Bear Hunt" also features the first appearance of characters who figure prominently in subsequent fictions on the subject, particularly Major de Spain and Uncle Ike McCaslin. According to Joseph Blotner, the story was written very late in 1933, after Faulkner himself had experienced a severe case of hiccups at General James Stone's hunting camp (1974, 822). Faulkner sent the story directly to the *Saturday Evening Post*, asking his agent, Morton Goldman, to facilitate the subsequent negotiations (*Selected Letters* 76). The *Post* published the story in its issue of 10 February 1934. Faulkner chose not to include "A Bear Hunt" in *Doctor Martino* (1934), but in 1948 he agreed with Robert K. Haas's suggestion that it be numbered among the *Collected Stories* and asked for a copy of the story "for a correction of locale" (*SL* 274). Although he made no change in the setting, he did change "Suratt" to "Ratliff" and "Bush" to "Ash" before placing "A Bear Hunt" fourth within the section he called "The Country." In 1955 he revised the story further for *Big Woods*, now specifically identifying Quentin Compson as the open-frame narrator and changing Lucius Provine to Lucius Hogganbeck, a name he would use again in *The Reivers* (1962). The reworking of his material is a hallmark of Faulkner's technique; in this case, he seems to have been revising the story to bring it into a consistent relationship to his other published fictions. Sometimes he cared about such matters, and sometimes he most emphatically did not.

63:3 **buckboard** an open, four-wheeled carriage, the seat of which rested on a board attached to the front and rear axles

63:3 **mismatched team** a team of horses or mules of unequal weight, speed, strength, and/or color: "A matched team is worth more than two unmatched animals of equal or individual value" (Calvin Brown 126).

63:4 **model T Ford** automobile first produced by the Henry Ford company in 1908. Known for its dependability and the simplicity of its engines, the model T was affordable and popular; Ford wanted to produce a car for the masses, and they repaid him by buying over fifteen million cars with that engine over the next nineteen years. In 1914, assembly line production made the car even easier and cheaper to build.

63:8 **bazaars** events, usually sponsored by churches, to raise money by selling homemade goods

63:8 **sewing bees** gatherings of women to sew large projects, such as quilts, that were occasions for friendly competition and socializing as well as work

63:9–10 **all-day singings at country churches** special church meetings to recruit new members and bolster the spirits of the faithful; revival meetings

63:10 **barrytone** baritone

63:12 **annual hunting camp** a campground used during hunting season; in this case, one with a cabin used during bear season in the fall

63:12 **river bottom** low-lying alluvial land next to a river

63:20 **without** unless

63:20 **indefinite credit** credit with no specific terms for payment

64:2 **the square** the central business district of the town, usually a courthouse bordered on all four sides by streets

64:10–12 **There are other men among us now whose families are in want; men who, perhaps, would not work anyway, but who now, since the last few years, cannot find work** The Great Depression began in 1929 and lasted roughly until America's entry into the Second World War.

64:19–20 **it contained whisky in pint bottles. Major de Spain extricated him somehow** The prohibition of liquor by the federal government lasted from 1920 until 1933, so Luke Provine was in violation of federal law and in danger of going to the penitentiary until Major de Spain intervened on his behalf.

64:23 **Roman gesture of salute and farewell** a salute made by extending the right hand, fingers together, with the arm straight and raised forward at about a 45–degree angle from the body

65:3 **celluloid collars** Men's shirts of the time seldom had attached collars, so a separate collar could be attached to "dress up" a shirt and then removed to be laundered or replaced. These collars were often paper, but celluloid styles appeared in the mid-1870s. Celluloid is highly flammable, and there is no way to demonstrate whether having it burned around one's neck would in fact be "painless" (65:4).

65:9 **cane and gum and pin oak** "Cane" can refer to any bamboo-like plants; the gum (genus *Liquidambar*) and pin oak (*Quercus palustris*) are trees common to North Mississippi.

65:10 **Indian mound** a mound or earthwork erected in former times by Indians as a burial place or fortification, which might well contain artifacts

65:3–4 **literate, town-bred people** the narrator's class. See 63:1–66:25.

65:17 **dime novels** cheap, sensationalistic novels, usually paperback

65:22 **Chickasaw tribe** one of the so-called Five Civilized Tribes of Indians, native to Mississippi and Alabama, and resettled in Oklahoma beginning with the Indian Removal Act of 1830

65:23 **Government protection** living on federally owned land, an Indian reservation

66:7 **Sherman's march** Union General William Tecumseh Sherman's devastating "March to the Sea" from the conquered and burned Atlanta to Savannah in November and December of 1864, during which 60,000 Union troops destroyed what they could of the Confederacy's supplies and supply lines, including civilian lands and homes—a swath sixty-one miles wide and 250 miles long

66:7–9 **Negroes among us living in economic competition who bore our family names** either the "shadow families" or mixed-race descendants of white men in the town (see Williamson) or descendants of freed slaves who had taken their former masters' names

66:26 **When I got back to town** This is the beginning of Ratliff's narration. His subject and style owe much to the humorists of the Old Southwest.

66:28 **bear hounds** the pack of dogs that track and tree quarry, in this case, bear

66:29 **cattymount** short for *catamountain*: a cougar, puma, mountain lion (Brown 48, 145)

66:31 **be dog** short for "I'll be dogged," euphemism for "I'll be damned" (Brown 108)

67:9 **swurging** perhaps a combination of *swinging* and *surging*. Faulkner uses the word to describe the act of running with no real control over one's arms and legs.

67:10 **skeered** scared

67:18 **set of threes in his hand** in draw poker, a hand of cards containing three threes, which will beat hands containing one pair and two pair

67:19 **a right smart** a considerable amount (Brown 163)

67:21 **fahr** fire

67:23 **tarnation** damnation. Brown says that "in the expression 'what the tarnation hell,' it is a pure intensive" (197).

68:3 **get shed of** from "get shut of," meaning "get rid of" (Brown 91)

68:9–10 **the biggest present gathering of men in the county** An archaic definition of "present" is "readily available," and that seems to suit Ratliff's meaning here.

68:14 **teching** touching; in this case, drinking from

68:17 **possum-rich bear pork** Brown explains that because bear meat is "somewhat greasy," it is "sometimes called bear-pork. Possum meat is rich and greasy. Hence the meaning is 'pork-like bear meat as rich and greasy as possum meat'" (154).

68:21 **clock bombs** a bomb with a timer that makes a ticking sound

68:31–32 **them shotgun fellows on the deer stands** men with shotguns at certain hunting stations in the woods, often platforms or seats in trees

68:33 **strike** catch the trail of the prey

69:2 **log-line levee** "an embankment to prevent the overflow of a river" (*OED* online)

69:6 **keep to the open** stay out of the cover offered by the woods

69:8 **mizzable** miserable

69:15 **varmint** a troublesome animal or person (from *vermin*)

69:15 **hay baler** a machine that packages loose hay into a bale

69:24–25 **one-cylinder gasoline engines** a simple, gasoline-powered engine containing one piston. Engines with more than one cylinder can usually run if one piston doesn't fire, but a one-cylinder obviously cannot; small engines like these are common on farms and homesteads—in lawn mowers, for instance.

69:32 **canebrake** dense thicket of cane; see 65:9

71:10 **cut-out** in an internal-combustion engine, a valve through which exhaust gases can escape without passing through the muffler. The result is loud, explosive bursts of sound.

71:19 **sujest** suggest

71:21–22 **automobile tahrs they used to advertise with** In the 1910s and 1920s, the Firestone Tire Company advertised its products in print with large images of a tire, inside which an illustration would speak to the various excellences of the product.

71:33 **dodges** scams; in this case, folk cures

72:1–7 **them pore aborigines would, because the white folks have been so good to them—not only letting them keep that ere hump of dirt that don't nobody want noways, but letting them use names like ourn and selling them flour and sugar and farm tools at not no more than a fair profit above what they would cost a white man** Ratliff is sarcastically summarizing the history of local white exploitation of the Indians.

72:33 **lantrun** lantern

73:7 **gwine up dar** going up there

73:17–19 **I hadn't never even seen a pair of shoes, let alone two stores in a row or a arc light** Ratliff is saying that he was so young and unworldly that he could never have anticipated what would happen to Luke. **arc light** = electric lamp with an incandescent bulb.

74:1 **Deal the cards** In poker, the dealer passes out either five or seven cards to each person and play progresses clockwise, beginning with the player to the dealer's left.

74:8–9 **Queen bets a quarter** If they are playing five-card stud poker (as they do in "Was" of *Go Down, Moses*), one card has been dealt face down and one face up; the person with the highest card showing (Ike, in this case) has the first bet.

74:27 **demijohn and fixings** The Major is going to make a toddy, a drink made from whisky, water, and sugar.

74:31 **to'ds** towards

75:4 **bust-skull whisky** cheap, hurriedly distilled whisky

75:15 **out on stand** See 68:31–32.
75:20 **harrycane** hurricane
75:24 **the Jackson a-sylum** the Mississippi state mental institution, located in the capital city of Jackson
76:1 **put my foot in hit** either a shortened version of "I opened my mouth and put my foot in it" or a euphemism for accidentally stepping in animal droppings
76:23–24 **my duty to my honor to call him outen the back yard** challenge him to personal combat in retaliation for being jumped unawares
76:24 **as the fellow says** a common phrase among Faulkner's folksy narrators like Ratliff, who use it to invoke an unspecified authority or common sense; an equivalent to the more commonly heard "they say"
76:25–26 **Major de Spain wasn't the only man that caught a bear on that hunt** the title passage of the story: Ash has "caught" Luke Provine
76:27 **hitched up my Ford** started his car
76:30 **nekkid** naked; in this case, unaided
77:7–8 **oiling Major's boots** lubricating to keep the leather soft and water-resistant
77:11 **ca'tridges** ammunition cartridges; the tubular container of powder, primer, and bullet
77:14 **frizzle-headed** frizzy-haired
77:21–22 **So then I changed my tone, like a fellow has to do to get anything out of a nigger** Ratliff's understanding of the history of white exploitation of other races (see 72:1–7) apparently does not extend to Ash, or to himself.
77:26 **Mr. Provine** Ratliff's racial ideology requires him to call white men "Mister" in the presence of a black person, regardless of the white person's social standing or class.
78:8 **jest dodged him** just avoided him
78:9 **revenue agent** an agent of the U.S. Treasury Department, which policed the manufacture and sale of illegally distilled whisky; also called revenuers (Brown 162)
78:11 **skeer** scare; fright
78:14 **take a back seat for you** assume a subordinate position

78:17–18 **a-hickin' en a-blumpin'** Ash is conflating the hiccupping sounds Luke makes with his awkward running, which Ratliff called "swurging" at 67:9.

78:31 **kyo** cure

79:9 **en nudder** and another. The man is Jack Bonds (64:34).

79:10 **cotch** caught

79:16 **fo' bits** fifty cents; a bit is one-eighth of a dollar.

79:17–18 **de race betwixt de Natchez en de Robert E. Lee** Brown explains the race itself: "The race between these two boats was the most famous and the greatest of all the Mississippi River steamboat races. It was prearranged as a sporting event. (Most races were simply impromptu affairs when two boats found themselves in the same reach of river and raced to the next port to get the freight waiting there.) The race was followed with close interest and frequent telegraph reports, both nationally and internationally, and it is said that friends of the two captains alone bet over a million dollars on it. The two side-wheelers left New Orleans at 5:00 pm on June 20, 1870, with St. Louis as the goal. The captain of the *Natchez* treated it as a normal trip except for a furious insistence on speed. But the captain of the *Lee* stripped his boat down to a bare minimum of superstructure in order both to lighten her and to reduce wind-resistance. He also had a small steamboat waiting at intervals to bring coal barges alongside and unload them while he merely reduced speed, instead of having to stop and lash them together—an early instance of refueling in flight. These stratagems enabled the *Lee* to win the race and set a record of 3 days, 18 hours, 14 minutes. This record stood until some sixty or seventy years later, by which time changes both in boats and in the river itself were so great that to break it was really meaningless" (136–37). We have not been able to find evidence, however, that anybody ever sold celluloid collars with drawings or pictures or designs of any kind on them, let alone of the *Natchez* and the *Robert E. Lee.* Ash's joke might therefore be on us, too.

79:12–13 **"And you waited all this time and went to all this trouble, just to get even with him," I says** Another title passage: Ratliff interprets Ash's actions as revenge for Provine's ill treatment of him and his friends, but Ash claims to miss the collar he loved and could easily afford to buy today (see 79:14–21). Because the story ends with Ash's voice and not Ratliff's, it is impossible to tell how we are meant to evaluate what he says. Did he really miss the collar, or is Ratliff right and is Ash lying in order to cover his racial insubordination? If the latter is true, he would be doing what Ralph Ellison called "changing the joke to slip the yoke" of racial oppression.

"Two Soldiers"

Faulkner spent some time anticipating World War II, and, even before America became involved, he sought for ways he might contribute to the war effort himself, telling Robert Haas that he might try to regain his commission in England, or try the U.S. air corps: "I could navigate, or teach navigation, even if I could not fly service jobs because of my age" (*Selected Letters* 139). And in March 1942, between the time "Two Soldiers" was written and published, Faulkner told Haas he was trying for a commission and a post to the Bureau of Aeronautics. Although these hopes were frustrated, Faulkner nevertheless articulated his support for American troops. In the 1940 short story version of "Delta Autumn," Don Boyd expresses doubts that Americans have the will to stop Hitler or other potential dictators: "How?" he asks. "By singing God Bless America in bars at midnight and wearing dime-store flags in our lapels?" Ike McCaslin responds quickly, "I ain't noticed this country being short of defenders yet when it needed them" (*Uncollected Stories* 269); and the passage recurs in *Go Down, Moses* (1942). "Two Soldiers" and "Shall Not Perish" manifest related though differing expressions of patriotism, largely through the agency of the Grier family.

"Two Soldiers" combines a number of elements often prominent in Faulkner's fiction. Frenchman's Bend itself—often the scene of violence, as in *Sanctuary*, "Barn Burning," and portions of *The Hamlet*—is here rather more benign, as in "Shingles for the Lord" (which also features another version of the Grier family). The Griers have neither telephone, radio, nor, probably, electricity. Their remote, isolated, and patently rural ways contrast pointedly with the ways of Jefferson and Memphis. By choosing the young boy as both his subject and narrator—"a type which I admire," Faulkner said, "not only a little boy, and I think little boys are all right, but a true American: an independent creature with courage and bottom and heart" (*SL* 184)—Faulkner wrote in a tradition that he called, in another context, "a sort of Huck Finn" (*SL* 123). This boy also undertakes the perilous journey to Memphis, as do characters ranging from Bayard Sartoris in *Flags in the Dust* (written in 1926–1927 and published in 1973) to Lucius Priest in *The Reivers* (1962). "Two Soldiers" may also be called an initiation story and a *bildungsroman*, forms to which Faulkner returned again and again.

Predictably, evaluations of this story vary widely. The story was bought immediately by the *Saturday Evening Post* and was soon selected for inclusion in an anthology aimed at high school students. Faulkner, however, resented the request of an anthologist to censor the story for younger readers, writing sarcastically to Harold Ober, "This [censorship] may be good for the children in fact; it will be teaching them at an early and tender age to be ever on guard to protect and shield their elders and teachers from certain of the simple facts of life" (*SL* 191–92). Compared to many other Faulkner short stories and novels, "Two Soldiers" is at once simple, straightforward, and clear, as well as positive in its sentiments, so it has had many appreciators and advocates. Perhaps for these same reasons, it has also had more than its share of detractors. James Ferguson, for example, says that these Grier stories are "marred by an altogether offensive jingoism" (42), and Edmond Volpe seems to agree that "Though it is obviously the work of a fine craftsman, the tale is a slick magazine story that offends with its gushing sentimentality and its cuteness"; "Faulkner's craftsmanship," he concludes, "is not sufficient to prevent his story from sinking into a bog of sentimentality" (259–60). Robert Brinkmeyer disagrees and asserts that the brothers' determination to enlist "is not mindless jingoism but deeply felt civic loyalty and responsibility, both to community and to nation" (311–12), while Frederick Karl pronounces the story "meretricious" and "a piece of patriotic fluff" (661, 662) and Michael Millgate calls attention to the boy as "the chief embodiment of those qualities of simple determination, endurance, and courage which Faulkner finds so admirable" (271). "Two Soldiers" remains popular with many teachers and students, not only for its simplicity and its sentiments but also because of the engaging figure of the Grier boy. After an extensive review of the critical responses to the story, Diane Brown Jones suggests that "we ought to return to 'Two Soldiers,' interpretive tools in hand, to see if more thorough scrutiny reveals something as yet seen only by its creator" (70–71).

This story first appeared in the *Saturday Evening Post* on March 28, 1942, and Faulkner placed it as the fifth story in "The Country" section of *Collected Stories,* immediately preceding "Shall Not Perish." Thus, with "Shingles for the Lord," exactly half of the stories in Faulkner's opening section center on the Grier family, and these three, with "The Tall Men," make for a preponderance of "positive" stories in this section, though all are overshadowed by the violent and dark workings out of Sarty Snopes's ethical and Oedipal dilemmas in "Barn Burning." "Two Soldiers" has twice been adapted for film (in 1985 and 2003), and the latter earned an Oscar for Best Short Film (Live Action).

81:2 **supper** the evening meal

81:9–10 **Japanese? What's a pearl harbor?** the event that brought the United States into World War II; the bombing on Sunday, 7 December 1941, of Pearl Harbor and other installations on Oahu, Hawaii

81:11–12 **the fellow in the radio** the radio announcer or evening newscaster

81:12 **make no heads nor tails** make sense

81:13–14 **Then the fellow said that would be all for a while** the announced end of the broadcast

81:16 **the Consolidated** as Calvin Brown explains, a "consolidated school, a name used when local rural schools began to be abandoned for big complexes to which students were bussed" (58)

81:19–20 **that Government reservoy** Sardis Reservoir (Brown 162)

82:8 **vetch** a legume planted after harvest in order to replenish the nitrogen in the soil and then plowed under in the spring prior to planting their cash crop

82:15 **it** the war news

82:26–27 **Pap give him ten acres** as a reward for graduating from high school

82:29–30 **Pete had them ten acres all sowed to vetch and busted out and bedded for the winter** See 82:8: Pete has already broken the soil of his new acreage and prepared it in beds, plowed it into rows and middles for the planting of his cash crop in the spring (Brown 27, 42).

82:32–34 **they was at it in the Philippines now, but General MacArthur was holding um** marks the progression of time to late December 1941; the Japanese occupied Manila on 31 December 1941, and General Douglas MacArthur was forced to abandon the islands, famously claiming "I shall return"; the Army surrendered on 9 April. MacArthur was appointed Supreme Commander of the Southwest Pacific area in 1942; the islands were retaken in October 1944, and MacArthur returned in 1945 (see "MacArthur, Douglas")

83:8 **the wood tree** presumably a downed tree to be chopped up for firewood

83:13 **When we going to start?** the first of several title passages

83:17–18 **I reckon we got to go** see 83:13

83:22 **You'll whup the big uns and I'll whup the little uns** title passage; see also 83:13

83:26 **sparking them girls** courting those daughters

84:9 **shirttail** "a very small quantity" (Brown 176); hence, a small farm

84:13 **Only I made sho from his own mouth** I made him tell me himself, so I could be sure

84:31 **that other war** World War I, 1914–1918, with official American involvement 1917–1918

85:3 **the one** the one who objected to Pete's going to war

85:4–5 **You ain't old enough for the draft, and the country ain't being invaded** The Selective Service Act of 1917 required men between twenty-one and thirty to register for military service; the age range was later changed to eighteen to forty-five. Pete is "nigh twenty years old" (88:11). Hawaii, a U.S. territory in 1942, did not become a state until 1959.

85:18 **Them Japanese—** "bombed us!"—and perhaps followed by an epithet, such as "sons of bitches," which would account for his mother's reaction at 85:19: "You hush your mouth!"

85:27–28 **a shoe box of vittles** a small box of food

85:29 **grip** small suitcase (Brown 95)

86:4 **Them Japanese—** see 85:18

86:22 **Is that what you'll ask for? Where to join the Army?** how the narrator learns how to trail Pete in Memphis, which he does at 93:21

87:11 **Frenchman's Bend** nearest village to their farm

87:24 **1942** the present time of the story

87:30–31 **wound the door shut** turned the crank that closes the bus door

87:32 **humming and grinding and whining** the noises of the shifting gears as the bus pulls away

88:6 **I never had no good chance** to pack his bag in preparation for joining the Army

88:9 **holp** helped

88:13 **shikepoke egg** the egg of a little blue heron (Brown 175)

88:14 **wropped** wrapped

88:21 **drapped** dropped

88:22 **clumb** climbed

88:23–24 **tomcatting around** chasing women (Brown 200)

88:31–32 **twenty-two miles to Jefferson** situates Frenchman's Bend in relation to Jefferson; see 87:11

89:4 **square** "surrounding the courthouse of a Southern county seat" (Brown 187)

89:5–6 **that Law looking down at me** a law enforcement officer, identified as Mr. Foote at 89:34

90:12–13 **You go and set down on the bench now, like Mr. Foote—** told you to

90:16 **whupped** whipped

90:29 **their faces already painted** their makeup on

91:12 **overhalls** overalls

91:13–14 **he—hope to breakfast** "The Law starts to use the standard *from hell to breakfast,* but out of deference to the ladies changes in mid-word to a nonce-euphemism" (Brown 101); "How far is it from hell to breakfast? Out in the cow country a man upon returning from a trip might say that he had traveled from hell to breakfast. Nobody could tell you in miles just how far he had been, but everybody would know that he had traveled a far piece and covered a lot of territory" (Boatright).

91:21 **artermatic writing pen** automatic; a fountain pen (Brown 22), as opposed to a pen dipped in a separate jar of ink

91:24 **case history** documentation of the boy's identity and condition; the language of the social worker or orphanage official

91:34 **da—I mean, fast enough to suit any man** "damned fast"; "the beginning of *damned,* which is suppressed out of deference to the ladies" (Brown 67)

92:6 **city board** Board of Aldermen or city council

92:13 **Wellum** Well, ma'am

92:32 **the signal arm** the marker that tells the train's engineer what to do

92:34 **plumb** "entirely, completely" (Brown 151)

92:34 **I couldn't resk it** risk falling asleep

93:3 **sholy** surely

93:9–10 **It** the Memphis skyline

93:12 **ara** any

93:14 **ever'** every

93:21 **Where do folks join the Army?** see 86:22

93:34–94:1 **big arrerhead** arrowhead; the chevron on the soldier's sleeve

94:6 **Pete Grier** Pete's full name

94:19 **where Pete—** is

94:20 **I be dog** I will be a dog (Brown 108), a euphemism for "I'll be damned"

94:30–31 **a belt with a britching strop over one shoulder** To the young narrator, the soldier's Sam Browne belt looks like "a breeching strap, which goes around a harness-horse's buttocks and takes the thrust when he backs up" (Brown 73). A Sam Browne belt has a supporting strap that passes diagonally from the left hip over the right shoulder and down across the back to the left hip.

94:33 **little son** euphemism for "son of a bitch"

94:34 **When he said that I tried to get at him again** to retaliate for what the soldier says at 94:33

95:2 **backing strop** see 94:30–31

95:9 **I came to—** join the Army with him

95:16 **stropped** strapped

95:32 **durnation** "durn" (or "damned") combined with "tarnation" ("damnation") (Brown 75)

96:2 **It** being separated from his brother

97:6–7 **the soldier throwed back in his chair, looking out the window and coughing** to hide his emotional reaction to the scene between the brothers

97:16–17 **she smelled all right, she never had no artermatic writing pen nor no case history neither** unlike Mrs. Habersham and her young friend at 91:20–22

97:30–31 **if all that was her house, she sho had a big family. But all of it wasn't** Mrs. McKellogg (identified at 99:9) and the boy have arrived at a hotel or apartment building.

97:31–32 **a hall with trees growing in it** perhaps a hallway lined with potted palm trees, or a lobby

97:32–33 **a little room without nothing in it but a nigger dressed up in a uniform** an elevator with a uniformed operator

98:5–6 **another soldier, a old feller, with a britching strop, too, and a silver-colored bird on each shoulder** see 94:30–31; the "silver-colored bird" is an eagle, which identifies the man as a full colonel

98:16–17 **eight and ten months. Going on eleven months** hence, born in 1933

98:18 **She telephoned then** called room service

98:23–24 **a nigger, another one, in a short kind of shirttail coat, rolled a kind of wheelbarrer in** a waiter pushing a food service cart

99:4 **that 'ere little moving room** the elevator; see 97:32–33

99:5 **a big car with a soldier driving it** probably Colonel McKellogg's personal car and driver

99:20–21 **I thought about me riding up to Frenchman's Bend in this big car with a soldier running it . . .** and Pete not there to see it

“Shall Not Perish”

“Shall Not Perish” tells the story of the Grier family’s reactions to the death of their older son in the Pacific during the early part of World War II; his father, mother, and younger brother—the narrator, nine at the time of the story—each must come to terms with the loss. Mrs. Grier proves especially energetic, determined, and strong in her efforts to share her understanding of grief with others who are also bereaved by the war, including the wealthy Major de Spain, who loses a son three months after she does. Claiming that she does not understand why either young man went to war, she respects her son’s decision “because there is nothing in him that I or his father didn’t put there” (109). The Grier family visits a Jefferson art museum before returning to Frenchman’s Bend, and the story closes with the boy’s long reflective coda on his great-grandfather, once jarred into reliving a Civil War battle by a Western movie gunfight. Again, Mrs. Grier justifies the old man’s behavior, which had been amusing or embarrassing to the other Grier males, as an act of leadership and bravery. Such solidarity of courage, presumably, is what “shall not perish,” whether found South or North. The story’s title sounds a similar note, coming as it does from Lincoln’s famous speech at Gettysburg, which promised that the “new birth of freedom” for the Union would endure so that “government of the people, by the people, for the people, shall not perish from the earth.”

“Shall Not Perish” seems to continue the action of “Two Soldiers,” which immediately precedes it in this volume, and to concern the same family in “Shingles for the Lord.” We say “seems” because “Shingles” mentions no brother Pete; the first-person narrator of “Perish” is an adult, that of “Shingles” and “Two Soldiers” a child, for example. While some attention has been given to the relations among the "Grier stories" and although de Spain's presence incorporates other Yoknapatawpha texts by reference, much of the commentary on the two war stories focuses on questions of tone. Arthur A. Brown, for example, says "Shall Not Perish" "moves from a quiet and personal point of view to a statement that seems simplistically nationalistic" (Peek and Hamblin 350), and James Ferguson notes "the saccharine inanities" and the "didactic and sententious" qualities of "Two Soldiers" and "Shall Not Perish" (42). Edmond Volpe, by contrast, differentiates "Shall Not Perish" from "Two Soldiers," calling the former "a deeply felt and imaginative declaration of faith in humanity and in America" (260) and the latter "a slick magazine story that offends with its gushing sentimentality and its cuteness" (259). Robert Brinkmeyer endorses Faulkner's writing and stands with Mrs. Grier, who believes that "the heroes of the present stand undiminished, every bit as tall as their forefathers; their actions mirror those of previous generations. The line remains intact; men themselves may perish in war but not the heroic force that drives them. That force remains vital, passed on from generation to generation" (314).

"Shall Not Perish" was received by Faulkner's agent less than a month after "Two Soldiers" appeared in the *Saturday Evening Post* on 28 March 1942, but the *Post* declined the sequel, even after Faulkner submitted a simplified revision (Skei, *Reading* 100–101). The story was further rewritten subsequently and rejected numerous times before finally appearing in the July-August 1943 issue of *Story*, which paid Faulkner $25 for it (Volpe 261). At first doubtful that the story merited inclusion in *Collected Stories*, Faulkner wrote to Robert K. Haas that "Two Soldiers" was an emphatic "YES" but "Shall Not Perish": "No. Topical, not too good" (*Selected Letters* 274). Nevertheless, he eventually placed it as the sixth and last story in "The Country" section, where it echoes and extends themes and techniques first presented in "Barn Burning," including issues of loyalty to family, self, class, and the narrator's position among others of his community. He adapted the story for television, which aired it on 11 February 1954.

101:8–9 **the little pale envelope that didn't even need a stamp on it** a Western Union telegram, used to notify the next of kin of the death of a member of the U.S. armed services during World War II

101:16 **Japs** a popular contemporary manner of referring to the Japanese, who, on 7 December 1941, attacked Pearl Harbor, an American naval base on Hawaii, and so propelled the U.S. into war

101:18 **wrastle** wrestle

101:22–102:2 **one morning Mother stood at the field fence with a little scrap of paper not even big enough to start a fire with, that didn't even need a stamp on the envelope, saying, *A ship was. Now it is not. Your son was one of them*** We have a copy of one typical death notice telegram, which illustrates that Faulkner never exaggerated governmental bureaucracy or incompetence:

> The Navy Department deeply regrets to inform you that your son Ensign Elmer Leroy Parkes US Naval Reserve was killed result plane crash 30 July in the performance of his duty and in the service of his country the Department extends to you it's sincerest sympathy in your great loss no information received as to recovery or disposition of body if further details are received you will be informed to prevent possible aid to our enemies please do not divulge the name of his ship or station.
> Rear Admiral Randell Jacobs The Chief of Naval Personnel

101:24–102:1 **that didn't even need a stamp on the envelope** see 101:8–9

102:3–4 **hardest middle push of planting time** the height of spring planting season, when the most physical labor is required in order to get a crop sown on time

102:12–13 **until the day finally came when there would be an end to it** the end of the war

102:13–14 **when we saw Pete's name and picture in the Memphis paper** the Memphis *Commercial Appeal*

102:19 **Pete was going to be all** the only soldier from Yoknapatawpha County to die in World War II

102:23 **light sweep** according to Calvin Brown, a "light plowshare" for the "shallow cultivation of row crops," "after the plants have come up and attained some size" (194–95)

102:23 **stalling the mule** putting the mule in its stall for the night

103:2 **dasher** the part of a butter churn that aerates milk, turning it into butter; its handle, with two crossties, that is plunged into the churn (Brown 53)

103:7–10 **"It's Major de Spain's boy," he said. "In town. The av-aytor. That was home last fall in his officer uniform. He run his airplane into a Japanese battleship and blowed it up. So they knowed where he was at"** Robert Harrison points out the resemblance between the de Spain boy's action and the heroic self-sacrifice attributed to Captain Colin P. Kelly, Jr., in *Life* magazine for 22 December 1941: "Kelly dove his plane straight the Japanese battleship, *Haruna,* released a stick of high explosives almost into the mouths of flaming guns, and then vanished himself in the mighty explosion that ushered the 29,000-ton ship to the bottom of the sea" (183).

103:12 **almost come** begun to form

103:34 **Manila** capital of the Philippines, occupied by the Japanese on 31 December 1941

104:8 **little wooden box** a radio

104:9–14 **Then Mother called me back to the kitchen. The water smoked a little in the washtub, beside the soap dish and my clean nightshirt and the towel Mother made out of our worn-out cotton sacks, and I bathe and empty the tub and leave it ready for her, and we lie down** an odd tense shift, invoking an eternal present like the one the narrator says his brother inhabits at 104:2–7

104:17–18 **shoes and stockings I hadn't even seen since frost was out of the ground** because he's been barefooted, with the shoes and stockings saved for special occasions (see Brown 190)

104:18–20 **in yesterday's overalls still I carried the shoes back to the kitchen where Mother stood in yesterday's dress** Mrs. Grier and the boy wear the previous day's work clothes rather than soil another set before they dress to go to town.

104:26 **the blacking-box** the set of shoe-shining tools, including the polish

104:29 **monkey nigger** a uniformed black servant, as Brown says, "from the resemblance between a bell-hop's uniform and the costume worn by an organ-grinder's monkey" (132); so a reference to his clothing and not only to his race

104:29 **the jar** the spittoon for expectorant produced by chewing tobacco

105:6–7 **the San Francisco drugstore where Pete bought it** probably where Pete embarked for the Pacific

105:17 **carbide headlight** "a light worn on the forehead for night hunting" (Brown 45–46)

105:23 **bottle of cattle-dip** "any of various compounds used to treat cattle for ticks and other skin infestations" (Brown 47)

106:11–12 **concrete streets began** the outskirts of Jefferson

106:30 **find the right door by ourselves** In leaving the Griers to locate the room where Major de Spain is, the servant demonstrates the presumption of his own superiority to them; he does not deign to announce their presence, as he would with the Major's social equals.

106:31–34–107:1 **rich man's parlor that any woman in Frenchman's Bend and I reckon in the rest of the county too could have described to the inch but which not even the men who would come to Major de Spain after bank-hours or on Sunday to ask to have a note extended, had ever seen** because the men have either been sent to the back door or met outside

107:1–2 **a light hanging in the middle of the ceiling the size of our whole washtub of chopped up ice** a large crystal or leaded-glass chandelier

107:8 **the medal** awarded posthumously for bravery; given the nature of the act (103:7–10), presumably the Medal of Honor, the nation's highest honor

107:9 **big blue automatic pistol** a standard-issue service revolver

107:10–11 **Major de Spain standing at the end of the table with his hat on** not only indoors but in the presence of a woman, an indication of the degree of his distraction

107:18 **that look on his face** of despairing grief

107:20–21 **altar of unpreparedness and inefficiency** the war

108:4–5 **two hands locked together on the big blue pistol** Mrs. Grier moves to take the gun; de Spain moves to prevent her from doing so.

108:7 **that old flag** the Confederate flag

108:11–18 **For his country! He had no country: this one I too repudiate. His country and mine both was ravaged and polluted and destroyed eighty years ago, before even I was born. His forefathers fought and died for it then, even though what they fought and lost for was a dream. He didn't even have a dream. He died for an**

illusion. In the interests of usury, by the folly and rapacity of politicians, for the glory and aggrandisement of organized labor! For de Spain, the dream that the South could achieve and sustain the autonomy of an independent nation ended when the South lost the Civil War. His son died merely for the sake of the capitalist greed and political ambition of others.

108:22–23 **poltroonery** cowardice

109:6 **What is your Negro's name?** Mrs. Grier wants to summon de Spain's black servant, and she wants to use his name; note her respectful use of "Negro" rather than her son and husband's "nigger," even though she refers to him as de Spain's.

109:16 **the war** World War I

109:18 **that old one there** the Civil War, conjured to memory by the Confederate flag on the table

109:24–25 **must be all right, even if I couldn't understand it. Because there is nothing in him that I or his father didn't put there** an honorable man, raised honorably

110:11 **it** what his parents "put" in him at 109:24–25

110:24–111:8 **There was an old lady born and raised in Jefferson who died rich somewhere in the North and left some money to the town to build a museum with. It was a house like a church, built for nothing else except to hold the pictures she picked out to put in it—pictures from all over the United States, painted by people who loved what they had seen or where they had been born or lived enough to want to paint pictures of it so that other people could see it too; pictures of men and women and children, and the houses and streets and cities and the woods and fields and streams where they worked or lived or pleasured** The museum described resembles the Mary Buie Museum in Oxford, Mississippi, opened in 1939 "with a collection of fine art, decorative art and historical memorabilia related to the town and the [S]kipwith family, who financed its creation" ("University Museum: History"). Faulkner expressed in various places, most notably at Stockholm, that art sustains all people. In this passage, he pays tribute to the philanthropy of the "old lady" who left the money to the town; the Griers' appreciation reflects the human need for aesthetic experience, regardless of the immediate circumstance of their grief and the general circumstances of their life.

111:4 **without let** freely

111:14 **egg-money** money earned by raising chickens and selling their eggs (Ruppersburg 19)

111:25 **by Grandfather** with Grandfather as an example

111:33 **Genesis and Exodus** the first two books of the Old Testament, containing most notably the creation story and the Ten Commandments

111:34 **him** God

112:6 **mulberry** common tree, often growing around houses (Brown 134)

112:14–16 **Forrest, or Morgan, or Abe Lincoln, or Van Dorn, or Grant or Colonel Sartoris himself, whose people still lived in our county, or Mrs. Rosa Millard** Grandfather calls out the names of identifiable Southern patriots, historical figures, and characters from Faulkner's own fiction: General Nathan Bedford Forrest (1821–1877), Confederate cavalry leader; John Hunt Morgan (1825–1864), Confederate general; Abraham Lincoln (1809–1865), sixteenth president of the United States and president during the Civil War; Confederate General Earl Van Dorn (1820–1863); Union General Ulysses S. Grant (1822–1885), later the eighteenth president of the U.S.; Colonel John Sartoris, a Confederate officer from Yoknapatawpha County; Mrs. Rosa Millard, John Sartoris's mother-in-law.

112:17 **Yankees and carpetbaggers** Northerners and profiteers (Brown 46), the latter so called because of the cheap, carpet-like material of the one bag in which they brought their possessions South after the war

112:21 **what it was** what Grandfather's outbursts meant

112:22 **a continued picture, a Western** a serial film shown in weekly installments, a device to encourage people to come to the movies

113:2–3 **could have set a watch by** prompt

114:9 **clods** dull and/or insensitive people

II. THE VILLAGE

"A Rose for Emily"

The first of Faulkner's short stories to appear in a magazine with national circulation, "A Rose for Emily" is by far his best-known, most reprinted, most widely read, and most discussed short story. It has been the means by which many readers have encountered Faulkner's fiction for the first time, and the memory of the first reading of its final paragraph remains indelible. If that reading of "A Rose for Emily" yields the shocking discovery that Miss Emily Grierson has not only murdered the man she was to have married but also that she has slept in the same bed with his corpse, subsequent readings allow meditation on why she was driven to these extremes and what implications her story has for us. Among these, probably the first question is why Emily felt compelled to commit murder. Some have accepted Faulkner's own explanation, that Homer Barron refused to marry her; others have seen her act as one of desperate revenge against her father, who had "thwarted her woman's life so many times" (127); still others have seen her violent gesture as directed toward all men, the community in which she lives, a Northerner, or a man of lower social class. Hal Blythe began the speculation that Homer Barron is homosexual and that Emily "poisons him to save face" (49). Such readings place heavy emphasis on the narrator's comment that Homer Barron "liked men" and "was not a marrying man" (126), but ignore Faulkner's careful delineation of the figure who seduces Emily and expects to abandon her—much as those who try to make the case for Homer Barron as a black or mulatto man call attention to the passage that describes him as "a Yankee—a big, dark, ready man" (124). Such speculations reach for easy answers where Faulkner insists on ambiguity and complexity. The questions the story raises invite repeated and subtle consideration, not least because much of the story concerns Miss Emily's evolving position in the Jefferson community, from sought-after young woman to orphan to "fallen" woman to recluse. Intricately structured, framed by a report of her death at the beginning and at the end by a description of the macabre discovery in the upstairs bedroom after the funeral, the story of Miss Emily's life emerges in sketches and tableaux that do not follow a strict and perfectly consistent chronology (see Moore, "Of Time"). The narrative voice of the story—an unidentified citizen of Jefferson—provides an intelligent, detailed, sometimes humorous perspective on a significant range of events, all the while withholding the story's unforgettable *dénouement* until the absolute last moment, guaranteeing that it will hit readers as hard as it hit the men who opened Miss Emily's bedroom. While the sheer quantity of commentary on "A Rose for Emily" is daunting, and perhaps excessive, the story remains one of Faulkner's most engaging texts, and, like Miss Emily herself, "a tradition, a duty, and a care" (119).

Reviewing *These 13* for the *Nation* in 1931, Lionel Trilling called the story "trivial in its horror," describing it as "pure event without implication" (492). In the critical landmark *Understanding Fiction*, Cleanth Brooks and Robert Penn Warren stressed Miss Emily's position within the community as "a combination of idol and scapegoat" (353): "They admire her, even if they are disappointed by her refusals to let herself be pitied, and the narrator, who is a spokesman for the community, recognizes the last grim revelation as an instance of her having carried her own values to their ultimate conclusion" (354). As Brooks later elaborated, "Miss Emily turns out to be not a Southern lady; she is a Clytemnestra, a figure out of tragedy" (161). "The members of the Jefferson community," he concluded, "might well have felt that in some sense Emily Grierson was more sinned against than sinning. She had not willed the great warping of her life; it had been imposed upon her. They would have felt, too, that her insistence on meeting life on her own terms had something heroic about it" (163). These arguments are typical of the community-based close readings of the New Critics, but other approaches to Emily and her plights soon appeared. Irving Malin, for example, provided an early psychological reading of the story, contending that Miss Emily's "repression of her sexual needs leads to perversion." "Her passionate, almost sexual relationship with her dead father," he argued further, "forces her to distrust the living body of Homer and to kill him so that he will resemble the dead father she can never forget" (37).

More recently, critics have successfully brought paradigms from gender studies to "A Rose for Emily." John N. Duvall argues that "because people categorize Emily as a lady, the passive and decorative object, they constantly misread her." Her murder of Homer Barron, he says, "creates a most bizarre alternative couple," standing necessarily outside the community, and the story provides "a strong critique of a system of sociosexual relations that denies a social space to the woman not claimed through marriage by a man. Miss Emily becomes the icon turned iconoclast" (*Marginal Couple* 128). Similarly, Minrose C. Gwin emphasizes the creative yet "morally ambiguous" aspects of Emily's response to the system that has repressed her. Emily, she says, "'plays' creatively by breaking down paternal and societal restraint. She subverts the Law of the Father. Within her own physical space, the bedroom, she subverts the culturally defined signifiers of marital love. . . . She thereby creates a play of signifiers which undermine their own referentiality, even within the repressive margins of patriarchal order—inside the Father's House" (26). The psychological elements of the story remain attractive to critics today. Noel Polk, for example, concludes that Miss Emily's necrophilia "is more than necrophilia": "Homer Barron, whose name signifies not just 'barren home' but also blindness—the blind poet, perhaps blind Oedipus himself—is also a father-surrogate. . . . She thus completes with Homer's body the gesture she began when her father died, of refusing to give up the body to the authorities. After his death she 'consummates' the Oedipal dream, at least to the extent of lying with him in bed" (*Children* 82).

Still other readers focus on Faulkner's craftsmanship in the story. Hans Skei pays special attention to the role of the story's narrator: "The reason for telling the story is the fact that Miss Emily has died; this is the first information that is given in the story, and it is the starting point for a story to which episodes and incidents are added as they, by way of association, implication, or closeness to the narrator, come to his mind." "All this is of course an illusion," he continues, "but it is an extremely carefully and skillfully arranged illusion. The seeming casualness with which the story is told should not be allowed to deceive us into believing that this is a straightforward reminiscence about a lady who has just passed away" (*Reading* 155–56). James Ferguson says time is handled in a more complex way in "A Rose for Emily" than in any of Faulkner's other short stories, in significant part because Faulkner's narrative method requires the reader to participate in the creation of the *fabula,* "the basic narrative, the actions of the story in strict chronological order" (126): "By employing this circuitous and oblique approach to the *fabula,* Faulkner *implicates* careful readers more fully than he could possibly do by using a more straightforward chronology. This kind of narrative manipulation of time calls attention *to* time, to the encroachment of the past on the present, to the complexity of causative factors, because we can make no real sense out of the story unless we confront these issues. We are involved more actively and intensely in the narrative process because it is up to us to recreate the *fabula*" (130). For readers like Edmond Volpe, the story is fundamentally about the South: "a brilliantly wrought, emotionally charged, haunting portrait of the Southern psyche—a psyche tormented by conflicting feelings, impulses, and needs" (98). He calls the title "superimposed, Faulkner's expression of affection for what he hates. What he hates is not so much the South's morbid, pathological attachment to the dead glory of the past but the ghoulish power of the past on the consciousness of the South. And what he loves," Volpe contends, "is the tragic figure of the Southerner, trapped by his pride in his heritage and tormented by conflicting needs to conform and to defy, struggling vainly and helplessly to escape from the past and exist in the present" (99). In such readings, Emily Grierson emerges as a kind of precursor to Quentin Compson of *Absalom, Absalom!* (1936), whose anguished ambivalence about his homeland closes the novel that many consider Faulkner's greatest.

Some have speculated that "A Rose for Emily" may have been written as early as 1927, when Faulkner told his publisher, Horace Liveright, that he was working on "a collection of short stories of my townspeople" (*Selected Letters* 34), but we can be certain only that it existed by 7 October 1929, when *Scribner's* magazine rejected it. Whether Faulkner revised the story between this date and its acceptance by *Forum* on 20 January 1930 is unclear, but "A Rose for Emily" in its present form was published in the April 1930 issue of *Forum.* The story was reprinted with what Jones calls "minimal and minor" changes in *These 13* (1931), the contract for which, at one point, referred to the volume as "A ROSE FOR EMILY And Other Stories" (Jones 89; Blotner 1974, 692). Cowley included the story in *The Portable Faulkner,* Saxe Commins chose it for *The Faulkner Reader,* and hundreds of anthologies contain reprints of it. In addition to the critical approaches outlined above, Faulkner's possible literary and local sources for the story have come in for a good bit of attention, and the story's title has prompted several interpretations. Diane Brown Jones, whose own summary of the criticism runs forty-seven pages, says "the critical canon of 'A Rose for Emily' has become as bloated as the character herself," and she observes that "there is little evidence to suggest a tapering off of published responses to the text" (133). We may conclude, then, that the story and its commentary, also like Miss Emily herself, promise to remain "dear, inescapable, impervious, tranquil, and perverse" (*CS* 128).

119:TITLE Enigmatic at least, the title seems to anticipate the "rose-shaded lights" (129:31) of the story's final pages. At the University of Virginia, Faulkner responded to a question about the meaning of the title: "Oh, it's simply the poor woman had had no life at all. Her father had kept her more or less locked up and then she had a lover who was about to quit her, she had to murder him. It was just 'A Rose for Emily'—that's all" (*Faulkner in the University* 87–88). The title, then, is metafictional, Faulkner's "rose," his tribute to his character.

119:1 **our whole town** Jefferson, Mississippi. The narrator's use of "our" might imply a communal narrative voice, but later passages seem to indicate a single narrator speaking on behalf of others in the town, since the narrator has some information (129:23–25) that the whole town does not.

119:7 **frame house** a wooden house, as opposed to a brick one or a shack; a marker of Emily's class status

119:8–9 **cupolas and spires and scrolled balconies in the heavily lightsome style of the seventies** ornate gingerbread-style trim typical of Victorian-era homes of the 1870s

119:11 **cotton gins** buildings in which the seeds are removed from raw cotton, by means of a cotton gin, the fiber then formed into bales

119:13 **coquettish decay** the house as a metaphor for its last mistress, whose brief life as a coquette decays into the final passages of the story

119:16–17 **cedar-bemused cemetery** so crowded with cedar trees that one could get lost or confused from the repetition of the trees and the cedar smell. According to James Crockett, many trees are informally known as cedars because of their aromatic smell, but there are only five "true cedars and only three [of these] grow in the United States" (*Evergreens* 91), all in Mississippi.

119:18–19 **Union and Confederate soldiers who fell at the battle of Jefferson** Faulkner may have been thinking of the Battle of Holly Springs, which occurred on 20 December 1863, about 30 miles north of Oxford. The battle involved CSA Major General Earl van Dorn, who "recapture[d Holly Springs] and [a] massive Union military supply depot, forcing Gen. Ulysses Grant to retreat to Tennessee" ("Bibliography—Military Actions in Mississippi").

119:23–120:1 **the edict that no Negro woman should appear on the streets without an apron** Slavery was abolished in 1865 with the adoption of the thirteenth amendment; five years later, in 1870, the fifteenth provided that rights, including the right to vote, were not to be denied on the basis of race or past servitude. In the South, and in Faulkner's Jefferson, these constitutional amendments made few changes to the reality of racial inequality and the local laws instituted to ensure this inequality. Colonel Sartoris's "edict" marks black women as inferior—and, in fact, as "black," regardless of their skin color—much as the *tigue* did in New Orleans.

120:7–9 **Only a man of Colonel Sartoris' generation and thought could have invented it, and only a woman could have believed it** Sartoris's generation was used to taking care of troublesome females, and they in turn were used to being taken care of by the man in charge.

120:17 **paper of an archaic shape** not a present-day, standard-size piece of stationery

120:23–24 **china-painting lessons** China painting, embroidery, musical training, and other "feminine arts" were particularly important in the eighteenth and nineteenth centuries, and were collectively known as "accomplishments," skills that young women of the upper and middle classes perfected to enhance their character and increase their marriage potential (see Theobald, for example). In Miss Emily's case, the occupation must serve as her source of income in the absence of a husband and his support.

120:33 **crayon portrait** not an oil painting but a chalk or conte crayon drawing; another indication of class pretense carried out with limited means

121:24 **by the—** "books" or "law"

121:27–28 **Colonel Sartoris had been dead almost ten years** Colonel Sartoris died in about 1917, according to this timeline.

121:30 **horse and foot** all of them, cavalry (horse) and infantry (foot) alike

122:19 **that nigger of hers** Tobe (121:29). The epithet characterizes Judge Stevens's racial views; the narrator has been scrupulous to use the then-current polite term "Negro," with the exception he makes at 124:16.

122:25 **graybeards** old men

122:28–29 **if she don't . . .** then we will fine/sanction her

122:31 **lady** In Faulkner's South, the term carries racial as well as class and gender connotations. A "lady" was by definition white, and the protection of her honor by (white) gentlemen a trap for both races and sexes. As Diane Roberts has argued, Faulkner was "fascinated" in the 1930s by "the white woman's burden" of repressed sexuality: "Miss Emily is an interrogation, a parody, and a celebration of the Confederate Woman . . . but above all she is a lady" (158, 160).

122:33 **slunk** past-tense version of *slink*; similar to *snuck* (instead of *sneaked*)

123:1–4 **one of them performed a regular sowing motion with his hand out of a sack slung from his shoulder. They broke open the cellar door and sprinkled lime there, and in all the outbuildings** The men are strewing quicklime on Miss Emily's property (the main house as well as the dependencies) in order to hasten the process of decomposition of whatever small animals they believe have died on the grounds and thus produced the offensive odor.

123:8 **locusts** trees, in this context, not insects

123:13–14 **held themselves a little too high for what they really were** an accusation that the Griersons are pretentious

123:15–19 **We had long thought of them as a tableau, Miss Emily a slender figure in white in the background, her father a spraddled silhouette in the foreground, his back to her and clutching a horse-whip, the two of them framed by the back-flung front door** a striking image of Emily's repression at her father's hands, and reminiscent of her appearance before the aldermen at 121:1–12.

123:28–29 **a penny more or less** being poor to the point that every penny makes a difference

124:10–11 **her hair was cut short** probably a result of being treated for a high fever. According to Dr. Victor Wilson and Dr. M. Wayne Cooper, during the eighteenth and nineteenth centuries physicians knew that fever patients radiated heat through their scalps; historian of medicine Sue Lederer adds that in the late 1800s there was a public health campaign to raise awareness of germ theory that included the shaving of men's beards. Her hair was probably cut in a belief that it would cool her brain, or as Dr. Wilson adds, to keep her hair from matting.

124:12 **colored church windows** stained glass windows

124:14 **let** awarded

124:16 **niggers** This passage is the first time that the narrator has used the word "nigger" to identify the black population in Jefferson; previously, the narrator has used "Negroes" (119:23; 120:25; 120:27; 120:29; 121:30; 122:7). He thus makes a class distinction between town-dwelling blacks, including house servants, and the gang of black laborers.

124:20–21 **the niggers singing in time to the rise and fall of picks** Possibly convict labor, the gang sings to relieve the backbreaking and monotonous work of breaking the earth for the sidewalks to be laid.

124:25–26 **the yellow-wheeled buggy and the matched team of bays from the livery stable** a flashy rented driving rig; the horse equivalent of a sports car, with two lookalike reddish-brown horses

124:30–125:2 **But there were still others, older people, who said that even grief could not cause a real lady to forget *noblesse oblige*—without calling it *noblesse oblige*. They just said, "Poor Emily. Her kinsfolk should come to her"** ***noblesse oblige*:** French term meaning "nobility obliges"; the moral obligation of those with high birth to treat the lower classes with kindness and generosity. The older folks seem to think that Emily is not a "real lady," that in consorting with Homer Barron at all she has revealed this fact and now, apparently sexually involved with him, stands in need of her kinfolks' protection.

125:8–9 **"Do you suppose it's really so?" they said to one another. "Of course it is. What else could . . ."** keep a man like that with her?; keep them together?; keep him seeing her? The townspeople believe that Emily and Homer are having a sexual affair at Homer's insistence; they never entertain the notion of Emily's desires.

125:14–15 **even when we believed that she was fallen** no longer virgin, and so lacking an important qualification for an unmarried lady

125:18 **arsenic** an easily obtained and common poison. According to Stewart Harvey, "the symptoms would be made to develop insidiously and to simulate disease; arsenic compounds have little taste and, consequently, could easily be administered in food without detection. . . . Arsenic is still used in certain insecticides and rat poisons" (Goodman 947). A potent capillary poison, arsenic affects the visceral area most dramatically; plasma seeps through the pores, blood volume drops, and, ultimately, "arteriolar damage occurs, and the blood pressure falls to shock levels. The heart muscle also becomes depressed and this may contribute to the circulatory failure" (946). It is a painful way to die.

125:30 **The druggist named several** According to David Fincannon, an expert on pest control and its history, the druggist would use the chemical names of these poisons, which would have included arsenic trioxide, strychnine sulphate, strychnine alkaloid, zinc phosphide, and thallium sulphate (see Truman). Emily seems to seize upon the arsenic, probably because she has heard it mentioned, but perhaps because he named it early in his litany.

125:31 **But what you want is—** Arsenic would indeed kill an elephant. He seems to want to sell her a less-potent poison for her "rat."

125:33 **Is . . .** He is trying to finish his sentence at 125:31, not listening to Emily.

125:33 **But what you want—** is something less strong

126:3–4 **the law requires you to tell what you are going to use it for** Fincannon (see 125:50) notes that the druggist might well have had arsenic in stock because, starting in 1910, it was an element in one cure for venereal disease.

126:8–9 **the druggist didn't come back** Perhaps embarrassed that he has compromised his professional ethics—and apparently broken the law—by selling her the poison without hearing her say what she will use it for, the druggist will not face her.

126:10 **the skull and bones** the symbol for poisonous materials, a skull with two crossed bones underneath

126:18 **a marrying man** the kind of man who wants to marry

126:23 **it** the unchaperoned buggy rides

126:26 **Baptist** denomination of Protestant Christians that believes in baptism only for its believers and practices baptism through total immersion

126:26 **Episcopal** members of the Episcopal Church, the Anglican church of the U.S.

127:1–2 **So she had blood-kin under her roof again and we sat back to watch developments** With the proper chaperones in place in Emily's house, the town settles into moral complacency and takes up its customary voyeurism.

127:5 **man's toilet set** grooming items, such as a mirror, brush, and comb

127:7 **including a nightshirt** They who watch Emily and Homer assume that an unmarried woman would not order sleeping garments for a man.

127:0–10 **more Grierson than Miss Emily had ever been** more "high and mighty"; see 123:13–14

127:13–14 **a public blowing-off** a dramatic, public break-up

127:27–28 **Then we knew that this was to be expected too** **this** = the abandonment by Homer Barron

128:10–11 **Meanwhile her taxes had been remitted** Emily is giving china-painting lessons in 1894 (119:22), when she is "about forty" (128:4); this would place her birth at around 1854 and her death, at age seventy-four (128:1), in 1928.

128:15–16 **pictures cut from the ladies' magazines** patterns for her pupils to copy onto the china

128:17–18 **When the town got free postal delivery** According to the United States Postal Service, free city delivery was begun in 1863, and free rural delivery was instituted in 1902. Clearly, it took a while to reach Jefferson.

128:26 **she had evidently shut up the top floor of the house** The townspeople must infer this from observing her only in the downstairs windows.

129:3–4 **a heavy walnut bed with a curtain** an old-fashioned four-poster bed, curtained for warmth and privacy

129:8–9 **He walked right through the house and out the back and was not seen again** Tobe, the only source of what "Already we knew" at 129:23–25, leaves the house because he knows what the town will find in the upstairs room, as a rejected passage from Faulkner's early manuscript and typescript drafts makes plain (see Millgate, *Achievement* 263–64; Volpe 103–04). He clearly wants to avoid the uproar, gossip, and possible danger to himself.

129:15 **brushed Confederate uniforms** The old war veterans have dressed up for Miss Emily's funeral and thus claimed her as their own, a remnant of the vanquished South.

129:23–25 **Already we knew that there was one room in that region above stairs which no one had seen in forty years, and which would have to be forced** see 129:8–9

129:25 **They** presumably the town elders or Board of Aldermen, but obviously including the narrator

129:30 **valance curtains** border of drapery around either the bed, the windows, or both

129:30–31 **faded rose color, upon the rose-shaded lights** the only hints in the story of its title

130:11–13 **the long sleep that outlasts love, that conquers even the grimace of love, had cuckolded him** Death, rather than another man, has taken Emily from Homer—an interesting inversion of what we might expect, since Emily sent death to him in the first place.

"Hair"

Told in the first person by an unnamed narrator of questionable reliability, "Hair" has often attracted readers interested in identifying and tracing various patterns of character, technique, and theme in Faulkner's fiction. The story contains one of the first appearances of attorney Gavin Stevens, tellingly in possession of a fact that topples the narrator's authority and perhaps even his self-assurance; Stevens, of course, comes to figure prominently in stories and novels of Faulkner's middle and later years as a writer—*Knight's Gambit* (1949), *The Town* (1957), and *The Mansion* (1959), most notably. A character named Susan, whose body is described as "reed-thin" (*Uncollected Stories* 500, 501), appears in "Moonlight," a 1928 revision of what Faulkner remembered as one of his very earliest stories (Meriwether, *Literary Career* 87); the Susan Reed of "Hair" numbers among the maligned women in Faulkner's canon. A barber named Hawkshaw also appears in "Dry September," to much different effect than in "Hair." Like so many of Faulkner's other fictions, the story treats of the vexed subject of female sexual desire and male reactions to that desire. The narrator and others who frequent the barber shop repeatedly assert stereotypical attitudes toward women in general and toward Susan Reed in particular. Story's end finds us in a problematic position, however. If we understand comedy as a narrative that ends with the largest and most comprehensive resolution of conflict, then the ending seems comic (unusual in itself in Faulkner's stories with similar subject matter): Hawkshaw's discipline, hard work, determination, selflessness, idealism, and patience pay off when Susan Reed agrees to marry him; and in return he takes her away from the town that has continuously and negatively judged her. Yet when we consider that he is forty-five and she seventeen or eighteen, and when we notice that we are never privy to Susan's thoughts and experiences, including how she feels about Hawkshaw, the happily-ever-after glow of the story's ending dims a bit.

Readers of "Hair" tend to emphasize either Hawkshaw or Susan Reed. Among those who search for character patterns, Joseph Blotner says the barber "displayed characteristics of a Faulkner type who would become more familiar: the good, decent, frugal, self-effacing man who is almost a victim but who is finally rewarded" (1974; 650). James Ferguson offers that "Hawkshaw seems, until the very end, one of those lonely souls doomed to empty, frustrated, and unfulfilled lives" (109). Judith Bryant Wittenberg compares the barber with his namesake in the better-known "Dry September." "Hawkshaw," she maintains, "delineated in 'Hair' as intensely devoted to personal values that include fidelity and compassion, subsequently reveals in 'Dry September' that those values cannot withstand the public assault represented by the irrational violence of the barbershop mob" (283). Edmond Volpe calls the portrait of Hawkshaw "static": "he seems to exist out of time, like a nondescript face in the background of a snapshot of a village barber shop." He also says that "Henry's thralldom to the dead girl explains his fixation as well as his lack of concern about Susan's history and character. It is not her but her Sophie-like hair that is meaningful to him" (131, 133). Susan herself has occasioned a variety of responses, ranging from Blotner's assessment of her as "a victim first glimpsed at age five" ("Children" 87) to Lisa Paddock's claim that "the sluttish Susan is an improbable successor to the nondescript Sophie" (40). Other commentators focus on the role of the narrator, in our view the principal character of the story. Hans Skei says "the story about Hawkshaw and Susan Reed is the product of the narrator's rather limited total understanding, and yet there is more to it than this. The narrator reveals some of his prejudice, and the *dénouement* shows that he has misinterpreted everything that he has watched and speculated upon" (*Novelist* 176). Ferguson maintains that "the viewpoint figure here is a real human being, a relatively individualized person, with a job, a family, health problems . . . and some very specific views of his own. In 'Hair' the narrator is something more than just a device" (110). Wittenberg says that the narrator "shares with the reader his efforts to assess a puzzling concatenation of events, and Faulkner gives the story additional complexity by introducing a series of secondary narrators who assist the principal in accreting detail" (286). Because we remain thoroughly grounded in this character's perspective and because he learns at story's end the one fact which he would never have entertained even as a possibility, we are equally blind-sided by the news.

As the echo in "Moonlight" implies, "Hair" may well have existed for some time before its first appearance on Faulkner's short story sending schedule at 20 March 1930. The story was rejected several times, and possibly revised, before it was accepted on a second submission to the *American Mercury,* which published it in the May 1931 issue. When Faulkner included the story in *These 13*, he revised it slightly, deleting the conventional periods after *Mr* and *Mrs* and the apostrophes in one-syllable contractions, for example. When the story was printed again, in *Collected Stories*—after Faulkner added it, along with other stories from *These 13* and *Doctor Martino,* to the list originally prepared by Robert K. Haas (*Selected Letters* 278)—the missing punctuation was restored and at least one apparent error was introduced ("clubhouse" for "courthouse" at 141:4). It appears as the second story in "The Village," right after "A Rose for Emily," perhaps Faulkner's most famous story about an imperfectly understood woman.

131:1 **This girl, this Susan Reed, was an orphan** The colloquial opening line of the story includes "Hair" among those Faulkner stories narrated in the first person by an unapologetic gossip and voyeur.

131:4–5 **others cast the usual aspersions on the character of Burchett and even of Mrs. Burchett: you know** the gossip that Mr. or Mrs. Burchett was Susan's biological parent; the first hint of the role that shared information plays in the story, and an implication of the reader in the gossip

131:7 **Hawkshaw** A newspaper cartoon, "Hawkshaw the Detective," created by Gus Mager, ran from 1913 until 1922 and then occasionally until the late 1940s. The name was taken from a stage production called "The Ticket-of-Leave Man" that featured a detective named Hawkshaw. As time passed, the name became slang for "detective" (see Markstein). See also 138:20.

131:8 **It was his first summer behind that chair** the story's chronological beginning

131:8–9 **barber shop** In small-towns and neighborhoods, the barber shop is one center of the men's socializing, as the local beauty shop is for women. Why Mrs. Burchett brings Susan to the bastion of male rather than female gossip remains an open question.

131:20 **me** the first direct revelation of the identity of the story's narrator, a clothing salesman who works a territory in North Mississippi and Alabama

132:3 **hair without any special name** see 131:12–13: "this straight, soft hair not blonde and not brunette"

132:6 **legs sticking straight out in front of her** Susan is so little that her legs stick out over the front edge of the chair.

132:8–9 **Saturday night shaving customer** men who would come in every Saturday, after the week's work, for a barber's shave (complete with hot towels, hot lather, relaxation, pampering, and gossip)

132:25 **five minutes to eight and to three o'clock came** that is, five minutes before the school day begins and ends

132:33 **No** an example of the narrator's catching himself in an error and correcting the record—or, perhaps, of changing matters to make a better story

133:9–11 **I guess maybe a talking man hasn't got the time to ever learn about anything except words** whereas a listening man learns about people, about life. This is an interesting pivot point in the narrative because our narrator is, for the space of this story at least, a talking man.

133:18 **it** Susan's "[getting] grown too fast" (133:18)

133:19–21 **Girls are different from boys. Girls are born weaned and boys don't ever get weaned** The narrator sees women as independent from their mothers and from each other and believes that men, however, always want to be—and might even need to be—mothered by women.

133:24 **they are all born bad** The narrator believes that women's natural sex drives are indications of the essential moral corruption of females; although this "badness" is no fault of theirs, it must be controlled by marrying them off before they have a chance to recognize what they feel and act out sexually. He thinks that the only sex women should have is married sex.

133:26 **natural head** the point at which she succumbs to her sex drive

133:32–33 **I think they can't help it. I have a daughter of my own, and I say that** The narrator is supporting his sexist ideology by acknowledging female "badness" in his own child. In doing so, he thinks he shores up the reasonableness of his case even as he acts like a reliable source of information; we wonder how old his daughter is and how she might describe her home life.

134:2 **rouge and paint** cosmetics, in this case colored powder on the cheeks and probably lipstick

134:9 **gingham** yarn-dyed, woven cotton cloth; a common and plain fabric

134:10–11 **pulled and dragged to show off what she never had yet to show off** She has shortened her skirt and somehow exposed some of her chest, like the older girls and adult women do, even though she isn't yet through puberty.

134:12 **silk and crepe** popular fabrics for fashionable adult dresses in the 1920s

134:21–23 **Why, nobody can be as gentle with them, the bad ones, the ones that are unlucky enough to come to a head too soon, as men** see 133:24 and 133:32–33; further evidence of the narrator's paternalistic sexism

134:24–25 **Even after folks knew, after all the talk began** Common gossip about Susan, in the narrator's mind, equates to "knowledge" of her character and her activities.

135:23 **gummed** styled and dressed to remain in place, probably with hair spray

135:32 **making out** pretending

136:2 **I made Jefferson** I got to Jefferson

136:8–9 **He stopped, the razor in his hand, the blade loaded with lather** Matt Fox's news about the wristwatch so surprises Maxey that he stops shaving his customer, an indication that what Matt says is so important yet so unforeseen that Maxey's routine comes abruptly to a halt.

136:10–11 **You reckon he was the first one, the one that—** "took her virginity"; Maxey's immediate suspicion

136:16–17 **trick one and then not even pay her nothing** Maxey insinuates that Hawkshaw tricked Susan into having sex with him and then did not pay her for it, which implies that Susan is in fact prostituting herself. Taken further, Maxey's logic implies that Hawkshaw—and by extension, all men who have sex with women to whom they are not married—must pay for sex.

136:21 **kin** a blood relation (or, more important in Hawkshaw's case, a spouse)

136:32 **worked Jefferson** finished meeting potential clients and selling wares

137:1 **I wanted to give him time** to finish cleaning up the house and leave town without knowing that I knew about his life there

137:5 **thirteen years ago** The chronology of this story isn't exact, and Susan's age in particular is ambiguous; in fact, it too is a part of community gossip (see 133:34–134:1, for instance). Susan was "about five" when Hawkshaw arrived in Jefferson (131:7), which is "a year later" after the narrator first met him in Porterfield "thirteen years ago" (see 137:15–16 and 17). Susan must be around seventeen or eighteen by the end of the story, which ends in 1930, because Hawkshaw arrived in Jefferson in 1917, before he made the first mortgage payment on the Starnes place (see 146:31), so Susan was probably born in about 1912.

137:5–7 **I had just gone on the road then, making North Mississippi and Alabama with a line of work shirts and overalls** Our narrator is a traveling salesman who sells work clothing, acting as the middle man between the manufacturer and general stores in his territory. By the logic at 137:5, we deduce that he has been in this line of work since 1917.

137:13 **serge suit** matching jacket and trousers made of very firm-textured and durable wool

137:16 **imitation leather suitcases** As a barber with income from small-town customers and paying off a debt of honor, Hawkshaw does not have enough money to buy genuine leather luggage, so instead he has a cardboard suitcase that probably has a printed leather design. See also 140:32–33.

137:21 **sixty miles away** the distance between Porterfield and Jefferson

137:22 **missing a lick** from "miss a beat": "hesitate momentarily," with specific reference to musical time and so in a regular rhythm (see Ammer 422). According to Calvin Brown, in Faulkner's South a "lick" is a blow, and "[t]o get (or get in) one's licks is to accomplish something or to have one's fair turn or chance" (119).

137:27 **It was three years after that before I found out about him** Our narrator discovered Hawkshaw's history with the Starnes family in 1920, three years after Hawkshaw got to Jefferson.

137:28–30 **a store and four or five houses and a sawmill on the State line between Mississippi and Alabama** Our narrator's job is to call on some very small "towns" indeed, like the appropriately named Division.

137:30 **I had noticed a house there** Our narrator is both observant of detail and unreliable in the conclusions he draws from what he observes, as the final line of the story reveals.

138:7 **pickets gone off the fence** While the usual meaning of "picket" is the pointed stake driven in the ground to support a fence, in this sentence and elsewhere Faulkner uses the word to describe the slats of the fence. As Calvin Brown explains, a "fence picket" in Faulkner is "one of the vertical and usually pointed slats . . . nailed, a couple of inches apart, to two horizontal rails to make a picket fence" (80). That definition makes more sense in this context; if neighbors had been pulling the supports out, there wouldn't be a fence standing for pickets to be "gone off" of.

138:11 **storekeeper** the proprietor of the store in Division, to whom the narrator sells his wares

138:13–14 **They were considered the best folks, because they owned some land, mortgaged** The passage implies that social status in Division is determined by land ownership, so if the Starneses are "the best," the other families there are probably tenant farmers, like Stribling. The fact that the land is mortgaged does not affect their class pretensions. See also 140:12.

138:20 **Stribling** Hawkshaw's last name, revealed in the story for the first time. T. S. Stribling (1881–1965) wrote hugely popular detective fiction for the popular magazines as well as serious fiction concerned with social issues, such as the future of African Americans in the New South. See also 131:7.

138:22–23 **went to Birmingham to learn barbering** The first school for barbers was established in 1893 in Chicago by A. B. Moler; an immediate success, "the parent school was rapidly followed by branches in nearly every principal city of the United States" ("History of Barbering").

138:31 **paid down on the furniture** left a down payment for furniture to be bought on the installment plan

138:34 **a right smart** "a considerable amount" (Brown 163)

139:8 **Cut them and shoot them: that's all right. But let them get a bad cold and maybe they'll get well or maybe they'll die two days later of cholera** The country people recover easily from knife and gunshot wounds, in the narrator's view, but not from common infections. He implies that they are used to the former, an indication of his class prejudice.

139:11 **They had to cut all her hair off** According to Dr. Victor Wilson and Dr. M. Wayne Cooper, during the eighteenth and nineteenth centuries physicians knew that fever patients radiated heat through their scalps; historian of medicine Sue Lederer adds that in the late 1800s there was a public health campaign to raise awareness of germ theory that included the shaving of men's beards. We speculate that in the backwoods South among ill-educated folk, Susan's hair was cut in a belief that it would cool her brain, or as Dr. Wilson adds, to keep her hair from matting.

139:20 **Henry Stribling** the first time Hawkshaw's full name appears in the story

139:31 **get shut of** get rid of

140:12 **being as she was better born than him** Mrs. Starnes is a snob who assumes that Stribling owes her his time and labor because she allowed her daughter to become engaged to him.

140:13 **parveynoos** from the French, *parvenu*: a social upstart; one who has moved up in class status

140:17–18 **Then he begun to pay the principal on the mortgage** Stribling is paying off the actual money owed on the house, not just the interest on the loan. Once he begins paying the principal, the debt will be reduced more quickly, since there will be less money owed on which to charge interest.

140:28–30 **He had been doing that for about five years when I saw him in Maxey's shop in Jefferson, the year after I saw him in a shop in Porterfield** a contradiction of the narrator's earlier account (137:27) of the three years that elapsed between seeing Hawkshaw in Jefferson and seeing him in Porterfield

140:32–33 **paper suitcase** see 137:16

141:3–4 **the loafers that pitch dollars all day long in the clubhouse yard** according to Brown, a game like horseshoes in which the players toss either silver dollars or washers toward a hole or a line on the ground (149)

141:4 **clubhouse yard** The *American Mercury* and *These 13* versions of the story read "courthouse yard."

141:8–10 **They said he was a detective, maybe because that was the last thing in the world anybody would suspect him to be. So they named him Hawkshaw** see 131:7

142:10 **Bolivar, Tennessee** town about 70 miles east of Memphis, TN; about 75 miles north of Oxford, MS

142:10 **Florence, Alabama** town located in the northwest corner of Alabama; about 125 miles northeast of Oxford, MS

142:29–33 **So Maxey and Matt and I reckon everybody else in Jefferson thought that he had saved up steam for a year and was now bound on one of these private sabbaticals among the fleshpots of Memphis** The line reflects the town's preoccupation with one another's sex lives, particularly those of its unmarried citizens like Susan and Hawkshaw. Here, they expect the abstemious Hawkshaw to spend his vacation in a brothel.

142:33 **depot freight agent** railroad agent who prices services

143:29–30 **Maybe that's her price** The narrator implies that Susan is prostituting herself.

143:31–33 **most of the talk about girls, women, is envy or retaliation by the ones that dont dare to and the ones that failed to** a curiously sympathetic comment from this narrator about the reasons that people gossip about women's sex lives. The absent phrase is telling: "don't dare to have sex" and "failed to have sex."

144:1 **got in trouble at last** got pregnant. Note that the only evidence for Susan's pregnancy is town gossip.

144:2 **doctor herself with turpentine** As at 144:1, gossip is the only source of information on the nature of Susan's illness. They believe that she either ingested turpentine or douched with it; both techniques were thought to facilitate miscarriage.

144:5 **some said in a hospital in Memphis** As at 144:1 and 2, gossip supplies the only explanation of Susan's absence.

144:18 **I used to be a bookkeeper in a Gordonville bank** a job that would help him appreciate Hawkshaw's meticulous ledgers

144:19 **my health broke down** perhaps an alcoholic or mental collapse; in any case, a breakdown serious enough to require hospitalization in a large city's hospital

144:22 **I told him about it two years ago** according to the most consistent chronology (see 137:5, for instance), about 1928

144:31–32 **the first man to tilt at windmills** an allusion to Miguel Cervantes' novel *Don Quixote*, the title character of which attacked a windmill because he thought it was a monster

145:26 **I got your letter** Stevens has the complete backstory on Hawkshaw's comings and goings in Division, so when he marries Susan, Stevens knows that he has discharged the debt he felt he owed the Starnes family. He therefore has no real need to ask the narrator, "Tell me about it" (145:27), because he already knows the outcome of their story. He seems to be interested in what the narrator's version of the story will be.

146:3 **apple shoot** young apple tree; a sapling

146:8–9 **The stove was polished and the woodbox filled** Stribling prepared the house for occupation, as he always has, but it is unclear for whose use he prepares it—the Alabama Starneses' or his own and Susan's.

146:12 **melodeon** a simple organ

146:14 **the bowl empty and clean too** Stribling has emptied the kerosene out of the bottom of the lamp, so that if it is knocked over it will not spill or catch fire.

146:17 **mortgage record** table listing payments made to the bank and money still owed on the loan

147:6 **copy book** penmanship primer

147:6–7 **old-time business colleges** schools at which pupils—men and women alike—learned secretarial skills such as typewriting, shorthand, transcription; professional preparation for support staff in business

147:18–20 **time and despair rushed as slow and dark under him as under any garlanded boy or crownless and crestless girl** Stevens seems to mean that Hawkshaw, upon discharging his debt to the Starneses, thought of the time that he had lost with Susan and despaired at the thought. Stevens is commenting sympathetically on Hawkshaw's age and how it could not cushion him from thoughts of mortality. The allusion is to A. E. Housman (1859–1936) and Lyric XIX of *A Shropshire Lad* (1896), more commonly known as "To An Athlete Dying Young":

And round that early-laurelled head
Will flock to gaze the strengthless dead,
And find unwithered on its curls
A garland briefer than a girl's.

Faulkner knew by heart and could recite long sections of Housman's poem.

"Centaur in Brass"

In "Centaur in Brass," Faulkner tells a richly complex trickster tale in which the would-be trickster, Flem Snopes—who in other fictions appears as one of Faulkner's arch-villains, on a par with Jason Compson—is himself tricked by the confederation of two African American men, Tom-Tom and Turl, whom he has set against each another as part of his scheme to steal brass from the Jefferson power plant where they all work. The story also features two adulterous triangles, the implied one among Snopes, his wife, and Major Hoxey, and the explicit one involving Tom-Tom, his wife, and Turl. Snopes apparently tolerates his wife's involvement with Major Hoxey in return for the plant superintendency, an arrangement that outrages respectable Jefferson. Tom-Tom and Turl behave more according to the town's expectations of adulterers (particularly black ones); when Tom-Tom catches Turl sneaking to meet his wife, he tries to kill him. The story's title refers partly to the scene of their wild confrontation in the dark, which leads to Turl's carrying the knife-wielding Tom-Tom on his back until they tumble into a ravine from which they eventually emerge in concert against Snopes, rather than as enemies of one another.

The narrative point of view of the story is a bit tricky, beginning with what seems to be the choric voice of Jefferson and recalling the opening line of "A Rose for Emily": "When Miss Emily Grierson died, our whole town went to her funeral" (*CS* 119). While the "Emily" narrator remains plural, anonymous, and distant, the unnamed "Centaur" narrator becomes imaginatively and rhetorically involved in the unfolding of the story. The narrator asserts in the opening paragraph of the story that "only four people, two white men and two Negroes, know that it is his monument, or that it is a monument at all" (*CS* 149). The four people are Tom-Tom, Turl, Snopes, and the power plant's night engineer, Harker. Although the narrator does not count himself among the knowing, he nevertheless joins their number as the story unfolds. This slight disparity has struck some as a flaw in the narrative. James Ferguson says that Faulkner's handling of point of view here is "a really egregious example of carelessness" and that the story is thus "rather thoroughly botched" (114). However we evaluate the success of Faulkner's method, it serves to invite us into a small circle of the knowledgeable, a discreet group privileged to contemplate the sexual peccadilloes of white and black alike and to appreciate the comic justice of Flem Snopes's defeat.

In spite of their role as originators of plot, the two women in the story receive scant treatment by the narrator and have occasioned little discussion among the interpreters of the story. As in other Faulkner stories, the narrative method draws on conventions of both gender and racial stereotyping. Neither woman, for example, bears her own name but remains instead defined as her husband's adjunct. Noting this frequent practice in Faulkner's delineation of a radically patriarchal society, Doreen Fowler concludes, "by pointedly omitting their names, Faulkner calls attention to the neglected state of women in this culture" (531). The conclusive articulation of Tom-Tom's cuckoldry contrasts with the town's conjecture regarding the relations between Major Hoxey and Mrs. Snopes, but even as Tom-Tom's wife is protected from direct exposure and humiliation, she nevertheless remains "shadowy and covert and unspeaking" (*CS* 165)—a mystery to all the men around her. The implicit and explicit confrontations between the black and white cultures of "our town," however, have evoked significant commentary. Charles H. Nilon, for example, argues that the story depends for its effects on both the articulation and subversion of racial stereotypes such as razors, watermelon, promiscuity, and butcher knives (*Faulkner* 51; "Blacks" 247–50). Because Tom-Tom and Turl are black, Snopes assumes their ignorance, even their stupidity, their willingness to steal, and their "natural" economic rivalry. He is wrong about all these things, of course, and his persistence in this condescension and manipulation leads to his downfall. While several commentators would agree with Joseph R. Urgo's assessment that the story is "a comic but pointed commentary on African American solidarity in the face of white efforts to divide the black community" (65), John T. Matthews argues that "this fable of black organization at the expense of white entrepreneurial mastery reflects the anxieties of the racially and economically advantaged in early thirties America" ("Shortened" 28–29). While this is true as far as it goes, it does not take into account the real-world, morally satisfying, and comically just victory that Tom-Tom and Turl achieve. A casual bigot himself, the narrator seems also to sympathize with Tom-Tom and Turl against Snopes. The story is as much a telling *against* bigotry as it is a telling *of* bigotry, and Edmond Volpe calls it "a moral comedy" (179).

The vast majority of the discussion of "Centaur in Brass" centers on its place in Faulkner's ongoing Snopes project. If we take *Father Abraham* (ca. 1927) as Faulkner's first treatment of the Snopes family, and if we note the Snopes material in *Flags in the Dust* (written by late 1927, published as *Sartoris* in 1929), we see that "Centaur" is only one text in what Faulkner once called a "chronicle" that had occupied him over a 34-year period (*Mansion* Preface). The chief texts of this chronicle, often called the "Snopes trilogy," are *The Hamlet* (1940), *The Town* (1957), and *The Mansion* (1959). "Centaur in Brass," probably written in 1930 or 1931, was published in the February 1932 *American Mercury*. Some have speculated that Faulkner turned to this story after *Scribner's* accepted the story "Spotted Horses" for publication in its June 1931 issue, but *Scribner's* editor Kyle Crichton rejected "Centaur," expressing a preference for stories in which Flem is triumphant rather than defeated (Meriwether, "Faulkner's Correspondence" 270–71). Faulkner saved "Spotted Horses" for *The Hamlet*, choosing not to include it in either *These 13* or *Doctor Martino*, and he similarly declined to collect either "Centaur in Brass" or "Mule in the Yard," eventually explaining to Malcolm Cowley in 1945 that both "are to fall in a later volume" (*Selected Letters* 197). He chose both for *Collected Stories*, however, placing "Centaur" as the third story in "The Village" section, between "Hair" and "Dry September." "Centaur in Brass" was thoroughly revised for Chapter 1 of *The Town* (see Towner, "'It Ain't Funny'"), and subsequent discussion has centered on the story's relation to the novel, although Diane Brown Jones observes that "sufficient differences between the texts warrant treatment of the short story as an independent writing"

(166). That observation is always true in reading Faulkner, and "Centaur in Brass" is, like "Mule in the Yard," an independent and authentic comic achievement.

149:TITLE **Centaur** mythological creature with the top half of a man joined to the bottom half of a horse; more figuratively, an unnatural hybrid or union

149:TITLE **Brass** alloy of copper and zinc, which at the time of this story and since has enjoyed popularity in the black market. Prior to ball bearings, brass bearings were used in engines because brass could be heated to a relatively high temperature for a long period of time before it would disintegrate or wear out. Once it had been worn down (or if it was stolen), brass could be resold to foundries that would melt down the brass and recast it into other forms.

149:1 **In our town** The "our" includes the narrator in the town's thinking and behavior, yet allows the possibility for differences in interpretation of what he sees.

149:4–5 **only four people, two white men and two Negroes** see Introduction

149:9–10 **a sewing-machine agent** traveling salesman specializing in sewing machines

149:10–11 **a half interest** half-ownership

150:31–32 **eating generations** The restaurant has been in Jefferson long enough for several generations of diners to have eaten there.

150:32 **the rich coloring of a calendar** a hand-tinted photograph or commercial print

151:6 **collarless shirts** Men's shirts of the time seldom had attached collars; so a separate collar, made most often of paper or celluloid, could be attached to "dress up" a shirt and then removed to be laundered or replaced.

151:6 **overalls** one-piece denim work clothing, with bib-and-strap top, favored by farmers and others who perform rigorous labor resulting in head-to-toe grime

151:7 **country-eating faces** the restaurant's usual clientele

151:9 **it** the town's sudden belief in an extramarital affair

151:15 **municipal power plant** City-owned and -operated, the site of electricity production. The production units in this story each consist of a firebox, boiler, steam tube, and generator. The coal-fed fires in the firebox heat the boilers, the steam from which goes through the tube and into the impeller of the generator. The pressure from the steam turns the impeller in the generator, which causes the generator to turn and create a magnetic field, which in turn creates the electricity for the town.

151:16–18 **one of those women the deeds and fortunes of whose husbands alone are the barometers of their good name** Flem's reputation will determine his wife's (see 151:27–28).

151:22–24 **Or perhaps what we knew or believed about Snopes was all; perhaps what we thought to be her shadow was merely his shadow falling upon her** With the information at 151:16–18, the narrator says that the town's belief in her affair with Major Hoxey derives from Flem's clear unfitness for his present position, not for anything she has done.

151:27–28 **walking and talking in amicable cuckoldry** see 160:24–25

151:28 **I** a distinction of the narrative voice from the voice of others in the town, like Harker, or the town itself, which is "outraged" by the amicability of the admittedly imagined cuckoldry

152:5 **third-rate grocery** grocery store selling goods of inferior quality, and usually liquor as well

152:8 **another woman that did that** Tom-Tom's wife, who fooled Snopes

152:9 **day fireman** one who feeds coal into the firebox of the power plant during the daytime shift; see 151:15

152:14 **the strictness of a Turk** The keeper of a harem would kill any man who entered it.

152:16 **shovel and bar** the shovel to load the coal and unload the ashes, and some kind of tamping bar or crow bar to arrange the coals in the firebox

152:17 **cleaning the fires** removing the ashes from underneath the firebox to allow oxygen to circulate

152:18 **coal-bunker** large compartment for storing coal, maybe open at the top to allow refilling from a railroad car. Coal burns at high temperatures unless treated with an accelerant of some kind, so Tom-Tom isn't in any danger of setting the place on fire.

152:20 **steam was up** strong pressure was powering the generator

152:21 **safety valve on the middle boiler was blowing off** see 151:15; a safety valve (which sometimes has a whistle) automatically opens and releases steam from the boiler into the room to keep the internal pressure from exceeding the maximum limit and so causing the boiler to blow up.

152:22 **potty** British slang for trivial or insignificant; perhaps here also slightly pot-bellied (see Calvin Brown 155)

153:5 **confounding his own shrewdness with his own cunning** cleverer than he needs to be to get what he wants; outsmarting himself

153:14 **setting hen** a hen in the process of laying or hatching eggs

153:17 **night engineer** overseer on the night shift; supervisor with some knowledge of how a steam engine operates, higher in rank than a fireman but not as high as the superintendent

153:18–20 **the vents stopped with one-inch steel screw plugs capable of a pressure of a thousand pounds** The one-inch-in-diameter screw plugs provide no way to let the steam out, as the safety valves did. It would have taken 1000 pounds of pressure per square inch to eject the bolts from the vents, but the boilers need only 100 p.s.i. to explode.

153:21–22 **And them three boiler heads you could poke a hole through with a soda straw** parts of the boiler where the steam enters the generator, which Harker implies are flimsy anyway, probably because they are subject to corrosion

153:23–24 **Turl, that couldn't even read a clock face, still throwing coal into them** The illiterate Turl can't read a steam gauge, either, and doesn't know what kind of danger he's in by continuing to fuel the fire.

153:26 **to even reach the injector** in time to get there to inject water into the boiler in order to cool the steam and reduce the pressure

153:27 **100** 100 pounds of pressure per square inch; the amount of pressure it would take to make a boiler explode

153:29–32 **they wouldn't even be able to find the job to give it to the next misbegotten that believed that live steam was something you blowed on a window pane in cold weather** Try the emphasis on *find*: If the gauge reaches 100 psi, the boilers will explode and take Turl (the present "misbegotten," a euphemism for bastard), job, and all with them.

154:4 **shut-off float in the water tank ain't heavy enough** If the float is similar to the mechanics of a toilet, then making the float heavier will open the valve that releases water instead of ensuring that it won't leak. Either Snopes has something backwards here, or he thinks Tom-Tom is too stupid to figure out the explanation for putting the valves in the water tank.

154:8–9 **"You mean—" I says. That's as far as I could get: "You mean—"** . . . he took them? We don't have any safety valves?

154:13 **catching forty winks** a brief nap; according to Christine Ammer, an expression supposedly first recorded in 1828 and relying on *wink* in the sense of sleep, which dates from the fourteenth century (223)

154:17 **after the load went off** after the demand for electricity diminished (the townspeople turned their lights off for the night)

154:19 **peanut parcher** machine for dry-roasting peanuts

154:25 **that** the fear that the boilers would blow up without the safety valves, killing them and blowing up the power plant

154:33–34 **an object which Tom-Tom said later he thought was a mule shoe** a magnet

155:3 **fittings, valves, rods and bolts** the small parts of the engine that might be brass

155:6 **runway** probably between the coal bunker and the boiler room

155:8–9 **sorting out the iron from the brass** iron is magnetic; brass is not

155:9–10 **then Snopes ordered Tom-Tom to gather up the segregated pieces of brass and bring them in to his office** a central metaphor of the central situation of the story, the segregation of the two affairs along race lines, as the metal is "segregated" by Snopes

155:21–22 **watching Tom-Tom, who looked at Snopes as steadily in turn; looked down at him** unlike Turl, Tom-Tom looks Snopes in the face (see 159:3), and down at him

155:28 **Turl was planning to steal some iron** Snopes apparently thinks Tom-Tom doesn't know the difference between brass and iron—which this section of the story belies—or that brass is more valuable than iron. He tries to mislead him as to the value of what he's asking Tom-Tom to hide.

155:32 **this stuff** the brass

156:2–3 **I knows a better way than that** "I'll just deal with Turl myself"; perhaps by the method mentioned at 162:9–11

156:10 **Ain't no man complained about my pressure yet** because he can shovel enough coal to maintain the steam pressure in the boiler, and no employer can complain; also a *double entendre,* a reference to his manhood

156:24 **a little piece of corn** a corn patch

156:33 **that little engine** the generator

156:33–34 **a right smart** a considerable amount (Brown 163)

156:34 **bushings and wrist pins** the metal lining in a wheel's axle-hole; the pin that joins a piston to its connecting rod; both are very small parts inside the engine

157:7–8 **Because by that time Turl had his own private temptations and worries** Although the chronology of the story is complex, this seems to refer to Turl's conversation with Snopes at 158:26–159:31, which brings him "temptations and worries, the same as Tom-Tom" (see 159:23–25).

157:18 **books** account books of assets and expenditures for the power plant

157:21–22 **one busted bib** broken tap (from *bibcock,* a faucet that curves downward)

157:26 **plumb** completely and entirely

157:31 **his chew** of tobacco

157:32–33 **hemmed and hawed a right smart** talked around the point a good deal (see Ammer 298 and 156:33–34)

158:1–2 **did he want me and Turl and Tom-Tom arrested right now, or would tomorrow do?** The blame shifts immediately to the black workers rather than to Harker or Snopes, a presumption behind which Snopes can hide and further maneuver.

158:3–4 **cup grease** calcium grease; a lubricant for high-pressure engines that has good water resistance and rust prevention (see "Lubricating Grease")

158:14 **then next Summer came** The narration of the story changes from second-hand first-person to first-person, as it remains until

160:11. It is difficult to locate the source of the narrator's information, which could be Turl as well as Harker.

158:14–17 **still laughing at and enjoying what he saw, and seeing so little, thinking how they were all fooling one another while he looked on, when it was him who was being fooled** He thought he knew everything that was going on at the time, but he didn't. This sentence provides some evidence for Harker's not being one of the two white men who know about Flem Snopes's "monument" (149:4–5). However, his final part of the narration in section V (166:14) shows that by the time he told the narrator the story, he had learned about the adultery and the brass-hiding. Given Harker's literal-mindedness as a narrator, we don't think he has the "high vision" that would allow him to see a symbol in the old water tower, but Flem and the narrator would.

158:18 **came to a head** reached a turning point or crisis; from "the medical sense of *head*, the tip of an abscess that is about to burst" (Ammer 83)

158:19 **to cut his first hay crop; clean the meadow for reseeding** harvest what was ready and prepare the field for another round of crops: call in the brass, sell it, and start over

158:21–22 **set the capital on his monument and had started to tear the scaffolding down** By bringing Turl into his scheme, Snopes has reached the height of his success, and yet he has unwittingly set the stage for the destruction of his own strategy; in other words, the game was over the instant he tried to profit from it.

158:24–25 **again two of them, white man and Negro, faced one another in the office** as Snopes and Tom-Tom had done at the beginning of Snopes's plot; see 155:21–22

159:3–5 **He looked briefly at Snopes's face; at the still eyes, the slow unceasing jaw, and down again. "I can handle as much coal as Tom-Tom," he said** Unlike Tom-Tom, Turl doesn't want to look a white man—his white supervisor, in any case—in the face. Race etiquette in this circumstance requires him not to do so.

159:6–7 **aside-looking face** see 159:3–5

159:10 **brass** Flem may think that Turl knows brass from iron and is therefore smarter than Tom-Tom, whom he misinforms at 155:28, or he may mention the brass so that Turl understands the high stakes involved in its going missing from the plant.

159:13 **Turl looked up** perhaps so shocked by the false allegation that he forgets race etiquette

159:23–25 **Buck Conner'll know that even a fool has got more sense than to steal something and hide it in his corn-crib** Flem insinuates that the marshal will think that Turl has framed Tom-Tom, since he will be the only one who claims to know where the brass is. Flem does not offer to support Turl's claim to the marshal, even though he's the one who passed on the information. Flem thus sticks Turl between the threat of punishment for something he didn't do and the promise of a job he hasn't asked for and doesn't deserve but would like to have nonetheless.

160:1–2 **no man could ever accuse him of having done anything that would aggregate forty years net** Turl hasn't got either Tom-Tom's pride or his experience; he's lazy.

160:4–7 **If Turl ever gets married, he wan't need no front door a-tall; he wouldn't know what it was for. If he couldn't come tom-catting in through the back window, he wouldn't know what he come after. Would you, Turl?** Harker's disparaging remarks about Turl's promiscuity ("tom-catting") foreshadow the importance it will have; the lines indicate that Harker told the narrator this part of the story after the main action finishes, and in front of Turl.

160:8–9 **So from here on it is simple enough, since a man's mistakes, like his successes, usually are simple** a kind of moral that the narrator seems to take as a motto, after which he turns the narration back over to Harker at 160:12

160:12 **pull his chestnuts** "out of the fire"; from the fables of a monkey that gets a cat to pull its chestnuts out of a fire, with the cat being a kind of pawn in the matter and the monkey the cleverer of the two (Ammer 89, 108–9); also, by implication, testicles

160:15 **high yellow** an African American of light skin tone, due to race-mixing

160:20 **wrastling** wrestling; in this context, firing the boilers

160:25 **like the fellow said** Harker's apparent imitation of the narrator's phrase "amicable cuckoldry" at 151:27–28 again raises the issue of who in this community tells what stories to whom, and on what authority.

160:25 **Colonel** Harker has promoted Hoxey from Major (151:4) to Colonel.

160:29 **It was bound to not last** the circumstances in the preceding lines 16–28 that Harker finds so amusing

161:4–5 **waiting for it to get along toward dark (it was already April then)** Because the days are getting longer, Turl can't approach the house until later and later; the longer days keep both Tom-Tom and Snopes waiting for him.

161:20 **iron** Snopes has previously told Turl that Tom-Tom is hiding brass, not iron (159:10).

161:28–29 **He would have to wait until along toward dark** see 161:4–5

162:1 **go-round** turn, chance, try

162:3 **shuck** seed hulls or corn shucks used to stuff the mattress

162:3 **bed tick** here, mattress rather than only the striped fabric ("ticking") covering it

162:4 **two audits** a detail that further obscures the chronology and narrative trades in the story: Harker means either the two auditors that came to see Snopes (see 157:10–158:13) or the initial audit and the audit that the reader has not encountered yet (167:16–33).

162:8 **strange tom-cat** Turl; see 160:4–7

162:9–11 **whenever a nigger husband in Jefferson hears that, he finds out where Turl is at before he even sharpens his razor: ain't that so, Turl?** see 160:4–7; Harker assumes Turl is the one who'll be first in line of anyone suspected of adultery, and so for vengeance. A straight razor, with a long blade that folded into the handle, was a formidable weapon and often the one of choice in a crime of passion, especially among blacks (see Perkins).

162:14 **brass hunting** Harker's sly euphemism for stalking Tom-Tom's wife

162:20 **dust-dark** dusk

162:21 **tom-cats up** creeps up quietly, as a tom cat would; see 160:4–7

163:6 **dosed** administered a dose of home remedies or patent medicines

164:11–16 **the two of them a strange and furious beast with two heads and a single pair of legs like an inverted centaur speeding phantomlike just ahead of the boardlike streaming of Tom-Tom's shirt-tail and just beneath the silver glint of the lifted knife, through the moony April woods** title passage; the unlikely hybrid brought together by brass and running hard and fast like the man-horses of legend, and "inverted" because Tom-Tom (on top) is so much bigger than Turl

164:17 **Turl said** This is the first time that Turl has spoken since Harker began speaking at 160:12. It is not clear whether Harker hears this portion of the story when the narrator does, since Turl and the narrator fill in the rest of the events of the evening, but he again takes over the narration at 166:14.

164:34–165:1 **runaway bareback mule** a stubborn, uncontrollable thing to ride

165:4 **nekkid air** only air, with nothing to hold on to or break their fall

165:7 **The first thing I wanted to know was** the first time the narrator has participated in drafting the shape of the story as it unfolds, by asking a question that anticipates the tellers

165:8 **used** to castrate or kill Turl

165:10–12 **Because there is a sanctuary beyond despair for any beast which has dared all, which even its mortal enemy respects. Or maybe it was just nigger nature** a doubly racist comment, equating Tom-Tom and Turl with beasts and locating them as members of a race to whom adultery in the final analysis just isn't that important; see Introduction. The passage is typical of much Faulknerian comic rhetoric in its juxtaposition of the grandiose abstract flourish with the crude colloquial phrase.

165:19 **getting their wind back** catching their breath

165:30 **unspeaking** not using speech; however, this does not mean that she was not communicating with them

165:33–166:1 **Harker's "amical" cuckoldry** see 160:25

166:9–10 **his scratched face wearing an expression of monkeylike gravity** Because the narrator has taken over the story at 165:7, this slur is his; he re-creates the scene and adds this detail.

166:14 **"And that was all he said," Harker said** Harker refers to the previous line (166:13), and the narrator retreats behind the second-hand narration.

166:30 **trimmed** criticized

167:6 **That's what whipped him** Tom-Tom and Turl are blackmailing Snopes in exactly the way he tried to use them: he can't tell anyone he stole the brass, and even though he has paid for it, he can't go get it out of the water tower because it is on the books as city property.

167:13–15 **them four loads of brass in it that now belonged to him by right of purchase and which he couldn't claim now because now he had done waited too late** see 167:6

167:27–30 **And there was Buck Conner with the warrant, all ready to arrest Turl and Tom-Tom when he give the word, and it so happening that Turl and Tom-Tom was both in the boiler-room at that moment, changing shifts** the same assumption at play at 158:1–2, only now Tom-Tom and Turl make sure to be present, to remind Flem of how matters stand

168:4 **him** Flem Snopes

168:11–12 **washed clay gullies and ditches filled with scrapped automobiles and tin cans** the undesirable edge of town, which nonetheless has quite a pull on Flem—the view of the water tank

168:17–18 **low smudge of the power plant** the visible smoke from the burning coal

168:19 **water had suddenly gone bad** It tastes bad, apparently from all of the brass in it, and is probably also contaminated from the lead in the brass.

168:23–24 **a quite liberal although anonymous offer to purchase and remove it** from Snopes, still trying to cash in on his monument

168:29–31 **for the very reason of its impermanence, was more enduring though its fluidity and blind renewal than the brass which poisoned it, than columns of basalt or of lead** Basalt is extremely durable rock suited for building columns, and lead is the heaviest of the base metals. Flem, like the columns of his monument, will not give way; but the real success of the monument belongs to Turl and Tom-Tom, who changed the way they saw each other and, then, the rules of the game in which Flem sought to trap them.

"Dry September"

Lynching began in the earliest days of colonial America as a swift way of administering punishment. As Trudier Harris explains, "The phrase 'Lynch Law' is said to have derived from the practices of Virginian Charles Lynch, who, during the Revolutionary War, summarily hanged Tories caught in the area" (197, n. 5). After the Civil War, however, "Blacks began to be lynched more frequently because of the increase in economic competition, in retaliation for crimes committed by a small element in celebration of new-found freedom, as a form of reprisal on the part of Southern whites for Northern interference, and as one of the 'sporting' activities of the Ku Klux Klan" (7). The years at the end of the nineteenth and beginning of the twentieth centuries saw appalling numbers of lynchings, most commonly in the South and in Mississippi in particular. Between 1882 and 1927, approximately 4951 people were lynched in the U.S., 3513 of whom were black (Harris 7); between 1882 and 1930, some 538 people, including 509 African Americans, were lynched in Mississippi, more than any other state in the nation (Tolnay and Beck 273). Faulkner's "Dry September" presents a vivid and chilling narrative of one instance of this horrific phenomenon, and offers subtle analysis of conditions under which such a thing might occur, including patterns of intense racial animosity, rigid gender roles, ritual scapegoating, extreme adverse weather, and the kind of communal moral wasteland in which, as Yeats put it, "The best lack all conviction, while the worst/Are full of passionate intensity."

The story begins in "the bloody September twilight, aftermath of sixty-two rainless days" and ends with "the cold moon and the lidless stars." In between, matters seem simple: at a Jefferson barber shop the occupants debate what to do about a rumor that Miss Minnie Cooper has been somehow assaulted by a black man named Will Mayes. Divided about how to proceed, they are finally goaded into action by the arrival of John McLendon, a hero of the Great War. Meanwhile, Miss Minnie dresses up and goes to the movies with her friends, where she has a hysterical breakdown. The cars of men come home without Will, and McLendon slaps down his wife. Within this simple plot, Faulkner manages to evoke "a particularized place redolent of universal as well as regional realities" (Watson, "Faulkner's Short Stories" 214). Among literary critics, discussion of those regional realities began with race and moved to gender. Irving Howe long ago contended that Faulkner tended to present black characters in terms both "sharply individualized" and abstract, as if over them "hangs . . . a racial aura, a halo of cursed blackness." With respect to "Dry September" in particular, Howe notes that "this tendency toward the abstraction of character is still clearer; like a paradigm of all lynching stories, it is populated not with men but with Murderer and Victim" (127). To the extent that such a "paradigm" can be said to exist, Don H. Doyle articulates another important element of it: "after Emancipation there was a widespread belief among whites that blacks, no longer subject to the discipline of slavery, would degenerate to primitive instincts, with black male sexual lust for white women regarded foremost as a danger" (Hamblin and Peek 238). In "Dry September," says Diane Roberts, "behind the reverence for white women lurks racial paranoia": "Miss Minnie's chastity is not the issue; her credibility is very low anyway. The white men of the town are more interested in maintaining the power structure in which they 'protect' women and terrorize blacks" (171). The world in which Faulkner found himself, according to Ellen Douglas, was one in which "women can impinge on the world and on men only through their sexuality. They have no weapon with which to control their destiny, to fight for themselves or their children except sex." Further, in this world, "women were unable to express their sexuality except in the framework of marriage, and frustrated old maids were known to make hysterical accusations of rape against innocent men" (163). "The force of male desire in a patriarchal society," John T. Matthews agrees, "seeks to deny and immobilize female desire" (*The Sound* 91). Writing here of Caddy in *The Sound and the Fury*, Matthews's observation applies equally well to Minnie Cooper, Emily Grierson in "A Rose for Emily," Susan Reed in "Hair," the title character in "Elly," and the unnamed daughter of the Tennessee mountain family in "A Mountain Victory," among others in *Collected Stories.* Anne Goodwyn Jones offers an apt summary of the sexual ideology of Southern culture, "a sort of unhappy marriage between Victorianism and slavery" ("Like" 56). In the particular case of "Dry September," she argues, that ideology appears in Hawkshaw's "defense" of Will Mayes: "Hawkshaw is appealing to dehumanizing clichés about women's sexuality in order to distract these men from their clichés about black men's sexuality and white men's manhood" (59).

Beyond these racial and sexual myths, "Dry September" also presents Will Mayes as a victim of ritual scapegoating. Citing Sir James Frazer and others, John B. Vickery early demonstrated that the lynching in "Dry September" follows both primitive and classical patterns; he argues that, along with Mayes, Minnie Cooper herself is also a kind of sacrificial victim. In this context, the drought mentioned in the story's opening paragraph reminds us that the scapegoat was sacrificed to prevent drought, thus assuring the continued prosperity of the community. The community of Jefferson, however, is not redeemed. As Hans Skei puts it, "The descriptions of the world as a wasteland are as powerful in 'Dry September' as in the war stories, and it is significant that two ex-soldiers are active in the vigilante group. The drought has created a world of dust and despair; the imagery in the story not only describes nature but also the spiritual malaise and violence which seem to be the only things growing and thriving under such circumstances" (*Reading* 90–91). Harris argues that such renewal was not possible because, unlike the peoples of antiquity, "white Americans" had "no regular ritual cycle" for cleansing but instead used lynching "to reinforce" racial beliefs (7). In that light, the contention of some critics that Hawkshaw, Mrs. McLendon, and even McLendon himself should also be understood as victims—as should, perhaps, the entire Jefferson community—seems counterintuitive to the sympathy and outrage that Faulkner invokes on behalf of this most sinned-against character, Will Mayes.

"Dry September" was first submitted for publication under the title "Drouth," first published in *Scribner's* in January 1931, and subsequently revised for publication in *These 13*. The same version appears in the

Collected Stories as the fourth story in "The Village" section and in *The Faulkner Reader* (1953). Often anthologized and consistently numbered among Faulkner's best short stories, "Dry September" remains powerful not only because of its sharply individuated characters but also because of its concise rendering of a universe of injustice of all kinds that we like to think we have left behind.

169:8 **pomade and lotion** styling ingredients for hair

169:12–13 **He's a good nigger** He follows the rules set by white (male) society for his behavior, especially around white folks.

169:14 **What do you know about her?** with emphasis on *know*, an attempt to tease Hawkshaw; with emphasis on *you*, an attempt to put him down as a source of authority

169:17 **That's why I dont believe—** that Will Mayes did anything to her

170:2 **niggerlover** While Calvin Brown would define this as "a term of opprobrium applied by REDNECKS to whites who try to protect Negroes from them" (139), the term in Faulkner knows no class boundaries among whites.

170:4–6 **I leave it to you fellows if them ladies that get old without getting married dont have notions that a man cant—** You men know that old maids have sexual fantasies that we can't explain or understand

170:17 **a woman that never—** had any man gets ideas (see 170:4–6)

170:21–22 **I—** don't need facts!

170:24–25 **a desert rat in the moving pictures** a stock character in early films; a miner, for instance, who doesn't shave or bathe

170:25 **Jack** Faulkner identifies the youth as Butch at 170:19. Brown notes that *Jack* is used as "a familiar and somewhat contemptuous form of address to one whose name the speaker does not know or does not bother to remember" (109), but the drummer seems to use it familiarly instead (see also 171:12).

170:27 **drummer** a traveling salesman (Brown 75)

170:31 **To think that a white man in this town—** would take a black man's word over a white woman's

170:32 **the second speaker** The difficulty in locating exactly who is speaking increases the anxiety of the story—some of these men seem to speak for everyone present—and if Faulkner is keeping strict track of who speaks and when, this speaker is the "second barber" of 169:14.

170:34 **the speaker** the "second speaker" of 170:32, who has support in the voice of "another" at 170:19

171:11 **Damn if I'm going to let a white woman—** be bothered by a nigger, get talked about that way: Butch's own bafflement makes exact interpretation difficult.

171:13 **By God, if they—** won't do it, I/we will

171:16 **felt hat** a city man's hat, perhaps in a fedora or paramilitary style; not a straw or canvas working man's hat

171:21 **son** son of a bitch (Brown 183)

171:23 **dark halfmoon** sweat marks in the armpits of the shirt

171:24 **That's what I—** said

171:26 **Hawkshaw** the first barber named. A newspaper cartoon, "Hawkshaw the Detective," created by Gus Mager, ran from 1913 until 1922 and then occasionally until the late 1940s. The name was taken from a stage production called "The Ticket-of-Leave Man" that featured a detective named Hawkshaw. As time passed, the name became slang for "detective" (see Markstein).

171:27 **kitchen roof** either a separate, detached one-story building ancillary to a main house, or a one-story room of the main house; given that Minnie lives in a "small frame house" (173:20–21), probably the latter

172:1–2 **get away with it until one really does it?** get away with their fantasies until they feel free to commit the act

172:18 **Why, you damn niggerloving—** see 170:2; maybe followed by a string of curse words, but also perhaps interrupted by the man who takes his arm at 172:19

172:19 **The third speaker** possibly the same speaker who tries to cast doubt on Miss Minnie's claims at 171:25–28

172:23 **The ones that aint—** an unfinished and implicit, but intense, threat

172:28 **if our mothers and wives and sisters—** are in danger, they can count on me to protect them

173:10 **I cant let—** this happen; them lynch Will Mayes; them get him

173:13–14 **It had a metallic taste at the base of the tongue** The base (back) of the tongue senses bitter tastes.

173:15 **the first said. The second one** "The first" barber seems to be the "second barber" of 169:14, who seems circumspect regarding Will Mayes; the second barber remaining seems to be "another [barber]" of 170:13, who seems content to crack jokes during the confrontation and afterward can only repeat "Jees Christ."

173:16–17 **I'd just as lief** "I'd just as soon" (Brown 119)

173:23–24 **a lace-trimmed boudoir cap** not an item of clothing usually worn outside the house; a cap worn over curlers or while applying makeup or dressing, to keep the hair in place (Brown 36)

173:25 **dinner** the mid-day meal; lunch

174:1–2 **still on the slender side of ordinary looking** not quite average in the looks department

174:6–7 **church social period** period of time in which the youths of Jefferson attend high school parties and church socials: "a social gathering or party, esp. one held by members of a club or association" (*OED* online)

174:11–12 **the pleasure of snobbery—male—and retaliation—female** By aging and not marrying, Minnie has become a fair target for both sexes: The men that she might have formerly snubbed now believe that they are too good for her, and the women she outshined or snubbed can now do the same to her.

174:17 **talking** gossiping about her

174:22 **"aunty"** Brown distinguishes between "aunty" as a term of respect for an older black woman and "miss" as an equivalent title for a white woman, coupled with her first name (22, 129). Those terms do not seem to apply to Minnie in her early middle age; her classmates use the term "aunt" to describe her to their children, as though she were a member of the family. In Minnie's case, "Aunty" also marks her age, which she tries to erase at 174:33.

174:26 **high-colored man** of rich or ruddy complexion, perhaps from alcohol

174:28 **runabout** sportscar

174:29 **motoring bonnet and veil** special headgear that women wore in early, open-air automobiles in order to protect their skin and keep their hair in place (see Brown 133)

174:33 **"cousin" instead of "aunty"** see 174:22; Minnie is trying to deny her real age

175:5–6 **over-the-way Christmas day visiting** social calls paid on friends and relatives; formal visits that often involved leaving small calling cards, the forerunner of the modern Christmas card

175:23 **serried** closely ordered files or ranks of armed men, a telling metaphor for Minnie's situation in town

175:30–31 **Below the east was a rumor of the twice-waxed moon** a not-yet-risen blue moon, which as Borgna Brunner explains, is "the second full moon in a calendar month. For a blue moon to occur, the first of the full moons must appear at or near the beginning of the month so that the second will fall within the same month (the average span between two moons is 29.5 days." The story therefore takes place near the end of September.

176:5–6 **when this town hears about how you talked tonight—** they'll run you out of here for sure

176:7 **the other ex-soldier said** "the third speaker" from 172:19 and 171:25–28, who has given up his defense of Will Mayes and joined McLendon

176:13 **and Miss Minnie anyway—** has said something like this before

176:16–17 **When we're through with the—** son of a bitch, then we can talk

176:18–19 **Do you want everybody in town—** to know what we're doing

176:20–21 **Tell every one of the sons that'll let a white woman—** "be bothered by a black son what we're doing"; he implies that the men who won't lynch are cowards, perhaps deserving of the same treatment as Will Mayes.

177:18–19 **vague noises began to grow out of the darkness ahead** McLendon, Butch, and Will coming toward the cars

177:31 **captains** "a vague term of respect, used to a man" (Brown 45); in this case, by a black man to a group of whites

177:32 **Mr John** in this context, as Brown explains, a term of respect "used in this way generally by Negroes for whites whom they know primarily by their given names" (130). Will clearly knows McLendon well enough to address him by his first name.

178:4, 9–10 **He spoke a name or two. He called another name** Will knows his attackers.

178:21 **running board** "a flat section of metal outside the doors of a car and joining the bases of the front and rear fenders," which one could ride upon or use as a step (Brown 165)

179:4–5 **an abandoned brick kiln—a series of reddish mounds and weed- and vine-choked vats without bottom** a site where an oven for baking bricks operated, including red clay mounds from which the bricks were made and pits in which the clay and water were mixed. Faulkner, who knew his Dickens, may have been remembering the manner in which Stephen Blackpool disappeared in *Hard Times.*

179:5 **It** the field containing the brick kiln

179:12 **Mr Henry** Hawkshaw; see 177:32

180:5 **the eternal dust** an echo of both Genesis 3:19 and the Book of Common Prayer: "For dust thou art, and to dust shalt thou return"; "Ashes to ashes, dust to dust"

180:7 **supper** the evening meal, according to Brown usually a light one because the main meal of the day was at mid-day (193)

180:9 **hooks and eyes** dress and lingerie fasteners; the hook fits into the loop of the eye

180:9–10 **her hair swirled crisp and crackling under the comb** In the specific terms of this story, the dry weather has produced greater static electricity in the air, which makes her hair crackle; but Minnie at her dressing table also has a literary predecessor in the upper-class woman in "A Game of Chess" in T. S. Eliot's *The Waste Land,* whose hair under the brush "Spread out into fiery points/Glowed into words, then would be savagely still."

180:11–13 **she donned her sheerest underthings and stockings and a new voile dress** see 173:23–24, 26

180:17 **the square** the town square, which is the center of activity and surrounds the courthouse; "Since it is almost invariably the only square in town, 'the square' [as a location and destination] is a specific expression that needs no further explanation" (Brown 187)

181:1 **Did they—?** kill him?

181:9–10 **There's not a Negro on the square. Not one** because they seem to know and seek to avoid Will Mayes's fate

181:11 **It** the movie theatre

181:12–13 **colored lithographs of life caught in its terrible and beautiful mutations** the movie posters in the lobby

181:14–16 **In the dark, when the picture began, it would be all right; she could hold back the laughing so it would not waste away so fast and so soon** a curious and ambivalent passage, the meaning of which hinges on the indeterminate pronouns. "It would be all right" might mean that when the movie starts, she will be able to control herself; "so it would not waste away" could be the laughter that fights its way out; laughter seems like a source of both pleasure and pain to her.

181:19 **the silver glare** the light coming from the black-and-white movie projection

181:25 **the silver dream** the film

181:30 **laughing on a high, sustained note** hysterically

181:33 **cracked ice** At the time, ice came in large square blocks from the ice plant (in this case, from the very plant where Will Mayes is watchman), and it had to be chipped apart for use in small quantities.

“Death Drag”

Faulkner’s fascination with aviation began in childhood, was confirmed by his experience as a pilot in training for the Royal Air Force in Canada in 1918, and continued through the 1920s and into the 1930s. His first published story, “Landing in Luck,” appeared in *The Mississippian* in 1919, and his first novel, *Soldiers’ Pay* (1926), has at its center the wounded and moribund aviator Donald Mahon. Fliers and flying figure prominently in a variety of his short stories, including “Ad Astra,” “All the Dead Pilots,” “Turnabout,” “Honor,” and “Uncle Willy,” and the subject receives its most extended treatment in *Pylon* (1935). “Death Drag,” like “Honor,” *Pylon*, and “Uncle Willy,” specifically describes an episode of barnstorming, the practice of independent fliers who performed aerial stunts in small towns that was so popular after the Great War.

“Death Drag” concentrates on a single day in which the military veteran Jock and his associates, Ginsfarb and Jake, arrange to perform a “death drag” stunt, during which Jock pilots a decrepit airplane from which Ginsfarb, suspended on a ladder, “swaps” to a moving car, driven by Jake, and back again. The spectators tend to worry about Ginsfarb, but Jock has the much riskier job in maneuvering the unsafe plane at low speeds and with little margin for error. As Robert Harrison puts it, “As for the death drag itself, Faulkner takes a pilot’s point of view: there is nothing remotely heroic in Ginsfarb’s hair-raising stunt; it is merely the way a desperate, frustrated man makes a living. Jock on the other hand displays considerable skill and courage in saving the wing walker’s life” (147)—and more than once.

Much of the discussion of “Death Drag” has centered on the Jewish stereotypes in the description of Ginsfarb (big nose, obsession with money, etc.). Ilse Dusoir Lind suggests that in constructing and subverting the comic stereotypical Jewish character, Faulkner may have drawn on his own performance as "Izzy Goldstein" in a September 1930 community production of *Corporal Eagen* (128–29). As is so often the case in his delineation of ethnic stereotypes, Faulkner's story not only presents the obvious popular prejudices, but it also subverts them: "the spectators saw that he, like the limping man, was also a Jew. That is, they knew at once that two of the strangers were of a different race from themselves, without being able to say what the difference was" (188). Ginsfarb in particular, for all of his scheming and complaining, emerges as a desperate man, ill-fitted for his sometimes-risky occupation and understandably outraged by its uncertain and often paltry rewards. Faulkner does not mean him for a hero but for a survivor.

"Death Drag" may have been written as early as December 1930. The story was rejected by several editors; Faulkner then revised it and, after a second reading, *Scribner's* published it in January 1932 as "Death-Drag." Faulkner chose the story for inclusion in *Doctor Martino*, as Malcolm Cowley did for *The Portable Faulkner*, though Faulkner spoke diffidently of the story ("That was just a tale, could have happened anywhere, could have been printed as happening anywhere") and suggested that it be dropped from the *Portable* if necessary in order to make room for "Appendix: Compson" (*Selected Letters* 205). It appears as the fifth story in "The Village" section of *Collected Stories*, between "Dry September" and "Elly," followed in turn by "Uncle Willy," the other story in this section featuring aviation. Nowhere in "Death Drag" is Jefferson identified as the locale, and the named characters of the story, except for Captain Warren, mentioned briefly in the title story of *Knight's Gambit*, do not appear elsewhere in the Yoknapatawpha chronicle. In fact, the narrator of "Death Drag" describes his town in deliberately anonymous terms: "a small town interchangeable with and duplicate of ten thousand little dead clottings of human life about the land" (197–98), where what happens "could have happened anywhere," as Faulkner said.

185:1–3 **The airplane appeared over town with almost the abruptness of an apparition. It was travelling fast; almost before we knew it was there it was already at the top of a loop** a loop-the-loop, an acrobatic stunt designed to draw spectators, in this instance, and gauge interest among them. According to Robert Harrison, "the slipshod, character-revealing loop" at the story's beginning was a standard practice by the barnstormers of that era (early 1930s) that was "used to 'buzz' the town" they had decided to "entertain" (147).

185:4–5 **in violation of both city and government ordinance** According to the Air Commerce Act of 1926, "No person shall acrobatically fly an aircraft—(a) Over a congested area of any city, town, or settlement" (Harrison 148).

185:12 **in order to save gasoline** Ginsfarb's mistaken belief that a well-done loop takes more gasoline than a poorly done one (Harrison 148)

185:13–15 **The airplane came over the loop with one wing down, as though about to make an Immelmann turn. Then it did a half roll, the loop three-quarters complete** named after the World War I German aviator Max Immelmann, reversal of direction executed by climbing steeply, flying upside down, and then flipping right side up; during a half roll, the plane turns 180 degrees longitudinally

185:22–23 **patched and shabby and painted awkwardly with a single thin coat of dead black** perhaps to cover up military markings (Harrison 148)

186:4–5 **an X-shaped runway** "a pair of runways set at right angles to one another" (Harrison 148)

186:17 **coverall** a one-piece denim suit often worn by mechanics to protect other garments

186:18 **breeches and puttees** protective, tight-fitting clothes that will not snag on any type of protrusion; as Harrison has it, "remnants of World War I uniform" (148)

186:34 **ship** airplane

187:3 **the Royal Flying Corps** the British Air Force

187:8–9 **in the diction of Weber and Fields in vaudeville** an American comedy team of Jewish vaudevillians, Joe Weber and Lew Fields. Fields was tall and aggressive, while Weber was short and the brunt of jokes. Performing together from 1875 to 1930, they were noted for slapstick comedy, dialect jokes, and burlesques of popular plays ("Weber and Fields").

188:35 **groundlings** those who do not fly; also spectators sitting in the pit of the Elizabethan theater. As Hamlet puts it, "Oh, it offends me to the soul to hear a robustious periwig-pated fellow tear a passion to a tatters, to very rags, to split the ears of the groundlings, who for the most part are capable of nothing but inexplicable dumb shows and noise" (III, ii, 8–13).

189:3–4 **the fuselage streaked with oil behind the rusting exhaust pipes** according to Harrison, a normal condition: "the stubby [exhaust] pipes of the Jenny routinely spat fumes and oil along the sides of the fuselage" (148–49)

189:8 **Wing-walking; death-drag** stunts performed on the wings of airborne planes, the latter "the promotional name for transfers between aeroplanes and surface vehicles" (Harrison 149)

189:31–32 **running boards** Calvin Brown explains: "flat section[s] of metal outside the doors of a car and joining the bases of the front and rear fenders . . . used as a step for getting into and out of a car" and riding while holding the car top (165)

191:5–6 **American Legion? Rotary Club? Chamber of Commerce?** The first is a community-service organization chartered by Congress in 1919 and open to retired members of the armed forces; the second a volunteer organization of business people dedicated to community service projects; the third an organization of business members to promote the interests of local businesses.

191:21–22 **in silver or in greenbacks** in coin or paper legal tender. In effect, Ginsfarb is saying to the taxi driver, "It doesn't matter which of us jumps, as long as one of us does, just as it doesn't make any difference to me what kind of money you use to pay me, as long as I get paid."

192:8 **Gruss Gott** idiomatic German expression: "Great God" (or "Good God" or "God's grace"), routinely used as a greeting in Bavaria and Austria

192:14 **that Republican Coolidge** (John) Calvin Coolidge (1872–1933), the 30th president of the United States. Although Coolidge chose not to run for reelection in the 1928 presidential election, many nevertheless believed the Great Depression (which began in October 1929) was a result of Coolidge's *laissez-faire* attitudes toward business during his administration.

192:18 **license** According to the Air Commerce Act of 1926, "It shall be unlawful . . . to navigate any aircraft registered as an aircraft of the United States, or any foreign aircraft, without an aircraft certificate or in violation of the terms of any such certificate" (see Harrison 149).

193:16–17 **I hadn't seen him in fourteen years, not since I left England for the front in '17** sets the story in 1931

193:18–19 **a twenty model Hisso smokepot** probably a 1920s model Jenny (a Curtiss JN-4) that has had its engine replaced with a more reliable Hispano-Suiza engine (a "Hisso") for purposes of barnstorming. Such planes often emitted large clouds of smoke. (See "The Curtiss JN-4 'Jenny,'" Harrison 149.)

193:26 **monkey suit** overalls; see 186:17

194:13 **inspectors** appointed by the Director of Air Regulation (Harrison 150)

194:19 **compound another felony** Jock has committed one of the few felonies specified by the Air Commerce Act of 1926 by taking the license off a wrecked airplane and using it on his own, which has been grounded by an inspector (Harrison 150).

194:20 **Jock had lost his license** his pilot's license

194:29 **parachute rigger's license** license to repair or pack a parachute (Harrison 150)

194:30 **they'd all go to the penitentiary** see 194:19

196:1–2 **a hundred dollars for the stunt** According to Harrison, "this was a cut-rate price, even in the leanest days of barnstorming" (151).

196:29–30 **a Ford or a Chevrolet running on three cylinders** of its four; underpowered, in other words, and consequently more dangerous for the stunt men

197:12–13 **seeing his money being blown out the exhaust pipes** more evidence of Ginsfarb's penny-pinching; see 185:11–12

197:17 **enough soup to zoom** "enough power to make a steep climb" (Harrison 151)

197:20–22 **held the ship in a climb with his knees, with the throttle wide open and the engine revving about eleven hundred** The engine was turning at 1,100 rpm—an extraordinarily high rate of speed for an older, poorly maintained airplane and Hisso engine: "The fact that twenty minutes elapsed before Jock had gained enough altitude to risk leaving the cockpit indicates how slow the rate of climb actually was" (Harrison 151).

199:2 **We're going to wring the old bird's neck** crank the propeller to start the engine

199:16–17 **He's got to turn into the wind** in order to take off

200:25 **death-colored airplane** see 185:22–23

201:12 **circular-saw drone which died into a splutter** because Jock has reduced the plane's speed in order to let Ginsfarb make the jump (Harrison 151)

201:27–28 **he was using words we had never heard him use** see 201:29–31—the language of flying and the language of poetry

201:29 **He's got the stick between his knees** the control that pushes the nose of the plane up or down, freeing his hands to argue with Ginsfarb

201:30–31 **Exalted suzerain of mankind; saccharine and sacred symbol of eternal rest** Captain Warren's admiration of the pilot's heroic flying: an invocation of God and the heavens in which a pilot flies, perhaps to his death

202:15 **It reared skyward** because it has been freed of Ginsfarb's weight (Harrison 151)

202:28 **cosmic balance** inherent justice of circumstances

204:19 **that crate** the obsolete and dangerous airplane

204:29 **Ground it** leave it

205:27–33 **That fellow never paid nothing down on it, like Mr. Harris wanted. He told Mr. Harris he might not use it, but if he did use it in his show, he would pay Mr. Harris twenty dollars for it instead of ten like Mr. Harris wanted. He told me to take it back and tell Mr. Harris he never used the car. And I don't know if Mr. Harris will like it. He might get mad** Ginsfarb's final triumph, at everyone else's expense

"Elly"

The title character of "Elly" comes to a violent and murderous solution to a dilemma common to a number of the women in Faulkner's fiction. As a young, respectable white woman, she is held to conventions dictating that she preserve her chastity until marriage, but her impulse is to rebel against those conventions. She appears as a kind of "flapper," flirtatious and overtly sexual, but she lives in a family and community that condemn such behavior. Elly not only defies the tradition of the virginal Southern belle—like Caddy Compson and her daughter of *The Sound and the Fury* (1929), Temple Drake of *Sanctuary* (1931), Emily Grierson of "A Rose for Emily," and, in a way, Minnie Cooper of "Dry September"—but, like Joanna Burden of *Light in August* (1932), she also deliberately flaunts the racial taboo, first by seeking to marry and finally by simply giving herself to a man of ambiguous racial origins. "Elly" contains a kind of female *doppelgänger* story, with Elly's modern aggressiveness and defiance juxtaposed with her grandmother's fierce adherence to the traditional female conventions. Elly's asserted willingness to violate sexual taboos, her narcissism, her manipulation of various suitors, her conformity to the "flapper" type, and her willingness to participate in a murder all might suggest that Faulkner's portrait constitutes a wholehearted disapproval of the young woman. However, the portrait that emerges of her family, her fiancé, her lover, and the town that watches them all might also work to make our final assessment of Elly's character, like the ending of the story itself, ambiguous.

The opening of "Elly" provides a narrative frame of a single significant day and features long flashbacks before returning to the violent conclusion of the day in question. As Elly and her companion, Paul, drive to the town of Mills City, Elly asks Paul whether there is anything "else" she can do to make him marry her; we discover that she has resumed their relationship on his terms in order to escape the prospect of a dull, conventional marriage and a dull, conventional life. Paul's refusal to marry her and her abject terror of her grandmother drive her to the suggestion of murder, which he rejects and she then acts on; at the end of the story, Paul and the grandmother are apparently dead, and Elly lies dazed, bleeding, and perhaps dying in the car wreck she has caused. "Stated simply," says Alice Hall Petry, "Elly's crisis is this: How (if at all) can the nationwide call for sexual freedom accommodate the persistent myth of the virginal Southern belle—let alone the personal situation of one Elly, age eighteen, of Jefferson? Hence her erratic behavior, especially in regard to sexual matters; hence also the confusion over her relationship with Paul" (226). "The need to defy and the need to conform," Edmond Volpe agrees, "are equally strong. There is no possibility of resolution. The forces pulling Elly apart are irreconcilable" (92). Noel Polk adds that Elly's initial decision to seduce Paul de Montigny "is a doubly intense sin, a doubly intense entry into the forbidden, a sin no less potent than incest. It is not just an act of rebellion against her grandmother and the mores of Jefferson, nor is it for her merely an attempt to escape from that life. Sex with the Negro, with the forbidden, is a chance to store up some excitement that she will have as a memory in the long, dull life to come" (*Children* 80). Elly's confrontations with her grandmother, Aurélie Guillain argues, "end in attempts at self-punishment and self-destruction." Her fantasies match the real, "instead of acting as screens against reality," so when they are fulfilled, they provide her "with a certain amount of perverse satisfaction" (30, 31). Early critics of the story tended to describe Faulkner's portrait of his title character as unsympathetic or essentially negative (see Malin and Kerr, for example), with M. E. Bradford providing the most damning judgment of Elly (see "Faulkner's Elly"). Hans Skei leavens such portraits by explaining the basic conflict of the story as one between "a young girl who naturally expects and hopes for more in life than what she has found her family and Jefferson can give, and, on the other side, a non-permissive society, which is depicted as injurious if not destructive" (*Novelist* 108). Petry and Lisa Paddock also present more sympathetic readings of Elly. Volpe suggests that Elly descends into madness by story's end, an idea that provides one means of negotiating the difficult choice between a repressive society, on the one hand, and a clearly narcissistic and possibly murderous protagonist on the other. "Elly," he says, "objectively presents an external drama to reflect an inner emotional state"; and the story, he concludes, is "a masterful work of art. Each character, each scene, each description, each image, each bit of dialogue is brilliantly and artfully used to render the internal drama of a personality unraveling" (87, 92).

"Elly," under the title of "Selvage," or "Salvage," appears several times in Faulkner's correspondence and sending schedule, and in various manuscript, typescript, and carbon versions, beginning no later than 23 February 1929, and presumably as early as December 1928. The story, as Joseph Blotner reports, began with a draft by Estelle Oldham, whom Faulkner would marry on 19 June 1929. Estelle, unsatisfied with her draft, turned the story over to Faulkner, who first suggested that the two of them collaborate on a revision, but he eventually took over the project as his own (Blotner, 1974; 604). Faulkner's version was subsequently refused by several editors, and "Elly" remained unpublished when Faulkner gathered selections for *These 13* (1931). After its publication in *Story* in February 1934, he included it in *Doctor Martino* later that same year. Robert Haas did not include "Elly" among his original suggestions for the *Collected Stories* volume, but Faulkner, supplementing Haas's list with stories from both *These 13* and *Doctor Martino*, placed "Elly" sixth among the ten Jefferson stories in the section he entitled "The Village." Elly and her wrecked life thus stand in the center of the hometown of Faulkner's imagination.

207:3 **passing the car in a flimsy blur** how the railing looks from Elly's perspective; a hint at the story's end

207:6 **Mills City** a fictional town some 200 miles away from the Jefferson (see 208:5–6)

207:11–14 **There was a man plowing in that field, watching us when we came out of those woods with Paul carrying the motor-robe, and got back into the car** Elly has just lost her virginity to Paul;

she remembers leaving the woods where it happened. **motor-robe** = a blanket to protect the clothing of the occupants of an open car or to keep them warm.

208:5 **She was eighteen** the beginning of an extensive flashback that ends at 216:23

208:8 **half lay** euphemism for engaging in sexual activity other than intercourse, including just kissing

208:13–14 **presently they all believed that they knew why** The men come individually to the conclusion that Elly will not go as far as intercourse because she does not want to get pregnant (208:24).

208:24 **So far, and no mother** see 208:13–14

208:25–27 **"Maybe." In the shadow now she would be alert, cool, already fled, without moving, beyond some secret reserve of laughter** Elly does not claim the easy reason for stopping the foreplay—pregnancy—but immediately distances herself emotionally from her partner.

209:18 **Paul de Montigny** The French surname is often a coded reference in Faulkner's texts to indeterminate racial identity, usually locating the bearer's origins in Louisiana or New Orleans, an allusion to that city's mixed racial and, decidedly non-Puritan, sexual history. The obvious example is Charles Bon from *Absalom, Absalom!*.

209:19–20 **like two swordsmen, with veiled eyes** Skilled fighters, with or without weapons, can read the intentions of their opponents in their eyes and can keep the same from appearing in their own; these are defensive and offensive strategies of great importance in mortal situations. These two girls are about to engage in a battle over Paul—a battle of a sort they obviously have engaged in before.

209:25–26 **You didn't notice his hair then. Like a knitted cap. And his lips. Blubber, almost** Elly's friend is pointing out the physical features that would "prove" Paul's identity as a black or racially mixed man. Given the one-drop rule of slave ownership and post-Civil War race-labeling, the options amount to the same thing: if she persists in pursuing Paul, Elly is going to cross a racially taboo line.

209:31–33 **How his uncle killed a man once that accused him of having nigger blood** Paul's family has a rumored history of reacting violently to accusations that they are not white. See also 209:25–26.

210:2 **his family** The girlfriend refers to a complex white social network that keeps track of the members of black and mulatto families to prevent them from passing into white life.

210:2 **Louisiana** see 209:18

210:21 **she** the grandmother, who is never far from Elly's thoughts

210:28 **bolt upright** straight up

211:1 **Mr. de Montigny! From Louisiana!** Elly shouts the barest elements of a formal introduction because her grandmother is deaf.

211:2–3 **start violently backward as a snake does to strike** Elly's grandmother has recognized either Paul's physical features (see 209:25–26) or his family's origins (209:18) and placed him racially as black.

211:8–9 **the very brink of surrender** of her virginity

211:16–17 **I am caught in sin without even having time to sin** Elly and Paul have not had sex, but she thinks her grandmother believes they have and will consequently tell her father.

211:23 **him** her father, to whom it would fall to confront Paul and demand that he marry Elly

212:10 **Ailanthia** feminization of *ailanthus,* also called tree of heaven or heaven tree, an invasive and fast-growing large tree

212:28 **I don't marry them** The line indicates that he has had more than one lover and holds certain principles regarding marriage, which could include refusing to marry ex-lovers or refusing to marry any woman at all.

212:31 **wan** usually, pale; but because Faulkner uses the word to describe the quality of Elly's voice, not her face, an obscure poetical definition of the word may be more applicable: "*transf.* or *fig.* sad, dismal; also awful, fearful, deadly, cruel, wicked, etc." (*OED* online).

213:12–13 **If I ever see you again, you know what it will mean** a sexual ultimatum

213:17 **Memphis papers** specifically, in the society columns there

213:18 **assistant cashier** one who handles the money at the bank, a position of some esteem in the community and one of the better paying jobs in small towns of the time. Elly's fiancé has been approved of as upwardly mobile.

213:21 **calling on her** formal visits made by a suitor to the woman he wishes to marry, usually supervised

213:23 **road shows** traveling carnivals, concerts, and plays

213:25 **and her mother** as a chaperone, and one whose company and favor he curries by doing so

214:13 **clematis** a genus of climbing and flowering vine

215:25 **His arm was without life** The sudden realization of Elly's duplicity has stunned her fiancé.

216:2 **And you'll let mother believe . . .** that I went with you

216:10–11 **This is the last trouble I'll ever give you, I expect** because she will either leave with Paul or come back and docilely marry her fiancé or has already formed the plot to kill her grandmother

216:24 **And then** the return to the opening time frame of the story

217:2 **Pausing at the turn of the stair** a time shift forward to the immediate present tense, with Elly, Paul, and the grandmother in Elly's uncle's house in Mills City

217:12–15 **littered with the frivolous impedimenta of a young girl . . . bottles, powder puffs, photographs, a row of dance programs suck into the mirror frame** **dance programs** = card bearing the names of a woman's prospective partners at a dance, which might well have included an attached pencil and been presented in a decorative case. The description recalls Alexander Pope's description of Belinda's table in *The Rape of the Lock*: "puffs, powders, patches, bibles, billet-doux" (Canto I, l. 138).

217:32–33 **one of the cards with its silken cord and tiny futile pencil** see 217:14

218:1–2 ***he went to Va. And Harvard and everywhere*** He attended Harvard University and the University of Virginia; she offers these institutions as proof of Paul's whiteness.

218:3–4 **I can understand Harvard, but not Virginia** She implies that the North might have relaxed the social rules separating the races, but such conditions would never occur in the South. See also 210:2.

219:16 **I'd hate to catch a train by you** The clock is inaccurate.

219:34–220:1 **tempered the drip of water to a minor but penetrating monotony** She is using the drip of water to mask the sound of her conversation with Paul.

221:20–24 **In the instant of striking her his hand, as though refusing of its own volition the office, opened and touched her face in a**

long, shuddering motion almost a caress. Again gripping her by the back of the neck, he assayed to strike her; again his hand, something, refused Elly has deeply insulted Paul by implying that he would willingly murder her grandmother for her, but even in the midst of trying to punish her physically for that insult, he cannot quite commit to the blows.

221:34 **single seat** The car Paul owns has a single bench-style seat, capable of holding three people, and possibly a small trunk or rumbleseat in the rear.

222:4 **then I will . . .** ask Paul again to marry me

222:7 **jockeyed** made slight adjustments with the wheel in response to the road conditions

222:9 **archaic black bonnet** from an earlier time; outdated, like her ideas

222:10 **a profile cut from parchment** in other words, like a silhouette, an old form of portraiture that traced the subject's profile, usually by means of a shadow, and filled in the outline with black. The outline could also be cut from black paper. It is ironic that the grandmother's archaic racial ideas "color" her own representation on the page.

223:4 **the robe** the motor-robe mentioned at 207:13

223:14–16 **You *hit* me!** Apparently a threat on his life removes Paul's scruples about hitting Elly (see 221:20–24).

223:17 **free** away from the crashing car

223:32–33 **And now they are dead; it's me that's hurt, and nobody will come** Elly's selfishness has become completely solipsistic.

"Uncle Willy"

"Uncle Willy" presents a profound conflict between the maverick individual, Uncle Willy Christian, and the respectable community of Jefferson, as told by a young narrator who sides completely with the title character. Uncle Willy, the town druggist, is a great favorite with the boys of the town, particularly the young narrator of the story, who defends him and accompanies him "on his last go-round" (225). Over the years, Uncle Willy has given the boys prizes and ice cream after their baseball games, and they, in turn, have watched fascinated as he satisfies his morphine addiction. The story that bears his name follows him as he thwarts the attempts of certain of the townspeople to cure him of that addiction and, as one puts it, "to see that he assumed that position in the world which his family's name entitled him to before he degraded it" (232). Faulkner's irony couldn't be more thickly laid: a group of Christians intends to make Willy Christian behave like a Christian, but he already is a "Christian"; if the do-gooders took morphine and married Memphis whores, too, then they would in some respects be like the named Christian in the story. Such layers raise a series of troubling questions. Should we accept without question the narrator's judgment that Uncle Willy is "the finest man I ever knew" (225), or does Faulkner mean for us to see him instead as a drug addict, an alcoholic, and a whoremonger, who shamelessly exploits the young narrator's lack of judgment? Does the narrator himself consciously abet what some have called Uncle Willy's "suicide," or is he simply trying to help Uncle Willy have as much fun as he can for as long as he can? Does the story leave any hope for the narrator's future, or does he face a bleak choice between the examples of the addicted and irresponsible Willy and the satirically delineated, meddling killjoys of the Jefferson church?

The story ends with the narrator insisting, as he has done throughout the story, on the rightness of his own actions—"I did help Uncle Willy. He knows I did. He knows he couldn't have done it without me" (247)—but just exactly what the narrator claims to have helped Uncle Willy do remains in doubt. Does he help him commit suicide, however unwittingly, or does he just help him do whatever he wants to do? Answers seem to hinge on each reader's interpretation of the tone of the story's events. Edmond Volpe, for example, emphasizes its comic elements: "Faulkner effectively creates the feeling of a child's joyous response to life with ebullient comedy; at the same time he conveys the threat the adult world poses to that joy through his narrator" and "makes the reader champion the old man's gleeful immorality and his defiance of Mrs. Merridew's brand of Christianity" (217, 218). He says the story is "fundamentally a traditional comic fable built around the familiar character of a beloved fun-loving old drunk" (219). Hans Skei denies that Uncle Willy is "presented as any sort of ideal," but argues that "Faulkner (or the implied author, rather) seems to suggest that those who know best and feel that they have a normal supremacy have no right to meddle with other people when no wrongs are performed" (*Novelist* 223–24). Edwige Pluyaut considers Uncle Willy as Jefferson's scapegoat who "incarnates all the desires, all the aspirations of a section of the community whose aim is to show off its propensities towards spiritual matters and brandish the flagship of morality, whereas its unique goal is to become sole and own proprietor of a human being, body and soul included" (271–72). James Ferguson also sees the story as "a kind of initiation" for the narrator, "perhaps as much the central figure as the title character" (113). Skei makes a related point: "The boy who tells the story hopes to discover some secret about the good life, about a meaningful existence, and the only lesson he may have learnt is that it must be sought in himself and that it ultimately depends on his strength to withstand the pressure to conform and accept the rigid rules and regulations of life in a modern, urbanized world" (225). Offering a corrective to these views of Uncle Willy as quixotic hero, Noel Polk calls attention to Willy's open practice of his morphine addiction. The narrator, he maintains, does not understand that a community that cares about the well-being of its children cannot tolerate such behavior: "He deliberately and selfishly involves them in crime; he distorts all of their values, virtually equating ice cream cones and heroin [*sic*] injections and making them believe that having 'fun' is the only important thing in life; and he makes them help him commit suicide" ("Respectability" 115, 118). Skei considers "Uncle Willy" among Faulkner's best stories (*Short Story Career* 131, n. 70), and Diane Brown Jones notes that it "offers a compelling if not complimentary view of the Jefferson community" (246). The controversies inspired by the story arise precisely because "Faulkner does nothing to resolve the tension established by the conflict between these two polar extremes" of Willy Christian and those who would reform him (Polk 119).

"Uncle Willy" may have been partially inspired by the automobile death of Oxford druggist Bob Chilton in September 1934 (Blotner 1974; 882). It was probably written in the early months of 1935, perhaps after Faulkner finished writing *Pylon* in late March. In this period, desperate for money, Faulkner turned to writing short stories in hopes of immediate sales, claiming to his agent, Morton Goldman, that he was now writing "two stories a week" (*Selected Letters* 91). While the story apparently did not meet his need for a high-priced sale, it was nevertheless accepted by the *American Mercury*, which published it in its October 1935 issue. In 1948 Faulkner agreed with Robert K. Haas that "Uncle Willy" should appear in the projected short story collection, remarking, "Yes. I like this one" (*SL* 274). Faulkner recalled the character and plot over twenty years later when he wrote *The Town* (1957), reusing much of the story's material. As the seventh story in the section of *Collected Stories* called "The Village," its ambiguous tone and mood serve as a bridge between the tragedy of "Elly" and the hilarity of "Mule in the Yard."

TITLE **Uncle** As Calvin Brown explains, "a title of respect applied (with the given name) by both white and black to an elderly Negro man or, less commonly, to an elderly white one" (206). "Uncle" suggests a greater degree of familiarity and affection than the more formal "Mr. Christian" would.

225:2 **tolled away** lured away with the promise of something, as animals are lured with food (Brown 200)

225:7 **on his last go-round** set of evasive maneuvers, as in "run-around"; figuratively, perhaps his last lap in life

225:14–15 **even women couldn't beat him** The young boy narrating the story thinks of women as Uncle Willy's enemies and, by extension, his own.

225:21–22 **He wasn't anybody's uncle, but all of us, and grown people too, called him (or thought of him) as Uncle Willy** see explanation at Title

225:24 **oil millionaire** Uncle Willy's sister probably lives near the Gulf Coast or in west Texas, where the most and the most productive oil reserves exist. The Lucas Gusher, located in the Spindletop oil field outside Beaumont, Texas, blew on 10 January 1901, and began a new economic boom in the state. Continued drilling in the Gulf Coast area of Texas and in west Texas during the 1920s and 1930s produced more oil wells and increased revenue for fortunate property owners and drilling companies (see "Spindletop Oilfield").

226:4 **porter** the one who did the physical labor involved at the store

226:7–8 **used dope** took narcotic drugs for pleasure; we learn at 232:10 that Uncle Willy is addicted to morphine

226:13–14 **patent medicines that were already in bottles** brand-name remedies, usually cheap and ineffective and often consisting of alcohol and so slightly narcotic in effect. Because they are "already in bottles," Uncle Willy doesn't have to read a prescription and measure or mix drugs for customers, which is a generally good thing for everybody involved.

226:21 **it** Job's unsteady hands and bad eyesight

226:25 **ball** baseball

226:32 **alcohol stove** small, lightweight portable stove that uses alcohol for fuel

226:32 **fill the needle** with "dope" (morphine)

226:33 **little blue myriad punctures** Willy has shot up liquefied narcotics so often and for so long that one can see the needle marks in the main veins of his arm.

227:8 **clean collar** some men's shirts had detachable collars that could be changed out or replaced; see 240:7

227:9–10 **his eyes behind his glasses kind of all run together like broken eggs** the surface of the eyeball is blurry, perhaps bloodshot or with cataracts; see also 231:24–26

227:15 **his blue arm** blue from the puncture marks; see 226:33

227:17 **they** the church members, including Reverend Schultz and Mrs. Merridew

227:27–29 **that tone in which preachers speak to fourteen-year-old boys that I don't believe even pansy boys like** with condescension; **pansy boy** = a sissy, an effeminate boy, as contrasted to the boys who play baseball and watch Uncle Willy shoot up

227:29 **Brother Christian** Uncle Willy's last name revealed—ironically so, with the invocation of Christian brotherhood, which is the last real motive in the Reverend's behavior

228:5 **fixing to** getting ready to

228:22–26 **one day last summer when they took a country man named Bundren to the asylum at Jackson but he wasn't too crazy not to know where he was going, sitting there in the coach window handcuffed to a fat deputy sheriff that was smoking a cigar** In *As I Lay Dying* (1930), Darl Bundren's family commits him to the state asylum. He fights this, but at his brother Cash's betrayal, his personality splits finally in two: Cash says, "I tried to tell him, but he just said, 'I thought you'd a told me. It's not that I,' he said, and then he begun to laugh" (221). The horror of Darl's own awareness of his broken personality emerges when he reflects, "Our brother Darl in a cage in Jackson where, his grimed hands lying light in the quiet interstices, looking out he foams" (236). The likely present of that novel, July of 1929, could date the first episode of "Uncle Willy" in the summer of 1930, and our narrator as born in 1917.

229:6 **lemonade** a pointed choice: a nonalcoholic, non-addictive drink

229:14–15 **like Darl Bundren and the deputy on the train** see 228:22–26

229:16 **she never needed any handcuffs** The force of her personality seems to be enough to restrain him.

229:21–22 **he couldn't even get the key into the lock** Uncle Willy is having withdrawal symptoms, including the extreme shaking associated with delirium tremens.

229:30 **vacation** The beginning of Uncle Willy's forced rehabilitation seems to be at the start of the boys' summer vacation from school in 1931.

230:12–13 **they had the marshal break in the door** an indication of the power that the Reverend and his "respectable" ladies have in Jefferson, because no legal orders for the marshal's action seem to exist

230:17–19 **hollering Mr. Christian and Uncle Willy and Willy, according to how old they were or how long they had lived in Jefferson** The oldest would be calling him by his first name, the youngest and most newly arrived by his surname, and the others by his nickname.

231:2–3 **Won't you please go to hell and just let me come on at my own gait** He is damning the church ladies and promising to join them there when he is good and ready.

231:9–10 **one of those sheep they would sacrifice back in the Bible** Ironically, in the narrator's view, the most Christian trait of the women who rehabilitate Willy "Christian" is their willingness to sacrifice him, like a sheep in the Old Testament.

231:24–26 **his eyes blinking and all run together behind his glasses so you couldn't even tell where the pupil was like you can in most eyes** see 227:9–10

231:30–232:1 **they would not trade with the clerk that Mrs. Merridew and Reverend Schultz put in the store** probably because they do not know him personally, as they do Uncle Willy; perhaps also because they don't trust the contingent from the church. See also 232:20–233:20.

232:4–6 **she was going to give him a complete rebirth, not only into real Christianity but into the practical world too** Deliberately comparing herself to Christ, in whom Christians are "reborn," Mrs. Merridew says she's going to save Willy, whether he likes it or not, spiritually and secularly. See also 232:13–14.

232:13–14 **position in the world which his family's name entitled him to before he degraded it** Mrs. Merridew is the town's biggest snob; not even Uncle Willy's sister wants to keep up the appearance of "Christian" respectability as much as she does.

232:16–17 **letters to the church** letters of introduction or recommendation from a third party known and respected by the church officials, perhaps from officials in another church

232:33–34 **swore out a warrant** got an legal restraining order to keep Job out of the store

233:4 **I ghy** I am going to

233:6 **new town trade** white middle-class customers, as opposed to the black and poor white country folks who regularly trade with Uncle Willy

233:19 **whipper-snappin' trash** young, insignificant upstart from a low class of people; Brown offers "quality" as an antonym to trash (202)

233:20 **Marse Hoke Christian** Uncle Willy's father's name: Mr. Hoke Christian, who started the business

234:16 **get a holt** take hold; hold on to

234:21 **neated up** tidily organized

234:32 **Nigger Row** Brown does not explain this reference, but we speculate that the narrator refers to a street with businesses that cater primarily to black customers in the black area of town.

234:33 **Jamaica ginger** appearing as "jamaica ginger" in the *American Mercury* version of the story; Old Jamaica Ginger Beer, a non-alcoholic beverage

235:6 **can of alcohol** see 236:2; the fuel for the alcohol stove

235:19–22 **then I knew that the clerk knew who got the alcohol before but I didn't know why he hadn't told Mrs. Merridew until two years later** The clerk knows Uncle Willy took the alcohol, but he doesn't tell Mrs. Merridew, and we never hear why. The story's timeline suggests that the narrator found out why about the time of Uncle Willy's death.

235:23–24 **Uncle Willy a year now** the second phase of the narrator's relationship with Uncle Willy, during which year Willy visits the whorehouses in Memphis

235:32 **burr-headed** having very short, spiky hair (Brown 41); a racial slur. Blacks were literally burr-headed; whites called this were burr-headed metaphorically because of their behavior.

236:2 **corn whisky** Because Uncle Willy goes into the hill country to buy the whisky, we know it's made illegally; he's visiting a bootlegger.

236:5–7 **smelling of that smell whose source I was not to discover at first hand for some years yet** the smell associated with adult sexual activity

236:8–9 **little notebook full of telephone numbers and names like Lorine and Billie and Jack** names evocative of the Memphis underworld. Lorine is similar to Lorraine, the name of the prostitute Jason Compson keeps in *The Sound and the Fury* (1929), and in *If I Forget Thee, Jerusalem/The Wild Palms* (1939), Charlotte Rittenmeyer observes to a woman named Billie that "It's a perfect whore's name, isn't it?" (150).

236:18 **bib** from "bibcock," a faucet with the handle bent downward

236:24–25 **over the wire** the telephone line; she is shouting so loudly that even someone elsewhere in the room can hear her

237:1 **house dress** dress meant to do housework in rather than public visiting

237:15 **young men and the boys that didn't work** loafers with leisure time to watch the spectacle unfold

237:24 **spring triggers** animal traps that catch the prey up in a net when it steps on a trigger point

237:29 **the wire** telegram; distinct from the telephone wire at 236:25

237:32 **laugh that off** try to ignore this

237:32 **Manuel Street** Like Ruby in *Sanctuary* (1931) and Nancy in *Requiem for a Nun* (1949), Uncle Willy's wife has worked as a prostitute in one of the brothels on Memphis's Manuel Street. Brown, seconded by Arnold and Trouard, identifies the fictional Manuel Street as Mulberry Street in Memphis's red-light district (Brown 125; Arnold and Trouard 18).

237:33 **high-nosed** stuck-up; snobby (figuratively, with their noses in the air)

238:6–7 **the thousand dollars came and they had to give Uncle Willy's wife the car too** Uncle Willy's sister has met the extortion demand for one thousand dollars, which Reverend Schultz and Mrs. Merridew deliver to her in exchange for her return to Memphis. When she gets the car, too, the Memphis woman has made all of the profit off Uncle Willy that she can.

238:11–12 **waiting at the post office for the afternoon mail** Before house delivery, customers picked up their mail at the post office.

238:13–15 **I will show you hicks what you can do to yourselves and one another** **hicks** = backwards, unsophisticated country people. Given her profession, it seems clear that she's telling the citizens of Jefferson not only that they can go fuck themselves but also that they are too backward to know how to do it.

238:24 **Keeley** according to Brown (113), a Keeley Institute, probably one on the southern edge of Memphis. Dr. Leslie E. Keeley claimed to have found a cure for alcoholism that involved injections of bichloride of gold; called the "gold cure," it became extremely popular after the first Keeley Institute was founded in 1879. The bus stop at 239:11–13 supports Brown's location.

238:26–28 **papers from Texas declaring that Uncle Willy was incompetent and making Mrs. Merridew his guardian and trustee** In order to avoid future shakedowns, Uncle Willy's sister turns his legal affairs over to Mrs. Merridew.

239:5–7 **any man who could sell Jefferson real estate for cash while shut up in a Keeley institute wasn't crazy or even drunk** Uncle Willy has sold his house and given them the slip again.

239:33 **cut some grass** mowed lawns to earn money

240:1 **Ford now without any top on it** Uncle Willy's first car was therefore not a Ford, and the new one is a convertible, perhaps a Cabriolet or Highboy roadster—early hotrods that would appeal to Uncle Willy's sense of adventure.

240:2 **chalk letters, $85 *cash*** the sign from the used car lot where he bought the car

240:6–7 **with the bill turned round behind and a pair of goggles cocked up on the front of it** Early motorists wore goggles to keep the dust out of their eyes, and Uncle Willy is also wearing a baseball cap, with the bill turned to the back so the goggles can perch on his forehead when he's not wearing them.

240:7 **celluloid collar** detachable collar made from a kind of common plastic; see 227:8

240:30 **Nemmine** never mind

241:3 **a little airplane with a two-cylinder engine** probably the Aeronca C-2, which was originally produced in 1929. The plane was "flying at its most basic . . . priced at a low $1495, bringing the cost of flying down to a level that a private citizen could aspire to and perhaps reach." Moreover, "it was almost impossible to make a hard landing with an Aeronca because the pilot could easily see his wheels touch the runway." It's thus not inconceivable that Secretary could learn to fly it so easily; pilots often took to the skies in its successor, the C-3, after only five hours of instruction. (See "Aeronautical Corporation of America.")

241:7 **tourist camp** also known as tourist courts and tourist cottages. The popularity and affordability of the automobile during the 1920s gave rise to the modern American road trip; people took to camping along roadsides, first in farmers' fields and then in areas designated for the purpose. Facilities in tourist camps became increasingly modernized throughout the 1930s; from a section of land with a privy and sites to pitch tents evolved elaborately landscaped grounds with individual cottages with their own private bathrooms. Tourist camps became today's motels. (See Grace and Towne.)

241:14 **permit from a doctor** Perhaps because of Uncle Willy's age, Captain Bean wants medical proof that he is physically fit to fly.

241:15–16 **Republicans and Democrats and XYZ's** During the Depression, the federal government instituted many public works programs known popularly by their initials. The Works Progress Administration (WPA), founded in 1935, is perhaps the most well-known; but by 1933, the year of Uncle Willy's death, the country had already seen the FDIC, TVA, and FHA, for starters. Uncle Willy seems less upset with a particular agenda than at the notion of regulation of his privacy by anyone.

241:29–32 **Then we would head west. When we ran out of the house money we would stop at a town and take up passengers and make enough money to buy gasoline and food to get to the next town** They have become amateur barnstormers, taking paying passengers up for short flights for a fee. Barnstorming began in the U.S. shortly after World War I and remained popular throughout the Great Depression.

242:15–18 **Because I was the other white one. I was white, even if old Job and Secretary were both older than me, so it would be all right; I could do it all right** As a white person, the narrator has the power to stop Uncle Willy's scheme, which he doesn't want to do. He can play along with this doomed plan and "do it all right," with the accent on "do," as in "get that job done."

242:18–22 **It was like I knew even then that, no matter what might happen to him, he wouldn't ever die and I thought that if I could**

just learn to live like he lived, no matter what might happen to me I wouldn't ever die either the reason the narrator goes along with Willy's plan even though he knows it has no chance of succeeding: he sees a kind of immortality in Uncle Willy's grand gestures of defiance toward Jefferson. See also 242:15–18, 244:10–12, and 247:3–8.

242:24–25 **a license to go away** a pilot's license

243:15 **Captin** captain; a term of respect for unknown white men

244:3 **like Uncle Willy was trying to take the short cut to China** like he was trying to get to the other side of the world by going through the earth instead of over it

244:6–7 **field hands** farm laborers

244:7 **folks in wagons** passersby

244:10–12 **looking exactly alike, I don't mean in the face but exactly alike like two tines of a garden fork look exactly like just before they chop into the ground** To the narrator, who fears conformity above all else, the locals look like automatons come to stare at Uncle Willy.

244:18 **outer dar** out of there

244:34–245:1 **about me being the white one, almost a man, and Secretary and old Job just irresponsible niggers** The narrator's father has indirectly blamed his son for Uncle Willy's death by reminding him of the adult status supposedly conferred by his whiteness, as opposed to the childlike, "irresponsible" black folks.

245:8–16 **"Didn't you learn to run it in two weeks?" he said. Secretary said yes. "You, a damn, trifling, worthless, ignorant, burr-headed nigger?" and Secretary said yes. "And me that graduated from a university and ran a fifteen-thousand-dollar business for forty years, yet you tell me I can't learn to run a damn little fifteen-hundred-dollar plane?" Then he looked at me. "Don't you believe I can run it?" he said. And I looked at him and I said, "Yes. I believe you can do anything"** In remembering this exchange, the narrator implicitly admits that there was a moment at which he might have stopped Uncle Willy, whose flying is so bad that Secretary deliberately takes the full measure of Willy's rage (with its racial insults) rather than let him keep trying to learn something that he obviously will never learn to do. The cost of the airplane accords with our identification of it as an Aeronca C-2 (241:3).

245:17–20 **And now I can't tell them. I can't say it. Papa told me once that somebody said that if you can know it you can say it. Or maybe the man that said that didn't count fourteen-year-old boys** We have not been able to identify a source for Papa's truism. More important to our reading is that the narrator is one of Faulkner's alienated children, who know that the adult world means to exclude the validity of their experience in the world.

245:22–27 **It was like we had both known it and we didn't even have to compare notes, tell one another that we did: he not needing to say that day in Memphis, "Come with me so you will be there when I will need you," and me not needing to say, "Let me come so I can be there when you will"** a passage that raises the possibility that the narrator assists in Willy's suicide

246:8 **him** Job—not Willy

246:11 **Uncle Job** the only time Job is referred to by this title

246:11 **she gonter git** she's going to get

246:34 **with the hearse in front** Uncle Willy has crashed the airplane, and now they are returning his body to Jefferson.

247:3–8 **Because the dying wasn't anything, it just touched the outside of you that you wore around with you for comfort and convenience like you do your clothes: it was because the old garments, the clothes that were not worth anything had betrayed one of the two of us and the one betrayed was me** a difficult passage because either Uncle Willy or Papa could be the betrayer—Willy for dying, or Papa for not understanding that Willy's physical life was not as important as the quality of life lived the way he chose—or perhaps, in deliberate ambiguity, both

247:10 **I didn't mean that** what he said at 244:34–245:1

247:12 **That was it** the end of the episode

247:15 **That's it** the essence of what the story of his life with Uncle Willy means to him

247:17 **there is only me to try to tell them** because the other one who could, Uncle Willy, is dead

"Mule in the Yard"

"Mule in the Yard" concentrates on one eventful day in Jefferson when the mule trader I. O. Snopes's mules run amok in the yard of Mannie Hait, the widow of his former employee. Such scenes happen regularly, and Mrs. Hait can neither prevent these episodes nor retaliate against them until the morning of the story at hand, when Snopes's responsibility for the burning of her house puts him at her mercy. The story may be read as a trickster contest in which Mrs. Hait proves herself the superior trickster; as a feminist fable; as a mock-epic; and as another story in which the apparently powerless and marginalized succeed in making a place for themselves. Mrs. Hait's battle is not only against the mule, but also against the man who owns them, the railroads, the banks, and, by extension, all men everywhere. As Hans H. Skei observes of Faulkner's short stories in general, "Even when the conflicts seem to be between individuals, these individuals must also be understood as representatives of a class, a race, or a culture [or a gender], and the conflicting interests must be viewed in this broader perspective" (*Novelist* 215). Mrs. Hait lives in a male-dominated world that she ignores until directly threatened by it; her very clothing is both a matter of thrift and a means, as John T. Matthews suggests, by which "she defines a position for herself in the marketplace" (30). She is joined on this day by the poor old black woman Het, of whom Skei notes her "presence and exclamatory nonsense, her zest for life, and her indomitable endurance through all tragic events" (*William Faulkner* 220). Mannie Hait is one of a number of masculinized women in Faulkner's world who have led Ilse Dusoir Lind to conclude that "It would appear that Faulkner, like Shakespeare, arrived early at an awareness of the androgyny of the creative mind, as well as a perception of the infinite shadings of the masculine and feminine in human beings" ("Faulkner's" 102). Perhaps, then, Mannie Hait and old Het are Jefferson's Rosalind and Celia, with Mrs. Hait donning masculine apparel as an expedient disguise that allows her to survive—and in the present case, thrive—in a hostile masculine world.

The confrontation over the mule in the yard is neither trivial nor amusing to Mrs. Hait and Snopes, who are fiercely engaged in their battle, but Faulkner's prose is elevated, ornate, and richly comic. "Mule in the Yard" constitutes a short story mock-epic, an oxymoronic achievement, perhaps, but one recalling "The Nun's Priest's Tale," *Don Quixote, The Rape of the Lock, Tom Jones,* and numerous passages from *Ulysses,* to name but a few. To Snopes and Mrs. Hait, the thrice-yearly escape of the mules is exasperating in the extreme, but life in the town literally stops to watch what happens every time they get loose; the mule in the yard is as good as a paid-for picture show. However comic the prose and entertaining the action, the story has serious moral purposes. Mrs. Hait's shrewd intelligence and direct action enable her to achieve a just revenge on both Snopes and the mule, and she achieves a place of safety, autonomy, and comparative freedom for herself within Jefferson's margin—as the "real hero" of the work (Skei, *William Faulkner* 220). Mock-epic forms from *Don Quixote* to *Ulysses* not only ridicule their subjects but also ennoble them, and "Mule in the Yard" continues this tradition.

While the exact date of composition for "Mule in the Yard" is uncertain, it may have been written in the late winter or early spring of 1933–34. The story was published in August 1934 by *Scribner's,* whose editor Kyle Crichton had earlier enthusiastically accepted "Spotted Horses" but later rejected "Centaur in Brass." The story was included as the eighth story in "The Village" section of *Collected Stories,* between the unhappy comedy of "Uncle Willy" and the grimly ironic "That Will Be Fine." Writing to Malcolm Cowley in 1945 and to Robert Haas in 1948, Faulkner announced his intention to use "Mule in the Yard" in "a later volume" (*Selected Letters* 197, 274). As *Collected Stories* neared publication, Faulkner assessed his achievement in the short story form: "It's all right; the stuff stands up amazingly well after a few years, 10 and 20. I had forgotten a lot of it; I spent a whole evening laughing to myself about the mules and the shingles" (*Selected Letters* 304). By rewriting

"Mule in the Yard" for Chapter 16 of *The Town*, however, Faulkner drew many readers' attention away from the story and toward the novel. It has not received the attention as an autonomous text that it deserves, and "Mule in the Yard" remains one of Faulkner's comic masterpieces.

249:1–2 **though not cold because of the fog** Clouds and fog can keep the air temperature from dropping: "Heat is absorbed by the earth's surface during the day and then slowly radiated into our atmosphere from the earth's surface. This is ultimately how our atmosphere warms. Sometimes with overcast skies, most of this heat energy emitted from earth remains relatively close to the surface due to that thick layer of clouds. So, the heat cannot continue to rise into space, and the surface temperature may remain relatively warm during the night" (Templeton).

249:11 **headrag** according to Calvin Brown, "a cloth worn wrapped around the head like a turban," usually worn by black women at work (Brown 100)

249:14 **ten-cent stores** like the original Woolworth's, retail stores with a wide range of products, none of which cost more than a dime

249:18 **Miss Mannie!** "a title with various special uses when employed with the given name rather than the surname" (Brown 129), here as a marker of Het's racial deference to Mrs. Hait

249:19 **Mrs. Hait** Miss Mannie's married name

249:20 **a scuttle of live ashes** "a bucket (usually of galvanized iron) with a flaring top and a handle" used to bring coal into the house and dead ashes out (Brown 171). Miss Mannie's still has some fire in it.

250:1–3 **indomitable yet relieved bereavement, as though that which had relicted her had been a woman and a not particularly valuable one at that** a curious passage, since an old form of the noun *relict* denotes a widow, but the term also describes an organism that has survived considerable change in its environment—a leftover, of sorts, as Miss Mannie is of I. O.'s mule schemes. Faulkner seems to suggest her relief at being left behind by something no more important than another woman.

250:5 **they in the town knew** the people in town have been taking note of Mrs. Hait's purchases since her husband died

250:10–12 **as though there lay supine and prisoned between earth and mist the long winter night's suspiration** see 249:1–2

250:14 **it** the fog

250:29 **Dar hit!** There it (is)!

251:5 **unmundane** not of this world; extraordinary

251:15–16 **Of course it did not take this long, and likewise it was the mule which refused the gambit** **it** = the furious running of 250:30–251:15. In chess, a gambit is an opening move involving the sacrifice of another piece; here, the mule declines to confront Mrs. Hait at all.

251:24 **unhasteful celerity** an exemplary Faulknerian paradox: unhurried speed

251:25 **brick coping** the top layer of brickwork, probably sloped to help with drainage

251:29 **Rhode Island Red** hardy breed of chicken used more for egg than meat production; a "good choice for the small flock owner" (see "Rhode Island Red")

251:33 **sunless and dimensionless medium** Faulkner describes the mule as "hell-born and hell-returning" two lines above (251:31), but the gray, foggy surroundings of its appearance and disappearance suggest a moment of purgatorial in-betweenness.

252:8 **new Manila rope** rope made from Manila hemp, fiber from the abaca plant found in the Philippines

252:9 **hap** happenstance; chance location, in this case

252:20 **which item Snopes included in the subsequent claim** the claim Snopes files with the insurance company, to compensate him for his dead mules

252:23 **wag** wit; joker

252:23–24 **a printed train schedule for the division** a timetable of arrivals and departures for the area; used either to avoid or to time better the trains' collisions with the mules

253:6–7 **what might be termed foreign matter** that is, Mr. Hait

253:14 **adjuster** insurance adjuster; the person who decides the merits of a claim against the company

253:17 **the old halcyon days when even the companies considered their southern branches and divisions the legitimate prey of all who dwelt beside them** that is, the railroads and insurance companies don't try very hard to catch people trying to defraud them of money; perhaps because of the economic hardships faced by common people in the South then, or because the South just wasn't worth bothering about

253:25 **salt sack** sack originally containing a certain weight of salt for household use, here recycled as a bank (see Brown 166)

253:26–28 **that serviceable and time-defying color which the railroad station was painted, as though out of sentiment or (as some said) gratitude** According to Walter Berrett, train stations and railroad cars were sometimes painted in the signature colors of the rail line that operated them. The "William Faulkner on the Web" site identifies the Old Depot in Oxford as once belonging to the Illinois Central Railroad, which at the time of the publication of this story used a circumscribed red and black diamond to represent the company, but we have not been able to identify the color that the engines or buildings might have been painted. Even if the Oxford depot is the basis for Jefferson's, the one near Mrs. Hait's house might have been painted some other "serviceable" color, like gray, which wouldn't show much wear or dirt.

In Sherwood Anderson's *Winesburg, Ohio,* a book Faulkner greatly admired and early in his career reviewed, we find a literary precedent for the paint on the train station. In "The Philosopher," Doctor Parcival describes his abusive and controlling older brother:

> "My brother was a railroad painter and had a job on the Big Four. . . . With other men he lived in a box car and away they went from town to town painting railroad property—switches, crossing gates, bridges, and stations.
>
> "The Big Four paints its stations a nasty orange color. How I hated that color! My brother was always covered with it. On pay days he used to get drunk and come home wearing his paint-covered clothes and bringing his money with him. . . . About the house he went in the clothes covered with the nasty orange colored paint." (35)

The Big Four was the combined railroads of the Cleveland, Chicago, Cincinnati, and St. Louis companies, formed in 1889. Faulkner's review appeared in *The Dallas Morning News* 26 April 1925 (see *Winesburg, Ohio,* Norton Critical ed., 166).

254:22 **porches screened and not** perhaps a class marker; screened porches cost money to install and maintain, and they offer privacy as well as protection from insects and the elements.

254:22 **boudoir caps** a cap worn over curlers or while applying makeup or dressing, to keep the hair in place (Brown 36)

254:27 **handkerchief-sized plot** small area of land

255:8–10 **two heavy lines of shaven beard descending from the corners of it as though in alluvial retrospect of years of tobacco** his two lines of beard look like dirty streams of tobacco juice have made a kind of Delta topography out of his chin

255:10 **Fore God** before God (Brown 84)

255:25–27 **they being able to pass under the house and so on the chord of a circle while it had to go around on the arc** Like many houses of the day and region, Mrs. Hait's house is raised slightly above ground level, so the chickens run underneath it while the mule must run around it.

256:7–8 **as though buried to the armpits for a Spanish-Indian-American suttee** While suttee is a Hindu custom in which the widow immolates herself on her husband's pyre, we are hard-pressed to explain why Snopes would be a multi-racial widow in this scene—perhaps as an ironic inversion of his business relationship to Mr. Hait or in homage to Mrs. Hait, to whom suttee did not and would never occur.

256:13–14 **stern staff of a boat** flagpole on the back end of a boat, probably with the off-color sense of "stern" as "backside"—hence, ready to defecate

256:18–19 **a pile of coal and another of pitch pine for priming fires** Mrs. Hait would use the coal for heating her house (in a coal stove), and the pitch pine chips (highly resinous and so flammable) to start fires.

256:29 **burlesqued nun** coat swept over the back of his head and hanging over his forehead, like a parody of a nun's wimple

257:21 **had—** a day, which Old Het says in full at 264:29

257:28–29 **more than one had made a point of finding him there by that time** Since the town is aware of the connection between

Snopes and Hait, the resentment he feels over Mrs. Hait's $8500 settlement, and the running of the mules, the townspeople keep coming to watch another installment of the saga.

257:34 **mail-order coat** a coat ordered from a catalog company, instead of bought from a store or homemade

258:1 **fruit jar** a glass jar with a gasket seal to contain preserved fruit (see Brown 87)

258:1 **banknotes** promissory note given by a bank, as good as cash; but 253:19 specifies that Mrs. Hait took cash from the insurance company, so "banknotes" here would seem to mean paper money.

258:11 **It was you that opened the cellar door, though** "You have some responsibility for the fire"

258:14–16 **To catch your mule with, that was trespassing on her property. You can't get out of it this time, I. O. There ain't a jury in the county that won't find for her** Mrs. Hait is going to win this round of their rivalry, too, and I. O. can't do a thing about it. James Hinkle has pointed out that in the U.S. Army, "I. O." stands for "Initials Only" (195).

258:20 **hit's a few things I could tell a jury myself about—** Mannie Hait

258:24 **Mannie Hait** Mrs. Hait named

259:17 **law something outen me** "get something out of me by legal action" (Brown 117)

259:26 **a greenback** note of legal tender, so called because of the green ink used on the back of it, issued first in 1862; later applied to paper currency in general

260:15 **neated** neatened, tidied up

260:22–23 **strip dat cow** milk that cow

260:35 **vittles** "victuals, food" (Brown 209)

261:10 **aunty** "a respectful form of address used, without a proper name, to an elderly Negro woman" (Brown 22), and sometimes not all that respectful, patronizing as it is

261:19 **critter** creature

261:30–31 **Them sixty dollars a head the railroad used to pay you for mules back when you and Hait——** was in business together

262:2 **owed——** Hait? What do you mean what I owed Hait?

262:3 **For getting them five mules onto the tr——** track

262:12–14 **Hit was our agreement that I wouldn't never owe him nothing until after the mules was——** paid for by the insurance company

262:16 **—until hit was over** Snopes's revised version of events from 262:14

262:17–18 **I never owed nobody no money because the man hit would have been owed to wasn't nobody** "I didn't have to pay Hait because he was dead." Snopes thinks he has beaten Mrs. Hait logically.

262:22–23 **ere a living man** any living man (Brown 78)

262:23 **fire——** continued at line 262:25

262:33 **ravine ditch** a redundancy on Mrs. Hait's part

263:9 **I reckon that's far enough** far enough to take it just to kill it

263:27 **agoment** "apparently a blend of *agony* and *torment*" (Brown 19)

263:31 **nere a man** never a man; no man

263:33–34 **you never even knowed where he was at and what doing** to Snopes, a kind of cosmic injustice, because she didn't have the "agoment" of the scheming and still got $8500 when Hait died

264:15 **a gesture almost Gallic** a caricature of a French gesture; highly theatrical and mannered thrusting of the hand toward heaven

264:28–29 **Gentlemen, hush!** a phrase from Owen Wister's *The Virginian* (1902), a book well-beloved by the Falkner family (Blotner 1974, 93)

“That Will Be Fine”

Told by the greedy and nearly megalomaniacal seven-year-old Georgie, “That Will Be Fine” has elements of the traditional initiation story, including a child narrator in contact with adult themes of sex, violence, and death. However, in this story the supposed initiate remains oblivious to the significance of the action he narrates. Thus, the story proceeds with a kind of unflagging irony: Georgie observes and accurately reports a good many details, but his own self-centeredness blinds him to the perfidy of his thieving, check-forging, embezzling, womanizing Uncle Rodney. In the end, Georgie’s own character flaws allow the outraged husband of one of Rodney’s paramours to lure him into a trap, and the boy leaves the story unaware that his uncle has just been killed. In addition to Georgie and his uncle, the story treats of their family (materialistic and duplicitous to a person), its genuinely concerned and supportive servants, and those from the larger community whom Uncle Rodney has outraged, who in turn seek to expose Rodney’s misdeeds and to call him or his family to account for them. The story’s tensions derive from the contrast between Georgie’s peculiar combination of obsession and ignorance—he remains stridently naïve through the entire narrative—and his uncle’s increasingly dangerous situation. The story thus serves to initiate its reader, rather than Georgie or any of the other characters, into a world nearly devoid of positive ethical role models.

Critical discussion of “That Will Be Fine” has emphasized the story’s combination of dark comedy and violence, the unusual point of view of its uncomprehending young narrator, the parallels between the uncle and the nephew, and the parallels between its character, situation, subject, and theme and those of other Faulkner texts. Placing the story in the traditions of Southwestern humor, Hans H. Skei maintains that "the story remains comic even through its tragic end. This is so because the boy's greed is so single-minded and so much exceeds our expectations that human tragedy and death cannot do away with the exuberant comic tone of the story" (*Novelist* 226). Other critics have been harsher on Georgie and on his story. Edmond Volpe, for example, says the story exhibits several "elements of burlesque, and the comedy is heightened by the child's objective presentation of jokes, conversation, and action that he does not understand. The facts that we are gradually discovering, however, are not at all amusing; they are sordid in the extreme" (214). Georgie, Robert Sayre offers, "has chillingly internalized adult acquisitiveness and dishonesty . . . he even carries his mercenary pettiness into family relations" ("Romantic" 248); and Joseph Blotner calls him "both villainous and naïve" and places him as "one in a progression of unfortunate or evil children" ("Children" 87). James Ferguson calls Georgie "utterly corrupt, one of the most loathsome children in all of fiction," and he notes that "the central ironies of the story derive from the appallingly mercenary and self-centered character of the narrator. Hence, our reactions . . . are very complex indeed" (59, 77). The "grim humor" of the story, says Lisa Paddock, "grows out of the greedy narrator's naïve unawareness that his Uncle Rodney's 'business'—in which he serves as an accomplice—involves the seduction of married women so that he can relieve them of their money and jewelry" (164). Most intertextual analyses of "That Will Be Fine" cite parallels with *The Sound and the Fury* (1929): Georgie with the money-hungry Jason Compson, his father with Mr. Compson, Uncle Rodney with Maury Bascomb, and Mr. and Mrs. Pruitt with Mr. and Mrs. Patterson. "Turning the last page," Blotner adds, "the reader is likely to think not only of Maury Bascomb and Uncle Rodney but also of Georgie grown to manhood" ("Children" 87)—as Jason, in other words. We note too that Maury Priest of *The Reivers* (1962), like Georgie's father, runs a livery stable. Ferguson calls the story "this underrated piece" (77), and Skei believes "Faulkner has had a lucky hand in rendering this prodigious child with consistency and credibility, and he has avoided the risk of becoming banal" (226). Volpe's final assessment differs: "With a narrator who represents moral innocence but still provokes a shudder of revulsion, Faulkner fails to provide a moral guidepost. As a result, the story leaves a bitter aftertaste, a feeling of disharmony beyond the feeling of revulsion, which is skillfully evoked" (215). Taking place at Christmas, the story's multiple ironies must surely emphasize that the absence of "moral guideposts" has formed Georgie's character and, by extension, created the very basis of the story's action.

"That Will Be Fine" was apparently written in March 1935, when Faulkner sought desperately to write and sell short stories in order to pay his income tax (Blotner 1974, 882). Though the story sold rather quickly to the *American Mercury*, which published it in its July 1935 issue, Faulkner was disappointed with the $250 payment: "I need a thousand," he wrote his agent, Morton Goldman (*Selected Letters* 91). Edward J. O'Brien soon republished it in a volume entitled *The Best Short Stories 1936 and the Yearbook of the American Short Story* (*SL* 96). Robert K. Haas at Random House wrote Faulkner in March 1948 to propose a volume of Faulkner's collected short stories; Faulkner was initially reluctant to undertake the project, but in early fall of that same year he reconsidered and sent Haas an amended list of titles to include in the collection, with notes. In a letter to Haas dated late September or early October, Faulkner apparently added "That Will Be Fine" to the list and asked, "Have you a good reason for not including this?" (*SL* 274). The version from the *American Mercury* was published without change as the ninth of ten stories in "The Village" section of *Collected Stories*, between "Mule in the Yard" and "That Evening Sun," where it serves to darken the mood of what Faulkner called, in reference to the stories at the heart of *These 13* (1931), "a collection of short stories of my townspeople" (*SL* 34).

265:1 **We** Georgie and Rosie, the family's cook. Much of Georgie's narration reflects anxieties about which social group characters inhabit and concern over gossip.

265:4–5 **when he would take them off the tree** Christmas presents have traditionally been kept under the tree, but during the high Victorian age, tree-decorating became very lavish and included the gifts on the tree. British and German Christmas tree fashions made their way to parts of America with immigrant populations and at times were indications of class status (or pretension) (see "A Chronological History of the Christmas Tree").

265:13 **twell** till; until

266:3 **it** Christmas

266:3–4 **they would begin to shoot the fireworks** As Calvin Brown explains, "Christmas, not the 4th of July, [was] the traditional time for fireworks in the South" (82).

266:4 **it** Christmas

266:7 **livery stable** "business that rents horses, carriages, etc." (Brown 121). As Brown and others have noted, Murry Falkner ran such a business in Oxford.

266:13 **Grandpa's tonic** his stash of alcohol, perhaps of over-the-counter patent medicine containing a high percentage of alcohol

266:16 **mamma and us** Rodney is Susan's brother; "us" includes Georgie and his father George.

266:16 **we** Rodney and Georgie

266:17 **doing business with Mrs. Tucker** Rodney's euphemism for his sexual affairs, which Georgie has unwittingly helped him to conduct

266:18 **Compress Association** A cotton compress is "a place where cotton intended for distant shipment is compressed much more heavily" than at an ordinary gin (Brown 60). The Compress Association, in this context, would probably have been an organization of stockholders who underwrite and profit from the sale and transportation of cotton.

266:22 **hollered** yelled. Georgie has just taken the Lord's name in vain.

266:23 **cussing** see 266:22

266:33 **I bound** "I'm determined," as in "I'm bound and determined" to do something; Rosie is the only character in the story who cares much about Grandpa.

267:5–268:6 **So Rosie turned out the light and went out. . . . All right, all right; for God's sake, all right** the first extended example of indirect dialogue in the story. Like Huck Finn before him, Georgie has an infallible memory for what people say and how they say it, coupled with a very limited understanding of the full meaning behind either.

267:20–21 **his generosity was longer than his pocket book** Rodney spends more money than he earns.

267:27–30 **one man in the connection whose generosity, or whatever mamma wanted to call it, was at least five hundred dollars**

shorter than his pocket book **one man** = himself, in reference to the first theft that he helped cover up

267:35 **good name** honor, reputation; the first example in the story of the store that Georgie's mother sets by class status

268:14–17 **He said how I never went around telling people about papa's business and I said how everybody knew papa was in the livery-stable business and so I didn't have to tell them** a conversation that occurs because Georgie has tried to extort extra money from Rodney by threatening to tell about his "business"

268:28–29 **he would tell mamma how far we had walked that day** the lie Rodney tells, and Georgie implicitly supports, about what they've been doing

269:1 **dose** Georgie's perspective on Rodney's swig of Grandpa's stashed liquor

269:4–5 **Sunday suit** from *Sunday best*: "one's finest clothes. . . . This expression alludes to reserving one's best clothes for going to church; indeed, an older idiom is *Sunday-go-to-meeting clothes* (*meeting* here meaning 'prayer meeting') [Mid-1800s]" (Ammer 625).

269:6 **hack** a hired coach

269:14 **without even her hat on** not dressed to appear in public

269:16 **Yessum** yes Ma'am

269:19 **box** the driver's seat

269:21 **hired buggy** a carriage that she has rented, in her haste to get to Jefferson

270:6 **Sho** sure

270:11–12 **it would sholy take a whole association to compress Uncle Rodney** **sholy** = surely; John Paul makes this pun at Rodney's expense, and Georgie understands neither his humor nor the seriousness of his remark that "anything a man kept at all the time, night and day both, he would call it work no matter how much fun it started out to be" (270:6–8).

270:13 **Nome** no Ma'am

270:19 **Remember the nigger** The line reflects the racial ideology of Georgie's parents; the black servants all know what Rodney is doing anyway, as the previous material in the paragraph suggests.

270:23–24 **light road hack hitched up** see 269:6

270:26–28 **if we didn't get to Uncle Rodney before the others caught him, papa would just wear the clothes Uncle Rodney had on now** Rodney's most recent fraud scheme has just been discovered, as Louisa's hasty arrival and Georgie's family's departure indicates. This comment from Papa reveals how serious Rodney's crime must be: he risks punishment, perhaps death, at the hands of a mob.

270:29 **closed the curtains** the curtains on the hired carriage that would provide privacy and protection from the dust and elements

271:28 **it** Rodney's arrest and the subsequent family disgrace

271:32–272:1 **Mr. Pruitt showed her with her own eyes the check with Grandpa's name signed to it and how even Aunt Louisa could see that Grandpa's name had been—** forged

272:12 **dash pocket** The dash on a carriage is a shield that keeps mud from the horses' hooves from being splashed inside; the dash pocket is roughly analogous to the glove compartment in a car.

272:12 **few drops on the handkerchief** for her to smell as a restorative

272:19 **bond business** Rodney's present scheme

272:20 **road bonds** government-issued interest-bearing certificates sold to cover the cost of road-building projects

272:33–34 **Grandma put up her road bonds for security on the note** They took out a loan to pay Rodney's debt, and as his mother gave her road bonds to the lender in case Rodney defaulted on the loan.

273:1–8 **Uncle Rodney had redeemed Grandma's note and the road bonds from the bank with some of the Compress Association's bonds out of the safe in the Compress Association office, because when Mr. Pruitt found the Compress Association's bonds were missing he looked for them and found them in the bank and when he looked in the Compress Association's safe all he found was the check for two thousand dollars with Grandpa's name signed to it** Rodney has taken his mother's road bonds, worth two thousand dollars, out of the bank and left in their place bonds issued by the Compress Association, which makes the deal look legitimate. He has left a forged check in the Compress Association, so he has effectively stolen four thousand dollars—the original two thousand, plus his mother's redeemable bonds.

273:11–12 **Grandpa never had two thousand dollars in it** Obviously, the whole family lives beyond its means.

273:26–27 **white like a whitewashed fence that has been rained on** Whitewash, a kind of paint, is water soluble, so if rain fell on a whitewashed fence, the places where the water ran down would be left bare. Louisa has been crying so hard that her face powder is streaked. (See Brown 215–16.)

273:29–30 **papa said how even if Mr. Pruitt had only lived in Mottstown a few months** he would have known Rodney's reputation well enough not to hire him for a job where he could get to other people's money

273:34 **belt** a heavy blow

274:1 **Pruitt's married** In other words, Mrs. Pruitt got Rodney the job by influencing her husband.

274:3–4 **They shoot fireworks in Mottstown too like they do in Jefferson** another example of Georgie's self-absorption and attention to the details of his surroundings

274:6 **remember Georgie** an admonition to the women not to discuss Mrs. Pruitt's apparently loose morals in front of the child

274:7–9 **Painted common thing, traipsing up and down the streets all afternoon alone in a buggy** cheaply and garishly made up, belonging to a lower social class than they do. Brown observes that "When one woman accuses another of traipsing around, it always means going around giddily, brazenly, wantonly, and up to no good" (202).

274:11 **without corsets on** without the close-fitting undergarments that shape the torso; not dressed properly to receive company

274:14 **it was Mrs. Pruitt that did it** Louisa blames Mrs. Pruitt for seducing Rodney.

274:26 **Mandy, that was Grandpa's cook** Beginning here and continuing through 276:14, when "they went back to the house," Georgie describes a series of events that he either misinterprets or fails to understand. Rodney has convinced Mandy to leave her cabin so that he can hide in it; he locks it from the inside, and Uncle Fred and Georgie's father lock him in from the outside, using the hasp and lock from the woodshed. At Rodney's instruction, Georgie brings him the screwdriver so Rodney can begin prying his way out through the window (279:32–33).

275:8 **them** the bonds

275:10 **that check was dated ten days ago** Uncle Rodney has probably already sold the bonds.

275:11 **reared back in his chair** sitting straight up, as a horse rears on its hind legs

275:16 **go down and bring his mail** In the days before home postal delivery, mail was picked up at the local post office.

275:19–22 **he was laughing now because when he said that about Christmas before Christmas he always laughed, it wasn't until after Christmas that he didn't laugh when he said that about Christmas** Grandpa has had enough of his family by the time the holiday is over.

276:2 **woodshed** small building to store firewood

276:14–18 **it didn't matter if Mandy was in the house too and couldn't get out, because the train came from Jefferson with Rosie and papa's Sunday clothes on it and so Rosie was there to cook for Grandpa and us and so that was all right too** To Georgie and his family, the black servants matter only as functionaries; nobody seems to care that Mandy might be locked up with a notorious womanizer (or at least evicted from her home by him), as long as someone does the cooking.

276:19–20 **But they couldn't fool Uncle Rodney. I could have told them that** Georgie overestimates Rodney's cleverness, as the story demonstrates, and the tragedy of the narrative also turns on what Georgie "could have told" everybody, including Rodney.

276:33 **exactly what he wanted** the physical security and the alibi

277:3–4 **did I ever see ten quarters all at once? and I never did** Rodney's initial bribe, for $2.50, and the basis of Georgie's subsequent quarter-counting speculation

277:5 **screw driver** Georgie's father and Fred have nailed the windows shut, so Rodney probably plans to use the screw driver as a lever to pry the boards off of the windows, just as he prizes open Grandpa's desk.

277:10 **they couldn't fool me either** Georgie's estimation of his own cleverness as Rodney's partner

277:11 **the man** the detective from Mottstown who is also investigating Rodney's actions; see 277:15–18

277:17–18 **Mr. Watts at Jefferson that catches the niggers** a sheriff. Georgie seems to think that only black people commit crimes.

278:21–22 **that would be twenty-one quarters, except for the dime** If Grandpa gives Georgie a quarter in addition to the ten quarters he will receive from Rodney, then Georgie will have eleven quarters, not twenty-one. Because Georgie "never did" see ten quarters before at once (277:4), we surmise that Faulkner—not Georgie—has temporarily lost count of Georgie's quarters.

278:25–26 **powder on their faces where they had been crying** They have recovered enough composure to put on fresh face powder to cover up the marks of the tears.

278:26–27 **it was papa helping him take a dose of tonic every now and then all afternoon** Uncle Fred usually does this.

278:32 **them** the bonds

279:2 **a rig** in this case, a horse and carriage

279:3 **the main line** the major hub of the railroad

279:13 **straight ahead now, pa** Grandpa has had a few too many doses of tonic and needs to be guided to the supper table.

279:17 **pool hall** establishment that sometimes serves alcohol and is equipped with billiard tables for games of pool, sometimes played for money; a popular hangout for men

280:22–23 **I am going to give you twenty** Here, Faulkner's quarter-counting rights itself.

280:25–26 **there wasn't any paper to carry this time** At least one of Georgie's jobs entailed passing notes from Rodney to a woman.

280:27–29 **it was too important to put on paper and besides I wouldn't need a paper because I would not know them anyhow** Rodney cannot risk a paper trail of evidence in his plan to leave Mottstown, but his insistence that it doesn't matter that Georgie know the people involved leads directly to his death.

281:3 **never mind who it will be** see 280:27–29

282:14–15 **It's my horse now, only damn this moonlight to hell** Rodney has stolen the horse and doesn't want to be seen with it.

282:30 **Never mind who it will be** see 280:27–29

283:20–21 **And then he had told me I would not know them anyway** see 280:27–29

283:32–33 **'She says to come and help carry it.' Say that to him twice, too** Georgie's literal-minded parroting of what he's told leads to Rodney's death; he never tells his uncle that a man said to say this.

284:15–16 **She said for you to come and help carry it. For me to say that twice** see 283:32–33

284:21–22 **kind of squatting along the bushes** skulking so that he won't be seen

284:31 **in time** in time not to be hit by a very nervous Uncle Rodney

284:32 **it was a stick in his hand** Georgie seems to realize that Rodney very nearly hit him with the stick, and he backs off.

285:14–16 **all of a sudden they started shooting firecrackers back at the house where Uncle Rodney had gone. Only they just shot five of them fast** the gunshots that kill Rodney

285:31 **something long** Rodney's body

285:34 **window blind** a shutter

286:13–14 **No, if it belonged to anybody now it belonged to Grandpa** Rodney is dead, and his body belongs to the head of his family.

286:27–28 **somebody in the house that sounded like singing** Someone inside is keening, moaning in grief.

287:9 **You don't need to tell me that** Rosie knows that her job is to shield Georgie from what has happened.

287:13 **dodge** avoid

287:16 **gonter** going to

287:22 **holt** hold

287:25 **Yonder** over there

287:26–27 **possum. It was in a persimmon tree** an opossum. As Brown points out, nobody but zoologists ever says the "o." Possums are omnivorous and fond of persimmons; they also eat carrion (153).

288:2–4 **then when I got the twenty quarters from Uncle Rodney I would have twenty-one quarters and that will be fine** title passage; also occurs in modified form at 266:19, 269:10, 269:13, 270:32–33, 276:18, and 278:22–23. By the end of the story, Georgie's tag line drips with irony.

"That Evening Sun"

"That Evening Sun" remains one of Faulkner's most memorable, fascinating, and problematic stories, as the narrator Quentin, now an adult, recalls his own unflinching but seemingly uncomprehending gaze upon the facts of African American life in the story's time and place "fifteen years ago." Quentin, usually accompanied by his younger sister Caddy and his younger brother Jason, and occasionally by his father, learns, in a series of compelling scenes, that Nancy, the family's laundress and substitute cook, is a prostitute, a user of cocaine, and a would-be suicide; that she is pregnant by someone other than her husband, Jesus; and that she fears Jesus is going to murder her. On the last night that Quentin describes, Nancy, believing that Jesus lies in wait for her in the darkness outside her cabin, temporizes by trying to keep Quentin, Caddy, and Jason with her. When the children's father comes to retrieve them, it becomes clear that he does not take Nancy's fears seriously. The story ends at an impasse between Nancy and Father on this issue, but Quentin clearly believes that something either is about to change or has already irrevocably changed: "Who will do our washing now, Father?" (309). "That Evening Sun," which takes its title from W. C. Handy's "St. Louis Blues" (see entry at Title) is equally the story of Nancy's tragic life and the story of Quentin's developing understanding of her dilemma. Her unresolved fate becomes the means of his initiation into the world of racial division and the world of exploitation, sex, violence, and death.

The presence of Quentin, Caddy, Jason, Father, and Mother and the references to Dilsey, Frony, T. P., and Versh connect the story inevitably with *The Sound and the Fury* (1929), and Quentin, Caddy, and Jason appear in "A Justice," which Quentin also narrates. The chronology of

"That Evening Sun" is part of one of the greatest intertextual problems in reading Faulkner. The narrator Quentin in *The Sound and the Fury* commits suicide at age nineteen, and, later, in *Absalom, Absalom!* (1936), the narrator Quentin says he is "older at twenty than a lot of people who have died" (301). Faulkner does not include either the Compson surname or the character of Benjy Compson in "That Evening Sun," just as he does not include Mrs. Compson, Caddy, Jason, or Benjy in *Absalom*, in which Quentin again takes a major role as both character and narrator. A different version of Nancy's story appears, too, in *Requiem for a Nun* (1951), in which she is a principal character with the last name of Mannigoe. "In 'That Evening Sun,' " Diane Roberts says, "her sexuality, triggering the murderous jealousy of Jesus, destroys her. In *Requiem*, she is resurrected and rewritten, defusing the power of desire in favor of self-immolating motherhood" (219). Many believe that Nancy's "resurrection" in *Requiem* cannot legitimately be used to provide evidence for a given reading of "That Evening Sun." Hans Skei, for example, states flatly that "Quentin, first-person narrator and character in 'That Evening Sun,' first and foremost exists within the limits of the tale he tells, and he is clearly a different Quentin from the very troubled young man in *The Sound and the Fury* and *Absalom, Absalom!*" (*Reading* 180). Faulkner answered a question about the story and the novel in Charlottesville by saying Nancy was "the same person, actually" in both texts, though he qualified his comment by adding, "These people I figure belong to me and I have the right to move them about in time when I need them" (*FU* 79). To what extent and in what ways we ought to read Nancy, Quentin, and the others as "the same" from appearance to appearance thus remain issues open for debate.

Many of the complexities of an intertextual reading arise from the fact that we do not know precisely when Faulkner wrote his first version of the story. Some have speculated that the story was begun even before *The Sound and the Fury*; some have thought it to have been written about the same time as the novel; and still others have noted the lack of convincing evidence for either theory, pointing out that we only know for certain that the story existed by October 1930. It was rejected by *Scribner's* but quickly accepted by H. L. Mencken's *American Mercury*. Mencken, however, had qualms about using the name "Jesus" for such a menacing character, and he wished Faulkner to treat Nancy's pregnancy more circumspectly. Faulkner assented to both changes, though he did not modify the references to pregnancy as much as Mencken may have hoped he would, and the story was prominently featured when Mencken published Faulkner's revised version in March 1931. Faulkner restored Jesus's name—he had been "Jubah" in the *American Mercury* version—and the "vine business" (292) when he revised the story for inclusion in *These 13* later in 1931, and the *Collected Stories* version is substantially the same. Those who believe "That Evening Sun" antedates *The Sound and the Fury* point to the inconsistent handling of Quentin's age (twenty-four in the story, a suicide at nineteen in the novel) and the absence of Benjy and the Compson surname from the story. Over and against that, one could argue that references to T. P., Frony, and Versh, explicitly identified as Dilsey's children in the novel, are not developed as such in the story.

"That Evening Sun" reveals many disturbing divisions—black and white, male and female, child and adult, past and present, master and servant, respectable and "Other," to name some of the most obvious—a general pattern in which "The old order may be designated natural and serene, but it also predicates inequity and oppression" (Matthews, "Faulkner's" 77). Quentin's narrative method reveals these divisions without comment, often through juxtaposition of competing fragments of dialogue, in a kind of Yoknapatawpha County stichomythia. See, for example, 293:9–294:7 and 294:22–295:28, which establish the technique, and, among others, the intricately textured exchange at 307:21–30, in which each of the four speakers makes statements or asks questions that are deliberately or unintentionally ignored, contradicted, deflected, or misunderstood.

For many readers, the essential subject of the story is the racial division and its origins in the whites' condescending, abusive, and oblivious treatment of blacks. For Quentin, says Edmond Volpe, "the experience plants seeds of recognition that will blossom, many years later, into an understanding of the social, moral, and emotional horrors that the inhumane treatment of blacks by whites has created in Southern society" (76). Skei suggests that through the narrative method "we are almost without noticing introduced to a world of deep conflicts, violence, fear, and anxiety seen from children's points of view, so that their limited understanding and preoccupation with their own small problems underscore and emphasize the selfishness and indifference of the white world"

(*Reading* 184). As Theresa Towner has argued, "I cant hang around white man's kitchen," Jesus says. "But white man can hang around mine" (292) contains the essence of the racial reality in this story (*Faulkner* 20). Jesus's anger at Nancy, which possibly culminates in his determination to kill her, also signifies the male determination to dominate the female, regardless of race. The injustice of such division is perhaps most glaringly illuminated in Nancy's inability to collect her meager prostitute's wages from Mr. Stovall, an encounter that leads to his knocking her down and kicking her teeth out, for which *she* is arrested. In sum, the child Quentin observes the behavior that reflects divisions in identity as well as culture, and the adult Quentin, as narrator, reports them without direct comment or interpretation. "That Evening Sun," finally, joins the past and present in a tense, unstable, and deeply threatening equilibrium to produce certainly one of the best short stories—and perhaps the best—that Faulkner ever wrote.

289:TITLE: from the opening line of W. C. Handy's "St. Louis Blues":

> I hate to see that evenin' sun go down
> I hate to see that evenin' sun go down
> 'Cause my baby, he done lef' this town.
> Feelin' tomorrow lak ah feel today.
> Feel tomorrow lak ah feel today.
> I'll pack my trunk, make my getaway.
> St. Louis woman, wid her diamon' rings
> Pulls dat man around by her apron strings.
> 'Twant for powder an' for store-bought hair,
> De man I love would not gone nowhere.
> Got de St. Louis blues jes as blue as Ah kin be
> Dat man got a heart lak a rock cast in the sea.
> Or else he wouldn't have gone so far from me.

Faulkner originally made the reference more explicit by calling the story "That Evening Sun Go Down." The title resonates with Nancy's situation generally, and with her fear of the darkness in particular. Just how far the story depends on Handy's blues is, of course, subject to debate. If Jesus has left Nancy for Memphis, as she says (293:18), or even if he has gone all the way to St. Louis itself and has "another wife by now" (295:16–18), then her fears of his return are groundless, but her shift from jealousy (295:19–22) to abject fear (296:24ff.) contributes to the story's problematic ending (see Peek, "That").

289:4 **water oaks, the maples and locusts and elms** Generally, these are all long-lived trees, with the locust the fastest-growing and the oaks and elms the longest-living (see Crockett, *Trees* 93, 139). Water oaks grow chiefly along streams and swamps, and all of these trees signify to Quentin the old order of life, which the newer ways of doing things threaten. The American elm at the time of this story had also begun to come under siege by Dutch elm disease, which killed nearly half of the elms in the United States.

289:5–6 **iron poles bearing clusters of bloated and ghostly and bloodless grapes** the light poles, with their glass globes; an image evocative of Quentin's fine and rather macabre sensibilities

289:8–9 **bright-colored, specially made motor cars** laundry trucks with the business's name painted on them

289:15 **fifteen years ago** see Introduction

289:18 **cotton bales** Quentin exaggerates, but in the process sets Nancy in an almost iconic role: an average cotton bale is 54 inches long and 26.5 inches wide, and usually weighs about five hundred pounds.

289:19 **kitchen door of the white house** Only white guests of equal social status or family members used the front door of the house; servants and black people had to use the back or kitchen door.

289:21 **Negro Hollow** a section of town inhabited only by black folks. Calvin Brown explains that there were two such sections in Faulkner's own Oxford (139).

290:18–19 **father told us not to have anything to do with Jesus** The *American Mercury* version of this story, with Jesus's name changed to Jubah, would have had none of the rich ironies produced by lines like this.

290:20 **razor scar** thin, cordlike scar from a razor cut, most likely incurred during a fight

291:3 **it** Nancy's chronic tardiness for work

291:5–6 **cashier in the bank and a deacon in the Baptist church** i.e., a person of respectable stature in the community. A deacon is a sort of "elder" in the Baptist church, and deacons as a group act as the church's governing body, making recommendations about church actions to the congregation and in general setting a Christian example in moral and business matters.

291:24–27 **He said that it was cocaine and not whisky, because no nigger would try to commit suicide unless he was full of cocaine, because a nigger full of cocaine wasn't a nigger any longer** The jailer exhibits the kind of broadbrush racism that this story asks us to confront, but he knows what cocaine use does to people. According to the National Institute on Drug Abuse, cocaine is a powerfully addictive drug of abuse, and an individual who tries it "cannot predict or control the extent to which he or she will continue to use the drug" ("Crack and Cocaine").

292:6 **sitting behind the stove** a cook stove fueled by wood positioned away from the wall, perhaps to better heat the room

295:1–2 **aint but one thing going to lay it down again** Nancy's death

295:11–13 **that razor in his mouth. That razor on that string down his back, inside his shirt** Jesus carries a straight razor, a long blade that might or might not fold into a handle; he wears it around his neck like a backward-hanging necklace, so that to use it in a hurry he need only pull it around and off, as Rider does in *Go Down, Moses*: "The same motion of the hand which brought the razor forward over his shoulder flipped the blade open and freed it from the cord, the blade opening on until the back edge of it lay across the knuckles of his fist" (148–49).

295:20 **wropped** a term Nancy coins, probably from "wrapped"; euphemism for sexual intercourse

295:21 **that arm** euphemism for penis

296:9–10 **It was like singing and it wasn't like singing, like the sounds that Negroes make** The syntax could suggest either that the sound Nancy makes is like other sounds that Quentin has heard from black people or that it is not; her abject terror later and the ambiguity of the story's end suggest the latter.

296:13–16 **we could see Nancy's eyes halfway up the stairs, against the wall. They looked like cat's eyes do, like a big cat against the**

wall, watching us The first of three passages that locate Quentin's perception of Nancy's fear in her eyes (see also 296:22, 27–29). Too frightened to stay in the kitchen and too hesitant to join the white folks above stairs, she is literally stuck "halfway up."

296:18–19 **father came back up from the kitchen, with his pistol in his hand** in case an intruder is in the house

296:27–29 **I had looked so hard at her eyes on the stairs that they had got printed on my eyeballs, like the sun does when you have closed your eyes and there is no sun** the title passage of the story: Quentin's own eyes have been imprinted with Nancy's terror. See also 296:13–16.

297:13 **rack and ruin** destruction

297:29 **it's** the attack that Nancy believes will come from Jesus, resulting in her death

298:1 **a spreading adder's** according to Calvin Brown, a harmless snake that can inflate its body in a bluffing move when attacked (186)

298:8 **sploshed** onomatopoeic cross between "splashed" and "sloshed"

300:7–8 **not unsinging** still somehow melodious or harmonic

301:6 **The lane was dark** an abrupt shift in the characters' location; they have taken Nancy's suggestion and left for her cabin. That she doesn't wait for an escort from Versh and instead takes the white children to her cabin unescorted indicate her full belief in the power of whiteness to protect her and the relative impotence of blackness—even in the face of danger from other blackness.

301:14 **You talk like there was five of us here** Caddy notices that Nancy pretends that "father" is with them but cannot speculate on why; with Quentin, we understand that Nancy is trying to convince someone lurking about that she has a white man—in this case, "Mr Jason"—with her for protection.

301:20–21 **You're the one that's talking like father—** was here

301:23 **aguh** Caddie starts to say "again" but Nancy puts her hand over Caddy's mouth.

301:30 **lit the lamp** a kerosene lamp, consisting of a base to hold the oil, a burner that contains the wick, and a chimney or globe to protect the flame and magnify the light

301:31 **put the bar up** a piece of wood to keep the door from being opened; see also 303:1–3

303:21–24 **She looked at Caddy, like when your eyes look up at a stick balanced on your nose** cross-eyed

303:25 **I'll bang on the floor** throw a temper tantrum

303:31 **globe** see 301:30

304:1 **lamp chimney** see 301:30

304:11 **popper** According to Brown, "The old-fashioned corn popper for use over an open fire consisted of a solid metal box fitted with a screened top and mounted on a handle about 3′ long. The top slid in grooves at the top of the box and had a wire attached to it so that it could be pulled back to empty the corn after it was popped. It was presumably this wire which was missing and which Nancy replaced to 'fix' the popper" at 304:32–33 (153).

304:32–33 **She got a piece of wire and fixed the popper** see 304:11

305:4 **We shelled it** took the kernels off the cob

305:9–10 **The lamp was turned up so high it was beginning to smoke** see 301:30; if too much wick is threaded through the burner, it will burn too quickly and make the lamp smoke.

305:12 **I'll clean it** remove the soot from the inside of the chimney; see 301:30

305:33–34 **All we need to do is—** pop these

307:9–10 **It was a hog bone, with blood meat still on it, laying by the lamp** a threatening reminder of mortality, maybe of Voodoo or conjure origins. The passage adds another layer of ambiguity to the story: Is Nancy lying, or did she remove the hog bone before Quentin had a chance to see it?

307:24 **I reckon it belong to me** her death at Jesus's hands is her destiny; **it** = her death

307:25 **I reckon what I going to get ain't no more than mine** I deserve what's going to happen to me

307:34 **there I am, and blood—** all over everywhere

308:5–6 **"You mean you're going to sit right here with the lamp lighted?" father said** The remark indicates that Quentin's father might take Nancy more seriously than his other comments indicate.

308:12 **coffin money** burial insurance

308:14 **Negro insurance** money collected weekly or monthly to be recouped as funeral expenses; see 308:12

308:17–18 **He and the child went away. After a week or two he came back alone** Quentin either does not know or does not share the fate of this mysterious child, but the mention of the little girl adds to the ominous tone of the story's final passages.

309:17 **Who will do our washing now, Father?** see Introduction. Quentin's father never answers him, and the story ends in near-complete ambiguity concerning Nancy's fate. Quentin, as his question shows, senses that Nancy is somehow "finished."

III. THE WILDERNESS

“Red Leaves”

“Red Leaves” describes a brief eventful period in a tribe of Chickasaws who inhabit north Mississippi in the early part of the nineteenth century. The Chief, Issetibbeha, has died, perhaps poisoned by his son, Moketubbe, and the tribe's ritual requires that the dead chief be buried with his horse, his dog, and his African American body servant. The body servant, however, has no wish to be sacrificed with his chief, so he escapes into the swampy bottom between the tribal village and the river. The tribe pursues him, nominally led by the obese and indolent Moketubbe, himself almost immobilized by the pain of wearing of a pair of red Parisian slippers acquired by Issetibbeha on an earlier trip to Paris with the equivocal Chevalier Sœur Blonde de Vitry. On an important level, the story provides a subtle and detailed account of the politics of succession. “Doom,” Issetibbeha's father, was originally a subchief, but on the New Orleans riverboats he was able to pass himself off as the hereditary landowner, the “Man,” the Chief of the tribe. Also in New Orleans he impregnated the daughter of a “fairly well-to-do West Indian family” (318), and Issetibbeha was the product of this union. Between the pregnancy and the marriage, Doom also actually became chief, presumably by murdering his uncle and cousin. Issetibbeha succeeded Doom, and Moketubbe, as “Red Leaves” opens, is preparing to succeed his father, though he seems monstrously unfit for leadership. Moketubbe's moral and physical opposite, the body servant is strong, intelligent, and knowledgeable, but, “since there was nowhere for him to go” (332), he is eventually captured and returned to the village for execution.

Readers have generally agreed on the significance of the pursuit, capture, and execution of the body servant. For Edmond Volpe, his is "a terrifying existential confrontation with the reality of death" (146), and Hans Skei agrees that "we understand fully why he does not want to die and even, as he himself comes to realize, why his desire to live is so strong, so deep, so intense" (*Reading* 144). In the fourth section of the story, says James Ferguson, "We are with the slave all the time, *inside* him, identifying intensely with him until at the end of the section, when the moccasin strikes him and he hails the beast, ['Olé, grandfather'], we acknowledge with him our kinship with all of life, our sense of mortality, and our fierce desire to *live*" (93). The slave, surely among the most admirable of all of Faulkner's unnamed characters, possesses the classical attributes of the hero. His courage, dignity, determination, and perseverance earn him the admiration of even his captors, yet it is precisely this heroism in a slave of "the Man" that cause them to chase, capture, and ultimately kill him.

While the body servant's desperate and unsuccessful struggle to avoid his doom provides the immediate narrative focus for the story, "Red Leaves" also presents an extensive and intricate meditation on the relations among Native American, African, and Anglo-European cultures. Briefly, the Native Americans, in imitation of the whites, have begun to acquire slaves and clear the land, not to plant cotton, but to raise food for the slaves themselves, thus aggrandizing the system of chattel slavery in service of a capitalist economy, the essential product of which is not cotton, or corn, or grain, but more slaves. In addition to slavery and the capitalist economy, the tribal leaders have imported many artifacts from the white culture: a steamboat, an enameled snuff-box, "a gilt bed, a pair of girandoles" (320), a frock coat, a beaver hat, a broadcloth coat, linen underwear, an oriental fan, a mother-of-pearl lorgnon, dungaree pants, "stiff European finery" (331), shirts, trousers, and straw hats, and most especially the pair of patent-leather slippers with red heels. In addition to these manufactured articles, the Native Americans, having enslaved the Africans, have assumed the habits and language of racial and ethnic stereotyping. With such methods Faulkner not only contrasts Native American, African, and white cultures but also combines and so hybridizes them.

Not surprisingly, then, for many years the criticism of "Red Leaves" has concerned itself with what Diane Brown Jones calls "cultural impingement" (330), especially the ways in which the white culture changed both African and Native American culture for the worse. By taking up chattel slavery and its concomitant racial and ethnic prejudices and stereotypes, the Native Americans create insoluble problems for themselves, in addition to the horrors they perpetrate on the enslaved, of whom Faulkner's depiction of the body servant is eloquently representative. Some would have it that prior to the white man's "impingement," the Native Americans were Noble Savages, living as they did "in the center of ten thousand acres of matchless parklike forest where deer grazed like domestic cattle" (318). Many readers point to the white man's steamboat, his red slippers, his enameled snuffbox, his Parisian bed, and ornamental candlesticks as evidence of the corruption of the traditional culture. Robert Woods Sayre, for example, writing of the stories of "The Wilderness" section of *Collected Stories*, says, "These fictions embody, in symbolic/allegorical or legendary form, Faulkner's romantic perceptions of the nature of Indian versus white culture, and of the historical relationship between the two" (39). Others, however, point out that the "Noble Savage" reading itself depends on a radically limiting and demeaning stereotype, implying that the Native Americans are essentially weak and helpless against the white man's degrading influence; and still others even assume that Faulkner in "Red Leaves" juxtaposed the bravery and dignity of the body servant and the "progenitive vitality" of the black people with the decadent and compromised Native Americans who have enslaved them. Gene M. Moore suggests that "the slaves have preserved a far more natural and unified culture than the borrowed and degraded cultural trappings of their masters" ("'European Finery'" 265).

Moore also observes that "Faulkner's 'Indians' are often found to be historically inaccurate" ("Faulkner's Incorrect" 3; see also Dabney). That Faulkner was not especially knowledgeable about the Mississippi "Indians" (or, at the very least, not punctilious in representing them) has been long known, intermittently documented, and variously explained. Calvin Brown's mother, for example, a local Oxford historian, once asked him "where his Indians came from, and he frankly and simply replied, 'Mrs. Brown, I made them up'" (5). His early failure to distinguish clearly between the Chickasaw and Choctaw tribes drew queries from many readers, and fifteen years after "Red Leaves" was published, he answered Malcolm Cowley's question on the subject by saying "the Indians actually were Chickasaws, or they may so be from now on" (*SL* 197). Although Chickasaws were known to have enslaved other Native Americans after battle, Patricia Galloway informs us that "the Chickasaws were not notably involved in enslaving Indians for sale afterwards," and "it is not clear to what degree the Chickasaws had actually begun to think of Indian slaves traded to the British as commodities by the time the trade ceased" (22). Galloway also points out that "There is no verifiable record at all of Chickasaws' having killed black slaves to accompany them to the other world, and only a little evidence to suggest that they may on occasion have killed dogs or their much-prized Chickasaw ponies for this purpose" (21). Cannibalism "was *not,*" as Peter Mallios puts it, "socially practiced by the Choctaws and Chickasaws of antebellum Mississippi as a matter of history" (148) but was instead a part of the general stereotype of the "Indian," dating back to Montaigne's essay, which served as the source for basic stereotypes of the Native American. So Faulkner, in the end, sought neither historical accuracy nor simplistic politics in this story. Instead, as Charles A. Peek insists, "By transferring the institution of slavery to another culture, Faulkner gains a hearing for his exposure of slavery's effect on the slaveholder; by making that culture one in which ritual is given its due, he can explore universals regarding the passages of life" (315).

The precise date of the original composition of "Red Leaves" is uncertain. Some believe that the story may have been written as early as 1927, or perhaps in 1929. The story certainly existed by 24 July 1930, when Faulkner submitted it to the *Saturday Evening Post.* The *Post* accepted the story—only the second time it had chosen to publish Faulkner—and "Red Leaves" appeared in the October 25 issue. Faulkner revised the story for inclusion in *These 13* (1931). This revision was included in *Collected Stories* and it appears as the first story in "The Wilderness" section. Portions of this version were reworked for *Big Woods* (1955). Cowley included "Red Leaves" in the first section of *The Portable Faulkner* (1946). Although there have been many differences of opinion over what Annette Trefzer identifies as "historical accuracy, ethnographical authenticity, and political correctness" (69), "Red Leaves" remains one of Faulkner's most frequently anthologized stories, continuing to receive detailed critical attention, and almost universally regarded as one of his very finest.

313:1–2 **The two Indians crossed the plantation toward the slave quarters** Both the plantation system and slavery are white institutions adopted by the Indians, so this first sentence introduces all three cultures concerned in the story (see Skei, *Reading* 140).

313:2 **baked soft brick** clay soil and water mixed and shaped into bricks, then baked in the sun

313:10–11 **chinked and plastered chimneys** flues or chimneys that have had the cracks (chinks) filled in and plastered over

313:13 **the Man** hereditary term of honor for the male patriarch of a tribe (see 317:30–318:1)

313:19–20 **like carved heads on a ruined wall in Siam or Sumatra** In Indochina, which includes Thailand (Siam) and Sumatra Island, many Buddha images are carved in rock walls on cliffs, mountains, and other areas where large rocks are found.

313:22 **like sedge grass on burnt-over land** like dried grass

313:23 **an enameled snuffbox** According to Brown, "the snuff-box is a pocket-sized, round tin box in which snuff is sold, not an elaborate or permanent possession. [This one] is an exception, obviously being a European eighteenth-century one" (182).

314:4 **them who prefer sweating** the slaves

314:5 **They** the slaves

314:7–8 **They are worse than the white people** The Indians consistently attribute to the blacks the same stereotyped faults which the white man attributes to Indian and black alike; furthermore, because the Indians perceive the slaves to be more "beasts of burden" than men, they feel the slaves must be even worse than the white men they know. See Mallios on how the story examines the "triangulation" of the process of racial stereotyping (174–75).

314:15 **man was not made to sweat** evidence that the Indians in this, too, imitate the white man, by repudiating "sweat" or manual labor and leaving it to slaves, not "man"

314:17 **It has a bitter taste, too** Although Three Basket refers to eating the flesh of slaves, there seems to be no evidence of cannibalistic practices among the Choctaw, Chickasaw, or other related tribes. Cannibalism may be a myth regarding the Indian culture adapted by Faulkner, or his invention consistent with white ignorance of Indian customs (see Cushman, Mallios, Swanton).

314:26 **fetish-shaped objects** small objects believed to have magical or spiritual power

314:27 **patinaed doorsteps** with sheen, in this case from long use by many feet

314:33–34 **where at certain phases of the moon the Negroes would gather to begin their ceremonies** native African traditions and rituals, in this case performed according to certain celestial events. Many such traditions were brought by captive slaves from Africa and perpetuated (see Cole).

315:3–4 **the ceremonial records which consisted of sticks daubed with red clay in symbols** attempts by the slaves to preserve their cultural heritage. Sticks daubed with clay represent African tribal linguists' staffs. The inscribed clay at the end of the staff contains symbols or figures that represent proverbial sayings to remind the holder of the staff of tribal or personal morals and values.

315:8 **abashless** relentless

315:14–15 **That is black man's fear which you smell. It does not smell as ours does** see 314:7–8

315:21 **rank twilight** odorous fading daylight; a synesthetic image

315:24 **He whom we seek is gone?** a rhetorical question

315:31 **You know our errand** an indication that everyone, slave and Indian, knows the clan's customs

315:32 **thinking something** we are not their friends

315:34 **knowing something** we are not their friends; we mean to kill one of their own

316:5–8 **I see my horse and my dog. But I do not see my slave. What have you done with him that you will not permit me to lie quiet?** This passage, as many others in this story, suggests the slave, the horse, and the dog of the deceased chief were to be buried with him to ensure his safe passage to or comfort in a future life. In recorded Native American and European accounts, there are no such instances of burial; indeed, Choctaw and Chickasaw leaders were typically elected and given no special treatment or burial upon death (Swanton). In attributing these customs to the Yoknapatawpha Indians, Faulkner is not seeking a historically accurate rendering but instead calling attention to the horrors of slavery.

316:10–11 **A people without honor and without decorum** see 314:7–8

316:15 **But then, they are savages; they cannot be expected to regard usage** see 314:7–8

316:27–28 **He can wear the shoes with the red heels all the time now** Because his father is dead, Moketubbe is now the Man and can do as he pleases, and he pleases to wear the slippers.

317:6–7 **then Issetibbeha became dead, who was not old** a hint that Moketubbe killed his father

317:9–11 **"I don't think about it," Basket said. "Do you?" "No, the second said. "Good," Basket said. "You are wise"** Neither man wishes to acknowledge that Issetibbeha might have been murdered, which would be to question the legitimacy of Moketubbe's succession. Should he hear that they had articulated such suspicion, they too might die. Faulkner thus elliptically challenges the system of hereditary monarchy, another custom that this tribe may have imitated from the white culture. See 317:22–23.

317:13–14 **the deck house of a steamboat which had gone ashore** the large structure from the upper deck of a grounded steamboat

317:16 **cypress rollers** in this case, cypress trees cut down and smoothed to form primitive rollers on which an object, such as the steamboat, could be placed. By removing the rollers from behind and placing them in front of it as it moved forward, the slaves could move the steamboat over the uncompromising terrain.

317:21 **jalousied doors** finished with blinds or shutters

317:22–23 **merely a subchief, a Mingo, one of three children on the mother's side of the family** either a member of a separate northern tribe, the Mingo, who occasionally lived among the Choctaws; or a term used to refer to a lower-echelon leader of a local Choctaw community or clan; therefore, of lesser status. Also, the current tribe is patriarchal, which was not the rule in the Choctaw and Chickasaw nations (see Cushman, Reeves, Swanton).

317:24–25 **New Orleans was a European city** Founded by the French in 1718, New Orleans was one of the only ports, and certainly the largest, in the Gulf of Mexico at the turn of the nineteenth century. A "European city" until the Louisiana Purchase in 1803, the city boasted a great deal of trade, traffic, and European influence; hence, Ikkemotubbe's journey from his tribal village to New Orleans was culturally vast, if not geographically.

317:26–27 **the Chevalier Sœur Blonde de Vitry** literally, "Knight Blonde Sister from Vitry." A "chevalier" is a French nobleman of the lowest rank, though his claim to such a title may be completely spurious.

318:2 ***du homme*, and hence Doom** The Chevalier's French is bad, but Faulkner's wasn't. The French word for "man" is *l'homme*, and coupled with the preposition meaning "of" or "from" to denote origin, is *de l'homme. Du homme* ("Doo-um") is incorrect, which Malcolm Cowley pointed out to Faulkner when he was editing the Viking *Portable Faulkner*. Faulkner replied, "I know it's *de l'homme*. I made it incorrect mainly because I decided no one would care especially. That is, it seemed righter to me that Ikke., knowing little of French or English either, should have an easy transition to the apt name he gave himself in English, than that the French should be consistent. Maybe [the Frenchman who named him] deliberately warped his own tongue so Doom could discover his English name" (Cowley 43).

318:5 **Carondelet** Baron Francisco Luis Hector De Carondelet XV (1747–1807), the French-born Spanish governor of Spanish Louisiana from 1791 to 1797; a great planner and governor who forged many treaties with the native peoples of Mississippi and Louisiana and was thought of as an ally to many of them

318:6 **General Wilkinson** James Wilkinson (1757–1825), a colorful and possibly traitorous character whose career as a Brigadier General in the U.S. Army took him to the Louisiana Territory in 1791. He made secret treaties with the Spanish in exchange for large sums of money and plotted with Aaron Burr to invade Mexico and form his own country. He had a close relationship with Carondelet (see 318:5), who compensated him well for various "services" rendered. That the Chevalier knows both Carondelet and Wilkinson suggests that he understands both legitimate and *sub rosa* power structures.

318:15 **the St. Louis packet** a steamboat usually carrying mail or freight rather than passengers

318:20–22 **He never told her how he had accomplished it, save his uncle and cousin had died suddenly** a hint that Doom murdered them

318:29–30 **combination itinerant minister and slave trader who arrived on a mule** trader doubling as a minister and likely another official as needed; common on the frontier

319:1–2 **coursed them with dogs** used them as quarry for his hounds

319:7–8 **gathered in squatting conclave** met in tribal council

319:8 **the Negro question** that is, what to do with the newly acquired slaves; also a powerful echo of the issue of freed slaves in the post-Reconstruction American South

319:11 **We cannot eat them** see 314:17 and Mallios

319:24–25 **We must do as the white men do** Having adopted the ways of the white man, the tribe now lacks any other models for behavior, even that of common sense.

320:10 **quarters** slave quarters like those on the white man's plantations

320:12 **forty head** 40 slaves; another metaphor invoking beasts

320:18–19 **in return he introduced him into certain circles** perhaps the "equivocal haunts" of corrupt Parisian society that he frequented with Doom (318:7–8)

320:21–22 **Pompadour arranged her hair while Louis smirked** Madame de Pompadour was the mistress of King Louis XV of France from 1745 to 1750 and remained his close confidante thereafter. Politically astute and involved in the arts as well as in politics, she served as an important political advisor until her death in 1764 (see Lever). As Ikkemotubbe did before him, Issetibbeha chooses artifacts representing the wretched excess of corrupt models (Rhodes 73).

320:23 **a pair of slippers with red heels** The color red was incorporated into Choctaw dress—and red moccasins played a role in the ceremonial transition from puberty to manhood. As Patricia Galloway notes, "Oddly, Issetibbeha's coveted red-heeled Paris shoes in 'Red Leaves' could conceivably not be a complete fabrication: red shoes—red moccasins—were used in the ceremony of the making of a warrior among the Chickasaws and Choctaws, and their war chiefs often had the element 'red' as part of their names; among the Choctaws, they were even frequently called Red Shoes, and several famous chiefs by this name are well documented in readily available literature" (23).

320:27–28 **a pair of saddlebags filled with cedar shavings** well-cushioned and protected

320:30 **a broad, flat, Mongolian face** a hint that Moketubbe might be a congenital idiot, affected by what used to be called Mongolism, in which the child is born with a short, flattened skull, slanting eyes, and other features attributed to the ethnic groups of Asian Mongolia

320:33–34 **Moketubbe's mother was a comely girl whom Issetibbeha had seen one day working in her shift in a melon patch** a slave, in other words

321:16 **Issetibbeha's newest wife** In alluding to polygamy here (and see also 329:23–24), Faulkner again varies from received knowledge. The Five Civilized Tribes regarded women as near-equals and as such typically took only one wife (see Cushman, Swanton).

321:19 **I too like being alive, it seems** Issetibbeha recalls how his father, Ikkemotubbe, came to power and wonders whether Moketubbe might resort to murder to get the slippers. See 317:6–7, 317:9–11, and 318:20–22.

321:30 **it** wearing the slippers; Issetibbeha seems to sense and to fear Moketubbe's thinly veiled Oedipal desire to overcome and replace him.

321:32 **using snuff** ingesting tobacco powder; see 321:33–322:2

322:1–2 **how to put the powder into his lip and scour it against his teeth with a twig of gum or of alphea** To dip snuff as the Indians do, "One end of [a] stick is chewed until it is moist and soft; then it is dipped into a box or bottle of snuff, and the end is either chewed or rubbed about the teeth and gums" (Brown 96, 182). The gum twig here is from a black-gum, which grows in "river bottoms and swamp edges" and has *"bright red leaves in the fall"* (Brown 31–32; emphasis ours, to suggest that this may be a title passage). Alphea is probably a reference to althea, or Rose of Sharon, a blooming shrub (Brown 21).

322:6–7 **But Doom's uncle had no shoes with red heels** Issetibbeha fears that his son might be secretly plotting to kill him, as Doom (with less material motivation) might have his uncle.

322:8 **all that** Moketubbe's excessive bulk

322:9 **a splint chair hammocked with deer thongs** As Brown explains, a splint chair is one with the back and seat woven of wooden strips, so this one "is puzzling, since the thongs of deer-hide would have the same function as the wooden splints" (185). We agree with Brown that this seat has apparently worn out and been repaired.

322:11–12 **he and I are both frustrated by the same gross meat which he wears** Moketubbe because he can't wear the slippers; Issetibbeha because his own life is in danger because Moketubbe cannot wear them, either literally or legally, without the sanction offered by the title his father holds

322:15–16 **the doctor came in a skunk-skin vest and burned sticks** a tribal medicine man who used traditional remedies to try to heal Issetibbeha (see Swanton)

322:19 **baked dog** From ancient times, the North American Indians kept dogs for many reasons, including as a food source, and the white European explorers and settlers followed their example. The Lewis and Clark expedition, in fact, documented receiving such food from Indians on several occasions (see "History of the Native American Indian Dog").

322:25 **Louis Berry** Three Basket's companion

322:25 **He** the dead Issetibbeha

322:27 **They** the slaves

323:2 **in man's sight** in public, legitimately

323:4 **He will lead the hunt** He must lead the hunt

323:9–10 **There is even yet a price he must pay for the shoes** The red slippers come with certain responsibilities that Moketubbe would rather not face, the first of which is to lead the pursuit of his father's slave (323:4).

323:17–18 **"Yao. Man must die." "Yao. Let him; there is still the Man"** The King is dead; long live the King.

323:20 **texas** the structure on a riverboat that contains the pilot-house and officers' quarters

323:24 **dressing a fowl** plucking the feathers, removing the innards, and so forth to prepare it for cooking

323:25 **shelling corn** removing kernels from the cob

324:2–3 **He is fled also** like Doom's slave before him

324:11–12 **They went on and left him talking** The old man here exaggerates or misremembers the length of time needed to capture Doom's body servant, so the two hunters just ignore him.

324:15–16 **figures cabalistic and profound** with secret or hidden, yet important, meaning

324:18 **the fore part of the running gear of a barouche** the chassis of a four-wheeled carriage, "on which the body, seats, top, etc., are mounted" (Brown 165)

324:19 **C-springs** a spring, shaped like the letter C, used to support the body of a carriage

324:20–21 **a fox cub ran steadily and soundlessly up and down a willow cage** This suggests that the Indians have taken up fox hunting and raised cubs for the purpose, another decadent custom borrowed from the whites; as Brown notes, "Mississippi fox hunting is essentially a spectator sport" (85).

324:22 **gamecocks** roosters bred and trained for fighting

324:24–25 **a big room of chinked logs** see 313:10–11

324:25–26 **hinder part of the barouche** the rest of the carriage at 324:18

324:29 **game chickens** see 324:22

325:1 **newest wife** see 321:16

325:10–11 **while in the darkness beside her Issetibbeha quietly laughed and laughed** amused at her subterfuge in appearing to please him while observing her own preferences

325:20–21 **a stripling with a punkah-like fan made of fringed paper** a youth in the process of passing from boyhood to manhood, pulling the cord of an Asian Indian style of fan that hangs in a panel from the ceiling. As he pulls the cord, the panel moves back and forth to fan Moketubbe.

325:30 **like an effigy, like a Malay god** like a Buddha figure; see 313:19–20

325:33 **Not if I were you** a comeuppance for the boy; Basket has the authority to disturb Moketubbe, which the stripling servant does not.

326:1 **He** the body servant; see 326:25

326:10 **Why should he not wish it?** Basket and Berry cannot comprehend that the slave is a man like themselves. They reason, moreover, that, as Issetibbeha's body servant, he has lived a comparatively privileged life and must now pay the price for that "privilege." Hence, as Three Basket asks, "Why should he not wish to die, since he did not wish to sweat?" (326:15–16).

326:11–12 **"Because he must die some day is no reason," the stripling said. "That would not convince me either, old man"** see 323:17–18

326:15–16 **Why should he not wish to die, since he did not wish to sweat?** see 326:10

326:25 **The one who held the pot for him** presumably a chamber pot. In his degrading job, he also "ate of his food" in "the valuable service of being a food tester" (Rhodes 77).

326:28 **"This is not the first time," Basket said** the first of three reminders of Moketubbe's duty; see also 327:2, 14

326:33 **the journey** to the afterlife

327:25 **All that day** flashback to the day before the story begins

327:27 **a Guinea man** of the West African nation of Guinea, formerly French Guinea

327:29 **gums were a pale bluish red** perhaps one of Faulkner's bluegums; according to Brown, "a Negro whose gums are blue rather than pink. In folklore he is viewed with that mixture of reverence and fear which constitutes awe. He has many strange properties, such as a fatal bite, and he is a particularly adept and powerful conjuror" (33); see also 329:2–4.

327:30–328:1 **He had been taken at fourteen by a trader off Kamerun, before his teeth had been filed** kidnapped by a slave trader off the coast of the present-day West African nation of Cameroon before his adolescence had been formally marked by his tribe

328:12 **the headman** honorary title of leadership bestowed on a slave by his peers

328:13 **"Not dead," the body servant said. "Who not dead?"** an avoidance of the imminent death of the Man, and thus his own

328:18 **pickaninnies** condescending term for small black children; originating in West African slaves' use of the diminutive *pequeno* (Portuguese) or *pequeño* (Spanish), meaning "little"

328:19 **If he lives past sundown, he will live until daybreak** ambiguous: either "If Issetibbeha lives past sundown, he will live until daybreak" or "If the servant lives past sundown, he will live until daybreak" because the Indians will not pursue him at nighttime. The sense of 331:34–332:2 would seem to argue against the latter meaning.

328:23 **We know but one thing** the servant will be dead soon

328:26 **He knows. He knows it** he knows he will be dead soon

328:28 **Let the drums tell it** As Harriette Cole explains, "In ancient African cultures, . . . languages were formed and articulated through the drum, allowing messages to travel across vast distances with a sometimes simple, often complex, always specific beat—understood only by the appropriate listener. Using their cunning and creativity, our ancestors delivered information during the early days of Slavery through the beat of drums (until they were outlawed by English colonists), including escape routes and strategies, until slave owners got wise to them and destroyed this vehicle for getting the word out" (487).

328:31 **and the Negroes kept them hidden; why, none knew** None of the Indians know, that is; the slaves hid them to prevent their discovery and destruction by the Indians. See 328:27.

329:2–4 **about his neck a fiber bag containing a pig's rib to which black shreds of flesh still adhered, and two scaly barks on a wire** As Mallios explains, "The amulet that the Negro body servant wears as a kind of signature for his being also serves as the story's signature for this entire process [of the man's "return to nature"]. Partially comprised of the skull of the cottonmouth snake which he once devoured in the deep woods and would later recognize as a grandfatherly likeness of himself, and the other part consisting of a portion of a pair of French opera glasses—'one half of a mother-of-pearl lorgnon which Issetibbeha had brought back from Paris' (*CS* 330)—the amulet is both 'nature' and its disclosure as a purely fictive, Eurocentric strategy of conception" (169–170). Scaly barks are hickory nuts (Brown 170).

329:18–19 **the smudge against mosquitoes** thick smoke produced by a fire contained for the purpose in a smudge pot

329:23–24 **Issetibbeha lay dying among his wives** see 321:16 and 325:1

329:25 **He** the body servant

329:28 **he** Issetibbeha

329:31–33 **"Who not dead?" "You are dead." "Yao, I am dead"** continuation of exchange at 328:12–13

330:2–6 **But he could not do that, because man leaped past life, into where death was; he dashed into death and did not die,**

because when death took a man, it took him just this side of the end of living. It was when death overran him from behind, still in life Were he to reveal himself, he would be captured and executed. Death seems ready for him before he is ready for it; it "overruns" him while he is still alive. See also 335:6–10.

330:8–20 **They had lived ninety days in a three-foot-high 'tween-deck in tropic latitudes . . . and he spoke then only his native tongue** a description of the brutal deprivations on the ships of the Middle Passage, "the term coined to describe the transatlantic slave voyages between Africa and the Americas that claimed the lives of approximately 1.8 million [of the 12 million slaves transported] over a period of about 350 years." The quarters on board were "no more than six feet long and not high enough to allow an individual to sit upright," and slaves endured unbearable heat, disease, stench, and malnutrition (Robinson 1302). The body servant spent his Middle Passage in a crawl space ('tween-deck) intended for cargo.

330:22 **amulet** see 329:2–4

330:33–34 **it seemed strange to him that he still breathed air, still needed air** because the man thinks of himself as already dead

331:5 **their Sunday clothes** white clothes from the white custom of wearing one's best clothing on Sunday; see 331:9, 339:5–6

331:9 **in their stiff European finery** their Sunday clothes of 331:5

331:16 **entered the spring branch** got in the creek to avoid leaving footprints

331:21–22 **an actual boundary between two different worlds** the world of the living and the world of the dead

331:29–30 **He had run thirty miles then, up the creek bottom, before doubling back** Why he does so is open for debate; see 332:14–15

331:30 **a paw-paw thicket** group of North American tree of the custard-apple family with edible fruit and purple flowers

331:31–32, 34 **There were two of them. . . . They were middle-aged, paunchy** Three Basket and Louis Berry

332:4–6 **he thought how he ought to be hungry, since he had not eaten in thirty hours** see 331:1–2 for a contradiction

332:14–15 **since there was nowhere for him to go** Skei argues that the slave cannot escape "because he is in a sense already dead.

Even his own people consider him dead, and the demands of ritual as well as of myth and genre cannot let him get away" (*Reading* 145); see also 332:30. In addition, his escape may be made impossible by the terrain; see 336:13–14.

332:23 **When he stood among them the drums did not cease** so the drums are not calling to him but telling others the news of Issetibbeha's death

332:30 **The dead may not consort with the living** his fellow slaves, "the living," will not protect or hide him, "the dead"

333:1–2 **I caught a rabbit this afternoon, and ate while I lay hidden** either a polite lie, or a fact that Faulkner doesn't report

333:4 **cooked meat, wrapped in leaves** meat cooked in leaves for flavor, wrapped for preservation, or both

333:6–8 **"I have twelve hours," he said. "Maybe more, since the trail was followed by night"** his calculation of the time he has left to live, which might be longer since his pursuers might have lost the trail at night

333:16 **he saw the two Indians** Three Basket and Louis Berry (331:33–34)

334:12–13 **That man whose body has been dead for fifteen years, he will go also** Moketubbe

334:15 **a footlog across a slough** a fallen log used as a bridge (Brown 84)

334:23 **a line of ants** perhaps Faulkner's acknowledgment of the famous passage in Hemingway's *A Farewell to Arms,* beginning "Once in camp I put a log on top of the fire and it was full of ants" (327–28). While Frederick Henry could save the ants but doesn't, allowing them to die for no purpose, Faulkner's character makes use of them in service of his own life.

334:32 **cottonmouth moccasin** according to Brown, "a dangerous venomous snake" whose "name comes from the dead-white lining of the inside of the mouth and the snake's habit of opening the mouth wide when confronted by an enemy" (60–61)

335:3 **Olé, grandfather** He hails the snake with reverence, a respect born of his knowledge of the cottonmouth moccasin and its capabilities. According to Brown, *olé* is "presumably the Spanish exclamation, which could have gotten into Chickasaw" (142).

335:4–6 **He touched its head and watched it slash him again across his arm, and again, with thick, raking, awkward blows** an ironic and possibly suicidal action, given his desire at 335:6–10

335:14 **fawnskin** skin of a young deer; hence, quite soft

335:19 **the crime and its object, on the business of the slain** Moketubbe (the murderer) and the red slippers (his prize); Issitebbeha and his body servant

335:26–27 **his face at once peaceful for the instant and filled with inescapable foreknowledge** peaceful because the slippers are off his feet; foreknowledge of how he will feel when he puts them back on

336:13–14 **By sunset he will reach Mouth of Tippah. Then he will turn back** The Tippah River is a tributary of the Little Tallahatchie River in north-central Mississippi, which, in turn, empties into present-day Sardis Lake. If the geography of the story is that of Faulkner's country, at the headwaters of the Tippah, the man will be forced to turn back. His attempt to escape is doomed, either by his own defeatism or by the river bottom, since he cannot swim the river that forms one boundary and cannot evade the Indians whose settlement forms its opposite.

337:5 **pickets** guards

337:16 **Tomorrow is just another name for today** Here, as elsewhere in Faulkner, there is an expression of time as continuous duration.

337:24–25 **we could smell something else** probably gangrene

337:27–28 **the face** the face of death, or the face of the one who killed him

337:28 **it was not that** the desire to die

337:30–31 **But it was not that which we smelled then** the gangrenous infection of his arm

338:1–2 **tomorrow is today also . . . Tomorrow is today** see 337:16

338:3 **We feared for a while** that the slave would maim or kill himself and so be unfit to join his master

338:9 **The Man says that it is good** the progress of the hunt and the condition of the servant

339:1 **tainted bright morning** contaminated by the present events

339:5–6 **bright, stiff, harsh finery** their European Sunday clothes

339:16–17 **the six suspended and desperate days** the days during which he has avoided capture

339:26 **Will you eat first?** the ironically humane offer of a last meal (Matthews, "Shortened Stories" 20–21)

340:32–34 **where today no fire burned, no face showed in any door, no pickaninny in the dust** Knowing that the man has been captured, no slave has ventured outside today.

"A Justice"

Through the confrontation of several Mississippi Choctaws with a pair of their African American slaves who are husband and wife, "A Justice" meditates on several of the broader implications and consequences of chattel slavery and the economic systems that slavery supported. Readings of this apparently humorous story, with its complex double frame, have often emphasized its relations to other Faulkner fictions ranging from *The Sound and the Fury* (1929)—based particularly on the identification of the narrator as Quentin Compson, though neither his first nor his last name appears in this story—to the later development of Sam Fathers in *Go Down, Moses* (1942). In addition, "A Justice" contains links with "Red Leaves" and "A Courtship," both through named characters like Herman Basket and Ikkemotubbe ("Doom") and through narrative episodes, such as the movement of the steamboat through the wilderness to the Plantation. The crisis of the story concerns the fathering of a male child on an unnamed slave woman by the Choctaw called Crawfishford (or "Craw-ford"), her husband's natural objection, and Doom's ingenious solution. This episode is held in place by the inner of the double frames: Sam Fathers, who like Tristram Shandy has learned the stories of his own conception and birth from someone else, has related them in turn to the twelve-year-old boy. The boy could not understand what he heard at the time, but he has clearly assimilated the story's significance by the time he takes up the narration himself, thus providing the outer of the two narrative frames. "A Justice" also describes how Ikkemotubbe became "Doom," using murder and intimidation to gain the chief position of the tribe for himself. Finally, the story shows Doom's reasoned wisdom in protecting the female slave (and her husband) from future *droit de seigneur* encroachments by Crawford—or, for that matter, by anyone else. Unlike Solomon, he does not threaten to "divide the living child in two" (I Kings 3:25) but rather affirms the life of the child and establishes conditions for subsequent procreation within his parents' union.

As with other Faulkner stories featuring Native Americans, "A Justice" has prompted some readers to characterize the Native American culture as corrupt precisely to the extent that it imitates the worst vices and practices of the white man, while others have questioned the accuracy of Faulkner's representation of the "Indians." By contrast, James Ferguson calls "A Justice" "a strange, grotesque, dark, but wickedly funny tale of sexual rivalry and murder," and he describes the story as "technically virtually flawless" (57, 147). Most critics read the episode of Sam Fathers's begetting and naming as central to the story's themes. "The adult Quentin," says John T. Matthews, "seems to use the frame to introduce his sympathetic effort to establish the closer facts of Sam's heritage and history." "The narrator," he continues, "seems to structure his story as an initiation into knowledge about his culture. Not then, but now, Quentin implies, I see the unjustness of racial categories like white and Negro" ("Faulkner's Narrative" 83). Edmond Volpe concurs: "Beyond the rich humor of the story is the real anguish of the black slave whose wife Crawford takes," while the story of Doom's rise to power and his rule is "subsidiary" (111, 112). Volpe offers a particularly positive reading of Ikkemotubbe's order that Craw-ford build the fence that will restrain him: "By forcing his childhood friend to build a fence around the slave's house, Doom acknowledges the humanity of the blacks, recognizes the slave's love for his wife and his right to her" (112). Other readers see Ikkemotubbe's rise to power as the principal matter of the story. Lisa Paddock argues that "the centerpiece of 'A Justice' is a social comedy about how Doom settles a dispute between Crawford and a black slave over Sam Fathers's mother, but it is framed by a narrative device that counteracts its overt levity" (168). Max Putzel agrees that "the core of the matter" is the story of the genesis of Sam Fathers, but "while this account touches at the very root of Sam Fathers's existence, it tells less about himself or his parents than about the formal monster Ikkemotubbe" (234). "A Justice," according to Robert Woods Sayre, "tells the tale of the Fall itself, and the crucial, disastrous transformation" is the direct result of

"Doom's preoccupation with private property." "All in all," he concludes, "the 'doom' of the People seems to stem most fundamentally from the introduction of the related evils of private property and inequality, and Rousseau is perhaps hovering in the wings" ("Faulkner's Indians" 40, 41).

We do not know when Faulkner first wrote "A Justice," although we know he significantly revised it in several versions. Some have speculated that this story, as well as "That Evening Sun," was written before *The Sound and the Fury*, because both short stories feature an adult Quentin as narrator, which cannot be reconciled with his suicide, in the novel, at Harvard at the end of his freshman year. Others believe "A Justice" was written in 1930, when Faulkner had not yet considered in detail the desirability of reconciling his various texts with one another. The story certainly existed by 29 November 1930, when it was submitted to the *Saturday Evening Post* under the title of "Indians Built a Fence" (Skei, *Short Story* 37). Rejected at least five times, the story saw its first publication in *These 13* (1931), under its present title. Faulkner added "A Justice" to Robert K. Haas's list of suggestions for the *Collected Stories* volume (*Selected Letters* 274–75, 278), and it appears as the second story in "The Wilderness" section of the volume. The section describing the movement of the steamboat from the River to the Plantation was significantly reworked for inclusion in *Big Woods* (1955).

343:3 **dinner** the noon meal (Brown 70)

343:3–5 **I in the front with Roskus, and Grandfather and Caddy and Jason in the back. Grandfather and Roskus would talk** Unnamed in this story, the narrator is Quentin, who also narrates "That Evening Sun," which also features Caddy and Jason. Although their last name does not appear in either story, they are three of the Compson children from *The Sound and the Fury*; the youngest child in that novel, Benjy, does not appear in either story, nor do any of the other children or their mother appear in *Absalom, Absalom!* (1936), the other novel in which Quentin is a principal actor and narrator. Racial protocol dictates that Grandfather be in the back seat, obviously chauffeured, while Quentin's age exempts him from the same rule; he can sit up front until he's old enough to understand the full meaning of the story he will soon hear from Sam Fathers.

343:8–9 **on some of the hills Roskus and I could smell Grandfather's cigar** In other words, some of the hills were so steep that the horses had to walk, and the cigar smoke floated forward.

343:11 **not painted but kept whole and sound** Unpainted or untreated wood will deteriorate after prolonged exposure to the elements, so although the house doesn't have the luxury of paint, it is in excellent repair.

343:12 **the quarters** slave quarters

343:13 **smokehouses** according to Calvin Brown, "a tight building with small vents at the top, in which meat was cured by woodsmoke" (181)

343:17 **blue-gum** Brown explains that a bluegum is "a Negro whose gums are blue rather than pink. In folklore he is viewed with that mixture of reverence and fear which constitutes awe. He has many strange properties, such as a fatal bite, and he is a particularly adept and powerful conjuror" (33). In *The Sound and the Fury*, Versh tells Benjy that his family has changed his name because "*They making a bluegum out of you. Mammy say that in old time your granpaw changed nigger's name, and he turn preacher, and when they look at him, he bluegum too. Didn't use to be bluegum. . . . Possum hunters found him in the woods, et clean. And you know who et him. Them bluegum chillen did*" (69). These are Faulkner's only two references to bluegums, and we note that Faulkner set them both in stories narrated by the Compson children.

343:18–19 **But he wasn't a Negro. That's what I'm going to tell about** Our narrator is now ready to explain or "tell about" how he learned that Sam Fathers "wasn't a Negro," which signals us to ask also what Sam Fathers is—or, more accurately, who he is and how much of his identity is personally, as opposed to culturally, constructed. The end of the story focuses on the narrator's age and how it keeps him from understanding the importance of Sam's name, and it remains an open question as to whether he now does.

343:20 **the manager** the property manager; one who oversaw the upkeep of the farm

344:1 **breast-yokes** Brown explains: "a piece of iron-bound wood used to support the tongue of a wagon or carriage." In turn, the tongue is "the pole projecting from the front of a two-horse wagon, to which the animals are attached, one on each side"; the breast-yoke "is fastened to the end of the tongue by a swivel-eye at its center, and each end is suspended from the collar of one of the horses by a short strap or chain" (37, 200–201).

344:4 **creek clay with a reed stem** He would form the bowl of the pipe from clay taken from a local creek and fit it with a water-reed straw through which to draw the smoke.

344:5–10 **He talked like a nigger—that is, he said his words like niggers do, but he didn't say the same words—and his hair was nigger hair. But his skin wasn't quite the color of a light nigger and his nose and his mouth and chin were not nigger nose and mouth and chin. And his shape was not like the shape of a nigger when he gets old** Quentin is trying to categorize Sam Fathers racially on the basis of physical traits—his speech and features—associated "naturally" with African ancestry. The fact that Sam's features are "not" racially explicable troubles Quentin, and the rest of the paragraph finds Quentin describing some of the things Sam is. His repeated use of the racial epithet indicates his own defensiveness and uncertainty.

344:13–14 **when people, even white people, talked to him, or while he talked to me** Sam's attention is where he wants it to be at all times; he does not acknowledge racial protocols that constrict black people in his community, and Quentin seems to be setting himself as a child outside those protocols as well. This line thus raises the issue of whether the narrator Quentin ever considers his own place in the culture (see the last lines of the story).

344:22 **They call me Uncle Blue-Gum** see 343:17

344:27 **whisky trader** itinerant middle-man who traded whisky to the Indians, probably in exchange for furs, skins, baskets, or crops, who would in turn barter those items elsewhere along the frontier

344:27–28 **Plantation** the land occupied by Sam Fathers's People. The adoption of "plantation" instead of "land" or even "home" indicates the extent to which these Native Americans have internalized white institutions and ideas, particularly racial ones. See 344:33.

344:28 **the Man** the chief of this group of Choctaws. His name is fully explained at 345:23–348:13.

344:33 **Choctaw** Originating in southern Mississippi and Alabama, the Choctaw were one of the so-called Five Civilized Tribes, which included the Cherokee, Chickasaw, Creek, and Seminole. Before they confederated under this name in 1859, the Tribes were known for absorbing and adapting the cultural practices of white European settlers, including raising livestock, dressing in European style (see "Lo!"), and owning slaves. Intermarriage existed between the Tribes and whites, and sexual liaisons between the Tribes and blacks were doubtless as common as those between blacks and whites—with, as this story suggests, similarly complicated racial implications. Sam Fathers is not original to Faulkner, then; there are significant numbers of descendants of black freedmen of these tribes, popularly known as Black Indians. (See "Five Civilized Tribes.")

Some of this information can help to set the story chronologically. If Quentin was born in 1891, as *The Sound and the Fury* suggests, then the date of this story is 1903, when Quentin is twelve. The Five Civilized Tribes were removed from east of the Mississippi River and settled in what is now Oklahoma in 1830, with the Indian Removal Act. Sam's birth and naming thus had to have happened before 1830, when the Choctaws were still in Mississippi. Doom sold Sam's mother to Quentin's great-grandfather, so it would follow that Sam and Quentin's grandfather are in the same generation. The farm workers "said that he was almost a hundred years old" (343:15–16), and even allowing for their exaggeration and a disparity in the older generation's ages, Sam could easily be eighty years old, born in 1823.

345:1 **because I was a warrior too then** by virtue of his sex or his age, Sam does not say. When Faulkner revised Sam's history for use in *Go Down, Moses* and moved it into Isaac McCaslin's life and out of Quentin's, he made Doom Sam's father.

345:6 **This is how Herman Basket told it** Sam Fathers takes over the first-person narration of the story and holds it through 358:2. He speaks not from firsthand knowledge (since this is the story of his own conception and birth) but from Herman Basket's, who directly observed the events. Very likely it is a story that Sam himself did not fully understand when he first heard it, until, like Quentin, he got old enough to understand exactly what and why the adults were doing and for what stakes. Faulkner uses this secondhand method of first-person narration again in *The Town.*

345:11–12 **Sometimes they would run the black men with dogs, like you would a fox or a cat or a coon** Fox hunting in Mississippi, as Calvin Brown explains it, "is essentially a spectator sport. It is done at night, and the participants my ride horses . . . but usually they simply build a fire on a commanding hilltop and stay by it with a jug of whiskey" and listen to the dogs pursue the prey (85). Wildcats and raccoons might be hunted a bit more enthusiastically, but Faulkner's point is that the Indians are casually and unquestioningly treating the slaves like beasts.

345:17 **New Orleans salt** poison, clearly, that looks like salt to the Indians and came from New Orleans; probably arsenic

345:25 **a coat with gold all over it** ornately embroidered with gold thread

346:1–3 **he was not born to be the man, because Doom's mother's brother was the Man, and the Man had a son of his own, as well as a brother** In this patrilinear arrangement, Ikkemotubbe, the son of the Man's sister, is third in the line of succession. The Choctaws, like most tribes in the Southeast, were matrilinear; according to historian R. David Edmunds, they were also matrilocal: "the mother and her adult daughters formed the household unit, living together—their husbands moved in after they got married," which is "common among tribes who rely upon their women for agricultural production" because "it maximizes the cooperation among the women since all are related" (e-mail response to an inquiry, 10 June 2004). What and how much Faulkner knew, or deliberately or not got wrong, about Native American culture and practices has been discussed by critics as diverse as Dabney, Hönnighausen, Kinney, and Doyle.

346:6–7 **your eye is a bad eye, like the eye of a bad horse** Your evil spirit shows in your eyes, like an untrainable and unmanageable horse's does. Even when Ikkemotubbe was a child, the Man literally "saw Doom."

346:10–12 **He used to like to play mumble-peg and to pitch horseshoes both, but now he just liked mumble-peg** mumblety-peg, as Brown explains: "a boy's game in which a knife must be thrown and stuck into the ground from each of a standard sequence of positions. The loser has to dig a wooden peg out of the ground with his teeth" (135). Horseshoes is a game in which players throw horseshoes at a stake in the ground and try to ring it with them. Given the rampant phallic imagery in the story and the cock contest later (354:17–356:31), we think Faulkner is using the Man's game preference to indicate his loosening hold on his title.

346:18 **Big River** the Mississippi River

346:18–19 **the white man's fight at New Orleans** the Battle of New Orleans, fought in early January of 1815; General Andrew Jackson's brilliant defense of the city under attack by the British in the last days of the War of 1812. Doom seems to have left the Plantation near the onset of the war, which would account for the Man's repeated inquiries.

346:21 **he had been gone seven years** If Doom left for New Orleans in 1812 or 1813 (see 346:18–1), then he returned to the Plantation around 1819 or 1820, which would accord with the calculations of Sam's age and the time of the story at 344:33.

346:22 **a written stick** a message to meet

346:24 **our river** probably the Tallahatchie of Faulkner's map of his county, at the northern boundary of Yoknapatawpha County; in any case, a smaller tributary to the Mississippi

346:26–27 **high water, about three years after Doom went away** a flood; major floods occurred along the Mississippi in 1813, 1815, and 1816 (see Trotter). Our math suggests that Sam refers to the 1815 flood.

346:31 **People** how this group of Choctaws thinks of and names itself; non-Choctaws, then, are at least not Our People and at worst not human

346:33–34 **the white man who told the steamboat where to swim** the captain

347:18–19 **a pine knot** a torch made of pine wood

347:20 **bullet of bread** a portion with poison added and kneaded and reshaped to form a small pill

348:9–10 **In French talking, Doo-um; in our talking, Doom** Doom's French is bad, but Faulkner's wasn't. The French word for "man" is *l'homme,* and coupled with the preposition meaning "of" or "from" to denote origin, is *de l'homme. Du homme* ("Doo-um") is incorrect, which Malcolm Cowley pointed out to Faulkner when he was editing the Viking *Portable Faulkner.* Faulkner replied, "I know it's *de l'homme.*

I made it incorrect mainly because I decided no one would care especially. That is, it seemed righter to me that Ikke., knowing little of French or English either, should have an easy transition to the apt name he gave himself in English, than that the French should be consistent. Maybe [the Frenchman who named him] deliberately warped his own tongue so Doom could discover his English name" (Cowley 43). We note that in the Compson Appendix (to which Cowley referred) Ikkemotubbe was a Chickasaw.

348:13 **the Man** see 348:9–10

348:30 **My ghost is still walking** an expression that seems to mean either that Herman Basket's loyalty has not yet been given either to the Man or to Doom or that Herman Basket is still alive

349:13–14 **burned a stick and covered his head with the blanket** perhaps incense to purify the home or make an offering to whatever god might protect him, and an obvious withdrawal from competition to be the Man

349:17–18 **before the doctor could get there and burn sticks** in other words, very suddenly; the doctor didn't have a chance to perform healing ceremonies

349:18 **the Willow-Bearer** in this context, the messenger in charge of summoning the new ruler; more generally, probably a bearer of important messages. Native Americans made much use of willow wood; the trees grow quickly near water and have strong yet flexible branches, ideal for use in arrow shafts and baskets, and the bark is medicinal in the same sense that aspirin is (see "Willow Branches and Other Twigs and Roots").

349:31 **pappy's ghost would not be easy** his mind was troubled

350:1–3 **before the Man and his son had entered the earth, before the eating and the horse-racing were over** before the burials and the celebration of life associated with a funeral or the succession of a new Man

350:20 **House** residence of the Man

351:3 **I wish you could advise that to my ghost** I wish that could ease my troubled thoughts

351:13–14 **though they had guns, Herman Basket said they did not look like men who would own a boat** They are at least squatters and probably looters of the abandoned steamboat.

351:20 **Will you give ten black people** Even though the People have "more black people in the Plantation than they could find use for" (345:10–11), Doom can use them here as currency to buy the steamboat because they are valuable to the white men.

351:30–31 **pappy said to go aside and talk** Craw-ford cannot stand to see the slave woman leave; he hatches the plan in the following passage.

351:31–352:1 **Pappy talked, but Herman Basket said that he did not think it was right to kill white men, but pappy said how they could fill the white men with rocks and sink them in the river and nobody would find them** Perhaps because of the People's long association with white folks and their adoption of so many white ways, including now slaveholding, Herman Basket draws a line at killing white people. With the suggestion that the bodies can be concealed, however, Craw-ford's plan prevails, and he keeps the black woman with the People.

352:7–8 **"This woman is my wife," one of the black men said. "I want her to stay with me"** the first assertion in the story of the black man's right to stake his claim to family and status as a man. Such moments are telling in all of Faulkner's work (see Towner, "How Can").

352:12–13 **There are two of you, and nine of us** another indication (with 352:7–8) of the slave viewing himself as an agent rather than as property, adding the suggestion that the slaves cooperate with their enslavement exclusively because they are outnumbered

353:2 **Hot Spring** a wellspring of hot water, often containing high amounts of salts and minerals, in which one could bathe as a curative measure. Craw-ford is making an excuse to stay with the women and the slave wife.

354:2 **river bottom** "the floodplain . . . often heavily timbered and overgrown" (Brown 36)

354:3–4 **they had to cut down the trees to make a path for it** see 354:2

354:5 **the steamboat could walk faster on the logs** The Indians place the cut and trimmed timber in front of the boat and perpendicular to its intended path and then haul the steamboat forward, so the logs act like makeshift wheels, turning under the boat and moving it forward.

354:8–9 **the front porch of the steamboat** maybe the foredeck, but more likely (given Doom's love of the trappings of office) the pilothouse

354:11 **flying beasts** insects: most probably and annoyingly, mosquitoes

354:18–19 **adjust it by a cock-fight, pappy's cock against the black man's** the beginning of an extended episode of double-entendre in which the assertion of Craw-ford's manhood against that of the black man, for the possession of the black wife, is controlled and monitored by Doom, the Man. The story ends at 356:30–31, with the black man jumping on Craw-ford's "dead cock until it did not look like a cock at all."

355:3 **pit** enclosed excavation in which the animals fight to the death

356:21–22 **the black man's eyes looked red in the dark pit, like the eyes of a fox** another instance of Herman Basket comparing the black people to animals

357:3 **an eating** a feast

357:15 **a new man** a newborn baby boy

357:22–23 **Do I get justice?** the question answered by the story's title

357:24 **yellow man** from "high yellow," to describe a mulatto of African parentage; the product of Craw-ford's liaison with the slave's wife

357:25–26 **I don't see that justice can darken him any** what's done is done

357:28 **copper snake** copperhead, a poisonous snake

357:29 **pappy would not come forward** because he is afraid to face the slave woman's husband

357:32 **melon patch** figuratively, his wife's womb

357:33 **wild bucks** young men

358:8–9 **at that moment, as though he had felt my gaze, Grandfather turned and called my name** Faulkner's deliberate obscuring of the narrator's name; more important, the narrator's interest in Sam's story has been so piqued that he ignores his grandfather's summons to hear the answer to "What did your pappy do then?" (358:10).

359:11–12 **the dogs found him and pappy about noon the next day** a reiteration of events introduced at 358:11–21. As they did during childhood when Ikkemotubbe bossed them around, Herman Basket and Craw-ford ran away rather than build the fence, but Doom found them by setting the dogs after them.

359:23 **palisade fence** a fence made of stakes set in the ground, in this case with horizontal railings, with the upper ends sharpened to points as a deterrent to one who might try to climb (or jump) over it

359:30 **What do you think about this for color** The second child, unlike Sam, is the dark-skinned product of the slave man and his wife. The line shows the slave's power to taunt Craw-ford on the subject of his manhood. While Craw-ford and Herman have worked on the fence "all that winter and all the next summer" (359:19–20), the husband has been inside with his wife. As we note in the Introduction, the passage has widely been recognized as Faulkner's playful take on the judgment of King Solomon in the case of two women claiming to be a child's mother (I Kings 3:16–28).

359:32–34 **I was just twelve then, and to me the story did not seem to have got anywhere, to have had point or end** see 360:22–25

360:11 **chip** small part of something larger, like a wood chip from a log, or perhaps in this context a comparison to a dried animal dropping

360:22 **preservative bath in a museum** solution (such as formaldehyde) to prevent decomposition of organic material in sealed jars

360:22–25 **That was it. I was just twelve then, and I would have to wait until I had passed on and through and beyond the suspension of twilight. Then I knew that I would know** Quentin senses that the full significance of Sam's story lies in the adult's and not the child's world, and in order to understand it he needs only to grow up, as Sam has. (The young Lucius Priest has a similar revelation in *The Reivers.*) The "point or end" (359:34) is that Sam had no "justice" as a child, neither from Doom nor from either of his fathers, one of whom wouldn't acknowledge him and the other of whom bragged on the color of Sam's younger brother after demanding "justice" of Doom for Sam's "yellow" color. Moreover, since we discover at 344:33–34 that Doom had sold Sam's mother, with no mention of either her husband or Craw-ford, we are left to wonder how much of Sam's identity has been forged by absences—a question reinforced by the absence in the present time of his whole last name, "Had-Two-Fathers," and the shortening of his pappy's name from "Crawfish-ford" to "Craw-ford."

"A Courtship"

"A Courtship" seems to be, on the most obvious level, a comic prose mock-epic in which two men—the Indian, Ikkemotubbe, and the white man, David Hogganbeck—engage in a spirited rivalry to determine which of them shall marry a lovely Indian maiden, known only as "Herman Basket's sister." In the course of this rivalry, the two men grow in respect, admiration, and affection for each other, but, at the moment Ikkemotubbe seems to have triumphed, Herman Basket's sister has already married another man, Log-in-the-Creek, whom both of the rivals had ignored or disdained. Ikkemotubbe and David Hogganbeck commiserate with each other and lament the failure of women to live according to the masculine code that has guided their behavior. Ikkemotubbe is so devastated by his failure in courtship that he leaves the Plantation for several years and returns utterly changed, a formidable and murderous man whose goals now are exclusively political rather than domestic. In spite of the dark future portended for Ikkemotubbe, the story of the failed courtship remains a comic tale, proving that "male ignorance about the female is not limited to any one culture or time" (Volpe 270). Many readers discount the "universal" themes of the story, however, preferring to read it as part of Faulkner's continuing meditation on the ways that Native American culture was corrupted by the capitalist economy. Certainly, steamboats and slaves and fancy clothing are prominent in the story, and "A Courtship" is not a simple *joie d'esprit.*

"A Courtship" is narrated somewhat elliptically: an unnamed "present" voice recounts events that were, in turn, recounted to him by his unnamed father. Both father and son extol the masculine values of Ikkemotubbe and, to a lesser extent, of David Hogganbeck: "there were men in those days" (*CS* 373). Taken at face value, the judgment of father and son reinforces the notion that the story champions the masculine virtues of the two rivals and disparages the apparently unfathomable choice of Log-in-the-Creek by Herman Basket's sister. The story, thus, in many readings, celebrates male bonding and, perhaps, homoeroticism over romantic heterosexual courtship: "Ostensibly about two rivals for the affections of a beautiful girl, 'A Courtship' is essentially the story of the intense manly love that develops between Ikkemotubbe and David Hogganbeck, who seek to impress one another in a symmetrical rivalry that culminates in their mutual rescue from the (Freudian) Cave" (Moore 57). In this regard, "A Courtship" seems to take place before "the Fall," which is often understood as the corruption of Native American culture by the whites, and Ikkemotubbe's behavior after he loses Herman Basket's sister certainly supports such a reading. Many contemporary readers also contend that Faulkner shows throughout his fiction that the Native American culture is brought down precisely as its people adopt or imitate the vices and values of the whites. While this works well for "Red Leaves," it accounts less satisfactorily for "A Courtship." The most immediate point of this story, rather, is that, because Ikkemotubbe and David Hogganbeck have become so caught up in their masculine friendship and rivalry, they have lost sight entirely of Herman Basket's sister, their ostensible quarry. Their equestrian, gustatory, and Olympian contests preoccupy them to the point that, for Ikkemotubbe, at least, she has become "that damned sister of Herman Basket's" (*CS* 376), a rejected pretext for their competition. In entering the Cave first, firing the pistol, and helping David Hogganbeck to escape, Ikkemotubbe has achieved superiority in the competition that he had proposed to "win" Herman Basket's sister. He has failed, however, to secure the agreement of Herman Basket's sister and aunt. Meanwhile, Log-in-the-Creek, who is beneath not only the contempt but even the attention of the rivals, chooses not to enter their manly competition. Log-in-the-Creek stays close to the girl (and her aunt) and plays his harmonica. His eventual, unexpected, and—to Ikkemotubbe, Hogganbeck, the narrator, and the narrator's father, at least—*incomprehensible* triumph is surely the triumph of the artist over the warrior.

The natural inclination of many readers is to accept the values of the narrator, and of the defeated rivals themselves, but this foregrounded "moral" requires qualification. "The moral of this courtship fable," says Edmond L. Volpe, "is the basic unity of all peoples throughout time. Though David and Ikkemotubbe are of different races and from different cultures, they instinctively trace patterns of loving, wooing, and grieving that transcend time and social and racial differences" (270). Others decline to accept the "one wisdom for all men" conclusion. They would have it rather that the story demonstrates, once again, the vulnerability of the Indian culture to corruption by the whites, one that even explains Ikkemotubbe's desire for Herman Basket's sister as essentially economic rather than romantic or erotic. For still others, "A Courtship," is essentially a humorous story, showing the extraordinary masculine excesses of Ikkemotubbe and Hogganbeck corrected by the confederation of a young man, a young woman, her guardian, and music. The story achieves a comic resolution, in the traditionally renewing and regenerating custom of marriage, a custom that transcends cultural differences.

The setting in time of the story is not specified, though various scholars have attempted to establish a date from historical inferences or other Faulkner texts. As elsewhere, however, Faulkner is more concerned with telling his tale than with achieving a minute fidelity to facts than can be confirmed by detailed reference to history or archaeology, and it is often simply impossible to import and reconcile the "facts" from one Faulkner narrative to another. Nevertheless, the first steamboats traversed the Mississippi in 1812, getting no farther than Natchez. Steamboats were running regularly from New Orleans to St. Louis by 1820, and Gene M. Moore locates Ikkemotubbe's Plantation "in the Big Bottom of the Tallahatchie, a sub-tributary of the Mississippi which merges with the Yoknapatawpha River and eventually flows into the Yazoo" ("Faulkner's Indians" 59). Likewise, the first treaty signed with the Choctaw was the Choctaw Treaty of 1820, though the Treaty of Fort Jackson in 1814 might well be the vague reference in the opening lines (361:5–7). Although the story clearly emerges from the matrix that had earlier produced "Red Leaves," "A Justice," and "Lo!," inconsistencies between "A Courtship" and these other texts suggest that Faulkner was more concerned here with spinning a yarn than with extending a tightly developed saga of Native American life. It is one of many cases in his career that he found comic material in characters and a situation that had also prompted tragic meditation.

Faulkner submitted a typescript of "A Courtship" to his agent Harold Ober on 2 June 1942. It remained unpublished until 1948 when it appeared in the October issue of the prestigious *Sewanee Review*, which paid Faulkner a mere $200 for the privilege. Writing to his Random House editor, Robert Haas, about the projected contents of *Collected Stories* in the fall of 1948, Faulkner agreed that "A Courtship" should be included in the volume. "Yes," he wrote, "I like this one" (*Selected Letters* 275). The following year, "A Courtship" was awarded the O. Henry short story prize and was reprinted in the O. Henry *Prize Stories of 1949*. Faulkner placed it as the third of the four stories in "The Wilderness" section of *Collected Stories*. Soon after "A Courtship" was published, Faulkner personally realized $40,000 from the sale of *Intruder in the Dust* to MGM, a financial juxtaposition that may explain why he ceased writing short stories for magazine sales. It was thus the last-published of the 42 stories gathered in *Collected Stories* and also among the last to be written. If it does mark the virtual end of Faulkner's short story writing career, he managed to quit on a good one.

361:2 **the Man** hereditary term of honor for the male patriarch of the clan

361:3–4 **the white man who told the steamboat where to walk** the pilot

361:4 **Herman Basket's sister** Never named in her own right, she and the other women of the story are perceived by the men here in terms of their relationships to men.

361:5 **The People** the tribe, "Chickasaw" according to 365:1–2. As Patricia Galloway argues, Faulkner's Indians "are an amalgam, in space and time, of features of the Chickasaws, Choctaws, and Natchez of Mississippi" (28). In that sense, "he did pretty much make them up, in the sense that he assimilated the practices of several tribes into his alleged 'Chickasaws' and was very far from presenting ethnographic accuracy" (10). According to H. B. Cushman, "the ancient traditional history of the Choctaws and Chickasaws claims for them a Mexican origin, and a migration from that country at some remote period in the past, under the leadership of two brothers, respectively named Chahtah and Chikasah both noted and influential chiefs to their possessions east of the Mississippi" (18). And Faulkner himself, writing to Malcolm Cowley, said that "the line dividing the Chickasaw and Choctaw nations passed near my home; I merely moved a tribe slightly at need, since they were slightly different people in behavior" (*SL* 197).

361:5–8 **Issetibbeha and General Jackson met and burned sticks and signed a paper, and now a line ran through the woods, although you could not see it** likely a reference to the Treaty of Fort Jackson in 1814 or the Choctaw Treaty of 1820. **General Jackson** = General Andrew Jackson, one of the commissioners to the Chickasaws ca. 1818 (Moore, "Faulkner's Indians" 59n15) and seventh President of the United States, 1829–1837. "This reference to boundaries is historically important," Bruce Johnson explains, "because it alludes to the treaties signed between the United States government and the Chickasaw and Choctaw tribes—treaties that were routinely broken by the U.S."; "Moreover, this 'line' symbolizes the tension of a relationship between these cultures based on land ownership [see 361:11–14]: 'So now when something happened on one side of the line, it was a bad fortune for some and a good fortune for others, depending on what the white man happened to possess (361[:11–14]'" (109).

361:22 **because of a delusion that he had been eaten** There is no anthropological or anecdotal evidence whatsoever of cannibalism ever taking place within any of the southern tribes, including the Choctaw. Such a claim seems to be discounted in this instance (Mallios 151).

361:22–362:1 **As if any man, no matter how hungry, would risk eating the flesh of a coward or thief in this country where even in winter there is always something to be found to eat** Drawing on the folk belief that one ingests the spirit or character of the food one eats, the narrator satirizes what he considers the prototypical white man—cowardly and/or dishonest—while praising the abundance of the land upon which the Indians live and thrive.

362:5 **Great Spirit** principal deity of the People

362:17 **chew his bitter thumbs too, aihee** an expression meant to emphasize the heartbreak that men share when they cannot attain the woman of their dreams; see 380:4

362:18–19 **Because she walked in beauty. Or she sat in it, that is, because she did not walk at all unless she had to** Faulkner uses the title and opening lines of Lord Byron's "She Walks in Beauty" (*Hebrew Melodies* [1815]) to comic effect:

She walks in beauty, like the night
Of cloudless climes and starry skies;
And all that's best of dark and bright
Meet in her aspect and her eyes:
Thus mellow'd to that tender light
Which heaven to gaudy day denies.

362:33–34 **suns passed and then moons and then three high waters came and went** Days passed, and months, and finally three years.

363:3–4 **the Chevalier Sœur-Blonde de Vitry** "Knight Blonde Sister from Vitry." A "chevalier" is a French nobleman of the lowest rank.

363:3 **named Doom** from a corruption of the French for "the man": *du homme* elided instead of the correct *de l'homme*, which Malcolm Cowley pointed out to Faulkner when he was editing the Viking *Portable Faulkner*. Faulkner replied, "I know it's *de l'homme*. I made it incorrect mainly because I decided no one would care especially. That is, it seemed righter to me that Ikke., knowing little of French or English either, should have an easy transition to the apt name he gave himself in English, than that the French should be consistent. Maybe [the Frenchman who named him] deliberately warped his own tongue so Doom could discover his English name" (Cowley 43).

363:6 **the little gold box of strong salt** poison

363:7 **containing the four other puppies which were still alive** see 363:6

363:8 **Moketubbe's little son was dead** presumably poisoned by Ikkemotubbe

363:18–20 **After Ikkemotubbe looked at her, my father and Owl-by-Night and Sylvester's John and the other young men looked away** **my father** = the unnamed narrator's father. When Ikkemotubbe notices Herman Basket's sister, the other young men resign their interest in her.

363:23 **bear's grease** "grease rendered from the fat of bears—a standard multipurpose grease in the early days" (Brown 26); used to decrease wind resistance, the honey added to make it smell sweeter

363:28–30 **the silver wine pitcher which her aunt had inherited from her second cousin by marriage's great-aunt who was old David Colbert's wife** The Colbert family were actual historical figures, white settlers in northern Mississippi whose men sometimes married into prominent Chickasaw Indian families (Galloway 14). According to Moore, "the Colberts were a large family, but apparently none were named 'David'" ("Faulkner's Indians" 61n21). The "David" Colbert that Faulkner created for "A Courtship" has become the leader of one of the tribe's sections (see 365:1–2), much as the men of the historical Colbert family were said to have done. That Herman Basket's aunt inherited this pitcher from Colbert's wife implies—to Herman Basket's aunt, at least—that the Basket family has a privileged status among the tribe. The fact that this "inheritance" passes from female to female is also noteworthy in positing a matrilineal character to the People (see also 364:34–365:1).

364:5 **gaited mare** horse with a showy step

364:11 **blew into the harmonica** the first allusion to a skill unique to Log-in-the-Creek

364:16–17 **blowing into the harmonica** suggests that Log-in-the-Creek, much like Herman Basket's sister, remains unfazed and unimpressed by the antics of the men who are trying so hard to woo the young woman

364:18–19 **invited Log-in-the-Creek into the woods until they became tired of carrying him** kidnapped him to get him out of the way

364:28–29 **So it seems I want this girl even worse than I believed** It was customary in Choctaw courtship for the suitor to give presents to the parents of the intended bride. In this case, Herman Basket's aunt is the parental figure, and Ikkemotubbe's gift is extraordinarily lavish (Cushman 310).

365:2–3 **she looked upon Issetibbeha's whole family and line as mushrooms** She thought of them as upstarts, newly and quickly sprung up from rot.

365:9–12 **there was no horse in the Plantation or America either between Natchez and Nashville whose tail Ikkemotubbe's new pony ever looked at** an exaggeration meant to convey the unmatchable speed of Ikkemotubbe's pony. "The phrase 'between Natchez and Nashville,'" writes Calvin S. Brown, includes the two terminals of the Natchez trace, "an early road (at first merely a trail) leading from Nashville, Tenn., to Natchez, Miss. Since much of it passed through Chickasaw lands for a generation before these lands were ceded to the whites, arrangements were made with this tribe (in 1801) providing for friendly treatment of travelers and guaranteeing to the Indians a monopoly of stopping-places along the route" (Brown 137).

365:18 **gamecocks** roosters bred and trained for fighting

365:31–34 **we would begin to watch the mark which David Hogganbeck had put on the landing to show us when the water would be tall enough for the steamboat to walk in** Spring rains would raise the river's water level high enough for the steamboat to navigate this far upriver.

366:1–2 **the steamboat would cry** its whistle would blow

366:11–12 **the upstairs and the smokestack moving among the trees** From the People's vantage point, the upper deck and the chimney of the steamboat are visible, while the bulk of the steamboat is hidden by the trees.

366:13 **walking fast in the water too when it was not crying** When the steamboat is running under full power, it moves rapidly, but when its whistle is sounded, steam that would otherwise drive the paddlewheel is released, so the boat slows down ("Firing the Steam Yacht Lady Hopetoun").

366:112–13 **its feet walking fast in the water too** the slats of its paddle wheel turning

367:8–14 **And then it did not go away. The river began to grow little, yet still David Hogganbeck played his fiddle on Herman Basket's gallery while Herman Basket's sister stirred something for cooking into the silver wine pitcher and Ikkemotubbe sat against a post in his fine clothes and his beaver hat and Log-in-the-Creek lay on his back on the floor with the harmonica cupped in both hands to his mouth** perhaps Faulkner's play with the cliché that "Nero fiddled while Rome burned," a description of how Hogganbeck neglected his opportunity to leave during the high water

367:32–34 **not to make it walk but to make its voice cry while Captain Studenmare leaned out of the upstairs with the end of the crying-rope tied to the door-handle** repeatedly sounding the steamboat whistle to get David Hogganbeck on board so they can leave

368:18 **dead uncle's shotgun** According to Moore, in this story, "guns serve only symbolic (and blatantly Freudian) purposes: Herman Basket's aunt appears with 'Herman Basket's dead uncle's gun' (379) in an effort to intimidate her niece's suitors" ("Faulkner's Indians" 55).

369:24–25 **at my father's house** that is, the house of the nameless narrator's father

369:30–31 **Ikkemotubbe and David Hogganbeck were both asleep in David Hogganbeck's bed in the steamboat** The two men stay together ostensibly to ensure that neither revisits Herman Basket's sister in secret. More significant is the bond that develops between them in the process, making the title of the story not so much "a courtship" of Herman Basket's sister but of one another (see Mallios 163).

370:1 **buckboard** "a light four-wheeled carriage with the seat mounted on a long, flexible board connecting the front and rear wheels, instead of on a sprung body" (Brown 39)

370:12–14 **they still had not found where Herman Basket's aunt had hidden the pony** Ikkemotubbe gave the pony to Herman Basket's aunt to secure her favor in his pursuit of her niece. The aunt, who has not asked for this gift and does not accept its implications, hides the pony to prevent Ikkemotubbe from retrieving it. See 378:14.

371:7–9 **If I am to truly win, it will be necessary for you to be there to see it** Ikkemotubbe would take no satisfaction in killing Hogganbeck. To be complete, his victory must be observed by his rival.

371:10–12 **lying wrapped in a blanket on a platform in the woods, waiting to enter the earth** According to Cushman, Choctaw burial customs consisted of draping the corpse with a blanket and placing it on a scaffold made from timber, where wild dogs and wolves could not reach it, prior to the mourning ceremony in the wooded area chosen by the mourners. Cushman cites manuscripts handwritten by Choctaw descendants themselves, one of which reads, in part, "When anyone died a scaffold was made in the yard near the house, put high enough to be safe from the dogs. On the top of this the body was laid on its side; and then a blanket or bear skin was thrown over it; and there it remained until it perished. Then the bone-pickers came and picked the flesh off and put the bones in a box" (330). Galloway notes that the "platforms" (or "scaffolds") upon which the bodies were placed were "the bed platforms they had occupied in life within their houses" (21). "The ancient Chickasaws, unlike the Choctaws," writes Cushman, buried their dead soon after life became extinct, placing in the grave with the corpse, if a man, his clothes, war and hunting implements, pipe and tobacco, and a few provisions" (404). As established at 361:5, Faulkner's Indians are an amalgamation of the Choctaws, the Chickasaws, and possibly the Natchez, which ostensibly accounts for his use of the burial customs of the Choctaws, rather than those of the Chickasaws, in this story.

371:13–15 **If that could satisfy me, we would not be squatting here discussing what to do. I think you see that** If I could win by killing you, I would have already done so

371:22–23 **I had been saving them, like a man with two hole-cards** Ikkemotubbe had been holding the pony and the coat in reserve, like two cards dealt face down (and so to the holder's advantage) in a poker game; they had been what he considered his two greatest strengths in winning over Herman Basket's sister.

371:29–30 **So there is just one other thing," he said. "And I am already beaten at that too before we start"** the race to the cave, as described subsequently, which David Hogganbeck's superior strength and endurance should win

372:19 **bird chitterlings** small intestines of birds (Brown 52)

372:27 **tallied the shells** counted the shells to see who ate the most

372:28 **melt** spleen (Brown 127)

373:2–3 **tallied the bones** see 372:27

373:3–4 **shote** shoat; a young pig

373:11–13 **Ikkemotubbe put the gourd down and raised the tail of his shirt before his bowed face and turned and walked away as the People opened aside to let him pass** Flashing the crowd, Ikkemotubbe cedes the eating contest to Hogganbeck.

373:28–34 **"Then what do you suggest now?" David Hogganbeck said. And now my father said how they loved David Hogganbeck at that moment as they loved Ikkemotubbe; that they loved them both at that moment while Ikkemotubbe stood before David Hogganbeck with the smile on his face and his right hand flat on David Hogganbeck's chest, because there were men in those days** Hogganbeck's gesture here is a magnanimous and worthy response to Ikkemotubbe's assertion at 371:13–15. Having bested Ikkemotubbe in the eating contest, Hogganbeck does not claim victory, but rather now asks his rival what other contest he would propose in order that his honor be satisfied, and the People acknowledge Hogganbeck as a worthy peer, one of the "men in those days," of Ikkemotubbe. The phrase echoes the description in Genesis of the men who populated the earth before the great flood: "There were giants in the earth in those days" (6:4).

374:1 **Once more then, and then no more** the last test in the courtship

374:5–7 **a hundred and thirty miles away, over in the country of old David Colbert** As Moore notes, the story "requires us to suspend our disbelief that the rivals can race one hundred thirty miles [see 374:5–6]—the equivalent of five marathons—in four consecutive days: indeed 'there were men in those days' (373[:34]" (52), and tall tales, too, it would seem.

374:7 **the spoor** the track

374:9–12 **where the boys from among all the People would go to lie on their first Night-away-from-Fire to prove if they had the courage to become men** the site of a solitary coming-of-age ritual

374:18–19 **drew the loads and reloaded them** replaced the gunpowder in the pistol cartridges and put them back in the pistols

374:29–33 **another charge of powder, with a wadding and bullet, into each of two small medicine bags, one for himself and one for David Hogganbeck, just in case the one who entered the Cave first should not lose quick enough** the means of suicide to end suffering, should they not be immediately killed and thus face starvation or other suffering in the cave

375:3 **It was evening then. Then it was night** marks the first of the four nights during which Hogganbeck and Ikkemotubbe rest in their race toward the cave. The subsequent nights, marked by references to sundown, sunset, night, and dark, are noted at 375:18–19, 376:8–9, and 376:24–26.

376:28 **He told how he stopped** **He** = Ikkemotubbe, an indication that he will survive to tell his tale. See also 377:6, 377:18–19, and 377:22.

377:5–7 **a noise, and a rushing, and a blackness and a dust, and Ikkemotubbe told how he thought, *Aihee. It comes.*** Part of the cave collapses and Ikkemotubbe thinks his death is imminent (see also 378:4–5).

377:13–14 **Between my legs. I can't—** You must crawl out between my legs. I can't hold this position much longer; Noel Polk has argued that "the athletic competition is a thin, a veritably gossamer, veil for the homoerotic or at least homosocial elements in their friendship" (*Children* 145).

377:31 **Then I can't move** either because he has been temporarily paralyzed or frozen from his exertions, or because he will not go because the weight has been taken from him

377:34 **the meat** the genitals

378:6 **flung him face-down too across David Hogganbeck** So does Ikkemotubbe survive winning the contest for Herman Basket's sister, fulfilling the conditions agreed to at 374:19–21.

378:9 **by the second day** after the cave-in

378:11–12 **my father met him with the horse for David Hogganbeck to ride** The narrator's father here serves as ambassador for the People, who assume that Ikkemotubbe will beat David Hogganbeck to the cave and be killed, making Hogganbeck the exhausted survivor in need of a horse.

378:14 **So you found the pony** He thinks the news is that they have found the racing pony that he gave to Herman Basket's sister's aunt, but the narrator's father reiterates the point, and Ikkemotubbe regroups well enough to hear it at 378:19.

379:5–6 **Log-in-the-Creek's wife** Herman Basket's sister. Her marriage to Log-in-the-Creek is the "news" that the narrator's father had communicated to Ikkemotubbe at 378:19.

379:8–9 **Presently Ikkemotubbe was gone completely away, to be gone a long time before he came back named Doom** Ikkemotubbe's response to his loss of the girl to Log-in-the-Creek is to leave for New

Orleans. He returns a changed man, as "Doom," summarized briefly at 362:32–363:10.

379:10 **either** the Chevalier Sœur-Blonde de Vitry (363:3–4)

379:12–14 **because at times someone would have to get up and walk somewhere to find something for the ones we already owned to do** All of the slaves on the Plantation, another of the corrupting influences that the Indians accepted from the white culture, are a constant source of trouble and irritation to the Indians.

379:24–27 **"But not for her!" Ikkemotubbe said. "And not even because it was Log-in-the-Creek. Perhaps they are for myself: that such a son as Log-in-the-Creek could cause them to wish to flow"** Wronged in love, Ikkemotubbe weeps but claims that he does so because he feels sorry for himself for being bested by a son of a bitch rather than by an honorable competitor.

379:34 **where a horse has stood** urinated

379:35–380:1 **a wise man of ours named Solomon who often said something of that nature too** possibly Proverbs 11:22: "As a jewel of gold in a swine's snout, so is a fair woman which is without discretion."

"Lo!"

"Lo!" is a comic story, juxtaposing an American President, obviously Andrew Jackson, and a Chickasaw chief named Frank "Weddel or Vidal" who has brought his people to Washington, D.C., where they occupy the White House in an ultimately successful effort to recover rights to a disputed ford on their Mississippi land. Like other Faulkner "Indian" stories, "Lo!" dramatizes the conflict between American ideals and political realities, especially as the latter reveal the vast disparity between white stereotypes of Native American "primitivism" and the shrewd and patient Native American persistence on behalf of their own interests. One of comparatively few Faulkner stories the understanding of which depends significantly on their titles, "Lo!" in cultural context "involves not only 'high' but also popular literature. In particular, 'Lo!' can be seen as a heavily ironic and explicit response to a particular formulation of the notion, popular in Faulkner's youth, that Indians were doomed to pass from the earth. This idea, part of the whole Manifest Destiny ideology, came to be connected with the famous verses from Alexander Pope's *Essay on Man*" (Galloway 24–25). Pope's verse not only provides Faulkner's title, but also the general formulation of a simplistic and archly condescending view of Native Americans:

> Lo! the poor Indian, whose untutored mind
> Sees God in clouds, or hears him in the wind;
> His soul proud Science never taught to stray
> Far as the solar walk, or milky way;
> Yet simple Nature to his hope has given,
> Behind the cloud-topped hill, an humbler heaven;

> Some safer world in depth of woods embraced,
> Same happier island in the watery waste,
> Where slaves once more their native land behold,
> No fiends torment, no Christians thirst for gold!
> To be, contents his natural desire;
> He asks no angel's wing, no seraph's fire;
> But thinks, admitted to that equal sky,
> His faithful dog shall bear him company. (2245–46)

Pope's version of "the poor Indian" consists of several interconnected assumptions, all of which are refuted by the behavior of the "Indians" in "Lo!" The Chickasaws in this story have minds exquisitely "tutored" by close observation of and generalization from the behavior of their white oppressors. They not only adapt the fancy clothing of the white men while maintaining a sense of the ridiculousness of their appearance, but they also prove that they have learned force, intimidation, and legal subterfuge, showing that they have become highly competent participants in what Thadious Davis, in another Faulknerian context, has called the "games of property." They ask "no angel's wing, no seraph's fire" but rather control of the land that the President and his people have taken from them. Their goal is not an otherworldly haven beneath the "equal sky," but instead a separate place here on earth, unmolested by white men who would control the ford. Paradoxically, the Chickasaws gain through civil disobedience (with frequent intimations of violence) what they could not gain through battle with the General's overwhelming numbers of troops.

"Lo!" is more a tall tale of the trickster sort than a mimetic account of a particular Native American victory over the American President who propounded and enforced the policy of Removal. Nevertheless, the story has historical precedents in Pushmataha's 1824 visit to President James Monroe and especially the part Choctaw, part French Greenwood Leflore's 1831 contention with Jackson (Howell, "President Jackson" 255). Several have seen the story as Faulkner's oblique commentary on the failed Bonus Expeditionary Force march of World War I veterans on Washington in 1932. The marchers were routed by a military force that included Douglas MacArthur, Dwight Eisenhower, and George Patton. Two details from the story have convinced readers that Faulkner mounts a critique of such political maneuvering: Peter Lancelot Mallios, who studies Faulkner's Indians in the context of "the poetics of cannibalism," argues that the gnawed rib at 381:17 reveals that "at some level the governing motif of this story is one of Weddel's 'having' Jackson 'for lunch'—a cannibalistic idea pretty clearly being figured and foreshadowed here in the images of the 'bone' and 'rib' and 'flesh' gnawed by human teeth, which are presumably so arresting for Jackson because he sees in them a metaphor for his own fears and fate" (161n20); and Bruce G. Johnson argues that the hand mirror at 381:22 "functions iconically on several levels. First the President's use of the mirror here underscores how this story is 'reflected,' or mediated, through the President's point of view and not through the Native Americans'. In this sense, Faulkner's American Indian chronicle begins as a form of Orientalism because Weddel's people are denied a voice in relating their own story; thus begins a trope of silence that continues to resonate throughout this chronicle" (105). For such readers, Faulkner's imagined triumph for Weddel and his people represents not an exercise in wish-fulfillment or "Edenic nostalgia" but rather a satire of American politicians who pretend to lofty ideals but employ force and farcical ceremony to crush their opposition (Hönnighausen, "Faulkner Rewriting" 337).

Faulkner seems to have written this story in 1933 (Skei, *Short Story* 79), and it appeared in *Story* magazine in November 1934. It was honored with reprints in *The Best American Stories of 1935* and *The Yearbook of the American Story*, but the initial printing did not pay well and Faulkner remarked ruefully to his agent, Morton Goldman, "I suppose 'Lo' is another dud" (*Selected Letters* 75). When he selected and arranged the *Collected Stories* years later, however, Faulkner specifically linked "Lo!" to "Mountain Victory," the concluding story in "The Middle Ground," where Saucier Weddel explains, "[My father] was a Choctaw chief named Francis Weddel, of whom you have probably not heard. He was the son of a Choctaw woman and a French émigré of New Orleans, a general of Napoleon's and a knight of the Legion of Honor. His name was François Vidal. My father drove to Washington once in his carriage to remonstrate with President Jackson about the Government's treatment of his people" (*CS* 759). If one reads *Collected Stories* in order, one has in fact "heard of" Saucier's father. By revisiting and expanding material alluded to in a previous fiction—"Mountain Victory" preceded "Lo!" by about two years—and by finding comic or humorous implications in matter that he had originally treated as grim or tragic, Faulkner showed, as in his composition and juxtaposition of "Red Leaves" and "A Courtship," both his extraordinary range and his modernist sense of narrative possibility.

381:1 **The President** Andrew Jackson. As Edmond Volpe notes, "to convey the abstract and impersonal facade of the government," Faulkner refers to the officials "solely by their functions" and names only Weddel individually; however, he provides "sufficient clues to make clear that he has, with obvious irony, modeled his president upon Andrew Jackson, the soldier who achieved sufficient national prominence as an Indian fighter to become, from 1829 to 1837, the nation's seventh President. In this figure, Faulkner embodies the power and the blindness of white America" (188).

381:6 **lean height** one of the "sufficient clues" noted at 381:1; Jackson was almost invariably described as tall and slim (*Grolier's Encyclopedia Online*).

382:6–9 **He did not know the faces, though he knew the Face, since he had looked upon it by day and dreamed upon it by night for three weeks now** the face of the leader, Weddel

382:9–10 **a squat face, dark, a little flat, a little Mongol** the face of an undifferentiated "savage," as foreign to him as a man from Mongolia, and resembling one

382:17 **beaver hats** a top hat, not necessarily made of beaver fur (Calvin Brown 27; Hinkle and McCoy 68)

382:17 **new frock coats** knee-length, double-breasted dress coats (Brown 86)

382:22–23 **Pickwickian England** Victorian England; after *The Pickwick Papers* (1837) by Charles Dickens (1812–1870)

382:23 **smallclothes** woolen underwear (see 384:8)

382:24 **Hessian boots** man's high boots, with a tassel in the front, popular in England in the early nineteenth century; hence, the style of the day, the flouting of which causes the outraged sensibility at 382:20–21; Hessians were German mercenaries in the British army during the American Revolutionary War.

382:29 **whiteoak withes** lattice work of twigs of white oak, a very tough wood (Brown 215)

382:31 **a game cock** a rooster bred and trained for fighting

383:7 **without a gun or anything** "Among the most strange of the many strangenesses of Faulkner's Indians," notes Gene M. Moore, "is the fact that in all the 'Wilderness' stories they are portrayed as *unarmed,* and as *unaccustomed to using firearms.*" "This 'gun-shyness' stands in stark contrast," he continues, "with ample historical evidence of conditions on the frontier"; by numerous accounts, the Chickasaws and Choctaws were armed with rifles, often specifically for the purpose of deer hunting, as "in the heyday of the deerskin trade" ("Chronological Problems" 55–56).

383:10 **It's for honor** a complex pun: "honorary," because unarmed, guards; an "honor guard" for the President

383:21–22 **no accounting for taste** smug condescension to the presumably inferior "Other," echoed by the President and the Secretary of War (389:5 and 389:12)

383:33–34 **by them to whom he was, by legal if not divine appointment, father** "The Great White Father in Washington"

384:5–7 **the very rotunda itself of this concrete and visible apotheosis of the youthful Nation's pride** the Capitol building in Washington, D.C.

384:20–22 **the hand glass on the dressing table, among its companion pieces of the set which the new French Republic had presented to a predecessor** the first French Republic, established in September 1792 after the Revolution abolished the monarchy; the "predecessor" would have been George Washington.

384:27 **Yes, General** respect paid to the President's military career rather to than his present political one

384:28 **Good. Did you . . .** bring a cloak for me, also?

384:30 **Now the . . .** hat

385:16–17 **these two words** "scuttled" and "ducked," from the previous sentence

385:23 **that Avenue** Pennsylvania Avenue, which runs between the White House and the Capitol

386:11 **I gave strict orders. . . .** that they were not to be permitted guns (see 387:28–29)

386:14 **the Secretary** of War, in the President's Cabinet, in charge of Indian Removal

387:4 **plug hats** top hats (Brown 151; see 382:17)

387:14–15 **Hessian soldiers** see 382:24

387:18–19 **That's something else I want. . . .** to say a word about (see 387:26)

387:32 **But I saw myself . . .** the deer that they had killed

387:33 **They use knives** Some readers have said that, because both Choctaws and Chickasaws were proficient with firearms by this time, Faulkner must have been ignorant of their hunting techniques. He seems rather to imply that their superior hunting skills make guns unnecessary.

388:5 **Then the President ceased and the Soldier cursed steadily for a while** The President has been saying "Damn. Damn. Damn"; he now resorts to the stronger language he had used as a soldier.

388:18 **Chickasaw Indians** "Faulkner was aware that the Choctaws—or 'Chocktaws,'—as he spelled the term in his letters to [Malcolm] Cowley—were geographically to the south of the future Lafayette County and thus historically more closely linked with the French than with the English. This French connection helps to explain Francis Weddel's transformation from 'a Choctaw chief' (*CS* 759) in 'Mountain Victory' to a Chickasaw in 'Lo!' " (Moore, "Chronological Problems" 51 n1).

388:21 **has nothing to do but . . .** eat breakfast at his own home

389:12–15 **"Yes," the Secretary said, "there's no accounting for taste. Though it does seem that when one has been presented with a costume as a mark of both honor and esteem, let alone decorum, and by the chief of a well, tribe . . ."** "he should wear it" (a jab at the President)

390:15–16 **"Have your joke," the President said. "Have it quickly. Are you done laughing now?"** the line the Secretary leaves unfinished at 389:15; the suggestion that the President wear the ensemble presented to him by Weddel

390:30 **a pair of steel-bowed spectacles** pince-nez, glasses without temples that are fixed to the bridge of the nose by pressure from the bowed frame. In explanation of "steel-bowed"—"*U.S.*, (of spectacles) having steel frames"—the *OED* cites this very passage.

391:7 **I don't see . . .** what that has to do with my problem now

391:10 **The man who was mur . . .** murdered

391:31 **a game of mumble peg** "mumblety-peg, a boys' game in which a knife must be thrown and stuck into the ground from each of a standard sequence of positions. The loser has to dig a wooden peg out of the ground with his teeth" (Brown 135)

392:10–11 **But I still don't see . . .** what this has to do with my problem (see 391:7)

393:13 **the agent** the "Indian agent," sent by the U.S. government to oversee Native American affairs in Mississippi

393:21–22 **Keep the rest of them from . . .** coming along?

393:29–30 **I would just declare a national thanksgiving** a playful and ironic anachronism: although George Washington declared November 26, 1789, as "a day of national thanksgiving and prayer," it was not until 1863 that Abraham Lincoln designated the last Thursday in November as an official holiday ("The History of Thanksgiving Day"; "Thanksgiving Timeline"). Whereas the earliest and continuing traditional thanksgiving celebrates, among other things, the Native American contribution to the survival of the white Pilgrim community, the President's imagined "thanksgiving" would be for the lessening of the perceived threat to his own "civilization."

394:31–32 **a metropolitan museum of wax figures** a collection of figures made of wax, portraying famous people; the first wax museum, Madame Tussaud's, opened in London in 1835.

395:2–3 ***café-au-lait*-colored jowls above a froth of soiled lace of an elegance fifty years outmoded and vanished** *Café au lait,* French for "coffee with milk," suggests racial mixing. As Robert Dale Parker argues, "Jackson's problem with Weddel is not simply that he is effeminate, but that his effeminacy is *café-au-lait.* His mixed blood and gender-bending suggest illicit sexuality and boundary breaking. A story about removal, racial conflict, and illicit sexuality has everything to do with boundaries, for Weddel will not keep to his supposed place" (92).

395:6 **the almost feminine mannerisms** Early white settlers frequently noted the effeminate ways of Chickasaw, Choctaw, and Cherokee men: "Sometimes, ruffled shirts of fine linen were worn, belted or hanging loose," wrote a white man named Adair who lived among these tribes from 1736 to 1744 ("Cherokee Clothing and Adornment"). As Galloway writes, "White visitors to Chickasaw country did report colorful dress on the part of Chickasaw men, who had a distinctive style of their own and adapted European articles of clothing and jewelry to their own uses" (22–23). Similarly, according to H. B. Cushman, Chickasaw men "used little beads in ornamenting their leather garments, intermingled with fancy embroidery" (395)—hence the conclusion by one writer that "The Chickasaw men are very effeminate and dressy" (quoted by Galloway 23).

395:21 **inkstand, quill, and sandbox** writing materials of the time period; the sand was used to blot the wet ink.

395:27–28 **Is this the man who . . .** stands accused?

395:33–396:1 **We do not think that it is right to slay white men like a confounded Cherokee or Creek** a complex sentence with two possible meanings: "We don't kill white men like the Cherokee or Creek do," or "We don't kill white men the way we kill Cherokee and Creek."

396:22–24 **What does it matter by what name the White Chief calls us? We are but Indians: remembered yesterday and forgotten tomorrow** part of Weddel's manipulation of the stereotypes originating in Pope's "Lo!" (see Introduction)

396:29 **He sanded what he had written** He dusted the paper with sand to set the ink; see 395:21

397:11–12 **I had thought. . . . But no matter** thought finished at 397:27–28

397:16–17 **To me, my Indian and my white people are the same** a lie, both in the framework of the story and in history: Andrew Jackson was a leading proponent of Removal, the government policy of driving Native Americans westward beyond the Mississippi River, made official by the Indian Removal Act of 1830.

397:22–24 **In my ignorance I had thought that even our little affair would have been concluded in. . . . But no matter** thought finished at 397:27–28

397:27–28 **In the big white council house beneath the golden eagle** the Capitol building

397:29 **In the . . .** Capitol?

398:6–7 **there is also a town in our country with the same name** Mississippi was admitted to the Union as the twentieth state on

December 10, 1817, with Washington, Mississippi, near Natchez, its first capital.

398:9 **poor, ignorant Indians** see 396:22–24

398:22–24 **For is it not well said that the graves of a man's fathers are never quiet in his absence?** This constitutes another instance in which the President assumes the clichés of Pope's "Lo!" (see Introduction). Here, he attempts to apply what he believes to be "Indian" religious beliefs about the afterlife to the situation at hand, but he has misconstrued those: "The Chickasaw believed in a hereafter in which the good would go to their reward somewhere in the heavens while the evildoers would wander forever in the land of the witches" ("The Chickasaw People").

398:27–28 **a council of chiefs who are more powerful there than I am** the U.S. Congress

399:6 **that Avenue with a high destiny** see 385:23

399:14 **the Speaker's desk of that chamber** the desk of the Speaker of the House of Representatives

399:26–27 **they have not been fired since Washington shot them last at Cornwallis** In 1781, George Washington effected the surrender of the British under Cornwallis at Yorktown, bringing the Revolutionary War to a close.

399:31 **it was Petrarch's Sonnets** sonnets of the Italian poet (1304–1373), as opposed to a legal volume

399:33 **law Latin** Latin phrases used in legal documents and casebooks. Moore notes that Petrarch's sonnets were written in Italian, rather than Latin (62n23). We account for the error by noting that the sonnets had been translated into English in 1931, which might have put them in the forefront of Faulkner's imagination.

400:25 **That is all** the end of the series of instructions or dictated letters to the secretary

401:19–23 ***For what can money be to me, whose destiny it apparently is to spend my declining years beneath the shade of familiar trees from whose peaceful shade my great white friend and chief has removed the face of every enemy save death?*** an apparent compliment, but a stinging barb at the effects of the policy of Removal itself

401:29–31 ***this cursed ford against a few miles of land, which (this will amuse you) this wild nephew of mine did not even own*** But

Weddel did own the land, by right of a grant from his father (391:1–3).

402:10 **And so again we see him** the revelation of a narrative gaze and voice joined identically with that of the reader in the present tense, as in a filmed scene

402:20 **that damned agent," he said** a return to the simple past tense of unmediated narration

402:28–29 **"Strike out *The United States*, then." The Secretary did so** and leaves a notice of complete meaninglessness in the process, with no agent for enforcement; an empty threat

402:30 **the two papers** the letter granting Weddel the ford and the notice to the Indian agent to post warnings each end of it

IV. THE WASTELAND

"Ad Astra"

"Ad Astra" looks back from the vantage point of an anonymous narrator recalling his experience of Armistice Day, 11 November 1918. Along with a captured German pilot, a small but diverse party of Allied soldiers—the narrator, his fellow Americans Bland, Monaghan, and Sartoris, an unnamed military policeman, the Irishman Comyn, and an East Indian subadar—spends the evening drinking first on the road to Amiens and then in a bar there. Although the war has just ended, there is little of the truly celebratory in the gathering. Instead, they drink heavily, argue among themselves, and threaten one another. The wounded German captive and the subadar provide a detached intellectual commentary on the just-concluded war and on the men celebrating that conclusion, while the narrator attempts, with little personal comment, to comprehend the "maelstrom" of the story's immediate scene. His inability to do so at the time seems to have stayed with him to the present day, twelve years afterward, when he recounts the various arguments of the evening. The final exchange between Bland and the subadar seems particularly troubling to him, and it anticipates Isaac McCaslin's ethical dilemma in *Go Down, Moses* (1942): the subadar believes that by "removing" himself from an unjust social structure, he "undid in one day what it took two thousand years to do," while Bland thinks the subadar merely left the problem to someone else. Although he says he "saved my destiny" by staying alive during the war, Bland also seems to take the subadar's comment that "your destiny" is "to be dead" quite to heart (427–29).

The narrative tension of "Ad Astra" derives from the juxtaposition of, first, the crude physical action with the abstract philosophical exchanges and, second, the narrator's memories with his 1930 perspective. As Max Putzel puts it, "the serene dignity of the two alien noblemen, both scions of military families, sharing a belief in the brotherhood of man and the paradoxical ennobling effect of war, is set off in high relief by the drunken cacophony of the rest" (134). Carvel Collins, who has identified many of the story's characters with individuals Faulkner knew in New Haven in 1918, finds in "Ad Astra" the themes of "voluntary renunciation of power," "victory in defeat, the Lost Generation, and . . . favoring such understandable preferences as love instead of force, justice instead of hierarchy, brotherhood instead of fatherland" ("Ad Astra" 121). Judith Bryant Wittenberg says "the composite voice" of the subadar and the German "is undermined by the pessimistic, cyclical vision of [the narrator], and their counterpoint becomes a rich polyphony with the addition of the angry, despairing voice of Bayard Sartoris, the pointless words of Bland, and the aggressive statements of Comyn and Monaghan" (286). The war has wounded these men, psychologically as well as physically; but no matter how horrible life in combat was, surviving it to war's end has doomed them to a kind of death-in-life ever after. Putzel notes "this has been an unnatural war. Those who fought it and survived are as if dead, their era, their function abruptly ended. Each is an Othello with his occupation gone" (135). "Ad Astra," says James Ferguson, "is really concerned with the cosmic injustice that the carnage of World War I seemed to reveal and with the consequent disillusionment and anguished attempts to adjust to that new view of life" (82). The overall merit of the story remains in dispute. Lisa Paddock calls it "a masterpiece of short story construction that manages to convey . . . the existential significance of war" (17). Hans Skei says it is "a concentrated, almost painful, portrayal of loss and decay, and of the futility and waste of war" (*Reading* 12). Sanford Pinsker calls the story "essentially a mood piece" (5), and Ferguson uses the same phrase but deems it "a somewhat flabby work" (31, 137). Edmond Volpe calls "Ad Astra" "a sententious expression of the bewilderment and despair of the lost generation and an attempt to explain why young men who fought in World War I died on November 11 when peace came" (37). Less willing to settle for traditional explanations of "Ad Astra," John N. Duvall points to the homosocial and homoerotic implications of the story, arguing that Monaghan is, in a sense, "seducing" the German: "what Comyn and Monaghan literally do with the prostitute, they figuratively do to the German. We see in this moment women devalued in a sexual economy; the prostitute will serve primarily as an agent to effect a displaced homoerotic consummation" (57).

With its evocation of the Lost Generation at the precise moment that killed it, "Ad Astra" stands at an interesting juncture in Faulkner's early career. He had written it some time before he acknowledged the *Saturday Evening Post's* rejection of it on 21 December 1927 (Skei, *Short Story* 29, 36). A brief reference to its plot occurs in *Flags in the Dust*, published as *Sartoris* in 1929 but certainly under composition in late 1926 (Day, "Introduction" vii). As the story of young Bayard Satoris draws to its doomed conclusion, Bayard meets Monaghan in Chicago: "Say," Monaghan says, "you remember that night in Amiens when that big Irish devil, Comyn, wrecked the Cloche-Clos by blowing that A.P.M.'s whistle at the door?" (*Flags* 414–15; *Sartoris* 289). The episode has provocative parallels to *The Sound and the Fury* (1929), in which a Southerner named Bland attends Harvard; "All the Dead Pilots," which features Bayard's brother John and closes "The Wasteland" section of *Collected Stories* that "Ad Astra" opens; and "Honor," in which an ex-pilot named Monaghan appears as narrator and barnstormer. Faulkner submitted the story, unsuccessfully, to the *American Mercury* in 1930, and *American Caravan* finally published it in March of 1931. Thus, "Ad Astra" was the first of Faulkner's World War I short stories to be published commercially—the only one of the four he collected in *These 13* (1931) to have that distinction. Faulkner revised the *American Caravan* version for *These 13*, and Cowley used this revised text in *The Portable Faulkner* (1945). Like the other war stories (or, for that matter, the entire contents of *These 13*), "Ad Astra" did not appear among Robert K. Haas's original suggestions for the *Collected Stories* volume, but to Faulkner these stories were important enough to comprise an entire section of the project. As he worked out the table of contents, he wrote to Saxe Commins, "something about it nagged at me." That something was the original heading "Indians" to describe the third section of the proposed volume, but almost in the same breath he seems to have arrived at the title for the war material: "Then I thought, not *Indians* but *Wilderness*, and then suddenly the whole page stood right, each noun in character and tone and tune with every other and I imagine that now you have divined the word for the war section too: The Wasteland" (*Selected Letters* 277). In that moment, he joined his work with Ezra Pound's and T. S. Eliot's apt assessments of the cultural and psychological costs of the Great War.

407:TITLE **Ad Astra** Latin meaning "To the stars." The motto of the Royal Air Force is *Per Ardua ad Astra,* "through adversity to the stars." Faulkner used "Per Ardua" as the title of one of his unpublished stories (see Harrison 63, 85).

407:1 **I** the unnamed American soldier who narrates the story

407:3–4 **we had started out Americans, but after three years, in our British tunics and British wings and here and there a ribbon** They are a motley group of Americans in the British air force, occasionally decorated for conduct, who began service in 1915, well before the U.S. entered the war in 1917.

407:6 **that day, that evening** 11 November 1918; see 428:33

407:9 **subadar** in the British Indian services, the chief native officer in command of a company of native troops (Harrison 85); Anglo-Indian word made from *subah* ("a province of the Mogul empire" and *–dar* ("master")

407:10 **trick major's pips** shoulder insignia indicating his rank in the Indian colonial army (and so "trick"); Robert Harrison explains that native officers could not hold regular British commissions (85). See also 409:9–10.

407:17 **Amiens** a town in northeastern France about halfway between Calais and Paris and a strategic point in the Western front of the War

407:19 **tackling dummy** in football, a stuffed bag mounted on blocks and used for practice in tackling

408:3 **But after twelve years** 1930, the present time of the narrator's reflections

408:11 **it** the experience of war

408:13–14 **the storm which we had escaped** the war

408:13–14 **and the foreign strand which we could not escape** France; perhaps an allusion to Sir Walter Scott's "My Native Land":

Breathes there the man, with soul so dead,
Who never to himself hath said,

This is my own, my native land!
Whose heart hath ne'er within him burned,
As home his footsteps he hath turned
From wandering on a foreign strand!

The poem goes on to promise that the man who has not felt this way "doubly dying, shall go down/To the vile dust, from whence he sprung,/Unwept, unhonour'd, and unsung."

408:23 **the Union** the Oxford Union, founded in 1823; a highly prestigious debating society dedicated to the free expression of ideas

408:27–28 **in the five months he had been out, no one had ever found a bullet hole in his machine** "The mark of either a very great pilot or a very timorous one. Although René Fonck was never wounded and used to boast that no German bullet had ever pierced his aeroplane, most pilots returned from engagements with numerous bullet holes in their machines" (Harrison 86).

408:29 **an Oxford battalion** made up of Oxford University students or coming from Oxfordshire County; during the First World War, seventeen battalions existed under the Oxfordshire and Buckinghamshire Light Infantry division, and these battalions fought across the French, Italian, Macedonian, and Mesopotamian fronts ("Oxfordshire and Buckinghamshire Light Infantry").

408:29 **Rhodes scholar** endowed by and named after British magnate Cecil Rhodes (1853–1902), scholarships awarded annually since 1902 to students from the U.S., British Commonwealth, South Africa, and Germany for study at Oxford University in England ("Rhodes, Cecil John").

408:30 **a barnacle and a wound stripe** "Barnacle" is "military slang for a *bar*, a silver rosette somewhat resembling a marine barnacle which was affixed to the ribbon of a British decoration to signify that the decoration had been awarded more than once" (Harrison 86). A wound stripe is a bar signifying that the wearer has been injured in hostile action.

408:30 **tight** drunk (chiefly British slang)

409:9–10 **he cannot hold their commission** see 407:10

409:16–17 **this one was being fought to end war forevermore** Although the description of the Great War as "the war to end all wars" is most famously attributed to President Woodrow Wilson, the phrase actually originates with British writer H. G. Wells (1866–1946), who published *The War That Will End War* in 1914.

409:19 **it** fighting in the war

409:23–25 **A man sees further looking out of the dark upon the light than a man does in the light and looking out upon the light. That is the principle of the spyglass** A spyglass is a refracting telescope, which "produces images by refraction using a lens. The advantage of this over reflection by a mirror is that the aperture remains completely unobstructed, thus yielding images of the highest contrast and brightness" (see "Refracting Telescope"). As a spyglass magnifies an object in the distance, the viewer's surroundings are obscured (made dark), allowing the viewer to focus on the object.

409:26 **the sense that suffers and desires** sight

409:31 **a hidden dog quartering a wheat field** a hunting dog slinking across the wheat field first one direction and then doubling back to recross the field, bisecting it at right angles

409:33 **Not hunting bitches** A curious phrase that can be read two ways: with emphasis on *hunting*, that word becomes an adjective; Bland seems to say that female hunting dogs would not behave in the way Comyn describes. With emphasis on *bitches*, that term becomes a pejorative and *hunting* becomes a verb; Bland says that Comyn's description does not apply when one hunts females. Although either reading can be defended, we believe that the first is more nearly what Bland means. Bland and Comyn both have experience hunting, and both would know that female dogs "come into season twice a year . . . and are therefore somewhat difficult to keep at home during those days. A bitch at this time might be a bit inattentive with game, and definitely cannot and may not be taken out working where there might be other dogs. Another drawback for people who want wide ranging dogs is the fact that, sometimes . . . bitches become short ranging and less avid for game when they reach four or five years old" (Desmonts). At the least, Bland's statement calls Comyn's expertise into question and possibly his sexual preferences, since comparing Comyn to the female dog implies that Comyn would be distracted from the prey (the women) by the other dogs (men). In either case,

Comyn takes offense to what Bland has said, and it inspires his "offer" to Bland at 410:4.

410:2 **Dolphin** the 5.F.1 Dolphin, intended as a replacement for the Sopwith Camel. Harrison explains that the "greatest complaint with the Dolphin had to do with its seating arrangement. The upper wing was set so low on the fuselage that a tall pilot's head projected above the center section. Surrounded by longerons, spars, cross-bracing wires, and tie rods, the engine at his knees and the fuel tank at his back, a Dolphin pilot had little chance of surviving a hard landing if the machine tipped over on its back" (86).

410:3 **emergency bolster** extra pillow

410:4 **shilling** unit of British currency; a coin worth twelve pence

410:23 **R.F.C.** Royal Flying Corps

410:23–24 **and an American tunic with both shoulder straps flapping loose** Monaghan's motley uniform is not solely the result of drunkenness, as Harrison notes: "Such improvisations in military attire were not uncommon in France. Thus [Victor M.] Yeates":

> There was a queer mixture of uniforms; or rather there was no uniform; and the new R.A.F. outfit was intended to impose order on this chaos; but as no outfit allowance had been made, and the uniform was generally disliked, progress was not rapid. The typical R.F.C. bloke still wore his wings on his dirty regimental tunic edged with leather at the cuffs and scented and stained with castor oil, a pair of oily but elegant breeches or slacks, a soft topped cap pulled on with infinite negligent rakishness, and an expression of hard-bitten, sardonic wisdom. (223–224) (Harrison 86)

His shoulder straps are "flapping loose" because Monaghan has cut off any insignia that would reveal his rank (Lieutenant).

410:25–26 **a tunic shorter and trimmer than ours** more fully described at 411:26; the uniform of a German soldier

410:34 **sovereign** unit of British currency; a coin worth about ten or eleven shillings

411:12 **Cloche-Clos** French: literally, "closed bell"; here, the name of the bar

411:26 **breeks** breeches; trousers

411:29–30 **using him pretty hard** wearing him out, perhaps even beating him

412:4 **Anthony** the first Christian monk (c. 250–350)

412:10–11 **rolling cigarettes from a cloth sack** making cigarettes by rolling loose tobacco, poured from a cloth sack in which it was sold, into individual cigarette papers

412:33 **Beyreuth** city in Bavaria famous as the home of German composer Richard Wagner (1813–83) from 1872 and of the annual Richard Wagner Festival, which started in 1876 ("Beyreuth")

413:1–2 **one spring** Although the Wagner festivals have always taken place from late July through early September, the subadar may have gone to visit Wagner's opera house, the *Festspielhaus,* which was built according to his design and funded by King Ludwig II, a great admirer of Wagner's. It is known for its sunken, covered orchestra pit and exceptional acoustics. Beyreuth also has an excellent concert hall dating from the eighteenth century.

413:4 **The music** Wagner's renowned operas; by the time of the first Beyreuth festival in 1876, Wagner had been recognized as the most famous composer in the world.

413:14 **Defeat iss good for art; victory, it iss not good** a debatable proposition; Harrison argues that "the German, by maintaining his dignity in defeat, enjoys a moral superiority over Monaghan, who, though quite possibly the better pilot, has not as yet learned humility" (85).

413:25 **patronne** proprietress (French)

414:1 **shanty Irish** belonging to the Irish lower class

414:5 **Camel squadron below us** attack squadron of Sopwith Camel airplanes. By this point in the war, their primary duty had become trench strafing (Harrison 89). It is "below us" because "in the great 'stacked' formations of fighters that roamed up and down the lines in 1918, the various types of machines cruised at the altitudes at which they fought best. Since Camels were no good above 12,000 feet, they usually made up the bottom layer. Above them would be a formation of S.E.5s at around 15,000, and Dolphins at 18,000" (Harrison 87). Trench strafing usually occurred from treetop level—rather, where that level would have been were there any trees left near the trenches.

414:8 **tanks and drums** fuel tanks and ammunition drums (Harrison 87)

414:10 **Ak.W.** an Armstrong Whitworth F.K.8, "used for light bombing, artillery observation, and reconnaissance in the final two years of the war . . . known as the 'Ack.W.' because of the bold company initials stamped in steel on its engine cowling," "Ack" being military slang for the letter A (Harrison 87)

414:11–12 **Hun patrol leader's crate** German patrol leader's airplane

414:26 **monkey cap** identified by Harrison as an overseas cap (87); a soft, visorless, envelope-shaped cap introduced to the American army uniform in 1918 and modeled after the French *bonnet de police,* that was easy to store in the pockets when the helmet had to be worn (see "Doughboy Center")

414:28–29 **his pistol was hunched forward onto his lap** His pistol is not on his hip but instead within easy reach on his lap.

415:1–4 **At the base of each flapping shoulder strap there was a small rip; there were two longer ones parallel above his left pocket where his wings and ribbon had been** see 410:23–24

416:5 **his damned king—** King George V of England

416:19 **gentlemen's school** Yale, mentioned at 415:25

417:11–12 **My people are of Prussia little barons** His family are lower-ranking nobility in Prussia, a state in northern Germany with a duchy dating from the fifteenth century that in 1871 successfully united Germany under Otto von Bismarck. Prussia made up 65 percent of this new empire and was its leading state until World War I ("Prussia"). Faulkner often captures the rhythm of another language by distorting English syntax to approximate that of the original.

417:14 **cadet of dragoons** a student in training to be a cavalry officer

417:17–18 **to witness a period quick like a woman with a high destiny of the earth and of man** in other words, at the beginning of a great moment in history

417:18–21 **It iss as though the old trash, the old litter of man's blundering, iss to be swept away for a new race that will in the heroic simplicity of olden time walk the new earth** The German seems to think that by eradicating old ideologies and hierarchies, a simpler, more heroic people will emerge.

417:22 **blut** blood (German)
417:34 **that one** the third brother
417:34–418:1 **that one** the second brother, named at 418:4
418:3 **like court-martial** as though on trial for breaking military law
418:4 **Franz** the second-oldest brother named
418:7–8 **the daughter of a musician who wass peasant** of a lower social rank and not of the nobility
418:10–12 **the most humble of the Army may eat meat with our Kaiser; he does not need to be baron** The German army ranks on a social par with royalty. Kaiser Wilhelm I (1859–1941) helped lay the foundations for the Great War, primarily by building the German military and not exerting enough control over Austria-Hungary, and lost his throne with it.
418:16–17 **he iss in Berlin newspaper dead of a lady's husband** A Berlin newspaper printed the news of his death at the hands of his lover's husband.
418:19–20 **it will not be long, since it was not long before** Prior to World War One, the Prussians were involved in the Franco-Prussian War, which lasted for six months (July 1870–January 1871) and ended in German victory.
418:20–21 **The fatherland in its pride needed us of the schools, but when it needed us it did not know it** Germany needed the intelligence and guidance of its scholars to prevent the coming of the Great War. Instead, As Richard Holmes explains, it got a bigger standing army, the move toward which had begun years earlier. In 1858, Albrecht Theodor Emil von Roon "submitted a memorandum [to Prince Regent William of Prussia] warning that the [Prussian] standing army was too small, while the Landwehr, the citizen militia which provided the reserve, was both 'politically false' because it no longer impressed potential adversaries and 'militarily false' because it was poorly trained and lacked discipline." Roon was appointed as war minister, but it was not until 1862 that "Roon got the army he wanted: a conscript was liable for seven years' service, three with the colours and four with the reserve, and he remained in the Landwehr, a second-line reserve to the regular army, for another five years. Roon created the instrument which won the Austro-Prussian and the Franco-Prussian wars" (Holmes). Kaiser Wilhelm

II built on that foundation and practiced saber-rattling politics that inflamed matters in Europe.

418:23 **And so—** I went to war

419:11 **snake-charmer** a derogatory reference to the subadar's ethnicity; like a sideshow snake-charmer, he wears a turban.

419:14 **frogs** derogatory term for French people

419:19–20 **the round-headed boy part of a gun** the bolt (Harrison 87), which positions the cartridge in a rifle and then ejects it when spent

419:20–21 **ace with iron cross by the kaiser's own hand** Prussian decoration instituted in 1813, a blackened equiform cross with a silver rim, awarded only for war service (Harrison 87), in this case awarded by Kaiser Wilhelm himself

419:21 **1916** the year of the battles of Verdun, a German offensive, and the Somme, an Allied attack, both of which caused heavy casualties on both sides

419:22 **your Bishop—** William Avery Bishop (1894–1956), Canada's leading ace of the war. Harrison describes him as "every inch the professional soldier" and "a superb lone hunter. To Bishop the aeroplane was preeminently a weapon of surprise attack. Typical of his exploits was the action of 2 June 1917, for which he was awarded the Victoria Cross. Alone he attacked a German aerodrome just at dawn, as the aircraft were being rolled out of their hangars, destroyed several on the ground, shot down the three which managed to get airborne, and brought his riddled Nieuport back to base safely. His record was little short of miraculous. In one 12–day period he shot down 25 enemy aircraft, and after a little over a year at the front his total was 72" (87–88). He was the first Canadian to receive the Victoria Cross, Britain's highest award for courage, and "he was also awarded the Distinguished Flying Cross (DFC) after scoring 25 victories in just twelve days . . . . Before the war ended, he found time to write *Winged Warfare*, an autobiographical account of his exploits in the air over France" (see "William Bishop").

419:29 **until our kaiser fled** Kaiser Wilhelm's abdication was forced on 9 November 1918, and he fled to Holland with his family, where he died in 1941 (Caddick-Adams).

419:34 **this morning** the morning of the Armistice, 11 November 1918

420:1 **seven years** since 1911, when he repudiated the title of baron

420:8 **identity disk** dog tag

420:9 **tunic—** because baron I will not be

420:27–28 **Ireland has had no king since the Ur Neill** the last of the O'Neill clan to reign as High Kings of Ireland; Máel Sechnaill macDomnail O'Néill was restored in 1014–1022: "in practice, descended as they were from the prominent Ulster Ui Neill/O'Neill Clan, the only territory under their command without dissent was Ulster" (Kessler Associates). The rule of Irish kings ended when Henry II declared himself Lord of Ireland in 1175.

420:28 **stern** Irish slang for backside

421:18 **four years rotting out yonder** the length of the war

421:32 **that** the German soldier

422:1–2 **make desagreable for France, monsieur** French *désagréable*: "make things unpleasant for France, sir"

422:7 **brassard** armband with the letters MP (Harrison 88)

422:24–26 **He said "dehvil-dahg" between his teeth, with no motion of his dead face, in itself insult** According to Harrison, a "devil-dog" is a U.S. Marine (88); said sucked between the teeth like this, a double insult.

422:28 **Boche!** French slang, specifically an insult to Germans; loosely translated as "blockhead" or "jerk"

422:30 **obus** French *obus*, an artillery shell; as Harrison notes, "Amiens was shelled by the Germans steadily from the beginning of April through mid-August 1918" (88).

422:33 **centimes** French coin worth a hundredth of a franc

422:34 **patrons—** drink from them!

423:6–7 **the specter which for four years we had been decking out in high words** the ghastly reality of the war

423:14 **poilus** slang for French infantrymen, called so by their shaggy appearance (*poilu* means "hairy" or "shaggy")

423:26–28 **tranquil as a squat idol, the both of them turbaned like prophets in the Old Testament** traditional headgear of the Jewish priests (from Exodus 28:4, in which God decrees the clothing)

423:31 **the old where we knew we had not died** the time during the war

424:2 **chop** choppy

424:12 **the sound of a band** probably playing patriotic music

424:30–31 **This spear is too short and too heavy** probably a rifle with an attached bayonet

425:8–9 **a traverse of the enemy's front line** a pair of right-angled bends in a trench in German territory

425:16 **sahib** sir; in colonial India, used by natives to an Englishman or European

425:23 **By God, I—** won't stand for this insult

425:25 **obligated—** "me to you"; a formal attempt to brush off Monaghan's attention

426:4 **A.P.M.** Assistant Provost Marshal (Harrison 88); assistant to the head of the military police

426:9 **fush** see 426:10

426:10 **yez midnight fusileers** fusilier; originally, a soldier armed with a light musket; designation still retained by some regiments in the British army. However, more pertinent here is a popular song among the British troops. Faulkner may have known it because he heard it sung or because it appears in the first unexpurgated bawdy songbook published in America, *Immortalia* (1927). Also known as "The Midnight Fusileers," "The Foreskin Fusileers," and "The Skinback Fusileers" (the latter two allusions to the military's frequent inspections for venereal disease), in *Immortalia* the song is called "*Battle Hymn of the 58th" and goes like this:

Eyes right! Assholes tight!
Foreskins to the front!
We're the boys that make the noise
And we're always after cunt.
We're the heroes of the night,
And we'd sooner fuck than fight,
We're the heroes of the foreskin fusileers!

The asterisk in the title directs readers to a note: "*At the time of the signing of the Armistice the 58th had been in the trenches without relief for ten weeks. Ordered back to their base at Laon they entered the town out of control of their officers singing this hymn" (Smith 108).

427:2 **he-beds** beds for men to have sex with other men

427:7 **Since seven years** since 1911; also the year that the German gave up his claim to the baronetcy; see 420:1

427:17–18 **foreigners who will treat the people like oxen or rabbits** imperial colonizers

427:19–20 **two thousand years** India existed as a thriving civilization since at least the third century B.C.; its classical period was the seventh century A.D. The British established their Empire there in 1757, which lasted until 1947. At about the time Prussia was amassing its great military power, then, the dynasties of India had fallen to colonization (see 417:11–12 and 418:20–21). (See "India.")

427:27–28 **Let England be glad that all Englishmen are not so wise** in effect, calling Bland a "wise guy"

428:25 **son** son of a bitch

428:27–28 **"Twice," he said in a quiet, detached tone. "Twice in an hour. How's that for high?"** a curious line that seems to refer not to Sartoris's drunken vomiting, which only happens once, but to Bland's being cursed by his comrades: first by Monaghan at 426:15 and then by the narrator at 428:25

428:33 **Twelfth** 12 November 1918, the first day of the rest of life without the war

"Victory"

"Victory," certainly the longest and probably the first of Faulkner's World War I stories to be written, has received intermittent and mixed reviews from readers. The multiple but obvious ironies of the title, the central character's unquestioning and insistent desire to rise within the class system that takes advantage of him and then casts him aside, and the pathos of the concluding scene have all drawn disparaging remarks. The fact that Faulkner drew in this story not on direct experience but rather on post-war tourist observations may have also contributed to the relative neglect of "Victory," as well as of other stories in "The Wasteland" section of *Collected Stories.* The story, nevertheless, works through a complex narrative structure and provides a substantial portrait of the effects of war (and peace) on a particular individual.

Faulkner plotted "Victory" in great episodic detail. Alec Gray, the son and grandson of Scottish shipwrights, determines to go to the Great War, in spite of his father's opposition, and early in his term of service is disciplined by his commanding officer for a minor infraction. The petty tyranny of the sergeant-major sends him to a seven-month term in the penal battalion. When he returns from this punishment, Gray finds an opportunity for particularly gruesome revenge on the sergeant-major, during a battle in which he subsequently demonstrates great valor, earning the Distinguished Service Medal. After a hospital stay, Gray returns to the battalion in the rank of subaltern-captain and leads his men to capture a German machine gun post, for which he earns the Military Cross. After another hospital stay and the signing of the Armistice, Gray chooses to go to London, where he finds a position in business and assumes the clothes, habits, and associations of a gentleman. In 1922, he takes leave from his London position and returns to France, visiting the scenes of some of his war experiences. After his return, losing his job and lacking both formal education and family connections, Gray begins a decline that brings him finally to destitution and homelessness. Through all this, he steadfastly refuses to consider a return to his Scottish home or to his shipwright's trade, as he had earlier declined to follow a fellow officer to seek post-war opportunity in Canada. He chooses instead to maintain the pathetic vestiges of his gentlemanly and military life—his regimental scarf, his walking stick, his fierce sense of personal superiority among his no-less-impoverished companions.

Such a straightforward summary does imperfect justice to the multiply episodic and anachronistically structured narrative of "Victory." James Ferguson remarks the story's exceptional length in its original form. Calling it "too novelistic," he notes its "very gradual expository development" and "its complex use of a double flashback" (124). The story actually begins with Gray's 1922 return to France, showing the mystification of those who observe him. It continues with a description of the minor breach of discipline that leads to Gray's incarceration in the penal battalion, followed with a further flashback to his original decision to enlist. The structure of "Victory" resembles that of many other Faulkner stories: the opening scene presents a mysterious or incomprehensible situation; next comes a reconstruction and recapitulation leading up to and clarifying the opening scene; the remainder of the narrative explores the consequences and conclusion of the previously presented material. "Wash," "Red Leaves," and "Mule in the Yard" among Faulkner's best stories demonstrate this narrative method, as do "Honor," "Fox Hunt," and "Beyond" among his less-appreciated. In light of Faulkner's use of this very structure in *The Sound and the Fury*, *As I Lay Dying*, *Absalom, Absalom!*, and *The Mansion*, to name a few, Ferguson's "novelistic" label seems not only apt but actually complimentary. The structure of "Victory" also depends upon a definite but little-noticed pattern of references to writing. For example, as James G. Watson argues, Alec Gray's correspondence with his family serves to reveal the contrasts between the Gray family's life at home and Alec's life in the military, but Alec's letters themselves also "conceal him in formulaic phrasing that, like the title 'Victory,' is ironically expressive" (*Letters* 98). Much the same could be said of the Bible that Alec takes to war and puts to uses other than spiritual comfort and guidance. Other writings include the memorandum taken by the sergeant-major in Gray's insubordination, the calling cards Alec has printed in his post-war London phase, the encyclopedias he attempts to sell, the letter the blind man has written from the hospital, and, finally, the blank card given to the blind man to replace the lost photograph of the woman who abandoned him. The story also incorporates a generous range of literary references, including allusions to Homer, Keats, Joyce, and Eliot that complement and underscore the highly metafictional quality of the story.

The overall evaluation of "Victory" remains in dispute. Edmond Volpe, for example, calls the it the weakest story in "The Wasteland" section (170) and criticizes especially what he calls Faulkner's failure to account for Gray's inability to return to his home and trade after the war: "An unappeasable hunger for social status is hardly a credible vehicle to dramatize the malaise of a war-induced trauma" (172). Lisa Paddock, by contrast, appreciates the way that Faulkner organizes "Victory" by the "counterpointing of scenes depicting Gray's lower-class Clydeside background . . . with images of his pertinacious commitment to the aristocratic pretensions he assumes along with the officer's rank he achieves" (20). More to the point, Douglas Day defines Gray's dilemma as his "unwilling[ness] to descend to his former social level; and the war, while it has allowed him to live as a gentleman for the duration, has not equipped him to live as a gentleman in peacetime" (391). Thus, he is one of "the humbler people who are elevated to the mock-aristocracy of the officer-class"; the war "creates its own artificial set of values, which are no more to be depended on than those of the aristocrats" (392). In this last point, Day isolates one of the issues of the story often ignored by critics. It is not simply the case that Alec Gray, in peacetime, is betrayed by the class system that his military service has successfully defended and preserved; it is far more important to see that in battle Gray has demonstrated the abilities and qualities of a true warrior, but the peacetime world to which he returns offers him no market whatsoever for those skills. Combat experience, especially including command, has allowed him to realize and demonstrate abilities greater than those expected of his class. The war fulfills him in a way that his civilian opportunities do not. Alec Gray, like the characters of "Ad Astra" and "All the Dead

Pilots," loses something vital to his innermost self when the Armistice is declared.

"Victory" apparently had its origins in Faulkner's observations on his "walking tour" of Europe, especially France and England, in 1925, and it may have specific literary sources as well. In his tour of the battleground of the great German offensive of spring 1918, Faulkner saw the places that Alec Gray observes on his own return to France. On 3 October 1925, Faulkner wrote to his mother, "Compiegne and Montdidier were 8 miles behind the front for 3 years, so they are not damaged much. But beyond that eight miles it looks as if a cyclone had passed over the whole world at about 6 feet from the ground. Stubs of trees and along the main roads are piles of shell cases and unexploded shells and wire and bones that the farmers dig up" (*Selected Letters* 28). In London he saw men like Alec Gray selling matches on the street corners. He described London in a letter to his mother on 7 October 1925: "the streets full of beggars, mostly young, able-bodied men who simply cannot get work—just no work to be had. They sell boxes of penny matches, play musical instruments, draw pictures on the pavement in colored chalk, steal—anything for a few coppers" (*SL* 29). "Victory" may also have been influenced by F. W. Bewsher's *History of the 51st (Highland) Division, 1914–1918*. While Alec Gray's adventures in the war bear some striking parallels to those of Bewsher's 51st, the differences and omissions indicate that if Faulkner used the *History of the 51st* as a broad outline to construct Alec Gray's story, he was not slavishly bound to it, nor was he constructing a *roman à clef*. Another plausible source for the general outline of Gray's wartime experiences is Neil Munro's introduction to *The 51st Division War Sketches*, by Fred A. Farrell. Most who have studied the typescripts agree that the earliest versions of "Victory" were probably written by 1926 or 1927, although no absolutely convincing evidence exists to support that conclusion. Neither is there evidence that Faulkner attempted to publish the story at that time, perhaps recognizing that its length made it unsuitable for most magazines. Constructing *These 13*, Faulkner revised earlier typescripts and excised one entire episode from "Victory," which he then revised and published as "Crevasse" in the 1931 collection. "Victory" thus had its public, if partial, debut in *These 13*, and it appears as the second of the five stories in "The Wasteland" section of *Collected Stories*, followed by its outtake. Hans Skei, who now rates the story among

Faulkner's best, concludes: "In 'Victory' the waste, futility, and cruelty of war are extended into postwar Europe, where unemployment and dishonor face those who helped win the war so that everyone could maintain at least one dream, the most important of them all: the dream of peace in our time" (*Reading* 205).

431:1 **him** the story's protagonist, identified at 439:7 ("Gray") and 441:19 ("Alec")

431:1–2 **the Marseilles express in the Gare de Lyon** the train from Marseilles, arriving at "Lyon Station," a train station at the intersection of Boulevard Diderot and Rue de Chalon, in the southeast part of central Paris

431:4–6 **"A milord," they said, remarking his sober, correct suit, his correct stick correctly carried, his sparse baggage; "a milord military"** Faulkner's literal translation of Anglicized French, *milord militaire,* or military my Lord (military man); a traveling aristocrat, complete with walking stick

431:9 **since four years now** 1922, four years after the end of the Great War

431:13–14 **the Legation offices** in this case, offices of a British diplomatic minister

431:14 **the Boulevards** Paris's grandest thoroughfares

431:15 **in the Bois** the Bois de Boulogne, a 2200–acre reserve on the western edge of Paris; the city's largest and most legendary park, especially popular with the upper class

431:17 **Gare du Nord** "North Station," a major train station in Paris, from which trains depart to the north of France and Europe

431:17–18 **returns home by haste** Faulkner's translation of the French *hâter de revenir,* to hasten to return, to hurry back. Faulkner often captures the rhythm of another language by distorting English syntax to approximate that of the original.

431:22 **the boat train** the train running from Paris to Dieppe, the port for the trans-channel crossings by boat

431:23 **Amiens** French town approximately 103 kilometers north of Paris, and the site of considerable fighting during World War I

432:1 **Rozières** Pozières, a town approximately thirty-five kilometers northeast of Amiens, virtually obliterated during the Battle of the Somme; **rosière** = virtuous maiden (French)

432:3–9 **through a gutted street between gutted walls rising undoored and unwindowed in jagged shards in the dusk. The street was partially blocked now and then by toppled walls, with masses of masonry in the cracks of which a thin grass sprouted, passing empty and ruined courtyards, in one of which a tank, mute and tilted, rusted among rank weeds** "Not only in terms of human life, but in loss of and damage to property, [France] had come out of the war the great loser among the Allies" (Marshall 460).

432:13–14 **a village of harsh new brick and sheet iron and tarred paper roofs made in America** rather than in war-torn Europe

432:25 **zinc bar** not of hardwood; a cheap bar

432:28 **"Bong jour, madame," he said. "Dormie, madame?"** Gray has trouble with *bonjour*, or "good day," and his French is even more fractured when he tries to ask if there is a place for him to sleep, or *dormir*. "Dormie, madame" would sound to his French hostess like "Slept, ma'am?"

432:29 ***C'est ça*** "That's so," "Yes"

433:4–6 **"Regardez, Monsieur l'Anglais," the man said. He took the bag from the newcomer and swept his other arm toward the ceiling. "La chambre"** "Look, Mister Englishman, the room," accompanied by an elementary pantomime to overcome Gray's fractured French

433:22–23 **a patent three-minute dessert** JELL-O gelatin

433:24 **slop basin** container for human excrement

433:29 **"Dîner, monsieur?" he said** literally, "To dine, sir?" (probably because of Gray's ineptitude with French)

433:33–34 **the patterned coloring of a Scottish regiment** necktie with distinctive diagonal stripes in the colors of Gray's old military unit, each of which had its own colors and pattern

433:34 **Manger?** literally, "To eat?" (see also 433:4–6 and 433:29)

434:14–15 **But he should have come four years ago** "when we needed help," probably a reference to the great German offensive in the spring of 1918 that finally failed on 8 August (see "Ludendorff Offensive")

434:23–24 **He is too cold to ever have had a son** an insult to Gray's masculinity; see also 437:4–5

435:11–12 ***Faites-moi l'honneur, monsieur*** Do me the honor, sir (to serve the soup, the first course); a polite gesture of deference and respect

435:13–14 ***Vous venez examiner ce scène de nos victoires, monsieur?*** You come to examine the scene of our victories, sir?

435:15–17 ***Monsieur l'Anglais a peut-être beaucoup des amis qui sont tombés en voisinage*** The English gentleman has perhaps many friends who are buried in this neighborhood

435:18 **A speak no French** I speak no French

435:21 **langue** literally, "tongue" (French); languages

435:27 **What deplorable, that man who ave** How deplorable (*quel déplorable*) that men have lost sons

436:9 **Arras** approximately sixty-seven kilometers northeast of Amiens, a center of fighting for almost the entire war. Dominated by German-occupied high ground to the north and threatened with encirclement by German positions to the south, the British constantly attempted to improve their situation at the cost of tens of thousands of lives.

436:24–29 **nothing to see save an occasional shattered road and man-high stump of shattered tree breaking small patches of tilled land whorled with apparent unreason about islands of earth indicated by low signboards painted red, the islands inscrutable, desolate above the destruction which they wombed** see Introduction

437:7 **That is why they drink whisky. Otherwise . . .** they would never beget children

437:21 **The battalion stands at ease** **battalion** = part of a division, a large body of military troops, usually consisting of two or more companies, here standing formally "at ease" because they are not called to "attention." The narrative verb tense here shifts for the first time from past to present, an indication of the importance of the scene in Gray's life.

437:21–22 **rest billets** the place behind the lines where units from the front line are sent to recover and have their losses in men and material repaired

437:28 **A.D.C.'s** aides-de-camp; secretaries and confidential assistants to a superior officer

437:30 **Para-a-a-de— 'Shun!** "Parade, attention!"; an order to assembled troops to stand formally at attention, an erect military posture with shoulders back, eyes forward, and heels together

437:25 **sergeant-major** In the British army, there are regimental and company sergeant-majors. Both ranks are warrant officers, setting them above the ranks but still below the commissioned officers. Gray's sergeant-major is in charge of a battalion inspection, which makes him a battalion sergeant-major.

438:6 **guide file of the first platoon** **guide file** = a line of troops, usually at either the extreme right or left, one behind the other in a marching column, to control alignment, direction, and pivot of the marching; **platoon** = a small body of infantry, detached from a larger body, such as a company, and operating as a organized unit

439:7–10 **024186 Gray** his serial number and last name

439:9 **"Sir!" the sergeant-major thunders** a reminder to follow military etiquette by addressing the superior officer as "Sir"

439:14 **A dinna shave, sir-r** I do not shave, sir

439:16 **A am nae auld enough tae shave** I am not old enough to shave

439:19 **You are not . . .** You are not old enough to shave?

439:21 **Take his name, Sergeant-major** for future punishment

439:30–31 **that damp and sullen clash which dies borning** the sound of their boots as their heels come together in unison, fading away as soon as it's made

440:12 **Double out 'ere** Step out here right away (on the double)

440:13 **Gray appears without haste** see 440:12

440:14 **kilts** Scots regiments in World War I, though under the command of the British Army, wore traditional kilts in service.

440:21 **a first-class warrant officer** intermediate rank between commissioned officers, such as the Colonel, and noncommissioned officers

440:23 **his vizorless bonnet** a cap without a brim, worn by Scots with the kilt

440:31 **the penal battalion** In the British Army, the punishment for some forms of insubordination was a tour in a penal battalion, with inadequate food, shelter, and clothing and a rigorous work regimen. Penal battalions mutinied, and suicides were not uncommon. Whereas the colonel presumably expects that Gray will be given some mild punishment for a minor breach of discipline, the sergeant-major elevates Gray's petty infraction to a serious offense. To send a man to the penal battalion for failing to shave is the act of an extreme bully; the punishment is grossly disproportionate to the "crime."

441:7 **"But why did ye no shave?" the corporal asked him** tense shifts back to past, a lowering of dramatic intensity

441:8 **leprous walls** scaling, perhaps moldy walls

441:9 **ammoniac air** pungent with the odor of urine

441:10–11 **Ye kenned we were for inspection thae mor-rn** You knew we were (scheduled) to have an inspection this morning. **ken** = chiefly Scots, "to know"

441:12 **"A am nae auld enough tae shave," Gray said** the same explanation he has given to the colonel at 439:14 and to the sergeant-major at 440:18

441:17–18 **a hull rising on Clyde or a hull going out of Clydemouth** a ship being built or a ship being launched. The River Clyde is in western Lowland Scotland, flowing by Glasgow into the Firth of Clyde, which opens into the Irish Sea a short distance from Northern Ireland. "Clydemouth" is a generic term meaning simply the mouth of the river or the firth.

441:21 **godless Sabbath hammering and sawing** The Grays, probably strict Presbyterians and unlike other present shipbuilders, refuse to work on Sunday: "Remember the sabbath day, to keep it holy" (Exodus 20:8).

441:27 **Whisht** Hush

441:28 **as mony a nail a day as yersel** as many nails in a day as you can

442:1 **John Wesley** the founder of Methodism

442:1–2 **not old enough by two years** two years too young

442:6 **in the parish house** buried in the church cemetery

442:8–9 **a Gray, a shipwright, has no business at an English war** Although armed Scottish resistance to English rule ended with the Battle of Culloden in 1746, many Scots maintained a fierce sense of independence from England.

442:17–18 **a medal, a bit of bronze on a crimson ribbon: a Victoria Cross** Great Britain's highest award for gallantry, available to all ranks; inaugurated in 1856 and made retrospective to the Crimean War

442:19–20 **while your uncle Simon was getting this bit of brass from the Queen** probably in the Boer War (1899–1903), and from Queen Victoria, who ruled from 1837–1901

442:24 **winna** will not

442:25 **gang** go along

443:4–5 **gazing south and eastward** toward the European continent

443:9 **Kinkeadbight** a certain bay (Faulkner's invention)

443:15 **Clydeside** the working-class districts of Glasgow, in which returning soldiers, dissatisfied with their prospects in "a land fit for heroes," staged a strike in January–February 1919. The strike was put down by troops called out by Lloyd George, and the district gained the name "Red Clydeside" (see *BBC Homepage History*). Although this strike occurred after the immediate present time of Alec Gray's first letter home, the episode may be how the area came to Faulkner's attention.

443:18–19 **Then they did not hear from him for seven months** his time in the penal battalion

444:4–5 **they were now well beyond Lamentations** We have been told Gray has a New Testament (442:31), but since Lamentations is in the Old Testament, Gray apparently has the entire Bible. The book of Lamentations consists of the prophet Jeremiah's bitter complaint about the condition of the Jews under Babylonian captivity.

444:13–14 **We ha a new sair-rgent-major too, A doot not?** We have a new sergeant-major too, I doubt not?

444:18 **Am auld enough tae shave noo** I'm old enough to shave now

444:24 **lap-robed** with a short blanket covering his lap and legs; once again, a return to the past tense

444:25 **motor** car

444:27 **Bapaume road** town some twenty kilometers south of Arras; often the site of heavy rains and resulting mud

444:27 **taking the ditch to pass** getting in the ditch to let the general's car go by

444:28 **"A's a cheery auld card," a voice says** "He's a cheerful old guy." As Michael Millgate has pointed out, the soldier is quoting from Siegfried Sassoon's "The General," in which a "cheery old card" of a general greeted his troops on their way to battle, but "Now the soldiers he smiled at are most of 'em dead," specifically because of his incompetent strategy (see "Faulkner on the Literature" 100).

445:1–2 **"Aweel," a third says, "thae awfficers wud gang tae thae war-r too, A doot not"** Oh well, the officers would go along to the war too, I doubt not

445:3–4 **"Why dinna they gang then?" a fourth says. "Thae war-r is no back that way"** Why don't they go along then? The war isn't back that way

445:8–10 **"A says tae me, a says: 'Fritz has a new gun that will carry to Par-ris,' a says, and A says tae him: ' 'Tis nawthin: a has one that will hit our Cor-rps Headquar-rters' "** "He says to me, he says: The Germans have a new gun that will fire as far as Paris, and I says to him: That's nothing: I have one that will hit our Corps Headquarters"; Fritz was the German nickname for *Friedrich* (Frederick), used by the Allies to refer to all Germans collectively, as well as to individual soldiers. Whether the gun in question was the "Big Bertha" or the "Long Max," the soldier is referring to the highly advanced (and terrifying) long-distance artillery developed by the Germans. The second soldier's black humor implies that any weapon might best be used against their own officers.

445:14 **They are in the trench** shift to present tense; see 437:21

445:25 **in the corpse glare** the flares portending death for those illuminated by them

445:27 **the next traverse** the barrier of earth alongside the trenches

445:28 **the fire step** the step or ledge in the trench from which soldiers fire their rifles

446:13 **duckboard** a board to lay across mud

446:17 **Blow your whistle, Sergeant-major!** The Officer commands the signal to assemble the troops, not knowing that the sergeant-major is dead.

446:18 **In the citation it told how Private Gray** shift to past tense; see 441:7

446:20 **N.C.O.'s** noncommissioned officers

446:27–29 **overcame the Officer and took from him his Very pistol and fired the colored signal which called for the attack Very pistol** = a flare gun carried by officers to send signals by shooting off a flare of a prearranged color. In one sense, this passage charges Gray and his companions with mutiny—disobeying orders, using force against a superior officer, sending an unauthorized signal, etc. In another sense, it describes precisely the kind of initiative and courage that culminate in effective and decisive action—heroism, in other words.

446:30–31 **or put down a barrage** launch heavy artillery fire, in this case a German defensive action

447:6 **when he was sitting up again** in the hospital, during convalescence

447:7–8 ***I have been sick but I am better now. I have a ribbon like in the box but not all red. The Queen was there*** the Distinguished Service Medal, available to all ranks. King George V, not a queen, was on the British throne during the Great War.

447:30 ***going for an officer*** trying to earn a higher rank

447:30–448:1 ***Never miscall your birth*** Never lie about where you came from

448:1 ***You are not a gentleman*** British Army tradition had reserved the ranks of commissioned officer for members of the aristocracy and squirearchy, or "country gentlemen." Only after battle had depleted the number of men suitable for officers' rank did the Army begin accepting men of the middle class into the officer corps—a temporary military expedient, which the civilian establishment did its best to ignore after the war.

448:5–6 **new tunic with the pips and ribbon and the barred cuffs pips** = shoulder insignia indicating rank. Gray has outfitted himself in an officer's uniform.

448:7–9 **He returned to Flanders in the spring, with poppies blowing in the churned beet- and cabbage-fields** Flanders is an area of northwestern Europe including parts of Belgium, France, and the Netherlands. It was the scene of the three devastating battles of Ypres (1914, 1915, 1917), the last of which (commonly known as "Passchendaele") resulted in the deaths of an estimated 250,000 men. The Flanders poppies were made famous by John McCrae's poem, "In Flanders Fields," written after the second Battle of Ypres in 1915. Related to the opium poppy, poppies flourish only when there is no other living vegetation to compete with them; they are thus traditionally associated with sleep and death.

448:14 ***and a voice said, Peter, raise thyself; kill—*** Acts 11:7: "And I heard a voice saying unto me, Arise, Peter; slay and eat"; God's word to Peter while he was on a mission to convert Gentiles as well as Jews. Gray presumably read the biblical passage on his last day in the penal battalion (during which time he tore the pages to light cigarettes), in a kind of *sortes bibliae,* "a religiously and culturally sanctioned practice of radical misprision—'mis-taking' the divine Word from its original Scriptural context and reinserting it, in a manner that itself seemed divinely ordained, into the narrative of one's own life" (see "Romantic Circles Praxis Series"). See also 455:13–15.

448:15 **batman** a British military officer's orderly or servant

448:17 **ranker** commissioned officer who has risen through the ranks from enlisted status

448:20 **like a mout be Haig hissel** "like he might be Haig himself." As part of the British Expeditionary Force sent to France, General Sir Douglas Haig became Commander-in-Chief of the British Expeditionary Force in 1915 and oversaw the bloody losses of the Somme and Passchendaele; he had a reputation as a stern, standoffish leader.

448:25–26 **It has lost** another shift to present tense to mark another significant stage in Gray's development

448:26 **subalterns** British military rank just below captain

448:31–32 **subaltern-captain** still holding the official rank of subaltern but now functioning as a captain

449:3 **trenching tool** a short-handled tool with a shovel blade set at right angles to the handle on one side, and a sharpened blade, like that of a pick, on the other

449:4 **Blawn—** blown

449:10 **Take his name, Sergeant** see 439:21

449:14 **010801 McLan, sir-r** see 439:7

449:15 **Replacement?** for a killed or wounded soldier; not fresh from battle

449:17–18 **Take his name, Sergeant. Rifle's filthy** Although Gray seems to repeat the kind of petty discipline that led him to the penal battalion and to murder, he is, in fact, administering appropriate discipline here. The first soldier should have been able to replace a lost trenching tool in four days, and the replacement has no excuse for standing for inspection carrying a filthy rifle.

449:19 **The sun is setting** see Introduction

449:23 **the captain** now officially promoted to that rank, called for by the losses in his battalion. Although Faulkner is careful not to locate Gray's experiences too specifically within the history of the war, such losses suggest the Passchendaele campaign in August–September 1917, in which the British armies suffered hundreds of thousands of casualties.

449:27 **Huns, sir-r** "Germans, sir." The Huns were a nomadic people who invaded Europe in the fourth and fifth centuries AD, with one famously barbarous leader, Attila. Their name was applied to the Germans as a derogatory and contemptuous epithet. The modern use of the term dates to the Boxer Rebellion (1899–1900); in despatching his troops to China, Kaiser Wilhelm II instructed them to behave like the Huns of old and to wreak vengeance ("let the Germans strike fear into the hearts, so he'll be feared like the Hun") (see *FirstWorldWar.com*).

449:27–28 **A ken their-r helmets** "I know (them by) their helmets" (which were rounded)

450:4 **Fix bayonets** Attach bayonets (to your rifles)

450:6 **Wull A stay wi thae hur-rt lad, Sair-rgent?** Will I stay with the hurt lad, Sergeant?

450:7–8 **"Nay," the sergeant says. "A'll tak's chance wi us. Forrard"** "No, he'll take his chance with the rest of us. Forward (march)"

450:13 **the bridgehead** a fortified position at the entrance to a bridge, used as a position of defense or as a stage for advance

450:17 **a short, guttural word** in German; perhaps "ach," uttered in disgust or frustration

450:22 **not a shot** because they have used bayonets

450:24 **a hand that tastes like brass** bloodied, either by his own or that of the man hushing him

450:32 **coalhod helmets** rounded, bell-shaped helmets, like those worn by coal miners; British ones were flat

451:4 **sappers' tools and explosive** Sappers—combat engineers—traditionally build covered trenches or dig tunnels by which troops may enter an enemy position, but they also build and repair fortifications and execute other field works. In this case, the squad with sappers' tools is presumably preparing to blow up the bridge, to prevent the further advance of Allied troops.

451:25–27 **something sears along his arm and across his ribs, dust puffs from the right side of the window** Gray has been shot. The dust is the result of the bullets from the machine gun's hitting the structure (mortar or stucco) in which Gray is temporarily housed, pulverizing it from his left to right in the pattern of the gunfire.

452:1–2 **that these troops wear khaki and that their helmets are flat** British troops

452:2–3 **there is no one to see** see 452:5

452:3 **when a party mounted** shift to past tense mid-sentence; see 441:7

452:5 **they thought that he was dead** Because he is found apparently lifeless by the advancing British troops, rather than by one of his own men, Gray is, presumably, the only member of his party who survives, unless the wounded man also survives. Farrell's Plate 15, and the associated prose, describes the heroism of 51st Division officers and men defending a bridgehead against the advancing Germans.

452:6 **the citation** the public notice of the award and the basis for it, listed in the *London Gazette*; see 455:23

452:24–25 **Gas cases? They don't send gas cases out again. They have to be cured** Gray has apparently recovered from the wound he incurred at 451:25–27 and has returned again to combat, where he has been gassed. Gray's gassing, given that he is still in hospital on 11 November 1918 (453:5–6), may have occurred either during the Third Battle of Ypres, or "Passchendaele" (July–November 1917), or during the great German offensive beginning in spring 1918, perhaps at Givenchy.

453:2 **almost white hair** While hair will normally turn gray or white with age, several things can accelerate this process, including great stress. Dermatologists believe that in cases of instantaneous whitening, persons probably have some white or gray hair mixed in with their pigmented hair, and, following a very stressful event, the pigmented hair selectively falls out, leaving only the white or gray hair. One of the most famous of these cases is that of Marie Antoinette upon learning of her death sentence (see Hanjani and Cymet).

453:4 **I'll meet you in Givenchy on Christmas Day** If Gray was gassed at Givenchy, his remark suggests that he believes no progress will have been made in the fighting during his convalescence. Givenchy-en-Gohelle, fourteen kilometers north of Arras and five kilometers northwest of Vimy Ridge, is the site of the cemetery and monument for the Canadians who died in the attack on Vimy Ridge on 12 April 1917.

453:5–6 **eleventh of November** 1918; Armistice Day, the formal end of the Great War

453:12–13 **I could hear a nightingale** The medical officer cheerfully looks forward to hearing the songbird as a sign of returning, perhaps romantic, life. Faulkner is surely also invoking John Keats's "Ode to a Nightingale," the bird in which

> . . . among the leaves hast never known,
> The weariness, the fever, and the fret
> Here, where men sit and hear each other groan;
> Where palsy shakes a few, sad, last gray hairs,
> Where youth grows pale, and spectre-thin, and dies;
> Where but to think is to be full of sorrow
> And leaden-eyed despairs,
> Where Beauty cannot keep her lustrous eyes,
> Or new Love pine at them beyond to-morrow. (22–30)

453:13–14 **He thumped Gray's chest. "Not much: just a bit of a murmur"** a diagnostic method to gauge the healing of Gray's lungs. The doctor listens for a hollow sound rather than a solid one, the latter of which would mean the lungs contain fluid.

453:24–25 **I could not—I did not . . .** I could not recognize you—I did not expect you

453:26 **You have two ribbons now** the Distinguished Service Medal and the Military Cross (see 446:18 and 447:7)

453:29–454:2 **Then Alec Gray reverted for an instant. Perhaps he had not progressed as far as he thought, or perhaps he had been**

climbing a hill, and the return was not a reversion so much as something like an avalanche waiting the pebble, momentary though it was to be Gray briefly considers rejoining the family's shipbuilding business, which takes him by surprise.

454:9 **No, I—** perhaps "No, I chose not to." Many combat veterans chose not to show off their veteran status by wearing their uniforms when they returned to civilian life. Young William Faulkner, who did not see active service during the war, bought a full RCAF officer's uniform and wore it around Oxford after his return from flight training in Canada (Blotner 1984; 66).

454:15 **ye should have—** worn your uniform home

454:17–19 **who had long since found out that no man has courage but that any man may blunder blindly into valor as one stumbles into an open manhole in the street** a silent contradiction of his father's earlier assertion "Ye hae shown courage" (454:14–15). He believes that acts of bravery are accidental.

454:23 **Bristol** a port on the west coast of England, just south of Wales

455:13–14 **We'll see what the Book will say** As Alec had done at 448:14, Matthew Gray here chooses a biblical passage apparently at random to guide a present course of action.

455:17–18 ***". . . and the captains of thousands and the captains of ten thousands . . . ["]* A paragraph of pride** Faulkner is not quoting from a clearly identifiable biblical text. Of several choices, the most relevant would appear to be I Samuel 8:12: "And he will appoint him captains over thousands, and captains over fifties; and *will set them* to ear his ground, and to reap his harvest, and to make his instruments of war, and instruments of his chariots." Other possibilities include Exodus 18:25, Numbers 31:14, Deuteronomy 1:15, and I Samuel 22:7. The failure to close the quotation marks after the italics makes ambiguous the speaker of the phrase "A paragraph of pride." Faulkner's typescripts show that the phrase should be understood as coming from the story's narrator, rather than from Matthew Gray.

455:19–20 **You will go to London, then?** The practice of *sortes bibliae* (see 448:14) would seem to be relatively congenial to those, including Scotch Presbyterians, who believe in predestination.

455:23 **M.C., D.S.M.** Military Cross, Distinguished Service Medal. The Military Cross is awarded to junior commissioned officers (not above a captain) for gallantry in the field, the Distinguished Service Order to officers with meritorious service during enemy combat who had been specifically mentioned in the dispatches by the Commander-in-Chief. Public notice of both appeared in the *London Gazette.* Those holding the Distinguished Service Order were allowed to list those initials after their name, and we do not know why Faulkner used "D.S.M." rather than "D.S.O."

455:24 **the Officers' Association** charity founded in 1919 to assist those who have retired from British military service and their widows and orphans; provides employment training, residential accommodation, and benevolent funding

455:29–30 **giving his coppers to blind and maimed in Piccadilly** giving pennies to the beggars in Piccadilly Circus, a famous traffic junction and meeting place in central London

456:3–4 **a gift of plate** a set of silverware or silverplated dishes

456:5–6 **he believed too firmly in the Empire to do that** Gray believes that the British Empire, for which he has fought, will in turn assist him in age or infirmity.

456:9 **the dead scenes of his lost and found life** the battlefields

456:10 **That was three years later** Assuming that Gray had been discharged in early 1919 and had spent three years at his employment, the year would be 1922; see also 431:9

456:13 **he did not bear eastward at once** that is, go directly to the battlefields

456:13 **Riviera** the northern coast of the Mediterranean, extending from France to Italy, and famous as a venue of the wealthy

456:16 **svelte kept women of all Europe** expensive prostitutes

456:25–26 **Conditions, the manager told him** Assuming Gray's battlefield tour took place in the autumn of 1922 and that he returned to London shortly thereafter, his dismissal occurs a bit early for postwar conditions to have thoroughly deteriorated. The recession began in earnest in Britain in 1924 when, for example, housing starts fell to an all-time low, there were numerous homeless and unemployed persons, and miners were in trouble because Germany was paying some of its reparations in coal. Gray's dismissal, like Whiteby's fate (457:1–3), suggests that those "gentlemen" without aristocratic family connections were the first to feel the effects of the coming economic decline.

457:14–18 ***Gentleman with social address and connections*** contacts in higher society

457:17 **the fleshpots of the West End** the bars, brothels, and denizens in Central London

457:18 **Birmingham and Leeds** visitors from the manufacturing towns in England's Midlands

457:23 **Surrey** one of London's Home Counties, south and east of the city

457:24 **on commission** a percentage of the sales rather than a salary; a dead-end job

457:30 **The man in the smoking jacket looks up** shift to the present tense; see 437:21

458:3 **HAWKERS** lower class of salesman, trying to peddle goods on commission

458:10 **In the fall he returned** the return to past tense

458:11–14 **Perhaps it was beyond any saying, instinct perhaps bringing him back to be present at the instant out of all time of the manifestation, apotheosis, of his life which had died again** Gray unconsciously returns to London for the ceremonies on the Day of Remembrance, marking the time that his "life" in the war "died" with the Armistice. At 11:00 A.M., 11 November, the formal end to World War I (and, later, World War II) is solemnized by military turnouts of the King's Guards in London. The center of these ceremonies is the Cenotaph, the national monument to the First World War dead, located in Whitehall, near the Houses of Parliament, Horse Guards Parade Grounds, and Westminster Abbey.

458:14 **he was there** among the diverse assembly at the Day of Remembrance; see also 458:11–14

458:16 **Household troops** troops that guard the royal household

458:17 **Guards in scarlet tunics** the famous Scots regiment that guards Buckingham Palace

458:18 **Church militant** Christian church on earth, as opposed to the Church triumphant in heaven; here, the Anglican clergy in full vestments ("stole and surplice")

458:18–19 **Prince defenders of God in humble mufti** other clergy, in civilian clothes

458:20 **shillings** unit of British currency; one-twentieth of a pound

458:22 **It is one of those spurious, pale days** In this paragraph, the verb tense shifts to present (458:22–459:2), reverts to past tense (459:3–10), and changes again to present tense (459:10), in which it remains through the entire remainder of the section (463:9). The rapid alteration of tenses here suggests that, as James G. Watson has it in another context, "multi-faceted events in time and place are presented with the semblance of simultaneity" (*Letters* 98–99).

458:31 **celluloid collar** a detachable collar made of celluloid, cheaper than a cloth one but more durable than paper

459:9 **frank or stubborn cast-offs** old clothes the wearers of which had attempted to darn, patch, fit, and clean—so "stubborn" ones—or those "frank" ones that have been allowed to deteriorate

459:11–12 **that echo as of bitter and unheard laugh[t]er of a hunchback** The typescripts indicate that "laugher" is a typographical error; the hunchback's laughter is Quasimodo's self-mockery and-loathing, in Victor Hugo's *The Hunchback of Notre Dame* (*Notre Dame de Paris,* 1831; English tr., 1833).

459:14 **the embankment** the Victoria Embankment on the Thames. Extending from Westminster Bridge to Blackfriars Bridge, it was built beginning in 1856 primarily to cover the great sewer draining London to a point below the city. Now a park, the areas near and under the bridges along its length were formerly the haunt of the homeless, partly because of the shelter provided and partly, one supposes, because the sewers underneath the pavement provided some warmth. George Orwell, in *Down and Out in London and Paris* (1933), describes life on the Embankment.

459:25 **a shell** Although according to Boswell, a "shell" is Scots for a glass for serving whisky, the shells in this passage are military ordnance.

459:27 **They'd give him the shell, all right** presumably to kill himself

459:31 **Mons** The Mons battle, beginning on 23 August 1914, the first engagement of the British and Germans on the Western Front

459:31 **dispatch rider** a messenger, not a combatant

460:5 **so we could—** sell it

460:8 **the Brighton Road** running south from Westminster through South London and its suburbs to Brighton Beach; the site for lower-middle-class shops and services

460:22 **everything sounded different since** since his blinding

460:24–25 **I would touch the scar and it would be like I—** was before the war

461:8 **her other hand** her right hand

461:17 **buggering off** sneaking away

461:26 **Courtplaster** cloth, usually silk, coated with adhesive and used to cover superficial skin cuts or wounds

462:16 **they turn their faces quickly aside, save the blind man** in embarrassment, or deference

462:19 **Yer stones is ot** "Your stones are hot," with which to press the suit

463:10 **demobilized** discharged from military service

463:26 **the colors and pattern of a regiment** see 433:33

464:9 **matches** see Introduction

"Crevasse"

"Crevasse" is not so much a short story as what Stephen Crane would call "An Episode of War." The episode features a literal and figurative descent into the underworld, a metaphorical death followed by an ambivalent rebirth. Thus, in high modernist fashion, the story implicitly recalls the *topos* prominent in texts of classical mythology. The central character, the Captain, is identified by his rank only, and only one named character appears in the story. Faulkner presents the action exclusively in the present tense, and the narrative is surely among the most tightly unified in place, time, and action of any of his stories. A barren No-Man's Land between the German and Allied forces, the landscape into which the men have wandered is not being contested, for it cannot be held; it cannot support structure, cultivation, or even—as the men discover too late—tentative exploration on foot. The story begins when the military "party" enters this alien landscape, continues to describe their harrowing experience in which almost half of them are killed in a cave-in, and ends when the survivors have returned to the "life" of the war itself. Those fortunate enough to escape from the chalky cavern (and inadvertent tomb) are, apparently, grateful for what meager hope remains to them. Their survival results from both random fortune and the clear-headedness of the Captain.

The cave-in narrative probably owes a good deal to Henri Barbusse's *Under Fire: The Story of a Squad* (Millgate, "Faulkner on the Literature" 100–01), and Fred A. Farrell's *The 51st Division War Sketches* may have provided a visual source. In composing and arranging *These 13*, Faulkner extracted "Crevasse" from an early typescript of "Victory," in which it appeared as an episode in the career of Alec Gray. The manuscripts of the parent story might date to 1926 or 1927, and there is no evidence that "Crevasse" existed as a separate story prior to Faulkner's work on *These 13*. Faulkner's manuscript notation "Crevasse" appears on page 22 of the 51-page typescript of "Victory" and concludes on page 36 of this typescript. Thus, the narrative we now know as "Crevasse" originally occurred between the scene in "Victory" in which the commissioned Alec Gray inspects his troops (448:25–449:18) and the scene in which Gray and his men capture the German machine gun post and secure the entrance to the village for the advancing Allied troops (449:19–452:5).

The relationship between "Victory" and "Crevasse," therefore, has often dominated the discussion of the latter story. The two have been inevitably linked in critical analyses, and although many have discussed the story's placement in both *These 13* and *Collected Stories* (where it follows "Victory" as the third story in "The Wasteland"), Faulkner's choice to publish "Crevasse" as a separate story has seldom been understood or respected. Edmond Volpe, for example, regrets the excision of "Crevasse" from "Victory," arguing that the episode helps to explain how Alec Gray's war experiences contribute significantly to his unsuccessful post-war experiences (170–71). Lisa Paddock disagrees, contending that "Crevasse" was quite rightly cut from "Victory," "where it would have been not only gratuitous but extraneous," and suggests that "Alec Gray's life would have followed a far different course had he undergone the ghastly experience of the troops in 'Crevasse' " (23). Judith Bryant Wittenberg focuses on the effects Faulkner achieved in *These 13* by revising "Crevasse" out of "Victory" to create "a version at once more restrained and more horrifying, and in so doing enhanced the role of 'Crevasse' as providing an effective reminder of the section's first story. Both the disorientation experienced by the soldiers at the outset and their terrified responses to the death-in-life represented by the Senegalese corpses amplify the reader's sense of Alec Gray's nightmarish war experiences as depicted in 'Victory' " (284).

Some critics have seen a profound sense of gender anxiety, perhaps misogyny, in this story, and others have emphasized the apparent irony and despair of the final scene. Anne Goodwyn Jones, for example, elaborates on what she sees as the sexual symbolism of the deadly cave into which the soldiers fall during the central incident: "Here, in a worst possible case, that woman shaped space is not even a moist depression: it is a horrible cave filled with the bodies of dead soldiers." Throughout the story, she notes, "Faulkner uses language that rather explicitly connects the landscape with the woman's body." In the end, the men "perform their own birthing, scraping and scrabbling at the dirt" (Skei, *William Faulkner's* 46); Noel Polk agrees and notes that "they are merely trading one kind of death for another, a physical for a spiritual" ("William Faulkner's 'Carcassonne' " 38). James Ferguson cites the same passage (*CS* 471) as one of the "low places" in Faulkner's writing which suggest "chaos, corruption, death—and female sexuality" (65). Of the story's final scene, Skei says, "the world of the living outside the cave cannot offer any hope of rebirth; and if the soldiers have any dreams, they are dreams of survival. The war-scorched landscape is moribund, and summer seems far away" (*Reading* 205). The Captain, however, thinks "soon it will be summer, and the long days," arguably a more optimistic response to the harrowing experience. The other survivors kneel while one of them intones "monotonously" from a Bible, and the wounded man's "gibberish" sounds the final note (474). These competing attitudes suggest the complexity of the situation. The Captain's comparatively positive attitude is juxtaposed with the men's recourse to ritual and with the wounded man's cries. If the descent into the bowels of the earth is a brief visit to a metaphorical hell, then the soldiers' reemergence is a kind of salvation. While Faulkner grants the wounded man the final cry, his inclusion of the other perspectives argues against a simplistic reading.

465:1 **barrage** heavy artillery fire, a regular firing of guns with the shells dropping along a line, usually used to hold back attackers. The party has gotten behind enemy lines.

465:10–11 **upon clumps of bitten poplars** Poplars are large, rapidly growing trees, so in this instance, such clumps indicate trees partially destroyed by fighting. This passage reflects Faulkner's direct observation in his walking tour of the battle scene of the great German offensive of spring 1918. On 3 October 1925, he wrote his mother: "Compiegne and Montdidier were 8 miles behind the front for 3 years, so they are not damaged much. But beyond that eight miles it looks as if a cyclone had passed over the whole world at about 6 feet from the ground. Stubs of trees, and along the main roads are piles of shell cases and unexploded shells and wire and bones that the farmers dig up" (*Selected Letters* 28). For a striking illustration of a scene on the road to Arras, see Farrell, Plate 16.

465:13–14 **the churned soil, among scraps of metal and seething hunks of cloth** battlefield upon which lie the spent machinery of war and the dead bodies of soldiers

465:15 **It** the party

465:15 **comes to a canal** Although Faulkner seems to have quite deliberately avoided locating this story in a particular area, the identification of the Zouave soldiers at 472:17 indicates a site in the Beaumont Hamel region, defended at the Battle of the Somme by troops from Newfoundland (see the subaltern's error at 469:29). There are many drainage canals in the area, and the landscape features the unusual topography described throughout the story.

466:3 **The captain, the subaltern and the sergeant** **captain** = a military officer above the rank of lieutenant and below that of major; **subaltern** = a British commissioned officer of a grade inferior to a captain; **sergeant** = a noncommissioned officer of the grade above the rank of corporal. This trio constitutes the party's chain of command.

466:6 **pallid strata** the pale layers of chalk in horizontal sheets, exposed through weathering

466:7 **speaks the men to their feet** orders the men to resume marching

466:21 **bonnet** hat; a soft cap worn by Scots with the kilt; the wounded man's delirious reference to his bandage

466:25 **A's pickin at's bandage, sir-r** "He's picking at his bandage, sir;" the accent identifies him as a Scot

467:1–5 **They gain the crest of the ridge. The ridge slopes westward into a plateau slightly rolling. Southward, beneath its dun pall, the barrage still rages; westward and northward about the shining empty plain smoke rises lazily here and there above clumps of trees** As high ground was always heavily defended, this passage suggests that the Germans have retreated.

467:6 **powder** gunpowder

467:9–11 **in a high, thin voice; "it's houses burning! They're retreating! Beasts! Beasts!"** evidence of the subaltern's youth and inexperience as a soldier; the German practice of destroying things rather than leaving them behind for the enemy's use shocks him.

467:15 **"For-rard"** "Forward"; the accent identifies him as a Scot

467:16 **slope arms** pick up their rifles to carry them with the butt of the rifle resting in the right palm and the stock of the rifle resting on the right shoulder

467:17 **gorselike grass** prickly grass; gorse is a spiny shrub native to Europe

467:18 **fall to slatting** make vertical patterns in the air

467:22 **close up** resume their regular interval in the march

467:25 **a broad shallow depression** see 467:30–31

467:30–31 **"Queer," the subaltern says. "What do you fancy could have made it?"** as we discover, a cave-in of a tunnel (the trenches of war) beneath the battlefield

468:5–8 **the ridge sheers sharply downward stratum by stratum of pallid eroded chalk. A shallow ravine gashes its crumbling yawn abruptly across their path** The landscape here, as well as at 468:31–469:6, describes a *karst,* a terrain formed by the natural acidic action of groundwater on limestone. Such terrain is often characterized by sinkholes (the "vaguely circular basins") and barren ground, often with caves beneath.

468:12 **shelving wall** sloping wall of the ravine

468:15 **debouched** moved from a close, narrow area into an open, wider place or space; military term taken from the French *déboucher,* "to go out of the mouth"

468:31–469:6 **The valley, the depression, strays vaguely before them. They can see that it is a series of overlapping, vaguely circular basins formed by no apparent or deducible agency. Pallid grass bayonets saber at their legs, and after a time they are again among old healed scars of trees to which there cling sparse leaves neither green nor dead, as if they too had been overtaken and caught by a hiatus in time, gossiping dryly among themselves though there is no wind. The floor of the valley is not level. It in itself descends into vague depressions, rises again as vaguely between its shelving walls** see 468:5–8

469:7–8 **whitish knobs of chalk** see 470:6–7

469:10 **Jolly** splendid, excellent

469:16–17 **"Topping hole-up for embusqué birds and such," the subaltern says** "a great place for snipers to wait"; ***embusqué*** = French for "ambush." Perhaps an echo of Hemingway's "Chapter IV" from *In Our Time,* in which a barricade is described as "absolutely topping" (*The Complete Short Stories* 83). Almost certainly a marker of the subaltern's class status; he speaks with no Scots burr but with upper-class diction and slang (see also 469:10 and 470:29).

469:21 **"But no birds here," the subaltern says. "No insects even"** The Germans used chlorine gas in the March 1915 attack (see 472:19), and the ground is now highly acidic and will support only the hardiest of plant growth and not even much of that. Unlike persistent toxic substances such as lead or mercury, chlorine gas is unstable. Upon contact with moisture, it reacts to form both hydrochloric acid and hypochlorous acid, chemicals that will "corrode" moist lung tissue and cause it to blister. Even though chlorine gas is heavier than air, because it is a gas, it disperses over a large area in a matter of a few days, rendering it relatively harmless to living things (a fact that the Germans used to their tactical advantage). Thus, it is very unlikely that it would persist long enough to enter an environmental food chain. It would do its major damage within a few days; however, the effects of its presence would linger for a period of time, especially in a war zone (see "ATSDR—ToxFAQs"; "Chemical Warfare"; "Trenches on the Web").

469:29 **Ross** the Ross Rifle, named for Sir Charles A. F. L. Ross, a Scottish-born engineer and soldier and manufactured in Canada, the standard weapon with which Canadian troops were equipped at their arrival in France in late 1914. The rifle was too long and too heavy for combat use, and it tended to jam during rapid fire; hence, the Canadian troops began discarding it, if they could, after the battle of Ypres, during which it proved quite unreliable. The Ross was abandoned in 1915 in favor of the British Lee-Enfield (see "Ross Rifle").

469:30 **"French," the captain says; "1914"** the captain's correction of the subaltern's error at 469:29; identifies the weapon as French, probably a Lebel, made in 1914 and used when Ypres fell (see 472:19)

469:32 **The bayonet is still attached to the barrel** indicating that the rifle was dropped during combat

469:34 **chalky knobs** see 470:6–7

470:6–7 **its earth-stained eyesockets and its unbottomed grin** one of the "chalky knobs," or human skulls

470:12 **All in the same position, do you notice, sir?** see 472:19

470:13–14 **Queer way to bury chaps: sitting down. Shallow, too** The subaltern does not realize that these men have not been buried but are sitting where they died; see 472:19

470:18 **"Dinna stop to gi's sup water," one of the bearers says. "A'll drink walkin"** "Don't stop to give him a drink of water. He'll drink walking"; i.e., "Let's get out of here"

470:24 **What's this?** The captain notices the unusual and awkward attempt to give the wounded man a drink.

470:27 **Wind-up** Nerves are high; They're on edge

470:29 **Feel it myself** "I am, too"; the clipped diction another marker of his upper-class status

471:8 **Then a crack springs like a sword slash** the story's first title passage

471:14 **cake** clot of dirt

471:25 **A'm no dead! A'm no dead!** "I'm not dead! I'm not dead!" With the earth collapsing, the delirious wounded man seems to believe he is being buried alive.

472:1 **pocket torch** small flashlight (see Calvin Brown 201)

472:1–4 **"McKie?" the captain says. For reply the sergeant turns the flash upon his own face. "Where's Mr. McKie?" the captain says. "A's gone, sir-r," the sergeant says in a husky whisper** The captain inquires after his second in command, the subaltern McKie who has previously been identified only by his rank, only to learn that he is dead ("gone").

472:8 **Twelve missing. We'll have to dig fast** The captain assumes that the missing men are buried under the avalanche of dirt and immediately starts a rescue effort (see 473:4–5).

472:17 **skeletons in dark tunics and bagging Zouave trousers** The French government asked for Moroccan volunteers after the French Conquest of Algeria in 1830. The first regiments were raised from volunteers of the Zouagha tribe (hence, the name "Zouave")

on 1 October 1830. They formed an elite unit, and their spectacular uniforms, consisting of black tunics and baggy scarlet trousers, and drills were such that Zouave units performed on stages around the world, inspiring many militia units, particularly in the United States, to imitate both uniform and drill (*Probert Encyclopaedia*).

472:19 **Senegalese troops of the May fighting of 1915** refers to the second Ypres offensive and places the party's location. Ypres was taken by the German army at the beginning of the war, but the British regained the town. The Germans made their first poison gas attack on Moroccan and Senegalese troops near Langemarck on 31 March 1915, an attack that developed into the Second Battle of Ypres, 22 April–25 May. This marked the first French use of black troops in combat. In April 1915, the Germans launched another offensive. A preliminary bombardment was followed by the use of chlorine gas against the French and Algerian troops defending an area north of the town. Heavy fighting and gas attacks continued until 25 May 1915 (see Hossack).

472:24 **trenching tools** short-handled tools with shovel blades set at right angles to the handle on one side, and a sharpened blade, like that of a pick, on the other; in this case, to dig for survivors

473:4–5 **There is nothing, no arm, no hand, in sight. The air is clearing slowly. "We'll get on," the captain says** With no sign of life in the pile of earth, the captain assumes the missing twelve soldiers dead and abandons his earlier hope of digging for them (see 472:8 and 472:23–24).

473:10 **"The cave-in threw us forward," the captain says** The captain confers with the sergeant, his new second in command, now that the subaltern has been buried alive.

473:21–22 **The air grows heavier; soon they are trotting, gasping, then the air grows lighter** "heavier" as the men near the rotted corpses and "lighter" after they have passed them

473:28–29 **He shows them the fissure through which air seeps in small, steady breaths** the story's second title passage

474:20 **After you, sir-r** a deference to the captain's superior rank

474:21 **Out wi ye, man!** vernacular repetition of his order at 474:19

"Turnabout"

"Turnabout," one of Faulkner's most popular stories and the best-known of his World War I fictions, has elicited a good deal of commentary and a wide range of critical judgments over the years. Set, most likely, in Dunkirk in World War I, the story concentrates on two pairs of servicemen, the American fliers Captain Bogard and Lieutenant McGinnis, and the British midshipmen Claude Hope and Ronnie Boyce Smith. Puzzled to account for Claude's drunken behavior, Bogard learns that Midshipman Hope is assigned to an unusual vessel, one on which he cannot berth at night. McGinnis and some of the other Americans are contemptuous of Hope, but Bogard displays a paternal and protective attitude toward him. When he and McGinnis take Hope along on a night bombing raid in their Handley Page bomber, the young Englishman is volubly appreciative of the novelty and danger of the expedition. McGinnis, believing that Hope knows little or nothing of actual combat (and perhaps displaying an Irish-American antagonism toward the English) mocks the boy in several ways. The airmen reach their target and release their bombs, and Hope watches, afterward anxiously calling out "Bomb." When Bogard lands the plane at the airfield, the Americans are astonished to discover that Hope has been trying to tell them about an unexploded bomb, lodged in the plane's undercarriage. Like Cadet Bessing of Faulkner's first published short story, "Landing in Luck" (1919), Bogard has managed to land a radically threatened plane, without being aware of the danger.

Impressed with Bogard's hospitality and skill, Hope arranges for the American to accompany him and Ronnie on one of their own raids. And now Bogard discovers precisely what the young Englishmen do that drives them to their nightly intoxication. They operate Coastal Motor Boats, high-riding launches carrying torpedoes under them. The midshipmen aim their craft directly at an enemy target, release the torpedo ahead of them, and then veer quickly away. They are constantly at risk, from German mines, enemy fire, or their own inability to get out of the way of the torpedo. As in the previous day's flight, the torpedo, like the bomb, fails to release the first time, and Bogard, literally sick with fear, can only barely comprehend the skill and courage the young men show in dealing with the crisis. Meanwhile, the torpedo launches successfully on the second effort and detonates the freighter, while Hope, Ronnie, and their crew escape the fire of an enemy cruiser and return to port. Thus, the "turnabout" is complete: the older Americans inadvertently escape disaster while the insouciant young Englishmen cope consciously and effectively with an equipment malfunction that threatened their vessel and their lives. No wonder they drink.

While novice readers of Faulkner may be inclined to appreciate the relative simplicity, directness, and moral posture of "Turnabout," professional critics are more skeptical, and usually divided. For some of the latter, the story is *too* neat, too perfect a reversal or inversion of plot, with corresponding contrasts of nationality, age, and attitude. "Turnabout," Hans Skei writes, "is close to being a formula story, which may be part of the explanation why critics have not found it to be of the highest merit." Pointing to Faulkner's immediate success in selling the story to the high-paying *Saturday Evening Post* and to Hemingway's choice of it for *Men at War,* he concludes that the story was "without doubt a great success as far as money, prestige, and popularity are concerned" but finally finds redemption in the story's last paragraphs, where he says some of Faulkner's "more general moral concerns" become prominent (*Story Writer* 73, 74). Edmond Volpe, by contrast, finds this ending "pure Hollywood" but the story itself a "satisfying tour de force: dramatic, intriguing, and exciting" (184). Robert Harrison, too, disdains the ending: " 'Turnabout' is a fine story, yet it is almost ruined by its closing paragraph. . . . Bogard's display of childish bravado is an embarrassment to both traditions from which it springs: anti-war propaganda and the pulp flying story" (98). In James Ferguson's view, the characterization of Bogard, "sensitive, quiet, controlled, aware . . . gives the work the kind of solidity that most commercial fiction lacks" (100).

Frederick Karl calls "Turnabout" "a considerable contribution to war fiction [that] deserves to be resurrected" (413). Karl also connects the material of the story with Faulkner's own labors within his chosen profession: "Here he was historian of a particular sensibility which would otherwise be lost amidst traditional heroics. There was also the quiet of their activity, the fact so few people seemed aware of these men's sacrifice, and the further fact that their work consumed their lives—they died or barely survived by day and then drank themselves into oblivion at night. It was a cycle Faulkner recognized" (461).

"Turnabout" had its origins in a story Faulkner heard from Robert Lovett in New York late in 1931. Lovett, who had been in Dunkirk with the Royal Naval Air Service, described the bravado, courage, and nightly dissipation of the young British sailors who operated the Coastal Motor Boats, aiming their light and virtually defenseless torpedo craft against German vessels. Faulkner, according to Ben Wasson, was quite taken with their story and crafted "Turnabout" soon after hearing Lovett's account (see Blotner, 1974 732–734; also Harrison 97). The story was published 5 March 1932 in the *Saturday Evening Post* as "Turn About," under which title Faulkner also collected it in *Doctor Martino.* In *Collected Stories,* entitled "Turnabout," it appears as the fourth story in "The Wasteland" section. "Turnabout" is also the basis for *Today We Live,* a much different version of the story directed by Howard Hawks and starring Joan Crawford, Gary Cooper, Robert Young, and Franchot Tone. The film premiered in Oxford on 12 April 1933. Hemingway chose the story for inclusion in his anthology, *Men at War* (1942), and the story remains popular with anthologists in general and with beginning readers of Faulkner in particular. Faulkner was still engaged with the story when he appeared at West Point in April 1962, less than three months before his death. Speaking of Bogard's rage in the final scene of the story, he said. "Any soldier would feel that toward the brass safe back in the dugouts and the chateaux that didn't have to run those little boats, or didn't have to ride the aircraft low enough to bomb the chateau" (*Faulkner at West Point* 75).

475:1 **pink Bedfords** corduroy made in Bedford, England, and used in the British military's officer's uniforms; Robert Harrison observes that, with the details at 475:3 and 7, this is "What every well-dressed young air service officer was wearing in 1918 London" (98).

475:3 **long London-cut skirts** see 475:1; finely tailored, stylish uniform coat

475:3–4 **Sam Browne** Sam Browne belt, part of the uniform worn by commissioned officers of the British Army and named for Sir Samuel James Browne (1824–1901). The belt also has a supporting strap that passes diagonally from the left hip up over the right shoulder and down across the back to the left hip. Browne designed the shoulder strap to help carry the weight of a sword or pistol holster. Having lost his left arm in the British attempt to quell Indian uprisings in Punjab in 1857, Browne had difficulty drawing his sword one-handed. The belt's accommodation of a holster allowed pistols to be carried more safely, without the risk of accidental discharge.

475:7 **Savile Row** see 475:1; the name of a street in London known for its upscale tailoring establishments

475:8 **ordnance belt** the Sam Browne belt at 475:34 (Harrison 98)

475:9–10 **the pilot's wings on his breast were just wings** His insignia was not overly ornamental.

475:10 **the ribbon beneath them was a good ribbon** according to Harrison, the ribbons attached to medals "awarded only for acts of valor in the face of the enemy," including the Victoria Cross and Distinguished Service Cross (99)

475:14–15 **not Phi Beta Kappa exactly, but Skull and Bones perhaps, or possibly a Rhodes scholarship** intellectual honor societies, from the United States, Yale University, and Oxford University, respectively; Bogard apparently has an elite, but not pretentious, education and air.

476:5 **M.P.'s** Military Police (officers)

476:16 **Cheer-o** abbreviated "cheerio," British slang for goodbye

476:16 **Name's not Beatty, I hope** Sir David Beatty, later 1st Earl Beatty (1871–1936), at the onset of the war one of the youngest admirals in the Royal Navy and succeeding as commander of the Grand Fleet in December 1916 (see French); in other words, "my boss"

476:22–24 **he wore the pink breeches, the London boots, and his tunic might have been a British tunic save for the collar** dressed very fashionably, although in a high-collared American coat as opposed to the shawl lapels of the British uniform (Harrison 99)

476:25 **eggs** kids; brats

477:18–19 **You mean to tell me they use officers just to—** run errands?

478:2 **'sure you** I assure you

478:4 ***pavé*** French for pavement, street

478:5–6 **Visiting lads jolly well deserve decent field to play on, what?** Claude's rhetorical question likens the British troops in France to a visiting sports team.

478:23–24 **He'll just call it a thrush or a robin or something** Presumably the American M.P. is parodying the British expression "lark," meaning spree or adventure, which Claude must use habitually (see 486:20, 502:4).

478:33 **this egg here laying—** this guy lying in the gutter

479:22 **a copy of their articles of war—** sentence continues at 479:24; see 479:23

479:23 **King's Regulations** military code of conduct in Britain and the Commonwealth; Queen's Regulations when a woman is the sovereign

479:27–28 **His Majesty's wet nur—** "nurse"; an insult to the King and to Claude

479:29 **That'll do, corporal** "That's enough out of you." A corporal ranks above private first class and below sergeant; Bogard outranks him and so can dismiss him, even though they are in different branches of the service.

480:22 **Captain Bogard's driver? I'll take care of Mr. Hope** The request for the car and driver identifies himself and the Englishman by name to the policeman and to us.

480:31 **aerodrome** the military air base. Before the arrival of a large contingent of American troops (and before America entered the war), Americans shared bases with the French and British. "The Americans assigned to [a] British or French airfield shared the facilities with the veteran Allied pilots. After the trench lines had solidified, the Allied personnel at these airfields improved the poor conditions with permanent barracks possessing such comforts as heated running water, stoves, gas or electrical interior lighting, and mess halls that prepared hot meals in an atmosphere reminiscent of hunting clubs" (Durden). New American airfields, on the other hand, "usually consisted of tents and corrugated tin buildings in any area level enough to allow aircraft to take off and land" (Durden). Harrison locates this one near Dunkirk (99).

481:4–6 **embroidered with a club insignia which Bogard recognized to have come from a famous preparatory school** Claude seems to have been a cricket player at a prestigious boarding school like Eton (see 478:5–6, 502:18–19), or another famous enough for an American to recognize.

481:10 **straight as a bird dog** immediately, and in a straight line, like a dog stalking prey

481:23 **limey** American slang for a British person; "an abbreviation of *limejuicer*, a U.S. term derived from the practice of serving lime juice on British ships to prevent scurvy" (Fergusson 130)

481:29–30 **You mean, there's a male marine auxiliary to the Waacs?** WAAC is the acronym for the Women's Army Auxiliary Corps, volunteers who moved into France in March 1917 and formally under the command of the British Army; they assisted with "unglamorous tasks on the lines of communication: cooking and catering, storekeeping, clerical work, telephony and administration, printing, motor vehicle maintenance" (Baker). The speaker calls Claude an assistant to women's work, a double insult, compared to the manly work the pilots do.

482:16 **color was high** red-faced from drink

482:19 **Won't you chaps join—** me (in a drink)?

483:1 **beaver** a simple game in which players see a bearded man, a "beaver," and claim a point, once scored as tennis is; see 483:3 and 491:18–19

483:3 **No beaver?** a *double entendre* to the Americans, who hear a sexual pun, but not to Claude

483:4 **basket masts** not single-pole masts but cage masts; a new kind of mast in the Great War "designed to take multiple direct hits from enemy fire without collapsing. One drawback to this design was its flexibility, which gave the spotters a wild ride in heavy seas or when the guns were fired" (Hartwell)

483:11 **She's German. Interned. Tramp steamer** an enemy ship with no regular route or ports but instead trading where it can, that has been confined to port by the Allies

483:11 **Foremast** the forward lower-mast of a ship

483:19–20 **You and Ronnie run about in the launch, playing beaver. H'm'm. That's nice. Did you ever pl—** play beaver with anyone else? play beaver with a woman? (see 483:3)

483:23–24 **Has yours and Ronnie's boat got a yellow stern?** an implication that they are cowards ("yellow")

484:5–6 **Here we are, spending our money and getting shot at by the clock, and it's not even our fight** These Americans have enlisted before the United States joined the war (on 3 July 1917). The fact that the pilots are flying Handley Page airplanes (British bombers; see 486:33) supports this interpretation; Harrison notes that beginning in March 1917 the Handley Page squadrons at Dunkirk "carried out extensive night raids against the submarine and seaplane bases in Belgium, the railway network of France and Flanders, and the Flanders bases of the big Gotha bombers used for the raids on England" (99).

484:7–8 **these limeys that would have been goose-stepping twelve months now if it hadn't been—** these Brits would have been marching like Germans for a year if it hadn't been for us (see 481:23)

484:9 **Liberty Loan** introduced in 1917, a savings bond that helped to finance the Great War by moving private funds into the hands of the government; also, the series of propaganda campaigns begun by U.S. Secretary of the Treasury William G. McAdoo to promote their sale

484:10 **—taking** treating

484:15 **Jenny** the Curtiss JN, produced first in Canada and used to train the pilots of the British, Canadian, and U.S. armies (Harrison 48)

484:20 **out front** In the Handley Page O/400 (see 486:33), "the nose gunner's pit was located immediately forward of the cockpit (Harrison 99), which gave him "a wide field of fire, but his position was rather uncomfortable" (Gustin).

484:20 **Lewis** a Lewis machine gun, located on the Handley Page in the nose and behind the wings (Harrison)

484:22 **channel-marker light** a light on a buoy indicating the depth of the water, or the route that ships should take

485:7 **Switzerland had been spoiled by 1914** "The tripwire that set off the century's first global conflict was Austria's declaration of war against Serbia on July 28, 1914, a month after Archduke Franz Ferdinand (the heir to the Austro-Hungarian throne) was assassinated in Sarajevo by a Serbian fanatic. A war between Austria and Serbia meant a war between Austria and Russia—Serbia's traditional ally. That meant war between Russia and Germany. And that meant war between Germany and France. And that meant war between Germany and Great Britain. In a flash, the whole continent was at war" ("Europe in 1914"). Although Switzerland officially stayed out of the fighting, its location between Austria-Hungary, Germany, Italy, and France made it difficult to reach and an unsafe place to visit—hence, the "spoiling" of Claude's travel plans.

485:10–11 **had got pretty high** that is, had gone high up in the mountains

485:24 **togs** in this case, flying clothes

485:26–28 **a vague rank of short banks of flickering blue-green fire suspended apparently in mid-air** Since many of the Handley Page runs took place at night, the planes would be lined up on the dark tarmac and appear invisible except for the flames from the exhaust stacks of the engines (see 484:5–6), which Harrison describes as a full twelve feet off the ground (99).

485:30 **Sidcott suit** one-piece coverall lined thinly with fur and airproof silk, to wear while flying

486:3 **Cold upstairs** Harrison explains that at 20,000 feet, the temperature "would be well below zero" and "death from exposure could be measured in hours" (100).

486:5 **a do** a party; Claude's typical sort of understatement

486:8 **teatime** traditionally in Britain, a light meal taken at 4 PM

486:20 **Lark** see 478:23–24

486:26–27 **Coffee makes such a confounded stain on the wings** when you vomit it up—another jab at Claude

486:33 **Handley-Page** a large bomber manufactured by the British, "a big twin-engined biplane that carried a crew of four and a payload of sixteen 112-lb. bombs." Planes of this make entered service in

November 1916; because of their large fuel tanks, they could fly for up to eight hours. The O series also included the Handley Page O/400, which was introduced in 1917 (Harrison 99).

486:34 **Pullman coach** a large and luxurious railway carriage used as a sleeping car, named after its inventor, George Pullman (1831–97); the comparison provides another indication of the Handley Page's size (see 486:33).

487:3 **cruiser** warship used in the protection of commerce. The Handley Page (see 486:33) had a wingspan of 100 feet, length of 62 feet 10¼ inches, and height of 22 feet. The largest of the armored cruisers in the British Fleet were only 60 feet across, but were substantially longer than the airplane (Milford).

487:9 **Big lark, eh? Buzzard, what?** McGinnis ridicules Claude in the same way the American M.P. does at 478:23–24.

487:20 **Not overside. Don't spew it overside** Don't vomit over the side of the airplane

487:22–23 **It'll blow back in Bogy's and my face. Can't see. Bingo. Finished. See?** Along with predicting that Claude will vomit, McGinnis is also imitating his clipped style of speech: "We can't fly the plane with your puke in our eyes, and we'll crash."

487:26 **Just duck your head and let her go** vomit inside the plane

487:28–29 **the front pit** the nose gunner's place (Harrison 100); see 484:20

487:34 **Cut** hurry

488:25 **the drum** the container of cartridges for the machine gun (Harrison 100)

489:1 **unload** drop the bombs

489:2 **Maybe in the dark—** he won't be able to see anything

489:10 **bomb toggles** the controls that drop the bombs, "situated below and behind the cockpit" (Harrison 100)

489:10–11 **the searchlights found them** used from the ground to illuminate enemy aircraft at night

489:18 **watching the pinpoint swing into the sights** a "complex instrument" to help the pilot account for "altitude, airspeed, wind drift, and wind velocity" that, according to Harrison, Bogard is not using properly but "merely as a rude pointing device, like a shotgun sight" (101)

489:28 **it** combat; see 489:31

489:29–30 **looking back to pick up the rest of the flight** locating the other planes on the mission with them

489:31 **it** the bombing run, with its anti-aircraft fire

489:33 **the office** the cockpit

489:34 **the colored pistol** a Very flare (signaling) gun, firing white flares to mean "Return to aerodrome" (Harrison 101)

490:3 **I counted all four of them** the other planes on the mission

490:5 **bomb release** the mechanism that lets the bomb go from the plane

490:13–14 **Hun channel group on top of us in thirty minutes** German fighter group patrolling the English Channel. Harrison argues that the time frame suggests "their objective must have been no further distant than Antwerp" (101).

490:18–19 **the noise of the still-unthrottled engines on either side of the fabric walls** "The Handley Page fuselage, made of wooden trusswork covered with fabric, responded to the vibrations of the engines and the buffeting of the propeller wash like an enormous drumhead" (Harrison 101).

491:1 **I'm flying on the right aileron and a little rudder** flying to compensate for the extra weight on the right wing "caused by the 112-pound bomb lodged in the gear strut" (Harrison 101)

491:4–5 **Wire somewhere, I guess. I didn't think any of those shells were that close** Bogard and McGinnis assume that the right side of the airplane is heavy because a control wire has been damaged by enemy artillery.

491:18–19 **provided the devil has a beard** provided that the pilot of the enemy aircraft has a beard, so that he can call "beaver"; see 483:1 and 483:3

491:29–30 **He blasted the port engine** another compensation for the weight on the right wing: a "crosswind landing" with "his left wing low" into the wind and "touch[ing] down first on the left main gear, the right settling down gently as the plane loses speed" (Harrison 102)

491:30 **the riggers—** the mechanics take a look at the right wing

491:31 **some** bullet holes; see 491:29

492:1 **tracer** special bullet that leaves a luminous trail

492:15 **they** the bombs

492:15–16 **Or maybe they aren't like ours—don't load themselves as soon as the air strikes them** British bombs did arm in just this way, with the freed propellers in their tails immobilized during transport and freed to turn and arm the bomb upon release (Harrison 102).

492:23 **the trap** trap door of the cockpit

492:25–26 **The bomb, suspended by its tail, hung straight down like a plumb bob** Harrison points out that had Bogard dropped the bomb during a level flight rather than in a dive (see 489:18), the bomb might well not have lodged in the plane's "rather complicated" undercarriage (102). A plumb bob is the weight that holds a mason's plumb line perpendicular, so this bomb hangs very precariously indeed.

493:2 **the boat** one of the Royal Navy's Coastal Motor Boats, described by Harrison as "21-foot-shallow-draught shells powered by Thornycroft engines, each carrying beneath its hull a single huge torpedo which was aimed by the boat itself" (97)

493:8–9 **It was quarter-decked forward** has a small raised deck above the main one and set toward the front

493:10 **engine—** then that is one powerful boat

493:13 **free-board** the space between the ship's flotation line and the outer edge of the top deck

493:24–25 **It's steel. It's made of steel** not of wood and cloth, like his airplane (see 490:18–19), or of wood, like other boats

494:22–23 **Balaclava helmet** wool covering for the head and neck

495:3 **warmer** long overcoat

496:9 **good gad** euphemism for "Good God"

496:24 **them** waves, and perhaps mines, which would explain why he says "That's why, you see"; the boat skims over the top of the water without setting off the mines, so that they can get close enough to the ships in the harbors to bomb them

496:28 **thwarts** rower's benches in a boat

497:8 **Silly business** the formalities of 497:1–6

497:8–9 **when silly fourstriper—** when a captain in the Royal Navy "is going to show up"

497:10 **to fetch—** an oilskin for you

497:22 **That's Muriel** the name of their torpedo

497:24–26 **The one before that was Agatha. After my aunt. The first one Ronnie and I had was Alice in Wonderland. Ronnie and**

I were the White Rabbit. Jolly, eh? In Lewis Carroll's classic, Alice falls into Wonderland when she follows the White Rabbit down a very deep rabbit hole; when this White Rabbit let Alice out of her "hole," Wonderland was a blown-up ship.

497:35–496:1 **the speed at which the Handley-Page flew** about fifty miles an hour (Harrison 102)

498:6 **It's the air in her, I suppose** Bogard seems to think that the rough ride is due to an air pocket in the tube on the boat's bottom; he hasn't figured out that it holds a torpedo.

498:22 **We're outside** outside of the harbor, in open sea

498:26 **it** the rough ride

499:12 **Courtesy, *noblesse oblige*—all that** the proper response to Bogard's favor to Claude

499:13–14 **I've been there. I've seen it** the front

499:15 **Strewth** "God's truth," an oath like "by God"

499:24 **But there's Kiel** Rejecting Berlin (a thousand-mile round trip) as too far to go by boat in one day, Ronnie suggests the famous port city, even more improbable a destination because it lies on the Baltic rather than the North Sea (see Harrison 102).

499:24 **I knew—** that he was right to think of it

499:28 **Zeebrugge** German submarine base in Belgium

499:30 **My Gad! Berlin** Ronnie is convinced that Bogard took Claude to Berlin, but see 490:13–14.

500:30 **just say—** there's no need to take me to Kiel

500:31 **ratting off on him again** revealing just how scared he is, in spite of his effort to control it

501:3 **I just—** don't want to go to Kiel (an evasion of the truth)

501:8 **You see, I—** will be fine right in the harbor (an attempt to find an excuse to get out of the boat)

501:9 **No vacations in wartime** (unwarranted) credit for Bogard's work ethic, which won't allow him the "vacation" to Kiel

501:32 **trawler** fishing boat

501:34 **Lightship** ship used as a lighthouse

501:34 **Theirs** the enemy's

502:1 **a low, flat mole** a breakwater or pier. The harbor at Zeebrugge had such a mole, "40 miles from Dunkirk, an hour's run" in a Coastal Motor Boat (Harrison 103).

502:3 **Mines** underwater explosive devices that detonate on contact: "Mines are small, relatively inexpensive, easily laid down, and require little maintenance. Yet they have the explosive ability to sink or badly damage even large vessels by blowing open their hull below the waterline. Consequently, smaller naval powers have often used them to impede the larger fleets of major powers. . . . Major use of underwater mines began in World War I with the British and later Americans planting tens of thousands of mines to contain the German surface and submarine fleets, and the Germans laying mines in British coastal waters" (Chambers).

502:7 **the screw** the boat's propeller

502:9 **it** the engine

502:13 **Might stop a stray** might get hit by a stray bullet

502:18–19 **Give them first innings. Sporting. Visitors, eh?** a metaphor from cricket meaning "visitors go first"

502:22 **freighter** cargo ship

502:22–23 **Painted midships of the hull was a huge Argentine flag** Argentina remained neutral through most of the First World War, choosing to trade with both the Allies and the Central Powers; see also 507:16–19.

502:23 **stations** battle stations

502:31 **gadget** at 500:11, the device that drops the torpedo into the chute

503:11–12 **the other lifted and extended at the height of his head** like Bogard at 489:18–20, ready to signal a bomb release; see also 509:15–17

503:13 **the hand would never drop** Ronnie's signal to Claude to fire the torpedo, like Bogard's own to Mac (489:18–20)

503:18 **poop** the poop deck, the aftermost part of a ship

503:26 **Get a broadside, this time** get hit on the boat's side

504:6 **me—** I can get to work

504:8 **Mac would say they had a telephone on board** Apparently the crank handle looks like the attached crank on an old telephone; Mac would take any opportunity to call the men soft and pampered.

504:19 **It didn't— The torpedo—** It didn't fire? The torpedo didn't fire?

504:22 **like engineers—** could make things that work

504:24 **But the nose, the cap!** the part of the torpedo that houses the detonator

504:27–29 **If we should stop or slow up it would overtake us. Drive back into the tube. Bingo!** He seems to mean that the boat would overtake the torpedo and jam it in the tube, right before it explodes.

504:34–505:2 **Mustn't draw her back too fast. Jam her into the head of the tube ourselves. Same bingo! Best let us. Every cobbler to his last, what?** 504:27–29 more fully explained, with the caution that it's best to let them do the jobs that they've been trained to do while Bogard should stay out of their way. As Christine Ammer explains, "This adage comes from an ancient story about a shoemaker criticizing a work by a Greek painter named Apelles, saying that the shoe in the picture was not correctly portrayed. After the painter corrected it, the shoemaker pointed out an error in the leg, whereupon the painter said, 'Shoemaker, do not go above your last.' Over the centuries the story was repeated, and the expression still is sometimes put as **cobbler, stick to your last**, even though cobblers are nearly obsolete" (616).

505:10 **spanner** wrench

505:12–15 **Bogard saw a long, drooping thread loop down from somebody's mouth, between his hands, and he found that the thread came from his own mouth** drooling, as a prelude to vomiting at 505:29–30

505:21–23 **the cruiser which had not dared to fire and the freighter which had not been able to fire** The cruiser, which is most likely a German vessel, does not want to fire on Claude and Ronnie's boat for fear of hitting the freighter, and the freighter can't shoot at them because they are circling just next to the ship's hull, directly underneath their guns.

505:29 **a pursuit ship going into a wingover** a plane's steep turn in which the bank is past the vertical—backwards, in effect (Harrison 103)

505:33 **Steady all** from a seaman's command to "make all fast and steady all"—that is, to secure items for a voyage; "you're all right now"

506:2 **starboard** "the right-hand side of a ship, as distinguished from the LARBOARD or PORT side; the side upon which in early types of ships the steering apparatus was worked" (*OED* online)

506:7 **I—** got sick; vomited in your ship

507:16–18 **In there. How do you suppose it got past us here? Might have stopped here as well. French would buy the wheat** see 502:22–23

507:19 **Machiavelli** Italian statesman and political theorist (1469–1527) whose most famous claim was that a state's or ruler's end justifies the means taken to that end (see Milo)

508:17 **English Gazette** may refer to a newspaper printed in English, or to the *London Gazette* (which published promotions and honors during the war)

508:21 **R.N.R.** Royal Naval Reserve

508:21 **Boatswain's Mate** assistant to the man in charge of summoning sailors to posts

508:22 **Able Seaman** second grade of three in the Royal Navy

508:22–23 **Channel Fleet, Light Torpedo Division** see 493:2

509:7 **Blank** the name of a town, censored

509:15–17 **until McGinnis, at the toggles below him, began to shout at him, before he ever signaled. He didn't signal until he could discern separately the slate tiles of the roof** like Ronnie at 504:12–13, who pilots the boat so closely to the ship that Bogard can "see the rivets in the plates"

"All the Dead Pilots"

On 5 February 1930, Faulkner submitted a story called "Per Ardua" to the *Saturday Evening Post,* which rejected it, as did four other magazines. The story appears as "Dead Pilots" on his short story sending schedule, and some have written erroneously that it appeared in *Woman's Home Companion.* On the contrary, it went unpublished by the magazines; he last offered it for publication on 23 April 1931, and by May of that year he was busy assembling his first collection of short stories, *These 13* (1931). He included "All the Dead Pilots" in that volume as the third story, following "Victory" and "Ad Astra" and preceding "Crevasse," which he had excised from "Victory." The plot concerns Johnny Sartoris's misadventures with two women and his commanding officer, Spoomer, who, though decorated, has no pilot's combat experience and owes his command to his brigadier general uncle. At a thirteen-year remove from the Armistice, an unnamed narrator tells the story. He heard about and also observed firsthand some of the story's main events in 1918 during his assignment to Wing Headquarters, where he worked as a military mail censor as he got used to his new artificial leg. His narrative technique, he says, "is composite" (512), which nicely describes the story's place in Faulkner's work as well. The Sartoris twins figure prominently in *Flags in the Dust* (published as *Sartoris* in 1929); Bayard's fate there attaches to the Benbow family's of *Sanctuary* (1931); and the letters that the narrator ultimately reads from Johnny and his family also connect this story to "There Was a Queen." "All the Dead Pilots" also explores in broadly comic and briefly tragic narrative the same theme explored discursively by the subadar, the wounded German, and others in "Ad Astra." The original title of the former even appears with the latter's in the motto of the Royal Air

Force, "Per ardua ad astra," or "Through struggles to the stars" (Harrison 85; "Royal Air Force Motto"). Yet such connections do not provide much help in interpreting individual works. In "Ad Astra," for example, Johnny's death serves more to illustrate Bayard's tenacity in seeking vengeance for it than to muse on the ironies of war. All of this intertextually related material highlights the "composite" quality of Faulkner's own imagination, which focused always on the demands of the story at hand rather than seek consistency among details.

Faulkner himself apparently thought very highly of "All the Dead Pilots." He inscribed "This is the best one" in an acquaintance's copy of *These 13* over the story's title, and he told another that he liked it best among his own stories (Blotner, 1974; 731–32, 777). Few recent critics have shared his enthusiasm for it, and it has received relatively little attention. Many who do comment on it have been struck by its humor, and this quality may well account for Faulkner's high regard for it. Douglas Day says the story "is, at best, a prime example of Faulknerian humor," but he argues finally that the war described therein is "so meaningless, so unimportant, that it can be overshadowed by a ridiculous quarrel between a fool and a neurotic" ("War" 389, 391). Edmond Volpe agrees, calling the story "a slap-stick comedy, a bedroom farce in a wartime setting" and concluding that "the narrative frame for the comedy does not serve to evoke sufficient reader sympathy, to adopt the author's view of the protagonist and to share his sentiments for the grim recklessness of the World War I pilot" (115, 116). Other readers discriminate more scrupulously between author and narrator: "The narrator's attitudes," according to Hans Skei, "are crucial to an understanding of the story's significance. The lack of personal involvement on the part of the narrator and the distance in time . . . gives another distorted impression of what the pilots were like, seen in retrospect thirteen years later" (*The Novelist* 133). James Watson observes that the narrator, as censor, is "one of the many voyeurs in Faulkner's fiction: the letters he reads and ruins give him access to the private lives in the story he tells and, finally, provide him a way of telling the untellable" (*Letters* 99). By extension, some readers have seen storytelling itself as the subject of the narrator's tale. "All the Dead Pilots," says Judith Bryant Wittenberg, "is perhaps the most explicitly metafictional tale in the volume [*These 13*], standing synecdochically for the work as a whole" (286–87). The last paragraph of the story, Robert Sayre concludes, "intimates that the only salvation—and a precarious one at that—comes from the writer preserving the memory of manifestations of human value in writing—in story-snapshots of its existence and the deed that express it" ("The Romantic" 251). In the hands of critics schooled in gender theory, the story reveals another level of meaning. John Duvall, for example, argues that "The Spoomer who returns to England may be a male heterosexual, but he isn't a man. Again, heterosexuality appears neither as a sufficient (or apparently necessary) condition of masculinity because the assertion Sartoris makes about masculinity devalues heterosexual fornicating in favor of homoerotic fighting" (60)—an insight that could apply equally well to "A Courtship." Answering a question at the University of Virginia, Faulkner himself said of the pilots who survived the war: "In a way they were dead, they had exhausted themselves psychically . . . anyway, they were unfitted for the world that they found afterward. Not that they rejected, they simply were unfitted, they had worn themselves out" (*Faulkner in the University* 23). Any of these readings return us to the title of the story, to the beginning that lies in the ending and, as Ralph Ellison's Invisible Man describes the paradox, "lies far ahead" (6). As the last of the five stories in "The Wasteland" section of *Collected Stories*, "All the Dead Pilots" closes one door and opens another, to "The Middle Ground."

511:2 **thirteen years** The present time of the story is 1930 or 1931. Virginia Sartoris indicates in her letter that the Americans had just joined the war (1917), and the Sopwith Camel that Sartoris flies was introduced in 1917; John Sartoris is killed on July 4, 1918 (see 530:7).

511:3 **brass and leather martial harness** Sam Browne belt, part of the uniform worn by commissioned officers of the British Army and named for Sir Samuel James Browne (1824–1901). The belt also has a supporting strap that passes diagonally from the left hip over the right shoulder and down across the back to the left hip. Browne designed the shoulder strap to help carry the weight of a sword or pistol holster. Having lost his left arm in the British attempt to quell Indian uprisings in Punjab in 1857, Browne had difficulty drawing his sword one-handed. The belt's accommodation of a holster allowed pistols to be carried more safely, without the risk of accidental discharge.

511:4–6 **esoteric shapes of wire and wood and canvas in which they flew without parachutes** the notoriously unsafe airplanes of the day

511:10–11 **the eleventh of November, 1918** Armistice Day, when the treaty ending the Great War was signed

511:13 **cowlings** the removable covering over or around the engine or other parts of an airplane

511:14 **slotted wings** a gap in the wing parallel to the leading edge that allows air to pass from the lower to the upper surface of the wing thus increasing the airplane's lift; in short, they get the plane in the air faster and more safely.

511:16 **saxophone age** what F. Scott Fitzgerald christened the "Jazz Age," the post-war period of prosperity following the Armistice, during which the popularity of piano-based ragtime music gave way to the brass and woodwinds of jazz

511:19 **miniature brass bowlers** probably the cup-shaped mute of a trumpet or trombone player

511:22–23 **welded center sections and parachutes and ships that would not spin** A "ship" is an airplane and a "spin" is a tailspin, or corkscrewing flight, usually downward and often resulting in a crash. The narrator means that modern airplanes are safer than the old and, consequently, those who fly them less talented than the war pilots were.

512:2 **crates** airplanes

512:4 **ack emma** military slang for ante meridian or for aviation mechanic—in this case, the latter. However, as Robert Harrison explains, "All the enlisted men attached to a squadron—fitters, riggers, armorers and gunners, as well as mechanics—were known as ack emmas" (91).

512:5 **warrant officer pilot** an officer ranking above noncommissioned officers and below commissioned officers. A warrant officer's authority derives from a warrant issued by the military, usually on the basis of some sort of technical ability or skill, such as the ability to fly an airplane.

512:5 **M.C.** Master Commander

512:20–24 **I was at Wing Headquarters, trying to get used to a mechanical leg, where, among other things, I had the censoring of mail from all squadrons in the Wing. The job itself wasn't bad, since**

it gave me spare time to experiment with a synchronized camera on which I was working The first-person narrator has been wounded in the war and subsequently assigned a desk job while he gets used to his prosthesis. His diction, vocabulary, and apparent ignorance of American ways (513:34–514:6) mark him as British. **Wing** = a unit of several squadrons; **censoring of mail** = During wartime, correspondence between troops in the field and home is censored to protect sensitive information such as troop activity and location; **squadrons** = basic tactical units of an air force; **synchronized camera** = Harrison explains that the British used box cameras during air reconnaissance but the Germans used a "(sequence) camera which held 50 meters of continuous film, making exposures automatically at regular intervals by means of a synchronizer driven by a small windmill propeller mounted in the airstream" (91). He implies that the narrator is trying to build one of these. Other commentators believe that he is working on an early version of a flash camera that fired the flash when the shutter was opened. If he is, then the narrator is somewhat ahead of his time, since cameras were not fitted with such devices until 1935 (see Watson, *Letters* 99; "A Flash of Light").

512:31 **play horse** play games with other people's lives

513:1 **Camel squadron** squadron composed of Sopwith Camel F-1 airplanes. The Camel held a crew of one and two machine guns; its name comes from the humped fairings over the guns. Although Camels were well-regarded as fighter planes because of their maneuverability, almost as many pilots died in accidents during takeoff and landing as in combat. Australia's top ace of the war described the Camel's problems: "Its main trouble was that owing to its very small wingspan, and its purposely unstable characteristics, coupled with the gyroscopic effect of a rotating engine and propeller, it flipped into a spin very easily at low speeds. Consequently, in landing and taking off, a tremendous number of fatal accidents occurred, and a general feeling of dislike for the machine was prevalent. It really had people frightened" (Cobby).

513:2 **Amiens** town in northeastern France about halfway between Calais and Paris and a strategic point in the Western front of the war

513:2 **gunnery sergeant** noncommissioned officer in charge of maintaining the squadron's machine guns

513:3 **synchronization of the machine guns** In a forward-firing fighter plane, the machine guns are synchronized with the propeller so a pilot can fire forward without destroying the propeller. This type of airplane was devised for the Germans by Anthony Fokker in 1915 and came to the Western front that summer.

513:4 **K.G.** Knight of the Order of the Garter, the oldest and most prestigious Order of Chivalry in England, dating from 1348 and the rule of King Edward III

513:5 **Guards' Captaincy** probably the 1st King's Regiment Dragoon Guards, dating from 1685 and the reign of James II; a regiment dedicated to the protection of the monarch

513:6 **Mons Star** popular name for the 1914 Star, decoration awarded for service in France or Belgium between 5 August and 22 November 1914. The Star was awarded to those who fought in the Battle of Mons (23 August 1914) and also to troops who did not participate in that engagement but served in those countries during the specified time. To earn the Star, one had to be on French or Belgian soil; this explains Ffollansbye's joke at 513:22–23.

513:6 **D.S.O.** Distinguished Service Order. An award not generally given to officers lower than Captains and almost always awarded for gallantry in action. The D.S.O. is the second most prestigious award in British military medals.

513:6–7 **pursuit squadron of single seaters** a squadron of fighter planes designed and equipped to pursue and attack the enemy and flown by one man who also fired the machine guns on board

513:7–8 **third barnacle on his tunic was still the single wing of an observer** The three decorations on Spoomer's uniform include an observer's wing and not the double wings of a pilot, indicating that Spoomer has not actually flown any aircraft.

513:9 **Sandhurst** in 1914 and now, the Royal Military College, a training site for officers of the British Army and the usual route to a military commission

513:9 **chap** upper-class British slang for "man"

513:12 **brigadier** brigadier general, the rank above colonel

513:13 **Indian service** In 1661, King Charles I received Bombay from Portugal as a wedding present; he then rented the city to the East India Company. By 1848 the British had consolidated power in

India, but there was a general rebellion in 1857, and the following year the Crown took over the Indian government. The British remained in power in India until 1947, but during the Great War the British military was needed in Europe.

513:15 **by gad** by God

513:18 **the Hun** derisive name for the Germans, called after the nomadic Asian people that toppled the Roman Empire

513:18–19 **the Home Office** department of the British government responsible for internal affairs and security of the populace

513:22–23 **since it was going to be one decoration you had to be on hand to get** See 513:6. Ffollansbye implies that Spoomer got his medals secondhand, or fraudulently, rather than earn them.

513:25–26 **to tap the stream where it came to surface** to get to the source of something

513:28 **pro patria** for one's country (Latin)

514:6 **came through Canada** Sartoris enlisted in the Canadian Royal Air Force before the United States entered the war.

514:7 **Pool** "A sort of limbo where pilots awaited posting to squadrons at the front. In France pilots' pool was located at the base depot of St. Omer (later Marquise); in Britain, it was at Ayr" (Harrison 92).

514:11 **the fourth of August, 1914** the date the war began

514:13 **Kitchener** Horatio Herbert Kitchener (1850–1916), British Secretary of State for War appointed in 1914. His face appeared on recruitment posters, but he became increasingly unpopular among other members of the Cabinet and was removed from real authority in 1915. He vastly expanded the British Army (from twenty to seventy divisions) and was responsible for funneling thousands of troops into unwinnable and costly battles at the Somme and Passchendaele.

514:23 **aerodrome** airport

514:25 **kit** set of articles assembled for a particular use, like a travel or mess kit

514:26–27 **barnacle ribbon** see 513:7–8

515:9 **in the spring, just before Cambrai fell** The Battle of Cambrai, which introduced the modern era of tank warfare, began in late November 1917; by its end on 7 December, the Germans had regained almost all of the ground they had lost to the surprise

Allied offensive, and the British had lost 316 air crew to Germany's 116. During the spring of that year, however, when the narrator first sees Sartoris, the British lost fully a third of their aircraft to the German Jasta pilots. The life expectancy of a pilot in the RAF in what is known as "Bloody April" was about seventeen hours in the air (see United States Centennial of Flight Commission; "The History of Aviation").

515:14 **afternoon patrol** squadron looking for enemy aircraft

515:16 **petrol** British term for gasoline; **tins** British usage for metal containers

515:24–25 **that terrible and omniscient inquisition of those in an inferior station** an example of the class conflict behind not only Spoomer and Sartoris's rivalry but also the narrator's interest in the situation. See also 516:30–35.

515:30 **Wing** Wing headquarters. See 512:20.

516:26 **an estaminet, a "bit of a pub"** a small café (French); **pub** = public house; tavern (British slang)

516:29 **furore** British spelling of *furor*

516:30–35 **the contest between the squadron commander and one of his greenest cubs was the object of general interest and the subject of the warmest conversation and even betting among the enlisted element of the whose sector of French and British troops. "Being officers and all," he said** another example of the class conflict in the story. See also 515:24–25. **greenest cubs** = least experienced novices

517:6 **What the girl was** Sartoris's love interest is at least promiscuous and perhaps a prostitute.

517:12–13 **a third-form lad in Harrow** A form is a level in the British school system roughly equivalent to the grades above kindergarten in American elementary school. Harrow is one of England's oldest and most prestigious boarding schools for boys; it was founded in 1572 by a royal grant from Elizabeth I, and its graduates include famous poets and statesmen.

517:18 **centime** a French coin worth one-hundredth of a franc. Sartoris has bought her very cheap jewelry.

518:9–10 **the machines were coming up to the line** The returning aircraft are lined up for refueling and maintenance prior to the next day's patrol.

518:14–15 **golf stockings** knee-high stockings for men, worn with knickerbockers or Bermuda shorts

518:23 **timers** devices carried by pilot to record length of flight and times of important events during it

519:10 **hand gallop** slow, gentle gallop

519:17 **lorry** large truck (British usage)

519:23 **I had imagined the scene, before he told me** The narrator is highly imaginative and has anticipated Sartoris's reaction to the public humiliation in the pub. He makes a point of the fact that they have talked only twice, and both conversations confirm his speculation.

519:25 **pips** shoulder insignia of officers (British usage)

520:3 **cashiered** dismissed from command

520:3 **clinked for life** put in prison for a life sentence. A clink is a British slang term for jail, so named after a London prison.

520:4 **articles of alliance** treaties signed between governments stipulating the terms of their behavior in a joint venture

520:10–11 **gone out six and come back five** a squadron of six has lost one of its planes and pilots

520:15 **they have got Cambrai!** See 515:9. Since Cambrai had been under German occupation since 1914, this passage is curious; it might reflect the constantly shifting and terrifying reality of life on the ground during wartime and not strict historical accuracy on the patrol leader's part.

520:17 **Jerry** chiefly British slang for the German soldiers

520:24–25 **tear out the cockpit and rig the duals myself** While learning to fly, observers sat in the front seat of a two-person airplane; a set of dual controls allowed the novice to practice and the pilot to teach by example or take over in an emergency or during difficult maneuvers. The Sopwith Camel was a single-seat aircraft, so Sartoris is offering to install a double cockpit and dual controls in order to teach Spoomer how to fly for himself—and then beat him in a contest of skills.

520:27 **S.E.** Scout Experimental 5, a fighter plane introduced in 1917 that was in several respects (such as safety and handling at high altitudes) superior to the Sopwith Camel

520:28 **Ak.W.** an Armstrong Whitworth F.K.8, "a big, slab-sided biplane known as the 'Ack.W.' because of the bold company intitials stamped in steel on its engine cowling" and "a doughty if unspectacular performer" (Harrison 87)

520:28 **Fee** a Fighting Experimental, British F.E. 2 airplane that by 1917 was obsolete as a fighter and used primarily for bombing missions (Harrison 93)

521:14–16 **a week after the patrol had told that Cambrai had fallen, a week after we heard the shells falling in Amiens** Cambrai was recaptured by the Germans in a counteroffensive that began on 30 November 1917, and was over by 7 December. See 515:9.

521:19 **broken front** the penetrated Allied offenses

521:20 **overall leg** the pants of his one-piece flight suit

521:22 **Base hospital** the hospital at headquarters (rather than the field hospitals at which secondary triage and initial treatments would be made)

521:23 **interdict** forbidden by military decree, in this case because Amiens is enemy territory

521:29 **light ambulance** At the beginning of the war, ambulances were wagons drawn by animals and generally could not accommodate more than two wounded, prone soldiers. Used to the convenience of the automobile and in concern for the wounded troops, Paris's Automobile Club originally modified cars for use as ambulances. The automobile could get more of the wounded to surgical help much more quickly, and the Ford Company Model T proved especially sturdy and reliable in field conditions. These light ambulances could hold as many as eight seated patients.

522:8 **operations officer** officer who oversees flight plans and controls flights from the airfield

522:10 **La Fayette** Escadrille Lafayette was a fighter unit under French command composed of U.S. volunteers and French soldiers; it was formed in 1916, prior to America's entry into the war.

522:10 **Santerre plateau** part of the landscape of the Battle of Amiens

522:16–17 **diving at it as they do in American football** In this sport, defensive players attempt to stop the advancement of the ball by grabbing the player carrying it and carrying them both to the ground. This is called "tackling," and it might be the most senseless way to try to open a door ever recorded.

523:1–2 **quicksilver** the element mercury; in Latin, *argentum vivum*, or "living silver," so called because it is silver in color and liquid at ordinary temperatures

523:17 **Où est-elle, 'Toinette?** Where is she, where is 'Toinette? (French; proper name probably short for Antoinette)

523:21 **wound-up toy** a toy with a mechanism inside it that makes it move in some way, usually with a key attached directly to the toy. With this reference and the one at 523:13–14, the narrator emphasizes the mechanical quality of 'Toinette's movements.

524:6 **Maman?** Mama (French)

524:22 **ordnance belt** a belt to hold ammunition and weapons; in this case, probably a Sam Browne belt (see 511:3)

524:31–32 **Que faites-vous en haut?** What did you do up there? (French)

525:2 **Descendez** Come down (French)

525:18 **like a Gilbert and Sullivan pirate** William S. Gilbert (1836–1911) and Arthur Sullivan (1842–1900) were British composers who collaborated on comic operas in the late nineteenth century, Sullivan writing the music and Gilbert the lyrics. Their opera *The Pirates of Penzance* premiered in 1879 and in its London engagement the following year ran for 363 performances. It remains their most well-known opera.

526:1 **inkstand** a tray or rack for holding pens and bottles of ink, into which the pens were dipped to write

526:9 **Anzac** acronym for Australian and New Zealand Army Corps

526:11–12 **helped him to start his engine, and held the wings for his tight take-off** cranked the engine to start it and stabilized the airplane to give it a better chance of a successful takeoff in the small space of the meadow in which he had landed

526:19 **strafed** According to Webster's, "*Gott strafe England*," meaning "God punish England," was a common greeting during the war; and according to the OED, the Germans were called "*Gott strafers*" or "God-punishers." The word entered English at first as a comic word but soon became adopted to mean what its origin suggests—fierce, punishing attacks—and specifically those caused by machine gun fire from aircraft.

526:25 **slow roll** an aerobatic maneuver in which the pilot turns the aircraft upside down and then rightside up without changing either altitude or direction

526:26 **valve stems** small tubes that allow the tires to be inflated and keep the air inside

526:28 **he stalled** The airflow to the engine was interrupted, causing the airplane's forward flight to halt slightly.

526:29 **he held the Camel mushing on its back** moving forward (in this case, while upside down) at a very slow speed, just above a full stall

526:32–34 **dived at the dog and then looped, making two turns of an upward spin, coming off on one wing and still upside down** He flew directly at the dog, as if to fire on it, and then pulled the airplane up and flew it in a vertical circle, after which he flew upward, turning the plane over twice, and then pulled level with the ground upside down.

526:35 **set back the air valve** allow the right amount of air into the engine

527:1 **conked** pilot slang for "quit"

527:2 **the only two poplar trees we had left** The incessant combat, with tanks and machine-gun fire and trench warfare, has destroyed the landscape.

527:15 **ox cart** The Great War was notable for its contrasts and its position as the last war of the nineteenth century and first of the twentieth. Here, the wagon pulled by oxen belongs to a local farmer, but it could easily have been an ambulance in the early days of the war (see 521:29).

527:19 **temporary colonel at ground school** Spoomer has been promoted within the ranks but sent to serve at flight school in England because of his humiliating return to the unit.

527:23–26 **second lieutenant, for dereliction of duty by entering a forbidden zone with government property and leaving it unguarded, and he had been transferred to another squadron** Sartoris has been demoted in the ranks, allegedly for going to Amiens with the airplane but more likely for humiliating Spoomer and his uncle, and assigned to another unit.

527:27 **B.E.** British Experimental, with a "heritage from an era when stability was regarded as the cardinal virtue of an aeroplane," which one veteran pilot claimed "that even Attila himself could not have fought from it" (Harrison 95)

527:27 **the Laundry** "where pilots got 'washed out'" (Harrison 95). In Air Force slang, to "wash out" is to be killed in a crash or to crash an aircraft (see 528:16). Grider writes that "Six American Naval pilots . . . thought that Camels were as easy to fly as the Hanriots they had been flying in France and they wouldn't listen to any advice from the instructors here. Three of them were washed out one week." For the B.E. pilots to call a squadron "the Laundry" despite their own high mortality rate would mean that an exceptional number of airmen were being killed in Sartoris's new squadron.

528:1 **the gun** the machine gun on board

528:3–6 **setting the air valve and flying it into the ground. Then you count ten, and if you have not crashed, you level off. And if you can get up and walk away, you have made a good landing** Sartoris is exaggerating the instability of the Camel during takeoff and landing, but not by much. See 513:1.

528:7 **ace** an expert pilot; in the military, one who has shot down five or more enemy aircraft

528:9 **night-flying squadron** See 528:18–19. Sartoris might well be implying that part of his punishment is not to be with women at night (see also 528:23–25).

528:16 **wash out** crash. See 527:27.

528:16–17 **wing flares explode. I've got that beat. I'll just stay up all night, pop the flares** signal lights on the wings that, when ignited, would show the position of the aircraft. To "pop" one would be to set it off.

528:23–24 **England, where all the men are gone. All those women, and not a man between fourteen and eighty to help him** British casualties by 1917 were horrendous. Sartoris is both satirizing Spoomer's appetite for women and casting aspersions on his manhood.

528:28 **paper cutter, a pot of glue and one of red ink** the tools of his trade as a mail censor

529:6 **batman** a British orderly or an officer's servant

529:17 **Malbroucks** John Churchill (1650–1722), the first Duke of Marlborough, known for embezzlement and taking bribes (see

"John Churchill"). The Château de Malbrouck still stands near what is now Luxembourg in the Alsace-Lorraine area of Europe, which has been a source of contested territory by both France and Germany. The perversion "Malbrouck" seems to come from a French nursery song sung to the tune of "For He's a Jolly Good Fellow," called "Malbrouck s'en va-t-en guerre" ("Malbrouck went off to war"). (See "John Churchill.")

529:26 **crank shaft** a shaft in a machine that converts movement into rotary motion

529:27 **wrist pins** a pin that joins a piston to its connecting rod

530:4 ***R.A.F.*** Royal Air Force

530:7 ***your son*** John Sartoris was Jenny's nephew. Major Kaye has clearly written a great many of this kind of letter. See 530:25.

530:7–8 ***yesterday morning*** 4 July 1918

530:10 ***E.A.*** enemy aircraft

530:18 ***side slipping*** flying sideways and downward at the same time

530:19 ***stabiliser*** generally, any of the plane's airfoils that keep it steady in the air, including the rudder and wings (British spelling). Since Major Kaye seems to have a specific piece of equipment in mind and since Sartoris's controls are simultaneously shot away, an educated guess would define the stabilizer in question as the lever that controls the wing flaps.

530:25 ***cemetary*** an alternative spelling often used by Faulkner, but perhaps an indication of the major's haste or unfamiliarity with the conventions of written expression; see 530:7

530:25 ***Saint Vaast*** While there are several sites named after St. Vaast in France, we believe that Sartoris has been buried in the cemetery north of the village of Neuville-St. Vaast, just west of the village of Vimy. The nearest large town, Arras, the capital of Artois, lies just to the south. At the same time the British air force was engaged in Bloody April (see 515:9), the Canadian army had an important victory at Vimy Ridge, securing the area for the Allies. A case could be made for the Louverval Military Cemetery near Cambrai, which contains war dead from 1917 and 1918 as well as a memorial to those who died at the Battle of Cambrai. In 1918, when Sartoris is killed, that ground was still mightily contested; Arras, while always near the front, was an Allied base and would seem to

Major Kaye to be a secured area. We also think that a soldier like Kaye would be more likely to refer to battle sites than abbeys or seaport towns (other St. Vaast namesakes) when describing the location of a grave on foreign soil, even if the survivor might not understand the reference.

530:27–28 ***by our padre since we were just two Camels and seven E.A. and so it was on our side by that time*** The passage is unclear on many levels. "Padre" is Spanish for "father" and could refer to the priest in charge of religious services for this squadron, or the Major could be invoking God without naming him. The three indefinite pronouns at 530:26–28 complicate interpretation as well. "[W]e hope it will not be shelled again" refers to the cemetery; "we hope it will be over soon" refers to the war. But "and so it was on our side by that time" could refer to the cemetery, to the bad luck of battle, or to something that rests with Major Kaye. It is also possible that Major Kaye has just written a Faulknerian sentence beginning with "*He was buried*" (530:25) and then interrupted and finally finished with "*by our padre.*"

531:3–4 ***I lived through a war myself*** the American Civil War

531:9–10 ***The Yankees are in it now*** Jenny equates all federal entities with the Yankees, or with an illegitimate invading and occupying force.

531:21 **sixpence** British coin worth six pennies, or half a shilling

V. THE MIDDLE GROUND

"Wash"

Probably because of its significant intersection with *Absalom, Absalom!*—which many believe to be Faulkner's greatest novel—"Wash" has received considerable attention for the way it resembles and differs from the novel in subject, focus, and narrative method but comparatively little as an independent short story. In intensely dramatic prose, the story at once represents Wash Jones's sudden disillusionment with Thomas Sutpen and the consequences of class stratification among Southern whites, and by extension, it offers a mythic parable of why the South lost the Civil War. In particular and memorable scenes, "Wash" also reveals and interrogates significant aspects of the rigid hierarchies of race and gender.

The opening paragraph of the story establishes Sutpen in an attitude of dominance over Wash's granddaughter Milly, their new-born child, and the African American midwife, Dicey, while Wash himself stands holding the reins of Sutpen's horse outside the cabin where Milly has just given birth. This "stages," as John T. Matthews puts it, "a moment of masterly assertion that expresses indivisible domination over the poor white, over women of both races, and over a black servant. Subtly, Faulkner suggests the entanglement of race and gender relations with class structure in the South" ("Faulkner" 171). The narrative then casts back to the twenty-year relationship in which Wash Jones has given to Thomas Sutpen abject loyalty, service, and worship, though the two men are "the same age almost to a day" (*CS* 538). "In characteristic Faulknerian fashion," says Lisa Paddock, "the story opens with the protagonist's moment of crisis, fills in the events leading up to it by means of flashback, and then circles back to the story's climax" (100). Wash, during the time leading up to the Civil War, had accepted his marginal and debased place in the social order. "It is a world of class and caste," David Minter observes, "in which race and gender loom large as shaping forces" (94). Sutpen owns the plantation, the big house, the slaves; Wash lives in "a crazy shack on a slough in the river bottom" by Sutpen's sufferance. When Sutpen goes away to the war, Wash claims to be "looking after the Kernel's place and niggers" (536) and explains his own absence from the war to the taunting slaves with "I got a daughter and family to keep" (537). "Who him?" the slaves respond, laughing, "calling us niggers?" (537). When Sutpen returns from the war, Wash continues to serve him unquestioningly. For him, says Edmond Volpe, "the figure of the patriarch assumes a cosmic dimension. The Southern legend and the Edenic myth merge when Wash's image of Sutpen on the black stallion is fused with his conception of God" (196). In this attitude, Jones unquestioningly accepts the system that gives pre-eminence to Sutpen and men like him, but he also assumes that he shares with Sutpen an innate superiority to women and black people.

"Reality for Jones," Volpe says, "is that mythical figure that is impervious to time and change. And that is why Wash is astonished when he discovers that Sutpen has fathered a female child" (198). When he hears Sutpen's casual remark comparing Milly to a mare, Wash for the first time sees Sutpen plain, and he simultaneously understands the profound cultural deception which has previously sustained him. Thus Sutpen's remark is epiphanic in two ways, showing Sutpen to others and Wash Jones to himself: "He heard what Sutpen said, and something seemed to stop dead in him before going on" (544). The remainder of the story articulates the radical revision in Wash's understanding and the apocalyptic consequences of his new vision: "*Better if his kind and mine too had never drawn the breath of life on this earth. Better that all who remain of us be blasted from the face of earth than that another Wash Jones should see his whole life shredded from him and shrivel away like a dried shuck thrown onto the fire*" (548–49). Critics have sometimes questioned the eloquence of such expressions by uneducated characters in Faulkner's work, but as H. R. Stoneback points out, "The poetry in the interior monologue of such a character recognizes that all human beings *feel* lyrically and poetically" (432). "Wash discovers," as Hans Skei puts it, "that his basic mistake has been to think that Sutpen was born a superior human being, and Sutpen discovers that he has made a fatal mistake in assuming that Wash always and in all circumstances will bend and yield and be subservient" (*Reading* 208). "The motivational forces behind Wash's new understanding," he continues, "and the actions that inevitably follow must be described as social and historical" (216)—in other words, as Faulkner's representation of Southern reality.

Written in the summer of 1933, "Wash" first appeared in the February 1934 issue of *Harper's.* It was subsequently published in *Doctor Martino* (1934), *The Portable Faulkner* (1946), *Collected Stories,* where it appears as the first story in "The Middle Ground" section, and later in *The Faulkner Reader* (1953). Faulkner reused the materials of the story in Chapters VI and VII of *Absalom, Absalom!* (1936), but with different techniques and to different purposes. Faulkner's use of certain of his stories in novels led him to exclude them from *Collected Stories,* so some critics have expressed mystification at the inclusion of "Wash" in this volume. However, the Sutpen family materials in the story are deliberately differentiated from the matter of *Absalom,* just as only traces of "Barn Burning" can be found in *The Hamlet.* Faulkner for a time even considered using both "Wash" and "Barn Burning" in what he called an "induction toward the spotted horse story" in *The Hamlet* but soon "discovered had no place in that book at all" (*Selected Letters* 197). Virtually every critic who has examined the short story as a short story, rather than as a paving stone on the road to Sutpen's Hundred, would agree with James Ferguson that "Wash" is "in its own right, a superlative story—moving, evocative, beautifully written" (162), a fine example of characters who cast shadows.

535:1 **the pallet bed** as Calvin Brown explains, "a bed made by laying bedding directly on the floor, without any bed-frame or legs" (114)

535:2 **shrunken planking of the wall** unsealed wood, swollen in wet weather and shrunken in dry

535:17 **Griselda** in Chaucer's Clerk's Tale, the patient and longsuffering wife of Marquis Walter

535:23 **Rob Roy** a novel by Sir Walter Scott (1817), a romance set in the Scottish highlands just before the Jacobite uprising of 1715. The historical title character, a "member of a proscribed clan, was once an honest drover; embittered by misfortune and injustice, he is now an outlaw, the ruthless and cunning opponent of the government's agents, but capable of justice and even generosity" ("Rob Roy").

535:23–24 **rode him North in '61** at the outbreak of the Civil War

536:1 **Marster** master

536:8 **scythe** not, as some have thought, a sickle, but "a two-handed implement with a curved handle, two projecting hand-grips, and a wide, slightly curved blade, used for reaping grain, cutting weeds, etc." (Brown 171)

536:12 **Kernel** Wash's pronunciation of "Colonel," different from the Sutpen slaves' pronunciation, which Faulkner writes as "Cunnel"

536:14 **gaunt, malaria-ridden man** Wash suffers from two ailments common among poor whites in the South—malnutrition and malaria. The latter is a mosquito-borne infectious disease that came to the U.S. with slaves and colonists alike and became especially devastating in the South: "The ravages of the most severe type of malaria (falciparum) influenced the choice of African slave labor for plantations in Carolina and Virginia, because African workers tolerated the disease and remained at work after European field hands had become incapacitated. Malaria also played an important role on the early frontier, since the principal form of transportation, river travel, dictated prolonged exposure to wetland areas. By the twentieth century, malaria, for a variety of environmental reasons, had retreated largely to the southern states. British physician Ronald Ross's discovery in 1897 that the anopheles mosquito transmitted malaria prompted southern towns in the early twentieth century to the destruction of mosquito larvae. . . . Still, rural malaria persisted in the South because the cost per capita for malaria control in the sparsely populated countryside was so high" (Humphreys).

536:18 **the few remaining men between eighteen and fifty** those who were not off fighting in the war

537:19 **the big house** in this case, Colonel Sutpen's house; "the main house, where the owners of a plantation live, as distinguished from slave quarters, Negro cabins, or tenant houses" (Brown 29)

537:19–22 **This was after bitter news had come down from the Tennessee mountains and from Vicksburg, and Sherman had passed through the plantation, and most of the Negroes had followed him** significant Confederate defeats; Vicksburg was besieged for fourteen months before it fell and so split the Confederacy geographically in two, and General William Tecumseh Sherman began his devastating March to the Sea after he burned Atlanta. Sherman moved from Vicksburg through Memphis on his way to the Battle of Chattanooga in the southeastern part of Tennessee. Following such losses slaves often deserted their plantations.

537:24 **scuppernongs** a type of muscadine grape grown for wine (Brown 171)

538:19–21 **whom the Bible told him had been created and cursed by God to be brute and vassal to all men of white skin** the belief that the African nations are "the sons of Ham" cursed by Noah for seeing him naked, in the book of Genesis: "These are the three sons of Noah: and of them was the whole earth overspread. And Noah began to be an husbandman, and he planted a vineyard: And he drank of the wine, and was drunken; and he was uncovered within his tent. And Ham, the father of Canaan, saw the nakedness of his father, and told his two brethren without. And Shem and Japheth took a garment, and laid it upon both their shoulders, and went backward, and covered the nakedness of their father; and their faces were backward, and they saw not their father's nakedness. And Noah awake from his wine, and knew what his younger son had done unto him. And he said, Cursed be Canaan; a servant of servants shall he be unto his brethren. And he said, Blessed be the Lord God of Shem; and Canaan shall be his servant. God shall enlarge Japheth, and he shall dwell in the tents of Shem; and Canaan shall be his servant" (9:18–27).

538:27–29 **the book said also that all men were created in the image of God and hence all men made the same image in God's eyes at least** "And God said, Let us make man in our image, after our likeness" (Genesis 2:26)

538:34–539:1 **His son had been killed in action the same winter in which his wife had died** most likely the winter of 1863. The war ended in April 1865, the year of Sutpen's return, and his daughter has received "meager bounty" from Wash for a year (539:4).

539:2 **General Lee** Robert E. Lee (1807–1870), head of the Army of Northern Virginia, who surrendered the Confederacy on 9 April 1865 at Appomattox Courthouse, Virginia

539:12–13 **the next five years** until 1870, the present year of the story; see 540:3–4

539:14 **stoneware jug** according to Brown, "the standard container for illicit whiskey" (112)

539:16 **highroad** main thoroughfare

540:3–4 **Lincoln, dead now, and Sherman, now a private citizen** Lincoln was assassinated on 14 April 1865, five days after the surrender at Appomattox Courthouse, but Sherman did not retire from the Army until 1884, which slightly contradicts the story's internal timeline. Sutpen went North in 1861, when Wash's granddaughter was eight (see 536:16–17). At the time of her pregnancy, she is seventeen; nine years have elapsed, making the date of the current action about 1870. See 569:12–13.

540:26–27 **Miss Judith** a title of respect "used by servants for the daughters of their employers" (Brown 129)

541:1 **fifteen** around 1868; see 536:16–17 and 540:3–4

541:2 **her kind** that is, her class—"white trash"; see 536:33

541:3 **he had been seeing it and its kind daily for three years** at Sutpen's store (539:19)

541:23 **ara** any

542:1 **ticket** the "citation for gallantry" mentioned at 539:2 and 541:33

542:8 **two years later** in 1870, the present time of the story

542:23–24 **his granddaughter's voice came steadily as though run by a clock** the cries of her labor

543:3 **the bitter cup in the Book** Before the soldiers take him in the garden of Gethsemane, Jesus prays to God, saying, "O my Father, if it be possible, let this cup pass from me: nevertheless not as I will, but as thou wilt" and, a second time, "O my Father, if this cup may not pass away from me, except I drink it, thy will be done" (Matthew 26:39, 42). Similar passages appear in Mark 14:36 and Luke 22:42.

543:21–22 **"Gittin a gal," he thought in that astonishment** "and not a boy"; to Wash a sign of Sutpen's weakness and age

543:31 **gawn** go on

544:9 **I be dawg if you ain't as old as I am—** "after all"; see 543:21–22
544:12 **He heard what Sutpen said** see 535:10–11
544:28 **Dicey** the name of the midwife
544:28 **You better—** "get to your chores," or some other trivial order
545:26 **'Twarn't nothing** It wasn't anything
546:7–9 **Women. Hit's a mystry to me. They seem to want em, and yit when they git em they cry about hit. Hit's a mystry to me. To ara man** Wash shares the gender biases of men of his time; see 543:21–22. Here he stands amazed that women would cry after giving birth.
546:17 **them** Sutpen's peers; see 547:1
546:28–29 **fatback it was, and cold corn pone** food of poor people; salt pork or bacon and corn bread, made without milk or eggs (see Brown 60, 79)
547:1 **men of Sutpen's own kind** the white upper class; see 546:17
548:4 **Hit** the certain confrontation between Wash and Sutpen's peers
548:11 **that** the ideas expressed at 548:7–11
548:24 **thinking was going smoothly on** a continuation of his remarks to Sutpen at 548:11
549:7 **the sounds of underbrush** the rustling of horses and men walking through the underbrush
549:32 **What is . . .** the matter?
549:32 **What is . . .** going on?

"Honor"

"Honor" is framed by an opening and closing section set on a single day in the present (circa 1930), when the story's narrator, Buck Monaghan, abruptly quits his job as an automobile salesman. To account for his restlessness and his inability to find satisfactory long-term employment, he takes us back to his service in World War I and the years immediately after the Armistice. In civilian life, Monaghan became a wing-walker and now works part-time as a member of a barn-storming air circus. Here he meets the pilot Howard Rogers and Howard's wife Mildred. The three of them develop a curious domestic friendship, and eventually Mildred and Monaghan begin an affair. The crucial episode of the story takes place when Rogers and Monaghan are teamed for performance for a large crowd at an amusement park. Monaghan believes that Rogers will exact the traditional *crime passionnel* revenge by maneuvering the plane so that he will fall to his death, but when he does indeed fall off the airplane, Rogers performs the extraordinary maneuver of catching his falling rival on the airplane's top wing and then hauling him into the cockpit. At this point the immediate narrative is interrupted, as Monaghan reminisces about his World War I experiences, including the night of the Armistice, when the events of "Ad Astra" took place, including the subadar's philosophizing: "something else he said, about breathing for a long time yet, some kind of walking funerals; catafalques and tombs and epitaphs of men that died on the fourth of August, 1914, without knowing that they had died, he said" (562). The night of the mishap, Monaghan leaves the couple, and we finally learn that the husband and wife have had a son together and named Monaghan as his godfather.

The title of the story has given many readers pause, although Diane Brown Jones observes that "critics generally agree that Howard Rogers achieves honor" (407). Buck Monaghan himself seems an unlikely candidate to recognize, value, and practice that quality of character, especially when we consider his apparent willingness to break up Howard and Mildred's marriage. In this case, says Max Putzel, "honor overrides desire, and despite his failure to adjust to civilian life, Monaghan is redeemed" (135). Robert Dale Parker calls the story "an elaborate sexual pantomime that the title tries to contain as merely a duel of honor" ("Sex" 89). James Ferguson develops a similar point: "This is one of the clearest statements in Faulkner's short fiction of his equation of heights and masculine sexuality and of the opposition, in his terms, between the clean, cold, simple world of men and the 'hot and dirty' world of women" (72). Edmond Volpe says that Monaghan's comments on women "have the effect of isolating the male, setting him off in an Edenic garden where the female is the temptress and corrupter of male innocence." Monaghan's story, he continues, is "a confession, a record of moral discovery and of expiation for moral weakness and moral inadequacy" (127). "Honor" is one of a number of Faulkner's stories, says Robert Sayre, that presents a critique of modernity: "What is yearned after are qualitative values and experiences that were possible or that were prized in earlier times, but that have become irrelevant and even self-destructive in the modern era." The war, in this reading, allows for demonstrations of "honor, courage, pride, love, sacrifice," and Monaghan "continues to live according to a code inherited from the war" ("Romantic" 248, 250). As a barnstormer, according to David Minter, Monaghan is one of those who "express themselves in acts and deeds rather than words. As a result they embody heroic if not tragic potential" (*William Faulkner* 147). Jones correctly observes that "Honor" has been "marginalized" among Faulkner's short stories because of readers' emphasis on the Yoknapatawpha fiction (407), and Minter and others have pointed out that the story might be overshadowed by Faulkner's subsequent treatment of similar materials in *Pylon*.

Faulkner sent "Honor" to the *American Mercury* on 22 April 1930, and it appeared in the July issue of that magazine. Faulkner chose not to include it in *These 13* (1931) but did use it to conclude *Doctor Martino* (1934). Like the other stories in *Doctor Martino*, it was not listed among

Robert K. Haas's original suggestions for the volume that became *Collected Stories*; however, Faulkner included it in his 1 November 1948 letter to Malcolm Cowley in which he presents his own selections and arrangement (*Selected Letters* 274–75, 278). The *Collected Stories* text is identical to that of the *American Mercury* version, restoring the word "handwriting" (which had appeared as "hand writing" in *Doctor Martino*). "Honor" appears as the second story in "The Middle Ground" section of *Collected Stories*. Placement there rather than in "The Wasteland" might well have contributed to the relative obscurity of "Honor," as Hans Skei has argued regarding the uncollected story "Thrift," neglected "simply because it was never canonized or institutionalized by being collected in a book" (*Short Story* 102). Whatever its current critical fortunes, "Honor" is another of Faulkner's highly intertextual productions that also sustains individual scrutiny quite well. The presence of Monaghan invites us to look back chronologically to *Sartoris/Flags in the Dust* (1929) and "Ad Astra" (composed in 1927), and forward not only to "Death Drag" but even as far as *A Fable* (1954), Faulkner's self-described "magnum o" set in the Great War. The barnstorming fliers and the love triangle anticipate *Pylon* (1935), and the triangle involving a tolerant husband recurs in *If I Forget Thee, Jerusalem/The Wild Palms* (1939) and *The Town* (1959). Beyond the various ironies of its title, the story explores the masculine ideal of heroism and honor in a post-war world complicated by the disturbing presence of women, the questionable conventions of domesticity, and the disagreeable exigencies of the contemporary economy. "Honor" not only provides one of Faulkner's treatments of the veterans' death-in-life but also attempts simultaneously to articulate the supreme values of the life that has been ended by the Armistice, to expose the shallow hypocrisy of the modern world, and to demonstrate the challenge of living by those values in that world.

551:2 **He's** Mr. Reinhardt, the narrator's boss; Miss West is his secretary.

551:2 **in conference** not to be disturbed

551:5 **write me off** take me off the payroll

551:8 **frog-eyed** with bulging or protruding eyeballs

551:8–9 **Isn't our car good enough for you to demonstrate** Our narrator, Buck Monaghan, has a job as a car salesman, which involves taking potential customers out in the automobiles to show them how the car operates. Mr. Reinhardt's first words in the story alert us to the patronizing way that Buck treats everyone, regardless of their sex or class status.

551:10 **the size of a tail-light** Since Buck sells cars, he reaches easily for a car metaphor to describe Mr. Reinhardt's gaudy ring.

551:12 **that word on the door** probably "Private," but perhaps "President"

551:14 **the record** the longest amount of time that Buck has been employed in civilian jobs

551:14–16 **And if three weeks is a record with him, he could have shaken hands with the new champion without moving** If Mr. Reinhardt has had no employee for longer than three weeks, he can congratulate himself on having employed Buck for this long.

551:18 **those days** the years before America's involvement in the First World War

551:18–19 **even the college campuses full of British and French uniforms** Buck seems to be implying either that college students were young men of privilege who would not ordinarily put themselves in harm's way or that, on campus, they were isolated from the "real world" he knows; "even" they were so anxious to become pilots that they joined the British and French armies to do so.

551:19 **us** another indication of Buck's inauspicious class status

551:20–21 **swank a pair of pilot's wings** With a hint of ostentatious swagger about it, the word *swank* indicates that Buck thought it would be easy to become a pilot; he seems to have cared only about getting and wearing the symbol of that status (the wings he would wear on his uniform).

551:22 **something that suited you right down to the ground** a line of work for which you were ideally suited

551:24 **Armistice** 11 November 1918, the day upon which the Great War formally ended

551:24 **stayed in** remained employed by the military

552:1 **wing-walking** Providing both private competition and public entertainment, wing-walkers were "the most extreme and intrepid" of the daredevil barnstormers. Wing walking involves stunts performed on the wing of an airplane in flight; wing walkers tried to one-up each other with stunts, and both they and the promoters of barnstorming events (see 553:1) were "both capitalizing on sudden death" or the chance of it. Stunts included handstands, hanging by one's teeth from a rope ladder, transfers between planes and between cars, boats, trains, and planes. (See "Wing Walkers.")

552:3 **hide out at about three thousand** three thousand feet above ground, in a location where the officers in charge couldn't see the risk they were taking with the aircraft and each other

552:3 **Nine** possibly the British-manufactured Airco D.H. 9 or D.H. 9a, a biplane with large wings and 2–person capacity that could fly as high as 18,000 feet (see "Airco D.H. 9a")

552:3–4 **muscled around on top of it** did physical stunts on the topmost of the two wings (see 552:1)

552:6–7 **And isolation is bad for poker. You lose on tick, and on tick you always plunge** "On tick" is a British expression meaning "on credit," and one vernacular meaning of "plunge" is to gamble extravagantly. Buck seems to mean that if one plays poker on credit, one is doomed to lose; moreover, playing on credit seems to doom one to making increasingly bad bets. The anecdote of the "fellow named White" at 552:8–24 demonstrates Buck's theory.

552:10 **plunging** making increasingly reckless bets; a metaphor that suggests flying, when an aircraft's plunge could be fatal

552:10–11 **losing every pot** the pot of money at stake in a given hand of poker

552:14 **yellow** a coward

552:16 **I'd cut him, double or quit, one time** Buck offered White the opportunity to cut the deck in any place; the shown card would have to be beaten by Buck's drawing a higher one from the remaining deck. Should Buck win, he would get double the money he has won; should White win, all of his losses will be called off.

552:18 **flipped his cut over and riffled them** Buck turned over the cards underneath the queen that White drew and shuffled them in order to make his own cut.

552:18–19 **gob of face cards and three of the aces** Buck is shuffling the remainder of the deck face up, and the spectators see that it contains a good many high cards.

552:21 **case ace** When three of the aces in a poker game have been seen ("are dead"), the remaining unseen ace is the case ace.

552:25 **speed ship** speculatively, a fast experimental aircraft

552:29–30 **dived the wings off at two thousand with a full gun** At five thousand feet up, White took the plane into a dive; the wings came off at two thousand feet, and he had the throttle (gun) fully open.

552:31 **So I was out again after four years, a civ again** Buck does not explain why White's death resulted in his discharge from the military or whether that discharge was voluntary or involuntary, honorable or not. "Civ" is short for civilian.

552:33 **bird** a guy (also slang for an aircraft)

553:1 **barn-storming circus** traveling air show. These became very popular in the years following the Great War and remained so throughout the Great Depression. Also called flying circuses (see 559:10).

553:6 **So is your old man** slang to express boredom with the situation at hand, in this case the description of his future mistress's marriage

553:15–19 **one of these long, dark, snake-like women surrounded by ostrich plumes and Woolworth incense, smoking cigarettes on the divan while Rogers ran out to the corner delicatessen for sliced ham and potato salad on paper plates** Buck expected that Rogers's wife would look like a caricature of an "exotic" woman imitating her idea of a high-culture lifestyle, lazily smoking and inhaling cheap (Woolworth, after the dime stores) fragrance and expecting her husband to wait on her.

553:20 **one of these little pale squashy dresses** The 1922 Montgomery Ward's catalog features a pink voile dress with the loose sleeves and waistline typical of the popular style that seems to us much like the ordinary housedress worn by Mrs. Rogers (see "History of Fashion 1920–1930").

553:22–23 **Howard—that was Rogers—had just told her about me and I said, "What did he tell you?"** She means that she has just received notice of the extra dinner guest, and he tries to make a clever remark in return, which she ignores until 553:30.

553:30 **Oh, don't you?** Her retort insults Buck's appearance and takes his attitude to task.

554:6 **Are you sorry?** No, he's not, and she knows it. Here begins their flirtation.

554:7–8 **By that time she had bought one for me to wear** The time frame of the story is unclear because Buck, of course, has no need to explain it to himself; he skips between important moments in his memory. It is fascinating to consider this line from Mrs. Rogers's point of view: she succeeds in feminizing a thoroughly sexist character, apparently without his knowledge.

554:11 **We're just an aviator** Mrs. Rogers repeatedly emphasizes her partnership in marriage as though the couple is one person, even as the flirtation with Buck escalates.

554:14–18 **'My Lord, a wing-walker? When you were choosing a family friend,' I said, 'why didn't you choose a man we could invite to dinner a week ahead and not only count on his being there, but on his taking us out and spending his money on us?'** She comments not only on Buck's small income but also the danger inherent in his profession.

554:20 **Buck** Buck Monaghan, the narrator, named here for the first time. His last name appears at 564:9.

554:32–555:1 **when I would come in that night I'd find traces of powder on my dresser or maybe her handkerchief or something, and I'd go to bed with the room smelling like she was still there** Mrs. Rogers is steadily moving toward Buck's bed, where she and Rogers end up at 555:7–8.

555:1–2 **She said: "Do you want us to find you one?"** the end of a conversation that Buck recalls in disjointed bursts at 554:20–21, 554:26–28, and 554:29

555:10: **I am—** Howard and Mrs. Rogers have been arguing, and he is probably calling to break off the evening's plans with Buck: "I am sorry, but we have to cancel."

555:13 **Well, what** do you want me to tell him?

555:16–17 **If this is not the night—** Buck senses that Rogers doesn't welcome his presence on this evening, and he tries to offer him a way to cancel the engagement; but the attempt is half-hearted at best: "I'll come another time."

555:21 **So if you'll just—** tell me when you'd like me to come

555:24 **stick it** stay in the marriage

555:26 **insurance rates** premium rates for life insurance; as an aviator, Rogers is in a high-risk profession and so would pay high premiums, a heavy drain on a household budget.

555:28 **tenement woman** poorer, lower-class woman

556:3 **stake** saved money. From 556:4–7, Buck offers Rogers money, which insults him as a man and as the head of a household.

556:12 **Mildred** Mrs. Rogers's first name, appearing here for the first time

556:16 **out on top I'd look back at his face behind the goggles** The cockpit of the Airco D.H.9a sat slightly behind and underneath the top wing, where Buck does his wing-walking. Although neither man discusses Mildred, both clearly think about her, and Buck tries to read Howard's face for information about her.

556:20–21 **hopping passengers** taking passengers short distances from one place to another; also the slang term for sight-seeing in a barnstorming airplane

556:25 **It** Buck's decision to go to Mildred while Howard is busy with passengers

556:27 **It** the first moment of physical passion between them

556:29 **It** the situation in which Buck finds the three of them

556:30 **windscreen** the glass in front of the cockpit that protects the pilot's face

557:6–9 **And when I'd unfasten my belt and crawl out I'd look back at his face and wonder what he was thinking, how much he knew or suspected** At his most psychologically vulnerable, the moment when he must take off his safety belt and get up on the top wing to perform his stunts, Buck wonders whether Howard might know about the affair. Should he know, what might he do about it? The passage implicitly invokes the principle in the story's title.

557:14 **cut the gun** turned off the throttle (see 552:29–30)

557:17 **last hop** final passenger trip of the day (see 556:20–21)

557:17 **monkey suit** coveralls to protect his clothing from the sun, dirt, and wind

557:20–21 **one of those little squashy dresses** like she wore when they first met (see 553:20)

557:30–31 **Do you know what I was thinking?** a direct address to Buck's auditor and Faulkner's reader; see also 551:17, 558:18, and 558:28

557:31–558:1 **I was thinking that he and I were upstairs and me out on top and I had just found that he had thrown the stick away and was flying her on the rudder alone and that he knew that I knew the stick was gone and so it was all right now, whatever happened** The rudder on an airplane controls changes in horizontal directions; the stick controls vertical changes. At the moment the three of them acknowledge the affair, Buck immediately imagines Howard and himself in another contest of honor (see 557:6–9), in which both know the stakes. Buck grants Howard enough honor to give him a fighting chance in the attempt to kill him but never questions his own assumption that Howard will in fact try to do so.

558:2–3 **So it was like a piece of wood with another piece of wood leaning against it, and she held back and looked at my face** **it** = Buck and Mildred's embrace; she notices that he is not thinking about her.

558:19–23 **Like nobody is anything in himself: like a woman, even when you love her, is a woman to you just part of the time and the rest of the time she is just a person that don't look at things the same way a man has learned to. Don't have the same ideas about what is decent and what is not** With his questions to Howard at 558:33–559:3, this comment suggests that Buck thinks of women in sexually commodified terms. She is a woman when he wants sex and an amoral nuisance otherwise.

558:25–27 **God damn it, if you'll just keep out of this for a little while! We're both trying our best to take care of you, so it won't hurt you** **it** = the contest between the two men; the adultery they try to settle between them

559:18 **laid for me, sucked me in** set a trap for him by withholding the fact that they had another job together scheduled for the next day

559:20 **mealy-mouthed** unwilling to speak directly

559:22 **"Take the stick yourself," he said. "I'll do your trick"** an indication of Howard's sense of honor

559:23 **Have you ever done any work like this before?** an indication of Buck's sense of honor

559:26 **grin on the outside of your face** in other words, show outside the grin you feel inside; let your face reflect how happy you are to have me in this situation.

559:27 **crate** airplane

560:1 **Because I want to hit back once** Buck implies that he won't be alive after this flight to hit Howard back.

560:4–5 **Let me have your shoes, will you? I haven't got any rubber soles out here** a reiteration of the offer to do Buck's stunt and let him fly the plane; the rubber soles would keep the wing-walker from slipping.

560:9 **them** spectators

560:12–13 **balancing me against side pressure** taking into account the pressure of the wind across the wing

560:20 **the loop** a loop-the-loop, in which the plane makes two successive 360–degree circles perpendicular to the earth and the stuntman (or -woman) is some of the time upside down, kept in place by centrifugal force. The stunt is described from Buck's point of view at 560:28–561:7.

560:28–29 **center section** of the top wing, where he will be in place for the loop-the-loop

560:30 **forward jury struts** the braces that attach the wings to the diagonal braces of the wings. Buck is getting into position to do the loop-the-loop.

560:34 **the wires began to whine** the wires holding the wings together and to the body of the airplane, singing as the result of centrifugal force operating on the looping plane

561:2 **he gunned her** suddenly increased the fuel with the throttle, in order to bring the plane back level with the earth

561:5–7 **Then I let go one end of the rope and jerked it out and threw it back at his head and held my arms out as she zoomed into the loop** Buck threw his safety rope at Howard just as the plane went into its second loop.

561:10–11 **Give him something he must fail at like he had given me something I failed at** Buck failed the test of honor involving another man's wife; he wants to besmirch Howard's honor as a pilot.

561:16 **first turn of a flat spin** His body has begun to rotate like a corkscrew, parallel to the ground

561:22 **camber** the slight curve in the airplane's wing

561:25 **slip stream** in this instance, the heavy force of the air sent backward by the propellers

562:7 **over the lines** into enemy territory

562:8 **blowing valve** a device that controls the air supply to the fuel line, in this case a malfunctioning one

562:9 **Hun** a German airplane or pilot

562:12 **Camel** Sopwith Camel, a notoriously unstable yet maneuverable plane used in combat in the Great War

562:13–16 **Not like when you're on the center section and he's at the stick, and just by stalling her for a second or ruddering her a little at the top of the loop** Buck doesn't finish his sentence: "he has you at his mercy"; "he can throw you off the wing"; "he can kill you." Pulling slightly back or forth on the stick, which controls vertical direction, Howard could dump Buck off the wing; slightly moving the rudder, the horizontal control, would shake him off. And unlike the case of the Camels, Buck has no power to control or change his situation.

562:18 **Armistice night in '18** see 551:24

562:19 **Amiens** French town on the Somme River, 75 miles north of Paris

562:19–20 **brought down that morning on an Albatross** Correctly spelled Albatros, this German-designed plane was produced in five different versions during World War I. All of them were single-seat fighter planes, armed with two machine guns; they were plagued by wing failures ("Aircraft of Germany"). Buck clearly sympathizes with any soldier trying to operate with shoddy equipment, as his experience with Camels would attest.

562:20 **frog M.P.'s** French military police

562:22–23 **a pen full of S.O.S. and ginned-up cooks and such** a makeshift prison containing mostly service personnel drunk from celebrating the Armistice. S.O.S. is Service of Supply, the division of the Army ("those damned infantrymen" of 562:21–22) that provides support services for fighting troops. Buck sees the captured German aviator as superior to these enlisted men.

562:26 **trick major's pips** the insignia on his shoulder indicating his rank; Buck seems to be insulting them as cheap or inauthentic.

562:25–35 **We were all young. I remember an Indian, a prince . . . . He was a card, queer. A good little guy, too** With Buck's allusion to the Indian subadar and paraphrasing of his comments in "Ad Astra," we can identify Buck's presence in that story as well. See 410–412, and for the comments on the "dead" surviving soldiers, see 421:4–5, 18–19. **fourth of August, 1914** = the day that Britain declared war on Germany and Austria-Hungary and that Germany invaded Belgium; the common date of the onset of the Great War; **card, queer** = odd, eccentric

563:2 **Standard** probably the famous Standard J-1, used extensively for pilot training in World War I, flying the mail, and for barnstorming in the 1920s. The J-1's large forward cockpit held two passengers to double the pilot's revenue per flight. It was also the aircraft used by Otto Timm in 1922 (the year in which the Rogers-Monaghan affair occurs) to give a young Charles Lindbergh his first taste of flying.

563:3 **Rogers grabbed me** Howard not only caught Buck on the wing of the plane, he also crawled out of the cockpit and onto the top wing to pull him to safety. Buck owes him his life twice.

563:5 **he brought me a letter from her, the first I ever had** We don't know what Mildred wrote to Buck, but that doesn't seem to matter as much as the fact that he refuses to read it. Howard has effectively beaten him on the field of honor, and she was the occasion of that defeat; his extreme dislike and distrust of women stem from the episode with the Rogers couple.

563:9–10 **Don't be a fool** don't throw away my wife's love

563:17 **buzzer** the alarm on the intercom system to alert his secretary

563:19 **dairy place** an ice cream parlor

563:20 **They are the worst** Buck seems to have had a camel's-back moment with at least one potential female customer on the day he goes to resign—an encounter that triggered the extended flashback to his involvement with Mildred and Howard Rogers. By extension, we reason that his attitude toward women has resulted in his job-hopping.

563:30 **one** a car

563:31–32 **I couldn't sell hair straightener to the widow of a nigger railroad accident** He is such a bad salesman that he wouldn't be able to sell a black woman a beauty product at a time when she needed it most—to look "respectable," which is to say whiter, at the negotiations for the settlement of the accident claim.

564:2–3 **without sticking** without staying employed in any of them

564:5 **crates were more general** less unpredictable and unstable; more universally specified and produced

564:6–8 **like women will. You know: urgent and sympathetic, and you can't shut them up like you could a man** Buck's misogyny is beginning to aim at Miss West, the "good kid, only" of 564:1.

564:9 **Monaghan** Buck's last name finally revealed

564:10 **cashier** to be paid his final wages

564:11 **hoop** child's toy, rolled along the ground with a stick

"Dr. Martino"

"Dr. Martino" focuses on the mysterious relationship between a young girl, Louise King, and her older mentor, Dr. Jules Martino. This relationship puzzles young Hubert Jarrod, who takes an interest in Louise. He takes this interest initially because of what he assumes is her forthright determination to fulfill her sexual desires, and that belief leads him to pay particular attention to what his psychology instructor at Yale has to say about "young girls" who experience "a time, an hour, in which they themselves are victims of that by means of which they victimize" (568). Less academically informed but just as determined as Jarrod, Louise's mother perceives Dr. Martino as a dangerous rival for control of her daughter, while the Doctor himself seeks to encourage Louise to overcome her fears and to live life with passion and independence. In this process, he fascinates her and earns her loyalty, while prompting her to undertake a series of often-dangerous challenges. His most recent project is to help Louise overcome her physical fear by learning to ride a dangerous horse, as he had earlier encouraged her to overcome her fear of swimming in a snake-infested river. His lesson for her, we are told, is "When you are afraid to do something you know that you are alive. But when you are afraid to do what you are afraid of you are dead" (574). The crisis comes when Mrs. King, partially abetted by Jarrod, seeks to remove her daughter from Martino's influence once and for all. Mrs. King presses her advantage, tricking Martino into believing that Louise chooses marriage to Jarrod over his continuing influence. Martino recognizes his defeat and gives up Louise, and his life as well. Thus, the domineering mother vanquishes her opponent and forces her daughter to acquiesce to the conventional matrimonial expectations for young women of her class. Jarrod, in the end, is a manipulated fool, who will, presumably, have hell to pay in his marriage to the young woman he has half-wittingly helped dupe. And Dr. Martino, who aimed at something better and higher for Louise, suffers a Quixotic defeat, reminiscent of the end of Miss Jenny in "There Was a Queen."

Faulkner's use of "Doctor Martino" as the title piece in his second short story collection has probably stimulated more interest in the story than might have otherwise been the case. James Ferguson, for example, refers to Faulkner's "undeservedly high opinion of this piece" which nevertheless "*is* a complex work containing many themes found in other stories in the volume, and in this sense it serves as a rather effective introduction to the rest of the book" (153). While many readers take the side of Dr. Martino in his efforts to serve as mentor for Louise, some share her mother's apprehension of the relationship; in Edmond Volpe's words, "Though one can readily feel animosity towards a manipulating, domineering mother, it is difficult to have strong negative feelings about a mother who would prefer that her nineteen-year-old daughter marry rather than associate with an old, dying man who urges her to risk her life" (163). Béatrice Lang maintains that "the reader must decide which, of the mother or Martino, exerts a thwarting influence on the young girl," and that "a closer look at [Martino's] role in the process of Louise King's initiation to womanhood leaves no doubts as to its negative quality" (23). Lisa Paddock sees both sides: "Martino's tutelage of Louise is in many ways dangerous and deleterious—preeminently in the way it makes her dependent upon him to such an extent that she is unwilling to relinquish him and accept the inevitable responsibility of maturity." "We come to see him," she continues, "not so much as a sinister, manipulative figure, but as a dying old man whose attachment to Louise and incipient death render him a sympathetic character" (85). Hans Skei, while expressing reservations about the behavior and values of Mrs. King—"the principle of choking parental authority and dominance"—and endorsing Dr. Martino's belief that "it takes courage and initiative and risks to stay alive and to prove to yourself that you are living," observes that Dr. Martino "remains a static centre about which everything seems to revolve. His power to control and lead the movements of other characters is nevertheless great, even if it is clearly on the decline" (*Novelist* 115–16, 180). The Yale psychology instructor, whose description of women sounds suspiciously like that of the barber-narrator in "Hair," has come in for a good deal of criticism. Lang says the instructor's comment "does not sound too scientific an explanation of human comportment—and as, without reason, he attributes [to young girls] a natural propensity to evil—which for him is inherent to action—we should discard his view of women" (24). Ferguson (mistakenly) speaks of Faulkner's "simple ignorance" about what might be said in a college classroom but grants that the instructor's speech "is a most peculiar disquisition for a teacher of psychology" (145), and Skei says the story presents "some very bad psychological understanding of how young girls tend to behave" (116). In some ways, Louise King learns well the lessons that Dr. Martino has taught her. Her return of Jarrod's ring shows that she is not frightened of not being married; she has the courage to reject the "opportunity" that he represents, as well as to reject her mother's scheme. In spite of Lang's assertion that Louise is directed by her mother to "marriage and the true force of life" (30), what Louise needs, as much as anything else, is not to be married: "Her eyes looked as if they were blind; her face was pale, white, her mouth open, shaped to an agony of despair and a surrender in particular which, had he been older, he would have realized that he would never see again on any face" (583). Faulkner's final description of her shows her hurtling toward a marriage she fears, with Jarrod along for the ride through a very uncertain "Middle Ground."

A story called "Doctor Martino" appeared on Faulkner's short story sending schedule for 5 March 1931, when the story was sent to the *Saturday Evening Post.* After the *Post* rejected it, and before it was accepted by *Harper's* magazine for publication in its November 1931 issue, the story was significantly revised (see Skei, *Short Story Career* 69–70). There was, thus, a version of "Doctor Martino" available to Faulkner as he selected and arranged the stories of *These 13* in 1931, but he chose not to publish it in that volume, presumably holding out hopes for its eventual acceptance as a magazine story. In producing his second collection of short stories in 1934, Faulkner chose "Doctor Martino" as the first story in that collection and called the book *Doctor Martino and Other Stories.* Robert K. Haas, who does not seem to have had either *These 13* or *Doctor Martino* at hand when he compiled his suggested list for stories for Faulkner's comment in 1948, does not mention the story, but Faulkner's later revision of the list included it as "Dr Martino" (*Selected Letters* 279). The *Harper's* version was published in *Doctor Martino* with one correction, and this version was further emended—the title is "Dr. Martino" and the word "Negro" is consistently capitalized—for *Collected Stories*, where it appears as the third story in "The Middle Ground."

565:3 **aura of oil wells and Yale** markers of his class status—and of the sister's snobbery and class pretensions

565:8–9 **swamp angel** a term of endearment that also reveals Hubert Jarrod's snobbery and class pretensions

565:10 **That** Louise King

565:13 **sex appeal** a clarification of the "it" that Louise has—or, in this case, does not. In 1927, the writer Elinor Glyn (1864–1943) coined the term "it" to describe sex appeal. "It" was a story first serialized in *Cosmopolitan*, then published in a collection with four other of Glyn's stories, then commissioned as a film starring Clara Bow (all in 1927). The silent film star Bow became widely known as the "It Girl." (See Anthony Glyn 299–300; "Glyn, Elinor.")

565:15 **the right clubs** upper-class campus social organizations at Yale

565:16 **a little on the epicene** a little feminine and a little masculine; not particularly sexualized. Cleanth Brooks (125, n. 13) suggests that Faulkner borrowed the term from T. S. Eliot's "Mr. Eliot's Sunday Morning Service," in which the bees' role in cross-pollination of flowers is the "Blest office of the epicene."

565:21–22 **which he immediately took to himself** Hubert notices Louise's apparent interest in him and credits himself for attracting it.

565:24 **They had not yet been introduced** not been formally introduced to one another by a third party, as was socially proper

566:23–24 **Your mother won't let him come to call on you?** Jarrod assumes that Louise is meeting a lover of whom her mother would not approve.

567:5 **I believe you really mean it** Jarrod thinks Louise is proposing a *ménage à trois.*

567:27–28 **The old girl is after me, anyway** Mrs. King is interested in Jarrod as marriage material for her daughter.

567:32–33 **natural prey of all mothers of daughters** Jarrod believes that his money and upper-class education have made him an irresistible candidate for matrimony.

568:1 **stalking horse** a decoy, used to conceal her real purposes

568:6 **New Haven** city in Connecticut in which Yale University is located

568:7 **prom** short for *promenade,* a formal dance

568:17 **psychology** Jarrod attends the class at Yale in 1930 that Quentin Compson cuts at Harvard in 1910 (see *The Sound and the Fury* 101).

568:19–27 **The instructor was talking about women . . . "A time, an hour, in which they themselves are victims of that by means of which they victimize"** The psychology instructor gets Jarrod's sudden attention because he needs an explanation of Louise's behavior and his own responses to it; the instructor says that for a time women are subject to the kind of sexual desire that they arouse in men. Jarrod seizes on this misogyny at 568:29.

568:21–22 **a blind spot, like that which racing aviators enter when making a fast turn** According to Robert Harrison, "Pilots of closed-circuit racers were subjected to brutal g-loads in turns, as time and again they slammed their machines over in a steep bank and hauled back on the stick"—in other words, they accelerated sharply while turning, an action which caused near-blackouts in the pilot (171).

568:29–30 **"We've got to be married soon," he said. "Soon"** Because he believes that Louise "needed looking after" (568:10–11) and has just "learned" the explanation for women's erratic sexual behavior, Jarrod thinks the only way to save Louise is to marry her and give her a legitimate (or at least socially acceptable) sexual outlet.

570:4 **town** New York

569:7–8 **They were allies now, not yet antagonists** Before a daughter is married, her mother and her future husband work together to make sure the wedding happens. After the wedding, each contends for the daughter's affections to the exclusion of the other's.

570:8 **the cheering throngs at the Dean's altar** the crowd at the commencement ceremony the next week

570:10 **business woman** prostitute

570:13 **Beano** another name for bingo, the game, and saying the word when one wins; here, equivalent of "I know what you mean" or "Got it"

570:20 **the iron-impregnated waters** the water at the hot mineral springs, in which one also bathed for health

570:26 **crepe myrtle copse** small thicket of flowering trees

571:1 **a dead man and a horse** the first allusion to what Jarrod later learns of Dr. Martino and the horse that Louise plans to ride

571:3–4 **flannels and a tweed jacket** winter clothing marking Jarrod as an outsider

572:2 **They looked like shoe-buttons** very small and dark, like the buttons on old-fashioned high-button shoes

572:16–17 **What rivers has he made *you* swim, I wonder?** see 573:21–574:28

573:11–12 **marquee above the spring** a large, open-sided tent under which the people gather to take the spring waters

574:6–7 **Every time he wakes up in the morning he does what I had to swim the river to do** Doctor Martino is in such physical pain that just getting out of bed requires courage, determination, and a commitment to life.

574:13–15 **A rabbit: don't you see? But it's brass now; the shape of being afraid, in brass that nothing can hurt** a totem of fear, the symbol of triumphing over it

574:17–18 **" 'And if you are afraid?' I said, 'then what?' " 'Then I'll give it back to him' "** see 582:33

574:31–32 **Doctor Jules** an affectionate address for Dr. Martino

575:1–2 **and that that fool mother of hers anyway . . .** would have forbidden her to write to him

575:34 **I know who's in the blind spot now** see 568:21

576:31 **strychnine** chemical that stimulates adrenaline production, thereby the heart and heart-rate

576:31 **Florence Nightingale** the founder of modern nursing (1820–1910)

577:5 **he will be . . .** dead

577:7–8 **a match box full of dynamite caps in your breast pocket** nitroglycerin pills, in easy reach. Nitroglycerin, the same chemical used in dynamite, has been a standard treatment for chest pain and heart attack symptoms since 1879. Converted to nitric acid in the body, the chemical relaxes the blood vessels and allows more blood to reach the heart (see Adams).

577:17–19 **And I can wait, because I haven't got a match box of dynamite caps in my shirt. Or a box of conjuring powder, either** Jarrod means that he doesn't have the claim on Louise's attention or affection that Dr. Martino has, nor any magic by which to attract them.

578:14 **the stained tumblers** glasses used at the spring, stained from the iron and mineral deposits in the water

579:1–2 **He has no one to fear here** an insult to Jarrod's manhood

579:5 **Mrs. King watched him go on down the path** Here the perspective of the story shifts from Jarrod's to Mrs. King's, where it remains until 583:3.

579:11–12 **Since you don't seem to have any private affairs where he is concerned; don't appear to desire any—** privacy from him

581:1–2 **like it might have come from Woolworth's** Woolworth's was the country's first dime store. Founded in 1911, it also offered inexpensive goods directly for the public's examination and selection rather than employ clerks to fetch and wrap merchandise. The snob Jarrod seems to feel as though Dr. Martino has snubbed him.

581:9–10 **that he knew he could always get between us before—in time . . .** another example of Jarrod's fear that Dr. Martino stands higher in Louise's esteem than he does

581:16–17 **his eyes closed and the sweat popping out on his face** the effects of some sort of heart pain or palpitation

581:17–18 **Now, strike me** the doctor's concession to the chivalric code Jarrod has invoked by claiming her as his fiancée

581:24–26 **"Louise is asleep," she said, for no reason that Jarrod could have discerned, even if he had been listening** Mrs. King is lying, and Jarrod is not paying attention to her anyway. Both things allow Louise to get caught in her mother's trap.

581:31 **Meridian** city in east central Mississippi, twenty miles from the Alabama border

581:33 **Has Louise—** "changed her mind" or "sent him a sign," repeated at 582:3

582:3 **And Louise has—?** see 581:33

582:23–26 **Young Mr. Jarrod, you have been conquered by a woman, as I have been. But with this difference: it will be a long time yet before you will realize that you have been slain** Dr. Martino recognizes Mrs. King's manipulation of Jarrod and Louise, even though Jarrod does not yet.

582:29 **And I said, "Dead"** Jarrod says this three times, as though incredulous at his own taunting of the gravely ill Dr. Martino.

582:33 **with tears or with sleep** Since she has been locked in her room, Louise might well not have known that her mother has taken the rabbit; she might be crying at its loss as well as because of her mother's betrayal and the doctor's note. Since we learned at 574:17–18 that Louise was to give the rabbit back to Dr. Martino if she was ever afraid, we know that his receiving it sends that message; it is as if Louise has told him that she has given up on life, and he can no longer depend on her to try to be brave.

582:34–583:1 **He was just making a fool of you** Here Mrs. King finishes off her scheme to separate Louise and Dr. Martino for good.

583:3 **The car was going fast** another shift in the story's perspective, from Mrs. King back to Jarrod

583:9–10 **Are you that glad?** Jarrod mistakes Louise's crying as evidence of her relief at not having to ride the horse.

583:15–16 **His foot lifted; the car began to slow. "Why, you sent . . ."** Jarrod takes his foot off of the accelerator and the car begins to slow down as he realizes that Mrs. King is the one who sent the rabbit to Dr. Martino, not Louise.

583:31–33 **an agony of despair and a surrender in particular which, had he been older, he would have realized that he would never see again on any face** Louise's mother has blasted her daughter's moorings and her belief in her own bravery, and even the man that will soon be her husband does not understand the magnitude of what has just happened to her.

583:34 **set the lever back into gear** switched the gearshift from a neutral position into first gear

584:7 **In that gathering of wide summer dresses** the story's final shift in perspective, from Jarrod's to Lily Cranston's

584:17 ***about*** The proprietress's focus on the preposition is curious, as is the repetition of "Don't worry about me" twice in Dr. Martino's three-line note. One interpretation of both suggests that Dr. Martino doesn't want anyone near (about) him, and though concerned, Mrs. Cranston respects his wishes.

584:21 **cyar** car

584:22 **outen** out of

584:23 **patter-roller** patroller; one who searched for runaway slaves or slaves off their master's property without a written pass

"Fox Hunt"

Faulkner knew two types of fox hunting. In his native Mississippi, hunters gathered at night, often around a fire and nearly certainly with some whiskey handy, and listened to the hounds chase the fox in the darkness (see Calvin Brown 85–86). This kind of fox hunting was practiced by ordinary people, such as Old Man Pettigrew in "Shingles for the Lord." The traditional English fox hunt was an aristocratic ritual, involving elaborate costumes and numerous conventions. The fox hunt in this story draws on both types. Harrison Blair represents himself as a kind of American aristocrat; he has inherited some money, married some more, and bought a large estate in Carolina as a wedding gift for his wife. He uses this estate only two months out of each year, for gentrified fox hunting. On the day of the story, Blair finally manages to ride down the fox he has been pursuing for three years, and his guest Steve Gawtrey also manages to "run down" Blair's wife, as witnessed by two poor white men from the neighborhood. We learn, eventually, that the tangle of plots in the story has been created by Blair's "valet," Ernie, for reasons of his own. Ernie thus functions as the traditional wily servant, manipulating his master for his own ends, some psychological and some financial.

There are many possible "fox hunts" in this story, not the least of which is Gawtrey's pursuit of Mrs. Blair. Never named in her own right, she remains trapped by all of the men around her, including the two who watch; indeed, Nicholas Fargnoli and Michael Golay speculate "that Mrs. Blair is no adulteress but, rather, a respectable woman trapped in a difficult marriage who continues to fight off the unwelcome advances of her unpleasant pursuer" (91). The story has a complex narrative structure and mostly unsympathetic central characters, and it has attracted very little critical attention. Certainly written by 1930 and maybe as early as 1929, "Fox Hunt" was published in *Harper's* in September 1931 and could conceivably have been included in *These 13*, but Faulkner chose to save it for *Doctor Martino*. In *Collected Stories*, "Fox Hunt" appears as the fourth story in "The Middle Ground," among six consecutive stories set outside Yoknapatawpha County. Lisa Paddock says "The Middle Ground" itself is "a kind of no-man's-land where the only true constant is the lowest common denominator of existence: death itself" (180). The stories of "The Middle Ground" in general, and "Fox Hunt" in particular, tend to feature some of the more squalid aspects of human nature. Edmond L. Volpe says Ernie's "shoddy moral values establish the aura of immorality that Faulkner seeks to create about the society of the urban rich" (119), and he might have extended the remark to include Blair and Gawtrey as well.

587:15 **that Jup'ter horse** that horse named Jupiter

587:16 **Clay-eaters** "a term of contempt for poor rural whites. It comes from the fact that one of the symptoms of a heavy infestation of hookworms is a craving for clay, which is frequently actually eaten" (Brown 54)

587:21 **patent** patented, presumably mechanized

588:14 **burr-starred mules** mules with coats matted by sticking burrs

588:19 **in boots and red coats** Fox hunters after the English fashion (see Introduction) often wore such elaborate costumes as part of the ritual of the sport. Faulkner himself liked to dress in hunt regalia and was photographed in his Farmington Hunt Club regalia by Oxford photographer J. R. Cofield in 1961 (see Williamson 327–28; photograph reproduced facing 249).

588:22–23 **owned the house and the dogs and some of the guests too** Blair, a very wealthy man, may have loaned some of his guests money or provided other favors to further his own financial advantage; he may also buy their company through his lavish entertainments, as Jay Gatsby does. The house and land, the immediate setting of the story, however, belong to Mrs. Blair (see 593:20–24).

588:24–26 **big, vicious-looking black horse, and they watched another man lift Harrison Blair's wife onto a chestnut mare and then mount a bay horse in his turn** Blair's is the "big, vicious-looking black horse" (the "Jup'ter horse" at 587:15); his wife sits a female horse that has reached breeding age; Gawtrey's reddish-brown, male horse is less formidable than Blair's.

589:6–7 **Don't believe anything you hear, and not more than half you see** paraphrase of an adage variously attributed to Mark Twain and Will Rogers

589:13 **That fellow don't own no horse** By "holding the bay horse against the chestnut mare's flank" (589:14–16), Gawtrey places Mrs. Blair, himself, and both horses in a potentially dangerous situation, as either horse can strike out violently against this confinement. To the speaker, Blair's behavior suggests that he cannot be the owner of a horse, because he endangers valuable property. Gawtrey's primary concern here, as at 592:4–7, is to keep Mrs. Blair and her mount under his direct, immediate control.

589:27 **pink coats** "A typical hunt is a ritualistic event. Riders wear traditional hunting costumes. The coats worn by hunting officials are often called 'Pinks,' a reference not to their color, which varies, but to an early tailor named Pink. The act of blooding began with King James I. This was a ceremony in which the huntsmaster smeared the blood of the quarry onto the cheeks of a newly initiated hunt follower" (TutorGig.com).

589:28 **vixen** both a female fox and a shrewish, ill-tempered woman

589:31–32 **Don't you know that ain't no way to catch a fox?** see Introduction

589:34 **spo'tin** sporting

590:2 **gempmuns** gentlemen

590:13–14 **That's something else about gempmuns you won't never know** a smug endorsement of the sophistication of his wealthy employer and condescension toward the white countryman

590:21–22 **the dogs were at fault** off-track; had lost the fox's scent

590:32 **he** Blair

591:5 **untangle** sniff out, find

591:21 **winy** like wine; rich, mellow, intoxicating

591:22 **their gaunt, yellow faces** suggests not only malnutrition but also the aftereffects of malaria, which was endemic in the South from the eighteenth century until World War II (Breeden 1337–43)

591:28–29 **like a double or hermaphroditic centaur with two heads and eight legs** A centaur is a mythical creature with a man's head, chest, and shoulders joined to the body and legs of a horse. This particular centaur is "double" or "hermaphroditic," combining male and female characteristics, because the woman's and man's heads appear to be joined to the legs of their two (male and female) horses—an image that suggests an unnatural intimacy or a forced union between Gawtrey and Mrs. Blair.

591:31 **unbobbed** not cut short in the fashion of the 1920s

592:4–7 **The man was holding the bay horse against the mare's flank at full gallop. His hand lay on the woman's hand which held the reins, and he was slowly but steadily drawing both horses back, slowing them** the same position at full gallop that he held at 589:15–16, a remarkable and dangerous feat of horsemanship

592:11–12 **with that semblance of a thrush and a hawk in terrific immobility in mid-air** like a smaller songbird and a larger (predatory) bird

592:16–17 **That one don't seem to need no dogs neither** an earthy and explicit parallel with the gentrified fox hunt

592:19–20 **I be durn if I see how that skinny neck of hern . . .** can hold up all of that hair

592:22 **brush** the fox's tail

592:24–25 **something to her that a man don't say to a woman in comp'ny** an obscene remark; a comment out of place in mixed company of men and women

593:4–5 **ditch-bank** bank of the dyke

593:7 **that ere leather riding-switch** Blair's riding whip

593:12–13 **a Ford car with a light truck body** a truck body set on a Ford automobile frame, customized and designed to drive around the countryside over rough terrain

593:14–15 **a man in a derby hat** Blair's valet/secretary/bodyguard, identified as "Ernie" at 594:34

593:20 **This all belongs to her, house and all** contradicts the earlier assertion that "Blair . . . owned the house" (588:22), raising the possibility that Ernie doesn't know as much as he thinks he does

593:30 **on Lenox Avenue? You don't have to drink the gin** a principal thoroughfare in Harlem of New York City, where bootleg gin was available for purchase; perhaps the only context in which the bodyguard, almost certainly a New Yorker, would have encountered "Nigras" (593:28)

593:34–594:1 **Fourteenth Street** Fourteenth Street in New York City was and is the location of Union Square and, at the time of the story, marked a significant division between "uptown," with its major department stores and theaters, and "downtown," where lower-class people lived, including the bohemian settlement of artists and writers in Greenwich Village.

594:6 **jack** slang for "money"

594:6–7 **of this Oklahoma Indian oil** Between 1820 and 1840, over 50,000 members of the Five Civilized Nations (Cherokee, Choctaw, Chickasaw, Creek, and Seminole) were forced to relocate from their southern lands to the Oklahoma territory, significant portions of which were then designated "Indian Territory." Considerable portions of the Oklahoma lands were intended for Indian occupation, but not assigned. These lands were taken up by whites who immigrated in the land rushes of 1889–1907, when the Oklahoma territory became a state. The first big Oklahoma oil strike was at Tulsa in 1905, making the Indian lands once again desirable to the whites. Congress passed the Indian Oil Leasing Act in 1924, so Mrs. Blair's mother was cheating the Indians out of their land between those two dates. Allen, Mrs. Blair's youthful sweetheart, along with his father, became an "oil Indian" (see 598:22–23).

594:19–20 **put the bee on you boys** gave you a hard time; made you a raw deal

594:34 **Ernie** Blair's valet/bodyguard; previously introduced, but unnamed, at 593:14–15

595:2 **skirts** slang for "women"

595:5–6 **I know which one of her and her husband it was that had took them oil wells off the Indians** the implication that Mrs. Blair's conniving, manipulative mother swindled the Native Americans out of their land; one of several important narrative strands of exploitation and greed in the story

595:18 **He used to ride me** He regularly abused Ernie.

595:20–21 **"When?" he says. "When you get back from the hospital?" "Maybe before I go there," I says** Ernie seeks to impress the chauffeur with his own masculine self-determination. In spite of their differences in wealth and in spite of the master/servant relationship, Ernie claims to have reacted with threatened violence of his own when Blair purportedly makes as if to manhandle him. See 601:5–9 for the context of this encounter.

595:28 **Ty Juana** Ernie's dialect pronunciation of Tijuana, a town in extreme northwest Mexico on the U.S. border south of San Diego, with the reputation as a center for vice

595:31–32 **Maybe he quit riding you because he had something else to ride** a pun on the sexual meaning of "ride"

596:4 **horse Pullman** a train's passenger car equipped for sleeping, named for its inventor, George Pullman; here, a boxcar

596:6 **a lower** Pullman sleeping compartments (see 596:4) conventionally had both a lower and an upper berth, the lower being more desirable because of its comparative ease of access.

596:14 **Callaghan** Mrs. Blair's riding instructor and operator of a New York City riding stable

596:14 **practice plugs** older, presumably placid, horses used for training inexperienced riders

596:15–17 **chorines that have took up horse riding to get ready to get drafted from the bushes out in Brooklyn or New Jersey to the Drive or Central Park** chorus girls who take up the aristocratic pastime of horseback riding in order to make themselves attractive to wealthy men who will take them from the streets of Brooklyn or New Jersey to wealthy areas such as Riverside Drive or Central Park

596:25 **one or two head of Zigfield's prize stock** Florenz Ziegfeld, Jr. (1869–1932), a New York theatrical producer famous for his annual productions from 1907 to 1931 of "Ziegfeld's Follies," an extravagant musical revue featuring scantily clad or nude women. Rich patrons of these shows would sometimes pick out particular dancers in the hopes of making them their wives or mistresses. The women were, thus, like prize cattle. At Callaghan's riding stable, Mrs. Blair is incongruous in the company of children and Ziegfeld chorines. In an article attributed to the producer himself, Ziegfeld tells "What Makes a 'Ziegfeld Girl'" (Musicals101.com). Beauty was the first consideration, and the chosen beauties were rigorously trained in dance and song, performing dressed in elaborate costumes that generally included a large headpiece.

596:27 **with that black face of his** a reference to Blair's habitual anger rather than to his skin color

597:1 **dump cart** a vehicle with two wheels and a body or bed that tilts or opens at the back for unloading materials

597:4–6 **My old man tried all his life to make a banker out of me, but your old woman done it in two months** By asking for money all the time, Mrs. Blair's mother has made Blair into a cash dispenser.

597:10–11 **you would have thought she was a conductor on a Broadway surface car** By the way she had her hand out for money all the time, Mrs. Blair's mother looked like a ticket salesman on a streetcar.

597:12–14 **Sometimes she wouldn't even wait until I could get Blair under a shower and a jolt into him before breakfast, to make the touch** According to Ernie, Mrs. Blair approaches her husband to ask for money early in the morning, before breakfast and, apparently, before Blair has had his morning alcoholic "eye-opener."

597:14–15 **Park Avenue** a street on the east side of Manhattan with many wealthy residents

597:18 **Burke** Mrs. Blair's maid

597:19–20 **this Yale college boy, this Indian sweetheart** Allen, the young man first named at 598:8–9, with whom Mrs. Blair remains jealously infatuated; not necessarily a Native American, but from Oklahoma

597:22 **ward school out at Oklahoma** Before their families became wealthy through oil dealings (see 597:24 and 598:22–23), Allen and Mrs. Blair, as youngsters, attended school together. A "ward school" was a public school for children living in a particular district.

597:23 **Swapped Masonic rings or something** went steady; the decidedly unsentimental Ernie, who would not understand such youthful feeling, likens their relationship to that of initiates of the Masonic order, a large fraternal order with secret rituals and signs, which he also doesn't understand.

597:27–28 **marry a gal out of a tank show that happened to be in town** Allen, presumably on the rebound from Mrs. Blair's marriage, marries a girl from a traveling show or carnival. Allen chooses his wife just as other men pick out "prize stock" from the Ziegfeld chorus line (596:25). A "tank show" takes its name from "tank town," a small town important only for the trains that stop there to take on water.

597:29 **that Callaghan has give her up** see 596:30–31

598:3 **swell** elegant, pretentious

598:8–9 **So now the old dame digs up about this boy, this Allen boy that the gal** The mother learns of Mrs. Blair's earlier infatuation.

598:12–15 **"You mean Columbia."**
"No. Yale. It's another college."
"I thought the other one was named Cornell or something," the chauffeur said. the class pretensions of the rich satirized, and the two servants' regional prejudice revealed: neither Ernie nor the chauffeur knows anything about American universities other than the two found in New York State, and Yale only by hearsay.

598:16–18 **Where these college boys all come from when these hotchachacha deadfalls get raided and they give them all a ride downtown in the wagon** "Hotchachacha" is slang from the Jazz Age used to describe a hot nightspot (Brown 106), and a deadfall is a trap that crushes its prey. In this context, a deadfall is also a low drinking or gambling establishment in which unwary customers are separated from their money. During Prohibition, these speakeasies were often raided and closed by the police and the patrons taken to the downtown police station in a paddy wagon.

598:18–21 **"Don't you read no papers?"**
"Not often," the chauffeur said. "I don't care nothing about politics" Ernie continues to condescend to the chauffeur, who would know about the arrest of college boys in police raids if he read the newspapers. The chauffeur's non sequitur reply suggests that he thinks newspapers principally publish news of politics. There may also be a suggestion of political corruption, as a raid on a speakeasy was thought to indicate a failure to pay illegal police "protection."

598:23 **lousy with it** very, very rich

599:6 **lyron** Ernie's dialect pronunciation of lion

599:16–17 **The other man, the valet, secretary, whatever he might have been** This line not only calls attention to the fact that Ernie's role as servant is an unconventional one, but also signals the uncertainty of the implied narrator of the story, an important issue in a story that features multiple narrators of limited credibility.

600:15–19 **but me and Callaghan are all right too; I done Callaghan a little favor once too, so about a week after we come back from Connecticut, I have Callaghan come in and tell Blair about this other swell dog, without telling Blair who owned it** Ernie has enlisted Callaghan to tell Blair about a "swell dog"—a fine horse—that Gawtrey supposedly owns but that a wealthy "Mr. Van Dyming" (see 600:19) wants to buy. The favor that Ernie had done for Callaghan is not specified, but it may involve bringing Mrs. Blair to Callaghan's stable for her riding lessons (see 596:14).

600:33–601:2 **"Leave your wife do the talking," I says. "He'll listen to her." That was when he hit me** for the implication that his wife has sexual influence on Gawtrey

601:18 **fired him off the college for losing his amateur's standing** Ernie's cruel description of Allen's dismissal from Yale because of his marriage. In the 1920s, Yale undergraduates were not allowed to marry; presumably, a Yale undergraduate's amorous adventures before marriage were not proscribed, as long as they followed "the recognized rules of gentlemanly conduct" (*Yale College* 6). By marrying, Allen put his lovemaking "on a professional basis," as a prostitute was said to have "lost her amateur standing."

601:20 **this Burke kid** the Irish maid, first mentioned at 597:17–18

601:25–26 **here is Gawtrey and her like a fade-out in the pitchers** Burke caught Gawtrey and Mrs. Blair in an embrace. In movie pictures of the time, sexually explicit scenes were prohibited; hence, the picture "faded out" on the embrace, leaving only a suggestion of further developments.

601:31–32 **some dog still finishing last year's Selling Plate at Pimlico** If Gawtrey ever owned a horse, according to Ernie, it was a worthless horse, unable to place in a selling plate race, in which the winner is to be sold at a predetermined price. Pimlico is a racetrack in Baltimore. Thus, Ernie triumphantly announces that the "swell plug" that Gawtrey presumably owns is imaginary; he also confirms the young man's comment earlier in the story, "That fellow don't own no horse" (589:13).

602:11–14 **". . . it got to where I wasn't no more than one of these Russian droshkies or something."**
"A Russian what?"
"One of these fellows that can't call their own soul." At this stage, Ernie must hustle to keep up the charade of his scheme. Grasping for a term specifically connoting indentured servitude, he confuses "droshky" (a small horse carriage) with "dusha," a "serf" as well as a "soul" in the religious or moral sense. Faulkner may well have been thinking of Nikolai Gogol's Tchitchikov, whose grandiose manipulations form the basis for his 1842 novel, *Dead Souls.*

602:17 **soap him down** calm him down

602:20 **Out of the Sunday school paper** conventional moral lessons from childhood, which would have included "these golden rules" (see 602:26–27), like "Do unto others as you would have others do unto you"

602:32 **for a Rockefeller quarter** equivalent to "in a New York minute" or "in a heartbeat." A "Rockefeller quarter," more frequently a "Rockefeller dime," is an insignificant amount of money to a fabulously wealthy man. John D. Rockefeller, Sr., the founder of Standard Oil, was in the habit, in his later years, of giving out dimes to schoolchildren (Chernow 614).

603:1 **So he don't . . .** finished at 603:13–14

603:24 **around to the crank** to start the car, the equivalent of turning the key to start the ignition in a contemporary vehicle

603:34–35 **Do they have to keep soldiers here?** Ernie mistakes the bugle signaling the capture of the fox for an Army bugler's flourish.

604:5–6 **The two men on the mules recrossed the rice field and mounted the ridge into the pines** The final section of the story brings into focus the rude initiation of the younger countryman as to the ways in which women like Mrs. Blair are hurt and abused by ruthless men. As noted by Frederick Karl (427), "Fox Hunt" recalls many aspects of D. H. Lawrence's "The Fox" (1922), in which an aggressive man resembling Blair and Gawtrey earnestly pursues a fox until its death, much as he pursues a woman.

604:14–15 **I reckon that's something about gentle-men you won't never know** an echo of the groom's language at 590:13–14, implying that the point of Blair's activity is not simply to kill a fox

605:5 **he began to whistle** presumably to warn Gawtrey and Mrs. Blair of their approach

605:29 **her hands arrested for an instant in her hair** perhaps because she understands the older man's allusion to herself as a kind of quarry

606:10–11 **you ain't never been married none to speak of** a dry comment on Gawtrey's bachelorhood

607:10 **She was crying** Mrs. Blair's tears suggest much: her regret for her acquiescence in an adulterous liaison, her lack of fulfillment in the surrender, her plight as a woman in a loveless marriage, and her profound despair. She is deeply and multiply unsatisfied, as are the men in the story—even the scheming Ernie, who may never know the degree to which his plan has succeeded, if it has.

607:12–14 **"Come on," the older man said. He did not look back. "I reckon them hunt breakfast hoe-cakes will be about ready time we get home"** The older man knows enough about gentrified fox hunting to refer ironically to the "hunt breakfast," a lavish brunch held after the hunt—in his own case, the pancakes waiting at home, which take their name from the blade upon which they were originally cooked.

"Pennsylvania Station"

"Pennsylvania Station" is one of only two Faulkner short stories set in New York City—the other is "Mr. Acarius," which appears in *Uncollected Stories* (1979)—but it follows several familiar patterns of structure. Like "Black Music," the story presents a conversation between an older man who knows the principal characters in an incident and a younger man who knows them only through his temporary companion's narration. Not only homeless but also transient in an immediate sense, they face eviction from the vast train station that gives the story its title. Their respite from the winter cold might end at any moment, taking the narrative with it, and the venue gives an ironic resonance to the tale of the older man's nephew's life of crime—itself a tale of home and family. As in "Barn Burning" and "That Evening Sun," a kind of initiation occurs in this story, but the discovery of evil is vouchsafed only to the younger man and through him to the story's readers. Although Danny's treachery, culminating in the theft of money his mother had been saving for her own coffin, apparently kills his mother, the older man remains oblivious to the perfidy he describes, just as Georgie fails to grasp his Uncle Rodney's scandalous and criminal behavior in "That Will Be Fine" and the title character of "Elly" fails to recognize the destructive potential of her own headstrong ways. The tone of the older man's final speech recalls Old Het's childlike optimism in "Mule in the Yard": "Half past one already. And a half an hour to get there. And if we're lucky, we'll have two hours before he comes along. Maybe three. That'll be five o'clock. Then it will be only two hours more till daylight" (635). On the whole, with its big-city setting, impoverished characters, and sordid and desolate conclusions, the story might fruitfully be read as a Faulknerian experiment in a kind of urban realism or naturalism appropriate to the tone of the other stories in "The Middle Ground."

James Ferguson describes "Pennsylvania Station" as "a tale of ingratitude and duplicity on the part of the boy and of self-sacrifice and incredible naiveté on the part of the mother and the uncle." Faulkner, he says, "does not achieve an effective balance here between the telling and the told; the former almost swallows the latter" (106). Noting that Faulkner "struggled arduously" with this story, Ferguson dismisses the result: "the work that was to emerge from all this travail—the story of a small-time hoodlum and his stupidly devoted mother and uncle—is dull and turgid" (32). At the other end of the critical spectrum, Edmond Volpe argues that "'Pennsylvania Station' is an interesting story because it offers an early example of Faulkner's talent for broadening perspective, for turning a mundane situation involving insignificant people into a metaphor of the human condition" (69). In a similarly macrocosmic approach, Robert Sayre observes that the setting of the story, the arcade of the building designed by McKim, Mead, and White, stands as a kind of metonymic structure for the society that it serves, but also exploits: "The economic system, the mentality it encourages, and its human consequences not only recur as practical thematic strands . . . but are also central organizing principles." "That economic system," he continues, "is central to 'Pennsylvania Station,' which shows the narrator's sister working her life away, cleaning office buildings at night, her salary drained away in paying for her coffin on credit. She lives only to pay for her own death, in effect, and she is cheated systematically in the transaction" ("Romantic" 246, 246–47). Other cultural markers besides the station dot the story. For example, the older man makes much of Danny's "generosity" in sending an expensive memorial wreath by air mail to his mother's funeral, and both of the men notice the airplane that hangs in the station, "motionless, squatting, with a still, beetling look about a huge bug preserved in alcohol" (624). This celebrates and advertises the first transcontinental air-rail service, in which Lindbergh figured prominently. At the time of the story, air mail was an opportunity available only to the extremely affluent, so Danny's crime has apparently paid very well. The plane, as Diane Brown Jones points out, "does not appear in early versions of the story" (435), an indication of how Faulkner revised the story to make it more nearly contemporary. Looking at another kind of cultural evidence, James G. Watson maintains that the story "turns largely on complications deriving from letters" (*Letters* 95). This comment raises again the issue of the two stories presented simultaneously in "Pennsylvania Station": the "murky" story of Margaret Gihon-Danny Gihon-Mr. Pinckski-Mrs. Zilich, to which Watson refers; and the straightforward story of the two men who spend their night in the clean, well-lighted confines of the Pennsylvania Station arcade. Hans Skei takes a more favorable view of the complex achievement of the story. The old man, he explains, "tells long and intricate stories to establish his own importance and to prove that nothing but bad luck and a combination of strange coincidences and circumstance have brought him to his present situation." But, he maintains, "the need to tell, the almost desperate urge to spin a tale, which in part is fabricated by his own imagination . . . all these elements reveal a man who tries to deceive himself as a means of survival" (*Novelist* 141). The older man's determination to live, says Jones, "represents survival for another day. Although [he] retains a certain astonishment that he continues to survive, he does not express a wish for death. Despite the squalid conditions of his life, he would rather continue marking his time." It is, she concludes, "a story about enduring" (438–39, 439)—an aspect and quality of life that Faulkner explored variously throughout his career.

An early version of "Pennsylvania Station," apparently entitled "Bench for Two," was rejected by Alfred Dashiell of *Scribner's* on 3 November 1928. Faulkner submitted this or another version to the *Saturday Evening Post* on 22 September 1930, but this, too, was rejected, and *Scribner's* rejected it again soon afterwards. Over two years later, Faulkner's agent, Morton Goldman, finally placed the story with the *American Mercury*, which published it in February 1934, paying $200 that Faulkner desperately needed at the time. In the same period, Faulkner wrote Goldman about selling "A Bear Hunt" to the *Saturday Evening Post*, "And for God's sake, get the money to me as soon as possible. Of course, if they dont want it, get what you can and where you can, and quick" (*Selected Letters* 76). Skei has identified and established a sequence of the seven versions of this text, including two complete typescripts, a complete manuscript, and four fragments (*Short Story Career* 40–41). Faulkner did not choose to include "Pennsylvania Station" in either *These 13*

(1931) or *Doctor Martino* (1934). He also expressed skepticism about Robert K. Haas's 1948 suggestion to include it in the proposed short story collection, and later that fall he did not list the story among the contents of the book that seemed to take shape as *Collected Stories* as he outlined it in a letter to Malcolm Cowley (*SL* 274). However, he later added "Pennsylvania Station" as the fifth story in "The Middle Ground" section, following it with "Artist at Home" and "The Brooch," which were also omitted from the outline he sent Cowley (*SL* 279). The *American Mercury* version was published in *Collected Stories* without change.

609: TITLE Pennsylvania Station was an enormous train station in New York City that occupied two city blocks between Seventh and Eighth Avenues and 31st and 33rd Streets. Commissioned by Alexander Cassatt, the president of the Pennsylvania Railroad, and designed by the firm of McKim, Mead, and White, it was the largest train station ever built. It was constructed of pink granite and its exterior decorated by twenty-two three-ton eagles designed by sculptor Adolph Weinman. Its ceiling soared to 150 feet, and its arcade and waiting rooms were modeled after sites in Milan and Naples; its main waiting room took its inspiration from the Roman baths at Caracalla. After entering the main concourse at Seventh Avenue, passengers chose to go to the north carriageway, leading to trains to Long Island, or to the south, to Pennsylvania. Pennsylvania Station opened in 1910 and was demolished in 1964. A new Pennsylvania Station opened at the same site in 1966. (See Diehl.)

609:2 **Seventh Avenue** a main north-south thoroughfare in Manhattan in New York City; sometimes called "Fashion Avenue" because it has been the center of the garment industry in New York and hence the U.S.

609:4 **arcade** See 609:title. The metal-faced, elaborate arcade in Pennsylvania Station contained shops and was intended by Cassatt to prepare people to experience New York City; it was designed to resemble the arcades in Naples and Milan and it led to the station's main entrance. (See Diehl.)

609:6 **serried** pressed close together, like files or troops ranked in line

609:7–8 **like the eyes of people drugged with coffee, sitting up with a strange corpse** Particularly in the South, the dead body was watched over by family before burial, usually in the family home.

609:9 **rotunda** See 609:title. Pennsylvania Station had an immense concourse from which stairways led down to train platforms. Architect Charles McKim modeled it on the old train sheds of Europe, with their high, arching beams and panes of glass. Faulkner's mention of the "steel girders" at 609:11 locates the men in the concourse and not in the main waiting room of the station.

609:15 **quiring** archaic variation of *choiring*, as in music sung by a choir

609:20–21 **a cap with earflaps like the caricature of an up-State farmer** "Upstate" refers to the state of New York, north and west of the City. The cap is one with extra material that can be turned up or pulled down to cover one's ears in order to protect them from extreme cold.

610:2–3 **soup kitchens and Salvation Army homes** a detail that sets the story during the Great Depression, still going on when the story was published. The needy and hungry often ate at publicly and privately funded places called soup kitchens because of the inexpensive and easily made food offered there.

610:9–11 **I used to think that if you sat somewhere about the middle, he might skip you. But I found out that it don't make much difference where you sit** The two men are strategizing in this passage because the smoking room is in the area reserved for paying passengers. A railroad deputy checks the waiting areas periodically and asks to see tickets in order to make sure tramps and vagabonds aren't taking shelter there.

610:14 **so-called army stores** stores that sell military-issue clothing, shoes, belts, coats, etc., to the general public

610:28–30 **"Until I—" He settled himself. Into his face came that rapt expression of the talkative old, without heat or bewilderment or rancor** Something in the memory of craving a cigarette has caused the older man to lose track of the present moment and thrown him back to his memories of Danny and of his sister's death. From this point on, he stops all pretense of conversation with the younger man and begins telling him the story, oblivious to his listener's comments or sarcasm.

610:31–32 **burying money** money set aside each week or month with a third party, not necessarily an insurance agent or funeral director, intended to be prepayment for funeral costs

610:33 **Danny's trouble** revealed in full beginning at 619:1: grand larceny and killing a police officer

611:20–24 **No. He's a good boy. He's in Chicago now. Got a good job now. The lawyer in Jacksonville got it for him right after I come back to New York. I didn't know he had it until I tried to wire him that Sister was dead. Then I found that he was in Chicago, with a good job** The sequence of events and precise chronology are difficult to sort out here. When the older man went from Florida to New York City, he left Danny, broke, in the Florida jail (see 620:10–12), and they "fix up" the letter read to his mother at 625:2–3. Where he gets the money for the funeral wreath (611:24–26, 624:19–22) is unclear, as are the circumstances under which he goes from Florida to Chicago. **wire** = send a telegraph message to someone, so called because the message went through a wire

611:24–26 **He sent Sister a wreath of flowers that must have cost two hundred dollars. Sent it by air; that cost something, too** Danny's job is paying him well. See 611:20–21.

611:29–31 **that trouble come up about that woman on the floor below that accused him of stealing the clothes off her clothes-line** Danny could have stolen either men's or women's clothes from the line where the woman had hung them to dry. In a city, the clothesline could be stretched out above a balcony, on a rack, or across the airshaft between two buildings and then operated with pulleys.

612:1 **low-life boys around the saloons** loafers and hangers-on at the local taverns; the unemployed, under-employed, illegally employed, or alcoholic

612:3–4 **Mr. Pinckski** name of Eastern European or Jewish origin

612:4 **pay on the coffin** see 612:25–613:2

612:9 **'tend** attend

612:11–12 **And especially with Danny already too busy to see if she was buried at all, himself** Even with its unmistakable jabs at the character and intelligence of his companion's family, the younger man's sarcasm does not faze the older one's memory or his storytelling.

612:25–613:2 **to see Mr. Pinckski . . . six minutes wouldn't—** Mr. Pinckski's coffin money scheme. Neither the old man nor Sister understood the scheme, which is typical of Faulkner's interest in complex financial matters and deals. Pinckski seems to be comparing a minute of Sister's life to a percentage point of interest; he convinces her that banking her money with him rather than an insurance company will save not only money but years of her life. See also 613:16–19.

613:4–5 **She scrubbed in them tall buildings down about Wall Street somewhere** Sister was a cleaning woman who worked at night in New York's financial district.

613:16–19 **If I was paying the insurance companies to bury me instead of you, I would have to live three years and eighty-five days more before I could afford to die?** an unintentional joke that gives Pinckski pause

614:8–10 **Then they examined me and the only policy they would give me was a thousand dollars at the rate of fifty years old** At the agent's insistence, the older man tried to get a life insurance policy, which required a medical exam to determine the state of his health. The exam revealed that medically he was fifty years old and according to actuarial tables not likely to live much longer, so he was eligible only for a thousand-dollar payout and would have to pay the higher premiums paid by a fifty-year-old, regardless of his own age.

614:16–17 **We paid the money to the man that his job was to look after the boys that Danny run with** They paid off Danny's boss, who was a member of the city government and arranged to keep Danny from being charged with theft.

614:32–33 **the buildings messed up with confetti and maybe flags** the aftermath of a tickertape parade

615:16–17 **The landlady kept the room a week for me** The landlady held the room empty at no charge to the older man, giving him (or Danny) the option of renting it.

615:18–19 **the refusal of it** another chance to rent it

615:32 **Mrs. Margaret Noonan Gihon** names of Irish origin; Sister's full name identifies the older man as Noonan

615:34 **the second fifty-two half a dollars** the second installment of twenty-six dollars, bringing her total payment to fifty-two dollars. Pinckski is convincing Sister to buy increasingly expensive coffins and charging her twenty-six dollars for each upgrade, meanwhile giving her the illusion that she is acting independently and in her family's interest.

617:1–2 **He must be in the poor-house now** A poor house is a lodging place for people receiving public charity, so the younger man is making a sarcastic remark about Mr. Pinckski's "generous" coffin deal; he can see the operation of the scam even though Noonan and his sister could not.

617:5–6 **settlement work** charity work; settlements were usually inner-city sources of social services to the poor.

617:14 **checked** reined-in

617:14 **long-broken** trained to the saddle and bridle for a long time

617:14 **slacked off** unreined; given its head and allowed to resume motion

617:28 **Augustine** St. Augustine, Florida

617:29 **Mrs. Zilich** name of Russian or Eastern European origin

618:10–12 **So when she would read the letters to Sister she would put in something about Danny was all right and doing fine** one of the many references to the fact that Mrs. Zilich adds good news about Danny to the narrator's letters to his sister. Illiterate even though her brother says otherwise (615:6–8), she has only these letters for news of her family; Mrs. Zilich's fabrications are epistolary complications that further obscure the Mrs. Gihon-Danny-Mrs. Zilich plot line of the story.

618:21 **without no collar on** wearing a collarless shirt; very casually dressed

618:23 **jack** slang for money

619:5–6 **That woman was lying about him. After we paid the money, she admitted she was probably mistaken** The woman might have been paid off to ensure her silence. See 614:16–17.

619:8 **grand larceny and killing a policeman** the theft of a significant amount of money or goods, probably interrupted by the dead policeman, both crimes carrying heavy penalties, including capital punishment

619:15 **I made a joke** His joke is the pun between "air mail" and "high postage" in 619:12–13, and it's not much of one.

619:23–24 **a ticket from Orlando to Waycross that he had bought and missed the train** From Orlando, Florida, to Waycross, Georgia, is about 225 miles. Danny's ticket does not prove his innocence, since one of his friends could have given it to him as part of his alibi; besides, he says he missed the train.

619:25 **It had the date punched in it** To ensure that train tickets were not reused, the date of travel was stamped on each one, and would be stamped or punched by the railroad official during the trip. Danny claims that the date stamp proves that he could not have committed the theft or killed the police officer.

620:4–5 **she had ten words without counting the address** The minimum charge for sending the telegram allowed ten words or less.

620:15 **a voice came** announcements started from a loudspeaker in the station

620:23 **dummies moved by a single wire** puppets

620:30 **them** the tickets; see 610:10

620:31–621:2 **"He caught me the other night. The second time, too." "What about that? This time won't make but three. What did you do then?"** Laws against vagrancy make these two men vulnerable to arrest for repeated violations, but the younger man has apparently become interested enough in the older one's story to risk it.

621:8–9 **not knowing she had ten words** see 620:4–5

622:24 **with a note from Sister** the first clue of Danny's scheme coming to light, since Sister could not write

622:34–623:2 **Received of Mr. Pinckski a hundred and thirty dollars being the full amount deposited with him less interest. Mrs. Margaret N. Gihon** the written evidence of Danny's treachery against his mother

622:5–6 **Interest? What interest?** Mr. Pinckski stated earlier that he does not charge interest on his coffins like the insurance companies do (612:27–613:2), so his taking out the cost of the nameplate before giving Danny the remainder of the money marks him as a hypocrite as well as a businessman.

623:7 **that made the coffin second-handed** used before, and an obvious lie

624:11–15 **There was an airplane in it, motionless, squatting, with a still, beetling look like a huge bug preserved in alcohol. There was a placard beside it, about how it had flown over mountains and vast wastes of snow** The airplane is a Ford trimotor monoplane, powered by Wasp engines and named *City of New York.* On 26 June 1929, the *New York Times* announced that the "flagship of the fleet that is to carry passengers on the air divisions of the Transcontinental Air Transport, Inc., line between New York and Los Angeles, was placed on exhibition yesterday in the main waiting room of the Pennsylvania Station" ("Coast Service Plane Here"). Transcontinental, under the sponsorship and promotion of Charles Lindbergh (1902–1974), developed an airplane-train system to deliver passengers between the coasts in forty-eight hours. The first leg of the first west-to-east journey was flown by Lindbergh himself, who also pressed a button to signal the departure from Pennsylvania Station of the first east-to-west journey, and among that party was Amelia Earhart ("Lindbergh Signal"). Lindbergh's popularity derived from his status as the first pilot to fly solo nonstop across the Atlantic Ocean on 20–21 May 1927. The placard mentioned in this story doubtless contains information about Lindbergh's history and the plans of the company to offer coast-to-coast transportation to the public; the reference to snow is to the first leg of the east-west journey, from New York to Montreal ("Air Route Rider"). **beetling** = looking like a beetle; insectlike

624:16–17 **"They might have tried it over New York," the young man said. "It would have been closer"** His sarcasm has returned; he refers to the bitter cold in the City at the moment.

624:18 **it** air mail

624:34–625:1 **The priest was already there** One of the Catholic sacraments is Last Rites, which are administered to the dying; the priest has heard Sister's confession and blessed her in the name of God, and she has slipped into unconsciousness by the time her brother arrives.

625:2–3 **we read the letter from Danny that we had fixed up in the jail** Mrs. Zilich and Noonan have forged a letter to give the dying mother a little comfort.

625:7 **Grand Central** the Grand Central railroad terminal in New York City, located at 42nd Street and Park Avenue, near Times Square, a walk of at least thirteen city blocks

625:10 **the clock** a New York landmark, suspended from the arch at the main entrance of the station

"Artist at Home"

"Artist at Home," among the most overtly and playfully metafictional of Faulkner's short stories, is thought to owe a good deal to Faulkner's relations with Sherwood Anderson and his wife, Elizabeth Prall, perhaps not so much for the romantic triangle that develops in the story but for Faulkner's exchange of personal fictions with his early mentor. Before her marriage to Anderson, Elizabeth Prall hired Faulkner as a clerk at Lord & Taylor's bookstore in New York in 1921 (Blotner 1974, 318); and Faulkner knew the couple in New Orleans, where Anderson encouraged Faulkner but also used him as fictional material in his story, "A Meeting South" (1925). Faulkner's story features Roger Howes, a formerly successful but presently unproductive writer who lives in the Shenandoah Valley in Virginia and is frequently visited by aspiring writers. One of these, a poet named John Blair, arrives suddenly, to the great resentment of Roger's wife, Anne. When Anne becomes romantically involved with Blair for a time, Howes observes the situation and uses it as the subject for a novel. Ultimately, Blair fulfills both his promise as a poet and his role as a tragic romantic hero: he leaves the Valley, writes his great poem, sends it to Roger, and finally dies after contracting pneumonia after standing in the rain pining after Anne (an echo of James Joyce's "The Dead"). "Faulkner's relationship with Sherwood and Elizabeth Anderson," Joseph Blotner writes, "had scarcely been as intimate as that of Blair with Roger and Anne Howes, but it seems likely that Faulkner was once more extrapolating from what had been to what, under certain circumstances, might have been" (1974; 689). Faulkner's narrative method in this story has drawn comment, in part, because the verb tense shifts frequently from past to present, with the present-tense narrative provided by an unidentified colloquial voice, perhaps a version of Howes, and perhaps not.

"There's a lot of wear and tear to just being a poet," Roger tells Anne; "I don't think you realize that" (631) and, indeed, the artistic subject of "Artist at Home" has made the story intriguing for many readers. Joseph W. Reed, for one, comments that "Artist at Home" is "the story its central character is writing" and Howes himself the first-person narrative voice of the story: "What seemed at the outset to have been rather shallow third-person satire has become the self-irony of a first-person involvement" (42). Tony J. Owens stresses that "Howes has not only condoned his wife's actions, but perhaps instigated the situation and certainly used it for stimulation, to provide inspiration and subject for his art." And even if Howes did not instigate his wife's involvement with the poet, "his vicarious use of it indicates the degradation of his actions. The story thus represents the dissociation and debasement of art and experience in a diminished, wasteland setting" (399). James Ferguson disagrees with the identification of Howes as the first-person "Ratliff-like" narrator, and concludes that "the pleasure Faulkner took in employing the first person, particularly if it suggested oral storytelling, got him into some rather serious trouble in the composition" (115, 115–16). Several readers have not only commented on the Faulkner-Anderson relationship on which Faulkner draws but have also seen the story as Faulkner's own comment on his artistic situation. "Faulkner looked back," says James G. Watson, "to a period of his creative life when he was turning from poetry to fiction, affirming in the person of John Blair his own early aspirations, his limited achievement, and his ultimate end as a poet" (*Self-Presentation* 109). Similarly, according to Lothar Hönnighausen, "the double portrait of novelist and poet in the story belongs with Faulkner's other double portraits of artists. . . . Apparently, Faulkner used the two caricatures of the hack writer and the poet in "Artist at Home" to define his own status as a writer and to exorcize vocational uncertainties, doubts, and temptations" ("Pegasusrider" 278). For Noel Polk, "the title and what we know of the external circumstances of Faulkner's life invite us to believe that at least at one level the story springs from a conscious recognition of the ways in which he had been exploiting his own psychic life." In his reading, "Faulkner, at least in the early years of his marriage, felt himself, as artist, to be at best a voyeur, perhaps at worst a pimp" ("Artist as Cuckold" 39). Among readers less concerned with autobiography, Stephen M. Ross and Robert W. Hamblin look at the role of imagination in the story. Ross fruitfully compares Blair's poem with Howes's fiction: Howes's commercial success with this fiction, he says, "is the target of Faulkner's irony. His production . . . makes money Howes can enjoy, whereas the more inspired artistic creation Blair writes for Anne grants the poet only posthumous success. Within the boundaries of the romantic image of the perishing young artist dying of unrequited love and in pursuit of self-expression, the story affirms Blair's art and mocks Roger's" (239). Hamblin sees the story more as "a satirical treatment of popular notions of artists and their behavior," but beneath the satire is Faulkner's parable of "the dilemma of any realist seeking to mirror a constantly changing life process." The story, he concludes, "ridicules the notion that art is mere copying and underscores Faulkner's emphasis upon the necessity of imagination in the fictive process" ("Carcassonne" 159, 160).

"Artist at Home" appears for the first time on Faulkner's short story sending schedule on 16 March 1931, when it was sent to the *Saturday Evening Post*, which rejected it. *Scribner's* also declined the story, and Ben Wasson eventually was finally able to place it with *Story*, which bought in for $25 and published it in the August 1933 issue. Robert K. Haas did not list "Artist at Home" among the stories to be considered for the volume that became *Collected Stories*, nor did Faulkner include the story in his 1948 plan for the volume, but he added it later, as the sixth story in "The Middle Ground," with two "minor corrections" to the magazine version of the text (*Selected Letters* 279; Diane Jones 441).

627:2 **Mississippi Valley** the area surrounding the Mississippi River, stretching from Minnesota to the Gulf of Mexico

627:4–5 **the Valley of Virginia** the Shenandoah Valley

627:8 **tea** social gathering, usually in the late afternoon, at which light refreshments and nonalcoholic beverages are served. The atmosphere, rituals, tablewear, and clothing for tea can range from the informal cup between friends in the kitchen to more formal occasions meriting invitations, RSVPs, and fine china. The ladies who visit Roger Howes seem to do so habitually but in no particular order.

627:10 **shoots and cuttings of flowering shrubs** Conventional ways of propagating plants of all kinds include planting recently cut branches or plant tips; shoots are recently sprouted young plants.

627:10–11 **jars of pickle or preserves** homemade jams and jellies and home-canned fruits and vegetables

627:16–17 **men with beards sometimes in place of collars** men who did not wear the detachable shirt collars of the time

627:19 **smocks** loose jackets worn over the clothes to keep them clean while working, usually worn by painters and sculptors, but also an archaic term for a woman's undergarment

627:20 **tymbesteres** tambourine players; in this case, those who make a great deal of lip service to Art instead of producing it—drum-beaters, as it were, for culture. The inimitable Edward Bulwer-Lytton used the word thus: "While Marmaduke, bewildered by this various bustle, stared around him, his eye was caught by a young maiden, in evident distress, struggling in vain to extricate herself from a troop of timbrel-girls, or tymbesteres (as they were popularly called), who surrounded her with mocking gestures, striking their instruments to drown her remonstrances, and dancing about her in a ring at every effort towards escape."

628:1 **wired** telegraphed; see 628:8–9

628:8–9 **telegraph agent and the station agent and Roger's kind of town agent all in one** A telegraph agent would be responsible for sending and decoding messages, collecting fees, and seeing to the delivery of messages sent over wire by means of a telegraph machine; because of the wires involved, *to wire* became the verb of choice to describe sending a telegram. The station agent is the person in charge of a railway station, whose duties might include anything from sweeping the floors to selling tickets. The town agent position began as one who would represent the town in legal proceedings but in this context seems to describe a kind of general factotum to the town's business with Roger—primarily directing visitors to his house.

628:11–12 **a little yellow station** building at which trains made regularly scheduled stops and departures for passengers and freight. According to Walter Berrett, train stations were sometimes painted the same color as the railroad that owned the line painted its cars; this one could be yellow because it is served by the Chesapeake and Ohio (C & O) Railroad, whose safety color was bright yellow.

628:25 **It's forty-eight cents to pay on it** Because all of the telegrams cost forty-eight cents, we assume all of the visitors send the same message and that the message does not exceed the ten-word minimum charge: perhaps something like, "arriving today Blair."

628:34 **sky-blue coat** see 629:14

629:14 **switch frogs** places where a train switches to another track. The implication is that the poet would not know a simple thing like measurable distance any better than he would an insider's term for a section of track.

629:14 **dressing-sacque** a loose-fitting gown or robe worn in private. The poet's is sky blue, notably feminine, impractical, and unique in these parts.

629:30 **Anne stands there** the first of several odd tense shifts in the story. Stephen M. Ross explains the tense shifts thus: "The present tense invokes . . . an immediacy of telling, while the past tense is the conventional tense of written narrative. That both are at work here suggests a movement into and out of telling and writing, an oscillation appropriate to Howes's role as writer and teller, as artist and gossip" (241).

630:16–17 **hauled him over the coals** scolded him. From *rake over the coals,* an allusion to the medieval torture of pulling a heretic over red-hot coals (Ammer 532).

630:31 **Poverty looks after its own** We have not been able to find a credible source for this. Faulkner recalled the phrase in 1944, writing to Malcolm Cowley, "All the moving things are eternal in man's history and have been written before, and if a man writes hard enough, sincerely enough, humbly enough, [and, with the unalterable determination never never never to be quite satisfied with it] he will repeat them, because art like poverty takes care of its own, shares its bread" (*Selected Letters* 185–86).

631:25 **easy mark** easily taken advantage of; a mark is the victim or intended victim of a swindler or con artist.

632:5 **head-rag** bandana or head scarf worn to keep hair off the face and out of the way; in the South, chiefly worn by black women

632:13–14 **Something with an entrail in it** something with guts; something of substance

632:25–29 **Because it soon developed that Anne doesn't see this poet at all, hardly. It seems that she can't even know he is in the house unless she hears him snoring at night. So it took her two weeks to get steamed up again. And this time she is not even combing her hair** another notable series of tense shifts

633:1–2 **time to smell smoke in the wind** time to notice that something's up; another invocation of the phrase "where there's smoke there's fire," a common proverb dating from the mid-1500s (Ammer 440)

634:1–10 **I've learned recently on the best authority that I am not intelligent enough to get my poetry at first hand . . . because it seems that, being a woman, I don't want freedom and don't know what equality means** John and Roger do not show John's poetry to Anne, but in his idle time John lectures her on the abstract concepts behind it; she is insulted by his patronizing attitude and angry at her husband for allowing it (see also 634:11–12 and 634:13–14).

634:11–12 **show him in professional words how he is not so wise** use the language of a professional literary critic to demonstrate his errors

634:12–14 **except he is wise enough to shut up then and let you show both of us how you are not so wise either** an implication that her husband doesn't know as much about either poetry or people as he seems to think he does

634:15–16 **So Young Shelley has not crashed through yet** "So Blair hasn't written a poem worthy of his talent yet"; English Romantic poet Percy Bysshe Shelley (1792–1822), known for his radical social activism, who drowned while sailing in the Bay of Spezia in Italy

634:25 **Now get this** the narrator's turn toward the conspiratorial tone that recurs at several points

634:25 **it** the affair between John and Anne; the heart of the narrator's story

634:27 **doping along** walking foolishly (from *dope,* slang for fool)

635:1–2 **the next thing she seemed to know was his mug all set for the haymaker** Anne was so surprised by John's kiss that afterwards she remembered only his face set for her to slap it; a haymaker is a hard, wide-swinging punch.

635:3 **clinch** the embrace; the kiss

635:5 **a fair shot** an opening to slap him for kissing her

635:15 **spavined** stiff and swollen in the rear tarsal (ankle) joints

635:34 **Like narcissus smells** Plants in the narcissus genus include daffodils and jonquils and are among the earliest of the spring flowers; named after the legendary Narcissus of Greek myth, who fell in love with his own reflection and wasted away admiring it. Shelley's *The Sensitive Plant* seems relevant to this passage in particular and to the character of John Blair as a Shelley figure in the story:

> But none ever trembled and panted with bliss
> In the garden, the field, or the wilderness,
> Like a doe in the noon-tide with love's sweet want,
> As the companionless sensitive plant.
>
> The snowdrop, and then the violet,
> Arose from the ground with warm rain wet,
> And their breath was mixed with fresh odour, sent
> From the turf, like the voice and the instrument.
>
> Then the pied wind-flowers and the tulip tall,
> And narcissi, the fairest among them all,
> Who gaze on their eyes in the stream's recess,
> Till they die of their own dear loveliness. (Part I, lines 9–20)

636:9 **her face all fixed** ready to be kissed

636:11 **She has to tell him to hurry** Anne is worried about being caught kissing John.

636:13 **it** the juicy part of the story

636:17 **happen-so** chance or happenstance

637:27 **lace boudoir caps** caps worn over hair to keep it in place and clean while applying makeup and dressing. From the French *boudoir,* a lady's private room.

638:5 **yap** mouth

638:12 **one-syllable feeb** feeble-minded person; one with limited mental capacity, in this case able to utter only one-syllable words

638:22 **Now get this. This is it** a return to the conspiratorial tone

638:24–25 **by daylight he was sounding like forty hens in a sheet-iron corn-crib** Roger is typing very quickly and noisily on his manual typewriter. A corn-crib is part of a barn used for storing feed corn for animals; if forty hens were pecking for corn in one made out of sheet iron, it would make a real racket.

639:9 **sleeping-porch** a screened-in porch containing small beds or cots for sleeping in during warm weather

639:18 **Bull market** a financial market in which the stock is rising; in other words, a lot of typing

639:19 **bullish** see 639:18

640:25 **out of fix** out of service; broken

641:1 **this** Roger is assuming (or pretending) that John's letter is another poem.

641:6–7 **is still steady, so that when the rain came up** tense change within sentence

641:8–9 **he used two or three of them** the "hunt-and-peck" method of typing, rather than doing so by memory and with the four fingers of each hand on the middle row with the index fingers resting on *f* and *j*

641:28–29 **great guns** very successfully

642:2–12 **"There," she says. "Out there." . . . he sees Blair, standing in the rain, without any hat, with his blue coat like it was put on him by a paper hanger, with his face lifted toward Anne's window** This passage and Blair's fate are highly reminiscent of James Joyce's "The Dead," in which a woman's self-satisfied husband learns that she had a young love who, already "in decline," died a week after he stood in the rain to say good-bye to her. Her husband Gabriel is deeply moved by the revelation: thinking of his own life and the dead boy, "His soul swooned slowly as he heard the snow falling faintly through the universe and faintly falling, like the descent of their last end, upon all the living and the dead" (*Dubliners*, 220, 222).

642:11 **paper-hanger** someone who hangs (applies) wallpaper

642:13 **plute** from *plutocrat*, a person who has or exercises power over others because of his wealth

642:14 **dashing blade** vigorous and handsome man of action. The phrase invokes the eighteenth-century romantic hero, significant because of the allusion at 643:20–21.

642:17 **Here we are** a return to the conspiratorial tone

642:18 **green silk, female umbrellas** a parasol, used as protection from the sun rather than rain

642:26 **saw-dust doll** cheaply made doll with a cloth body that has been stuffed with sawdust; hence, limp and heavy

643:20 **Pope** Alexander Pope (1688–1744), English poet and essayist known for his scathing wit, sarcasm, and satire; Shelley's opposite in temperament and aesthetic

643:30 **the shot** the big chance; opportunity

643:31–32 **the magazines that don't have any pictures** the "little magazines" that print poetry and other matters literary, as opposed to the slick popular magazines

643:32–644:1 **stealing it from one another while the interest or whatever it was ate up the money that the poet never got for it** a pun on the financial and intellectual connotations of "interest." Interest in the poem from different magazines led to multiple publications of it, but since the magazines were "stealing it from one another," they did not pay a royalty to the author (who, in this case, was John Blair).

644:13–14 **jaw over** talk about

644:18–20 **live people do not make good copy, the most interesting copy being gossip, since it mostly is not true** a highly metafictional passage that blurs the distinctions between "live people" like John and Anne, who are "real" only on paper, and the creations of Blair and Roger Howes, which are ostensibly art. Moreover, the reminder that this story is a fiction further interrogates the role and stance of the narrator. Since the story has such a gossipy tone, and "[gossip] mostly is not true," why should we believe what the narrator says? **copy** = source material for a story

644:24–26 **with the rest of the money he bought Anne a fur coat and himself and the children some winter underwear** Roger buys Anne an extravagant gift—perhaps a payoff for her part in the story he sells—and only basic necessities for himself and the children. See also 646:2–3.

644:31–33 **"Shelley," he says. "His whole life was a not very successful imitation of itself. Even to the amount of water it took"** a reference to Shelley's death by drowning; see also 634:15–16. Roger implies that Shelley's romanticism and idealism didn't equip him to live in the real world, where flesh-and-blood wives had affairs with poets. Shelley left his first wife, who committed suicide, for Mary Godwin, the daughter of William Godwin.

645:4–8 **them making poets and artists and such pay these taxes which they say indicates that a man is free, twenty-one, and capable of taking care of himself in this close competition, it seems like they are obtaining money under false pretenses** The narrator is saying that artists are not capable of taking care of practical matters.

645:17 **gave it away** tense shift

645:18 **churning** making butter by repeatedly turning the handle of a butter churn containing whole milk

645:19 **wrist that looked like a lean ham** See 645:18. Farm life includes difficult physical labor, like churning, and Mrs. Crain has muscular arms with no fat on them.

645:20 **caint** cannot; dialectical pronunciation of "can't"

645:26–27 **go into a clinch on their own account** embrace and kiss because they want each other, not someone else

646:2–3 **Their children are bigger than ours, and even Mrs. Crain can't wear my underclothes** Roger has his family back and his moral accounts settled: the Crain children can't fit into the underwear he paid for by selling the story about the affair; Mrs. Crain has the fur coat he bought for Anne; nobody can wear the underwear he bought himself. See 644:24–26.

"The Brooch"

Like most of the stories in "The Middle Ground" section of *Collected Stories,* "The Brooch" is not specifically located within Faulkner's Yoknapatawpha saga through either geographical reference or named characters. Like many of the residents of Jefferson, however, Howard Boyd, his mother, and his wife, Amy, all come from "the little lost Mississippi hamlet" where the present action of the story takes place (648). The story shows Howard caught between his jealous and overprotective mother on the one hand and his apparently promiscuous wife on the other. Depressed and alienated by the death of their child, Howard struggles to balance the competing claims and needs of the two women in his life. When the events of one evening force him to choose between them, he cannot bring himself to leave his mother's house, and when Amy leaves because his mother has in effect banished her from it, he commits suicide. His dilemma recalls and inverts that of Sarty Snopes in "Barn Burning," with the form of the story resembling that of "Wash." Sarty, forced to choose between two irreconcilably opposed alternatives, seeks to accomplish both and fails, though he lives, while Boyd, faced with similarly difficult choices, refuses both and chooses to die. In both "Wash" and "The Brooch," an abrupt initial frame incident introduces a recapitulation of events leading up to this moment, and then Faulkner follows the implications of this incident to a fatal conclusion. "The Brooch" is unusual in that it deals overtly and extensively with a literary source and subject, W. H. Hudson's *Green Mansions,* a very late addition to the story that has a long and somewhat complex textual history of its own. The Hudson text, the Oedipal paralysis of Howard Boyd, and the fetal position he assumes in suicide all suggest an overtly Freudian presence in the story, while the brooch of the title objectifies the tenuous material connection among husband/son, wife, and mother.

"The Brooch" has not received extensive attention as a story in its own right but has instead usually been grouped with other stories containing similar character types and thematic resonances. Joseph Blotner describes it as "another tale of a girl harassed into profligacy by circumstances and an inflexible, malevolent older woman" (1984; 274). Edmond Volpe, citing Bayard Sartoris and Quentin Compson, maintains that "there is much about Howard that is reminiscent of other male characters that Faulkner was writing about during the period in which he wrote the original story" (157). Aurélie Guillain, comparing "The Brooch" with "Elly," sees Howard and Mrs. Boyd as "literary doubles," like Elly and her grandmother (29–34). Lisa Paddock connects the story with "Dr. Martino" and "Fox Hunt," in which "a young person's life is blighted by a malevolent and domineering mother" (179). The most comprehensive treatment of the story, that of Sharon Smith Hult, describes "The Brooch" as "a skilled early treatment of a characteristic Faulkner theme, that of the sexually crippled male, tormented and bewildered . . . by his fantasy of an ideal female" (291). She argues that the extended reference to *Green Mansions* "clarifies [Howard's] otherwise peculiar and erratic behavior," including his relationship with his mother and his wife, and "the bizarre pattern of his eventual suicide" (292). Mrs. Boyd's "timelessness," she says, "—in preventing Howard from motion and growth—*is* death. Similarly, Rima's existence in her bower of green mansions is a life freed from the exigencies of time, but her return to the cave of her birth results in her death" (295). James Ferguson agrees with Hult's emphasis on the Freudian character of the story, saying it shows "a most sophisticated awareness of Freudian theory" (143), and Noel Polk argues that the final published version of "The Brooch" "insists upon a Freudian reading" (*Children* 157). "In the revised story," says Volpe, "the central character . . . seems to have been ejected whole from a Freudian mold," which he characterizes as "obtrusive" (156, 160). He much prefers an earlier version of the story, which does not end with Howard's suicide. Other readers focus on the story's provocative details. Joseph M. Garrison, Jr., for instance, calls attention to another literary parallel, "The Love Song of J. Alfred

Prufrock" (55). James G. Watson analyzes the significance of the empty picture frame between the photographs of Howard and Amy: "the blank frame symbolizes the blank space in a family line broken across three generations: Boyd's surname suggests the boy he still is, and his suicide at the end of the story repeats the death of his child in a pattern of dissolution begun when Howard himself was a child and his father deserted the family" (*Self-Presentation* 39). "The Brooch," as Diane Brown Jones concludes, "still offers suggestive possibilities for critical inquiry" (464).

"The Brooch" has a long textual history, much of which includes inference and speculation. If, as Hans H. Skei reasons, the story first existed under the title of "Fire and Clock" (or "The Fire and the Clock," the manuscript version that Volpe prefers), then Faulkner first listed it on the short story sending schedule for 23 January 1930 (*Short Story* 36, 54–57). Blotner notes autobiographical elements in the story, including Estelle Faulkner's enjoyment of dancing and the couple's loss of their daughter in infancy. Alabama Faulkner died on 20 January 1931, nine days after her birth, and nine days later Faulkner sent a version of "The Brooch" to *Forum*, which rejected it, as did *College Humor* (Blotner 273–74; Skei 55). The story underwent subsequent rejection and revision before its eventual publication in *Scribner's* in January 1936 (see Jones 455–57). In 1948, when Robert K. Haas listed "The Brooch" among stories to be included in the projected collection, Faulkner connected it with "Monk" (collected the following year in *Knight's Gambit*) and "Pennsylvania Station," describing them as "Not too good, but will be included nowhere else, and there will probably not be enough more to make a volume, provided all my pieces are to be reprinted in book form" (*Selected Letters* 274). In time, he placed "The Brooch" seventh among the eleven stories in "The Middle Ground" section of *Collected Stories* with "incidental" changes in the text (Jones 457). The story has a footnote in popular culture as well: Faulkner adapted it for television, and the Lux Video Theatre production aired on 2 April 1953.

647:4 **the instrument** the telephone, ringing as the story begins

647:10–11 **Charlottesville, Virginia** the home of the University of Virginia

647:13 **travelling man** traveling salesman

647:14 **letters of introduction** letters vouching for the good character of the bearer

647:18–19 **sitting in front of the hotel with the lawyers and the cotton-planters** loafing rather than working, but with a high class of loafers—men whose income did not depend on steady hours or regular physical labor

647:24–648:1 **rolling onto empty spools the string saved from parcels from the stores** Mrs. Boyd was apparently a cheapskate who saved and reused common articles like string; her character is exactly opposite that of her social-climbing husband.

648:6 **Fauntleroy suits** velvet suits for boys, consisting of a long-sleeved jacket and short pants and a white shirt with lace collar and cuffs and a colored sash at the waist, so named after the hero of Frances Hodgson Burnett's novel *Little Lord Fauntleroy* (1886). That novel, with its elaborate illustrations of the suit, caused a fashion craze for boys in England and the United States driven primarily by mothers; American boys in particular were not fond of the rather fussy clothes. The suit was generally worn by three-to eight-year-olds.

648:11 **round jacket** boy's jacket with rounded edges on the bottom front openings, as in the Fauntleroy style

648:11 **man's hard hat** a bowler hat, made of stiffened felt

648:12 **impunity** without being punished or injured. Mrs. Boyd has made her son's educational choices based on her own fashion sense.

648:14–15 **a character out of Dante** Dante Alighieri (1265–1321), the Italian poet whose *Divine Comedy* combined Catholic theology with classical philosophy to represent the fates of the human soul after death. Dante was a Florentine exiled by a rival political party; his *Comedy* consists of one hundred cantos describing his journey with his guide Virgil through Hell and Purgatory and then his guide Beatrice through Heaven. Beatrice herself was Dante's lifelong platonic love. The passage in Faulkner's story seems to indicate that "the character out of Dante" lives in a kind of sexual hell or purgatory because of his mother's influence, unable even to look at women directly (648:16–20).

648:16–20 **who hurried with averted head, even when his mother was not with him, past the young girls on the streets not only of**

Charlottesville but of the little lost Mississippi hamlet to which they presently returned see 648:14–15

648:20–22 **an expression of face like the young monks or angels in fifteenth-century allegories** Faulkner seems to be thinking here of the Italian Renaissance visual artists, from sculptor Donatello (c. 1386–1466) to the great Michelangelo (1475–1564) and Leonardo da Vinci (1452–1519), who all brought classical training and an emerging humanist sensibility to religious subject matter. Da Vinci was born near Florence, and Donatello and Michelangelo were also Florentine. Given the earlier invocation of the Florentine Dante (648:14–15), it seems reasonable to assume that Faulkner means for us to visualize the serene faces of High Renaissance Italian martyrs and angels, creations that had known the world and renounced it.

648:30 **caste handicap** The town may be small, but it has rigid class distinctions, perhaps the more rigid and apparent because the size of the town makes everybody's behavior observable. Mrs. Boyd and her friends shore up their own sense of moral superiority by impugning the character of those in other socioeconomic circumstances. See also 648:32–649:2.

648:32 **more smoke than fire** more rumor or gossip than actual fact. From the saying "where there's smoke there's fire," based on the belief that rumors have a basis in fact, whether or not they do (Ammer 440)

648:32–649:2 **whose name, though she always had invitations to the more public dances, was a light word, especially among the older women, daughters of decaying old houses like this in which her future husband had been born** Mrs. Boyd and her friends do not take, and have never taken, Amy seriously even though she has a respectable reputation. See also 648:30.

649:11 **bolt upright** straight up

649:30, 31 **it's** and **it** insulting references to Amy

650:3–4 **Don't confuse the house with the stable** an insult, comparing Amy to an animal

650:32–33 **staid out dances with other men, in the parked cars about the dark lawn** did not dance some dances in order to drink, or perhaps engage in sexual activity, in cars with other men

651:2 **It's no fun with you** Howard obviously thinks that she might mean that sexual contact is no fun with him, but she could mean other things, like the excitement of drinking illegal liquor with a variety of men rather than dance with one's stuffy fiancé.

651:17–18 **except one, and that perhaps shocked out of her by surprise or perhaps by exultation** the "Mother" that Amy says on her last day in the Boyd house (657:17)

651:19–20 **the brooch: an ancient, clumsy thing, yet valuable** the first title passage; obviously, an ugly family heirloom

651:30 **vindictive incongruity** Amy purposely pairs the valuable brooch with inappropriate clothing as a way to spite Mrs. Boyd.

652:6–7 **I never saw Amy's father, that I know of. But then, I never travelled on a train a great deal** By deliberately overlooking the new parents and instead locating resemblance in an ancestor she has never seen, Mrs. Boyd is openly questioning the baby's paternity.

652:8 **The old—the old—** bitch

653:3 **jelly beans** in this case, pranksters; slang for frivolous young men

654:2–3 **the impotent intelligent** smart but powerless and ineffectual people

654:6 **the top of his mind** the rational part

654:8 **it** the rational statement of what he will do when his mother catches Amy sneaking in or out

654:15 **cerebration** action of the brain that produces intellectual results, the processes of which are not accessible to conscious examination, such as reasoning processes or the exercise of the imagination. The term *unconscious cerebration* was coined by Dr. William B. Carpenter and popularized in his *Principles of Mental Physiology* (1874), an important forerunner of modern scientific psychology.

654:16–17 **that faulty whole whose third the two of them had produced yet whose lack the two of them could not fill** The "whole" that Howard and Amy created between them is their family of three; the "lack the two of them could not fill" is their dead child and their inability to recover from their grief.

655:5–6 **We tried to get her to come on home with us and have some ham and eggs, but she—** wouldn't come with us; refused to leave the man

655:7 **Then the voice died away** Mrs. Ross has suddenly realized that Amy is not at home, even though she and her husband dropped her off there earlier.

655:9–10 **something instinctive and feminine and self-protective** the desire to lie to protect her friend and herself, for her own complicity in her friend's conduct

655:13 **Amy's in bed, I suppose** a deliberately duplicitous comment that allows Howard to lie for his wife

655:32 **five years ago** At 649:20, we learn that Mrs. Boyd had stopped the clock two years ago; consequently, Amy and Howard have now been married for three years.

656:26 **phials** variant of vials; small bottles

656:30 **the smaller one between them empty** the frame that held a picture of their baby

657:17 **It's me, Mother** the second time that Amy calls Mrs. Boyd "Mother" (see 651:17–18)

658:16 **last year's cotton bale** old and stale. Harvested and ginned cotton is packaged into large bales for transport and for sale.

658:27 **pleasure** specifically, sexual pleasure

658:33–659:4 **not of the face whose impeccable replica looks out from the covers of a thousand magazines each month, nor of the figure, the shape of deliberately epicene provocation into which the miles of celluloid film have constricted the female body of an entire race** not the popular images of female beauty found on popular magazine covers and in the films of the day. "The shape of deliberately epicene provocation" refers to the flapper ideal: a young, almost pre-adolescent, androgynous figure with slim hips and no discernible breasts, usually dressed scantily with the arms and legs exposed. Celluloid was the highly flammable substance upon which early films, which featured flapper stars like Clara Bow and Miriam Hopkins, were printed.

661:10 **crystal objects** the phials (see 656:26)

662:2 **careful evening face** the makeup she had applied to go out that evening; c.f. T. S. Eliot's "The Love Song of J. Alfred Prufrock": "there will be time/To prepare a face to meet the faces that you meet" (lines 26–27).

663:6–7 **the coat-pocket size, Modern Library *Green Mansions*** novel by English author William Henry Hudson (1841–1922), *Green Mansions: A Romance of the Tropical Forest,* published in 1904. The novel is a frame tale and the first-person, principal narrator is Abel Guevez de Argensola. Chapter Sixteen describes Abel's journey with his love Rima and her adopted grandfather Nuflo to find Rima's lost people, the Riolama. The cave they find is the place where Nuflo found and tended her mother after an injury, and there Abel steals a few kisses from the unconscious Rima. Modern Library published *Green Mansions* in 1916; that publisher is known for the portable sizes of its books.

663:8–30 **During that period . . . sound of birds** Chapter Nineteen of *Green Mansions* describes the death of the heroine: Rima was burned to death while hiding in a tree in a dense forest; her last words were the narrator's name, and to her murderers her voice sounded like "the cry of a bird." See 663:6–7.

663:14 **the cave-symbol** in Freudian terms, a vagina, or womb

663:33 **it** the rational part of his mind (see 654:6, 8)

664:7 **two-gallon keg of corn whiskey** whiskey distilled from corn rather than rye; also known as bourbon

664:17 **the young Italian novice** see 648:20–22

664:22 **report** the sound of the gun discharging

664:32–33 **it seems that it was right. It seems to have known us better than I did** it = the rational part of his mind; see 654:6, 654:8, and 663:33

"My Grandmother Millard and General Bedford Forrest and the Battle of Harrykin Creek"

A romantic farce in costume, the story commonly known as "My Grandmother Millard" has, by far, the longest title of any of Faulkner's short stories. It also stands in complex relations to his other texts. For example, from the characters in this story descends Melisandre Backus Harriss, who becomes Mrs. Gavin Stevens in *Knight's Gambit* (1949) and *The Mansion* (1959). In *The Unvanquished* (1938), drawing on a series of short stories written expressly for the *Saturday Evening Post*, Faulkner had traced the involvement in the Civil War of young narrator Bayard Sartoris and his family, from comparatively innocent and comic skirmishes through tragic, violent episodes of vengeance and murder. The Civil War material also connects the story to *Sartoris/Flags in the Dust* (1929/1973) and *Absalom, Absalom!* (1936), but here the war remains in the background, clearly subordinated to the central romantic plot involving Bayard's cousin Melisandre's courtship and marriage. As such, "My Grandmother Millard" offers a subtle comic commentary on the traditions of southern romance, trading for its humor on Cousin Melisandre's delicate sensibility about her body, her refusal to accept a suitor named "Backhouse," and her insistence upon playing the dulcimer during times of emotional upheaval. The story pokes fun at a variety of rituals, such as burying the silver and washing out swearing boys' mouths with soap, while developing others, such as Granny's formal summons of General Forrest and his "discharge" of the young man who will become "Cousin Philip," in order to advance the plot. When

Faulkner sent the story to his agent, he noted that "The Sat. Post bought five stories about these same people back in '35. They may throw it out because of the can motif" (*Selected Letters* 150). As the comment promises, "My Grandmother Millard" is exuberant, classic, and well-crafted comic *tour de force.*

The story, says Hans H. Skei, "is void of any deeper significance; it is a very simple story, broad in its outlines, based on outrageous events, and deliberately intended to evoke laughter" (*Novelist* 273). Edmond Volpe describes it as "a stylized comedy of manners," such manners "governing the conduct of ladies and gentlemen and governing the relations between the sexes in antebellum plantation society" (265, 266). In that same vein, John L. Longley, Jr. identifies Cousin Melisandre as "a Victorian pretending to be an aristocrat, with all of Victorian morality's morbid horror of the body and its physical functions." What he calls "the exquisitely subtle comedy" results from Faulkner's ability "to tell the story without ever saying *precisely*, in words, what the dreadful position was in which Cousin Melisandre found herself and which she thinks has so irrevocably disgraced her" (110). Although "duty and responsibility," according to M. E. Bradford, are important in the story, and although the final marriage is "comedy's traditional image for the promise that civilization will continue," it is important not to "distort the story's flavor and attribute to the author a heaviness of touch"; Rosa Millard's role, he concludes, is "high comedy surrounding a moment of low farce" ("Coda" 319). Similarly, Lisa Paddock describes the story's tone as "wry and understated, constantly steering around the 'delicate' issue on which the story hinges" while the plot, by contrast, "revolves farcically around the improbable coincidence linking Cousin Melisandre's prudish and hysterical reaction to her ordeal in the outhouse with the name of her savior-cum-suitor" (187, 187–88). James Ferguson disagrees on the merits of the story, classifying it as one the writer could not "bring . . . to life because of the diminution of his narrative drive late in his career" (127). The extent to which the story successfully combines high and low comic traditions and conventions with more "serious" issues it raises, such as race and class, remains to be considered. Although Granny refers to the Sartoris servants as "free folks" (669), for example, the story takes place before the formal Emancipation and amidst complex racial protocols. Ab Snopes, too, calling himself "father's horse-captain" (673), stands as an equivocal poor white figure in the Sartoris household—not as reprehensible a character as he is in *The Unvanquished*, but less sympathetic than in the opening pages of *The Hamlet* (1940).

"My Grandmother Millard" was probably written shortly before Faulkner sent it to Harold Ober on 30 March 1942. As it turns out, Faulkner correctly anticipated the *Post*'s reaction, as editor Stuart Rose wrote to Ober, "The turning point of the story destroys it for a family magazine" (Blotner 1974; 1100). Faulkner spoke of the piece as "a good funny story, and I think it has its message for the day too: of gallant indomitability, of a willingness to pull up the pants and carry on, no matter with whom, let alone what" (*SL* 150). The story was rejected seven more times before *Story* accepted it for publication in its March April 1942 issue (Blotner 1974; 1138). Robert K. Haas listed the story among possibilities for inclusion in the projected volume of collected stories in 1948, and Faulkner agreed, placing it between the darker "The Brooch" and "Golden Land" (*SL* 274). It appears as the eighth of eleven stories in "The Middle Ground," "a thoroughly comic exercise, the only one of its kind" in the section (Paddock 187). The *Collected Stories* version shows evidence of some editing at the level of "corrected spellings and word-choices" (Jones 467), but we do not know just who is responsible for this "corrected text."

667:TITLE **General Bedford Forrest** General Nathan Bedford Forrest (1821–1877), Confederate cavalry leader. As Calvin Brown summarizes, "He was successively a cattle-dealer, slave-trader, and planter before he volunteered in the Confederate army as a private and turned out to be a military genius. His activities of immediate concern in Faulkner's world are his fighting in the vicinity of Oxford at Hurricane Creek and Tallahatchie Crossing, his raid into Memphis when it was held by Federal forces, and the fact that at one time he had his headquarters in Oxford" (85). Forrest actually came through Oxford during 9–10 August 1864.

667:TITLE **Harrykin Creek** Hurricane Creek in Lafayette County, flowing "in a general northwesterly direction into the Tallahatchie River" and near the Sartoris plantation (Brown 107)

667:1 **supper** the evening meal (Brown 193)

667:3 **Yankees had taken Memphis** This happened on 6 June 1862, but Philip fires on the Yankees on 28 April 1862 (see 697:8); Faulkner nods.

667:7–8 **the regiment in Virginia voted Father out of the colonelcy** Officers were elected, not appointed.

669:2 **the free men** the slaves

669:3–4 **the rest of us that aint free** the white folks

669:14–16 **Memphis was already gone then, and New Orleans, and all we had left of the River was Vicksburg and although we didn't believe it then, we wouldn't have that long** see 667:3; the Battle of New Orleans took place over 25 April–1 May 1862, and Vicksburg was under siege for fourteen months before it fell on 4 July 1863, effectively splitting the Confederacy in two and giving the Union control of the Mississippi River.

670:19 **Sunday hat** her best one, to wear to church

670:19–20 **she had already sent her ear-rings and brooch to Richmond a long time ago** Granny has apparently donated her earrings and brooch and sent them to the Confederate capital to help finance the southern cause. Women were told "first [that] luxuries, then necessities were to be relinquished for the Cause. 'Fold away all your bright tinted dresses. . . . No more delicate gloves, no more laces,' one poem urged. Women 'take their diamonds from their breast/And their rubies from the finger, oh!' a song proclaimed" (Faust 1212).

670:26 **dulcimer** As Brown explains, "not the dulcimer of European musical history, but the Appalachian dulcimer, also known as the 'folk zither.' It is a long, narrow instrument with (usually) three strings: a melody string and two drone strings. It is played on a table or on the performer's knees, with the right hand 'picking' the strings and the left hand stopping them" (75).

670:26 **medallion** cameo

672:11 **it was all over** the events chronicled in this story that lead up to and include Philip and Melisandre's wedding

673:2–9 **thirty years later, and General Wheeler, whom Father would have called apostate, commanding in Cuba, and whom old General Early did call apostate and matricide too in the office of the Richmond editor when he said: "I would like to have lived so that**

when my time comes, I will see Robert Lee again. But since I haven't, I'm certainly going to enjoy watching the devil burn that blue coat off Joe Wheeler" General Joseph Wheeler (1836–1906), a Confederate army officer who after the war served as an Alabama Congressman for eight terms and, in the Spanish-American War in 1898, was given a commission as a major general of Army volunteers, eventually made regular Army brigadier general ("Wheeler, Joseph"). By contrast, Confederate General Jubal A. Early (1816–1894), was famous for his continuing and bitter loyalty to the Cause and his "invariable and picturesque profanity" (Brown 76). As Brown points out, the anecdote is historically impossible, but it does speak to the careers and characters of both men.

673:11 **Sartoris** the plantation, named after the family (Brown 168)

673:16 **General Grant** Union General Ulysses S. Grant (1822–1885), "important in Faulkner largely because of his movements in northern Mississippi in connection with the Vicksburg campaign. He made his headquarters in Oxford for most of December 1862" (Brown 94).

673:28 **dinner** "except on very formal occasions, the noon meal" (Brown 70)

673:31 **a strange horse as usual** As we see at 684:16, Ab has captured several Union horses and his self-designated status as a "horse-captain" is actually a euphemism for horse thief.

674:2 **in Tennessee with General Bragg** Confederate General Braxton Bragg (1817–1876), a West Point graduate in command, first, of the Army of Mississippi, reorganized as the Army of Tennessee in 1862, who resigned his command after the Confederate defeat at the Battle of Chattanooga in November 1863 (see Vandiver and "Stones River Campaign")

674:7–8 **he better not come to Granny's front door hollering that way** Brown notes that in the South of the story, "the front door was for visitors and social equals and the back (or kitchen) door was for tradesmen and social inferiors" (87).

674:9 **blown horse** horse completely out of breath from running

674:9–10 **U.S. army brand on it you could read three hundred yards** see 673:31; Ab is riding a horse belonging to the Union Army, which puts a large "U.S." brand on one haunch of its horses to mark ownership.

674:15 **she had copied from someone else** followed a common practice

674:19 **cup towel** dish towel (Brown 65)

676:2 **back house** privy; outhouse

676:15 **little tall narrow flimsy sentry-box** the privy: "because of its general size and shape, it is called a sentry-box" (Brown 23)

676:20 **in blue** the color worn by Federal (Union) troops

676:21–22 **as if they were not only yoked together in spans but were hitched to a single wagon-tongue** A span is "a team of two horses or mules, considered as a single unit, and a wagon-tongue is "the pole projecting from the front of a two horse wagon, to which the animals are attached, one on each side" (Brown 184, 200–201). The three sets of horses and their riders carry the battering ram between them, giving the illusion of animals hitched to a very long wagon tongue.

676:33 **three span** of men and horses; see 676:21–22

676:34 **peering** misprint for *jeering*

677:4 **in gray** the color worn by Confederate troops

677:11–12 **changing them from column to troop front at full gallop** moving the troops from riding in columns of men to a wider row of soldiers ready to engage in fighting, which would require those in the front of the column to slow down slightly while those in the back speed up to join them

677:27 **in the spread of her hoops** As Brown has it, "the hoops supporting a hoop-skirt. This absurd garment had a trick way of tilting up at the back to produce an indecorous exposure of its wearer. Hence 'spreading her hoops back' [at 695:21–22] was not merely the spreading of the skirt that frequently accompanied a curtsy, but a precautionary measure as well" (105).

678:1 **summer house** a small outbuilding, where the men might have gone to smoke, or where one could sit and enjoy the views and still be shielded from the elements

678:13 **elder-flower wine** a ladies' drink, wine made from the American elder, "a large bush or small tree growing along water-courses and the edges of swamps. A wine is made of its flat-topped 'pale clumps of tiny bloom,' and a different wine is made of its purplish fruits" (Brown 77).

680:13 **braid and sash** at his cuff and waist, the details that distinguish his rank as an officer. A lieutenant would have a single row of gold sleeve braid. Confederate regulations called for officers to wear a silk net sash that was wrapped twice around the waist and tied at the left hip.

680:22–23 **his full name, all three of them, twice** see 681:4

680:28 **He said his name again** see 681:4

680:34 **tea cakes** a light cookie to eat with tea, usually made with butter, sugar, eggs, flour, and some kind of flavoring (like lemon zest, caraway seeds, currants, or raisins); but with the shortage of foodstuffs during the war, Louvinia must improvise with what she has on hand.

681:4 **Backhouse** see 676:2

682:18–19 **at King's Mountain, with Marion all through Carolina** King's Mountain was the site during the American Revolution (1775–1783) of the defeat of British forces by "a coalition of frontiersmen"; occurring on 7 October 1780, the victory "marked the start of the American recovery in the South during the Revolutionary War and the beginning of the end for Britain's hopes of using loyalists to suppress the southern countryside" (Selesky). Francis Marion (1732–1795), a native South Carolinian known as the "Swamp Fox," was a daring commander who was promoted to brigadier general in charge of eastern South Carolina in 1781 (Frasché).

682:21–22 **Republican Abolitionists** The Democratic party was reformed from the Democratic-Republicans by Andrew Jackson in 1828, and its support of rural and agrarian interests dominated Federal elections until anti-slavery forces began to make their cause a national one. The Republican party was formed in 1854 as a third party to the Democrats and Whigs.

682:22 **Chapultepec** 12 September 1847, the fall of Mexico City to the U.S. in the Mexican War (1846–1848)

683:21 **Git the soap** to wash his mouth out for saying "damn" in the previous line

684:21 **They were chasing me before—** they got here

684:26 **tolled** "to lead (an animal) by holding food in front of him" (Brown 200)

684:26 **and-bush** ambush

684:27 **present—** I lay claim to them
685:12 **would . . .** rob
685:29 **better—** get on down the road
685:32 **near** "nigh, lefthand" (Brown 137)
686:2 **just—** be going
686:14 **smokehouse** "a tight building with small vents at the top, in which meat was cured by woodsmoke. The meat was hung from the rafters" (Brown 181).
686:21 **passel** "(parcel), considerable number or quantity" (Brown 145)
686:21 **infantry** soldiers who fight on foot, as opposed to the cavalry, who fight on horseback
687:28 **Granny was right** see 687:2: "She can't play it"
688:20 **patter-rollers** patrollers; people set to apprehend missing or runaway slaves (Brown 146)
688:23 **Yankees—** catch me?
688:27–29 **Do you think any Yankee is going to dare ignore what a Southern soldier or even a patter-roller wouldn't?** No one, Union or Confederate, is going to ignore her note to General Forrest.
689:11–12 **whuppin Genl Smith at Tallahatchie Crossing about that time** General Forrest plans to be defeating the troops of Major General A. J. Smith (1815–1897) at a creek crossing about twelve miles north of Oxford, a historically accurate detail (Brown 196).
689:29 **wasn't a patch on it** couldn't compare to it in any way
690:8 **by godfrey** euphemism for "by God"
691:13 **braid** see 680:13
691:23 **My plans have. . . .** changed
691:31 **boy—** has defied my orders
692:27 **provost** military police officer
693:14–15 **Johnston at Jackson** Confederate General Joseph E. Johnston (1807–1891), in charge of the large Department of the West and so of the defense of Vicksburg. He lost Jackson, Mississippi, to Union General William Tecumseh Sherman in the aftermath of Vicksburg's fall.
693:27 **Bragg's** see 674:2
694:2 **shavetail** a newly commissioned officer; more generally, an inexperienced person

694:19 **Make her** make her marry Lt. Backhouse despite his last name

694:26 **commander—** she will listen to me

695:25 **to cough** to laugh, that is

696:13–14 ***raised to the honorary rank of Brevet Major General*** promoted to higher officer status (just below lieutenant general, in this case) but not entitled to extra pay with the honor

696:14 ***Vice*** a substitute: "in whose place"

696:22 **To give Johnston** General Forrest has to account somehow for Philip's name change, but the only official way he can do so is to document Philip's "loss," as he does in the note to Johnston.

697:8 **this day 28th ult. April 1862** a reference to the day that Philip fired on the Yankees rather than the day of the citation: *ult.* is an abbreviation of the Latin *ultimo* (from *ultimus*, last), meaning "in or of the month before the present one"—in this case, May. See also 667:3.

“Golden Land”

Faulkner went to Hollywood for the first time in early May of 1932 and continued to work there, off and on, through September 1945 (see Blotner 1974; 771, 1191). “Golden Land,” his only “Hollywood” story, allowed him to vent a good deal of his disgust with what he found there. The story dramatizes a fundamental opposition between 1930s Hollywood, “that city of almost incalculable wealth whose queerly appropriate fate it is to be erected upon a few spools of a substance whose value is computed in billions and which may be completely destroyed in that second’s instant of a careless match” (719), and the Nebraska of the Ewing family’s roots, “the treeless immensity” that Ira Jr. fled at the age of fourteen (702). As the story’s central character, Ira Ewing, Jr., stands at the center of this opposition, between his unhappy wife and spoiled and perverse children—who see him mostly as a money machine—and his aged mother, who feels imprisoned in her house in Glendale and wants nothing more than to return to Nebraska. Events at the beginning and the end of an eventful day that finds his daughter embroiled in a trial with, as the tabloids have it, “ORGY SECRETS” (705) frame descriptions of the Ewing family members and Ira’s mistress. Significantly responsible for the family’s unhappiness, Ira is both deliberately and unwittingly controlling and abusive of each of them. A telegram reveals, for example, that he is manipulating the tabloid scandal for his own benefit, having bought thirty percent of the front page of one of the newspapers to show a photograph of himself, in a ploy to call attention to his real estate business. Only his mistress seems to escape his contempt, if not his critical eye.

Many critics have seen links between Faulkner and his main character. Heavy indulgence in alcohol and ambivalent attitudes toward

Hollywood and home certainly figure in both lives. Michael Grimwood reads the story as deliberately autobiographical, expressing Faulkner's profound ambivalence over his choice to leave Mississippi and his family for Hollywood, "sacrificing honor for money" (277). "The rhythm of his travels," Grimwood continues, "mirrors a fundamental tension in his writing—between domestic entrapment and escape to a disagreeable liberty, between the local and the cosmopolitan, between regional realism and international modernism, between concrete experience and rhetorical abstraction" (278). The story, he concludes, features both "a voice of hope" and "a voice of despair" (280). Bruce Kawin also sees the story as autobiographical: "It appears that Los Angeles struck him . . . [as] an imitation world without foundation, indifferent not just to the old truths but to truth itself"; "The place is ungrounded physically and morally. It's so corrupt that if it were a barn full of rats, Ira's father would burn it down to clean it out" (199–200, 201). Without addressing autobiography, some readers have dismissed the story's characters as superficial or stereotypical, while others have found the story nevertheless intriguing. H. R. Stoneback echoes Kawin in reading "Golden Land" as Faulkner's "definitive landscape study of California as anti-Edenic cacotope—the epitome of displacement, rootlessness, and corruption" ("Golden Land" 155). Similarly, James Ferguson, who calls the story "largely unsuccessful," says such coherence as it has is thematic: "at the most obvious level, Faulkner's contempt for Hollywood as a false and meretricious Eden; at a deeper level, the idea that we define ourselves as human beings only through our willingness to acknowledge and confront the harsher realities of life" (137). M. E. Bradford posits the story's central theme as "that suffering, struggle, effort, and 'endurance' are necessary to the formation in man of all those traits which give life meaning and dignity" ("Escaping" 73). In this scheme, the elder Mrs. Ewing and her late husband are admirable without qualification, "expressive of Faulkner's abiding agrarianism" (74). Edmond Volpe says that the story's characters are "static and stylized, representative rather than individual," but that Faulkner "transforms, through style, characters into archetypes" (206, 207). "Golden Land," he argues, "is like a moral fable. The characters, their relationships, their actions and reactions serve as dramatic illustrations for Faulkner's analysis of the corruption of the American myth" (208). It surprises us that a story treating so extensively of Nebraska has not been glossed for possible Willa Cather influences. Ira Ewing, for example, offers some suggestive parallels to Godfrey St. Peter of *The Professor's House.* Also, one expects that Ewing's sadistic violence toward his conspicuously homosexual son, reminiscent in some respects of Jason Compson's violence towards his niece Quentin in *The Sound and the Fury* (1929), and his attitude toward his daughter's sexuality will eventually attract more attention in studies of Faulkner's treatments of sexuality, including issues of homophobia and eroticism. Queer theory and gender studies have much to bring to this story and should move discussion of these issues beyond early assertions that claimed, for example, that the younger Mrs. Ewing has helped her son become a homosexual "by teaching him to hate and reject his father," while the young Samantha "is obviously a comment on what happens to beauty when it becomes a commodity" (Bradford, "Escaping" 75). Many have noted the ironies of the title of the story, which Grimwood says "ostensibly satirizes the utopian vision of Southern California" but does not merely embrace "the mother's Nebraska" in its place (277). Indeed, by story's end, warm climate or cold seems only to offer "grim and almost playful augury of the final doom of all life" (*CS* 703).

Faulkner likely had "Golden Land" in mind when he wrote his agent, Morton Goldman, in August of 1934, "I have a good story out of California I want to write," and January 1935 found him writing Goldman with "a suggestion I want to make in regard to GOLDEN LAND"—that the story be recalled so Harrison Smith could try to place it, "with its flavor of perversion," in the high-paying *Cosmopolitan* (*Selected Letters* 84, 88). Though this tactic failed, by 9 March 1935 the story had been accepted by the *American Mercury* and Faulkner had revised the galleys (*SL* 89–90). The story appeared in the *American Mercury* in May 1935. Robert K. Haas suggested in 1948 that "Golden Land" be included in the projected collection of Faulkner's short stories, and Faulkner responded simply, "Yes" (*SL* 274). The story appears as the ninth of the eleven stories in "The Middle Ground" section, where it was reprinted, with a few additions in punctuation. The themes of sex and death considered so intensely in "Golden Land" reflect similar preoccupations in "The Middle Ground," while the Hollywood setting has no doubt stimulated more than the usual interest in this story, which has no explicit connections with any of Faulkner's other fiction.

Ironically, Faulkner himself was able to escape Hollywood permanently only by selling the film rights to *Intruder in the Dust* (1948) to MGM.

701:2 **raw gin** undiluted gin

701:11 **he carried a little better than his weight** He can still drink a little more alcohol than others his size without becoming drunk, and he pays for rounds of drinks a little more often than do those with whom he drinks.

701:21–22 **the monument to almost twenty-five years of industry and desire** the Hollywood Hills, where many of the celebrities live

701:23 **canyonflank** the side of the canyon

702:1 **friezed** having the visual effect of a frieze, a broad horizontal band containing sculpture

702:2 **cypress** hardwood tree with very dense foliage, often symbolic of mourning

702:2 **façades of eastern temples** the formal and elegantly decorated fronts of the temples, featuring spaced columns, here likened to the cypress trees

702:2–6 **whose owners' names and faces and even voices were glib and familiar in back corners of the United States and of America and of the world where those of Einstein and Rousseau and Esculapius had never sounded** Owned by movie stars and entertainers, these ornate and pretentious homes underscore both the widespread nature of celebrity and its essential vapidity. The masses who "know" such figures remain ignorant of real individual achievement and cultural worth as manifested in people like Albert Einstein (1879–1955), the physicist who developed the theory of relativity; Jean-Jacques Rousseau (1712–1778), the French philosopher who posited the corrupting influence of "civilization" on human nature; and Esculapius (or Asclepius), the legendary Greek physician worshipped in ancient Rome.

702:10 **stock** ancestry

702:12 **brakebeam of a westbound freight** the beam connecting the brake controls of opposite wheels on a train carrying goods and not primarily passengers

702:18 **sodroofed dugouts** a house in the earth, generally dug into the side of a hill and so topped with grass, or partly dug so and then roofed with sections of cut earth and grass

703:10 **half tramp half casual laborer** alternating between traveling unemployed and taking jobs for quick wages, probably manual labor

703:16 **nineteen-twenty-nine** the year of Black Tuesday (29 October) and the stock market crash and the beginning of the Great Depression

703:20 **Filipino chauffeur** The California Gold Rush of 1848 brought many Asian immigrants to America, and "the Central Pacific Railroad recruited Chinese to work on the transcontinental railroad in 1865. Three years later the Chinese and the U.S. ratified the Burlingame Treaty which facilitated Chinese immigration. . . . Meanwhile, increasing contact with Japan prompted Japanese to move to Hawaii and California to work in agriculture. In 1869 the Wakamatsu Tea and Silk Colony was established in California. . . . In 1899, following the Spanish-American War, the Philippines came under U.S. control, prompting increased immigration. In 1902 the *pensionado* program, which allowed Filipinos to study in the U.S., was implemented" (David Johnson). The 1930 U.S. Census reported that out of 5,677,251 individuals residing in California, 168,731 (about 3%) were of Asian or Pacific Island descent, compared to 95.3% White; 1.4% Black; and 0.3% Native American or Eskimo (U.S. Census Bureau).

703:32–33 **select residential section of Beverley Hills** prime section of private homes in Beverly Hills, an upscale Los Angeles suburb

704:4 **dig a hole for his wife to bear children in** see 702:18

704:11 **Japanese gardener** see 703:20

704:23 **old strong harsh Campbellite blood** Alexander Campbell (1788–1866) left the Presbyterian church to pursue a religious life based strictly on scripture; he and his father founded a section of the Baptist church known as Reformers. After they were forced out, they became known as the Disciples of Christ but were most popularly known as Campbellites (*Columbia* online, Milner).

705:6–7 **the black headline flared above the row of five or six tabloid photographs** large capital letters positioned above either posed publicity still photographs or hurriedly taken paparazzi shots, in order to call immediate attention to the newspaper

705:8–9 **flaunted long pale shins** 1930s fashion was still heavily influenced by the 1920s flapper image, part of which included bared legs, in a direct repudiation of what "good" girls would or would not wear. As Yellis explains, "the flapper was the utter antithesis of the [Charles Dana] Gibson girl's long hair, high brow, thirty-six inch bust, narrow, anatomically precise waist, broad hips and well-concealed legs. As an ideal physical type the Gibson girl was contradicted in every particular by the flapper, who bobbed her hair, concealed her forehead, flattened her chest, hid her waist, dieted away her hips and kept her legs in plain sight" (44).

705:19 **the trial** see 713:11–23 for an explanation of why Samantha Ewing/April Lalear is being sued

705:20 **third tabloidal day** an implication that the case is being tried in the tabloid newspapers rather than in court

705:27–28 **burnt orange turtleneck sweater beneath his gray flannels** Ira is wearing upscale casual gentleman's clothing rather than a business suit; flannel trousers in particular were for sports like boating and playing cricket.

705:28–29 **Spanish staircase** wide staircase that slopes gently by virtue of several landings

705:33 **Voyd** a play on *void.* Ira "never knew" why his wife chose the name (706:2), but Faulkner uses it as a signifier for many important absences in the story, including but not limited to the apparent absence of moral values in the young man and the emotional absence of his parents from his life.

705:34–706:1 **mutual contemptuous armistice** They have suspended their mutual dislike of one another long enough to name their children.

706:13 **brassière and step-ins** underwear; a bra and panties

706:15–17 **a series of towels which a servant was steeping in rotation in a basin of ice-water** The heavy, cold towels will hurt Voyd more than either a simple blow of the fist or dry towels would. For whatever reasons, Ira is torturing his unconscious son.

706:23 **virago** a man-like, vigorous, possibly tyrannizing woman

706:29–707:5 **The sun, strained by the vague high soft almost nebulous California haze, . . . leaned intact against the sustenanceless lavawall by someone who would later return and take them away** the story's first title passage. Haze occurs when sunlight hits particles of pollutants in the air.

707:7 **depilatory** Voyd's removal of his body hair (another significant absence flagged by his name) is further evidence for Ira of the boy's homosexuality. See 708:35.

707:9 **straw beach shoes** skimpy sandals

707:10–11 **the highest class one of the city, yet there was a black headline across half of it too** probably the *Los Angeles Times.* Librarian Glenna Dunning writes that "most people would believe that [that paper] was more 'scholarly' and had a broader scope and vision than the *Los Angeles Examiner* or the *Los Angeles Herald,* newspapers which seemed to be more sensational in nature." Those three newspapers had the largest circulation at the time the story is set.

707:15 **white service jacket** Eton jacket; waist-length and with broad lapels, probably made of cotton duck or canvas material

707:20 **Mrs. Ewing telephoned** Ira's wife, herself a "Mrs. Ewing," refers to his mother.

707:26 **platinum hair** silvery blond in color; here, with the added connotation of a metal helmet

707:27–28 **a book of silver leaf such as window painters use** silver beaten out thinly into foil squares and put into books; used by window painters to apply signs to windows

707:30 **any of your women** Ira's wife implies that he has had multiple affairs, yet she also disparages Ira's mother by including her in the category of "his women," which by extension would include herself and their daughter.

708:3–4 **Or are you the same model son you have been a husband and seem to be a father?** the beginning of an oft-repeated criticism of Ira's drinking and lack of attention to her and their children; see also 708:33–35

708:16–17 **spent alcohol** alcohol that Ira has consumed but no longer intoxicates him

708:33–35 **I made my daughter a bitch, did I? Maybe you will tell me next that I made my son a f—** "fag" or "faggot"

709:2–3 **the five feet of irrevocable division** Ira and Mrs. Ewing are sitting at opposite ends of the dining table—which, like the table in *Citizen Kane*'s famous montage, represents the distances between them.

709:4–6 **Don't interfere with the girl's career. After all these years, when at last she seems to have found a part that she can—** "play"; Voyd implies that Samantha knows more about sex than about acting.

709:26 **French windows** floor-length windows with double casements that act as doors

709:28–29 **the skillful map of makeup standing into relief now** She wears so much makeup that Ira can see it as distinct from her face, as the topography appears in a relief map.

710:4 **Terriers** type of dog known for their ratting prowess

710:13 **icebedded glass** a glass embedded in ice to keep the juice cold

710:28–33 **MADE SETUP BEFORE I BROKE STORY LAST NIGHT STOP THIRTY PERCENT FRONT PAGE STOP MADE APPOINTMENT FOR YOU COURTHOUSE THIS P.M. STOP WILL YOU COME TO OFFICE OR CALL ME** Ira and his secretary have set up his appearance at the courthouse as a publicity stunt in order to create more business for his real-estate company. We now know that while Ira dislikes the scandal, he is not above using it (and his daughter) for his own gain. **MADE SETUP** = made the publicity deal **BROKE STORY** = told the press about Ira's connection to one of the scandal's principal players **STOP** = in a telegram, indicates the end of a sentence or thought **THIRTY PERCENT FRONT PAGE** = the story will occupy thirty percent of the front page

711:2 **half headline** sub-headline in smaller type under the one that appears at 705:9

711:9 **jacket of bright imitation tweed** Real tweed is woolen cloth originating in the south of Scotland and usually containing two or more colors in the same yarn; cheaper tweeds are made from poorer-quality wool and wool-and-cotton mixes. See also 715:20.

711:11 **Glendale** suburb about 10 miles north of Los Angeles, about 20 miles northeast of Beverly Hills

711:14–20 **pepper trees and flowering shrubs and vines which the Japanese tended, backed into a barren foothill combed and curried**

into a cypress-and-marble cemetery dramatic as a stage set and topped by an electric sign in red bulbs which, in the San Fernando valley fog, glared in broad sourceless ruby as though just beyond the crest lay not heaven but hell another invocation of the title, but with emphasis on Ira's mother's entrapment in California. **the Japanese** = see 703:20 **a cypress-and-marble cemetery dramatic as a stage set** = Forest Lawn Memorial Park, which contains the graves of many Hollywood stars and celebrities. Its art and architecture are famous in their own right. The mention of the "stage set" cemetery echoes the description of the celebrities' houses at 702:2–6.

711:17 **electric sign in red bulbs** probably an illuminated Pacific Electric Red Car line sign

711:18 **San Fernando valley** valley bordering Los Angeles to the north, containing many of its middle-class suburbs

711:20 **sports model car** We have no idea what kind of car this is, but here are the things we know about it: it has a long chassis ("the length . . . dwarfed [the house]" 711:20–21); it has running boards (715:18); it "move[s] quiet[ly]" and is "powerful and fast" (716:33–34); it has a small luggage area, back seat, or perhaps a rumble seat ("the Filipino . . . got himself into the back" 718:25–27).

711:21 **it** the house, rather than the crest

712:9 **beach burn** slight sunburn caused by exposure to the elements at the beach; Ira's features are marked not by hard physical labor but by leisure activities

712:10–11 **bright expensive suavely antiphonal garments** as at 705:27–28 and 712:9, markers of Ira's class status and leisure activity

712:33 **Kazimura** see 703:20

713:4 **extra parts** minor, uncredited parts in films

713:6 **all this** the scandal

713:17–18 **framed—tricked; that they were trying to blackmail him** The man in the scandal says that Samantha and her friend staged the raid on the house.

713:34–714:1 **they come here in droves on every train** With the rise of the film industry in the early 1900s and the establishment of Hollywood as the film capital of America, hopeful actors and actresses flocked to Southern California.

714:5–7 **She has made her bed; all I can do is to help her up: I can't wash the sheets** from *make one's bed*—to suffer the consequences of one's actions; and from *wash one's dirty linen in public*—to make private matters public (see Ammer); a play on the saying, "She has made her bed and now she'll have to lie in it," with Ira subtly bragging to his mother that he is helping his daughter, when in fact he's profiting from the scandal

714:14 **Do you want me to—** get you one now?

714:17 **That would be—** $7500

714:23–24 **Are you asking me again for money?** Ira has taken away Mrs. Ewing's financial independence by establishing credit with local merchants to make things "easy" for her. This is apparently not the first time Mrs. Ewing has asked for, and been denied, money from her son.

714:26 **You want to go away. You want to run from it** Ira means that his mother wants to run away from the scandal; as we see, she wants, and has wanted for some time, to go back to Nebraska.

715:7–8 **two others** either two other girls involved in some scandal for publicity or two other scandals

715:18 **runningboard** foot-board on the outside of an automobile's doors, between the wheels

715:20 **jacket of authentic tweed** contrasted with the chauffeur's jacket of imitation tweed; see 711:9

715:22–23 **dummy newspaper page** mock-up of how the page will look before it is printed

715:27 **WILSHIRE BOULEVARD** one of the most prestigious streets in Beverly Hills

715:28 **Is thirty percent all you could get?** Ira chastises his secretary for getting "only" 30% of the front page, revealing that Ira is behind some of the publicity surrounding the trial; see 710:28–33. In this instance his secretary has arranged for his photo to be taken at the courthouse, apparently "spontaneously," for the newspaper.

715:31–716:2 **They are going to print a thousand extra copies and use our mailing list. It will be spread all up and down the Coast and as far East as Reno. What do you want? We can't expect them to put under your picture, "Turn to page fourteen for halfpage ad," can**

we? The tabloid will print a thousand copies more than it usually does and send them directly to Ira's targeted audience of real estate owners; the passage indicates that Ira also advertises in the paper that is sensationalizing his daughter's trial. **Reno** = a city in Nevada approximately 450 miles north of Los Angeles

716:20 **magnesium** element formerly used in light-bulbs for flash-bulb cameras; when ignited, it produces a brilliant white light

716:24 **reporter in charge** in charge of arranging press coverage at the trial, in this case the photo of Ira arriving at the courthouse

716:26 **chief** nickname, not always used respectfully, for an important person

717:7 **beach cloak** swimsuit cover-up

717:7–8 **treated hair also** dyed hair; the "also" marks her as a woman of Ira's wife's age

717:28 **swell** first-rate

717:32 **clothes for the evening** The social circles in which Ira moves require more formal attire for evening events than for daytime activities; these evening clothes would include a black tuxedo and perhaps a white dinner jacket.

718:3 **cellarette** freestanding cabinet with locking doors and drawers; contains shelves for glasses, bottles, mixers, etc., and often a fold-down or slide-out counter top

718:3 **silver flask** a bottle intended to carry liquor while traveling

718:4 **wax female dummies** store mannequins to display clothing and accessories were made of wax before the days of *papier mâché*, plaster of Paris, or fiberglass

718:9–10 **unremitting and perhaps even rigorous care** Ira's mistress exercises to fight the inevitable aging process, and she seems as determined in that effort as in her efforts to take care of him.

718:24 **dip** swim

719:1–719:16 **from time to time, had he looked, he could have seen the city in the bright soft vague hazy sunlight, random, . . . that city of almost incalculable wealth whose queerly appropriate fate it is to be erected upon a few spools of substance whose value is computed in billions and which may be completely destroyed in that second's instant of a careless match between the moment of striking and the moment when the striker might have sprung and stamped it out** another invocation of the title; Ira is trapped in this beautiful environment and in a city that has been "erected upon" the medium of cinema. At the time, films were recorded on celluloid, which is highly flammable; a similar irony exists in the lives of Faulkner's Great War veterans in "All the Dead Pilots" (see 521:16–22).

719:24–25 **somehow she had contrived to become completely immobile** She has suddenly realized the truth of his mother's feelings but managed to control her physical reactions to it.

719:31 **What what . . .** is; a repetition of 719:27

720:12 **rollers** large waves rolling slowly in to the shore

720:13 **creaming** a reference to the white caps of the waves as they reach shore, with echoes of the emulsification process that changes either solids into less-dense matter or liquids into denser products

720:15 **the club** a social club with standards for admission and fees for use of its facilities. Ira's mistress seems to be trying to spare him the embarrassment of appearing in public during the scandal.

721:12–14 **the grained skin and temples, the hairroots showing where the dye had grown out, the legs veined faint and blue and myriad beneath the skin** Despite her efforts to exercise and to color her hair (whether to make it a more popular color or to cover gray, Faulkner doesn't specify), Ira's mistress shows unmistakable and irrevocable signs of aging; she has lines on her face and the beginnings of varicose or spider veins. She doesn't seem as savage about maintaining her appearance as his wife is about hers, though, and it says much about Ira that he has chosen a mature woman with a family, rather than a starlet or a younger woman, as a mistress. We do not know whether she accompanies him on his nights on the town.

721:21–22 **"You take," the Japanese said. "Read while I catch water"** The gardener seems intent on passing news of the scandal to the elder Mrs. Ewing. **catch water** = water the plants

722:16–17 **back in the early twenties when the railroads began to become worried and passenger fares began to drop** They were "worried" because of the increasing popularity of the automobile; Henry Ford first produced his Model T in 1908, and America (particularly youthful America) fell in love with individual motorized transportation.

722:19 **quotations** the fares, compared here to stock price quotations

722:20 **Then at last the fares became stabilized** By the end of the 1920s, the automobile market had become saturated. Of course, the Great Depression was right around the corner.

723:9 **puttysoft** Faulkner's compound adjective seems to suggest the malleability of the babies; Mrs. Ewing seems to feel that she can make an ally of one or both of them.

723:9–11 **she had said it was because they were babies yet and so looked like no one** She seems to be searching their faces for evidence that "they were Ewings too" (723:7–8) and hence potential allies, and "it" is the absence of that evidence—at least so far.

723:15–16 **it was not to begin then. It did not begin for five years** "It" seems to be the desperation of her desire to return to Ewing, Nebraska, since she has been patiently waiting for the children to become her allies. When they steal from their mother and deny it and their mother sides with them, the elder Mrs. Ewing realizes she has no ally in the family, especially not her son (see 724:24–25).

723:24 **moral enemies** The moral code by which each lives absolutely opposes that of the other. Ira's wife reaps and keeps the benefits of the "easy money" he earns, while his mother and father had to earn their money with hard physical labor (see 723:15–21).

724:1 **broken dollars** not torn paper currency but a reference to the old practice of cutting up silver dollars into eight equal "bits" in order to make change. The Spanish silver dollar, produced in the New World beginning in 1772 and the original "piece of eight," was legal currency until 1857. If Mrs. Ewing had real "bits," she wouldn't need her son's money to get home to Nebraska; rather, the dollars are "broken" because they're coins and not bills. (See "America's First Dollar.")

724:21 **blockhouse** three generations back from Ira's time, a military fort on the western frontier of the United States

724:28–30 **the first chair which the older Ira Ewing had bought for her after he built a house and in which she had rocked the younger Ira to sleep** The older Mrs. Ewing identifies exclusively with the male line of her family and seeks literally to sit in a time when they surrounded her.

724:32 **flour barrel** large wooden barrel in which flour is kept

725:3 **Spartan circumstance** metaphorically, circumstances like the harsh conditions under which the ancient Greek Spartan soldiers prided themselves on maintaining; stark, plain, self-disciplined

725:30–726:3 **It was still high, still afternoon; the mountains stood serene and drab against it; the city, the land, lay sprawled and myriad beneath it—the land, the earth which spawned a thousand new faiths, nostrums and cures each year but no disease to even disprove them on—beneath the golden days unmarred by rain or weather, the changeless monotonous beautiful days without end countless out of the halcyon past and endless into the halcyon future** the final and most clear invocation of the story's title

726:4 **"I will stay here and live forever," she said to herself** Her son's promised land of celebrity and sunshine is, for her, an eternal prison, in which she will eventually die.

"There Was a Queen"

Developing an incident described in Faulkner's first Yoknapatawpha novel, *Flags in the Dust* (published in a highly edited form as *Sartoris* in 1929), "There Was a Queen" expands Faulkner's saga of the Sartoris family. As the story opens, we hear a substantial recapitulation of some of its history, leading up to the present moment, when the surviving family members are the ninety-year-old Virginia Sartoris Du Pre, "Miss Jenny," confined to her bed and her wheelchair; Narcissa Benbow Sartoris, the widow of Miss Jenny's great-great-nephew Bayard; and Narcissa's son Benbow or "Bory" Sartoris. Another surviving Sartoris is the cook, Elnora, the daughter of Miss Jenny's long-dead brother John, though this "shadow family" relationship remains unacknowledged by (and perhaps unknown to) the members of the present household. The plot concerns Narcissa's ultimately successful attempt to recover some erotic letters written to and stolen from her years before. Discovered by a Federal agent, with whom Miss Jenny will not share a table because he is Jewish, the letters become fodder in an extortion scheme that Narcissa ends by trading her sexual favors for them. The story juxtaposes old and new codes of behavior, principally through the contrasts between Virginia Du Pre and Narcissa Benbow Sartoris, made much to Narcissa's detriment by Elnora. Moreover, "There Was a Queen" has special interest for those who are interested in epistolary matters in modern fiction, as well as for those who are interested in Faulkner's continuing meditations on ethnicity and female sexuality.

The story can be read as supporting unequivocally the traditional values articulated by and embodied in Miss Jenny. Edmond Volpe, for example, reads "There Was a Queen" as "a warm, moving tribute to a character that Faulkner greatly admired and respected." He sees Miss Jenny as "an embodiment of the finest qualities of the old South." Faulkner's "strong emotional commitment to the past," Volpe also notes, "was not an uncritical commitment" (95). Other readers have not necessarily shared Elnora's admiration of the regal Miss Jenny nor mourned her passing at story's end. According to Frederick Karl, Faulkner's description of Miss Jenny "presents her as someone not only caught up in the past and unable to escape but as someone redeemed by her relationship to the past" (421). For Karl, "the most unpleasant aspect of the story is its palpable anti-Semitism." Miss Jenny's "expression of anti-Semitism," he maintains, "becomes more than the voice of the character. It carries the weight of the author's approval" (421). Alfred J. Kutzik also identifies the Federal agent with what he sees as Faulkner's Jewish stereotype (215–16). In response to such readings, Ilse Dusoir Lind argues that "while Faulkner obviously admires Miss Jenny despite her anti-Semitism, it does not follow that he approves her bigotry" (131); and "in the story, it is not the lawyer [sic] who proposes a Memphis assignation, but Narcissa who first mentions such a meeting on the assumption that he demands it." Miss Jenny's encouragement that Narcissa marry again, she notes, "lends support to the interpretation that Narcissa's sexual initiative is being emphasized, rather than the lawyer's" (132 and n. 22). John T. Matthews reads the story as something other than an account of Aunt Jenny's "shocked retreat from the vulgarities of a world bereft of tradition, dignity, and a firm sense of hierarchy" (13). Her death has wider cultural significance: "The passing of queens like Aunt Jenny signals the break-up of an aristocracy whose pretense to exemption from the world of social change and economic exchange conceals their continued enjoyment of privilege as the product of oppression" (14–15). Others have emphasized Narcissa's new sense of the feminine erotic self. "It is significant," Susan V. Donaldson offers, "that Narcissa feels a certain freedom to pursue whatever course necessary to acquire those stolen letters because she lives in a world singularly empty of white male authority" (109). James Watson makes clear the difference between Miss Jenny and Narcissa on this subject:

> The letters themselves are central in a special way. In the "background," they are the source of Jenny's and Narcissa's differences

> about how a lady behaves; in the foreground, the laws of letters shape Narcissa's sexual attitudes and guide her sexual activity. The erotic force of the Snopes letters and Narcissa's sense of the anonymous Sender as a vicarious lover are much more fully developed here than in the novels. But stronger still is her sense of her own presence in the letters as named Receiver, and as the fascinated reader and re-reader who marked the texts with "the marks of my eyes where I had read them again and again." (*Letters* 101–2)

In other words, Narcissa deeply desires the world that the letters represent: "They were mine," as she says.

"There Was a Queen" went through several versions. The first, entitled "Through the Window," came back from *Scribner's* in 1929 with the note that it was "nearer to being publishable than most of your short pieces" (Jones 487). The second version was called "An Empress Passed," and the third gave the story its present title. The revisions among these three are many and substantial, but after the final version appeared in *Scribner's* in January 1933, Faulkner collected it without further change in *Doctor Martino* (1934) and placed it as the tenth story in "The Middle Ground" section of *Collected Stories.* The story has a few problems of fact. James Ferguson questions the plausibility of the premise, doubting that a Federal agent would have continued to pursue the embezzler after such a long period (144). More important, the story tells us that Miss Jenny had come from Carolina to Mississippi in 1869, "fifty-seven years this summer" (728, 738), which would suggest a narrative present tense of 1926. Narcissa and Bayard Sartoris, however, did not marry until some time after his return from the war, and since their son is either ten years old (728) or "almost twelve" (740), we can also reason a present tense of 1928–1931, so the chronology of the story is, at best, muddled. "There Was a Queen" continues to hold the attention of readers not because of its verisimilitude but because it dramatizes the ever-present conflict, regardless of the year, between "traditional" and "modern" values. While early readings of "There Was a Queen" chose to support Virginia Du Pre and to condemn Narcissa, more recent readings have called attention to the complex balance of claims within the radically circumscribed world of Southern women of the era.

727:1 **coming up from her cabin** from the servants' quarters behind the Sartoris mansion, the old slave quarters

727:20 **Beale Street** as Calvin Brown puts it, "famous as the high point of [Memphis's] low-life" (26)

728:4 **flower cuttings** small shoots used for propagation

728:17 **Cunnel** Colonel John Sartoris, Miss Jenny's brother

729:21 **Trash. Town trash** low-class whites; the opposite of "quality" (see Brown 202)

729:30 **I don't know'm** I don't know, ma'am

730:11 **Negress** Negro woman; now archaic (and almost invariably offensive) but at the time of the story's publication a neutral, formal descriptive word, like "Negro"

730:14 **Nome** No, ma'am

730:17 **traipsing around** "to gad about. When one woman accuses another of traipsing around, it always means going around giddily, brazenly, wantonly, and up to no good" (Brown 202).

730:18 **A right smart** "a considerable amount, number, period of time, etc." (Brown 163)

730:23–24 **A Sartoris woman, now** by virtue of having married into the Sartoris family

731:2 **Elnora stood a little behind the chair** in deference to Miss Jenny

731:10 **jasmine** "Cape-jasmine, a common name in the South for what is more widely known as gardenia (*Gardenia jasminoides*), a small evergreen shrub with large, white, very fragrant flowers" (Brown 110)

731:15 **caryatid** sculpture of a woman that acts as a supporting column in a building; originally, priestesses of Artemis, the ancient Greeks' virgin goddess of the hunt; see also 738:12

731:30 **(not honest cornbread, not even biscuit)** more traditional fare in the South than yeast-risen bread

732:10 **quality** "upper-class people, real gentlemen and ladies—usually contrasted, by implication at least, with 'trash' " (Brown 157); see 729:21

732:25 **Marse** Master

732:28 **nigher two thousand** depending on where in Carolina, actually between five hundred and a thousand miles

732:32 **Her mammy's** Miss Jenny's mother, the death of whom occasioned Jenny's departure from home to join her brother in Mississippi

733:4 **dusk-dark** "late twilight" (Brown 75)

733:5 **Marse John and the chillen** Master John and the children

733:11 **commonalty** "the common people" (Brown 57)

733:13–15 **after all them four thousand miles—" "It ain't four thousand miles from here to Cal-lina," Isom said. "Ain't but two thousand. What the book say in school"** see 732:26–28

733:25–26 **the food which she herself could not eat** presumably, an indication that Elnora has poor digestion

734:6 **that war** World War I

734:18 **Needings** deep-seated desires

734:26 **that coat** a waiter's jacket; see 743:2

735:8 **That was back in 1918** during the last months of World War I

735:20 **shortly before Bayard returned home** from World War I

736:19 **It's come** the time for Narcissa to move away

736:26–27 **a Phi Beta Kappa key on his watch chain** symbol of membership in the oldest and most prestigious of the academic Greek-letter societies in America, worn here on the chain attaching his pocket watch either to his vest or pants pocket

736:31 **Yankee** Perhaps Miss Jenny declines to insult the federal agent by referring to his ethnicity and instead chooses the stereotypical mask of the Southern lady who has never forgotten the Civil War, or perhaps to her "a Jew" is also inevitably a "Yankee."

737:4 **You can thank your stars** "Thank your lucky stars," a traditional reference to the guards of fortune

737:27 **Yessum** Yes, ma'am

738:12 **caryatid** see 731:15

738:13 **It was those let—** letters

738:18–19 **fifty-seven years this summer** see Introduction

738:20–21 **that first March I sat up all one night, burning newspapers about the roots** in order to keep the root zone warm and the plants alive in a month with radically changing temperatures

739:1–2 **unsourced of either mouth** disembodied because of the growing darkness

740:15 **a Federal agent** an agent of the Federal Bureau of Investigation. The FBI's jurisdiction in 1919, when the agent found Narcissa's letters, included enforcement of the Mann Act, which prohibited the transportation of women across state lines for immoral purposes and gave the Bureau a "tool" to "investigate criminals who evaded state laws but had no other federal violations" ("F.B.I. History"). This jurisdiction explains why a federal agency might well be involved in a local crime—if the man is in fact an agent at all.

741:2–5 **asked him if he would make his final decision in Memphis and he said why Memphis and I told him why. I knew I couldn't buy them from him with money, you see. That's why I had to go to Memphis** an offer to meet the agent in Memphis for a sexual liaison in exchange for the letters

741:6–8 **Men are all about the same, with their ideas of good and bad. Fools** Narcissa believes that in spite of their idealistic moral pretenses, all men are vulnerable, "foolish," to sexual advances.

741:13 **But I would have done more than that** Among the possible meanings of Narcissa's disturbing but otherwise undeveloped assertion must certainly be "I would have killed to get those letters back."

741:16–17 **They might even put him in the penitentiary** for withholding evidence in a felony and, perhaps, for blackmailing Narcissa

741:20 **Jordan** the river in which John the Baptist baptized Christ, so washing away his sins (Matthew 3:13–17; Mark 1:9–11; Luke 3:21–22; John 1:29–34)

741:28 **Johnny** Miss Jenny's insistence on calling him "Johnny" does not seem so much a function of her failing memory (which does not fail anywhere else in the story) but rather of her will to continue the Sartoris ways.

742:14–15 **his dead grandfather's place at the end of the table** as head of the family

743:2 **a duck jacket** a waiter's jacket made of densely woven cotton or linen

744:4 **her lighter face** that is, lighter than the shadows that surround her

"Mountain Victory"

In its rendering of an immediate post–Civil War confrontation featuring a Confederate officer and his servant and an east Tennessee mountain family with a Union history, "Mountain Victory" combines an extraordinary number of Faulkner's characteristic subjects, themes, and techniques. Organized in a series of vignettes related from different characters' perspectives, the story dramatizes the continuation of the regional, racial, and class animosities of the War. In late April, 1865, following Lee's surrender at Appomattox, Confederate Major Saucier Weddel and his servant, Jubal, seek shelter for the night on a Tennessee mountain. The major and his former slave are both casualties of the war, Weddel an obvious one, having lost an arm, and Jubal less obvious but perhaps more dangerously so because he remains controlled by the illusion that the two of them will return to an unchanged Mississippi plantation, the social structure of which he believes affords him safety and immunity in all times and places. Vatch, the Union veteran of the mountain family, is psychically wounded, haunted by his memories of a charge of Confederate soldiers yet savoring the memory of his own brutality during those awful years. His unnamed sister's immediate fascination with the aristocratic and presumed wealthy Southern stranger creates a kind of Capulet-and-Montague dilemma for Weddel, who claims to want no part of that drama even as it draws him further into it. Ultimately, he cannot escape her family's determination to protect her from him, especially because they mistakenly believe him to be a "nigra" (751). Throughout the brief but emotionally charged visit to the mountaintop, the family's youngest brother reveals his desire to escape it and the aging father desperately tries to maintain his status as the man, the head, of the family, as the wife and mother seems only to try to disappear. Racial stereotyping, including the fear of miscegenation, sexual tension, and class envy drive the story line of "Mountain Victory," with the victorious "Yankees" expressing and acting violently upon the prejudices and taboos usually attributed to white Southerners. Thus, the story both presents and calls into question what Malcolm Cowley early on called Faulkner's "Legend of the South" and, as John T. Matthews has recently reminded us, its "Lost Cause."

The story's combination of multiple subjects and techniques is reflected in the critics' analyses and evaluations. Edmond Volpe says that Faulkner's "skillful introduction of ironic juxtapositioning, contrast, imagery, and symbolism into the realistic narrative mode serves to broaden a story of action and suspense into an allegorical drama of the tragic war between the states and its aftermath" (150). James Ferguson lists a number of themes in this "most ambitious work": "alienation (in the portrayal of Weddel), a kind of abortive initiation in the characterization of the boy, a young woman at the focal point of conflict, and the attempt to achieve the quid pro quo in Vatch's murder of Weddel because of their differing allegiances in the Civil War and Vatch's concern about his sister's attraction to the older man" (154). Arthur Kinney, among others, notes specifically that the fear of miscegenation provides the motive for the murders, and is, thus, "a Confederate attitude, not the Unionist one to which they lay claim." The mountain family equates the Native American with the African American, and thus "Faulkner encodes the depravity of the white man" (202). Hans Skei, who calls "Mountain Victory" "among the best Faulkner ever wrote" (*Reading* 111), emphasizes Weddel's coming to life again on the mountain. As the story puts it, Weddel has regained "the power to be afraid again": "It means that I am still alive. Still alive, since I still know fear and desire" (*CS* 771, 772). Skei stresses Weddel's refusal to "trade with his newly won insights, with the humility and humanity that seem to be internalized in his character and which the brief encounter on the Tennessee hilltop puts into relief" (121). Weddel affirms the values of the culture which he has been defending, although he has become aware of its limitations, and he also knows that he will not go home to what he left. The girl, by contrast, embraces the plantation ideal that has produced Weddel, though her immediate concern is to escape the bleak, impoverished, and brutal life with her family, and she imagines herself as the chatelaine of Weddel's (now devastated) plantation, Contalmaison. She endorses the lost cause, not knowing how thoroughly it is lost, while Weddel remains true to his principles, though it costs him his life—perhaps an irony of the "victory" in the title. As Skei has it, "Victory appears to be an illusion: it may well be better to have been beaten if it means having been taught a lesson in humility and humanity" (121). He concludes by pointing to "the ruthless and sublime inevitability" of the story, in which "the treatment of a particular existential experience . . . transcends the limits of the story elements in the text." It is "a dramatic and tragic story . . . . It tells a story but signifies a lot more than the story it tells" (123).

"A Mountain Victory" was sent to the *Saturday Evening Post,* which apparently accepted it on 24 September 1930, suggesting revisions that Faulkner soon reported that he had completed, though other cuts and revisions followed (Meriwether, "Faulkner's Correspondence" 468, 470). Although these changes were made quickly, the *Post,* for reasons that remain unclear, did not publish the story until the 3 December 1932 issue. Faulkner further revised the story (an indication of his special regard for it) before publishing it as "Mountain Victory" in *Doctor Martino* (1934) (Skei, *Reading* 108–09). "Mountain Victory," like other stories in *These 13* and *Doctor Martino,* was not included in Robert K. Haas's original suggestions for the collected volume in 1948, but Faulkner added numerous stories from both collections, including what he recalled as "A Mountain Victory" (*Selected Letters* 274–75, 279). "Mountain Victory," with the text taken from *Doctor Martino,* ultimately appeared as the eleventh and final story in "The Middle Ground" section of that volume. The story was highly praised by such early readers as Stephen Vincent Benét, Malcolm Cowley, and Irving Howe and by more recent critics such as Skei and James Ferguson. As Skei notes, however, it has received comparatively little attention among Faulkner's better stories, perhaps because it is not directly linked to Faulkner's novels dealing most particularly with the Civil War—*Sartoris/Flags in the Dust* (1929), *Light in August* (1932), *Absalom, Absalom!* (1936), and *The Unvanquished* (1938)—or to the principal families of the Civil War fiction. In converting the rifle to a period at the end of the story, Aurélie Guillain suggests, Faulkner himself called attention to the metafictional aspect of "Mountain Victory." As Vatch is about to kill Jubal, his "gun is about to fire . . . and is also about to put an end to the short story itself. A gradual anamorphosis transforms the barrel into a full stop traced by a writer on a blank page" (36). That such a metafictional moment should also be violent speaks to Faulkner's clear belief in the power of art not only to represent the world or to meditate upon itself but to shape the world in its image—to do nothing less than change the face in the mirror by refusing to let it look away.

745:1 **the five people** the father, the mother, the oldest child Vatch, the nameless sister, and the youngest child and brother Hule

745:4–5 **weathered gray cloak** the gray marks him as a Southern soldier and the cloak as an officer

745:6 **silvermounted** studded, decorated with silver

745:7 **thoroughbred bay** As Calvin Brown explains, Weddel's horse is "not merely a purebred animal (as many people think), but a specific breed of horse developed in England around 1700 from native mares and Arabian stallions. Practically all race-horses and jumpers are Thoroughbreds" (198–99). Weddel's bay is reddish-brown with black legs and hooves; it's a color that helps a horse's durability because it does not "bleach out" or sunburn "from the rubbing of saddles, harness and the effects of sweat" as much as other colors do (Green 23).

745:8 **navy blue army blanket** a Northern blanket, a souvenir of war

745:9 **shortbodied, bigheaded, scrub sorrel** disproportioned horse of a light brown color and poor breeding ("scrub"), less durable than Weddel's thoroughbred; the inferior horse by far (see Green 81)

745:11 **army saddle** from which one, we don't know

745:12–13 **crouched a shapeless something larger than a child** the first of several dehumanizing references to Jubal, Weddel's black body servant; here seen from the point of view of the five people watching them approach the house

745:18 **"No, you don't," the older man said** "You won't shoot at/kill them"; our first indication that Vatch will kill the "rebel cloak" if he can

745:19–20 **"Don't you see that cloak?" the younger said. "That rebel cloak?"** part of the Southern officer's uniform; see 745:4–5. Vatch seems equally annoyed by both elements of it.

745:21–22 **They have surrendered. They have said that they are whipped** As Brown offers, "The story is set in the Tennessee mountains, probably in East Tennessee, where there were many Union sympathizers and members of the Union forces. The family presented here are genuine Appalachian mountaineers, using the language of the mountaineers (*you-uns,* etc.), which Faulkner sharply differentiates from that of his Mississippians" (133), black and white. The Civil War ended with General Robert E. Lee's surrender at Appomattox, Virginia, on 9 April 1865. As a condition of the surrender, Lee's men were allowed to keep their horses and side arms, but all other equipment was turned over to Union forces ("American Civil War: Timeline 1865").

745:24 **hickory** a common, hardy North American tree comparable to the walnut, with tough heavy wood and often edible nuts

745:24 **rock fence** probably made of fieldstones, so durable and low-maintenance

746:4 **the creature** Jubal, from the mountain family's point of view

746:9 **it** Jubal, from the mountain family's point of view; see 745:12–13

746:10 **it** see 746:9

746:16 **the dying April afternoon** location of the story in the weeks following Lee's surrender (see 745:21–22). Weddel and Jubal are about halfway home from Appomattox to Mississippi; making good time, they have gone west from Appomattox, probably to Lynchburg, and southeast in the valley between the Appalachians and the Blue Ridge, crossing into Tennessee at Bristol (see "Eastern Tennessee, 1865: Map"). See also 747:32–34.

746:20 **voluminous blue overcoat of a private in the Federal army** see 745:8

746:23 **hood of a sutler's wagon** the covering of a wagon of a trader who follows and sells provisions to an army

746:29 **Marster Major Soshay Weddel** "Master Major Saucier Weddel." While Brown claims that Jubal's "piling up of titles is not standard usage but indicates his pompousness and self-importance"

(126), the greeting is not unlike other elaborately formal introductions offered between members of the military, or other occasions in Faulkner where protocol is strict.

747:3 **him** her husband; the head of the household

747:4 **ghy** gonna; are going to

747:5–6 **Hit aint near a ho-tel on the mou-tin** "There isn't anything like a hotel on this mountain." See 745:20–21; in an aside worthy of Twain's comments on the accents in Huckleberry Finn, Brown adds that the Appalachian mountaineers speak differently than Mississippians, and "This fact should be noted by some critics who have confused the hill-men of Yoknapatawpha with Appalachian mountaineers" (134).

747:8 **We done stayed de night in worse places den whut dis is** an assumption of class privilege; an insult to the mountain family's home

747:13–14 **broad slouched hat bearing the tarnished wreath of a Confederate field officer** broad-brimmed officer's hat with a patch on the front crown showing a laurel wreath and the letters CSA in gold, in this case dirtied by long wear

747:20 **brushed again and again** to keep dirt and debris out of the weave of the fabric

747:23 **my boy** "a male Negro servant, regardless of age" (Brown 36)

747:30 **jean clothes** "clothes made of jean, a tough twilled cotton fabric long used for work clothes. Jean was originally used in solid colors or stripes. The plural, *jeans,* originally meant 'fabrics of the jean type'; then it came to mean 'pants of jean,' and now to most people it means 'pants of blue denim.' Faulkner's usage here is strictly accurate for the period at the close of the Civil War" (Brown 111).

747:32–34 **I am on my way home to Mississippi from Virginia. I am in Tennessee now?** Mississippi seceded from the Union on 9 January 1861, followed by five other states. On 12 April, the Confederate Army fired on Fort Sumter, which is generally noted as the first battle of the Civil War. Virginia seceded five days later, on 17 April, and Tennessee on 25 April. Despite their states' joining the Confederate States of America, citizens within these states were divided regarding decisions to secede and fight against the Union (which, for example, resulted in the creation of the state of West Virginia). Weddel has been fighting in Northern Virginia, the site of the surrender; he must be very close to the Virginia-Tennessee border, since this seems to be the first occasion he has had to inquire about whether he has crossed it. See also 746:16.

748:5–7 **with that swaggering arrogance which he had assumed as soon as he saw the woman's bare feet and the meagre, barren interior of the cabin** another of Jubal's assumptions of class superiority; see 747:8 and 752:7–8

748:17 **the room from which her father had driven her** the main room of the cabin, wherein Weddel would see her upon entering

748:21 **flour sacks** "When not bought in barrels, flour was bought in cloth sacks of from 20 to 50 lbs. These sacks, like some feed sacks, were often deliberately made with attractive patterns so that they could be used eventually for towels or even dresses. During the Civil War, coarse (unadorned) flour-sacking was often the only fabric available" (Brown 83).

748:25 **plank leanto built against the log wall of the cabin proper** a room made of boards, the roof of which is pitched against the existing exterior wall of the main cabin of logs set together with clay (see Brown 122)

748:27 **clay chinking** "material used to fill the chinks between the logs of a LOG HOUSE or similar structure. The traditional chinking is red clay, but mortar is sometimes used" (Brown 51).

748:31 **earthenware jug** according to Brown, "the standard container for illicit whiskey" (112)

748:31–749:1 **box of musket cartridges stenciled *U.S. Army*** see 747:32–34; Vatch has served in the Union army.

749:6 **crimping them** turning the ends of the paper casings in on themselves so that the cartridge can stand upright in its carton (see Brown 63)

749:9 **Vatch** perhaps a nickname for Vachel

749:27–28 **like a creature from another world with other air to breathe and another kind of blood to warm the veins** distinct from her world and so admirable; see 746:4 and 755:24 for other perspectives on such distinctions

750:8 **these** the cartridges on the table; see 748:31–749:1

750:9–11 **Why not? We used them too. We never always had the time nor the powder to stop and make our own. So we had to use yours now and then. Especially during the last** "days of the war"; the shortage of Confederate supplies included ammunition.

750:12–13 **Maybe you would know them better if one exploded in your face** a direct threat

750:22 **I am not afraid to show it** Weddel cannot show his other hand because he doesn't have one.

750:25–27 **It's my stomach. For three years of war I have had to apologize to my stomach; now, with peace, I must apologize for it** During the war, he went hungry; now that it's over, he is so ill (perhaps with stomach ulcers) that he cannot drink whiskey. He offers this elaborate excuse for declining Vatch's "hospitable" offer of a drink.

750:31–33 **the voices came, not yet raised yet forever irreconcilable and already doomed, the one blind victim, the other blind executioner: "Or maybe behind your back you would know it better"** each man's destiny in the tragedy foretold and foreclosed. The "it" is the Union cartridge; Vatch insinuates that Weddel ran away from the fighting, that he is a coward.

751:2–3 **Perhaps oftener, if he faced the Army of Northern Virginia** Weddel's expression of pride in his former corps. The Army of Northern Virginia was "the main Confederate army in the East during the Civil War" and was commanded by General Robert E. Lee from 1 June 1862: "At its peak in 1863, it numbered some 75,000 men. Under Lee's command the Army of Northern Virginia participated in the Seven Days', Second Bull Run, Antietam, and Fredericksburg campaigns of 1862; the Chancellorsville and Gettysburg campaigns in 1863; and the Wilderness, Spotsylvania, and Cold Harbor battles in 1864. Lee surrendered the Army of Northern Virginia to Union Gen. Ulysses S. Grant at Appomattox, Virginia, on April 9, 1865" ("Army of Northern Virginia"). No matter when or how long he was with Lee's troop, Weddel saw vicious and bloody fighting, and the immediate aftermath of the surrender frames his appearance in Tennessee on the way home to Mississippi.

751:11 **I thought perhaps this door—** led outside

751:18–19 **He's waiting for paw to tell him** the man of the house, in other words, and not the son

751:20–21 **You damn nigra** Weddel reveals his racial heritage and family history at 759:15–760–14. Brown's explanation that "nigra" is a "spelling [that] represents the normal pronunciation of many Southerners who do not say *nigger*" (140) seems dated and does not take into account the clear hatred that Vatch feels for Weddel on account of his Confederate allegiance and so easily transfers to racial taunts and slurs. In Vatch's mouth, "nigra" is just as vile an epithet as another Southerner's "nigger."

751:22–23 **"So it's my face and not my uniform," the stranger said. "And you fought for four years to free us, I understand"** Weddel understands the transference that Vatch makes and rather than correct his assumption seems to affirm it: "So you don't like the color of my skin even more than my fighting for the South. Didn't your side just spend four years of war to free us black folks, and now you treat me like this?"

752:1 **thin dancing slippers** As with the cloak, which has been brushed until the nap is worn off, Jubal takes care of Weddel's shoes to maintain his appearance as a gentleman. Although Jubal works in the stables back at the plantation, during the War he serves Weddel as a valet, a high-ranking position in the white construction of slave hierarchy: "The occupational ranking of plantation slaves was well known during antebellum times. Perhaps the best contemporary white account of this ranking system is presented in Daniel R. Hundley's *Social Relations in our Southern States.* Hundley states that a dual ranking system existed among slaves that minimally differentiated between house slaves and field slaves. Field slaves were considered to have less prestige than house slaves. According to Hundley, the 'chief ambition' of the house slave was 'to become master's waiting-man, or *valet*; or, in the case of a female, lady's maid' " (Orser 740).

752:7–8 **dese hyer mountain trash** "this here mountain (white) trash"; the latter term used by blacks and whites alike for lower-class whites (see Brown 202)

752:16 **Dat's water** The liquor Jubal usually drinks has color, like bourbon or whiskey; Weddel brings him moonshine, which doesn't.

752:24 **pizen** poison

752:32 **pater-roller nigger—** a slave trying to avoid members of a patrol set up to catch slaves off their owner's property without a pass, usually but not always at night (see Brown 146)

753:11 **Is dese folks Yankees?** "**1.** *n.* a member of the Union forces during the Civil War. **2.** *adj.* pertaining to the Union forces during the Civil War. **3.** a person from the northern part of the United States" (Brown 219–20). In senses one and two, the answer to Jubal's question is yes.

753:13 **No** see 753:11; in the third sense of "Yankee," Weddel is right; the family lives in Tennessee. Yet he seems to speak to a deeper sense of what "Yankee" means: if the family were Yankees who truly believed in the cause to free the slaves, he himself would not just have been racially insulted by Vatch. Weddel seems to indulge here in a moment of private irony regarding the family's principles.

753:15–16 **all disyer up-and-down land** mountains rather than the plains around Memphis; the Great Smoky Mountain range

753:18 **de Memphis country** Jubal's whole knowledge of the state of Tennessee consists of one trip to Memphis; he tries to process what Weddel has told him by comparing it to what he knows, but the two don't match.

753:19–20 **And now you telling me dem Memphis folks is Yankees?** see 753:18; in fact, Weddel has just told him that the Tennessee family are not Yankees (753:13), but Jubal pushes his usual pattern of relying on his own experience to generalize about the world.

753:24 **Caesar** the thoroughbred's name

753:26 **I is fawty en you twenty-eight** Weddel would thus have been born in 1837 and Jubal in 1825.

753:28 **cap-and-ball revolver** As Brown explains, "the common type of revolver in the Civil-War era. It used separate percussion CAPs. The CHAMBERS of the CYLINDER were loaded with powder and BULLETS from the front. At the back of each chamber was a raised, hollow 'nipple' over which the cap was fitted. The striking hammer detonated this cap, which in turn ignited the powder" (45).

753:29 **chuckled it** Although Brown says that when a cap-and-ball revolver is "cocked, it makes a series of clicks something like the sound of a ratchet," hence a "chuckling" noise here (53), the verb happens in this sentence before he cocks the revolver by drawing the hammer back. "Chuckled" here therefore refers to something Weddel does with the pistol, probably a gentle tossing and catching motion, up and down or back and forth in his one hand, to test the feel and weight of it.

753:32–33 **Dey tole us back dar at Ferginny it was done wid** the surrender at Appomattox Courthouse, on 9 April 1865, where Jubal and Weddel apparently were

754:1 **Is my shirt—** ready?

754:7 **Marster** here, Saucier's dead father

754:9 **well house** "a shelter over a well to protect a person using it from the rain and to protect the well-water from surface-drippings," sometimes with sides but usually just a cover, posts, and rafters that support the well pulley for the bucket to be lowered and raised (see Brown 213)

754:9–10 **Ask them to draw the curtain on that window there** perhaps Weddel's modesty, but perhaps also a self-defensive action, insisting that the kitchen window be covered so as to keep someone in the kitchen from seeing him bathe—or Vatch from claiming that he had put himself on display to the house. The father asks him to "Go out the front way and around the house" to find Jubal (751:24–25), so we know that the kitchen faces the rear of the property and its outbuildings. Although Weddel does not yet know about the girl, he knows that Vatch doesn't want him in the kitchen, and we know why.

754:16 **blue forage cap** everyday uniform cap of soldiers; in this case, a Union one

754:21 **dried Dyak trophy** The Dyaks, one of the aboriginal peoples of Borneo and Sarawak, were headhunters, and the "trophy" refers to a dried and shrunken head. The English naturalist Alfred Wallace, a colleague and contemporary of Charles Darwin's, chronicled the ritual of Dyak trophy hunting in 1857, but we have been unable to determine whether this description in the story is anachronistic. The description of Jubal's skin as resembling "a thin pallor of wood ashes" seems to indicate that Faulkner knew about the ritual drying and smoking of the captured heads, but when he discovered this, we do not know (see Wallace for a description of the ritual).

755:10 **you-uns** "you ones, a distinctive plural form of *you* used by mountaineers of the Southern Appalachians," like "you-all" and "y'all" in other parts of the South (Brown 222)

755:11 **de Domain** One French word for a country estate is *domaine,* and Weddel's father has obviously used that to describe his lands, which must rival in size those of Sutpen's Hundred in *Absalom, Absalom!*: "We are on the Domain," Rosa Coldfield says the night that Quentin Compson takes her to discover the house's secret (290).

755:12 **Countymaison** Jubal's mispronunciation of Contalmaison; see 759:16

755:14–15 **His grandpappy named it Countymaison caze it's bigger den a county to ride over** Jubal's interpretation of the family tree and meaning of the name are incorrect; see 759:16–23.

755:24 **folks** *my* people, as distinct from you lesser beings

755:31 **Marster Francis Weddel** Saucier Weddel's father; see 759:17

755:33 **yawl's president** the President of the United States, at that time Andrew Jackson; Jubal's further distinction of himself and the Weddels from the lower-class whites and Yankees, even in antebellum times

755:33–34 **he aint like de way yawl's president wuz treating de people** see 755:33. The Choctaws originally inhabited Mississippi, but most were forced out during the Great Removal. President Andrew Jackson drew considerable criticism for his treatment of Native Americans and was responsible for relocating thousands of them from their homes to the newly created "Indian Territory" in present-day Oklahoma by virtue of his Indian Removal Policy. See 759:22–23.

756:2 **heat de bricks to kept he foots warm** "When traveling by carriage or wagon in the winter, the gentry often kept their feet warm by resting them on hot bricks wrapped in cloth. When the bricks got cold, they would stop and have the servants build a fire and reheat them" (Brown 37).

756:18–19 **a stableman, in the domestic hierarchy a man of horses** see 752:1

757:3 **dat ere Tennessee spring water** the whiskey

757:6–7 **light-drinking kahysene** easy-to-swallow whiskey, which is clear and fiery like kerosene

757:11 **corn** moonshine whiskey (Brown 60)

758:15 **it** Vatch's behavior toward him

758:16 **And having to be a victor, too** an implication that winning a war doesn't necessarily produce peace of mind, and might be adding to Vatch's ill temper

758:23 ***hant*** a haunt; a ghost

758:23 ***Maybe I am*** see 747:24–25, when to the mother of the family he looks like "an apparition"

758:25 **Who are you?** In stories and cultures as diverse as the *Odyssey* and the Bible, guests are to be treated with kindness and not troubled, but instead given unstinting shelter and sustenance. The older man violates this tradition of hospitality, perhaps anxious not to treat a "nigra" as one of his own.

758:27 **Do you ask guests who they are in Tennessee?** see 758:25; an implication that in Mississippi, they do not do so

758:31 **I expect I felt that way once** hatred for his enemy

759:1 **Vatch said something, sudden and harsh** doubtless some sort of oath

759:14 **I think I told you once** the answer to the father's question at 758:25; Weddel has told him, at 747:32–34.

759:16 **Contalmaison** possibly another anachronism, since Contalmaison is the name of a town in Picardie that saw heavy fighting during the Great War, which Faulkner would have known from his walking tour of the early 1920s, and which might be the homeland of the original Vidals. Jubal has provided an incorrect translation of the name at 755:14–15. A literal translation of the name results in *conte à la maison*, "story of home" or "home story," perhaps a foreshadowing of 766:10–16. See also 759:18–20.

759:18–20 **the son of a Choctaw woman and a French émigré of New Orleans, a general of Napoleon's and a knight of the Legion of Honor** Weddel's paternal grandfather had been granted the lowest of four ranks of France's most prestigious award. Instituted by Napoleon in 1804, the Legion of Honor recognized civilians as well as military personnel (see "The Legion of Honor"). Faulkner used the historical figure Greenwood LeFlore as the model for Weddel's ancestor. LeFlore was "a French-descended Choctaw chief who, after helping arrange the Choctaw removal [to Oklahoma] had remained to become one of the richest cotton planters in the state." The name of his estate was Malmaison—literally, "Bad House" in French (Dabney 35; see also Galloway 19).

759:21 **François Vidal** the French name anglicized as Francis Weddel in the next generation

759:22–23 **to remonstrate with President Jackson about the Government's treatment of his people** see 755:33–34

759:25–26 **the native overseer, who was a full blood Choctaw and my father's cousin** Originating in southern Mississippi and Alabama, the Choctaw were one of the so-called Five Civilized Tribes, which included the Cherokee, Chickasaw, Creek, and Seminole. Before they confederated under this name in 1859, the Tribes were known for absorbing and adapting the cultural practices of white European settlers, including raising livestock, dressing in European style, and owning slaves.

759:27 **The Man** the head of this clan of Choctaws, the title passed from generation to generation. In this case, it seems to have come to Francis Weddel because of his Choctaw mother—in a matrilineal succession, in other words, unlike the patriarchal pattern described in "A Justice" and "Red Leaves."

759:28–30 **after we became Europeanised like the white people, we lost the title to the branch which refused to become polluted** see 759:25–26

759:31–32 **The Man now lives in a house a little larger than the cabins of the Negroes—an upper servant** the head of the clan now has less class status than the "polluted" Weddels

759:34 **Mexican War** from 1846–48, a war under President James K. Polk in response to Mexico's fury over losing Texas in 1845, as the result of which "the United States gained the territories that would become California, New Mexico, Arizona, Nevada, Colorado, and Utah, and stretched the Texas border to the Rio Grande. . . . Most importantly, the war heightened tensions over slavery, as a series of postwar measures granted slavery in California, abolished it in Washington, D.C., and created the new Fugitive Slave

Law, thus bringing the country closer to the Civil War" (see "Mexican War").

759:34 **two years ago, in '63** 1863; further evidence of the story's setting in April 1865

760:1–2 **burying some silver on a wet night when Federal troops entered the county** done in hopes of hiding the silver (and other valuables) from advancing Union soldiers

760:5 **Martinique coffee** the original source of coffee in the New World, brought first by a Frenchman, whose seedling was eventually responsible for ninety percent of the world's coffee (see "Special Coffee Fact File"); in other words, not the cheap coffee or coffee substitutes of wartime

760:5–6 **beaten biscuit** a labor-intensive kind of biscuit, the dough of which must be beaten vigorously with a rolling pin or special mallet (Brown 27)

760:12–13 **Mississippi infantry in the corps of a man named Longstreet** James Longstreet (1821–1904), a Civil War general who graduated from West Point and served in the Mexican War. He joined the Confederacy in 1861 and led the First Corps of the Army of Northern Virginia, established in 1862, until Lee's surrender in April 1865 (see Piston). See also 751:2–3.

760:20–21 **We had to stop there and lie down** because the unit was under fire

760:22 **Yes. I have water** given Vatch's vindictive and crude character, perhaps a reference to his own urine; see 760:23

760:23 **I couldn't stand up** because of the enemy fire, which might frustrate his desire to urinate on the Union major (see 760:22)

760:26–27 **"Didn't you have a bayonet?" Weddel said. "But I forgot; you couldn't stand up"** a bayonet knife with which to kill the major in close quarters, a technique that requires the attacker to stand quite close to the enemy and drive the blade upward through the belly or, from behind, across the throat

760:29 **where—** I had room to aim

760:32 **musket—** jammed

761:9 **I had to shoot three times** first, when he missed completely (761:2); second, when he hit the soldier in the throat (761:3); third, when he hit him between the eyes (761:9–11)

761:17–18 **His hands went to his bosom, disappearing into the foam of linen** (a typographical error: Weddel has only one hand); an automatic response, reaching for his hidden pistol

761:19–20 **I have seen too many of him for too long a time** I've seen too many angry men for too long to be surprised by him

761:24 **Damn the pistol** Forget about the pistol

761:33 **You go back** the father does not want his daughter near Weddel; see 748:17

761:34 **Me to go back?** the mother's subservience to her husband, again

762:1 **a name** his daughter's

762:15–17 **"I am stronger than you are, still," the father said. "I am a better man still, or as good." "You wont be always," Vatch said** the central Oedipal conflict playing itself out in a cabin in eastern Tennessee

762:24–25 **once more his hand was hidden inside his bosom** see 761:17–18

762:25–26 **the cold, Nordic face and the half Gallic half Mongol face** the father's Northern European as opposed to Weddel's half-French, half-Indian ancestry; the father's blondness contrasted with Weddel's darker features and hair

763:16 **Stock would get trompled to death, sho mon** because so many people would be trying to get to the "spring" to drink that they'd trample the animals "for sure, man"

763:27 **trash—** drink it themselves, because they're too dumb to know any better

764:7 **Jubal** the servant named; from the book of Genesis, a descendant of Cain and "the father of all such as handle the harp and organ" (4:21). General Jubal Anderson Early was an officer in the Army of Northern Virginia and "the preeminent authority on Confederate military affairs" in the nineteenth-century South (see "Early, Jubal Anderson").

764:12 **de Man** see 759:27

764:13 **Field hands. Field niggers** see 752:1

764:19 **Hule** the younger son named

765:7 **I have warned you** at 762:28–29

766:5 **If I leave the mountains** If I make it out of here alive

766:7 **it** the ability to feel fear, or any emotion in life

766:10 **thinking of home** with the lines at 766:15–16, an echo of Darl Bundren's musing, "How often I have lain beneath rain on a strange roof, thinking of home" (*As I Lay Dying* 81). Where Darl ponders existential reality, however, Weddel seems glad of the affirmation of his own presence among the living.

766:11 **summed up in sounds and made significant** an indication of the tenuous relationships between language and action, found everywhere in Faulkner, the most famous touchstone of which is Macbeth's worry that life "is a tale/Told by an idiot, full of sound and fury,/Signifying nothing" (V, 5, 26–28)

766:15–16 **To be whipped and to lie under a broken roof, thinking of home** See 766:10

766:19–20 **What would happen, say, a man in the lobby of the Gayoso, in Memphis, laughing suddenly aloud** Weddel's slight giddiness upon realizing that he still cares about life: "What if I were in the lobby of one of Memphis's choicest hotels, and had such a realization in public—how would other people see me?"

766:20–21 **But I am quite happy—** to realize I still want to live after all

766:21 **the sound** of someone scaling the ladder

766:34 **I could wish like Vatch wishes** I could want you dead

767:3 **he can still hear you uns yelling** vivid memories of the Confederate troops in battle; what we would now call post-traumatic stress disorder

767:6–8 **Without nothing but unloaded guns, yelling, Vatch said, like scarecrows across a cornpatch, running** outnumbered and outgunned, but still on the attack

767:13 **to—** continued at 767:15

767:24 **I—** continued at 767:29

767:29–30 **But I told her if you was a nigra and if she done that I would—** If you are really black like Vatch says and she has sex with you, I will kill her and you both

768:8 **older. . . .** and bigger than I am

768:13 **Not so loud** Hule has either begun to yell or is crying; he might wake the house.

768:19 **Vatch would be mad** because he didn't get to kill Weddel himself

768:24 **I told you before** at 768:4

769:14 **Your . . . I see** Your sister; so that's what this is all about

769:23 **She says different** perhaps her wishful thinking and fantasizing; perhaps an outright lie

769:32–33 **He believes that I still belong to him; he will not believe that I have been freed** a trifling, joking reference to his servant's perspective and his own duty toward Jubal, yet also a nod to the mutual bonds that slavery creates between master and slave

770:11 **Which one is it?** Vatch or your father?

770:26 **I cannot** I cannot leave my servant, and I cannot carry him as he is

770:26–27 **After four years I have bought immunity from running** After fighting for four years, I no longer have to prove that I am no coward

770:29–30 **I have had less than that in Virginia for four years. And this is just Tennessee** I had less time to live during the War, and now that's over

771:8–9 **yet there was between them, quiet and soundless, the copse, the sharp dry report, the abrupt wild thunder of upreared horse, the wisping smoke** premonition of what happens at 776:19–31

771:19 **it** see 771:20

771:28 **Hillbilly rednecks** class-based insults for poor white folks living in the hills; according to Brown, "it is an error to confuse the Mississippi hillbilly with the Appalachian mountaineer, as many critics have done" (103, 161). Jubal judges the world by what he knows of Mississippi.

772:4 **laurel** Mountain laurel (*Kalmia latifolia*) is native to the eastern Tennessee area, and although it is not the type of laurel foliage used in imagery of the victor, the passage helps to illuminate the various ironies of the story's title: What "victory," and whose?

772:5 **He said we must not pass that copse** The boy has told him not to go past the clump of laurels but to circle them to the left and find a path there.

773:16 **tother** the other

773:27–28 **So we have one guess and they have one guess** They have one chance to find us, and we have one chance to avoid them.

773:33–34 **So I have to choose between three things** We have arrived at two possibilities for the third of these. Weddel has thought he was choosing between going down the mountain by one way or the other, and the boy has told him which to choose. The third thing might be the boy's presence and his motives for being there at this time. Now that the boy has appeared, Weddel has to re-evaluate his initial alternatives and decide whether to trust any of the boy's advice. Alternatively, the third thing for Weddel to choose might be to return up the mountain and so escape either possible ambush, whether or not he takes the girl and her brother with him.

774:6–7 **are . . .** not there right now, because they're waiting in ambush in the copse

774:26–27 **I aint gwine ride down no. . . .** mountain

775:2 **playing Indian** playing a game of imagined danger, as in the game of cowboys and Indians; apparently telling himself not to let his imagination run wild

775:9–10 **whether I am playing Indian or not** whether I am imagining all the danger I seem to sense

775:22 **We could . . .** a repetition of 774:7–9

776:8 **They think you will be riding the good horse** the thoroughbred; see 745:9. Hule has just deliberately put himself in the line of his family's ambush.

776:10 **I told them you would be riding . . .** "the good horse," the thoroughbred (745:9 and 776:8). The boy has set Weddel up to be murdered, ostensibly because of his refusal to marry his sister and take both of them out of the mountains.

776:12 **Git outen the. . . .** path!

776:15 **rhododendron** genus of flowering shrub, including azaleas. The mountain rhododendron grows to about five feet and blooms pink in the early spring.

776:17 **rowelled** spurred

776:19 **It** the "thin grimace of exasperation and anger almost like smiling" (776:17–18)

777:20 **the sound** of the gunshot

776:25–26 **the boy's body where it lay in the path, the face wrenched sideways against a stone** Hule has either fallen or been thrown from the thoroughbred, dying when his head strikes the ground and his fall twisting the blanket saddle beneath the horse as it charges off.

776:33 **One of them was running** the father—Vatch is reloading his rifle (see 777:17)

VI. BEYOND

"Beyond"

"Beyond" is one of the relatively few Faulkner short stories with a source in Faulkner's immediate circle of acquaintance. The story itself amply sets forth its literary and intellectual origins, and we have, in addition, a genuine rarity—Faulkner's own explanation of the story at the time of its acceptance for publication. As the story opens, Judge Howard Allison, attended by Dr. Lucius Peabody, lies on his deathbed. Leaving the familiar scene, he finds himself at the crowded entrance of an afterlife, and there he encounters several people who might provide him with answers to questions he has asked his entire adult life—questions of love, religious faith, ethics, and grief, as answered (and avoided) by a virgin bridegroom, a profane suicide, a famous agnostic, and the mother of a child with stigmata. In the end, rather than take the chance offered him to see his only child, who died at the age of ten, the Judge returns to the world he knows and composes himself in his coffin.

Joseph Blotner has pointed to the parallels between Judge Howard Allison and Estelle Oldham Faulkner's step-grandfather, Henry C. Niles, a Republican federal judge and "a vehement agnostic" (1974, 654). He further notes that Estelle's parents, Lemuel and Lida Oldham, lost a son about the same age as the Allison boy and that Faulkner borrowed the Oldham boy's epitaph for young Howard Allison (1984, 259). Thomas McHaney has elaborated upon the possible connections between Estelle Oldham's family and the Allisons, and he calls particular attention to Faulkner's use of the works of agnostic philosopher Robert Ingersoll in the story. In fact, McHaney argues, Faulkner expresses something very close to Ingersoll's view in his preface to *The Faulkner Reader* in 1954: "The heart began to tell him, *You don't know the answer either and you will never find it*" (304). Faulkner's comments on the story, in a 1933 letter to Ben Wasson, explain the specific failing in the Judge's "logic": "The agnostic progresses far enough into heaven to find one whom his intelligence, if not his logic, could accept as Christ, and who even offers him an actual sight and meeting with his dead son in exchange for the surrender of his logic, agnosticism. But he naturally and humanly prefers the sorrow with which he has lived so long that it not only does not hurt anymore, but is perhaps even a pleasure, to the uncertainty of change, even when it means that he may gain his son again" (*Selected Letters* 71–72). "The father is searching for the son," James Ferguson concludes, "but he gives up the quest because, unlike so many of Faulkner's characters, he prefers a weltanschauung in which injustice is rooted in the very nature of things. If he were to find the boy, life would make sense, would add up, and the old man would therefore have to deny everything he has lived for" (203, n. 15). Mick Gidley says that in "Beyond," as in *As I Lay Dying*, "polar opposites are called into question . . . and the chief such categories called into doubt are the elemental ontological ones of life and death" (230). Edmond Volpe finds "Beyond" "a dense, complex story that demands very careful reading" (134). He interprets the Judge's four encounters as progressive challenges to his agnosticism and his rationalism, presenting him with an apparent need for faith: "What he has been doing is substituting one book for another, the book of a rationalist for the Bible" (136). In the end, however, his rationalism triumphs, for "the meaning of human existence is not to be found in death, in a belief in a hereafter. Death is meaningful only because it intensifies humans' awareness of being alive" (137). McHaney argues similarly, concluding that Faulkner realized "the search *was* the answer, a search by which the artist achieves the only immortality humankind can know, through writing something lasting that will remain just in front of the beyond, the 'wall of the final and irrevocable oblivion through which he must someday pass' " (304).

Faulkner submitted a version of this story entitled "Beyond the Gate" to the *Saturday Evening Post*, which rejected it in April 1930. Three years later he sent a revised version of the story to *Harper's*, whose editor, though accepting the story, queried several points, leading to Faulkner's exasperated gloss on his own story quoted above and his description of the piece as a "tour de force in esoteria" (*SL* 72). While he did not choose the unpublished version of this story for *These 13* (1931), as he had "Victory" and "Mistral," he included the September 1933 *Harper's* version in *Doctor Martino* (1934), with the title shortened to "Beyond." This story apparently did not appear on Robert K. Haas's original list for the proposed collection of Faulkner's stories in early fall of 1948, perhaps because Haas appears not to have had a copy of *Doctor Martino* available, but within a month or so Faulkner himself had chosen it as the first (and title) story of the final section of *Collected Stories* (*SL* 274–75, 277). The first of three stories in this section to explore the realm of the supernatural, "Beyond" sets the surreal tone and the essential method of the section by watching what happens when a person must confront incomprehensible circumstance, "like a man who, not a swordsman, has practiced with a blade against a certain improbable crisis, and who suddenly finds himself, blade in hand, face to face with the event" (*CS* 784).

782:1 **little toy telephone** the stethoscope

782:6–7 **a pandemonium of wailing** Milton's Pandemonium was the "city and proud seat/Of Lucifer" (*Paradise Lost,* X, 424); now the term more generally describes uproar and lawlessness.

782:12–13 **steamer siren** whistle powered by steam, found on a steam ship or locomotive; a very loud, piercing whistle

783:22 **That was to come later** see 785:32–34

783:26 **conventional morning dress** man's formal suit consisting of dark gray cutaway morning coat and striped trousers, often worn with a top hat

784:8 **And are you waiting here to. . . .** find her?

784:17 **a certain improbable crisis** in this case, his own death

784:32 **mine** my situation

784:34 **I came here to escape someone** most probably Chlory, and her "pandemonium of wailing"

785:27 **Mothershed** a name of complex possibilities: pronounced "mother-shed," a hint of the women the Judge has left behind; pronounced "mother's head," an allusion to the young mother of the story as well as to a source of something vital

785:32–34 **as the mesmerism left him, the shadow bewildered and wary and complete, touched his face** the wariness predicted at 783:22

786:1 **dea. . . .** dead

786:13–14 **if I am where I am beginning to think I am, I don't know whether I am here or not** an indication that he might be dreaming or, if not, that residence in this otherworldly anteroom might be voluntary

786:17 **Voltaire** François Marie Arouet de Voltaire (1694–1778), the greatest French figure of the Enlightenment and a rationalist in the tradition of John Locke. Voltaire was an ardent crusader against legal corruption and arbitrariness and "became famous as the implacable opponent of organized Christian religion," saying famously that "those who can make you believe absurdities can make you commit atrocities" ("Voltaire").

786:18 **Ingersoll** Robert Green Ingersoll (1833–99), a lawyer and Democrat-turned-Republican politician; a believer in free-thinking, he became known as "the great agnostic" and published many rationalist critiques of theology and the Bible. His lectures "had an important influence on American thought during the late 19th century" and his complete works were published in 1900 ("Ingersoll, Robert Green").

786:23 **I. . . .** worked hard on that theory!

786:33 **I heard that you had. . . .** "died" or "committed suicide"

787:4 **trigger. . . .** to pull

787:6 **token. . . .** "a suicide lies outside the Church." The Saints "Augustine and Thomas Aquinas stand out as the main shapers of Catholic thought on the subject of suicide. Both spoke forcefully against it, and both were instrumental in leading the church to adopt strict prohibitions and recriminations against the act. They considered it to be a form of murder, and thus a mortal sin. It ruled out any opportunity for repentance. It was further an attack upon society and upon the sovereignty of God. Protestants have been heavily influenced by these teaching[s], and may quite firmly believe them also" (Hewett 89–90).

787:12 **Agnosticism** term coined by T. H. Huxley (1825–95), the philosophical doctrine holding that first truth or first knowledge, such as the existence of God, is not demonstrable

787:29–31 **you don't seem to want to know as much as you want something new to be uncertain about** another dig at the Judge's agnosticism (see 787:12)

787:32 **have. . . .** talked to them?

787:34 **Paine** Thomas Paine (1737–1809), best known for his support of the American Revolution in *Common-Sense* (1776), the French Revolution in *The Rights of Man* (1791–2), and "deistic anti-clericalism" in *The Age of Reason* (1794–95) (see Bedau)

788:3 **Is he. . . .** here?

788:5–6 **the one that wrote the little women books** because of Mothershed's tendency to jump between subjects, a difficult reference to explain. At first blush, he seems to refer to Louisa May Alcott (1832–1888), author of books like *Little Women, Little Men,* and *Jo's Boys.* Also popular at the time of the story's setting was the "Two Little Women" series by Carolyn Wells (1862–1942). However, if the next sentence refers to a male author and not to Ingersoll, that author could be Edward Stratemeyer (1863–1930), who wrote under several pseudonyms many volumes of books for boys and girls, including the Hardy Boys and the Bobbsey Twins. (See "Stratemeyer, Edward").

788:6 **he** a reference either to Ingersoll or to the author of "the little women books" (788:5–6)

788:15 **Him** God

788:17 **your books** see 786:18

788:18 **Montesquieu** Charles-Louis de Secondat, baron de (1689–1755), one of the earliest figures of the Enlightenment and author of *Persian Letters* (1721), a satire of the contemporary French social, political, and religious scene, and *The Spirit of the Laws* (1748), a masterpiece of political science and sociology. Montesquieu, an advocate of the division and balance of governmental powers, allegedly had a "widely publicized" deathbed conversion to Catholicism ("Montesquieu, Charles-Louis de Secondat, baron de").

788:22 **still green hurt** fresh wound; the death of his son

788:23 **any straw** part of the longer idiom "grasping at straws," meaning to make a last desperate attempt (Ammer 270)

789:18–19 **Voltaire's *Philosophical Dictionary*** *Lettres philosophiques,* published in 1734, and consisting of chapters on various subjects, often in parable form. The entry on "Religion," for example, describes Voltaire's sojourn in a waste land containing the bones of those massacred for (any) religion's sake and a conversation that he has with the wounded Christ.

789:22–23 **I am a Republican officeholder in a Democratic stronghold** Joel Silbey summarizes the origins of the Republican party in the sectional conflict immediately preceding the Civil War: "The organizers of the new party brought together formerly hostile groups, including Northern Whigs, antislavery Free Soil Party members, and dissident Democrats—all affected by worsening North-South tensions unleashed by the struggle for control of the Kansas territory—along with nativist Know-Nothings reacting against the flood of Irish Catholic immigrants. Republicans portrayed the Democratic party as controlled by an expansionist Southern 'slavocracy' abetted in the urban North by immigrant votes, and the new party grew rapidly." As Jean Baker explains, "After the [Civil War], Democrats came to embody white racism as they opposed the Reconstruction amendments granting freedmen citizenship and voting rights. White southerners' disproportionate power in the party was perpetuated by a party rule that presidential nominations must be approved by two-thirds, not just a majority, of convention delegates. Using voting-precinct surveys and door-to-door leafletting (a campaign strategy developed by New York's Samuel Tilden), Democrats captured the House of Representatives in 1874, stunningly demonstrating their durability. As Reconstruction collapsed and the South returned to white domination, the party's future was assured, albeit with a dependence on the South and the increasingly Democratic border states that lasted until after World War II. Urban ethnic voters and white southerners formed the party's core constituencies." However, she adds, "from 1896 to 1932, Republicans overwhelmingly controlled the federal government." The Judge has thus been appointed by a federal government with values opposing the local Democratic one.

789:23–24 **Federal judge, from a Mississippi district** an appointed, not elected, position; see 789:22–23

789:27–28 **my one intellectual companion** Mothershed

790:9 **the carriage to. . . .** care for the horse once we'd arrived

790:22–24 **She died when I was fourteen; I was twenty-eight before I asserted myself and took the wife of my choice; I was thirty-seven when my son was born** Howard Allison II was born on 3 April 1903 (796:9), which means that Judge Allison was born in 1866, his mother died in 1880, and he married in 1894. See also 795:19–22.

792:23 ***Non fui. Sum. Fui. Non sum*** Latin: "I was not. I am. I was. I am not"

792:29–30 **Roman soldiers in various stages of dismemberment** According to the Christian gospels, Roman soldiers arrested Jesus and accompanied him to Pilate's court; they also tortured him before and during his crucifixion.

792:33–34 **On the exact center of each of the child's insteps was a small scar** stigmata

793:1 **third scar** see 792:33–34

793:4 **fourth scar** see 792:33–34

793:9 **Pilate** Pontius Pilate, the governor of Judea under the Roman emperor Tiberius Caesar who assented to Jesus's crucifixion: "When Pilate saw that he could prevail nothing, but that rather a tumult was made, he took water, and washed his hands before the multitude, saying, I am innocent of the blood of this just person: see ye to it" (Matthew 27:24; see also Luke 3:1).

793:29 **steamer rug** thick blanket to keep his legs warm, used on passenger ships and railways and in early automobiles

795:6–7 **Perhaps with this. . . .** you can buy him something new

795:13 **playthings. . . .** "he might be trusted with it," taking the coin itself as a toy

795:19–22 **You see, by that token, the pony would have to be thirty years old. That pony died at eighteen, six years unridden, in my lot. That was twelve years ago** If the pony was last ridden on the day that Howard II died, then it died in 1919. This means that the present time of the story is in 1931, and Judge Allison is sixty-five years old (as indicated at 781:6). See also 790:22–24.

796:1 **the raw and recent excavation** his own freshly dug grave

796:4 **Pettigrew** his executor and attorney; see 797:4–5

796:5 **the two of them** the graves of the Judge and his son

796:6 **at least I thought that he. . . .** would show respect for Howard's grave

796:9 ***1903*** see 790:22–24

796:10 ***1913*** see 790:22–24

796:10 **Gothic lettering** the name of the type commonly used for printing German and easily carved or set in hot-metal type

796:11 ***Auf Wiedersehen*** German: conventionally, "goodbye"; literally, "to see you again"

796:24 **that** immortality

796:28–30 **who is he who will affirm that there must be a web of flesh and bone to hold the shape of love** Who, living or dead, can prove that love exists only in the living world?

796:31–32 **Probably they are setting their clocks back at this very moment** Daylight savings time was not in effect in 1931, so this might refer to synchronizing a clock with the one in the square. Alternatively, the Judge may use "setting their clocks back" idiomatically, in the sense of "return to an earlier era" (Ammer 569), which would correspond with the Judge's request for his casket to be taken away on a horse-drawn hearse instead of an automobile (see 797:3 and 7).

797:3 **the vehicle at the head of the line** the hearse, an automobile

797:7 **decent pair of horses. . . .** an unfinished threat: "to carry me to the graveyard, then . . ."

797:34–798:1 **he lay in the close dark** inside the closed casket

798:2 **the moment** of his last conscious thought

798:4–5 **a last full exhalation had emptied his body of waking** his last conscious thought before falling asleep in life

“Black Music”

Faulkner’s first national publication was a poem in *The New Republic,* “L’Aprés-Midi d’un Faune,” or “Afternoon of a Faun” (1919). His first published book was a collection of poems he called *The Marble Faun* (1924), and in 1926 he hand-lettered and illustrated with fauns a tale of a young knight’s search for perfect love. He called it *Mayday* and gave it to Helen Baird after she had refused to marry him. The classical image of the faun, and the uses to which the French symbolist poets had put it, thus appeared early in Faulkner’s career and remained with him. Part man and part goat, the faun played the flute and chased women; he was poet-singer-lover all in one. To Faulkner, though, he was also often a tragic figure. In *Mayday,* for example, he presides from the endpapers over a tale in which the search for love leads only to death. Carvel Collins explains the “explicit twist toward sorrow” indicated by the title: the French military distress call “*m’aidez*” (“help me”) had become “mayday” to English speakers; moreover, folk belief in Mississippi held that “a young person looking into the water of a stream on May Day will see there the face of the one he or she will marry” (*Mayday* 38–39). Like Quentin Compson of *The Sound and the Fury,* this knight finds “Little Sister Death” in the faun’s song. The place of the faun in Faulkner’s early imagination suggests that “Black Music” has deeper implications than its premise might suggest to the contemporary reader. By turns funny and solemn, and ultimately ambiguous, the story brings together elements of myth, fantasy, the supernatural, and the psychologically perverse. An unnamed narrator visiting in the Latin American town of Rincon learns about Wilfred Midgleston, an old man from the United States who has lived there for twenty-five years. When the narrator queries him, Midgleston hesitantly claims that he has "done something. . . . Something that ain't in the lot and plan for mortal human man to do": "At one time in my life," he confides, "I was a farn" (805). When the narrator accepts this declaration with a straight face, Midgleston tells him the whole story, complete with documentary evidence from the newspapers, of how he became a faun and disrupted the wealthy Mrs. Van Dyming's plans to disfigure the Virginia countryside with colossal replicas of classical architecture.

In Midgleston's view—shaped by his early reading of "pirates and cowboys" (818)—this single strange day in his otherwise ordinary life justifies the tedium and servility that come before it and the alienation and poverty that come after it. The title, according to Lothar Hönnighausen, has "occult implications," and "as a persona of the artist, the faun is to make readers transcend the borderline between banal modernity and the visionary" (*Masks* 82). "The faun's epiphany, exploding Mrs. Van Dyming's pseudo-culture," he adds, "is characterized by pagan sensuality, closeness to nature, and vitalistic implications" (84). "Black Music," says John T. Matthews, "combines a criticism of upper class indulgent consumption with ridicule of an inadequate response to it. Van Dyming represents urban industrial capital," while Mrs. Van Dyming's project "will translate this wealth into a display of American imperial glory" ("Whose America" 76). Midgleston's brief gesture of rebellion against Mrs. Van Dyming, he points out, has no lasting effect on the *nouveau riche* woman, and Midgleston himself ends as a penniless outcast in an American oil "company town" in central America, where he "fails to recognize that his own dissatisfaction with American bourgeois life and his confinement to a service class put him in a position to identify with the alienated natives of Rincon" (77). According to James Ferguson, Midgleston's "discovery of this Dionysian side of himself constitutes his initiation" after which "he realizes that he cannot go back to his old life" (67). Edmond Volpe sees Midgleston's afternoon as a faun as a triumphant and transcendent act of the imagination. "The secret of Wilfred's success," he maintains, "is not, as he believes, his apotheosis into a faun, but his sudden transformation into an artist who transcribes, through an act of imagination, reality into a work of fiction" (40); and then "The suppressed male in him wreaks vengeance upon the emasculating female, threatening and terrifying her with all those male sexual symbols" (43). Noel Polk sees both Midgleston's pathetic limitations and his transcendence: "he becomes the marble faun made flesh who preserves the ancient grove from destruction through the accident of his first drink of alcohol when he unlocks the gate that constrains a bull—for Faulkner the quintessence of natural power—which scares the bejesus out of the citified Mrs. Van Dyming so badly that she abandons the project" ("Was Not" 22). And still none of us—Wilfred, Mrs. Van Dyming, the narrator, his readers—know exactly what happened on the day that changed several lives. "Black Music" thus lays bare the ambiguous processes by which stories come into the world.

While we cannot definitely establish that "Black Music" existed before 1931, when Faulkner submitted it to the *Saturday Evening Post,* its ties to "Carcassonne" have led to speculation that it was written as early as 1926. Those ties include the setting in Rincon, the large oil company, the character of Mrs. Widrington (Widdrington), and Midgleston's sleeping arrangements. Faulkner was unable to sell the story in the commercial fiction market, and in the fall of 1933 he wrote his agent, Morton Goldman, asking him to send the story to the "Revue Artistique Et Litteraire" *Minotaure,* in Paris: "I had a very nice letter asking for something, and as I like BLACK MUSIC and I don't believe anyone in America will want it, please send it to them" (*Selected Letters* 76). The story was published for the first time in *Doctor Martino* (1934). It was not among those first suggested in 1948 by Robert Haas for the volume that would be published as *Collected Stories,* perhaps because Haas did not have a copy of *Doctor Martino* at hand. Faulkner added it to the list, placing it as the second story in the "Beyond" section, where it certainly introduces us to a world beyond usual ken.

799:9 **Elijah** prophet of the Old Testament who ascended into heaven in a chariot of fire (II Kings 2)

799:10 **I** the unnamed narrator (who may be British; see 802:5 and 820:15)

799:10 **Rincon** "corner" in Spanish. Faulkner's Rincon has been located by Noel Polk in Puerto Rico ("William Faulkner's 'Carcassonne'") and by others in some vague Latin American locale

(Skei, *Reading* 75, for example). Here, it seems that Puerto Rico is more likely.

799:12 **Universal Oil Company** Although a company named "Universal Oil Products" has existed since 1915, this is probably a play on "Standard Oil Company," which was founded in 1870 by J. D. Rockefeller and quickly monopolized the development, production, and sale of oil. In 1911, the Supreme Court found the company in violation of the Sherman Antitrust Act and dissolved it; but the newly formed branch companies—existing in all of the 48 contiguous states and Canada and with additional refineries in Cuba and the Caribbean—retained the right to use the Standard Oil name.

799:16–17 **"He came from the States," they told me. "Been here twenty-five years"** See 819:17 for Midgleston's age; if he came to Rincon in the same year that the incident with Mrs. Van Dyming happened, then he is about eighty-one years old at the time of the story.

799:19 **Spanish** primary language of Puerto Rico (Riviera)

800:2 **George Ade fable** George Ade (1866–1944) wrote *Fables in Slang* (1899) and *More Fables* (1900), collections of satirical pieces "liberally salted with capital letters" and italics, that came to a facetious "moral" (Brenner 198). "The Fable *of the* Author *Who* was Sorry *for* What He did *to* Willie," for example, describes the plight of a serious writer who publishes a sappy poem and becomes famous for it; the moral is "*Refrain from Getting Gay with the Emotions*" (see Ade, *More Fables*).

800:2–3 **Presbyterian social charade in 1890** church social gathering from an earlier era

800:19–20 **I guess you are right** the projection of the speaker's prejudices onto the narrator

800:28 **pull his chestnuts for him** "out of the fire"; from the fable of a monkey that gets a cat to pull its chestnuts out of a fire, with the cat being a kind of pawn in the matter and the monkey the cleverer of the two (Ammer 89, 108–9)

800:34 **I—** "was, with none left"; catching himself before fully admitting to theft

801:3–4 **Wm. J. Burns** director of the Federal Bureau of Investigation from 1921–1924 who resigned in 1924 due to his part in the

Teapot Dome scandal and turned to writing detective and mystery stories (see "William J. Burns")

801:12 **Spigs** from *spic*, a derogatory term for Spanish-speakers, but sometimes also applied to Italians

801:14 **Spiggotties** see 801:12; a term current in the first years of the twentieth century

802:5 **drill** coarse twill

802:23 **the handleless bowl** coffee served in the Old World custom

803:9 **an architect's draughtsman** one who drew the architect's ideas for him

803:16 **the Company, and Mrs. Widrington** see 799:12

803:27 **tarred roofing paper** paper sealed by tar or asphalt which can be nailed to a roof, alone or under shingles, in order to waterproof it

804:11 **a right smart** as Calvin Brown explains, "a considerable amount, number, period of time, etc." (163)

805:23 **Pan** lesser Greek deity, half goat and half man, son of Hermes and favorite of Dionysus; the god of fertility, forests, wildlife, and flocks and herds; a musician whose instrument was the syrinx (pipe)

805:24–25 **them little fellows that was half a goat** see 805:26

805:26 **a faun** half-goat from the waist down, with the top half of a man and goat horns; in Greek mythology, the companions of Dionysus, god of wine associated with frenzied carnal indulgence

805:29–30 **the Bible says that them little men were myths** Midgleston has got the general idea that Christianity abolished the gods of the past, as in the first and second commandments: "Thou shalt have no other gods before me. Thou shalt not make unto thee any graven image, or any likeness of any thing that is in heaven above, or that is in the earth beneath, or that is in the water under the earth: Thou shalt not bow down thyself to them, nor serve them: for I the Lord thy God am a jealous God" (Exodus 20:2–5).

806:21 **I-talian** regional pronunciation of "Italian"

807:9 **them** the "Park Avenue folks" mentioned at 807:14

807:14 **Park Avenue** street in Manhattan in New York City; then as now a wealthy, upper-class neighborhood

807:15–17 **community house built to look like the Coliseum and the community garage yonder made to look like it was a Acropolis** shared house built as a meeting-place for guests, copied after the famous Roman amphitheatre that saw the bloody work of the gladiators, with a shared garage for housing automobiles, copied after the Athenian fortress—more particularly, the Parthenon, the most important temple in and symbol of ancient Greece

807:18 **a outdoors theatre** an amphitheatre; those of the ancient Greeks staged the plays in the contests at Dionysus's festivals and had excellent acoustics.

807:20 **Roman barges** large, flat-bottomed boat, in ancient Rome propelled by oars. Mrs. Van Dyming may imagine herself as Cleopatra from Shakespeare's *Antony and Cleopatra*:

> The barge she sat in, like a burnish'd throne,
> Burn'd on the water. The poop was beaten gold,
> Purple the sails, and so perfumèd that
> The winds were love-sick with them. The oars were silver,
> Which to the tune of flutes kept stroke and made
> The water which they beat to follow faster,
> As amorous of their strokes. For her own person,
> It beggar'd all description. (II, ii, 196–202)

807:28–29 **Westchester** affluent county suburb of New York City

807:29 **Poughkeepsie** working-class city in New York state, about 70 miles north of the City

808:16 **It belonged there, fitted** was compatible with the landscape

808:18–19 **Not to make anybody mad** like the gods

809:9–10 **I am not a man who believes that people have learned everything** a man who discounts the supernatural

809:13 **threescore and ten** seventy years, from Psalms 90:10: "The days of our years are threescore and ten"

810:6 **theatre prints** blueprints for the theatre building

810:32 **back to the ice water** back to the dining car, where he gets a drink of water

812:2 **ladies' temperance** organization of women engaged in the cause to ban the production and consumption of alcoholic beverages, like the Woman's Christian Temperance Union or, more generally, the Anti-Saloon League, which helped in the passage of the eighteenth amendment establishing Prohibition (see Tyrrell)

812:9 **it had already started then** the process of turning into a faun

812:11–12 **Like it was drinking out of the bottle and not me** The faun that has temporarily possessed Midgleston takes over here.

812:20 **Let her rip** "Go ahead"; Christine Ammer explains that "the use of *her* in the variant comes from a tradition of referring to vehicles as feminine" (380).

812:24 **the whistle—** Midgleston's attempt to copy Pan's syrinx, a set of graduated pipes bound together

812:31–32 **It was a tin one, with holes in it** a toy whistle

813:10 **by gummy** "by gum"; euphemism for "by God"

813:17 **It was clear like water** most probably, Blue Ridge moonshine

813:19 **I dont smell, you see. I dont know what they call it** Partial loss of the sense of smell is hyposmia, while total loss is anosmia.

814:21–22 **the broken seams glued carefully with strips of soiled cloth** Midgleston has glued the article to some cloth to keep the seams from tearing apart and destroying it with such repeated readings.

815:33 **a knife** actually the whistle

815:34–35 **a flat, square object in the other** the portfolio with the theatre blueprints inside

816:14 **Durham bull** a breed of shorthorn cattle

816:23–24 **take subscriptions to the *Police Gazette*, for premiums** sold subscriptions in return for prizes

816:24–25 **a little machine guaranteed to open any lock** a lock-pick, an ironic prize for selling the *Police Gazette*

816:32 **wump-wump-wump inside like a dray horse** breathing as hard and loudly as a horse pulling a heavy cart

818:1 **lock, stock, and barrel** all of something; expression deriving from the three main parts of a firearm (Ammer 392)

818:31–32 **Coney Island** resort and amusement park on the Atlantic coast on the south shore of Long Island, New York

818:32 **Washington Square** park in Greenwich Village in New York City, a neighborhood known for its artist and bohemian types

818:33–35 **that some day . . . that living wouldn't play a trick on him like getting him alive and then. . . .** lock him in a dull routine, with no chance to do something exciting

819:17 **56** see 799:16–17

820:15 **agony column** in British slang, an advice column

821:6 **I dont—Maybe you'd better tell me** I don't understand exactly; maybe you'd better spell it out for me

821:18 **Maison Payot** the name of the young man's place of employment; a French term meaning "House of Payot," which could be a play on *payer*, or "to pay," implying that he works for a financial institution; alternatively, "pay out," implying; bribery or blackmail

"The Leg"

Davy, the first-person narrator of "The Leg," opens with a deceptively simple scene of two friends boating on the River Thames before the beginning of World War I, takes us into the war in which one of them dies and the other is grievously wounded, and finally brings us into a surreal realm of violence, perversion, and death, which might be realistic, hallucinatory, or supernatural—or all of these at once. It is one of those stories in which the reader must first figure out what happens before addressing the questions of why it happened and what it all means. The story has three time frames: 1914, when Davy's friend George falls into a lock while apostrophizing the lock-keeper's daughter, Everbe Corinthia; 1915, when George dies and Davy loses his leg; and 1917, when the lock-keeper's son attacks Davy for seducing Everbe Corinthia and causing her death, while Davy at the same time has supposedly been in hospital or in flight training. In some sense a "war story," Davy's troubled contemplation of his own body, and the bodies of both George and Everbe Corinthia, suggests that "the Leg" is more in the tradition of the *doppelgänger* as practiced by such writers as Poe and Henry James. Too, though the opening of the story is filled with literary allusions—to Milton, to Keats and Spenser, and to classical mythology and the Bible—the story's exploration of perverse sexual desire, repression, and enactment may owe as much to Freud as to its specifically literary sources.

"Faulkner's text," Robert W. Hamblin writes, "leaves ambiguous the question of whether key incidents represent supernatural occurrences or merely the imaginary products of an unsettled mind" ("The Leg" 225), a familiar question regarding *doppelgänger* narratives. The principal ambiguity concerns Davy's apparent callous seduction and abandonment of Everbe Corinthia: did Davy himself somehow do this, or did his ghostly double, or is the whole narrative, in the end, the delusion of a permanently deranged mind? Hamblin calls "The Leg" "a ghost story based on the idea of reincarnation." Noting that Davy was in hospital talking with George's ghost at the time the incriminating photograph was made, he concludes that "the implication is that the lost leg has worked its frightful purpose" ("Carcassonne" 163–64). Describing all of the stories in the "Beyond" section of *Collected Stories* as "strange stories of the supernatural," Hans Skei calls "The Leg" "the best example of a story about the supernatural" (*Short Story* 125). Adding another layer of uncertainty, James Carothers suggests that the scene in which George falls into the lock "describes not merely a temporary and quickly rectified embarrassment by immersion for George, but actually his death by drowning, and that Davy's madness stems from this incident, rather [than] from, his later experiences in the war" ("Faulkner's" 221). Whatever the presumed or speculative plot, most who have discussed "The Leg" emphasize its psychosexual implications. Lisa Paddock, connecting "The Leg" with "Black Music," says both stories are "tales about *Doppelgängers*," and "the double is associated with sexuality." "Davy's leg," she maintains, "is fraught with demonic and Freudian significance" (102). Carothers describes "The Leg" as "a case study in sexual guilt and retribution, in which Davy's real or imagined attack on Everbe Corinthia constitutes an unconscious projection of his resentment over the fact that Everbe, as Circe, provokes 'swinish' behavior in himself and in George" (220). Most readers agree that "The Leg" is lesser Faulkner, with James Ferguson calling it "lurid, intense, and overwrought" (30). Edmond Volpe, however, calls the story "a fascinating display of imagination" and "a modern morality play in which Everyman discovers that the dark powers of evil lurk deep within his own being" (56). The end of the story, Volpe says, "conveys a profound sense of guilt. The part of Davy that is represented by the freed leg has committed a monstrous evil. . . . [T]he seduction of Corinthia and the destruction of the whole Rust family may be read as a symbol of the unleashed evil forces that have created the havoc and horror of war" (57).

Though the story certainly existed by 3 November 1928, when it was rejected by *Scribner's*, it was not published until Faulkner included it, as "Leg," in *Doctor Martino* in 1934 (Skei, *Short Story* 41). An early version of "The Leg" called its first-person narrator "David" (as did early versions of "Carcassonne"), which suggests an association with *Mosquitoes* (1927). Some have dated the story from Faulkner's 1925 European trip, citing the letter he wrote his mother on 15 October: "I've written a queer short story, about a case of reincarnation" (*Selected Letters* 31). "The Leg" was apparently not among the list of stories first suggested by Robert Haas at Random House for inclusion in *Collected Stories* (*SL* 274–75), but Faulkner's later version of the list includes it and places it in its present position as the third of the six stories in the "Beyond" section (*SL* 279). "The Leg" remains one of Faulkner's most enigmatic, little discussed, and rarely appreciated efforts.

823:2 **made two reaches below us** came into the lock two levels down from the level at which Davy and George's boat sits

823:4 **pile** heavy, pointed post driven into a riverbed to support another structure

823:4 **Milton** John Milton (1608–1674), English poet most famous for *Paradise Lost* (1667, 1674), "perhaps the greatest epic poem in English," who went blind in 1652. His other major works include *Lycidas* (1637), *Aeropagitica* (1644), and *Paradise Regained* (1671) (see "Milton, John").

823:5 **the final tack** the last change of course made by turning its head into and through the wind, to bring the wind to the opposite side

823:6 **Comus' second speech** Milton's first major work (performed in 1634). Enid Welsford describes it: "Although described as a 'masque,' *Comus* depends little on spectacle and may be defined as a pastoral drama. Comus himself is a pagan god invented by Milton, son of Bacchus and Circe, who waylays travellers and transforms their faces to those of wild beasts by means of a magic liquor"; he tempts a Lady and begs her "not to be 'cosen'd with that same vaunted name Virginity.' She defends herself and Chastity with such spirit that even Comus feels her possessed of 'some superior power.' " The goddess of the river Severn, Sabrina, arrives to free her from Comus's spell. Welsford notes that "the action has been justly but somewhat irrelevantly criticized as 'a dramatised debate' " (quoted in "Comus"). Comus delivers his second speech when he first sees the Lady:

Can any mortal mixture of Earths mould
Breath such Divine inchanting ravishment?
Sure somthing holy lodges in that brest,
And with these raptures moves the vocal air
To testifie his hidd'n residence. . . . ("A Mask Presented at Ludlow Castle" 244–48)

823:8 **Give way** yield

823:9 **glazed** worn smooth and shiny with repeated brushing

823:10 **the lock** a device that allows watercraft to move between water levels, consisting of watertight compartments into which water is either added or removed to raise or lower the vessel

823:11 **Sabrina** see 823:6

823:11 **Hebe** in Greek mythology, daughter of Zeus and Hera; the cup-bearer of the gods and Heracles' wife on Olympus; "the personification of the Greek word for youth" ("Hebe")

823:11 **Chloe** another name in the classical period of ancient Greece for Demeter, goddess of the harvest and fertility; also, from *Daphnis and Chloe*, a Greek pastoral romance describing "in formal style the wakening of passion in its two protagonists" ("Daphnis and Chloe")

823:13 **dairy-maid's complexion** wholesome; milk-fed

823:15 **the lever** the handle of the windlass or crank used to open the gates of the lock; see 823:10

823:18 **luffed and stood away** brought its head nearer to the wind and steered away from the lock

824:3–4 **apostrophised her in the metaphor of Keats and Spenser** made a flowery, ornately phrased speech (an aside from the main action of the punting) to her that copies the style of Romantic poet John Keats (1795–1821), whose brilliant career was cut short by tuberculosis, and the Elizabethan poet Edmund Spenser (1552–1599), best known for his epic *The Faerie Queene* (1590)

824:5–6 **aback and in stays** sails laid flat against the mast by the wind, with the vessel's head turned windward to tack (see 823:5)

824:10–11 **Circe's droves into the sea? Pull, then, O Super-Gadarene** two references to men turned into swine, which Circe did literally in Homer's *Odyssey* and which Jesus did figuratively when he cast the devils out of two men and sent them into the bodies of a herd of swine, which then charged into the sea and died (Matthew 8:28–32). Near the present border of Israel and Syria, Gadara was one of the ten cities in the ancient Decapolis and home to many Cynic and other philosophers and is associated with the story in Matthew.

824:27 **mate** assistant on a vessel; also, British slang for male friend

824:30 **towpath** path on the side of the lock where horses pull a boat through the lock by means of a rope

824:33–34 **his ugly crooked face and his round head now dark in the sunlight** features perhaps distorted by revulsion at the taste of the river water; his head "dark" because wet

825:2 **seeing 'is mate. . . .** If the fall into the lock kills George, the sentence might end with "drown" or "die." However, if George survives his fall into the river and dies at 829:10, then the sentence might end with "fall in the water" or "take a tumble like that."

825:4 **flannels** trousers made of flannel fabric

825:12 **Oxford young gentlemen** careless college boys; Oxford sits on the Thames River, and punting continues to be popular among the University's students.

825:15 **farthing** in British currency, a quarter of a penny

825:16–17 **tears over the accomplishment of your appointed destiny** see 824:10–11: "crying because you got what you wanted and saw me dumped in the water?"

825:24 **the lock mechanism** the device to open the gates; see 823:10 and 823:15

826:2 **dove-cote** a shelter for doves

826:29 **below a bit** lower down the river

826:30 **keb** a cab, or taxicab

826:33–827:1 **pull down** row

827:7 **the symbol of my soul** phrase appears in "O Star of France" (in some editions of *Leaves of Grass*) by Walt Whitman:

> Dim smitten star,
> Orb not of France alone, pale symbol of my soul, its dearest hopes,
> The struggle and the daring, rage divine for liberty,

Of aspirations toward the far ideal, enthusiast's dreams of brotherhood,
Of terror to the tyrant and the priest. (4–11)

827:7–8 **unshipped one scull** removed one oar from its mooring

827:13–14 **public servant who did not want his public charge cluttered up** the lock keeper and his lock, which would have been "cluttered" with George's body if they hadn't fished it out

827:21 **bunk** American slang for nonsense, with a slightly more earthy edge

827:21–22 **Why not use the river for a while? It's paid for** Why not let the current take us back instead of expending your energy?

827:23 **That is . . .** one way of looking at things

827:26 **outside her** on the opposite side from the towing animals

827:29 **goad** a pointed rod or stick, used to drive the towing animals

827:31 **freeboard** the distance between the water line and the top deck of the vessel

828:17 **I think—** you're a fool

828:23–24 **"O Thames!" he said. "Thou mighty sewer of an empire!"** The river that gave London its life and character from ancient times, the Thames has served simultaneously as thoroughfare, water source, and sewer.

828:32–34 **the old splendid bloody deeds, the spirits of the blundering courageous men, slumbered in every stone and tree** the memories of the ancient and medieval warriors and knights of England's history

829:1 **Valse Septembre** waltz written by Felix Godin in 1909, known by the first line of its chorus, "Oh! Listen to the band"

829:3 **Mister Moon and There's a Bit of Heaven** Several possibilities exist, including "Farewell, Mister Moon" by Arthur E Behim (1908), "Move on Mr. Moon" by Rose and Snyder (1912), "Hello, Mr. Moonman! Hello" by Albert H. Fitz (1909), "A Little Bit of Heaven (Shure They Call it Ireland)" (Music: Ernest R. Ball, Lyrics: J. Keirn Brennan, 1914)

826:4 **Christ Church** the largest college in the University of Oxford and the city of Oxford's cathedral

829:6 **Napier** possibly John Napier (1550–1617), a Scots theologian and mathematician who invented logarithms, or Arthur Napier

(1853–1916), a scholar of English literature at Oxford during the time of the story

829:6 **Ben Jonson** English Renaissance poet and playwright (1572–1637), the most famous author of his day, whose *Pleasure Reconciled to Virtue* (1618) gave Milton the idea for *Comus* (see 823:6; "Jonson, Ben")

829:7–8 **God Save the King** British national anthem

829:9 **sang Mademoiselle of Armentieres in the mud** popular wartime song written by Harry Carlton and Joe Tunbridge and often very crudely extemporized upon by soldiers, with some versions as follows:

Mademoiselle from Armentières, Parley-voo?
Mademoiselle from Armentières, Parley-voo?
Mademoiselle from Armentières,
She hasn't been kissed in forty years,
Hinky, dinky, parley-voo.
Oh, Mademoiselle from Armentières, Parley-voo
Oh, Mademoiselle from Armentières, Parley-voo
She got the palm and the croix de guerre,
For washin' soldiers' underwear,
Hinky-dinky, Parley-voo? (see Duffy, "Vintage")

"Parley-voo" is *parlez-vous*, or "'Do you speak' French?"

829:11 **gone out** been sent to France

829:11 **subaltern** junior officer in the British army

829:12 **hereditary colonels** high-ranking officers by virtue of their social status

829:14 **Givenchy** Battle of Givenchy, 18–22 December 1914, after which the front lines had not changed and which cost the Germans 2000 men and the British 4000 (Duffy, "Battles")

829:14–15 **a telephone strapped to his ears** George was a communications officer; field telephones and switchboards were developed during this war and significantly changed the way war could be conducted (see Danny Johnson).

830:17 **temporarily submerged in—** "the sewer of an empire" (see 828:23–24)

830:31 **it** Davy and George's chances to talk to each other

831:3–4 **Now, now. He's not going. Yes, yes; he'll come back. Lie still, now** the nurses' reassurances upon hearing Davy talk to George

832:3–4 **You jumped into the skiff and pulled away. So I came back here** the first indication of supernatural trouble because of the leg

832:20 **the wood-and-leather one** his artificial leg

832:22 **that's** the artificial leg

832:23 **Maybe now . . .** it will be at peace

832:24–25 **forgot to—** put it to rest

832:31 **Observers' School** school to train one for work observing enemy positions and directing forces and fire. Robert Harrison notes that "In the spring of 1915 a small wireless operator's school was opened at St. Omer to train men transferred from the army to the RFC. The first wireless school in Britain was opened at Brooklands the same year" (105).

832:32 **wireless key** a device for breaking and closing electric circuits in a telegraph system, thus sending Morse code

832:33 **gunner's piano stool** revolving seat in an aircraft for the gunner; see next two entries

832:33 **R.E.** As Harrison explains, the "Reconnaissance Experimental, a line of two-seat tractor aeroplanes"; The R.E.8 was perhaps the worst of the [Royal Aircraft] Factory aeroplanes, embodying virtually every major design flaw for which a remedy was already known" (105).

832:33 **F.E.** Fighting Experimental, in service in the R.F.C. since January 1916, in which the observer/gunner sat in front of the pilot in the airplane's nose (Harrison 81, 105)

833:12 **the dream** described in full at 833:13–834:11

833:13 **it** the amputated leg

833:21 **And then I was awake** Although he is awake in his dream, Davy is still asleep in the reality of the story; see 834:8.

834:8 **"Wake up," it said** evidence that Davy's encounter with George was just a dream; see 833:21

834:18 **to not observe what should not be observed** secret or sensitive Allied military operations

834:20 **the outcast's** the amputated leg's

834:22 **mother of dreams** possibly Queen Mab, queen of the fairies and maker of dreams, as described by Mercutio in Shakespeare's

Romeo and Juliet, and the title figure of Percy Bysshe Shelley's epic poem (1813)

834:25 **It** the leg

835:5 **it** the dream

835:15 **Devon** county in the southwest part of England

835:17 **Marlowe** English playwright and poet Christopher Marlowe (1564–93), most famous for the poems *Hero and Leander* (1598) and *The Passionate Shepherd* (1599) and the plays *Doctor Faustus* (1604) and *The Jew of Malta* (1633) and a significant influence on Shakespeare and Ben Jonson

835:18 **Thomas Campion** 1567–1620, English poet, musician, and doctor, who published four *Bookes of Ayres* (1601–1617), of which the following is a fair sample:

My loue hath vowd hee will forsake mee,
And I am alreadie sped.
Far other promise he did make me
When he had my maidenhead.
If such danger be in playing,
And sport must to earnest turne,
I will go no more a-maying.

835:18–19 **breath was not a bauble given a man for his own pleasuring** possibly an allusion to Alexander Pope's *Essay on Man* (1733–34), which observes that man adopts different playthings at each stage of life but remains "Pleased with this bauble still, as that before;/Till tired he sleeps, and life's poor play is o'er" (II, 274)

835:21 **Padre** army chaplain

835:21 **Poperinghe** town in Belgium that was the center for British military operations during the war

835:29 **three years ago** sets the present time of the story at roughly 1917

836:3 **Midlands** of England; the counties including Oxford and Cambridge as well as the working class cities of Birmingham and Nottingham

836:10 **Yet he . . .** At least two possibilities exist: either the padre refers to "man" in general, still in rebellion against God, or to Jotham Rust in particular, so the sentence might well end "refuses."

836:10 **seem . . .** to reach him
836:11 **stock** clerical collar
836:15 **night before last** when Rust tried to kill him
836:15–16 **the other was . . . two—three years ago** in 1914
836:18–19 **And if you hadn't told me his sister's name, I wouldn't have remembered him then** The padre has apparently known only one of her names; see 837:3.
836:22 **the—the other** the other funeral
836:24 **sexton** maintenance man in a church and its attached graveyard; formerly, gravedigger
836:24 **Abingdon** Abingdon on Thames, in Faulkner's day the county seat of Berkshire and today part of Oxfordshire; a town dating to ancient times
837:3 **"Was that her name?" he said. "Everbe Corinthia?"** The question indicates surprise at her whole name; the narrator knows her as Everbe Corinthia (see 823:4), and the padre seems to have known only one of them (see 836:18–19).
837:6 **major's crown** the shoulder insignia designating his rank in the army
837:9 **magneto case** the case in which a small generator of alternating current, produced by permanent magnets, was housed; in this instance, part of the ignition system for an aircraft
837:23–24 **a sense of social responsibility, integrity, that . . .** makes him sound credible
837:24 **And you say that you—** haven't seen her in three years
838:1 **now . . .** I certainly would
838:5–6 **to him who has sinned, that sin will come home to him** Any number of Bible verses could be combined to produce this Christian version of karma, including the parable of the prodigal son (Luke 15:11–32) and the warning in Exodus about worshipping other gods: "I the Lord thy God am a jealous God, visiting the iniquity of the fathers upon the children unto the third and fourth generation of them that hate me" (Exodus 20:5).
838:6 **Otherwise . . . God is at least a gentleman** . . . where would be the justice? God has a sense of *noblesse oblige* and would not let a sinner go unpunished.
838:7 **I am not—** making sense

838:12–14 **the still and sinister darkness in which the fine and resounding words men mouthed so glibly were the vampire's teeth with which the vampire fed** the surrounding war, which is "fed" with the bodies of men who die for the sake of oratory

838:28–30 **That was last summer, about the time I was completing my course at the Observers' School** the beginning of an explanatory flashback that ends at 840:17

840:8 **they dragged the lock** used nets and hooks to search the lock for the body

840:18–19 **He had now been absent from his battalion for a hundred and twelve days** sets the attack in autumn 1917; see 841:27

840:22 **B.E.F.** British Expeditionary Force, the professional British Army that went to France in 1914

840:32 **You'll not—** come any closer

841:5 **shovel hat** broadbrimmed hat with the brim turned up on the sides, worn by some clergy

841:12 **Is he—** dead?

841:12 **it** the execution

841:27 **June of the summer just past** fine-tunes the date of the present time of the story as October 1917; see 840:18–19

841:34–842:1 **an unprintable phrase** an obscenity; unprintable in respectable publications

842:11 **Pop** Poperinghe; see 835:21

"Mistral"

With its origins almost certainly in Faulkner's 1925 "walking trip" to Europe with William Spratling, "Mistral" is one of three early stories with the principal characters "Don and I." In each of these, the narrator and his companion encounter a kind of mystery and seek to solve it. "Mistral" employs a retrospective first-person narrator to offer a straightforward chronological account of a single eventful day in the lives of two young men *en promenade* in Italy. The story hints at several kinds of initiation for the two young Americans; they first learn of an apparent murder and seek to identify the murderer, but they subsequently encounter a succession of mysterious or contradictory revelations about a young priest, his ward, her dead fiancé, and her preferred suitor Giulio. The local people they meet seem either loquacious or fiercely tight-lipped, welcoming or forbidding, yet all with apparent opinions of this odd foursome. The two friends hear or try to discover these opinions in the grip of the ever-present mistral, the bitter cold wind that sweeps through the country and the story. They begin bantering easily and condescendingly about the people and the mystery they encounter in the Italian village above Milan, but by the end they have been drawn in to a situation that might well portend evil beyond their comprehension.

Summarizing the story raises more questions than it answers. Has the fiancé been murdered or not? If so, by whom? What, exactly, has been the priest's role in the town in the past, and what are his motives now? Lisa Paddock suggests first that "perhaps the impending prospect of his ward's marriage was ultimately too much for the possessive priest to bear," or, alternatively, that the girl murdered her fiancé on learning that Giulio was to be released from the army. Too, she speculates, perhaps Giulio himself might have returned surreptitiously to the village to do away with his rival

("Trifles" 415–16). A. Nicholas Fargnoli and Michael Golay suggest the murder may have been committed by Giulio's aunt, out of resentment of the priest's opposition to her nephew's relationship with the girl and his presumed conniving to get the young man drafted (161). If, however, we are not certain precisely what the priest *does*, it is surely impossible to explain why he does it. Some observers, within the story and without, speculate that he objects to the romance between Giulio and the girl not out of a desire to protect her but because of his own lust for her. His arrangement of the unsatisfactory betrothal, then, was his way to keep the girl near him. Is he in torment at the end because the girl and Giulio have finally achieved the consummation he had worked so long and nefariously to prevent, or does he give in to grief for his own denied and thwarted sexuality? Much of the difficulty of the story comes from the quick and casual way that the young travelers, especially Don, reach conclusions about matters of fact and impute motives to characters, but this glibness may be a consequence of the alcohol they consume from the beginning of the story to the end of it. While many have seen the affinities between "Mistral" and *Absalom, Absalom!*—two young male friends telling a story together of violent sexuality, for example—the short story answers its questions ambiguously and indistinctly at best. The narrator himself, in retrospect, notes his and Don's youth, hinting that the experience in Italy initiated them into a world they could not accept, in which murder goes undetected or unpunished, a priest behaves in a manifestly unpriestlike way, and carnal desire wins out over the romantic illusions of youth and the restrictive conventions of orthodox society, "as though," as Arthur A. Brown puts it, "its illegal consummation had been God's will" (253). Hans Skei says "Mistral" "may be overwritten and too long, but its intricate presentation of passion and murder . . . foreshadows narrative techniques Faulkner used later" (*Reading* 14). Ferguson calls the story "anything but a totally successful work of art . . . much too long and diffuse, and, in places, maddeningly obscure," but he also assesses it as a "powerful, complex, and richly atmospheric piece" (31). Edmond Volpe is perhaps most laudatory of "Mistral," calling it "technically a very competent story, with tight control of point of view and structure . . . an impressionistic evocation of the unappeasable desire, the dread and anguish of young people whose romantic, untempered imaginations can envelop love with love, human anguish with the terror of nightmare" (49).

On 3 November 1925, Faulkner wrote his mother from Paris: "I have just finished typing 6 short stories which I shall leave with an agent in New York" (Watson, *Thinking* 216). It is tempting to speculate that an early version of "Mistral" was among these, but we have no certain proof. At any rate, "Mistral" was rejected by *Scribner's* on 3 November 1928 and by the *Saturday Evening Post* after Faulkner's submission in June of 1930. In spite of these rejections, he included it in *These 13*, placing it first in the third section of that collection, with "Divorce in Naples" and "Carcassonne" following it. He arranged the same three stories in the same order at the end of *Collected Stories.* Both of the other "Don and I" stories, "The Big Shot" and "Evangeline," remained unpublished until *Uncollected Stories* (1979), as did "Snow," a later story with these characters. Although it lacks the supernatural elements of several of the other "Beyond" stories, "Mistral" places its narrator and his companion in circumstances beyond their experience and comprehension. It may also present readers with a narrative beyond certain interpretation, and it would not be the only Faulkner story to do that.

843:TITLE **Mistral** dry, cold, northerly wind that blows in squalls toward the southern coast of France. The fact that the travelers in this story experience it, combined with the drink mentioned in the story's first line, sets them in far northwestern Italy.

843:1 **Milanese brandy** brandy made in Milan, in northwestern Italy, the capital of the Lombardy region

843:1 **I** see Introduction

843:3 **leather jacket** a covering for the pocket flask

844:18 **Maybe there's a haystack at the bottom** to break his fall when he crashes

844:27 **cropping** nibbling

844:28–29 **a stone shrine** niche containing the statue of a saint, and perhaps candles, certainly flowers (see 845:12)

844:32 **signor** Italian for sir

844:32 **Is it far?** from here to the town

844:33 **signori** "sirs" in Italian

845:2–3 **then she made swift play with her fingers before his face** a kind of personal sign language; see 852:18–19

845:12 **mountain asters** flowers laid as an offering to the saint in the shrine

845:20 **prestidigitator's** sleight-of-hand magician

846:20–21 **He said something else, too swift for me** The narrator's Italian isn't good enough to allow him understand the old man when he speaks at his normal speed.

847:1 **banns** formal announcement in church of an intended marriage

847:3 **Tchk** a dismissive noise, like "tsk"

847:8 ***e bello*** incorrect Italian for "is good"; see 847:9

847:9 **he also said, *bello*** As Don does at 847:8, the native speaker uses the wrong gender of the adjective. "Life is good" in Italian is "*La vita e bella.*"

847:17 **for the child's—** sake

847:20 **1916** see 847:24

847:24 **Caporetto** 24 October–10 November 1917, a surprise attack by the Germans on the Italian front that resulted in 300,000 Italian casualties

847:25–26 **the mother had been seen in a house in Milano that was not a good house** a house of prostitution

847:27 **She was six then** She would thus have been born in 1901.

848:1 **red or a green dress for Sundays and feast days** On religious occasions, she wore a special dress; red, green, and white are the colors of the Italian flag.

848:3 **to be a crown to her husband** Proverbs 12:4: "A virtuous woman is a crown to her husband; but she that maketh ashamed is as rottenness in his bones"

848:5 **put such away** The full context of the Biblical passage reveals some of Faulkner's irony: "When I was a child, I spake as a child, I understood as a child, I thought as a child; but when I became a man, I put away childish things. For now we see through a glass, darkly; but then face to face: now I know in part; but then shall I know even as also I am known. And now abideth faith, hope, charity, these three: but the greatest of these is charity" (I Corinthians 13:11–13).

849:16 **an anonymous child** a child with no name; a bastard

849:17–18 **when you open it . . .** it contains obscenities

851:31 **I no spika** pidgin English, in imitation of the way a native speaker of Italian might say "I don't speak English"; however, the narrator does speak Italian, since he has understood the conversation and related it to us.

852:18–19 **The other we made lying in the bed in the dark** the sign language described at 845:2–3, which they have apparently invented together

852:32–853:4 **Then the wind began: a steady moving wall of air full of invisible particles of something. Before it the branches leaned without a quiver, as before the pressure of an invisible hand, and in it our blood began to cool at once** the first title passage

853:9 **He got in with a fast gang** a flippant pun

853:35 **Malbrouck** John Churchill, the First Duke of Marlborough (1650–1722); there is also a French nursery song dating from the eighteenth century popular throughout Europe, "*Malbrouck s'en va-t-en guerre*," or "Malbrouck Goes Off to the War," sung to the tune we know as "For He's a Jolly Good Fellow."

854:2–4 **Overhead the leaves streamed rigid on the wind, stippled black upon the livid translucent sky** title passage

854:11 **padrona** Italian for owner; lady of the house

854:22 **Cavalry** a joke: not infantry, because he has a mount

854:29–30 **It's because we are old. We lie in the draft. That's a joke too** a double pun, on "lie" and "draft," and a parody of the old woman's comment at 852:19–20, "The old lie in the bed and talk"

854:34 **No spika. I love Italy. I love Mussolini** more pidgin English to dodge the topics that Don would pursue

855:20 **the priest—** would take us in

856:7–8 **The leaves made a dry, wild, continuous sound** title passage

856:20–24 **The particles in the wind seemed to drive through the clothing, through the flesh, against the bones, penetrating the brick and plaster of the walls to reach us** title passage

856:33 **the black wind** title passage

857:14–15 **those harsh iron counts and bishops of Lombardy** After the Germanic Lombards' rule of the area, the region became part of Charlemagne's kingdom; around 887, a number of city-states emerged, ruled independently by counts or bishops (see "Lombardy").

857:22 **Beaver** a simple game in which players see a bearded man, a "beaver," and claim a point, once scored as tennis is
857:32 **the Host rose** the eucharist, lifted above the priest's head during the mass
858:8–9 **it seems like . . .** more people would be here, and it would be daylight
858:30 **you die too many times** you lose yourself every time you see one
858:33 **I said it was like fire** it = sexual desire
859:9–11 **Because when you reach reality, along about forty or fifty or sixty, you find it to be only six feet deep and eighteen feet square** The only reality is mortality, and its symbol the grave.
859:12 **it** the funeral mass
859:22 **presbytery** in the Catholic church, the residence of the priest
859:23 **mufti** civilian clothes
860:12 **This is October** we can't sleep outside
860:21 **Beaver** see 857:22
860:23 **Beaverette** because she's a girl; see 857:22, with a likely pun on her pubic hair
860:33 **that we might—** stay here
861:1 **en promenade** on a walking tour
861:12 **Maybe she won't have to, by then** because she'll be gone
861:27 **Must have heard—** he was in town
862:8–14 **The whisper in our ears seemed to fill the room with wind . . . the long dark fury of time** title passage
863:6 **pale, mahogany-colored face** an oxymoron to describe her ethnicity
863:12 **There come times—** that try a man's soul
863:25 **Firenze** Florence
863:30 **spirituel** the French form of the adjective; the Italian, *spirituale*
864:5 **There come times—** see 863:12
864:9 **There come times—** see 863:12
865:3 **If it were just summer** we could sleep outside and be out of this mess
865:18 **This house belongs to God: you can't have a lock on it** a reference to the Church's function as a sanctuary and haven

867:30 **he made the sign** of the cross, in blessing

868:3 **lee** the side sheltered from the wind

868:9 **skirling** shrill, piercing sound; usually said of a bagpipe

869:9–10 **Thaw and White and Evelyn Nesbitt** Stanford White (1853–1906), a prominent architect and libertine, seduced and took the virginity of sixteen-year-old Evelyn Nesbit (1884–1967), an artist's model and Gibson Girl. Her husband, Harry K. Thaw (1871–1947) subsequently shot and killed him in a rooftop theatre at Madison Square Garden on 25 June 1906.

869:30 **Grandfather Lust** the narrator's invention

870:22 **Cavalcanti's** possibly an allusion to Ezra Pound's translation *Sonnets and Ballate of Guido Cavalcanti* (1912)

870:24 **But she said—** at 855:16, that "there were none"

872:3 **made him** identified him

872:7–8 **I wonder why he didn't stop the . . . before they . . .** "funeral"; "could bury him"

872:26 **jack** money

873:8 **it** your money

873:24–25 **in the morning early—** we can leave

873:32 **a shooting coat of Harris tweed** jacket with leather or padding where the rifle rests against the front of the shoulders and elbow patches, of warm wool cloth made in the Hebrides of Scotland

873:32 **guineas** former unit of British currency; a gold coin worth one pound and one shilling

874:1 **the Tyrol** region in western Austria and northern Italy known as a hiking and skiing destination

874:2 **make** seduce

874:5–6 **with a green feather in his hat** a typical Tyrolean hat, a short-brimmed fedora style with a feather in the brim, usually made of green felt

874:26 **Let's go back—** to the cafe

876:2 **wouldn't—** need to hide it

876:26–27 **while we are . . .** out of the wind

876:29–32 **I could see past my shoulder his cigarette shredding away in fiery streamers upon the unimpeded rush of the mistral, that black chill wind full of dust like sparks of ice** the final title passage

"Divorce in Naples"

In "Divorce in Naples," Faulkner drew on observations and experiences he shared with William Spratling in sailing to Europe on the *West Ivis* beginning on 7 July 1925, and after arriving in Genoa on 2 August (Blotner 1974, 446–47). They celebrated their landing by going drinking with some of the ship's officers. After a brawl with some local pimps and prostitutes, Spratling was arrested, and he spent the evening in an Italian prison, during which time he had a homosexual encounter. He told his friend Faulkner about it the next day (Williamson 202). The incident found its way into several of Faulkner's fictions, particularly the 1925 novel fragment called "Elmer," "Divorce in Naples," and *Mosquitoes* (1927); the projection of homoerotic attraction onto the body of a young man's sister—the transition from homosexual desire to incestuous—appears most famously in *The Sound and the Fury* (1929) and *Absalom, Absalom!* (1936). "Interestingly," Joel Williamson observes, "in all of the early stories touching the matter of homosexuality, the protagonist was actually a young person searching for his or her sexuality. These characters were experimenting, and they seem to be heading toward heterosexual personalities" (389). As Williamson's focus suggests, gender studies and queer theory in criticism have given us other ways to understand Faulkner's often ambivalent, nearly always veiled representations of human sexuality of any kind. "Divorce in Naples" displays both raw sexual activity and the romantic idealism that exalts sexual purity, yet in typical Faulknerian fashion does not solve for us the tensions between the two.

The ending of the story, like the central relationship between George and Carl, seems unequivocal to some readers and ambiguous to others, and while the story deals with a young man's loss of innocence, many have called the initiation a comic one. Perhaps too delicately, Edmond Volpe suggests that the "divorce" of the title may represent Carl's "loss of innocence in Naples," or it may refer to George and Carl, whose relationship "seems to go beyond friendship" (65). By contrast, Hans Skei pays tribute to the "tender and gossamer" nature of the pair's union: "despite the frailty of the relationship, the tenderness and the genuine quality of the men's feelings should not be doubted" (*Novelist* 120). Carl's request for George to buy him the pink silk "teddybears" has been read by many to signal Carl's ultimate return to the woman in Naples, or, at least, to heterosexuality; but Robert Dale Parker says the story "keeps trying to deny homosexuality in ways that reassert it. The homosexual-heterosexual binary is too deeply intertwined with the binaries between masculine and feminine genders and between sex and gender for Faulkner to let go of it" ("Sex" 79). James Ferguson maintains that both "Mistral," another story about male friendship and forbidden sexuality, and "Divorce in Naples" "are obviously concerned with the archetype of initiation, but again the mood of the first story, with its pathos and intensity, can be sharply contrasted with the humor, slight as it is, of the second" (151). Similarly, Lisa Paddock sees "Divorce in Naples" as a "comic counterpoint" to "Mistral," "by focusing on the incongruities and humorous dynamics of an ostensibly homosexual relationship" (58). Williamson sounds a note that parallels recent studies in race theory: in his examinations of sex and sexual attitudes, "Faulkner could also be saying that the difference between men and women projected by society is not natural, not real" (389).

"Divorce in Naples" makes its first certain appearance in Faulkner's short story sending schedule on 21 May 1930, but there were two manuscript versions, one of them entitled "Equinox," which may date from much earlier. The story remained unpublished until Faulkner chose it for inclusion in *These 13* (1931). In the process that led to the selection and arrangement of *Collected Stories*, "Divorce in Naples," like the other stories in the "Beyond" section, was not included in Robert K. Haas's original draft of suggestions, but Faulkner had added it by early November of 1948, placing it as the fifth of the six stories in the final section. As we begin to ask why he would grant this story of seduction, betrayal, and tenuous reconciliation such an important place in his most important collection, we find ourselves at the beginning of serious study of "Divorce in Naples."

877:1 **We** Although the narrator identifies the other members of his party by name or position and he appears to be a member of the crew, we never learn his name, rank, or relationship to the other sailors.

877:1 **a table inside** European cafés often have seating available on the sidewalks and in courtyards as well as inside. Service is more expensive at outside tables.

877:2 **bosun** pronunciation of *boatswain,* the ship's officer in charge of the sails and rigging and of summoning the crew when necessary

877:3 **that abject glittering kind that seamen know or that know seamen** either prostitutes or women of easy virtue

877:5–7 **By that means they could speak constantly to us above and below the sound of our voices in a tongue older than recorded speech and time too** By not speaking, the women can concentrate on the men's body language, which will signal sexual desire.

877:12 **dark pairing time** the time for the men and women to couple, to pair off for sexual activity, probably after closing time at the café

877:20 **black** in this context, clearly not African-American, but the narrator's generalized impression of George's dark complexion, hair, and eyes

877:23 **classic Anglo-Saxon** eloquent swearing. Faulkner uses the phrase often to describe cussing that is particularly specific and extended and therefore eloquent in its own right. See, for instance, "Afternoon of a Cow," in which narrator Ernest V. Trueblood reveals that he has been writing "Mr. Faulkner's" books for years (*Uncollected Stories* 424–34).

878:1–2 **an eight-year-old by-blow of a vaudeville comedian and a horse, say** The narrator suggests that when George is not inspired to swear, he uses dull and simple language; by doing so in this way, he is also insulting George's parentage by comparing him to a half-animal bastard (a by-blow) and a performer on the cheap stage frequented by the vulgar.

878:4 **ginger beer** a nonalcoholic drink flavored with fermented ginger

878:6–7 **the temperature of a ship's showerbath** about room temperature. After thirty-four days at sea (877:8), the narrator seems to have mainly nautical terms of comparison and description.

878:7–8 **I sure wouldn't bring my girl to a dive like this, even if he did wear pants** The bosun raises the possibility of a sexual relationship between George and Carl, and the ambiguous final line of the story might indicate that one begins; but at this point, George seems most interested in protecting Carl's virginity for its own sake.

878:15 ***Èinnocente*** sexually "innocent," virginal

878:18–19 **slipped through a porthole on you any time these three years** George has been obviously protective of Carl since they came aboard ship together at the port of Galveston (879:4) three years ago, and the bosun implies that Carl might have sneaked out from under his watch during that time.

878:25 **Are you still pure?** The bosun has raised enough doubt in George's mind that he asks Carl directly whether he is still a virgin, a question that Carl seems to answer but actually avoids at 878:27–28.

878:27 **three per cent beer** very weak beer; beer with a 3.0% alcohol content

878:32 **second cook** not the head cook aboard but his assistant

878:32–33 **You damn lying little bastard** He could be addressing either Carl or the bosun; the bosun's next gesture suggests that George was speaking to him, and his response is to mimic Carl's effeminate style of drinking.

879:6–7 **Might as well be board ship if we're going to spend the evening in one place** The bosun realizes, as the narrator does at 879:8–9, that the sexual pairings for the evening have nearly been completed and do not include him.

879:9–11 **The third one had a lot of gold teeth. She could have been thirty, but maybe she wasn't** Apparently, the woman has been badly used over time and has tried, unsuccessfully, to cover up the evidence of her aging and experience.

879:14 **Galveston** Galveston, Texas; a port town on the Gulf of Mexico

879:15 **portable victrola** Victrola was the brand name of an early kind of record player that became enormously popular between 1906 and 1929. Manufactured by the Victor Talking Machine Company, the machine improved upon previous record players, which had external cones to transmit sound from a recorded disk, by moving the cone inside the cabinet of the machine. This change made the machines more stable, more attractive, and more like the rest of the furniture found in the public areas of homes; with the increased popularity of the Victrola, the company developed and sold cheaper and portable models. By the time George and Carl board the ship, electronic models called Electrolas had begun to supplant the Victrola, which was powered by turning a small hand crank. See "History of the Victrola" and Baumbach.

879:16 **well-known ten-cent store** a store selling inexpensive merchandise that the public could examine and select firsthand rather than with a clerk's assistance. Frank Woolworth opened the first dime store in 1879, and stores like it had their heyday in the years surrounding World War I. The F. W. Woolworth Company was founded in 1911 and would've been the most "well-known ten-cent store" of the day.

879:19–20 **Pullman section** the sleeping car on a train, named after its inventor, George Pullman (1831–1897)

879:20–21 **concatenant voice a little overburred with *v*'s and *r*'s** According to Noel Polk, Faulkner liked to make verbal adjectives by using the French equivalent of *–ing* (*-ant*), as a suffix. Thus *concatenate,* meaning linked in a series or chain, becomes *concatenant* to describe the movement in the sound of George's rough, run-together orders to Carl.

879:24 **drill serving jackets** jackets made of heavy duty cotton or linen (drill), worn while serving meals as protection against spills. Carl's are probably in the style of the Eton jacket, which has wide lapels and falls only to waist level. His meticulous care and wearing of them marks him in the narrator's eyes as distinctly feminine (879:25–29), as does his dancing with George.

879:25 **the next thirty-four days** Based upon this and the reference at 877:8, we infer that the sailor's usual tour of duty was thirty-four days.

879:26 **messboy** waiter in the dining room (mess) of the ship

879:28 **poop awning** protective overhang above the poop deck, the aftermost deck of a ship, which sailors used in the days before shipboard plumbing to relieve themselves

879:29 **galley** ship's kitchen

879:31 **after well deck** a lower level of the main deck near the rear of a ship, between the forecastle and poop deck. See also 881:3.

879:31–880:1 **hold full of Texas cotton and Georgia resin** Carrying cotton and resin, two products that must be changed in the process of manufacture in order to be useful, the commercial cargo ship on which they serve seems to be on a domestic leg of commerce when Carl and George join it, rather than embarked upon an international one as in the present tense of the story.

880:1–2 **one record for the machine and it had a crack in it** sound recording on a flat disk with the music scratched into it from the outer edge to the center; this one has a crosswise crack that causes the needle to skip, thus breaking the music.

880:16–20 **some ancestor long knocking his quiet bones together at the bottom of the sea (or perhaps havened by accident in dry earth and become restive with ease and quiet) had sent back to the old dream and the old unrest three or maybe four generations late** The slight Carl seems ill-suited to the physical life of a sailor; the narrator wonders whether doing so revealed a genetic predisposition for it. His description of the ancestor "knocking his quiet bones together at the bottom of the sea" recalls similar passages in *The Sound and the Fury*, with its allusions to Coleridge's *Kubla Khan* and T. S. Eliot's *The Waste Land*, and looks forward to "Carcassonne" (897:13–15, 899:21–24). The Eliot seems most relevant here, with one narrator hearing "the rattle of the bones" and another seeing the dead sailor Phlebas the Phoenician as "A current under sea/Picked his bones in whispers" (186, 315–16). (See also Ross and Polk, 51, 61, 96, for examples of these influences upon *The Sound and the Fury*.)

880:17 **havened** put into port, sheltered; again we see the narrator's tendency toward nautical metaphor

880:25–26 **down to the corner after the old man on Saturday night** Carl's father frequented the neighborhood bar, and his mother sent the boy after him to bring him home.

880:26 **Jeez** Jesus

880:28 **sawdust** strewn across tavern floors to absorb spills and tobacco juice; easily swept up and replaced for the next day of business

880:31 **berth** a job on ship

880:33–881:2 **a face that should have followed monstrances up church aisles, if not looked down from one of the colored windows themselves** Carl has an open countenance, the innocent face of an altar boy or saint.

881:9–10 **perhaps we didn't know the man** the man who knew what "virgin" meant. The narrator is patronizing George, as he did at 878:1–2.

881:12 **poop** poop deck, see 879:28

881:13 **two days out of Gibraltar** two days' sailing time out of the Spanish port

881:17 **the petite cleared** the certificate issued by the harbor master indicating that the ship was not in quarantine

881:26 **drag** inhalation of cigarette smoke. We speculate that George's next words would be "hits your lungs"; in any case, he revels in the first cigarette of the day and compares it to anticipating one's first sexual experience.

881:31 **a swipe, some West India Docks crum** The narrator is again patronizing another sailor, this time one who has joined the ship from the West India Docks, London's first commercial wet docks and site of London's first dockside warehouses, by calling him two kinds of lowlife. In the early nineteenth century, the West India docks were the largest in the world.

881:32 **lobbing the tongue** swearing

881:33 **Lymus mate laying into a fo'c'sle of bloody Portygee ginneys** an officer's assistant cursing the Portuguese sailors on the forecastle deck, which is at the front of a ship. The passage is another instance of the race and class prejudices among the sailors; this one, himself called a "swipe" and a "crum" by the narrator (881:31), uses the derogatory term "ginneys" (Italian or Spanish immigrants) to characterize other sailors. His use of the slang word "bloody" marks him as English.

882:6 **Then he paraphrased unwitting and with unprintable aptness Byron's epigram about women's mouths** The bosun's sensitivity to George's respect for virginity leads him into swearing about the inevitability of virginity's loss, and Faulkner seems to be invoking in this passage a stanza from *Don Juan,* by George Gordon, Lord Byron (1788–1824):

I love the sex, and sometimes would reverse
    The tyrant's wish, "that Mankind only had
One neck, which he with one fell stroke might pierce:"
    My wish is quite as wide, but not so bad.
And much more tender on the whole than fierce;
    It being (not *now,* but only while a lad)
That Womankind had but one rosy mouth,
To kiss them all at once from North to South. (Canto VI, stanza XXVII)

The bosun's paraphrase is doubtless more succinct, perhaps "I'd fuck 'em all."

882:13 **Now, you take Brussels sprouts** Monckton is studiously avoiding the discussion of sex. His name and the fact that he leaves the bar with the narrator (879:8) suggest that he might avoid sex—or at least sex while in port, perhaps out of fidelity to his wife.

882:14 **Old Man** the captain

882:29 **steward** officer in charge of the ship's stores and of arranging serving of meals

883:3–7 **one of those Columbia day students that go up each morning on the East Side subway from around Chatham Square. He was hatless, with an oiled pompadour. He had not shaved recently, and he spoke no English in a pleasant, deprecatory way that was all teeth** Columbia University is an Ivy League university with a prestigious history and reputation; Chatham Square, in Chinatown, was at the time of the story a seedy area of taverns and flophouses frequented by sailors and soldiers. The narrator seems to know both equally well, so we speculate that he is a well-educated native New Yorker. His snobbery and racism appear in these lines; he looks down on students who can't afford to live on campus at Columbia, and he sees no real difference between the Italian man with slicked-back hair in this passage and the Chinese in New York.

883:17 **a third-class European hotel** a cheap hotel, which might well be infested with vermin

883:20 **a-*tall*** at all

883:32 **suspicioned** suspected

884:3–4 **the bottom of George's glass had distorted their shapes enough to create in George the illusion** The narrator slyly insinuates that George is a drunk—one who sees the world through the bottom of his glass.

884:17 **three stacks of saucers** In Europe, drinks are served on saucers and the bill is calculated by the number of saucers accumulated; there is one stack each for Carl, George, and the woman.

884:20–21 **Porteus ahoy!** Probably an inside joke of the narrator's, and one that reveals again his contempt of George. Stanley Porteus, the inventor of an intelligence test, published *Race and Temperament* in 1926, which argued that intelligence was limited by race. His work with "feeble-minded" children had convinced him that their limitations lay in not being able to develop and follow long-range plans and goals; his intelligence test was therefore a maze on paper, in which one began in the center and plotted one's way out. In our narrator's view, George is wandering through the bar as though lost in a maze; yet his language and grammar elsewhere in the story mark him as nearly uneducated, so we believe the narrator supplies him with this allusion. Porteus's branch of social science was even in the late 1920s under fire as racist.

885:3–4 **paying the score; beaten the bill** left without paying the bar tab

885:16–18 **the two Napoleons in their swords and pallbearer gloves and Knights of Pythias bonnets** George is taken in hand by two armed guards, who wear formal uniforms out of place for the occasion of containing a drunken sailor. Depicted on the crest of the fraternal order of the Knights of Pythias are plumed hats. Faulkner also wrote a short story called "Damon and Pythias Unlimited," which was published in the *Times-Picayune* on 15 February 1925.

885:20 **Prefecture** the official residence of the local magistrate

885:21–23 **he was a political prisoner, having insulted the king's majesty by placing foot on the king's effigy on a coin** Just as he made fun of the formality of the local police, the narrator patronizes the corrupt local government, which he implies has fabricated charges against George and the other seven foreign prisoners in order to extort money from them.

885:26–27 **They taken my belt and my necktie and the strings out of my shoes** so that he would not be able to harm himself while incarcerated

885:30–31 **they had already been using it for that** to relieve themselves

885:33 **it** the bench

885:34–886:1 **it was like looking down at Forty-second Street from a airplane. They looked just like Yellow cabs** The bench is infested with vermin, probably lice.

886:2–3 **I used it with the end of me it wasn't intended to be used with** He vomited.

886:12 **lire** unit of Italian currency

887:16 **well deck** see 879:31

888:11 **bulkhead** an upright partition on the ship, in this case a division between parts below deck

888:18 **it** the water in the shower

888:26–27 **bridge deck** the raised deck running across the middle of the ship, from which the commanding officer directs the ship

888:31 **brightwork** metal-work on ships, including handles and trimming

888:31 **companions** companionways; staircases on a ship

888:33 **topside** on deck

888:34 **port side** looking forward, the left side of a ship

889:1 **starboard** looking forward, the right side of a ship

889:5–6 **George can't come up there** Only officers in charge of operating the vessel are allowed on the bridge, unless others are summoned there.

889:9 **binnacle; Old Man** nonmagnetic box or stand containing the compass; the captain of the ship. Monckton is complimenting George's courage.

889:11–20 **"But not for curiosity," . . . "Do you think so?" Monckton said** the exchange between the sailors that prompts the story's title. They all seem to agree that George and Carl are in one way or another married and that Carl has been unfaithful to the union.

889:26 **the Italian boys in bright, soiled jerseys and the venders of pornographic postcards** Of all the people and bustle taking place on the docks, the narrator focuses on these two things, as though they are what Carl seeks to avoid by staying on the port side of the ship.

890:10–11 **the rail midships or forward** protective railing around the edge of the ship. Carl will not willingly go to the rear of the ship, where George is playing the victrola.

890:17 **astern** the rear of the ship

890:19 **Gates of Hercules** also Pillars of Hercules; the promontories at the east entrance to the Strait of Gibraltar

890:20 **the River Ocean began to flow into the darkling sea** Okeanos, both Titan god and a presence on earth to the ancient Greeks. *Okeanos* translates as "River Ocean," the steady, calm current running south to north on the western side of the earth and the opposite way on the eastern, the source of all waters on earth. The narrator's use of the Homeric "darkling sea" gives the passage a further sense of the mythic.

890:21 **crosstrees** the timbers crossing the ship's masts

890:24–25 **The dog's gone back to his vomit** a curious passage, since it insults both George and Carl and comes from the usually uninvolved Monckton. Monckton calls Carl the dog and George his vomit—his known if nonetheless disgusting regurgitation—and implies that Carl is going to lick him up.

890:28–29 **George hasn't made the grade yet** Monckton implies that George hasn't yet proved himself worthy of his "marriage" to Carl.

891:1–2 **a man can't be a angel all your life** George's unwitting admission that he was living Carl's virginity vicariously

891:9–10 **something they would have paid you money for it in Siam** Alluding to Thailand's notorious reputation for peddling vice, George refers to Carl's virginity.

891:18 **wops** derogatory slang for Italians

891:18–19 **wouldn't give them a full breath if they was a toy balloon** a metaphor for stinginess

891:23 **Hatteras** Hatteras Island, a barrier island in North Carolina known for its dangerous storms

891:29 **watching the phosrus along the logline** probably George's corruption of *phosphorous*, referring to the phosphorescent algae churned up as a ship passes through the water. Before sailing ships had engines, the best way of slowing the ship in an emergency was to drop the sails and throw out a large log (attached to the log-lines). The log slowed the ship's momentum by providing a greater surface area for the water to push against.

891:32–892:2 **Didn't you make her show you her petite? Like she would have needed a ticket, with that face full of gold; Jeez, she could have rode the train on her face alone; maybe that was her savings bank instead of using her stocking** Prostitution itself was not illegal in Italy, although some forms of soliciting and providing it were (and still are). George refers, then, to the prostitute's license or "petite," the "ticket" like his own seaman's license, which he implies she got by paying off the police. Her "face full of gold" might mark her as the woman in the opening passage of the story whom the narrator avoids; in any case, he says she has money safely held in her teeth that another might keep hidden in a stocking top.

892:5 **So I knew what the trouble was** George believes that Carl is shocked by the woman's profession.

892:7–9 **'Oh,' I says, 'the smell. It don't mean nothing,' I says; you don't want to let that worry you. It ain't that they smell bad,' I says, 'that's just the Italian national air'** George gratuitously insults Italy in order to mask what he believes is Carl's reaction at 892:5.

892:14 **windlass** device by which to hoist ropes of anchor

892:24 **Gulf Stream** the great oceanic current of warm water beginning in the Gulf of Mexico and running parallel to the east coast of the U.S. to Newfoundland and then toward Europe

892:25–26 **bubbled with fire by night in the softening latitudes** The narrator could refer either to the reflected starlight of the southern latitudes or to various plankton glimmering in the water there.

892:26 **Tortugas** island group in the Gulf of Mexico, sixty miles west of Key West, once a pirate base, famous for bird and marine life

893:1–2 **Spit it out** say whatever you mean

893:3–5 **When we get to Galveston, I want you to buy me a suit of these pink silk teddybears that ladies use. A little bigger than I'd**

wear, see? Carl asks George to buy him a woman's undergarment that combines a chemise top with panties or short pants. He has shown a penchant for tight-fitting clothes and undergarments throughout the story, but it is far from clear why he asks George to do this or what he intends to do with the pink silk ones. Now that he has been introduced to heterosexual adult sexuality, perhaps he intends to seduce George. Perhaps he intends to send, or to give in person, the underwear to the Neopolitan prostitute, although the phrase "buy me" might suggest that he means to keep it. Perhaps he means to mark himself as a prostitute; perhaps he intends to finish feminizing himself; perhaps he is merely curious.

"Carcassonne"

Possibly the first of the *Collected Stories* to be written, certainly the shortest of them all, and perhaps the most difficult to interpret, "Carcassonne" holds a special and enigmatic place in Faulkner's work. He apparently revised this previously unpublished story to conclude *These 13* (1931), and he later chose it to conclude *Collected Stories.* Allusive and ambiguous, often cryptic, the piece has been called a "prose poem," "an esthetic declaration," "a poetic fantasy," "a poetic fable," and many similar variants. Long a favorite challenge for Faulknerians, "Carcassonne" has elicited many readings and many questions. Some questions center on the basic narrative components of character and plot; others concern the story's title and the welter of historical and literary allusions surfacing, sometimes to coalesce, in the protagonist's consciousness. Additionally, of course, there is the question of what it all means. For some readers, such challenges are mere obscurities that make the piece "virtually unreadable" (Karl 429), even "overwritten and clichéd" (Parini 167). Adding to the controversies, some readers insist that "Carcassonne," perhaps more than most of Faulkner's work, must be read in the context of the collections in which it appears: first of *These 13*, which, they argue, it was re-written to unify; and then in relation to *Collected Stories,* and especially to the story "Black Music," which also takes place in a town called Rincon. Moreover, "Carcassonne" contains one of Faulkner's most brilliant and memorable images, "that riderless Norman steed" (896), apparently a specific allusion, the precise source of which many have sought in vain. All in all, "Carcassonne" is a fitting final story for the "Beyond" section, for it may take us beyond life or beyond death, and it surely remains beyond certainty.

"The physical action in the story is the slightest of any in Faulkner's fiction," one commentator writes; "A young man lies down to go to sleep, allowing his mind to wander" (Carothers 81). But even such a simple declaration is open for debate: James Ferguson contends that "There is hardly the remotest suggestion of a narrative in it" (23). Faulkner himself called the protagonist a "young man in conflict with his environment" (*FIU* 22), "a young man who sees a horse" (Blotner, *Faulkner* 1974, 960), but the story does not actually indicate his age. He lies in the squalid garret of a cantina in a town called Rincon. In this impoverished venue, the protagonist "nightly perused the fabric of dreams" (896). The first of these is of himself "on a buckskin pony *with eyes like blue electricity and a mane like tangled fire, galloping up the hill and right off into the high heaven of the world*" (895). The protagonist reflects on the immediate relation between his skeleton (body) and soul or imagination (mind). At first, the skeleton lies still, then it groans, and eventually it "speaks" to the protagonist, who is imagining a Norman horse, severed by the sword stroke of a Saracen Emir, "wrapped still in the fury and the pride of the charge, not knowing that it was dead" (896). The ensuing conversation between the protagonist's skeleton and his mind or soul or imagination—"that part which suffered neither insects nor temperature and which galloped unflagging on the destinationless pony . . . neither flesh nor unflesh" (895)—recalls the medieval convention of *corpus spiritus*, perhaps familiar to Faulkner through Andrew Marvell's "A Dialogue between the Soul and the Body," or, at least equally likely, "The Immortal Part" from A. E. Housman's *A Shropshire Lad*, both of which articulate the irreconcilable claims of the divided self. In this conversation, the skeleton eventually reminds the consciousness that "the end of life is lying still" (899), which the protagonist refuses to believe. Thus, the skeleton insists on human mortality, while the young man imagines immortality. "*I want to perform something bold and tragical and austere*," he thinks (899). Significantly, he has been meditating on exactly that kind of performance as immortalized in imaginative literature, with direct or elliptical references to Eliot's "The Love Song of J. Alfred Prufrock" and *The Waste Land*, Shakespeare's *Hamlet* and *The Tempest*, tales of the First Crusade (such as those by Torquato Tasso, Sir Walter Scott, Benjamin Disraeli, or others), the Old and New Testaments, Homer's *Odyssey*, Byron, and, perhaps, Hemingway.

Returning to the image of himself on the buckskin pony, the protagonist approaches a final moment of consciousness before sleep or, perhaps, before death: "Steed and rider thunder on, thunder punily diminishing: a dying star upon the immensity of darkness and of silence within which, steadfast, fading, deepbreasted and grave of flank, muses the dark and tragic figure of the Earth, his mother" (900).

Given the dense texture of literary allusion and the protagonist's deliberate imaginative exercise, most readings of "Carcassonne" emphasize the story's metafictional nature. David Minter maintains that the story "explores a conception of life, a conception of art, and a conception of art in its relation to life" (91). Robert W. Hamblin generally describes the "curious paradox" of Faulkner's aesthetic: "One impulse in Faulkner, his desire to say No to death, moved him to celebrate life and experience, even tragic experience, and to seek to preserve the world through an aesthetic of memory. But a stronger impulse, deriving from the ultimate recognition that life is ever subject to death, led Faulkner to oppose life as it is given and to transform it through an aesthetic of imagination" ("Saying No" 23). Writing of "Carcassonne" particularly, Hamblin says the "dialogue between the poet and his skeleton" sustains the contrast between "the physical, inert, and earthbound values of the skeleton with the subjective, transcendent, and limitless fanciers of the poet's imagination." In the end, "the symbolic victory of the imagination in imposing its will upon the harsh reality of the setting represents one of Faulkner's strongest statements of the necessity and power of invention" ("Carcassonne" 152). Noel Polk offers a sharply divergent reading of the story, however, arguing that the character in the story is a *poet manqué*, a dreamer rather than a poet. Nothing in the story suggests that he has accomplished (or will accomplish) the "*bold and tragical and austere*" performances of his imagination. Rather, he remains "one of a long line of Faulkner's failed idealists . . . who are soundly defeated by those elements of the real world that they have to contend with" ("William Faulkner's 'Carcassonne' " 31). Although Faulkner himself commented that "there was the poet again" in the creation of this story, Polk, supported by Joseph Blotner, submits that we must distinguish between the poet Faulkner who wrote "Carcassonne" and the failed poet-dreamer-protagonist of the story. The latter, in Polk's reading, "is himself physically dead, or on the point of dying. Or rather he is . . . in an artistically arrested moment right in the crack between living and dying" (38). In this regard, "Carcassonne" evokes other ambivalent scenes in Faulkner's work of what may be death, or may not be. In *Collected Stories* alone one thinks of Abner Snopes and his older son in "Barn Burning," Nancy in "that Evening Sun," and, perhaps, Jubal in "Mountain Victory," while Gail Hightower in *Light in August* and Mink Snopes in *The Mansion* have similarly open-ended fates. Of such ambiguities, Hans Skei concludes, we need not despair: "The problematic nature of artistic creation is central" in "Carcassonne," he writes; "the text presenting the dream [of creation] indicates the validity of this kind of experience as a way of coping with the world and at the same time contributing to an understanding of it. The text is proof that the dream is valid: it produces the literary text in spite of the bareness of the surrounding world" (*Reading* 82). Most favorable commentary reflects this view. As James Watson puts it, "the story concludes with such a performance, both his and Faulkner's. The rider-writer is ascendant now, revived and strong" (*Self-Presentation* 111).

The story has a murky composition history, but one with provocative ties to Faulkner's other work early and late. "Carcassonne" was published for the first time on 21 September 1931 as the last story in *These 13*, though a version of it had apparently existed for quite some time before that. One version that may have been written in 1926 or 1927 names the protagonist "David," thus associating him with characters in *Mosquitoes* (1927), "The Leg," and "Out of Nazareth." The role given to Mrs. Widdrington in "Black Music" and the published "Carcassonne" was assigned in that version to "Mrs. Maurier," who figures prominently in *Mosquitoes*. Polk has argued that Faulkner revised "Carcassonne" to unify *These 13*, "the most complete and deliberate portrait of a waste land that Faulkner was ever to draw" (33), while Lisa Paddock argues that "Carcassonne" most appropriately concludes *Collected Stories* (which, we note, was a significant effort of his later years as a writer). She notes that "Faulkner chose to conclude this cumulative work with a piece that spoke to his sense of the limitations of language, but while in itself and in the context of *These 13* 'Carcassonne' may seem an expression of artistic failure, its place in *Collected Stories* helps to make that volume—and indeed, Faulkner's whole career as a writer of short fiction—a complete artifact which, like Keats's urn, can be "picked up and held in the hands at one time" (198–99).

When Faulkner outlined the proposed story collection to Malcolm Cowley in November 1948, he had settled on the six major divisions of the volume and placed "Carcassonne" as the last of the six stories in the last section, entitled "Beyond" (*SL* 279). Explaining his aesthetic to Cowley in that letter, Faulkner asserted that "to a collection of short stories, form, integration, is as important as to a novel—an entity of its own, single, set for one pitch, contrapuntal in integration, toward one end, one finale" (278). Whatever form or integration we may seek to impose individually on *These 13*, "Beyond," or *Collected Stories*, "Carcassonne" provides us with one dramatic and tantalizing end, one imaginatively splendid finale.

895:TITLE **Carcassonne** a walled city in Languedoc in southwestern France, with origins in prehistory and a strategic location in medieval Europe. Since the Middle Ages, Carcassonne has been occupied by the Muslims, Cathars, and Christians, and by a variety of rulers within those faiths. After the Fourth Crusade (1204), which saw the Christian armies turn to sack Christian Constantinople rather than restore the Holy Lands under control of the Muslims, a leader named Simon de Montfort, disgusted by the diversion from the original goal, left the city. Shortly afterward, Pope Innocent III dispatched troops under De Montfort in a sweep of Languedoc in order to put down the Cathar religion. It succeeded, and the city fell in 15 days (1–15 August 1209). This is known as the Albigensian crusade, distinct from what historians understand as The Crusades. Because our protagonist refers directly to battle in the First Crusade, it is difficult to tell whether the historical confusion is Faulkner's or his protagonist's.

895:1 **buckskin** yellowish gray (Brown 39)

895:4 **His skeleton** a point of debate in the story's interpretation; we think the young man's corporeal self, his body as opposed to his imagination that creates and then soars on the buckskin pony

895:4 **this** the image at 895:1–3

895:6 **he** the whole main character of the story, including "his skeleton" (895:4) and his imagination (see 895:9–11)

895:8–9 **unrolled strip of tarred roofing made of paper** paper sealed by tar or asphalt which can be nailed to a roof, alone or under shingles, in order to waterproof it

895:9–11 **that part which suffered neither insects nor temperature and which galloped unflagging on the destinationless pony** his mind or imagination; his soul

895:12 **cumulae** Latinized pluralization of *cumulus,* the high, mountain-like clouds present during unstable combinations of air masses; here, the literal site of the young man's imagination's galloping on the pony

895:13 **precipice** the hill at 899:31

895:13–14 **neither flesh nor unflesh** see 895:9–11

895:14–15 **its lackful contemplation** Because this part of him is not flesh, it is not burdened with the need to "contemplate" or think; not "unflesh" and so not dead, its "lack" frees it instead to dream.

895:17 **denning up** an odd metaphor for the main character to choose, unless he is distinguishing himself from what Mrs Widdrington might consider "human" sleeping habits (see 897:29:34)

895:19–23 **It was like those glasses, reading glasses which old ladies used to wear, attached to a cord that rolls onto a spindle in a neat case of unmarked gold; a spindle, a case, attached to the deep bosom of the mother of sleep** We have not been able to locate a brand name, but the style is common even today, with the glasses sometimes folded at the nose piece as well as the temples. The passage is the first evocation of the story's final line.

895:24 **this** the sensations and thoughts of 895:1–23

895:24 **Rincon** "corner" in Spanish. Faulkner's Rincon has been located by Noel Polk in Puerto Rico ("William Faulkner's 'Carcassonne' ") and others in some vague Latin American locale (Skei, *Reading* 75, for example). Faulkner might have had in mind Tampico, Mexico, an oil town that Jack London wrote about in *Collier's* in 1914. Anne Goodwyn Jones offers another intriguing possibility: Rincon is the name of a famous beach in Carpinteria, Santa Barbara County, in Southern California, located less than ten miles south of Summerland, which in 1894 saw the discovery of oil and, within a few years, an oil boom and the development of the first off-shore oil rig in 1896. The boom was over by 1920, but the discovery of a new field ten miles west of Santa Barbara in 1928 revived the industry. (See "Summerland" and "Summerland Oil and Gas Production.")

896:1–2 **its fatal, secret, nightly pursuits, where upon the rich and inert darkness of the streets lighted windows and doors lay** Skei notes the influence of T. S. Eliot in these lines, "'Prufrock' more than 'The Waste Land' " [*sic*] (75). Eliot's "Preludes," with its invocation of "burnt-out ends of smoky days" and "the lighting of the lamps," also seems relevant to the atmosphere of Rincon.

896:3 **oily strokes of broad and overladen brushes** like those in impressionist paintings, but here made to feel dirty and urban rather than lightsome

896:4 **unsourced** came forth from its unknown point of origin

896:8 **it** the sound of the unsourced siren (896:4)

896:11 **this** the information between the last "this" (895:24) and this point: his present environment in the garret above the docks

896:12–13 **the fabric of dreams** literally, what follows at 896:14–30; the young man's recurrent dreams in his garret, but highly evocative of Prospero's famous meditation in *The Tempest* (1611):

> Our revels now are ended. These our actors,
> As I foretold you, were all spirits and
> Are melted into air, into thin air.
> And, like the baseless fabric of this vision,
> The cloud-capped towers, the gorgeous palaces,
> The solemn temples, the great globe itself—
> Yea, all which it inherit—shall dissolve
> And, like this insubstantial pageant faded,
> Leave not a rack behind. We are such stuff
> As dreams are made on, and our little life
> Is rounded with a sleep. (IV, I, 148–59)

896:14 **the twin transparencies of the spectacles** the lenses of the tarred paper metaphor; his skeleton and his imagination

896:19–20 **He can see the saddlegirth and the soles of the rider's feet in the stirrups** The protagonist is standing behind and below the horse and rider and slightly to one side of them, looking up at an angle that allows him to see the underside portions of the riding gear.

896:20–22 **The girth cuts the horse in two just back of the withers, yet it still gallops with rhythmic and unflagging fury and without**

progression a trick of the observer's eye; the girth draws a line across the horse's body just behind its shoulder blades. Like the image of the lovers on the Grecian urn that Faulkner evoked so often in his career, this running horse appears paradoxically static. For a recent essay on the many presences of Keats in this story and elsewhere in Faulkner's career, see Koyama.

896:22–28 **he thinks of that riderless Norman steed which galloped against the Saracen Emir, who, so keen of eye, so delicate and strong the wrist which swung the blade, severed the galloping beast at a single blow, the several halves thundering on in the sacred dust where him of Bouillon and Tancred too clashed in sullen retreat** In the time of the Crusades, "Saracen" was a name for any Arab, any Muslim, the peoples who inhabited the Holy Land that the Crusaders sought to restore to the Roman Catholic Church. Normandy was a duchy of France on the north coast, along the English Channel. Godfrey de Bouillon, Duke of Lower Lorraine just east of Normandy, was a leader of the First Crusade; his success in battle led to his appointment as the king of conquered Jerusalem. He appears as a character in Tasso's *Jerusalem Delivered* (1580) and in Sir Walter Scott's *Count Robert of Paris* (1831). A few critics have noted Tasso's apparent influence in these passages, as in the tribute to De Bouillon's horse, of which Tasso says,

And had you seen the beast, you would have said
The light and subtile wind his father was;
For if his course upon the sands he made
No sign was left what way the beast did pass . . . (VII)

Faulkner's reference to lightness, however, is to the Saracen Emir, or ruler, who cuts the horse in two so quickly that it runs on "not knowing that it was dead" (896:30). It seems more likely that Faulkner would have found Bouillon in Scott, and "Tancred too" in a more contemporary literary place—the last novel in a trilogy by Benjamin Disraeli (1847) devoted to reconciling Judaism and Christianity. Louis Bréhier explains that Tancred, born in Antioch, led a breach of Jerusalem concomitant with De Bouillon's and became one of his principal knights after his selection as king; he also appears in *Jerusalem Delivered,* a work that also influenced

Spenser's *Faerie Queene* and the work of John Milton (see Bréhier, "Tancred"). Sir Steven Runciman describes one episode of a riderless horse and its effect on a battle. Close to Christmas 1097 during the First Crusade, the Crusaders were running out of food, and their leader De Bouillon was ill. The army leaders decided to raid several villages for supplies and split their troops. One group, led by Count Raymond of Toulouse, was attacked by a group of Turks, but he led his forces in a counter-attack: "So hotly did Raymond pursue them that for a moment his men obtained a foothold across the bridge before the gates could be swung shut. It seemed that Raymond was about to justify his belief that the city could be stormed, when a horse that had thrown its rider suddenly bolted back, pushing the knights crowded on the bridge into confusion. It was too dark to see what was happening; and a panic arose among the Crusaders. In their turn they fled, pursued by the Turks, till they rallied at their camp by the bridge of boats; and the Turks returned to the city. Many lives were lost on both sides, but especially among the Frankish knights, whom the Crusade ill could spare" (132).

896:28–29 **the assembled foes of our meek Lord** the Muslim fighters in the Crusades, a general term for the wars conducted to bring the Holy Lands back under control of the Roman Catholic Church. According to Bréhier ("Crusades"), we customarily divide the Crusades into eight major efforts. Faulkner seems to be thinking of the First (1095–1101, which included the fall of Jerusalem) and of the Albigensian, which he might or might not have distinguished from the Fourth (see 895:TITLE).

896:32 **the body consciousness** his awareness of himself as a physical, corporeal being

896:33–897:1 **his motionless body grown phosphorescent with that steady decay which had set up within his body on the day of this birth** a meditation on the notion that we begin to die at birth. Imagining himself as a kind of sea creature (see 897:13–15, for example), the protagonist visualizes the effects of chemicals involved in bioluminescence in certain deep-sea organisms (see "Luciferin n").

897:3–4 ***will never die for I am the Resurrection and the Life*** Before raising Lazarus from the dead, Jesus tells Lazarus's sister Martha, "I am the resurrection, and the life: he that believeth in me, though he were dead, yet shall he live; And whosoever liveth and believeth in me shall never die" (John 11:25–26).

897:4 **the worm** the maggot, a consumer of dead flesh and a potent symbol of common mortality. Examples from the Old and New Testaments that seem pertinent here are Isaiah 66:24: "And they shall go forth, and look upon the carcases of the men that have transgressed against me: for their worm shall not die, neither shall their fire be quenched; and they shall be an abhorring unto all flesh"; and Mark 9:44, 46, 48: "Where their worm dieth not, and the fire is not quenched." Given the story's many references to rats and specifically to Polonius at 898:18–20, Hamlet's comment that Polonius is "at supper" also applies: "Your worm is your only emperor for diet. We fat all creatures else to fat us, and we fat ourselves for maggots. Your fat king and your lean beggar is but variable service, two dishes, but to one table" (*Hamlet* IV, iii, 22–25).

897:5–8 **Of women, of delicate girls briefly like heard music in tune, it should be suavely shaped, falling feeding into prettinesses, feeding** **it** = the worm. The "Magdalen" figure from Faulkner's early work in New Orleans thinks similarly: "And lights and sultry music, and all the bright chimaerae of the brain! And ah! my body like music, my body like flame crying for silken sheens a million worms had died to make, and that my body has died a hundred times to wear them. Yes, a thousand worms made this silk, and died; I have died a thousand deaths to wear it; and sometime a thousand worms, feeding upon this body which has betrayed me, feeding, will live" (*New Orleans Sketches* 13).

897:7 ***what though to Me*** The protagonist seems to be wondering what relationship, if any, exists between Christ's life and death and his own, and the capital letter in the pronoun suggests a possible divinity in the mortal—perhaps by extension any mortal—man.

897:7–8 ***but as a seething of new milk*** The evocation of new life conjured by the image of fresh milk, with tiny bubbles of air mixed in during the milking process, stands in contrast to the images of rotting flesh and death begun at 896:33–897:1.

897:8–9 ***Who am the Resurrection and the Life*** see 897:3–4. The echo of the earlier passage creates a strong possibility that the protagonist has accepted the reality of mortality by also believing in immortality, whether Christ's or his own.

897:10–11 **The agony of wood was soothed by these latitudes** The dry wood is softened by the humidity in the air; "it did not creak and crack" (897:11).

897:13–15 **Bones might lie under seas, in the caverns of the sea, knocked together by the dying echoes of waves** more echoes of T. S. Eliot, including "The Love Song of J. Alfred Prufrock": "We have lingered in the chambers of the sea/By sea-girls wreathed with seaweed red and brown" (final stanza); and "Death by Water" from *The Waste Land*, in which Phlebas the Phoenician has drowned and "A current under sea/Picked his bones in whispers."

897:15–19 **Like bones of horses cursing the inferior riders who bestrode them, bragging to one another about what they would have done with a first-rate rider up. But somebody always crucified the first-rate riders** The mention of bones under the sea immediately calls to the protagonist's mind the bones of horses and their riders, the idea of the Crusades reinforced here with the threat of crucifixion. In "My Old Man" from *In Our Time* (1925), Ernest Hemingway had written of a first-rate rider crucified by crooked circumstance and the need to support his son in such a climate. After a fixed race in which a superior horse loses, the narrator's father says, "George Gardner's a swell jockey, all right. . . . It sure took a great jock to keep that Kzar horse from winning"; and although the narrator says, "I knew it was funny all the time, . . . I thought, I wish I were a jockey and could have rode him instead of that son of a bitch" (124). That same year, Faulkner published "Cheest!" in the *New Orleans Times-Picayune* (5 April), a first-person fictional account of how a tough jockey proves himself to a skeptical owner, with the barest hint of behind-the-scenes corruption at the end: "Yes," the owner says, "you done your best, and still come in ahead, didn't you?" (*New Orleans Sketches* 45).

897:20–21 **the caverns and the grottoes of the sea** see 897:13–15

897:22 ***where him of Bouillon and Tancred too*** see 896:22–28

897:23–24 **the twin transparencies of the glassy floor** the spectacles; see 896:14

897:25–26 **the barn where sleep was stabled** an as-yet-unreachable place of rest

897:27–28 **Standard Oil Company** Standard Oil was founded in 1870 by J. D. Rockefeller and quickly monopolized the development, production, and sale of oil. In 1911, the Supreme Court found the company in violation of the Sherman Antitrust Act and dissolved it; but the newly formed branch companies—existing in all of the 48 contiguous states and Canada and with additional refineries in Cuba and the Caribbean—retained the right to use the Standard Oil name.

897:29–34 **it was Mrs Widdrington's, the Standard Oil Company's wife's, darkness he was using to sleep in. She'd make a poet of you too, if you did not work anywhere. She believed that, if a reason for breathing were not acceptable to her, it was no reason. With her, if you were white and did not work, you were either a tramp or a poet** very possibly Faulkner's version of Mrs. John D. Rockefeller, Jr., both unusual last names having eleven letters and both wives patronesses of the arts. One of the founders of the Museum of Modern Art in New York, Abby Aldrich Rockefeller contributed many works to its collections and gave commissions to several artists during the Great Depression (see "Abby Aldrich Rockefeller"). Mrs Widdrington has Faulknerian counterparts in Mrs. Maurier in *Mosquitoes* and Mrs. Van Dyming in "Black Music" (see Introduction).

898:1–2 **Women are so wise. They have learned how to live unconfused by reality, impervious to it** a sentiment common to many of Faulkner's male protagonists of early middle age

898:3 ***and knock my bones together and together*** see 897:13–15

898:4 **fairy pattering of small feet. stealthy and intent** the first mention of the rats that live in the protagonist's garret

898:18–19 **Something of the rat about Byron: allocutions of stealthful voracity** The poet George Gordon, Lord Byron (1788–1824) was influenced by Tasso (see 896:22–28) and wrote "The Lament of Tasso" in 1817. The "allocutions of stealthful voracity" that would associate him with women, poetry, and ravenous rats might refer to Bryon's Don Juan, who wished "That Womankind had but one rosy mouth,/To kiss them all at once from North to South," *double entendre* intended by His Lordships Juan and Byron.

898:19–21 **a bloody arras where fell *where fell where I was King of Kings but the woman with the woman with the dog's eyes*** an important place in the story, at which the erstwhile artist gropes for connections ("where fell where fell") between other works of art to try to express a precedent for what he wants to do with his own vision of the pony. The passage recalls the arras through which Hamlet stabs Polonius and the rats in the attic of this story:

HAML. [*Drawing.*] How now, a rat? Dead for a ducat, dead!
[*Makes a pass through the arras.*]
POL. [*Behind*] Oh, I am slain! [*Falls and dies*]
. . .
HAML. [*Lifts up the arras and discovers* POLONIUS.]
Thou wretched, rash, intruding fool, farewell!
I took thee for thy better [Claudius]. (III, iv, 23–32)

"King of Kings" as a reference to the risen Christ occurs several places in the Bible, but two quotations from Revelations seem appropriate here: "These shall make war with the Lamb, and the Lamb shall overcome them: for he is Lord of lords, and King of kings: and they that are with him are called, and chosen, and faithful" (17:14); "And he hath on his vesture and on his thigh a name written, KING OF KINGS, AND LORD OF LORDS" (19:16). Recalling one king seems to lead to another, for the protagonist immediately thinks of King Agamemnon speaking to Odysseus in the underworld in Book XI of the *Odyssey*. Blotner quotes Faulkner quoting Homer: "As I lay dying the woman with the dog's eyes [his wife, Klytemestra, who murdered him upon his return from Troy] would not close my eyelids for me as I descended into Hades" (Blotner, *Faulkner* 1974, 634–35). The rats and dead kings come together in a garret in "The Fire Sermon" of Eliot's *Waste Land* (lines 187–95), and they all find their way into our protagonist's garret.

898:21–22 ***to knock my bones together and together*** see 897:13–15

898:23 **I would like to perform something** the protagonist's first articulation (if soundless) of his desire to create or to do something out of the ordinary

898:25–26 **He could see the saddlegirth and the soles of the rider's stirruped feet** see 896:19–20

898:27–32 **that Norman steed, bred of many fathers to bear iron mail in the slow, damp, green valleys of England, maddened with heat and thirst and hopeless horizons filled with shimmering nothingness, thundering along in two halves and not knowing it, fused still in the rhythm of accrued momentum** the "riderless steed" of 896:22–28. Note the protagonist's imaginative sympathy with the horse and not the riders involved, perhaps because he himself exists in "two halves," and knows it.

898:32 **mailed** covered in chain-link armor, with blinders (perhaps the plates of 898:33) to protect it and to keep it from panicking at the sight of the battle on either side

898:33 **plates** section of the plate armor on the horse's head; see 898:32

899:1 **Chamfron** metal plate armor to protect the front of the horse's head, sometimes with a spike or medallion on the forehead

899:3–4 **the ranks of the Lamb's foes** see 896:28–29; in contrast with the King of Kings (898:19–21), Jesus is also the meek and the Lamb of God.

899:13–14 **"Oh, I've learned it," he said. "I've had it dinned into me enough. It isn't that. It's just that I don't believe it's true"** The same distinction appears most famously in the beginning lines of Chapter Six of *Light in August*: "Memory believes before knowing remembers. Believes longer than recollects, longer than knowing even wonders" (119). There is an important distinction between Joe Christmas and this protagonist, however: for his entire life, Joe "believes" things that are "dinned into" him before he even develops the conscious thought represented by "knowing"; but this protagonist has had the idea of mortality "dinned into" him during his years of conscious thought and "knowing," yet still he resists "believing" what he's been told, by his skeleton and others.

899:21–24 **Again his body slanted and slanted downward through opaline corridors groined with ribs of dying sunlight upward dissolving dimly, and came to rest at last in the windless gardens of the sea** see 897:13–15; in architecture, *groined* is "a term applied to the curved intersection of two vaults meeting each other at any angle" (Burke 157)—the introduction of a man-made structure into the under-seascape

899:28–32 ***I want to perform something bold and tragical and austere*** **he repeated, shaping the soundless words in the pattering silence** ***me on a buckskin pony with eyes like blue electricity and a mane like tangled fire, galloping up the hill and right off into the high heaven of the world*** the culmination of the groping toward his desire and the unification of the disparate images that the protagonist has been chasing throughout the story (in order of this passage, see 898:23, 898:24, 898:4, 895:1–3)

899:900:5 **Still galloping, the horse soars outward; still galloping, it thunders up the long blue hill of heaven, its tossing mane in golden swirls like fire. Steed and rider thunder on, thunder punily diminishing: a dying star upon the immensity of darkness and of silence within which, steadfast, fading, deepbreasted and grave of flank, muses the dark and tragic figure of the Earth, his mother** The shift to the present tense indicates that the protagonist's vision has broken free of his earthly placement in the garret, whether because he has died and left the Earth his mother behind or because the vision has taken on a life of its own, or for some other reason, we leave for you to decide.

WORKS CITED AND CONSULTED

PRIMARY SOURCES

Absalom, Absalom! 1936. Corrected text. New York: Vintage International, 1990.

As I Lay Dying. 1930. Corrected text. New York: Vintage, 1987.

"The Brooch." Lux Video Theatre, 2 April 1953. *The Faulkner Journal* 16.1&2 (Fall 2000/Spring 2001): 149–80.

Collected Stories. New York: Random House, 1950; Vintage, 1977.

Faulkner at West Point. Eds. Jospeh L. Fant, III and Robert Ashley. New York: Random House, 1964.

Faulkner in the University. Ed. Frederick L. Gwynn and Joseph L. Blotner. New York: Random House, 1959; Charlottesville: University Press of Virginia, 1995.

Flags in the Dust. Ed. Douglas Day. New York: Random House, 1973; Vintage, 1974.

Go Down, Moses. 1942. Corrected text. New York: Vintage International, 1990.

If I Forget Thee, Jerusalem [The Wild Palms]. 1939. Corrected text. New York: Vintage International, 1995.

Light in August. 1932. Corrected text. New York: Vintage International, 1990.

Lion in the Garden: Interviews with William Faulkner, 1926–1962. Ed. James B. Meriwether and Michael Millgate. New York: Random House, 1968.

Mayday. Ed. Carvel Collins. Notre Dame and London: University of Notre Dame Press, 1976.

New Orleans Sketches. Ed. Carvel Collins. Jackson: University Press of Mississippi, 1958; rpt.2002.

The Reivers. New York: Vintage, 1962.

Sartoris. New York: New American Library; Meridian, 1983.

Selected Letters. Ed. Joseph Blotner. New York: Random House, 1977.

"Shall Not Perish: A Play for Television." Lux Video Theatre, 11 February 1954. *The Faulkner Journal* 16.1&2 (Fall 2000/Spring 2001): 181–215.

The Sound and the Fury. 1929. Corrected text. New York: Vintage International, 1990.

Uncollected Stories. Ed. Joseph Blotner. New York: Random House, 1979; Vintage, 1981.

Secondary Sources

(The entries below have been streamlined in order to limit the length of this list and to reduce clutter in website citations.)

"Abby Aldrich Rockefeller, 1874–1948." *The Rockefeller Archive Center.* http://archive.rockefeller.edu/bio/abby.php

"Abner." *Behind the Name.* http://www.behindthena!me.com

Adams, Cecil. "How Does Nitroglycerin Stop Heart Attacks?" 30 April 2004. http://www.straightdope.com

Ade, George. *Fables in Slang.* 1899. http://gaslight.mtroyal.ab.ca

———. *More Fables.* 1900. http://gaslight.mtroyal.ab.ca

"Aeronautical Corporation of America (Aeronca)." http://www.centennialofflight.gov

"Agnosticism." *The Concise Oxford Dictionary of World Religions.* Ed. John Bowker. 2000. http://www.oxfordreference.com

Agus, Stephen. "The Story of *Robert le Diable.*" *Meyerbeer Fan Club.* 17 September 2004. http://www.meyerbeer.com

"Airco D.H. 9a." 2003. http://www.theaerodrome.com

"Aircraft of Germany." 2003. http://www.theaerodrome.com

"Air Route Rider Speeds to North." *New York Times.* 24 June 1929: 2.

"Akan Linguists' and Family Staff Symbols." *Akan Cultural Symbols Project.* G. F. Kojo Arthu and Robert Rove—1998–2001. 2 August 2004. http://www.marshall.edu/akanart/poma.html

"All Info—About English Culture." 2 October 2004. http://englishculture.allinfoabout.com

"Allied Weapons—Colt." 5 August 2004. http://hoax2kone.tripod.com

"American Civil War: Timeline 1865." http://americancivilwar.com

"The American Legion: Who We Are." 3 September 2004. http://www.legion.org

"America's First Silver Dollar." http://www.collectsource.com

Ammer, Christine. *The American Heritage Dictionary of Idioms.* Boston: Houghton Mifflin, 1997.

Anderson, Sherwood. *Winesburg, Ohio.* New York: Bantam, 1995.

———. *Winesburg, Ohio.* Ed. Charles F. Modlin and Ray Lewis White. New York: W. W. Norton, 1996.

Andrew, A. Piatt. "The Light Field Service Ambulance." *History of the American Field Service Told by Its Members.* Boston: American Field Service, 1920.

Appiah, Kwame Anthony, and Henry Louis Gates, Jr., eds. *Africana: The Encyclopedia of the African and African American Experience.* New York: Basic *Civitas* Books, 1999.

Aquinas, St. Thomas. *Summa Theologica.* Second and Revised Edition, 1920. Trans. Fathers of the English Dominican Province. Kevin Knight. 23 November 2004. http://www.newadvent.org

"Army of Northern Virginia." In *The Oxford Essential Dictionary of the U.S. Military.*

Arnold, Edwin T., and Dawn Trouard, *Reading Faulkner: Sanctuary. Glossary and Commentary.* Jackson: University Press of Mississippi, 1996.

ATSDR—ToxFAQs: Chlorine, Agency for Toxic Substances and Disease Registry (part of the Centers for Disease Control in Atlanta). April 2002. 16 July 2004. http://www.atsdr.cdc.gov

Aubey, James A. "Charles Day." 2003. http://www.rcooper.ocatch.com

Baker, Chris. "Women's Organisations." *The Long, Long Trail.* 26 September 2004. http://www.1914–1918.net

Baker, Jean Harvey. "Democratic Party." In *The Oxford Companion to United States History.*

Barbusse, Henri. *Under Fire: The Story of a Squad.* Trans. Fitzwater Wray. London: J. M. Dent, 1917.

Baumbach, Robert. *"Look for the Dog." BBC Homepage History.* 30 October 2004. http://www.bbc.co.uk

"Bearings and Bushings from GlobalSpec." 3 July 2004. http://bearings.global spec.com

Bedau, Hugo Adam. "Paine, Thomas." In *The Oxford Companion to Philosophy.*

Bell, Haney H., Jr. "A Reading of Faulkner's *Sartoris* and 'There Was a Queen.'" In Kinney, *Critical Essays.* 164–70.

"Beverly Hills, California." 2003. http://themls.com

Bewsher, F. W. *History of the 51st (Highland) Division, 1914–1918.* Edinburgh: William Blackwood and Sons, 1921.

"Beyreuth." *The Concise Oxford-Duden German Dictionary.* Ed. Michael Clark and Olaf Thyen. 2004. http://www.oxfordreference.com

"Bibliography—Military Actions in Mississippi." *Mississippi Civil War Information.* 15 April 2001. http://www.misscivilwar.org

Blotner, Joseph. "Children in Faulkner's Short Stories." In Skei, *William Faulkner's Short Fiction.* 82–89.

———. *Faulkner: A Biography.* New York: Random House, 1974.

———. *Faulkner: A Biography: One-Volume Edition.* New York: Random House, 1984.

———. "Notes." In Faulkner, *Uncollected Stories.* 681–712.

Blythe, Hal. "Faulkner's 'A Rose for Emily.'" *Explicator* 47 (1989): 49–50.

Boatright, Mody C., and Donald Day. "From Hell to Breakfast." *University of North Texas Press.* 7 October 2004. http://www.tamu.edu/upress

"Boat Train." 30 October 2004. http://www.infoplease.com

Bradford, M. E. "A Coda to *Sartoris:* Faulkner's 'My Grandmother Millard and General Nathan [*sic.*] Bedford Forrest and the Battle of Harrykin Creek.'" In Kinney, *Critical Essays.* 318–23.

———. "Escaping Westward: Faulkner's 'Golden Land.'" *Georgia Review* 19 (1965): 72–76.

———. "Faulkner's 'Elly': An Exposé." *Mississippi Quarterly* 21 (1968): 179–87.

———. "The Knight and the Artist: Tasso and Faulkner's 'Carcassonne.'" *South Central Bulletin* LXI (1991): 88–90.

"Brass Bushings for the Mechanical Clock." *Mark Headrick's Horology Page.* 3 July 2004. http://www.geocities.com/CapeCanaveral/Hall/3934/Broach6/html

Breeden, James O. "Science and Medicine." In Wilson and Ferris. 1337–43.

Bréhier, Louis. "Crusades." http://www.newadvent.org

———. "Tancred." http://www.newadvent.org

Brenner, Jack. "Howells and Ade." *American Literature* 38 (1966): 198–207.

Brinkmeyer, Robert. "A Fighting Faith: Faulkner, Democratic Ideology, and the World War II Home Front." In Skei, *William Faulkner's Short Fiction.* 306–15.

Brooks, Cleanth. *William Faulkner: Toward Yoknapatawpha and Beyond.* Baton Rouge: Louisiana State University Press, 1978.

Brooks, Cleanth, and Robert Penn Warren. *Understanding Fiction,* 2nd ed. New York: Appleton-Century-Crofts, 1959.

Brown, Arthur A. "Mistral." In Hamblin and Peek. 253.

Brown, Calvin. *A Glossary of Faulkner's South.* New Haven: Yale University Press, 1976.

Brunner, Borgna, and Anne Marie Imbornoni. "Once in a Blue Moon." 2004. http://www.infoplease.com

Bulfinch, Thomas. *Age of Fable: Vols. I & II: Stories of Gods and Heroes.* 1913, 2003. http://www.bartleby.com

Bulwer-Lytton, Edward. *The Last Of The Barons, Volume 1.* Project Gutenberg Text. 6 May 2003. http://www.ibiblio.org/gutenberg

Burke, Arthur E., J. Ralph Dalzell, and Gilbert Townsend. *Architectural and Building Trades Dictionary.* Chicago: American Technical Society, 1950.

Byron, George Gordon Byron, Baron. *Byron: A Critical Edition of the Major Works.* Ed. Jerome J. McGann. Oxford: Oxford University Press, 1986.

———. *Don Juan by Lord Byron.* Ed. Leslie A. Marchand. Boston: Houghton Mifflin, 1958.

Caddick-Adams, Peter. "Wilhelm II." In *The Oxford Companion to Military History.*

Campion, Thomas. "My Love Has Vowed He Will Forsake Me." http://www.luminarium.org

Carothers, James B. "Faulkner's Short Stories: 'And Now What's to Do?' " In Fowler and Abadie, *New Directions.* 202–27.

———. *William Faulkner's Short Stories.* Ann Arbor: UMI Research Press, 1985.

Chambers, John Whiteclay, II. "Mines, Naval." In *The Oxford Companion to American Military History.*

Chaucer, Geoffrey. *The House of Fame.* In *The Modern Reader's Chaucer,* John S. P. Tatlock and Percy MacKaye, eds. New York: Free Press, 1912. http://www-rohan.sdsu.edu

Chernow, Ron. *Titan: The Life of John D. Rockefeller, Sr.* New York: Random House, 1998.

"Chemical Warfare." J. B. Calvert. 29 July 2004. http://www.du.edu/~jcalvert

"Cherokee Clothing and Adornment." Cherokee Culture Notes. Ed. Wendell Cochran. Ed. and Rev. 27 August 2000. 29 August 2004. http://www.yvwiiusdinvnohii.net

"Chickasaw Customs: Cultural Characteristics." 29 August 2004. http://www.redearth.webtol.com

"The Chickasaw People." 29 August 2004. http://www.utm.edu/departments/acadpro/library/departments/special_collections/wc_hist/chksaw.htm

"Christmas in the United States: 1700s-1900s." Instructional Materials Center. University of Missouri–Kansas City, School of Education. 22 May 2003. 7 August 2004. http://www.umkc.edu/imc/christmas.htm

"The Chronological History of the Christmas Tree." http://www.christmasarchives.com

Clark, Christopher. "Conscription." In *The Oxford Companion to United States History.*

Cleveland, Les. "Soldier's Songs: The Folklore of the Powerless." 1 November 2004. http://faculty.buffalostate.edu/fishlm/folksongs/les01.htm

Clifford, J. Garry, and Samuel R. Spencer, Jr. *The First Peacetime Draft.* Lawrence: University Press of Kansas, 2000.

"Coast Service Plane Here." *New York Times.* 26 June 1929: 2.

Cobby, Arthur. Quoted in "Sopwith Camel." www.theaerodrome.com

Cole, Harriette. *How to Be: A Guide to Contemporary Living for African Americans.* New York: Simon & Schuster, 2000.

Collins, Carvel. " 'Ad Astra' through New Haven: Some Biographical Sources of Faulkner's War Fiction." In Harrington and Abadie, *Faulkner and the Short Story.* 108–27.

The Collins English Dictionary. http://www.wordreference.com

The Columbia Encyclopedia, Sixth Edition. Columbia University Press: 2002.

Columbus World Travel Guide. Highbury Columbus Travel Publishing Ltd. 2 August 2004. http://www.travel-guide.com

"Comus." In *The Oxford Companion to English Literature.*

The Concise Oxford Companion to Classical Literature. Ed. M. C. Howatson and Ian Chilvers. 1996. http://www.oxfordreference.com

The Concise Oxford Dictionary of the Christian Church. Ed. E. A. Livingstone. 2000. http://www.oxfordreference.com

The Concise Oxford Dictionary of Politics. Ed. Iain McLean and Alistair McMillan. 2003. http://www.oxfordreference.com

Conway, David. "The Nun, The Dun and the Son of a Gun." *Jewry in Music.* 17 September 2004. http://www.smerus.pwp.blueyonder.co.uk

Cook, Sylvia Jenkins. *From Tobacco Road to Route 66: The Southern Poor White in Fiction.* Chapel Hill: University of North Carolina Press, 1976.

"Court Martial." In *World Encyclopedia.*

Cowley, Malcolm. *The Faulkner-Cowley File: Letters and Memories, 1944–1962.* NY: Viking, 1966; rpt. Penguin, 1978.

Crockett, James Underwood. *Evergreens.* Alexandria, Virginia: Time-Life Books, 1971.

———. *Trees.* Alexandria, VA: Time-Life Books, 1972.

———. *Vegetables and Fruits.* Alexandria, VA: Time-Life Books, 1972.

"Curtiss JN-4." http://www.theaerodrome.com

Cushman, H. B. *History of the Choctaw, Chickasaw and Natchez Indians.* Norman: University of Oklahoma Press, 1999.

Dabney, Lewis P. *The Indians of Yoknapatawpha: A Study in Literature and History.* Baton Rouge: Louisiana State University Press, 1974.

"Daphnis and Chloe." In *The Oxford Companion to English Literature.*

Dasher, Thomas E. *William Faulkner's Characters: An Index to the Published and Unpublished Fiction.* New York: Garland, 1981.

Davis, Thadious M. *Games of Property: Law, Race, Gender, and Faulkner's* Go Down, Moses. Durham: Duke University Press, 2003.

Day, Douglas. "Introduction." *Flags in the Dust.* vii–xi.

———. "The War Stories of William Faulkner." *Georgia Review,* 15 (1961): 385–94.

Desmonts, Henri. "Very Personal Opinions about Dogs for Game Hawking with Longwings." *UplandBirdDog.com.* 25 October 2004. http://www.uplandbirddog.com

Devlin, Albert J. "*Sartoris*: Rereading the MacCallum Episode." *Twentieth Century Literature* 17 (1971): 83–90.

A Dictionary of British History. Ed. John Cannon. 2001. http://www.oxfordreference.com

A Dictionary of First Names. Ed. Patrick Hanks and Flavia Hodges. 1996. http://www.oxfordreference.com

Dictionary of Psychology. Ed. Andrew M. Colman. 2001. http://www.oxfordreference.com

Dictionary of Superstitions. Ed. Iona Opie and Moira Tatem. 1996. http://www.oxfordreference.com

Dictionary of World History. 2000. http://www.oxfordreference.com

A Dictionary of World Mythology. Ed. Arthur Cotterell. 1997. http://www.oxfordreference.com

Diehl, Lorraine B. *The Late, Great Pennsylvania Station.* New York: Four Walls Eight Windows, 1996.

DiscoverFrance.net. "Le Bois de Boulogne." 30 October 2004. http://www.discoverfrance.net

"Dog Tags." *Digger History: An Unofficial History of the Australia and New Zealand Armed Services.* 1 November 2004. http://www.diggerhistory.info

Donaldson, Susan V. "Dangerous Women and Gothic Debates: Faulkner, Welty, and Tales of the Grotesque." In Skei, *William Faulkner's Short Fiction.* 106–16.

"Doughboy Center." http://www.worldwar1.com

Douglas, Ellen. "Faulkner's Women." In Fowler and Abadie, "*A Cosmos of My Own.*" 149–67.

"Douglas Haig: A Brief Biography." *Aftermath: When the Boys Came Home.* 30 October 2004. http://www.aftermathww1.com

Doyle, Don H. *Faulkner's County: The Historical Roots of Yoknapatawpha.* Chapel Hill and London: University of North Carolina Press, 2001.

Drabble, Margaret, and Jenny Stringer, eds. *The Concise Oxford Companion to English Literature.* Oxford: Oxford University Press, 1996.

Duffy, Michael. "Battles: The Battle of Givenchy, 1914." In *FirstWorld War.com*

———. "Vintage Audio: Mademoiselle from Armentieres." In *FirstWorld War.com*

Durden, W. Kevin. "World War I from the Viewpoint of American Airmen." *Air & Space Power Chronicles.* 2 October 2004. http://www.airpower.maxwell.af.mil

Duvall, John N. "Faulkner's Crying Game: Male Homosexual Panic." In Kartiganer and Abadie, *Faulkner and Gender.* 48–72.

———. *Faulkner's Marginal Couple: Invisible, Outlaw, and Unspeakable Communities.* Austin: University of Texas Press, 1990.

"Early, Jubal Anderson." In *The Oxford Essential Dictionary of the U.S. Military.*

"Eastern Tennessee, 1865: Map." http://www.ancestry.com

Eliot, T. S. *The Complete Poems and Plays, 1909–1950.* New York: Harcourt, Brace & World, 1971.

———. *Selected Essays.* New York: Harcourt, Brace, & World, 1950.

———. *The Waste Land and Other Poems.* New York and London: HBJ/Harvest, 1962.

Ellison, Ralph. *Invisible Man.* New York: Random House, 1952; Vintage International, 1990.

Encyclopedia of Farm Animal Behavior. 7 July 2004. 5 September 2004. http://www.depts.ttu.edu/liru_afs/efab/image.asp

"Europe in 1914." *The Great War and the Shaping of the 20th Century.* 28 September 2004. http://www.pbs.org

"Fargo, North Dakota, Keeley Institute." http://www.fargo-history.com

Fargnoli, A. Nicholas, and Michael Golay. *William Faulkner: A to Z. The Essential Reference to His Life and Work.* New York: Checkmark Books, 2002.

Farrell, Fred A. *The 51st Division War Sketches.* Edinburgh: T. C. 86 E. C. Jack, Ltd., 1920. 16 July 2004. http://www.lib.byu.edu

Faust, Drew Gilpin. "Altars of Sacrifice: Confederate Women and the Narratives of War." *The Journal of American History* 76 (1990): 1200–28. 2 November 2004. *JSTOR.* http://links.jstor.org

"F.B.I. History." http://www.fbi.gov

Ferguson, James. *Faulkner's Short Fiction.* Knoxville: University of Tennessee Press, 1991.

Fergusson, Rosalind, ed. *Shorter Slang Dictionary.* London: Routledge, 1994.

"Fire in North American Wetland Ecosystems and Fire-Wildlife Relations: An Annotated Bibliography." *USGS. Northern Prairie Wildlife Research Center.* 2 August 2004. http://www.npwrc.usgs.gov

"Firing the Steam Yacht Lady Hopetoun." David Taylor. 13 August 2004. http://home.swiftdsl.com.au

FirstWorldWar.com. Ed. Michael Duffy. 30 October 2004. http://www.firstworldwar.com

Fitzgerald, F. Scott. *Tender Is the Night.* New York: Scribner's, 1933.

"Five Civilized Tribes." http://www.shadowwolf.org

"A Flash of Light." http://photography.about.com

"Fog." *A Dictionary of Weather.* Storm Dunlop. 2001. http://www.oxfordreference.com

Folks, Jeffrey J. "Honor in Faulkner's Short Fiction." *Southern Review* 18 (1982): 506–16.

Fowler, Doreen. "The Nameless Women of Faulkner's *Go Down, Moses.*" *Women's Studies* 22 (1993): 525–32.

Fowler, Doreen, and Ann J. Abadie, eds. *"A Cosmos of My Own": Faulkner and Yoknapatawpha, 1980.* Jackson: University Press of Mississippi, 1981.

———. *Faulkner and Popular Culture: Faulkner and Yoknapatawpha 1988.* Jackson: University Press of Mississippi, 2000.

———. *Faulkner and Race: Faulkner and Yoknapatawpha, 1986.* Jackson: University Press of Mississippi, 1987.

———. *Faulkner and Religion: Faulkner and Yoknapatawpha, 1989*. Jackson: University Press of Mississippi, 1991.

———. *Faulkner and the Craft of Fiction: Faulkner and Yoknapatawpha, 1987*. Jackson: University Press of Mississippi, 1989.

———. *Faulkner and Women: Faulkner and Yoknapatawpha, 1985*. Jackson: University Press of Mississippi, 1985.

———. *Fifty Years of Yoknapatawpha: Faulkner and Yoknapatawpha 1979*. Jackson: University Press of Mississippi, 1980.

———. *New Directions in Faulkner Studies. Faulkner and Yoknapatawpha, 1983*. Jackson: University Press of Mississippi, 1984.

Frasché, Louis D. F. "Marion, Francis." In *The Oxford Companion to American Military History*.

Frederickson, Kari. *The Dixiecrat Revolt and the End of the Solid South, 1932–1968*. Chapel Hill: University of North Carolina Press, 2001.

French, David. "Beatty, Sir David, later 1st Earl Beatty." *The Oxford Companion to British History*. Ed. John Cannon. 25 September 2004. http://www.oxford reference.com

"Frequently Asked Questions about Air Pollution." *LA Times*. 2001. http://weather.latimes.com

"From Native Soil: American Indian Ingredients Are Ingrained in the Country's Cuisine." *Restaurants USA*, October 1999. 2 August 2004. http://www.restaurant.org

Furry, William. "Faulkner in a Haystack: The Search for William Faulkner's Television Adaptations of 'The Brooch' and 'Shall Not Perish.'" *The Faulkner Journal* 16.1&2 (Fall 2000/Spring 2001): 119–48.

Galloway, Patricia. "The Construction of Faulkner's Indians." *The Faulkner Journal* XVIII (Fall 2002/Spring 2003): 9–31.

Garrison, Joseph M., Jr. "Faulkner's 'The Brooch': A Story for Teaching." *College English* 36 (1974): 51–57.

"General Joseph Johnston." *The American Civil War*. 3 November 2004. http://www.swcivilwar.com

Genini, Ron. "Latin America in World War I." *Trenches on the Web*. 2 October 2004. http://www.worldwar1.com

Gidley, Mick. "Beyond 'Beyond': Aspects of Faulkner's Representation of Death." In Hönnighausen, *Faulkner's Discourse* 223–33.

"Glossary of Power Industry Terms." Alemeda Power and Telecom. 2 July 2004. http://alamedapt.com

Glyn, Anthony. *Elinor Glyn: A Biography*. London: Hutchinson, 1955.

"Glyn, Elinor." www.LitEncyc.com

Green, Dr. Ben K. *The Color of Horses: The Scientific and Authoritative Identification of the Color of the Horse.* Flagstaff, AZ: Northland Publishing, 1974.

Greene, A. Wilson, and Gary W. Gallagher. *National Geographic Guide to the Civil War: National Battlefield Parks.* Washington, D.C.: The National Geographic Society, 1992.

Grimwood, Michael. "Faulkner's 'Golden Land' as Autobiography." *Studies in Short Fiction* 23 (1986): 275–80.

Grider, J. M. *War Birds.* Texas A&M University Press, 1988.

Grolier's Encyclopedia Online. http://ap.grolier.com

Grote, David. *British English for American Readers.* Westport, CT: Greenwood Press, 1992.

Goodman, Louis S., and Alfred Gilman, eds. *The Pharmacological Basis of Therapeutics.* New York: Macmillan, 1965.

Guillain, Aurélie. "Waiting for the End: Eliminating Digressions and Representing Repression in Four Short Stories by William Faulkner: 'Elly,' 'The Brooch,' 'Red Leaves,' 'Hair.' " In Skei, *William Faulkner's Short Fiction.* 29–37.

Gustin, Emmanuel. "Defensive Armament." *The World War II Fighter Gun Debate.* 28 September 2004. http://www.geocities.com/CapeCanaveral/Hangar/8217/fgun/fgun-de.htm

Gwin, Minrose C. *The Feminine and Faulkner: Reading (Beyond) Sexual Difference.* Knoxville: University of Tennessee Press, 1990.

Halper, Donna. "Radio in 1941." 7 October 2004. http://www.old-time.com

Hamblin, Robert W. "Carcassonne in Mississippi: Faulkner's Geography of the Imagination." In Fowler and Abadie, *Faulkner and the Craft of Fiction.* 148–71.

———. "The Leg." In Hamblin and Peek. 225.

———. " 'Saying No to Death': Toward William Faulkner's Theory of Fiction." In Fowler and Abadie, "*A Cosmos of My Own.*" 3–35.

Hamblin, Robert W., and Ann J. Abadie, eds. *Faulkner in the Twenty-First Century. Faulkner and Yoknapatawpha 2000.* Jackson: University Press of Mississippi, 2003.

Hamblin, Robert W., and Charles A. Peek, eds. *A William Faulkner Encyclopedia.* Westport: Greenwood Press, 1999.

"Handley Page O/100." 28 September 2004. http://www.theaerodrome.com

"Handley Page Type O." 28 September 2004. http://en.wikipedia.org

Handy, W. C. "St. Louis Blues." 21 Oct. 2004. http://www.theonlineblues.com

Hanjani, Michelle N., and Tyler Cymet. "Gray Hair: Medical Explanations and Issues." *Clinical Geriatrics* 11 (March 2003): 36–42. 5 July 2004. http://www.mmhc.com

Hansen, Joyce, and Gary McGowen. *Breaking Ground, Breaking Silence: The Story of New York's African Burial Ground.* New York: Henry Holt, 1998.

Harrington, Evans, and Ann J. Abadie, eds. *Faulkner and the Short Story: Faulkner and Yoknapatawpha 1990.* Jackson and London: University Press of Mississippi, 1992.

———. *The Maker and the Myth: Faulkner and Yoknapatawpha, 1977.* Jackson: University Press of Mississippi, 1978.

Harris, Trudier. *Exorcising Blackness: Historical and Literary Lynching and Burning Rituals.* Bloomington: Indiana University Press, 1984.

Harrison, Robert. *Aviation Lore in Faulkner.* Amsterdam and Philadelphia: John Benjamins, 1985.

Hartwell, Joe. "ACR-5 USS West Virginia/USS Huntington." *Troopships, Battleships, Subs, Cruisers, Destroyers: A History of how the United States Navy moved the Army to the war in Europe during WWI.* 26 September 2004. http://freepages.military.rootsweb.com/~cacunithistories

Harvey, Stewart C. "Heavy Metals." In Goodman and Gilman. 944–75.

"Hawkshaw the Detective." *Don Markstein's Toonopedia, 2003.* 7 August 2004. http://www.toonopedia.com

"Hēbē." In *The Concise Oxford Companion to Classical Literature.*

Hemingway, Ernest. *The Complete Short Stories of Ernest Hemingway: The Finca Vigia Edition.* New York: Scribner's, 1987.

———. *A Farewell to Arms.* 1929. New York: Simon and Schuster, 1995.

———. *In Our Time.* New York: Scribner, 1996.

Hewett, John H. *After Suicide.* Philadelphia: The Westminster Press, 1980.

Hinkle, James. "Some Yoknapatawpha Names." In Fowler and Abadie, *New Directions.*

Hinkle, James, and Robert McCoy. *Reading Faulkner: The Unvanquished. Glossary and Commentary.* Jackson: University Press of Mississippi, 1995.

"The History of Aviation: The Pioneering Years." http://www.multied.com

"History of Barbering." 2003. http://www.barberpole.com

"History of Fashion 1920–1930." www.vintageblues.com

"The History of Thanksgiving Day." AAA Resources for Information and Entertainment. 8 September 2004. http://www.information-entertainment.com

"History of the Native American Dog." *Majestic View Kennels. Read More About It.* 2 August 2004. http://www.majesticview1.com

"History of the Victrola." The Victor Victrola page. http://www.victor-victrola.com

Hoffman, Frederick J., and Olga W. Vickery, eds. *William Faulkner: Three Decades of Criticism.* East Lansing: Michigan State University Press, 1960.

Holmes, Richard. "Roon, FM Graf Albrecht Theodor Emil von." In *The Oxford Companion to Military History.*

Hönnighausen, Lothar. *Faulkner: Masks and Metaphors.* Jackson: University Press of Mississippi, 1997.

———. "Faulkner Rewriting the Indian Removal." In Hönninghausen and Lerda. 335–43.

———. "'Pegasusrider and Literary Hack': Portraits of the Artist in Faulkner's Short Fiction ('Carcassonne' and 'Artist at Home')." In Skei, *William Faulkner's Short Fiction.* 275–80.

———, ed. *Faulkner's Discourse: An International Symposium.* Tübingen, Germany: Max Niemeyer Verlag, 1989.

Hönnighausen, Lothar, and Valeria Gennaro Lerda, eds. *Rewriting the South: History and Fiction.* Tübingen: Francke, 1993.

Hoover, Herbert. "Depression Papers." www.geocities.com/mb_williams/hooverpapers

Hossack, Anthony R. "Memoirs & Diaries: The First Gas Attack." In *FirstWorldWar.com*

Howard, Donald S. *The WPA and Federal Relief Policy.* New York: Da Capo Press, 1973.

Howe, Irving. *William Faulkner: A Critical Study.* 1952; 4th edition, Chicago: Ivan R. Dee, 1991.

Howell, Elmo. "Faulkner's Country Church: A Note on 'Shingles for the Lord.'" *Mississippi Quarterly* 21 (1968): 205–10.

———. "President Jackson and William Faulkner's Choctaws." *Chronicles of Oklahoma* 45 (1967): 252–58.

———. "William Faulkner and the New Deal." *Midwest Quarterly* 5 (1964): 323–32.

Hult, Sharon Smith. "William Faulkner's 'The Brooch': The Journey to the Riolama." *Mississippi Quarterly* 27 (1974): 291–305.

Humphreys, Margaret. "Malaria." In *The Oxford Companion to United States History.*

"The Hydraulic-Press Brick Company." *The Clayworking Plants of St. Louis.* In *Brick. Special Issues on St. Louis,* May and June 1904. Webster University. 7 August 2004. http://www.webster.edu/~corbetre/dogtown/history/hydraulic-main.html

"India." In *World Encyclopedia.*

"Ingersoll, Robert Green." In *The Oxford Companion to American Literature.*

"Insect Avoidance. *DiscoverTheOutdoors.com, Inc.* 2 August 2004. http://www.dto.com

"International Recipe Exchange." http://groups.yahoo.com/group/Intl_Recipe_Exchange/message/1037?source = 1

"James Wilkinson." *Encyclopedia Louisiana.* 2 August 2004. http://www.enlou.com

"John Churchill, First Duke of Marlborough." http://www.en.wikipedia.org

Johnson, Bruce G. "Indigenous Doom: Colonial Mimicry in Faulkner's Indian Tales." *The Faulkner Journal* XVIII (Fall 2002/Spring 2003): 101–27.

Johnson, Danny. "Telephone." In *The Oxford Companion to Military History*.

Johnson, David. "Asian-American History." 2003. http://www.infoplease.com

Jones, Anne Goodwyn. "'Like a Virgin': Faulkner, Sexual Cultures, and the Romance of Resistance." In Kartiganer and Abadie, *Faulkner in Cultural Context*. 39–74.

———. "Penetrating Faulkner: Masculinity and Discourse in Selected Short Fictions." In Skei, *William Faulkner's Short Fiction*. 38–48.

Jones, Diane Brown. *A Reader's Guide to the Short Stories of William Faulkner*. New York: G. K. Hall & Co., 1994.

Jonson, Ben. In *A Dictionary of British History* and *The Oxford Companion to English Literature*.

Joyce, James. *Dubliners*. Ed. Robert Scholes and A. Walton Litz. New York: Viking, 1969.

Judge, Edwin A. "Pilate, Pontius." In *The Oxford Companion to the Bible*.

Karl, Frederick R. *William Faulkner: American Writer*. New York: Weidenfeld & Nicolson, 1989.

Kartiganer, Donald M., and Ann J. Abadie, eds. *Faulkner and Gender: Faulkner and Yoknapatawpha, 1994*. Jackson: University Press of Mississippi, 1996.

———. *Faulkner at 100: Retrospect and Prospect: Faulkner and Yoknapatawpha 1997*. Jackson: University Press of Mississippi, 2000.

———. *Faulkner in Cultural Context: Faulkner and Yoknapatawpha, 1995*. Jackson: University Press of Mississippi, 1997.

Kawin, Bruce. "Sharecropping in the Golden Land." In Fowler and Abadie, *Faulkner and Popular Culture*. 196–206.

Keats, John. "Ode to a Nightingale." *John Keats: Selected Poems and Letters*. Ed. Douglas Bush. Boston: Houghton Mifflin Company, 1959. 205–06.

Keegan, John, ed. "MacArthur, General Douglas, 1880–1964." *Who's Who in World War Two*. New York: Routledge, 2002.

Kerr, Elizabeth M. "William Faulkner and the Southern Concept of Woman." *Mississippi Quarterly* 15 (1961–62): 1–16.

Kessler Associates. "The High Kings of Ireland." *The History Files*. 1 November 2004. http://www.kessler-web.co.uk

Kinney, Arthur F. "Faulkner's Other Others." In Kartiganer and Abadie, *Faulkner at 100*. 195–203.

———, ed. *Critical Essays on William Faulkner: The Sartoris Family*. Boston: G. K. Hall, 1985.

Knight, Kevin, ed. *The Catholic Encyclopedia, Volume IX*. Robert Appleton Company, 2003. http://www.newadvent.org

Koyama, Toshio. "'From Flora and Old Pan' to Human Agonies: Faulkner's Early Literary Career." *Faulkner Journal of Japan* 2 (June 2000). http://www.isc.senshu-u.ac.jp

Kutzik, Alfred J. 1965. "Faulkner and the Jews." *Yivo Annual of Jewish Social Science* 13 (1965): 213–26.

La Forte, Robert, and Ronald E. Marcello. *Remembering Pearl Harbor: Eyewitness Accounts by U.S. Military Men and Women.* Wilmington, DE: Scholarly Resources Inc., 1991.

Lahey, Michael E. "Narcissa's Love Letters: Illicit Space and the Writing of Female Identity in 'There Was a Queen.'" In Kartiganer and Abadie, *Faulkner and Gender.* 160–80.

Lang, Béatrice. "'Dr. Martino': The Conflict of Life and Death." *Delta* 3 (1976): 23–33.

"Latin American Foods: Livin' La Comida Loca." Weeks Publishing Company. December 2000. August 2, 2004. http://www.foodproductdesign.com

Leadbetter, Ron. "Gaia." *Encyclopedia Mythica.* http://www.pantheon.org

"LeadCheck AquaII." HybriVet Systems. Bud Evans. 3 July 2004. http://www.leadcheck.com

"The Legion of Honor." http://www.info-france-usa.org

Lever, Evelyn. *Madame de Pompadour: A Life.* Trans. Catherine Temerson. New York: Farrar, Straus and Giroux, 2002.

"Liberty Loan Campaigns." In *The Oxford Essential Dictionary of the U.S. Military.*

Lighter, J. E. *Random House Dictionary of American Slang.* New York: Random House, 1994.

Lind, Ilse Dusoir. "Faulkner's Relationship to Jews: A Beginning." In Fowler and Abadie, *New Directions.* 119–42.

———. "Faulkner's Women." In Harrington and Abadie, *The Maker and the Myth.* 89–104.

———. "The Language of Stereotype in 'Death Drag.'" In Hönnighausen, *Faulkner's Discourse: An International Symposium.* 127–31.

"Lindbergh Signal Opens Air-Rail Line." *New York Times.* 8 July 1929: 1, 3.

"Lombardy." Encyclopedia Britannica 2002.

"London Bridge Collector's Toys, Ltd. 22 July 2004. http://www.londonbridgetoys.com

Longley, John Lewis, Jr. *The Tragic Mask: A Study of Faulkner's Heroes.* Chapel Hill: University of North Carolina Press, 1963.

"Lubricating Grease" (table). http://www.nskaustralia.com.au/page/bearing2/J10/J10-3-4B.HTM

"Luciferin n." In *Dictionary of Psychology.*

"Ludendorff Offensive." 30 Oct. 2004. http://college.hmco.com/history/readerscomp/mil/html/mh_031000_ludendorffof.htm

Lyman, Lauren D. "Big Plane in Station Prompts Many Questions on Air-Rail." *New York Times.* 14 July 1929: 22.

"MacArthur, Douglas." http://www.bartleby.com

———. www.ww2db.com

"Magnolia Tree." 2003. http://www.bhg.com

Malin, Irvin. *William Faulkner: An Interpretation.* Stanford CA: Stanford University Press, 1957.

Mallios, Peter Lancelot. "Faulkner's Indians, or The Poetics of Cannibalism." *The Faulkner Journal* XVIII (Fall 2002/Spring 2003): 143–78.

"Marlowe, Christopher." In *World Encyclopedia.*

Marshall, S. L. A. *World War I.* Boston: Mariner, 2001.

Matthews, John T. "Faulkner and Proletarian Literature." In Kartiganer and Abadie, *Faulkner in Cultural Context.* 166–90.

———. "Faulkner's Narrative Frames." In Fowler and Abadie, *Faulkner and the Craft of Fiction.* 71–91.

———. "Faulkner's Stories and New Deal Interference." In Skei, *William Faulkner's Short Fiction.* 222–29.

———. "Shortened Stories: Faulkner and the Market." In Harrington and Abadie, *Faulkner and the Short Story.* 3–37.

———. *"The Sound and the Fury": Faulkner and the Lost Cause.* Boston: G. K. Hall, 1991.

———. "Whose America? Faulkner, Modernism, and National Identity." In Kartiganer and Abadie, *Faulkner at 100.* 70–92.

Matthews, Mitford M. *A Dictionary of Americanisms.* Chicago: University of Chicago Press, 1956.

McCarty, Kenneth G. "Depression and Hard Times in Mississippi: Letters from the William M. Colmer Papers." *Mississippi History Now.* http://www.mshistory.k12.ms.us.

McHaney, Thomas L. "'Beyond' and BEYOND and *beyond*: Faulkner and the Threshold of Human Knowledge." In Skei, *William Faulkner's Short Fiction.* 289–305.

"Medals, Decorations and Orders." 20 August 2004. http://members.shaw.ca/calgaryhighlanders/medals.htm

Meriwether, James. "Faulkner's Correspondence with *Scribner's Magazine.*" *Proof* 3 (1973): 253–82.

———. *The Literary Career of William Faulkner: A Bibliographical Study.* 1961; authorized reissue: Columbia, SC: University of South Carolina Press, 1971.

———. "The Short Fiction of William Faulkner: A Bibliography." *Proof* 1 (1971): 293–329.

———, ed. *A Faulkner Miscellany.* Jackson: University Press of Mississippi, 1974.

Mertz, Paul E. "Sharecropping and Tenancy." In Wilson and Ferris. 29–31.

"Mexican War." In *The Oxford Essential Dictionary of the U.S. Military.*

Milford, Darren. "Edgar Class First Class Protected Cruisers." *World War I Naval Combat.* 28 September 2004. http://www.worldwar1.co.uk

Millgate, Michael. *The Achievement of William Faulkner.* Lincoln: University of Nebraska Press, 1978.

———. "Faulkner on the Literature of the First World War." In Meriwether, *A Faulkner Miscellany.* 98–104.

———. *Faulkner's Place.* Athens: University of Georgia Press, 1997.

Milner, Vincent L. *Religious Denominations of the World.* Philadelphia: Bradley, 1860.

Milo, Ronald D. "Machiavelli, Niccolò." In *The Oxford Companion to Philosophy.*

Milton, John. "A Mask Presented at Ludlow Castle." http://www.dartmouth.edu/~milton/reading_room/comus

"Milton, John." In *World Encyclopedia.*

Minter, David. "'Carcassonne,' 'Wash,' and the Voices of Faulkner's Fiction." In Harrington and Abadie, *Faulkner and the Short Story.* 78–107.

———. *William Faulkner: His Life and Work.* Baltimore MD: Johns Hopkins University Press, 1980.

"Montesquieu, Charles-Louis de Secondat, baron de." In *The Oxford Dictionary of Philosophy.*

Moore, Gene M. "Chronological Problems in Faulkner's 'Wilderness' Stories." *The Faulkner Journal* XVIII (Fall 2002/Spring 2003): 51–67.

———. "'European Finery' and Cultural Survival in Faulkner's 'Red Leaves.'" In Skei, *William Faulkner's Short Fictions.* 263–68.

———. "Faulkner's Incorrect 'Indians'?" *The Faulkner Journal* XVIII (Fall 2002/Spring 2003): 3–8.

———. "Faulkner's Indians." *The Faulkner Journal* XVIII (Fall 2002/Spring 2003): 51–67.

———. "Of Time and Its Mathematical Progression." *Studies in Short Fiction* 29:2 (Spring 1992): 195–204.

"MOPP Level 4, Gas! Gas!" Rod Powers. "The Orderly Room." 2 August 2004. http://usmilitary.about.com/library/weekly/aa032603a.htm

Mossman, Jennifer, ed. *Acronyms, Initialisms, and Abbreviations Dictionary.* Detroit: Gale Research Company, 2002.

National Institute on Drug Abuse. "Crack and Cocaine." http://www.nida.nih.gov

Newton, M. B., Jr. "Dogtrot House." In Wilson and Ferris. 498–99.

"New Air-Rail Line Brings 2 in 46 Hours." *New York Times.* 11 July 1929: 4.

Nicolaisen, Peter. "William Faulkner's Dialogue with Thomas Jefferson." In Urgo and Abadie. 64–81.

Nilon, Charles H. "Blacks in Motion." In Fowler and Abadie, *"A Cosmos of My Own."* 227–51.

———. *Faulkner and the Negro.* New York: Citadel Press, 1965.

O'Brien, Edward J. *The Best Short Stories 1936 and the Yearbook of the American Short Story.* Boston and New York: Houghton Mifflin Company; Riverside Press Cambridge, 1936.

O'Donnell, George M. "Faulkner's Mythology." *Kenyon Review* I (Summer 1939): 285–99. In Hoffman and Vickery. 82–93.

The Old Farmer's Almanac. 7 October 2004. http://www.almanac.com

Orser, Charles E., Jr. "The Archaeological Analysis of Plantation Society: Replacing Status and Caste with Economics and Power." *American Antiquity* 53 (1988): 735–51. *JSTOR.* http://links.jstor.org

Owens, Tony J. "Faulkner, Anderson, and 'Artist at Home.'" *Mississippi Quarterly* 32 (1979): 393–412.

The Oxford Companion to American Literature. Ed. James D. Hart. Rev. Phillip W. Leininger. 1995. http://www.oxfordreference.com

The Oxford Companion to American Military History. John Whiteclay Chambers II, ed. 1999. http://www.oxfordreference.com

The Oxford Companion to the Bible. Ed. Bruce M. Metzger and Michael D. Coogan. 1993. http://www.oxfordreference.com

The Oxford Companion to English Literature. Ed. Margaret Drabble. 2000. http://www.oxfordreference.com

The Oxford Companion to Military History. Ed. Richard Holmes. 2001. http://www.oxfordreference.com

The Oxford Companion to Philosophy. Ed. Ted Honderich. 1995. http://www.oxfordreference.com

The Oxford Companion to United States History. Ed. Paul S. Boyer. 2001. http://www.oxfordreference.com

The Oxford Dictionary of Idioms. Ed. Jennifer Speake. 2000. http://www.oxfordreference.com

The Oxford Dictionary of Philosophy. Ed. Simon Blackburn. 1996. http://www.oxfordreference.com

The Oxford Dictionary of Quotations. Ed. Elizabeth Knowles. 1999. http://www.oxfordreference.com

Oxford English Dictionary. http://dictionary.oed.com

The Oxford Essential Dictionary of the U.S. Military. 2001. http://www.oxfordreference.com

The Oxford Guide to People and Places of the Bible. Ed. Bruce M. Metzger and Michael D. Coogan. 2001. www.oxfordreference.com

"Oxfordshire and Buckinghamshire Light Infantry." http://www.regiments.org

Paddock, Lisa. *Contrapuntal in Integration: A Study of Three Faulkner Short Story Volumes.* Lanham, Maryland: International Scholars Publications, 2000.

———. "'Trifles with a tragic profundity': The Importance of 'Mistral.'" *Mississippi Quarterly* 32 (1979): 413–22.

Parini, Jay. *One Matchless Time: A Life of William Faulkner.* New York: HarperCollins, 2004.

Parker, Robert Dale. "Red Slippers and Cottonmouth Moccasins: White Anxieties in Faulkner's Indian Stories." *Faulkner Journal* XVIII (Fall 2002/Spring 2003): 81–99.

———. "Sex and Gender, Feminine and Masculine: Faulkner and the Polymorphous Exchange of Cultural Binaries." In Kartiganer and Abadie, *Faulkner and Gender.* 73–96.

Peek, Charles A. "Red Leaves." In Hamblin and Peek. 315–17.

———. "'That Evening Sun(g)': Blues Inscribing Black Space in White Stories." *Southern Quarterly* 42:3 (Spring 2004): 130–50.

Perkins, Hoke. "'Ah Just Cant Quit Thinking': Faulkner's Black Razor Murderers." In Fowler and Abadie, *Faulkner and Race.* 222–35.

"Permaculture and Mosquitoes." *Permaculture Archives.* 2 August 2004. http://csf.colorado.edu/perma/lists/nov97/msg00312.html

Petry, Alice Hall. "Double Murder: The Women of Faulkner's 'Elly.'" In Fowler and Abadie, *Faulkner and Women.* 220–34.

Pinsker, Sanford. "Ad Astra." In Hamblin and Peek. 4–5.

Piston, William Garrett. "Longstreet, James." In *The Oxford Companion to American Military History.*

Plunkett-Powell, Karen. *Remembering Woolworth's: A Nostalgic History of the World's Most Famous Five-and-Dime.* New York: St. Martin's, 1999.

Pluyaut, Edwige. "'That One Man Should Die,' or The Figure of the Scapegoat in 'Uncle Willy' and 'A Bear Hunt.'" In Skei, *William Faulkner's Short Fiction.* 269–74.

"Poilu." In *The Oxford Essential Dictionary of the U.S. Military.*

Polk, Noel. *Children of the Dark House.* Jackson: University Press of Mississippi, 1996.

———. "Faulkner and Respectability." In Fowler and Abadie, *Fifty Years of Yoknapatawpha.* 110–33.

———. "Faulkner: The Artist as Cuckold." In Kartiganer and Abadie, *Faulkner and Gender.* 20–47.

———. "Was Not Was Not Who Since Philoprogenitive." In Kartiganer and Abadie, *Faulkner at 100.* 18–25.

———. "William Faulkner's 'Carcassonne.'" *Studies in American Fiction* 12 (1984): 29–43.

Pope, Alexander. "An Essay on Man." *The Norton Anthology of English Literature.* 4th ed., vol. 1. Ed. M. H. Abrams. New York: W. W. Norton & Company, 1979. 2243–50.

Probert Encyclopaedia. http://www.probertencyclopaedia.com

"Prussia." In *World Encyclopedia.*

Putzel, Max. *Genius of Place: William Faulkner's Triumphant Beginnings.* Baton Rouge: Louisiana State University Press, 1985.

"The Pythian Story." 2003. http://www.pythias.org

Railroad Dictionary: A Glossary of Railroad Definitions Plus. 24 September 2003; 5 September 2004. http://www.geocities.com/gold27ca/glossary.html

"Refracting Telescope." *A Dictionary of Astronomy.* Ed. Ian Ridpath. 2003. 25 October 2004. http://www.oxfordreference.com

"Rhode Island Red." *Poultry Breeds.* 27 August 2004. http://www.ansi.okstate.edu/poultry/chickens/rhodeislandred

Reed, Joseph, W., Jr. *Faulkner's Narrative.* New Haven: Yale University Press, 1973.

Reeves, Carolyn Keller, ed. *The Choctaw before Removal.* Jackson: University Press of Mississippi, 1985.

"Remembrance Sunday: Cenotaph Parade." *Army: Ceremonial & Heritage.* http://www.army.mod.uk

"Rhodes, Cecil John." http://www.bartleby.com

Rhodes, Karen. "The Grotesque Economics of Tragicomedy: Cultural Colonization in Faulkner's 'Red Leaves.'" *The Faulkner Journal* XVIII (Fall 2002/Spring 2003): 69–79.

Roberts, Diane. *Faulkner and Southern Womanhood.* Athens and London: University of Georgia Press, 1994.

Robinson, Alonford James, Jr. "The Middle Passage." In Appiah and Gates. 1302.

"Romantic Circles Praxis Series." 30 October 2004. http://www.rc.umd.edu

Ross, David, ed. *The Encyclopedia of Trains and Locomotives: The Comprehensive Guide to Over 900 Steam, Diesel, and Electric Locomotives from 1825 to the Present Day.* San Diego: Thunder Bay Press, 2003.

"Ross Rifle." In *FirstWorldWar.com*

Ross, Stephen M. *Fiction's Inexhaustible Voice: Speech and Writing in Faulkner.* Athens: University of Georgia Press, 1989.

"Royal Air Force Motto: Per Ardua Ad Astra." http://www.raf.mod.uk

Ruffner, Frederick G., Jr., and Robert C. Thomas, eds. *Code Names Dictionary.* Detroit: Gale Research Company, 1963.

Runciman, Sir Steven. *The First Crusade.* New York: Cambridge University Press, 1992.

Ruppersburg, Hugh. *Reading Faulkner: Light in August. Glossary and Commentary.* Jackson: University Press of Mississippi, 1994.

"Safety Valves." *The Boiler Book Online.* 2 July 2004. http://www.bhes.com

Said, Edward. *Orientalism.* New York: Random House, 1978.

"Saint Martin of Tours." *Catholic Online.* 27 October 2004. http://www.catholic.org

Sala, George Augustus. *London Up To Date.* London: Adam and Charles Black, 1895. 4 December 2004. http://www.victorianlondon.org

Sassoon, Siegfried. *Counter-Attack and Other Poems.* 1918. http://www.bartleby.com

Sayers, Alethea D. "Holly Springs, Mississippi: A Virtual Tour." 3 November 2004. http://www.civilwarweb.com

Sayre, Robert Woods. "Faulkner's Indians and the Romantic Vision." *The Faulkner Journal* XVIII (Fall 2002/Spring 2003): 33–49.

———. "The Romantic Critique of the Modern World in the Faulknerian Short Story." In Skei, *Willam Faulkner's Short Fiction.* 244–52.

Scholes, Robert. "Learning and Teaching." *Profession.* New York: Modern Language Association, 2004.

Scott, Sir Walter. "My Native Land." In *The Oxford Dictionary of Quotations.*

Selesky, Harold E. "Kings Mountain, Battle of." In *The Oxford Companion to American Military History.*

Serafin, Joan. *Faulkner's Uses of the Classics.* Ann Arbor: UMI Research Press, 1983.

Shakespeare, William. *The Complete Works.* Ed. G. B. Harrison. New York: Harcourt, Brace, & World, 1968.

"Siam Online." 2 August 2004. http://www.siam-online.net

"Siam Wanderer." *Thailand Travel Guide by Siam Wanderer.* 2 August 2004. http://www.siamwanderer.com

Silbey, Joel H. "Republican Party." In *The Oxford Companion to United States History.*

Skei, Hans H. *Reading Faulkner's Best Short Stories.* Columbia: University of South Carolina Press, 1999.

———. *William Faulkner: The Novelist as Short Story Writer.* Oslo: University of Oslo, 1985.

———. *William Faulkner: The Short Story Career: An Outline of Faulkner's Short Story Writing from 1919 to 1962.* Oslo: Universtetsforlaget, 1981.

———, ed. *William Faulkner's Short Fiction.* Oslo: Solum Forlag, 1997.

Skipton, Sharon, and DeLynn Hay. "Drinking Water: Lead." U.S. Department of Agriculture and University of Nebraska at Lincoln. http://ianrpubs.unl.edu/water/g1333.htm

[Smith, Thomas R.] *Immortalia: An Anthology of American Ballads, Sailors' Songs, Cowboy Songs, College Songs, Parodies, Limericks, and Other Humorous Verses and Doggerel* ["Now for the First Time Brought Together in Book Form by A

Gentleman About Town"]. New York: Macy-Masins, 1927. http://www.immortalia.com

"Spanish Governors of Louisiana: Francisco Luis Carondelet." *Encyclopedia Louisiana.* 20 December 2001. 2 August 2004. http://www.enlou.com

"Spanish Texas." 2 August 2004. http://users.evi.net/~gpmoran/chap1a.htm

"Special Coffee Fact File." 27 August 2004. http://www.firstscience.com

"Spindletop Oilfield." http://www.tsha.utexas.edu

Steam & Engine of Australia—The Steam Boiler. 2 July 2004. http:www.steamengine.com.au

Stoneback, H. R. "Carcassonne." In Hamblin and Peek. 59–60.

———. "Golden Land." In Hamblin and Peek. 155.

———. "Wash." In Hamblin and Peek. 432–33.

"Stones River Campaign December, 1862." 3 November 2004. http://americancivilwar.com

"Stratemeyer, Edward." In *The Oxford Companion to American Literature.*

"Summerland." http://www.santabarbara.com/community/neighboring_communities

Swanton, John. *Source Material for the Social and Ceremonial Life of the Choctaw Indians.* Birmingham: Birmingham Public Library Press, 1993.

Swift, Jonathan. "A Satirical Elegy on the Death of a Late Famous General." www.portablepoetry.com

"Swift, Jonathan." *Microsoft Encarta Online Encyclopedia.* 2004. http://encarta.msn.com

Tasso, Torquato. *Jerusalem Delivered.* http://sunsite.berkeley.edu/OMACL/Tasso

Templeton, Steve. "Clouds Affecting Weather." 19 September 2004. http://www.weathersavvy.com

"Thanksgiving Timeline, 1541–2001." 9 September 2004. http://memory.loc.gov/learn/features/thanksgiving

Theobald, Marjorie R. "The Sin of Laura: The Meaning of Culture in the Education of Twentieth Century Women." *Victoria* New Series 1. http://www.cha-shc.ca/jcha-rshc/issues/ab_90_12.htm

Thomas, Brian W. "Power and Community: The Archeology of Slavery at the Hermitage Plantation." *American Antiquity* 63 (1998): 531–51. *JSTOR.* http://links.jstor.org

Thoreau, Henry David. Letter to Ralph Waldo Emerson, 8 June 1843.

"Thumb-Sucking: Topic Overview." MeritCare Health System. 4 August 2004. http://www.meritcare.com

Thurber, James. *New York Post.* 29 February 1960.

Tolnay, Stewart E., and E. M. Beck. *A Festival of Violence: An Analysis of Southern Lynchings, 1882–1930.* Urbana: University of Illinois Press, 1995.

Towne, Douglas C. "As Subtle as Neon: Motel Signs of the Southwest." http://www.sem20.com/neonmotel/subtle.html

Towner, Theresa M. *Faulkner on the Color Line: The Later Novels.* Jackson: University Press of Mississippi, 2000.

———. "'How Can a Black Man Ask': Race and Self-Representation in Faulkner's Later Fiction." *The Faulkner Journal* 10:2 (Spring 1995): 3–21.

———. "'It Ain't Funny A-Tall'": The Transfigured Tales of *The Town.*" *Mississippi Quarterly* 44:3 (Summer 1991): 321–35.

Trefzer, Annette. "Postcolonial Displacements in Faulkner's Indian Stories of the 1930s." In Hamblin and Abadie. 68–88.

"Trenches on the Web—Armory: Gas Warfare. The Great War Society." Michael E. Hanlon. 29 July 2004. http://www.worldwar1.com

Trilling, Lionel. "Mr. Faulkner's World." *Nation* 133 (1931): 491–92.

Trotter, Paul S., G. Alan Johnson, Robert Ricks, and David R. Smith. "Floods on the Lower Mississippi: An Historical Economic Overview." http://www.srh.noaa.gov

Truman, Lee C. *Scientific Guide to Pest Control Operations.* West Lafayette: Purdue University Press, 1962.

TutorGig.com: Encyclopedia. 16 February 2003. http://www.tutorgig.com

"Underwood History." http://www.underwoodspreads.com

United States Census Bureau. "California—Race and Hispanic Origin: 1850 to 1990." Internet Release Date: 13 September 2002. http://www.census.gov/population/documentation/twps0056/tab19.xls

United States Centennial of Flight Commission. www.centennialofflight.gov

"University Museum: History." The University of Mississippi Museums History. 5 August 2004. hp://www.olemiss.edu/depts/umuseum/history.htm

Upton, Dell. "Farm Buildings." In Wilson and Ferris. 65–67.

Urgo, Joseph R. "Centaur in Brass." In Hamblin and Peek. 65.

———. "Shingles for the Lord." In Hamblin and Peek. 351–52.

Urgo, Joseph R., and Ann J. Abadie, eds. *Faulkner in America: Faulkner and Yoknapatawpha 1998.* Jackson: University Press of Mississippi, 2001.

Vandiver, Frank E. "Bragg, Braxton." In *The Oxford Companion to American Military History.*

Vickery, John B. "Ritual and Theme in Faulkner's 'Dry September.'" *Arizona Quarterly* 18 (1962): 5–14.

"Victoria Cross. Britain's Highest Award for Gallantry." http://www.victoriacross.org.uk

"A Victorian Christmas." *Celebrating a 19th C. Holiday.* Joanne Haug. 7 August 2004. http://www.victoriana.com

Volpe, Edmond L. *A Reader's Guide to William Faulkner: The Short Stories.* New York: Syracuse University Press, 2004.

Voltaire, François Marie Arouet de. *Philosophical Dictionary.* Selected and translated by H. I. Woolf. New York: Knopf, 1924. http://history.hanover.edu/texts/voltaire

"Voltaire." In *The Oxford Dictionary of Philosophy.*

"Voltaire, François Marie Arouet de." http://www.bartleby.com

Wallace, Alfred Russel. "The Dyaks." *The Alfred Russel Wallace Page.* http://www.wku.edu/~smithch/wallace/S034.htm

Watson, James G. "Faulkner's Short Stories and the Making of Yoknapatawpha County." In Fowler and Abadie, *Fifty Years of Yoknapatawpha.* 202–25.

———. *Thinking of Home: William Faulkner's Letters to His Mother and Father, 1918–1925.* New York: W. W. Norton & Company, 1992.

———. *William Faulkner: Letters and Fictions.* Austin: University of Texas Press, 1987.

———. *William Faulkner: Self-Presentation and Performance.* Austin: University of Texas Press, 2000.

Watson, Ken. "History of the Rideau Lockstations: The Basics of a Rideau Lock." http://www.rideau-info.com

"Wax Museum." 9 September 2004. http://www.free-definition.com

"Weber and Fields." 3 September 2004. http://www.encyclopedia.com

Webster's II New College Dictionary. Boston: Houghton Mifflin, 1995.

"Welcome to the Officers Association." www.officersassociation.com

Welsford, Enid. *The Court Masque.* Cambridge: Cambridge University Press, 1927.

"West India Docks." 2003. http://www.english-heritage.org.uk

"Wheeler, Joseph." www.bartleby.com

Whitman, Walt. "O Star of France." www.bartleby.com

"Why Did Unemployment in Britain Remain a Problem Throughout the Inter-war Period." http://www.courseworkbank.co.uk

"William Bishop." 1 November 2004. http://www.theaerodrome.com

"William J. Burns." *Directors, Then and Now.* Federal Bureau of Investigation. 30 November 2004. http://www.fbi.gov

Williamson, Joel. *William Faulkner and Southern History.* New York: Oxford University Press, 1993.

"Willow Branches and Other Twigs and Roots." http://www.nativetech.org

Wilson, Charles Reagan. "Tobacco." In Wilson and Ferris. 666–68.

———. "William Faulkner and the Southern Religious Culture." In Fowler and Abadie, *Faulkner and Religion.* 21–43.

Wilson, Charles Reagan, and William Ferris, eds. *The Encyclopedia of Southern Culture.* Chapel Hill: University of North Carolina Press, 1989.

"Wing Walkers." http://www.centennialofflight.gov

Winston, Jay S. "Going Native in Yoknapatawpha: Faulkner's Fragmented America and 'The Indian.'" *The Faulkner Journal* 18: 1 & 2 (Fall 2002/Spring 2003): 129–42.

Wittenberg, Judith Bryant. "Synecdoche and Strategic Redundancy: The 'Integrated Form' of *These 13*." In Skei, *William Faulkner's Short Fiction.* 281–88.

World Encyclopedia. http://www.oxfordreference.com

Yale College: Rules for Scholarship, Attendance, and Conduct. New Haven: Yale University Press, 1925.

Yellis, Kenneth A. "Prosperity's Child: Some Thoughts on the Flapper." *American Quarterly.* 1969; 21(1): 44–64. http://80–www.jstor.org.

"Zeebrugge Raid." In *A Dictionary of World History.*

Ziegfeld, Florenz, Jr. "What Makes a 'Ziegfeld Girl.'" http://www.musicals101.com/ziegspeaks.htm

INDEX